BIODIVERSITY CONSERVATION *in* COSTA RICA

BIODIVERSITY CONSERVATION
in COSTA RICA

*Learning the Lessons in
a Seasonal Dry Forest*

Edited by Gordon W. Frankie,
Alfonso Mata, and S. Bradleigh Vinson

UNIVERSITY OF CALIFORNIA PRESS
Berkeley   Los Angeles   London

University of California Press
Berkeley and Los Angeles, California

University of California Press, Ltd.
London, England

Library of Congress Cataloging-in-Publication Data

Biodiversity conservation in Costa Rica : learning the lessons in a
seasonal dry forest / edited by Gordon W. Frankie, Alfonso Mata, and
S. Bradleigh Vinson.
  p. cm.
  Includes bibliographical references.
  ISBN 0-520-22309-8 (cloth : alk. paper).—ISBN 0-520-24103-7 (pbk. :
alk. paper).
  1. Biological diversity conservation—Costa Rica. 2. Forest ecology—
Costa Rica. I. Frankie, G. W. II. Mata, Alfonso. III. Vinson, S.
Bradleigh, 1938–
QH77.C8 B56 2004
333.95′16′097286—dc21   2003000593

Manufactured in the United States of America
13 12 11 10 09 08 07 06 05 04
10 9 8 7 6 5 4 3 2 1

CONTENTS

PREFACE

THE IDEA OF PRODUCING this book resulted from several realizations for the editors in 1997. The first was an awareness that a large body of biological research from major regions of Costa Rica was available in the literature. In particular, extensive research had been carried out on the lowland Atlantic wet forest, the middle elevation cloud forest (1,400–1,800 m), and the lowland Pacific dry forest over a period of about 30 years. Further, the wet forest had just received a comprehensive biological review by McDade et al. (1994), and a biological review of the cloud forest was in progress (see later in this preface). Second, from the 1980s onward, many biologists and nonbiologists made enormous human and financial investments to protect biodiversity in all parts of the country, using modern conservation approaches and methods. Despite these efforts, little attention had been paid to assessing effectiveness of their work. Finally, in the more than 30 years that had passed since the first national parks and reserves were established in Costa Rica, including the dry-forest area, there had been no comprehensive assessments of whether these designated areas had been effective in protecting biodiversity.

We decided to focus on the seasonal dry forest in the northwestern region of the country because it lacked a review comparable to that of the lowland wet and cloud forests of Costa Rica. Furthermore, this type of forest was rapidly disappearing, in large part because it was so easily converted to agriculture. Daniel Janzen estimated that only 2 percent of the original Middle American tropical dry forest remained.

Building on extensive biological knowledge and modern trends for conserving biodiversity, we determined that the book should address three main questions: What do we know about the biodiversity and status of the most prominent groups of plants and animals in the dry forest? What have we learned biologically, socioeconomically, and politically about conserving these specific groups? What do we need to consider and do in the future to ensure improved conservation and protection of all biodiversity in the dry forest, as well as other major regions of the country?

Several major publications have influenced our thinking in developing the conceptual goals for the book. One of the first workers to investigate Costa Rican life zones was Leslie R. Holdridge of the Tropical Science Center in Costa Rica. Over a period of several years, he and his colleagues intensively studied many plant formations and their environmental determinants. This work established an ecological foundation that eventually led to a lengthy treatise on the life zone system (Holdridge et al. 1971). Daniel H. Janzen (1983) and numerous invited colleagues prepared an overview of the natural history of the country. His classic 1983 volume and its later Spanish translation (1991) also provided extensive lists of the plant and animal diversity found in several selected life zones countrywide.

More recently, in the 1990s, large scientific publications focused on compiling ecological papers from major life zones that have received extensive study. For example, McDade et al. (1994) presented a large series of edited papers on the ecology and natural history of a lowland Atlantic wet forest, La Selva. This is the site where researchers associated with the Organization for Tropical Studies first began to study the biota intensively, in 1968; research at La Selva has continued since that time. Nadkarni and Wheelwright (2000) published a dozen edited papers on the natural history and ecology of the Monteverde Cloud Forest and its several life zones. In addition, their book offers a limited view of conservation issues.

A publication by Bullock et al. (1995) on the seasonal dry tropical forests of the world also influenced the development of the current volume. Most papers in the Bullock volume are concerned with botanical information, with only limited coverage of the fauna. Further, there is surprisingly little mention of conserving biodiversity in any of the examined forests (Frankie 1997).

In the current volume we chose to focus on the lowland seasonal dry-forest region of Costa Rica, which includes several related life zones, according to Holdridge et al. (1971). The book represents the first effort to treat comprehensively the findings from a wide variety of plant and animal biologists investigating a highly seasonal tropical environment. We were also interested in whether modern principles of conservation biology had been put into practice to study and conserve dry-forest biodiversity. Thus, we asked the biological contributors to assess the status of the particular taxonomic groups they studied and, where applicable, to generalize for the entire country. In several cases, this request took some authors into other Costa Rican life zones and beyond into adjacent countries of Middle America. Further, because biodiversity conservation by definition encompasses more than just biology, we also invited several contributors to present socioeconomic, policy, legal, and political perspectives on biodiversity conservation to provide the important social contexts. Finally, all authors were asked to offer their personal recommendations on future directions, policies, and actions to better conserve and protect biodiversity. These recommendations form the final synthesis chapter.

The book begins with an introductory chapter, and the chapters that follow are divided into two parts. The final chapter presents conclusions and recommendations. Chapter 1 ("Introduction") is concerned with the physical, biological, human, and conservation environment of the dry forest. To exemplify these features, the chapter focuses on two prominent regions, the Tempisque Valley and Peninsula of Nicoya (see maps). In addition to the terrestrial environments, these major areas are ecologically connected with major riparian corridors from other ecosystems, coastal areas, and the marine environment.

Part I consists of biological and ecological studies of biodiversity in the dry forest and adjacent ecosystems. It is divided into three subparts, each based on different biogeographical considerations of biodiversity. The first of these consists of three chapters (2–4) on flowering phenology, breeding systems, pollination, plant-breeding structure in fragmented landscapes, and possible global changes in tropical plants and their pollinators. Chapters 5–7 in the same subpart are concerned with mammals, bees, and ants as bioindicators of environmental health and ecological/evolutionary adaptations of insects to the seasonal dry forest.

Chapters in the next subpart explore the ecological relationships between dry-forest organisms and other ecosystems in Costa Rica. Chapter 8 presents the diversity of butterflies that live in dry forests and migrate regularly to other habitats. Chapter 9 deals with hydrological resources in the dry forest and watersheds that connect the dry forest to upland ecosystems. This is followed logically by a critical examination in chapter 10 of the flow of sweet water into the marine gulf of Nicoya estuary, with all its biological and socioeconomic implications. Finally, in chapter 11, mangrove forests that form a transitional habitat between the dry forest and the marine environment are examined in terms of their ecology, uses to humans, and potential for conservation.

The third subpart examines selected dry-forest organisms over broad geographical areas, which include the Costa Rican dry forest. Chapters 12–14 deal respectively with birds, bats, and the herpetofauna. Each author develops a case for the necessity of evaluating the diversity—over a wide geographical area of Middle America—of the taxa he or she has studied. In chapter 15, sea turtle diversity, conservation problems, and projections for the future are offered for all of Costa Rica, Middle America, and beyond to open marine environments where these animals migrate. The final chapter (16) in this subpart deals with an ongoing bio-socioeconomic study to conserve valuable tree species in dry-forest agro-ecosystems of Middle America.

Part II explores transferring and applying biodiversity and conservation knowledge. The eight chapters in this part examine a wide range of experiences and projects aimed at applying accumulated biological knowledge to solve problems in conserving and protecting biodiversity and natural resources in general. In chapter 17 Costa Rica's rich inventories of biodiversity are described and actual and potential uses explored. Chapter 18 is the only contribution that does not deal directly with a Costa Rican experience. The author was invited to present a model that has wide potential use for bringing diverse stakeholders together to collaborate on projects of mutual interest and benefit. The next two chapters are concerned with transferring bioconservation knowledge to diverse audiences. In chapter 19 the transfer is from biologists and other professionals to elementary school children, high schoolers, and selected adult audiences. The importance of transferring information between biologists and the media and vice versa is emphasized in chapter 20.

The next four chapters form a loose unit of contributions dealing with threats to conservation (chapter 21); the environmental laws that are designed to protect the environment and penalize offenders (chapters 22 and 23); and the policy context for conserving all biodiversity in Costa Rica (chapter 24). These four chapters are considered to be extremely important for understanding the basic challenges that currently face biodiversity conservation and those likely to confront biodiversity protection in the future.

In the final chapter (25), a synthesis is provided of 12 of the major lessons that emerge from the 24 contributions. Some of these lessons are repeatedly mentioned or explained in more detail in several of the chapters. Some represent special cases, which the editors considered to be important, and still others could only be inferred from several authors. Minor lessons can be found at the conclusion of most chapters.

ACKNOWLEDGMENTS

We are grateful to the following colleagues for their time, interest, and helpful comments during the early stages of developing the book and for their reviews of many of the chapters: Mario Boza, Harry Greene, Bill Haber, Peter Kevan, Felipe Noguera, Sean O'Keefe, Paul Opler, Jerry Powell, Mauricio Quesada, Peter Ronchi, Mary Schindler, Stan Schneider, Kathryn Stoner, Robbin Thorp, and Jorge Vega. Several others who reviewed early manuscript drafts are cited individually at the end of each chapter. Collectively, the thoughtful and critical comments of reviewers helped greatly to improve the quality and clarity of the book. We also thank Pablo Mata for his excellent translations. Marilyn Tomkins, Genesis Humphrey, Margaret Przybylski, Megan Konar, and Mary Schindler greatly assisted the editors by keeping communications constantly flowing among all contributors. Special thanks are due to Mary Schindler, who assisted in editing several manuscripts prior to their final submission to the University of California Press.

GORDON W. FRANKIE
AND ALFONSO MATA

REFERENCES

Bullock, S. H., H. A. Mooney, and E. Medina, eds. 1995. *Seasonally dry tropical forests*. New York: Cambridge University Press. 450 pp.

Frankie, G. W. 1997. Endangered havens for diversity. Book review of S. H. Bullock et al., eds. *Seasonally Dry Tropical Forests* (1995). *BioScience* 47:322–24.

Holdridge, L. R., W. C. Grenke, W. H. Hatheway, T. Liang, and J. A. Tosi Jr. 1971. *Forest environments in tropical life zones: A pilot study*. Oxford: Pergamon Press. 400+ pp.

Janzen, D. H., ed. 1983. *Costa Rican natural history*. Chicago: University of Chicago Press. 816 pp.

———. 1991. *Historia natural de Costa Rica*. Chicago: University of Chicago Press. 822 pp. Spanish translation of Janzen's 1983 volume.

McDade, L. A., K. S. Bawa, H. A. Hespenheide, and G. S. Hartshorn, eds. 1994. *La Selva, ecology and natural history of a Neotropical rain forest*. Chicago: University of Chicago Press. 486 pp.

Nadkarni, N., and N. Wheelwright, eds. 2000. *Monteverde, ecology and conservation of a tropical cloud forest*. New York: Oxford University Press. 573 pp.

CHAPTER 1

Introduction

Alfonso Mata and Jaime Echeverría

THE CHOROTEGA REGION in northwestern Costa Rica is one of the most important areas of this republic; it covers primarily the Tempisque River Basin (TRB), Nicoya Peninsula, and other nearby lands (see map 1.1). The country's only seasonal dry forest is located here. Enjoying a climate of contrasts, varied geological formations, very attractive natural scenic areas, and a rich cultural heritage, the Chorotega region is perhaps the second most important economic region in the country, after the Central Valley (Mata and Blanco 1994), where the capital city of San José is located. Politically, this area constitutes the province of Guanacaste, with approximately 275,000 inhabitants distributed in 11 counties and an average density of 26 inhabitants per square kilometer. In addition, three counties of Puntarenas Province occupy the tip of the Nicoya Peninsula. The TRB is made up of nine counties of Guanacaste Province. The approximate population in this area is 157,000, with an average density of 30.6 inhabitants per square kilometer. Of this population, 43 percent is located in urban centers (~60 inhabitants per square kilometer), whereas 57 percent lives in rural areas and tends to move toward cities such as Liberia, Cañas, and Nicoya (see map 1.2).

There has been a slow migration of rural and urban residents toward other parts of the country, mainly owing to lack of employment and the mechanized monocultures that require less human labor. These activities involve seasonal crops (melons, sugarcane) and are primarily carried out by a large contingent of nonresident Nicaraguans. The tourism industry in this area is one of the most important of the country.

The entire region has been notably altered and transformed, undergoing substantial changes in land use and ownership, as well as in the quality and quantity of its natural resources. The impact is a cause of concern for the region's inhabitants, public institutions, and nongovernmental organizations, which are making efforts to prevent further damage and repair that which

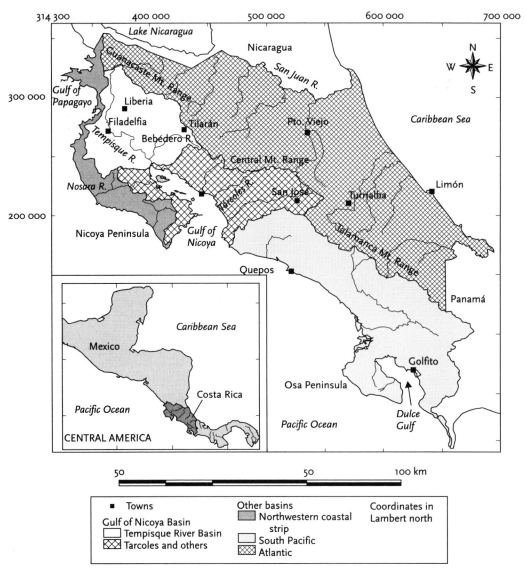

MAP 1.1. Principal river basins of Costa Rica.

has already been done. This introductory chapter presents the region's main physical, biological, and general environmental characteristics, as well as some anthropogenic environmental effects, topics discussed in subsequent chapters of this volume.

GEOGRAPHY

The massive mountain range system that runs along the length of Costa Rica, with a northwest–southeast orientation, creates two principal versants, or basins, with similar areas (map 1.1). The Pacific Basin covers a territory of 26,585 km² (Herrera 1985), modeled by a network of rivers whose flow and eroding behavior are determined by marked climatic seasons. This basin, particularly the northwestern part of Guanacaste, is characterized by a dry seasonal climate, represented by the tropical dry-forest life zone (sensu Holdridge 1967; see the section "Life Zones" later in this chapter and map 1.2) with its transitions and the tropical wet forest of atmospheric association, which is characteristic of the

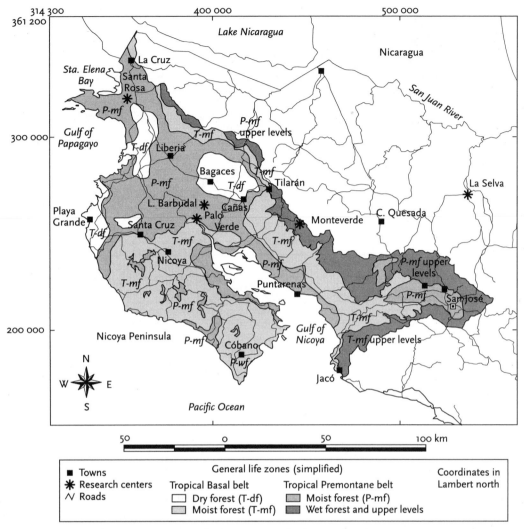

MAP 1.2. Life zones, river matrix, and important geographical points of northwestern Costa Rica.

Nicoya Peninsula. On the other side, the Caribbean Basin has a more homogeneous and much more humid climate for most of the year. This large basin is divided into two main watersheds; in one, the rivers empty into Lake Nicaragua and the San Juan River, which in turn reach the Caribbean Sea, and in the other, the rivers empty directly into the Caribbean.

The Guanacaste Mountain Range (Cordillera Guanacaste) separates the watersheds with a few rivers flowing to Lake Nicaragua and the San Juan River from those of the Gulf of Nicoya (Mata and Blanco 1994). The Nicoya Peninsula is located in the southern sector of Guanacaste.

Along with the continental northwest, the peninsula encloses the Gulf of Nicoya, one of the most important ecosystems in the country (chapter 10). The coastal hills and mountains determine the watershed of the northwestern coastal strip, which begins at the border with Nicaragua and ends at the southern tip of the peninsula (map 1.1).

The vast region around the Gulf of Nicoya, with this common drainage, is known as the Gulf of Nicoya Basin (GNB), covering approximately 12,000 km². The basin's land and estuarine fluvial components are hydrologically connected with a common receptor: the Gulf of

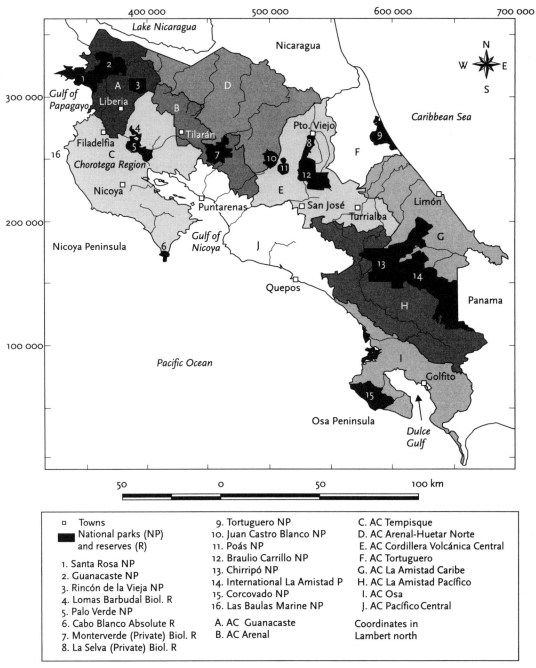

Map legend:

□	Towns		9. Tortuguero NP	C. AC Tempisque
■	National parks (NP) and reserves (R)		10. Juan Castro Blanco NP	D. AC Arenal-Huetar Norte
			11. Poás NP	E. AC Cordillera Volcánica Central

□   Towns

■   National parks (NP) and reserves (R)

1. Santa Rosa NP
2. Guanacaste NP
3. Rincón de la Vieja NP
4. Lomas Barbudal Biol. R
5. Palo Verde NP
6. Cabo Blanco Absolute R
7. Monterverde (Private) Biol. R
8. La Selva (Private) Biol. R

9. Tortuguero NP
10. Juan Castro Blanco NP
11. Poás NP
12. Braulio Carrillo NP
13. Chirripó NP
14. International La Amistad P
15. Corcovado NP
16. Las Baulas Marine NP

A. AC Guanacaste
B. AC Arenal

C. AC Tempisque
D. AC Arenal-Huetar Norte
E. AC Cordillera Volcánica Central
F. AC Tortuguero
G. AC La Amistad Caribe
H. AC La Amistad Pacífico
I. AC Osa
J. AC Pacífico Central

Coordinates in
Lambert north

MAP 1.3. Parks, reserves, and conservation areas of Costa Rica.

Nicoya (see maps 1.1–1.3). The surface area of the GNB constitutes half of the country's entire Pacific Basin (map 1.1) and represents nearly 25 percent of the entire country (Mata and Blanco 1994: 47). The GNB has a variety of land and aquatic ecosystems comprising nearly all the life zones that occur in Costa Rica. It also features the country's only tropical dry-forest zone. The TRB, which includes the Bebedero River, is situated here. It is the most extensive hydrological subregion of Guanacaste (5,460 km², which represents 54% of the province and approximately 10% of the total national area). The largest extant territory of dry forest in the Pacific-side ecoregion of Mesoamerica (World Wildlife Fund/World Bank 1995), which is protected (Boza 1999), is in this subregion.

GEOPHYSICAL ASPECTS

CLIMATE

Precipitation in the northwestern region of the country shows a marked seasonal variation, with an average of 1,800 mm annually; the TRB has 1,746 mm of rain per year. About 95 percent of the rainfall occurs from May to November, and the dry period extends from December to April. There are recurrent periods of prolonged rains that induce extensive flooding in the lowlands of the TRB (Asch et al. 2000). The southern region of Nicoya Peninsula has the most abundant annual precipitation, between 1,800 and 2,300 mm, and the least abundant is in the central and northwestern zones of the TRB, with around 1,400 mm per year. The monthly mean temperature lies between 24.6°C and 30°C. The highest temperatures occur in April and the lowest between September and December. Strong trade winds are predominant during the dry season, with speeds between 10 and 30 km per hour and gusts of roughly 60 km per hour. Winds from the Pacific are predominant during the rainy season, bringing humidity with them, with speeds between 3 and 8 km per hour, making the Nicoya Peninsula the most humid sector of the entire region.

GEOLOGY AND GEOMORPHOLOGY

The northwestern region of Costa Rica was formed through various processes. Notable are the volcanic and sedimentary rocks from the Mesozoic, which crop up extensively in the peninsula (Castillo 1984), as well as the Bagaces and Liberia formations and the sedimentary rocks of the Quaternary (Castillo 1983) in the TRB. The Nicoya complex, the Aguacate Group, and the Quaternary volcanic formations are included in this geological evolution, as well as recent volcanic structures that make up the Guanacaste

Mountain Range (map 1.1). The Nicoya complex consists of the oldest rocks in Costa Rica, formed around 74 million years ago. In addition, the region has sedimentary formations such as Rivas, Sabana Grande, Brito, and Barra Honda. Formations of intrusive rocks and fluvial, colluvial, and coastal deposits are common, as well as swampy areas. Three main formation processes contributed to the relief in the TRB. The first is volcanic, which occurred in the northern and northeastern sectors of the area. The second, denudation, occurred in different sectors but more toward the southwestern sector. The main alluvial sedimentation forms, the result of the third process, are located in the flat and lower parts of the TRB (Bergoeing et al. 1983).

Sulfur, clays, alluviums, limestone, and diatomite are among the geological resources of Guanacaste. There have been claims of illegal exploitation of alluvial material in public-access riverbeds, and there are authorized quarries for road maintenance and construction. Geothermal energy is generated on the volcanic mountain range slopes. Seismic activity is lively throughout the province, with local faults. The subduction process of the Coco's and Caribbean tectonic plates affects the whole country, and consequently the probability of a strong energy release is high in the entire Chorotega region.

SOILS

Soils vary from volcanic types in the upper parts of the mountain range to flooding alluvial in the lower part of the TRB. The region has valleys of varying sizes, with high-fertility soils (e.g., Tempisque, Curime, Nacaome, Nosara) and poor soils (ignimbrite deposits of Liberia-Cañas). Some soils are light in texture, such as the volcanic types, and others are heavy, such as soils with a high clay content in the floodplains. Among the soil orders in the TRB are alfisols (13%), entisols (26%), inceptisols (38%), mollisols, and vertisols (TSC 1999).

LAND-USE CAPACITY AND CONFLICTS

The soils of Guanacaste are shallow or stony, or both, and the long dry period and strong winds further limit their productiveness (Echeverría et al. 1998). Many sectors with small slopes are classified as lands for watershed protection, for example, north of Bagaces and Liberia and the hills of the Nicoya Peninsula. During the first half of the past century, deforestation was extensive in the entire region, but particularly in the lowlands during the period 1940–65, with the opening of the Pan American Highway. After the cattle-ranching decline, at the end of the century, and regardless of natural regeneration on many hills, the effects of tree cutting are still noticeable in the inner parts of the peninsula's coastal mountain range.

Official data indicate that the Chorotega area has some of the highest land-use imbalances in the country. In this region 38 percent of the land—almost 600,000 ha—is overused, only 16 percent is used sustainably, and the rest is underused. In the case of the TRB, which is the flattest land in the region, 30 percent of the area is overused, 40 percent used sustainably, and 30 percent underused. Overuse brings about deterioration of soils and other resources, as is the case when cattle are kept in lands with forest capacity. An example of underuse in the basin is raising livestock in lands with the potential for agricultural activity.

A considerable part of the Guanacaste floodplains is used for agricultural purposes and for some urban and semiurban areas (such as Filadelfia and Ortega); these zones are extremely vulnerable because they include wetlands and plains with recurrent flooding (see the section "Geohazards and Disasters"). There are no ordinances for the safe construction and location of urban developments in these areas.

The main erosive process in the region is hydrological, but eolian erosion is also a problem. Because of the inadequate use of soils, the sediment load in rivers is directly related to the erosion. The most abundant production of sediments coincides with the rainy season (May to November), particularly in the hills of the Nicoya Peninsula, which become microbasins producing large quantities of water during short periods. Landslides and fast floods are frequent during the strong and sustained rainfalls of September and October, particularly under the influence of the tropical storms in the Caribbean Basin.

HYDROGEOLOGY

Groundwater is used in the entire region for human as well as agricultural, industrial, and cattle needs. The Chorotega region has 62 percent of the country's rural aqueducts, which are supplied by wells (Echeverría et al. 1998). The principal sources are the volcanic aquifer of the Bagaces formation, which supplies water to the people of Liberia, Bagaces, and Cañas, and the colluvial-alluvial aquifer alongside the right-hand region of the Tempisque River, which supplies water to several towns and smaller population centers and may be the most important aquifer in the entire basin. Colluvial deposits in Nicoya Peninsula's valleys can provide effective flows of up to 65 liters per second (e.g., Nosara Valley and smaller ones). Their waters are generally potable and suitable for agriculture.

Several of these aquifers could supply coastal tourist projects between Culebra and Brasilito Bays, transporting water across the TRB's western divider and therefore diminishing risks of saline intrusion in those limited coastal aquifers. There have been documented cases of salinization from overexploitation of the northwestern coastal strip, specifically in Flamingo, El Coco, and Tamarindo and particularly in the area of Puntarenas (TSC 1983: 95), among other cases.

HYDROLOGY

The rivers of northwestern Costa Rica can be divided into three geographical sectors: the Lake Nicaragua Basin, to the north; the northwestern coastal strip; and the GNB. In the first sector, four rivers originate in the volcanic massifs of Cerro El Hacha and Orosi Volcano, the northern extreme of the Guanacaste Mountain Range (map 1.2). These are the Sapoa, Sabalos, Mena, and Haciendas, and they empty into Lake Nicaragua. The Haciendas is the boundary between the provinces of Alajuela and Guanacaste. The largest watercourse of Guanacaste is the Tempisque River, born in the southern flanks of the

Orosi volcanic massif. Together with the Bebe-dero River it forms the largest watershed in Costa Rica. The western sector of the Nicoya Peninsula has low coastal sierras (50 to 250 m above sea level) where creeks and a few rivers originate, their microbasins emptying directly into the Pacific Ocean along the entire northwestern coastal strip. Most of these small streams remain dried up during the summer but rapidly grow and flood with the strong and persistent precipitation of the rainy season. All of them are born in the driest life zones of the country (see map 1.2), such as the tropical dry forest, as well as in the tropical moist and premontane wet forests.

The northwestern coastal strip is narrow compared with the TRB, which empties into the gulf, and it widens heading south in the peninsula as its mountains become higher. For example, the Cerros La Carbonera and Cerro Vista al Mar (983 m above sea level) and Zaragoza later average between 200 and 500 m above sea level all the way to the extreme of the peninsula. Although most of the rivers are nearly dry during the summer, the Nosara and Ario Rivers, the two longest and most affluent of the entire northwestern coastal strip, keep a perceptible base flow, with a more noticeable decrease in April and May. Two of the most important wetlands of the coastal strip are the outstanding Tamarindo National Wildlife Refuge (mangroves and estuary), annexed to Las Baulas Marine National Park and the Ostional National Wildlife Refuge, at the mouth of the Nosara River (map 1.3).

Water is used in many ways in the region: public supply, domestic use, agricultural irrigation, hydroelectricity generation, tourism, and industrial activities. Water services to cities and large towns are provided by the national system of aqueducts. There are rural aqueduct councils in smaller population centers, but some are continuously mismanaged, and the dispersed population obtains its water supply from artesian wells. Groundwater resources largely supply industrial and agricultural activities.

Irrigation water, used for the extensive sugarcane, rice, and melon industries, is obtained primarily by detouring rivers and creeks through the Arenal Tempisque Irrigation System. When completed, the system will service about 45,000 ha, with a water volume of 45 m^3 per second. This project, the largest hydrological system in the country, consists of surface water for multiple purposes collected from the Arenal River watershed (Atlantic Basin), which passes through a tunnel to feed a cascade of three power stations on the Pacific Basin side. These power stations are part of the Arenal-Corobici-Sandillal Hydroelectric Project developed by the Costarrican Institute of Electricity. The presence of water of excellent quality in the dry-zone area has stimulated the invasion of the floodplains and many wetlands for agricultural purposes, without sufficient environmental studies. The entire area is subject to recurrent natural floods. Stream corridors are being altered, and levees, channels, and ditches have been constructed without a master plan. These and other activities are making the area highly vulnerable to environmental damage (see the section "Deforestation of Basins, Wetlands, and Stream Corridors" and chapter 9). Balance between ecological alteration and economic development of the entire region, although it seems to be positive, has not yet been studied.

GEOHAZARDS AND DISASTERS

The main geohazards of the region are hydrometeorological; they increase during times of strong rainfall and storms, which in some instances are indirect effects of hurricanes originating far in the Caribbean but which always have strong repercussions. As a result of the vulnerability caused by uncontrolled human activity (deficient urban planning, urban invasion of lands susceptible to the effects of these strong recurring phenomena), there are damages from floods, avalanches, and landslides, as well as from hydrological erosion. They occur in the floodplains of rivers and on steep slopes, and they affect crops, bridge infrastructure, roads, and urban areas, particularly in the wetland sectors of the Tempisque, Cañas, and Las Palmas Rivers. However, these lands have been overtaken by agricultural activities, settlements, neighborhoods, and even cities (case in point: the city of Filadelfia and areas nearby). Although the National Emergency Commission acts efficiently during disasters, there is no ordinance for appropriate and obligatory construction of houses (e.g., perched on piles) or for development of urban centers on more elevated lands. Levee construction continues along the Tempisque River without environmental studies or official restrictions.

There is a potential seismic threat throughout the entire Pacific region of the country. Volcanic hazards are present only in the sector of the Guanacaste Mountain Range, where the Rincon de la Vieja and Arenal are the only volcanoes currently having eruptions and fumaroles activity; other volcanoes show less activity.

BIOLOGICAL ASPECTS

LIFE ZONES

The great bioclimatic diversity of the Chorotega region (map 1.2) is divided into seven life zones with various transitions. The method of classification of plant formations, or World Life Zone System (Holdridge 1967), consists of three main levels of detail. The first is the main life zone category, which considers climatic variables of annual mean precipitation and annual mean biotemperature and the potential evapotranspiration defined by the first two variables and a constant empirical value. The biotemperature is an adjustment of the annual mean temperature, in the 0°C–30°C range, at which there is supposed to be a better development of life. Each life zone has a definite range for each variable, and the plotting of these factors on a graph forms a diagram of hexagons (Hartshorn 1983). The plant association, or ecosystem, is the second level. It considers local environmental factors, such as dry periods, soils, geological relief, and prevailing winds; therefore, associations such as hydric, wet and dry edaphic, cold and warm atmospheric, and combinations of them are found. The third level is the successional stage, referring to the degree of intervention, mainly due to

human activities, undergone by the original natural vegetation. It includes categories such as intervened primary forests, secondary growths and their initial successional stages, and agricultural and other matrixes in the landscape. Advantages of this system include the prediction of the type of natural vegetation that should exist in a deforested area, starting from local physical environmental factors; the prediction of carbon offsets by terrestrial biota in a determined life zone (Tosi 1997); and the analysis of possible changes in type of vegetation from climatic change.

The tropical dry-forest zones, which are strongly seasonal, and the related transitions to moist forest constitute around 30 percent of the Chorotega region. The largest remaining dry forest in the Pacific-side ecoregion of Mesoamerica (World Wildlife Fund/World Bank 1995), which is protected (Boza 1999), lies in this territory. The tropical moist forest predominates, particularly in the Nicoya Peninsula (map 1.2). The greatest biodiversity occurs in the Guanacaste and Tilarán Mountain Ranges, where several life zones are found as narrow elevational bands surrounding the volcanic mountain chain.

PROTECTION AND BIODIVERSITY CONSERVATION

The northwestern region of Costa Rica has three conservation areas: Tempisque (dry), Guanacaste (dry), and Arenal (midelevation/cloud forest) (map 1.3). The three manage a total of 35 wild areas that have varying protection categories, such as national parks and wildlife refuges. One of the most outstanding examples of protection is the Area de Conservación Guanacaste (ACG), covering 120,000 terrestrial and 43,000 marine ha (Janzen 2000; chapter 7). The second dry-forest conservation area, Area de Conservación Tempisque (ACT), consists of about 35,000 ha of terrestrial and wetland habitat and is still being defined and administered.

An essential part of the conservation process is maintenance of the biodiversity that is threatened by human activities. In the dry forest it is still necessary to increase the number of protected areas and to connect them with appropriate corridors, so that all existing ecosystems and biomes of the region can be encompassed. Conservation organizations have developed outstanding protected areas (e.g., Monteverde Cloud Forest Preserve) and have been making efforts to protect other important zones already targeted for development projects; a few are nearly established, and several corridors are under consideration.

WILDLIFE

In general, the Chorotega region still has a rich flora and fauna. The different life zones of the area have an ample diversity of plants and animals. In the past 25 years, important sectors of the forest habitat in the Nicoya Peninsula have naturally recovered (secondary growth) after the recession of cattle ranching (TSC/CIEDES/CI 1997); many species of mammals and birds have had noticeable increases in their populations (A. Mata, pers. obs.). This is an important development because Guanacaste is one region of Costa Rica where wildlife has suffered the greatest negative impact, resulting from loss of natural habitat, overexploitation through extensive cattle ranching and agriculture (chapter 21), and hunting/poaching, particularly during the middle years of the past century. Furthermore, the hunting of sea turtles (chapter 15) and dolphins, as well as overfishing in the Gulf of Nicoya (chapter 10), has prompted legal actions for environmental protection.

There are almost 30 endangered bird species in the region (chapter 12), 12 mammal species (chapter 5), and several hardwood tree species having commercial value. On the other hand, about 20 animal species—among them birds, rodents, and mammals—are considered pests because of alleged damages done to agricultural crops and domestic animals.

The creation of protection areas, such as the ACT and ACG, and wildlife refuges or private preserves (e.g., Monteverde Cloud Forest) has brought about a change in the consciousness of the population, resulting in a slow but effective

decline in faunal loss. Even so, poaching still exists, whether with temporary permits or illegally by unscrupulous people, and even fire is sometimes used to flush wildlife. Furthermore, political pressure to develop tourist facilities and hotels in national refuges is common, and there is illegal fishing during prohibited seasons. The National System of Conservation Areas (map 1.3) has recently become an instrument for implementation and interinstitutional coordination, with a geographical decentralization, and watches over integrated forestry management, wildlife, and areas for biodiversity protection. However, the system is not completely efficient, as it lacks appropriate finances and staffing.

WETLANDS

These productive ecosystems are abundant in Guanacaste, particularly around the Gulf of Nicoya. Wetlands alone represent 20 percent of the area of the TRB, that is, 1,025 km^2, not including the riparian area or uplands. These ecosystems present conditions of great ecological, economic, and social value, and the inhabitants of the region have exploited them throughout history. In the case of the middle TRB area, the continuous invasion of wetlands by agriculture has resulted in a large negative impact. There have also been cases of agricultural, domestic, and industrial contamination of wetlands, as well as overexploitation of their resources and the alteration of natural drainages.

The most extensive wetlands are those between 3 and 30 m above sea level, located in the floodplains of the rivers in the TRB, the so-called palustrine wetlands. Those influenced by tidal estuarine waters are located near the Tempisque River mouth (near Palo Verde; map 1.2) and surrounding the Gulf of Nicoya (Echeverría et al. 1998). Small lakes or lagoons cover a lesser area (e.g., Cañas River); the rest of wetlands are the banks of the stream corridors, which extend up to the headwaters. The natural vegetation includes herbaceous gramineae and cyperaceae shrubs, floating and submerged aquatic vegetation, rooted vascular plants, mangroves, and dry-forest trees in naturally drained areas. The wildlife supported by different wetland types is of great environmental significance to inhabitants of the area. The government protects a few of these areas, such as the wetlands in the ACG and Palo Verde in the ACT.

Although smaller in size, other important wetlands have diverse wildlife, such as those located on the northwestern coastal strip (map 1.1). On the southern coast of the Nicoya Peninsula some remain in protected areas such as in Tamarindo and at the mouth of the Nosara River (map 1.3); they are in national wildlife refuges.

ENVIRONMENTAL IMPACTS

DEFORESTATION OF BASINS, WETLANDS, AND STREAM CORRIDORS

The disappearance of extensive forest areas and fragmentation caused by human actions has strongly affected the ecosystem of the entire region, especially lowland areas subjected to agriculture and extensive livestock use. Damage to riparian systems, which had traditionally been protected, is visible in the majority of rivers in Guanacaste—as it is nationwide. The fluvial-riparian continuum is essential to maintain biodiversity of the ecosystem (chapter 9). However, each bridge, road, or crop established along a river zone results in various degrees of fragmentation, which could be prevented by protecting stream corridors and by environmentally sensitive construction, as well as through enforcement of current laws (chapters 22 and 23). Cattle grazing in wetlands and stream corridors, which is common, is even more damaging to understory vegetation. Slum settlements, as well as expanding urbanization from main cities, have reached the natural floodplains and banks of rivers and their wetlands, resulting in undesirable environmental effects and increasing the vulnerability of those same settlements.

Although outstanding advances have been made in fire prevention, thousands of hectares in the region were affected by fires from 1997 to 1998, in part as a result of the effects of the El Niño phenomenon (*Estado de la nación* 1999:

189); the old custom of slash-and-burn land clearance is still a problem during the dry season.

WATER EXTRACTION BY INDUSTRY, IRRIGATION, AND HUMAN POPULATIONS

There are several notable water consumers in the dry forest. Once they use this resource, those consumers become producers of contaminated water, in varying degrees of output. Among them are sugar industries, rice growers, coffee mills, fruit-packaging plants (melons), the Arenal-Tempisque Irrigation System, aquaculture, cities, and towns (Echeverría et al. 1998).

The sugar industry taps water from the Cañas, Liberia, and Tempisque Rivers, with volumes varying from 5 to 20 m^3 per second or more for industrial and irrigation purposes. There have been shortage problems during the dry season and when the sugar harvest is ending, and it has even been necessary to obtain water from the irrigation system to satisfy the industrial demands, to the extent that in some years the Tempisque River can be easily crossed on foot by the end of the dry season. Taxes for exploitation rights are quite low, and, according to municipal authorities, there is an evident lack of controls for the amount of water pumped.

MODIFICATION OF THE NATURAL COURSE OF THE TEMPISQUE RIVER

Near those same industries, fluvial morphology has been altered by channeling and dam construction for water deviation and containment, as well as by intervention of riparian forests. If sugarcane expansion in these fragile areas is not regulated, there will probably be more intervention with channels, levees, and fluvial detours, which would bring about certain alteration of nearly all wetlands in this region. Water consumption during the dry season drastically changes the volume of the river, which has already been tapped upstream. There is no legislation that regulates levee or channel construction, and some residents of the area who have experienced floodings feel that this infrastructure, built without specific environmental planning, is contributing to the prolonged containment of floodwater in the middle TRB.

POLLUTION: WATER AND SOLID WASTES

The entire dry-forest region, but particularly the TRB, is subject to various types of pollution; water pollution is the most relevant, in the form of sewage, wastewater from industry and urban centers, and water from agriculture activities. The initial capacity of urban sewage treatment plants was reached some time ago, and now they cannot handle wastes produced by new urban developments (Echeverría et al. 1998; chapter 9).

Point-source pollution is generally caused by the discharge of urban wastewater, tourist developments, industry (sugar mills), mining, pig farms, tilapia aquaculture, and garbage dumpsites, among others. Aside from routine government controls of bacteriological quality of water from aqueducts and sediment monitoring of some rivers by the Costarrican Institute of Electricity, there is almost no surveillance of surface-water quality in the entire region.

The legal frame for pollution control in the country is sufficient. However, the lack of regular monitoring, failure to reinforce laws, lack of application of new technologies, and limited capacity of governmental offices in charge work against improved control of emissions. Despite this situation, several agreements have been reached between the government and the sugar industry (as well as coffee mills and pig farms) regarding the control of these industries' liquid and solid wastes (chapter 9); a positive change has been noticed. Nonpoint sources of pollution include the use of chemicals in agricultural areas, such as in the extensive rice paddies. Almost no studies have been done on this subject. Along with the pollution from the Central Valley Basin, the contamination of the TRB has repercussions on the Gulf of Nicoya that are yet to be estimated (chapter 10).

ALTERATION OF THE TERRESTRIAL-MARITIME ZONE

Certain laws protect this coastal strip, which is made up of a public area and a restricted area.

The public zone consists of the first 50-m strip of land starting from the high-tide water level and all surface uncovered during low tide and includes any extension covered by estuaries, mangroves, coastal lagoons, and floodplains. The interior band of 150 m of continental or insular land constitutes the restricted zone. According to the law, both contiguous bands should be under protection and careful management with regard to urban, tourist, industrial, or agricultural developments. However, there have been serious transgressions. Several disasters have occurred since approval of the law, particularly as a result of ignorance, lassitude, or connivance involving the same municipalities in charge of surveillance of resources. Even worse, some of these disasters were the result of inaction on the part of the Ministry of Environment and Energy (MINAE) and the Tourism Ministry, which were perhaps afraid of hampering economic development. This lack of action may contribute, paradoxically, to the destruction of the natural attraction that is the driving force for tourist development and a reason for the country's overseas environmental prestige. The problem is of special relevance in the Chorotega region: of 484 official tourism concessions and permissions registered in 1999 for the country (*Estado de la nación* 1999: 191), 388 were for Guanacaste Province.

ASSESSMENT OF BIODIVERSITY CONSERVATION BY SPECIALISTS

Superimposed on today's complex dry-forest environment are the numerous biologists who have studied the extant flora and fauna, principally in Costa Rica. Working with them, directly or indirectly, are the specialists who have dealt with socioeconomic, political, and legal aspects of conserving this biota. In the chapters that follow, major players present their individual and interrelated stories on what has been learned about biodiversity and its conservation in the dry forest and beyond and what must be done in the future to better protect this biodiversity. The authors provide the first overall assessment of how well one Central American country has examined, valued, and conserved its biological heritage.

ACKNOWLEDGMENTS

We thank Gordon Frankie and Brad Vinson for their valuable commentaries and suggestions and Vladimir Jimenez at the Tropical Science Center for the preparation of maps.

REFERENCES

Asch, C., G. Oconitrillo, and J. L. Rojas. 2000. *Delimitación cartográfica y otras consideraciones sobre las áreas afectadas por las inundaciones de la cuenca baja del Río Tempisque, Guanacaste*. San José: National Geographical Institute of Costa Rica. 24 pp.

Bergoeing, J., et al. 1983. *Geomorfología del Pacífico Norte de Costa Rica*. San Pedro, Costa Rica: Oficina de Publicaciones Universidad de Costa Rica. 110 pp.

Boza, M. 1999. Biodiversity conservation in Mesoamerica. In *Managed ecosystems: The Mesoamerican experience*, ed. L. Hupton Hatch and M. E. Swisher, 51–60. New York: Oxford University Press.

Castillo, R. M. 1983. Geology of Costa Rica. In *Costa Rican natural history*, ed. D. H. Janzen, 44–62. Chicago: University of Chicago Press.

———. 1984. *Geología de Costa Rica: Una sinopsis*. San José, Costa Rica: Editorial de la Universidad de Costa Rica. 187 pp.

Echeverría, J., A. Echeverría, and A. Mata. 1998. *Plan de Acción para la Cuenca del Río Tempisque. Antecedentes del Estudio y Resumen Ejecutivo*. San José: Tropical Science Center/Association for the Tempisque River Basin Management. 39 pp.

Estado de la nación en desarrollo humano sostenible. 1999. 5° informe. Proyecto Estado de la Nación. Costa Rica: Editorama S.A. 338 pp.

Hartshorn, G. 1983. Plants. In *Costa Rican natural history*, ed. D. H. Janzen, 118–57. Chicago: University of Chicago Press.

Herrera, W. 1985. Clima de Costa Rica. In *Vegetación y clima de Costa Rica*, ed. L. D. Gomez, 2:15–19. San José: Editorial Universidad Estatal a Distancia.

Holdridge, L. R. 1967. *Life zone ecology*. San José: Tropical Science Center. 206 pp.

Janzen, D. H., ed. 1983. *Costa Rican natural history*. Chicago: University of Chicago Press. 816 pp.

———. 1991. *Historia natural de Costa Rica*. San José: Editorial de la Universidad de Costa Rica. 822 pp.

———. 2000. Costa Rica's Area de Conservación Guanacaste: A long march to survival through non-damaging biodevelopment. *Biodiversity* 1: 7–20.

Mata, A., and O. Blanco. 1994. *La cuenca del Golfo de Nicoya: Reto al desarrollo sostenible*. San José: Editorial de la Universidad de Costa Rica. 235 pp.

Tosi, J. A. 1997. *An ecological model for the prediction of carbon offsets by terrestrial biota*. Occasional Papers No. 17. San José: Tropical Science Center. 34 pp.

TSC (Tropical Science Center). 1983. *Costa Rica: Country environmental profile*, ed. G. Hartshorn. San José: Editorial Trejos Hnos. 124 pp.

———. 1999. Map of Soils of Costa Rica (scale 1:200.000). San José: Geographical Information Center of the Tropical Science Center.

TSC/CIEDES/CI (Tropical Science Center/Center for Sustainable Development Research/Conservation International and Fondo Nacional de Financiamiento Forestal). 1997. *Estudio de Cobertura Forestal Actual (1996/97) y Cambio de Cobertura para el período entre 1986/97 y 1996/97 para Costa Rica*. San José: Tropical Science Center, Center for Sustainable Development Research/University of Costa Rica and Conservation International/FONAFIFO. 20 pp.

Vargas, G. 1999. The geography of dryland plant formations in Central America. In *Managed ecosystems: The Mesoamerican experience*, ed. L. Hupton Hatch and M. E. Swisher, 88–97. New York: Oxford University Press.

World Wildlife Fund/World Bank. 1995. *Una evaluación del estado de la conservación de las ecorregiones terrestres de America Latina y el Caribe*. Map. Washington, D.C.: World Wildlife Fund/World Bank.

PART ONE

Biodiversity and Ecological Studies

Section A. Costa Rican Dry Forest

CHAPTER 2

Flowering Phenology and Pollination Systems Diversity in the Seasonal Dry Forest

Gordon W. Frankie, William A. Haber, S. Bradleigh Vinson,
Kamaljit S. Bawa, Peter S. Ronchi, and Nelson Zamora

WHEN COMPARING Neotropical life zones, one of the first generalizations to emerge is that seasonal dry forests have lower species diversity than wetter or more aseasonal life zones (Janzen 1983; Bullock et al. 1995). This pattern is easily recognized. The species-level count, however, is only one aspect of a much larger picture of biodiversity. Noss and Cooperrider (1994: 5) provide a useful definition of biodiversity that is relevant to this discussion: "Biodiversity is the variety of life and its processes. It includes the variety of living organisms, the genetic differences among them, the communities and ecosystems in which they occur, and the ecological and evolutionary processes that keep them functioning, yet ever changing and adapting."

In this chapter we focus on selected processes of plant reproduction in the highly seasonal dry forest of Costa Rica and their evolutionary implications. The chapter has three goals. First, we document the diversity of flowering phenologi-cal patterns and pollination systems in the dry forest. Second, we compare the diversity with that of other tropical forests. Third, we explore the significance of this diversity and how it might be affected by environmental disturbances caused by humans.

PHENOLOGY STUDIES

EARLY PHENOLOGY STUDIES, 1969–1973

Community-level periodicity patterns of leaf fall, leaf flushing, flowering, and fruiting were determined for Costa Rican dry forest trees and shrubs from 1969 to 1970 and from 1971 to 1973. Patterns were found to be closely associated with the highly seasonal dry and wet periods (Frankie et al. 1974; Opler et al. 1975, 1976, 1980). The major seasons are the long dry period from early November to early May and the wet period from late May to early November, with a brief, but variable, dry spell from July to August (Frankie et al. 1974). The forestwide patterns, as well as individual species patterns, have remained largely the same every year since 1969 (G. Frankie pers. obs.).

RECENT PHENOLOGICAL STUDIES, 1996 TO PRESENT

Early survey work provided a partial examination of dry-forest phenology, focusing on only tree and shrub life forms. Goals of the early work were limited to marking and monitoring a restricted number of plant species in replication in selected habitats. The approach was labor-intensive and tedious, but it provided the first forest overview of flowering patterns of the most common tree and shrub species. These findings also indicated that flowering patterns of the other plant life forms needed to be factored into the forest-wide picture.

In mid-1996 we began another flowering phenology study at a forest site in close proximity to the sites of the earlier studies. The goal of this new study was to survey flowering patterns of as many native angiosperm species of all forms as possible in a lowland dry-forest area (100 m elevation) that contained a variety of habitat types. The new site (Bagaces) was an area measuring 10 × 10 km with an approximate center at Hacienda Monteverde, just to the northwest of the small town of Bagaces (see map in Frankie et al. 2002: 329; maps in chapter 1). It consisted of mostly wooded savanna with two riparian forest corridors and several creeks (both with perennial water), limited dry deciduous forest, and scattered oak forest (70%). Some of the nonriparian habitats had experienced variable damage from wildfires during the past 20 years. The site also had regenerating second-growth forest (10%), cattle pasture (12%), cropland (6%), and the town of Bagaces (2%). With the exception of one notable grass species, exotic plants were rare in the wildland habitats (Frankie et al. 1997).

The survey was conducted by periodically visiting 14 different subsites within the Bagaces study area. Each was usually visited at least once a month, and several were visited more frequently. Field observations were made on all flowering plants from mid-1997 to project termination in mid-2003. Expected flowerings were based on cumulative experiences for each species by one of us (GF) from 1969 to 1995.

Expected flowering was expressed as the most likely month(s) of flowering for a given species. We also used three supplementary sources to determine expected flowering. These were field notes from one of us (GF) that had been collected yearly from 1971 to 1995; published accounts of selected flowering patterns (Janzen 1967; Frankie et al. 1974, 1983; Heithaus et al. 1975; Opler et al. 1975, 1980; Frankie and Haber 1983; Haber and Frankie 1989); and herbarium records from the Institute of Biodiversity (INBio) in Heredia (see chapter 17). Because we were assessing abundance and timing of floral resources for pollinators at the population and community levels, population and community constituted the levels of analysis for collecting phenological records in this study. (For discussion of analyses in phenology, see Newstrom et al. 1994a,b.) Therefore, data were not collected on individually tagged plants because this level of analysis was not pertinent to our question. Moreover, it would have been cost-prohibitive to attempt to collect for a long-term study of an entire community. By restricting the study to population and community levels, we were able to survey thousands of plants for more than six years.

The composition of plant life forms observed in the Bagaces study area is presented in table 2.1. Herbs were the most common plant life form (36%), followed closely by the trees. The percentages of shrubs (16.0%) and climbers (16.2%) (lianas and vines combined) were each about half that of the herbs. Epiphytes formed only a small percentage of plant life forms, and parasitic plants (mistletoes) were represented by only two species. A terrestrial cactus rounded out the list with only one species. The total number of flowering plants observed to date was 487 species. Based on the current rate of discovery, we expect the total to reach about 550 species. This projection is also based on the number of flowering plant species, about 1,000, that are known from the entire lowland dry-forest zone of Costa Rica (Janzen and Liesner 1980; D. H. Janzen pers. comm.).

TABLE 2.1
Composition of Plant Life Forms Recorded at the Bagaces Study Area

PLANT LIFE FORM	NUMBER OF SPECIES	PERCENT OF TOTAL
Herbs[a]	175	36.0
Trees	144	29.6
Shrubs	78	16.0
Vines	56	11.5
Lianas	23	4.7
Epiphytes[b]	8	1.6
Parasites	2	0.4
Other (terrestrial cactus)	1	0.2
Total	487	

[a]About 25 percent of herbs are woody based; the rest are herbaceous.
[b]Epiphytes are characteristically rare in the dry forest.

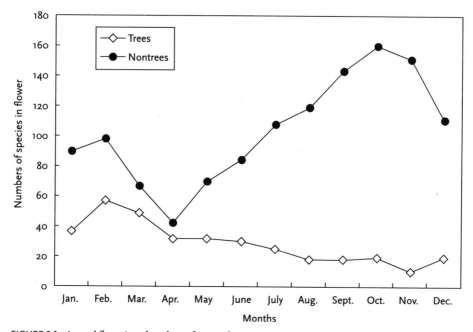

FIGURE 2.1. Annual flowering phenology of tree and nontree angiosperm species in the Bagaces study site. $n = 140$ tree species; $n = 343$ nontree species.

AREAWIDE FLOWERING PHENOLOGY

Flowering phenologies for tree and nontree species in our study area are presented in figure 2.1. A total of 140 tree species were plotted compared with 113 species in the 1969–70 study (Frankie et al. 1974). The addition of 27 tree species in this study changed the forestwide tree picture slightly by increasing the large number of February and March blooming species. The small second peak in flowering recorded in 1974 at the onset of the wet season did not appear with the new compilation (see also Janzen 1967). There was a wide diversity of flowering times (or patterns) among tree species, but most could be categorized as strictly dry-season or wet-season bloomers. Within these patterns, in both dry- and wet-season flowering species, duration of flowering ranged from brief through intermediate to extended. Most species had annual patterns, with one flowering period per year, but a few species had subannual patterns, with flowering twice a year in two separate seasons. A few species had a supra-annual pattern in which they skipped one or more years of flowering. Diverse patterns of flowering behavior have also been observed in wet-forest trees of La Selva in the Atlantic lowlands (Frankie et al. 1974; Opler et al. 1976, 1980; Newstrom et al. 1994a,b).

In every month, substantial flowering was observed at the community level consisting of herbs, shrubs, climbers, epiphytes, parasitic plants, and a terrestrial cactus ($n = 343$ species). In the lowest month, April, at least 42 nontree species were in flower (fig. 2.1). After April, the numbers of species in flower increased continuously each month until a peak of 160 species was reached in October, which is characteristically the wettest month of the year in the dry forest. Flowering in the nontrees declined sharply after November. A slight rise in flowering was recorded in February, which corresponds to the period when a high number of climber species bloom.

SURVEY OF POLLINATION SYSTEMS

Considerable community pollination work was conducted between 1970 and 1980 in the lowland dry forest of Costa Rica. Heithaus et al. (1974, 1975) analyzed foraging patterns and resource utilization in bats and the plant species they pollinate. He and his colleagues also studied the fruits consumed and seeds dispersed by the bats. Haber and Frankie (1989) and Haber (1984) developed detailed information on floral characteristics of dry-forest plants in relation to the hawk-

moths (family Sphingidae) that pollinated them. Frankie and Haber (1983) and Frankie et al. (1983) characterized the large- and small-bee pollination systems (see also Heithaus 1979). In each of the studies cited in this paragraph, one type of pollination system was described. No attempt has been made to investigate the various pollination systems as an interactive community of plants and pollinators in a given area.

In 1996, four of us (GF, SV, PR, and NZ) initiated a study to examine in detail the relationships of Africanized honeybees and native bees foraging on the flora at the Bagaces study site (Frankie et al. 2000, 2002). Although the study was focused on bees, which number about 250 species in this area (Frankie et al. 1983), the survey also provided an opportunity to reexamine most other pollination systems in the area. Griswold et al. (2000) calculated that the entire Costa Rican bee fauna consists of at least 98 genera and 785 species.

POLLINATION SYSTEMS OF THE DRY FOREST

In this section we provide an overview of the pollination systems in our study area and the most prominent characteristics of both the plants and their pollinators. We used three methods for categorizing a plant according to its pollination system. The most important was through repeated field observations of each plant in several different habitats. Secondarily, we used the classic floral and pollinator syndromes for guidance (Proctor et al. 1996). Finally, we called on published accounts and our general field experiences with pollinators and pollination that began in 1970 in this dry forest.

We found four prominent pollination systems in both tree and nontree life forms. These were large-bee, small-bee/generalist, moth, and bat pollination types (table 2.2). The large-bee system occurs frequently in the trees (26.4%) and about half as frequently (12.5%) in the nontrees. Large-bee flowers are usually large, brightly colored, and bilaterally symmetrical, and they commonly bloom during the long dry season (Frankie et al. 1983). They are mostly adapted for visitation and pollination by bees measuring 12 mm

TABLE 2.2
Pollination Systems of Dry-Forest Plants in the Bagaces Study Area

POLLINATOR GROUP	TREES		NONTREE PLANTS		ALL PLANTS	
	SPECIES	PERCENT OF TOTAL	SPECIES	PERCENT OF TOTAL	SPECIES	PERCENT OF TOTAL
Large bee[a]	38	26.4	40	12.5	78	16.8
Small bee/generalist[a,b]	39	27.1	206	64.2	245	52.7
Moth[c]	25	17.4	9	2.8	34	7.3
Bat	9	6.2	2	0.6	11	2.4
Hummingbird	0	0.0	10	3.1	10	2.1
Wasp	1	0.7	0	0.0	1	0.2
Beetle	4	2.8	1	0.3	5	1.1
Butterfly	0	0.0	4	1.2	4	0.9
General insect	14	9.7	5	1.6	19	4.1
Unassigned insect[d]	8	5.5	44	13.7	52	11.2
Fig wasp[e]	2	1.4	0	0.0	2	0.4
Wind	4	2.8	0	0.0	4	0.9
Total	144		321		465	

[a]See Frankie et al. (1983) for description of large-bee and small-bee systems.
[b]Small bees predominate in this category.
[c]Includes hawkmoths and perching moths.
[d]Limited opportunity for study.
[e]*Ficus* species are pollinated by specialized chalcid wasps in the family Agaonidae.

or more in length, however, small bees such as megachilids also visited many of these species and probably account for some of the pollination (Frankie et al. 1976). Large bees included mostly anthophorids in the genera *Centris* (the most abundant genus, with 12 species, in our study area), *Epicharis, Mesoplia,* and *Mesocheira.* Several species of *Xylocopa* and Euglossini (orchid bees) were occasional visitors to large-bee flowers (Frankie et al. 1983). With the exception of Euglossini, most large bees confine their breeding and nesting to the long dry season (Sage 1968; Frankie et al. 1983; S. Vinson and G. Frankie unpubl. data).

The small-bee/generalist system was more than twice as common in the nontree life form (64.2%) as compared with the trees (27.1%)

(table 2.2). This system accounted for slightly more than half of all pollination types. Small-bee/generalist flowers are usually small, often cream colored, and radially symmetrical and typically occur in inflorescences with numerous flowers (Frankie et al. 1983). The blooming periods of species within this system are spread throughout the year, and flowers are visited by a wide variety of small bees (less than 12 mm in length), social and solitary wasps, and several fly families. Some are also visited by certain groups of beetles. Common bee taxa included several genera of anthophorids, megachilids, halictids, and stingless bees (meliponines). Small bees are the most important pollinators in this system, although wasps and flies may account for some of the pollination.

The moth pollination type is common in the trees (17.4%) and noticeably less frequent in the nontrees (2.8%) (table 2.2). This system consists of flowers that are morphologically variable, mostly white or cream-colored and varying from narrow tubed to broad, open cup-shaped, or brush flowers. Pollinators consist of two basic types of moths, hawkmoths (about 70 species in the Sphingidae), which hover while feeding, and the smaller perching moths of several families (Baker and Baker 1983; Haber and Frankie 1989; W. A. Haber unpubl. data). Flowering times of moth plants are distributed throughout the year with a prominent peak in the wet season (Haber and Frankie 1982, 1989; Haber 1983, 1984). Wet-season concentration of moth flowers corresponds to the period when adult moths are most abundant and also coincides with the enormous flush of new leaves available to moth larvae shortly after the onset of the wet season (Frankie et al. 1974; Janzen 1988; Haber and Frankie 1989).

An interesting group of trees (e.g., *Albizia caribaea, Enterolobium cyclocarpum, Lysiloma auritum* [Mimosaceae], and *Guarea glabra* [Meliaceae]) with flowers adapted for perching moths bloom during mid- to late dry season well before the first rains. These trees are apparently pollinated by moths that are active as adults in the dry season, whose caterpillars take advantage of several tree species that flush new leaves before the rainy season begins; some species eat the flowers.

The bat pollination system was found in the trees (6.2%) and to a much lesser extent in the nontrees (0.6%). Overall, it accounted for only 2.4 percent of the systems in the study area (table 2.2). As with the moth flowers, bat flowers are morphologically variable (Heithaus et al. 1975). Compared with moth flowers, they are larger and supply their pollinators with more nectar per flower (and pollen in some cases). They are also structurally strong and often provide landing bases for bats. In contrast to moth flowers, flowering times of bat flowers tend to be spread out evenly over the year and are broadly overlapping. Heithaus et al. (1975) provide a par-

tial examination of bat floral resources and their interaction with seven flower-visiting bat species they studied.

Other distinct pollination types in this forest site, which are all rare, are also presented in table 2.2. The general insect type represents plant species that have a wide variety of visitors with no clear group as the primary visitor or pollinator. With more study, we expect that many of these species might be placed in the small-bee/generalist system. There has been insufficient time and opportunity to study those in the category "unassigned insect," but the flowers show morphological adaptation for insect visitors. Finally, plants adapted for wind pollination are rare in this forest.

Despite the relative ease of placing most plant species in a particular pollination system (table 2.2), there were many pollinator crossovers between systems. Examples include small bees (and wasps) commonly visiting large-bee flowers and, on occasion, large bees visiting small-bee/generalist plants (Frankie et al. 1976, 1983, 1997). Hawkmoths commonly visited bat flowers, although the reverse was rare (Heithaus et al. 1975; Haber and Frankie 1989). There were also several cases of large numbers of bee species visiting nocturnal bat and moth flowers in the morning for residual resources. Plants such as *Crescentia alata* (Bignoniaceae), *Bombacopsis quinata* (Bombacaceae), *Hymenaea courbaril* (Caesalpiniaceae), *Enterolobium cyclocarpum, Inga vera, Lysiloma auritum, Pithecellobium lanceolatum, Samanea saman* (all Mimosaceae), and *Manilkara zapota* (Sapotaceae) often attract high numbers of Africanized honeybees or native bees (or both) for relatively short periods (about 30 min.) during and just after sunrise. Some bee groups are also attracted to wind-pollinated plants such as *Quercus oleoides* (Fagaceae) and a few grass species for their pollen. The flowers of *Trigonia rugosa* (Trigoniaceae), a common liana, attract hawkmoths just prior to sunrise; then large bees arrive for brief foraging at sunrise only, followed for the next few hours by a mix of small bees, wasps, flies, butterflies, and beetles. Diverse visitor/pollinator assemblages at flowers of particular pollination systems have been known for some time (Baker and Hurd 1968). They have not, however, received enough ecological and evolutionary study (Johnson and Steiner 2000).

COMMUNITY STRUCTURE OF DRY-FOREST POLLINATION SYSTEMS

The recent and intensive phenological and pollination studies provide important insights on how most flowering resources and their pollinators (fig. 2.1 and table 2.2) are structured in diverse pollination systems within the dry-forest community. Overall combined flowering times (fig. 2.1) indicated that substantial floral resources are available every month, with a dry-season peak for trees and wet-season peak for nontree species. When large-bee, small-bee/generalist, and moth systems (table 2.2) are superimposed on the annual flowering pattern, three immediately new patterns emerge. First, large-bee flowers mostly bloom in the dry season. Nesting times of most large bees are also largely restricted to this season (Sage 1968; Frankie et al. 1983; S. Vinson and G. Frankie in prep.). A few *Centris* species and other large bees are occasionally observed in low numbers in the wet season, but their consistently low diversity and abundance are considered of minor importance for pollination.

The second pattern is that most moth-adapted plant species flower in the wet season. This is also the period when a peak in caterpillars feeding on new foliage leads to production of new wet-season adult moths for several months (Janzen 1988; Haber and Frankie 1989). The relationships of new foliage to larval feeding and the production of new moths is obvious and well based on fundamental biological needs of these lepidopterans. What is not yet clear is the relationship between moths and some moth-adapted flowers that bloom at the end of the dry season, when leaflessness reaches its extreme in the dry forest. Caterpillars of these moths may specialize on those plant species that flush new leaves before the rainy season begins. In addition, caterpillars of some Lepidoptera eat flowers of mass-flowering bee trees that are so abundant late in the dry season.

The small-bee/generalist system is the least charismatic of all the other systems (table 2.2). Yet, by its abundance and pervasiveness, the system plays a vital ecological role in the community of dry-forest pollinators and visitors. It is found commonly in trees and nontrees, and it is not restricted to any particular season. Further, a wide variety of small bees are probably the most important pollinators of the system, but other groups, such as flies, wasps, and beetles, may also contribute to pollination. At the community level, the frequent occurrence of this flower type in every month ensures that a wide variety of flower visitors will always have floral foods.

OTHER COMMUNITY POLLINATION STUDIES

Large community studies on tropical pollination systems are rare. In this section we present results of investigations on pollination systems of the Monteverde Cloud Forest Reserve and the lowland wet forest of La Selva (both of Costa Rica). These are followed by a review of recent pollination findings from an Asian Dipterocarp forest. *Pollination Systems of the Monteverde Cloud Forest.* Pollination systems of the dry forest (table 2.2) were compared with those from the nearby midelevation cloud forest at Monteverde (see maps in chapters 1 and 8). In this examination we were interested in similarities and differences in the systems and also in the diversity and composition of pollinators in this cooler, wetter environment. Monteverde was also chosen for comparisons because it is the only other location in the country where extensive community pollination work on trees and nontrees has been done (Haber 2000a,b; Murray et al. 2000).

The cloud forest study site consisted of about 40 km² ranging from 1,200 to 1,860 m in elevation. Three habitat types occur there: (a) Pacific slope wet forest, (b) Pacific slope, or leeward, cloud forest, and (c) Atlantic slope, or windward, cloud forest. The almost exclusively wind-pollinated families Cyperaceae and Poaceae were omitted from the species count, as well as the highly specialized, often nectarless, and poorly

TABLE 2.3

TABLE 2.3
Pollination Systems of Cloud-Forest Plants in the Tilarán Mountain Range near Monteverde

POLLINATOR GROUP	TREES		NONTREE PLANTS		ALL PLANTS	
	SPECIES	PERCENT OF TOTAL	SPECIES	PERCENT OF TOTAL	SPECIES	PERCENT OF TOTAL
Large bee	28	7.4	65	9.0	93	8.5
Small bee/generalist	146	38.5	248	34.4	394	35.9
Moth[a]	54	14.2	14	1.9	68	6.2
Bat	2	0.5	32	4.4	34	3.1
Hummingbird	11	2.9	95	13.2	106	9.6
Beetle	6	1.6	20	2.8	26	2.4
Butterfly	8	2.1	13	1.8	21	1.9
Wasp	10	2.6	8	1.1	18	1.6
Fly	0	0.0	2	0.3	2	0.2
General insect	49	12.9	0	0.0	49	4.5
Unassigned insect[b]	30	7.9	145	20.1	175	15.9
Fig wasp[c]	6	1.6	0	0.0	6	0.5
Arboreal mammal	1	0.3	0	0.0	1	0.1
Wind	26	6.9	31	4.3	57	5.2
Unknown[b,d]	2	0.5	48	6.7	50	4.5
Total	379		721		1,100	

Note: The study included only those plants occurring at elevations above 1,200 m. Species of Cyperaceae, Orchidaceae, and Poaceae were omitted.
[a]Includes hawkmoths and perching moths.
[b]Limited opportunity for study.
[c]*Ficus* species are pollinated by specialized chalcid wasps in the family Agaonidae.
[d]Includes 48 species of Piperaceae in which the distribution of insect versus wind pollination is unclear.

studied Orchidaceae, leaving a list of 1,100 plant species in the study area. Results presented here are based on more than 20 years of inventory, phenology, and pollination work by one of us (WH) and other researchers at Monteverde (Haber 2000a,b; Murray et al. 2000).

Many similarities in pollination systems between the two sites can be observed in tables 2.2 and 2.3. With rare exceptions (i.e., arboreal mammals), both sites have the same general pollination types. Three of these, moth, bat, and beetle systems, occur at approximately the same gen-

eral frequencies in both areas. The small-bee/generalist type is the most frequently observed system at each site; however, it is more common in the dry forest (52.7% versus 35.9%).

Distinct differences between the two forest types can be observed in the large-bee, bird, butterfly, and wind pollination systems (tables 2.2 and 2.3). The large-bee type occurs much less commonly at Monteverde (8.5%). In the dry forest this system is twice as abundant (16.8%). This difference may be due to the large-bee fauna of the cloud forest, consisting of 31 known species

(W. A. Haber unpubl. data), which is much less diverse and abundant than in the dry forest (Frankie et al. 1976, 1983; Heithaus 1979).

An example of dry-forest bee diversity and abundance was demonstrated in 1972 through intensive sampling conducted on the large bee-flower tree, *Andira inermis* (Fabaceae) at the southern limit of the town of Liberia (see maps in chapter 1 and Frankie et al. 2002: 329). At that time high numbers of *Centris* bees, consisting of several species, were sampled from several trees and shown to make intertree movements at rates that accounted for cross-pollination of this self-incompatible species (Bawa 1974; Frankie et al. 1976). Further, it was estimated that at peak foraging periods there could be up to 50,000 bees on a single large flowering crown of *A. inermis,* and most of these belonged to the genus *Centris.* A comparable legume tree at Monteverde might attract a maximum of 100–200 bees (W. A. Haber unpubl. data). With regard to bee flowers, it is also noteworthy that the small-bee/generalist system is more common in trees of the cloud forest as compared with the dry forest (38.5% versus 27.1%). This system occurs almost twice as frequently, however, in the nontree plants of the dry forest (64.2% versus 34.4%).

The hummingbird pollination system is extremely conspicuous in the cloud forest with its colorful yellow, orange, red, or blue flowers and abundant hummers. It accounts for 9.6 percent of the Monteverde species, with epiphytes or shrubs the most representative plants. In sharp contrast, the bird system is rare in the dry forest (2.1%). The difference between the two forests is also evident in the high species diversity and abundance of hummers in the cloud forest; 20 cloud-forest species versus 11 dry-forest species (see chapter 12; see also Feinsinger et al. 1986; Murray et al. 1987, 2000).

The general insect system occurred at about the same frequency in both forest types (4.1% in dry forest versus 4.5% in cloud forest). This pollination type has received more study in cloud forests and consists of two groups of plants: (1) those whose flowers are regularly visited by a wide variety of insects including butterflies,

beetles, and wasps, in addition to small bees; (2) those with very small flowers with unspecialized morphology presumably pollinated by small flies and wasps, with very low representation by bees (W. A. Haber unpubl. data). Finally, wind pollination occurs only rarely in both forests; however, it is more common in cloud-forest plants (5.2% versus 0.9%).

Pollination Systems of La Selva. Kress and Beach (1994) provide an overview of the pollination systems of a relatively high proportion of understory and overstory plants in this lowland wet-forest site (excluding epiphytes). They conclude that bees may pollinate as many as 60 percent of the canopy ($n = 51$ species) and subcanopy ($n = 74$ species) plants and almost 40 percent in the understory plants ($n = 151$ species). Other overall common pollination systems were, respectively, hummingbird, beetle, small diverse insect, and moth. As in the dry forest, Kress and Beach state that plants in the "small diverse insect" category may ultimately turn out to be pollinated by bees.

Pollination Systems of a Malaysian Forest. Momose et al. (1998) conducted a plant-pollinator survey in a lowland dipterocarp forest in Sarawak, Malaysia, where they monitored 576 individually marked plants (including trees, lianas, and epiphytes) from 1992 to 1996 to determine flowering periodicity, breeding systems, floral characteristics, and pollinator types. They recognized 12 pollination systems in 270 plant species (of 999 known species from the general study area). Slightly more than 50 percent of all pollination systems were bees. Further, they recognized five different bee systems, which they described in some detail. The beetle system was the second most common (20%), followed by two general insect systems (17%). The only other notable system was the bird system (9.5%). Together, these four major systems made up 95 percent of the known pollination systems in this forest.

POLLINATION IN THE CHANGING DRY FOREST OF COSTA RICA

Given that dry-forest plant communities show definite reproductive structure from a pollination perspective, one must wonder how this structure will endure present and future human disturbances (see also Johnson and Steiner 2000 and references therein). In this regard, Hamrick and Apsit (chapter 3) consider the effects of forest fragmentation on pollen and gene flow in the Costa Rican dry forest and conclude that, at present, fragmentation is not significantly affecting outcrossing. But what happens in the future as this forest becomes even more developed (chapters 1 and 16)? Bawa (chapter 4) considers the effects of local and global changes on pollinators and their ability to continue providing pollination services to plants (see also Janzen 1974).

Our past and ongoing monitoring studies of large bees in the Bagaces study area and nearby Liberia indicated that these important pollinators are progressively declining (Frankie et al. 1976, 1997, unpubl. data). This is understandable in the vicinity of Liberia, which is the fastest-growing town in the region. What is not clear is why large-bee numbers also seem to be declining in the Bagaces study area, which still has much intact habitat. Our recent assessments suggest that (1) loss of habitat due to agricultural development scattered throughout the region, (2) increased and intensified wildfires over the past 20 years (Frankie et al. 1997), and (3) reduction of preferred floral hosts (Frankie et al. 2002) all seem to be negatively and cumulatively affecting these bees (G. Frankie and S. Vinson unpubl. data).

FUTURE STUDIES AND APPLICATIONS FOR CONSERVATION WORK

Despite the threats that development poses (chapters 21–23) to the dry-forest plants, their pollinators, and other floral visitors, there is still much to be learned about the pollination ecology of lowland dry-forest plants, especially in areas that have largely intact habitats. We urge that these studies be initiated as soon as possible while valuable biological information can still be gathered and effectively applied to addressing conservation issues. In addition to the obvious value of this information, there is the recognition that lessons learned here have application in other

tropical and temperate regions as well (Frankie et al. 2000, 2002). These topics are briefly explored in this section.

MORE BASIC PLANT INVENTORY WORK

Plant inventory surveys in the Neotropics are extremely important in order to determine the full range of species present in given regions, ecosystems, or habitats. Dry forests of Mesoamerica especially need plant inventory work because of the many distinct habitats (Frankie 1997) that make up this forest type. In addition to species lists, these surveys help to (1) determine frequencies of species occurrence, (2) define geographical and habitat limits of species, (3) construct phenological patterns, and (4) identify which habitats are in urgent need of attention.

INFORMATION ON GENERALIZED VERSUS SPECIALIZED POLLINATION

Common occurrence of the small-bee/generalist and general insect systems in both the dry forest and cloud forest raises many questions about the effectiveness of each visitor type in pollination (Johnson and Steiner 2000). This system is also common in the La Selva site of the Atlantic lowland forest (see maps in chapter 1) (K. Bawa and G. Frankie pers. obs.). More specifically, we need to know the comparative capacity of each visitor type for carrying pollen and which visitors are moving between plants to promote outcrossing. We also need to know more about periods of stigmatic receptivity in relation to visitor activity.

MONITORING AND RESTORING POLLINATORS

There is little doubt that at least some pollinator types, such as large bees, are declining in the dry forest (Frankie et al. 1997) as habitat loss through human development continues (see chapters 1, 4, 7, 12, 13, and 21). In large areas that still contain substantially protected natural habitat, long-term monitoring programs need to be developed for the important pollinator groups, especially large and small bees, bats, and moths. At the same time, basic biological and ecological information must be obtained for use in restoring populations of pollinators where downward trends are obvious (Vinson et al. 1993; chapter 6). It is important to stress that this kind of work must start now, while appropriate habitat and pollinator populations are still extant (see also discussion on this topic by Janzen 1974).

APPLICATION OF BIOLOGISTS' KNOWLEDGE TO CONSERVE AND RESTORE POLLINATORS

Pollinator and pollination biologists are just beginning to recognize and document the decline of pollinators worldwide (Allen-Wardell et al. 1998). They are also the professionals who know best how to monitor declines and sound the alarm about impending losses to plants and eventually to humans, with their dependence on plants. But how does a classically trained biologist become involved in taking action on decline issues? There is no clear answer to this question, but it is certain that to do nothing will probably lead to pollinator population levels that are unable to provide vital plant reproductive services (Janzen 1974; Daily 1997, esp. chap. 8).

There are at least three courses of action that pollinator biologists could pursue to assist declining pollinator populations. First, they can collaborate with other biologists/land stewards who are also concerned about decline of specific organisms (e.g., birds, mammals) and habitat. Second, biologists could also work in a variety of ways toward conserving specific areas known to naturally harbor healthy populations of pollinators, preferably several types. Biologists are aware, through years of field experience, which areas have good diversity and abundance of bees and moths, for example. As in the first case, this kind of project will require that pollinator biologists collaborate with land stewards to ensure that high-quality habitats will be given special attention.

In areas where much is known about the requirements of pollinators and where decline is strongly suspected, a third possible course of action is restoration. In this case the goal of restoration should be to add known floral and other resources preferred by pollinators (see chapter 6). Hands-on work such as planting or actively enhancing other pollinator resources (e.g., nesting material for bees) has great appeal to private landowners and some public land stewards in contrast to just "setting habitat aside for wildlife."

In all three cases, the pollinator and pollination biologist must be an active member of the outreach effort. Further, the biologist will need to continue the outreach for an extended period, and this could mean employing follow-up professional monitors and perhaps training volunteers from local nongovernmental organizations to monitor, as well. The extended project period would provide the principal investigator of the project with many opportunities for transferring environmental knowledge to types of various audiences.

ACKNOWLEDGMENTS

We thank the California Agriculture Experiment Station and the Texas Agricultural Experiment Station for their support of this research. Several grants from the National Science Foundation and the National Geographic Society supported the early periods of this work. The David A. Stewart family kindly allowed us to use their property for our research. They also generously provided us with logistical help and were agreeable to setting aside sections of their land for long-term monitoring of bees and plants. Linda Newstrom and Robbin Thorp kindly read an early draft of this chapter.

REFERENCES

Allen-Wardell, G., et al. 1998. The potential consequences of pollinator declines on the conservation of biodiversity and stability of food crop yields. *Conservation Biology* 12:8–17.

Baker, H. G., and I. Baker. 1983. Floral nectar sugar constituents in relation to pollinator type. In *Handbook of experimental pollination biology,* ed. C. E. Jones and R. J. Little, 117–141. New York: Van Nostrand-Reinhold.

Baker, H. G., and P. D. Hurd Jr. 1968. Intrafloral ecology. *Annual Review of Entomology* 13:385–414.

Bawa, K. S. 1974. Breeding systems of tree species of a lowland tropical community. *Evolution* 28: 85–92.

Bullock, S. H., H. A. Mooney, and E. Medina, eds. 1995. *Seasonally dry tropical forests*. Cambridge: Cambridge University Press. 450 pp.

Daily, G. C., ed. 1997. *Nature's services, societal dependence on natural ecosystems*. Covelo, Calif.: Island Press.

Feinsinger, P., K. G. Murray, S. Kinsman, and W. H. Busby. 1986. Floral neighborhood and pollination success in four hummingbird-pollinated cloud forest plant species. *Ecology* 67:449–64.

Frankie, G. W. 1997. Endangered havens for diversity. *BioScience* 47:322–24.

Frankie, G. W., and W. A. Haber. 1983. Why bees move among mass flowering neotropical trees. In *Handbook of experimental pollination biology*, ed. C. E. Jones and R. J. Little, 361–72. New York: Van Nostrand-Reinhold.

Frankie, G. W., H. G. Baker, and P. A. Opler. 1974. Comparative phenological studies of trees in tropical wet and dry forests in the lowlands of Costa Rica. *Journal of Ecology* 62:881–919.

Frankie, G. W., P. A. Opler, and K. S. Bawa. 1976. Foraging behavior of solitary bees: Implications for outcrossing of a Neotropical forest tree species. *Journal of Ecology* 64:1049–57.

Frankie, G. W., W. A. Haber, P. A. Opler, and K. S. Bawa. 1983. Characteristics and organization of the large bee pollination system in the Costa Rican dry forest. In *Handbook of experimental pollination biology*, ed. C. E. Jones and R. J. Little, 411–47. New York: Van Nostrand-Reinhold.

Frankie, G. W., S. B. Vinson, M. A. Rizzardi, T. L. Griswold, S. O'Keefe, and R. R. Snelling. 1997. Diversity and abundance of bees visiting a mass flowering tree in disturbed seasonal dry forest, Costa Rica. *Journal of the Kansas Entomological Society* 70:281–96.

Frankie, G. W., S. B. Vinson, S. O'Keefe, and M. A. Rizzardi. 2000. Assessing impacts of Africanized honey bees in Costa Rica and California: A progress report. In *Proceedings of the Sixth International Conference on Apiculture in Tropical Climates, Costa Rica*, 157–61. San José: International Bee Research Association. 226 pp.

Frankie, G. W., S. B. Vinson, R. W. Thorp, M. A. Rizzardi, N. Zamora, and P. S. Ronchi. 2002. Coexistence of Africanized honey bees and native bees in the Costa Rican seasonal dry forest. In *Proceedings of the Second International Conference on Africanized Honey Bees and Bee Mites*, ed. E. H. Erickson, R. E. Page, and A. A. Hanna, 327–39. Medina, Ohio: A. I. Root Co.

Griswold, T., F. D. Parker, and P. E. Hanson. 2000. An inventory of the bees of Costa Rica: The myth of the depauperate tropics. In *Proceedings of the Sixth International Conference on Apiculture in Tropical Climates, Costa Rica*, 152–16. San José: International Bee Research Association. 226 pp.

Haber, W. A. 1983. Hylocereus costaricensis. In *Costa Rican natural history*, ed. D. H. Janzen, 252–53. Chicago: University of Chicago Press.

———. 1984. Pollination by deceit in a mass-flowering tropical tree, *Plumeria rubra* L. (Apocynaceae). *Biotropica* 16:269–75.

———. 2000a. Plants and vegetation. In *Monteverde: Ecology and conservation of a tropical cloud forest*, ed. N. Nadkarni and N. Wheelwright, 34–94. New York: Oxford University Press.

———. 2000b. Vascular plants of Monteverde. In *Monteverde: Ecology and conservation of a tropical cloud forest*, ed. N. Nadkarni and N. Wheelwright, 457–518. New York: Oxford University Press.

Haber, W. A., and G. W. Frankie. 1982. Pollination ecology of *Luehea* (Tiliaceae) in Costa Rican deciduous forest. *Ecology* 63:1740–50.

———. 1989. A tropical hawkmoth community: Costa Rican dry forest Sphingidae. *Biotropica* 21:151–72.

Heithaus, E. R. 1979. Flower-feeding specialization in wild bee and wasp communities in seasonal Neotropical habitats. *Oecologia* 42:179–94.

Heithaus, E. R., P. A. Opler, and H. G. Baker. 1974. Bat activity and pollination of *Bauhina pauletia*: Plant-pollinator coevolution. *Ecology* 55:412–19.

Heithaus, E. R., T. H. Fleming, and P. A. Opler. 1975. Foraging patterns and resource utilization in seven species of bats in a seasonal tropical forest. *Ecology* 56:841–54.

Janzen, D. H. 1967. Synchronization of sexual reproduction of trees within the dry season in Central America. *Evolution* 21:620–37.

———. 1974. The deflowering of Central America. *Natural History* 83:48–53.

———. 1983. *Natural history of Costa Rica*. Chicago: University of Chicago Press. 816 pp.

———. 1988. Characterization of a Costa Rican dry forest caterpillar fauna. *Biotropica* 20:120–35.

Janzen, D. H., and R. Liesner. 1980. Annotated check list of plants of lowland Guanacaste Province, Costa Rica, exclusive of grasses and non-vascular cryptograms. *Brenesia* 18:15–90.

Johnson, S. D., and K. E. Steiner. 2000. Generalization versus specialization in plant pollination systems. *Trends in Ecology and Evolution* 15: 140–43.

Kress, W. J., and J. H. Beach. 1994. Flowering plant reproductive systems. In *La Selva, ecology and natural history of a Neotropical rain forest*, ed. L. A. McDade et al., 161–82. Chicago: University of Chicago Press.

Momose, K., T. Yumoto, T. Nagamitsu, M. Kato, H. Nagamasu, S. Sakai, R. D. Harrison, T. Itioka, A. A. Hamid, and T. Inoue. 1998. Pollination biology in a lowland Dipterocarp forest in Sarawak, Malaysia. I. Characteristics of the plant-pollinator community in a lowland Dipterocarp forest. *American Journal of Botany* 85:1477–1501.

Murray, K. G., P. Feinsinger, W. H. Busby, Y. B. Linhart, J. H. Beach, and S. Kinsman. 1987. Evaluation of character displacement among plants in two tropical pollination guilds. *Ecology* 68: 1283–93.

Murray, K. G., S. Kinsman, and J. L. Bronstein. 2000. Plant-animal interactions. In *Monteverde: Ecology and conservation of a tropical cloud forest*, ed. N. Nadkarni and N. Wheelwright, 245–302. New York: Oxford University Press.

Newstrom, L. E., G. W. Frankie, and H. G. Baker. 1994a. A new classification for plant phenology based on flowering patterns in lowland tropical rain forest trees at La Selva, Costa Rica. *Biotropica* 26:141–59.

Newstrom, L. E., G. W. Frankie, H. G. Baker, and R. K. Colwell. 1994b. Diversity of long-term flowering patterns. In *La Selva, ecology and natural history of a Neotropical rain forest*, ed. L. A. McDade et al., 142–60. Chicago: University of Chicago Press.

Noss, R. F., and A. Y. Cooperrider. 1994. *Saving nature's legacy: Protecting and restoring biodiversity.* Covelo, Calif.: Island Press. 416 pp.

Opler, P. A., H. G. Baker, and G. W. Frankie. 1975. Reproductive biology of some Costa Rican *Cordia* species (Boraginaceae). *Biotropica* 7:234–47.

Opler, P. A., G. W. Frankie, and H. G. Baker. 1976. Rainfall as a factor in the release, timing, and synchronization of anthesis by tropical trees and shrubs. *Journal of Biogeography* 3:231–36.

Opler, P. A., G. W. Frankie, and H. G. Baker. 1980. Comparative phenological studies of shrubs in tropical wet and dry forests in the lowlands of Costa Rica. *Journal of Ecology* 68:167–18.

Proctor, M., P. Yeo, and A. Lack. 1996. *The natural history of pollination.* Portland, Oreg.: Timber Press. 479 pp.

Sage, R. D. 1968. Observations on feeding, nesting, and territorial behavior of carpenter bees genus *Xylocopa* in Costa Rica. *Annals of the Entomological Society of America* 61:884–89.

Vinson, S. B., G. W. Frankie, and J. F. Barthell. 1993. Threats to the diversity of solitary bees in a Neotropical dry forest in Central America. In *Hymenoptera and biodiversity*, ed. J. LaSalle and I. D. Gauld, 53–81. Wallingford, England: CAB International.

CHAPTER 3

Breeding Structure of Neotropical Dry-Forest Tree Species in Fragmented Landscapes

James L. Hamrick and Victoria J. Apsit

LANDSCAPES THAT ONCE featured continuously distributed, seasonal dry tropical forests are now characterized in much of Central America by a matrix of pastures and agricultural lands punctuated by occasional patches of remnant forest, secondary forests, and narrow riparian forest corridors. Fragmentation of these once continuous forests could adversely affect several aspects of the biology of tropical dry-forest tree species (Harris 1984; Bierregaard et al. 1992). In particular, changes in pollinator densities and behavior may disrupt or highly modify normal breeding patterns in remnant populations (e.g., Frankie et al. 1997). Such changes in breeding patterns can, in turn, modify levels and distribution of genetic diversity throughout local landscapes (Nason and Hamrick 1997).

Most tropical forest tree species are predominantly outcrossing (Bawa 1974; Opler and Bawa 1978; Loveless 1992; Nason and Hamrick 1997). Population genetic studies have demonstrated that, on average, tropical tree species have quite high levels of allozyme genetic diversity and that the majority (86.5%) of the genetic diversity is found within rather than among populations (Hamrick 1994). Indirect estimates of gene flow among populations (Nm = the number of migrants per generation) of tropical tree species indicate that historical levels of gene flow have been high enough to counteract the effects of genetic drift (i.e., $Nm > 1.0$). Contemporary measures of gene flow made in relatively undisturbed continuous forests indicate that pollen flow rates above 25 percent often occur over distances of several hundred meters (Hamrick and Murawski 1990; Chase et al. 1996; Stacy et al. 1996).

The question, then, is, Does forest fragmentation change pollinator behavior so that pollen movement is reduced to the extent that over several generations genetic diversity is lost via genetic drift and rates of inbreeding increase within the remaining fragments? In the following sections we first examine theoretical expectations of the effects of fragmentation on the genetic composition of tropical dry-forest tree populations. We then review case studies of the breeding structure of several Neotropical dry-forest tree species located in fragmented landscapes to determine if gene flow is sufficient to increase the low effective population sizes that often characterize fragmented tropical tree populations.

THEORETICAL EFFECTS OF FOREST FRAGMENTATION

IMMEDIATE EFFECTS

The genetic composition of forest tree populations immediately after fragmentation depends on several factors: (1) number, size, and distribution of fragments; (2) original density of the species; and (3) original distribution of genetic variation. If numerous fragments are left after disturbance and/or if fragments are large and close together, most of the genetic diversity in the original populations will be preserved. If, as is more likely, there are relatively few, small, widely dispersed fragments, some low-frequency alleles may be lost, but most genetic diversity present in the original population will remain (Young et al. 1996; Nason and Hamrick 1997). The density and dispersion of trees in the original forest will determine the number of individuals in fragments and fragment-to-fragment variation in population numbers. Finally, if genetic variation was distributed at random within the original population (i.e., low genetic structure), each of the fragments should retain a relatively high proportion of the overall genetic diversity and should be genetically similar to one another. On the other hand, if genetic variation was patchily distributed originally (i.e., high genetic structure), fragment populations will each contain less of the overall genetic diversity, and genetic differentiation among fragments will be higher. Overall genetic diversity for the total landscape will be maintained, however. An exception would occur if deforestation was not random with remnant forests occupying particular habitats (e.g., steep hillsides, ridgetops, riparian areas). Alleles that preferentially occur in the deforested areas would be lost, decreasing overall genetic diversity.

SUBSEQUENT EFFECTS

With little gene flow via pollen or seeds between fragments (i.e., $Nm < 1$) and with low effective population sizes within fragments, in subsequent generations genetic drift would decrease genetic diversity within fragments, and genetic differentiation among fragments would increase. Inbreeding would also increase because of either increased self-fertilization or matings between related individuals. However, most of the original genetic variation will be maintained within the region; the genetic variation is only distributed differently. If individual fragment populations are destroyed or become extinct after drift has restructured genetic diversity, overall genetic diversity will be reduced.

In contrast, with gene flow between fragmented populations, the effects of genetic drift and inbreeding will be reduced—that is, genetic diversity will be maintained within each fragment, and genetic differentiation among fragments will be relatively low. Thus, as a result of gene flow, subsequent loss of fragments will not appreciably reduce the region's genetic diversity.

In many highly disturbed landscapes, isolated, freestanding trees are located in pastures, agricultural fields, and fence rows. Such lone individuals are reservoirs of genetic diversity and may also play an important role in local breeding populations (Levin 1995: chap. 16). Pollinators or seed dispersal agents that might not move between fragments because of distance or their inability to perceive the fragment might move from a fragment to an isolated individual and then to a second fragment. Such movements would increase gene flow among fragments, increase genetic diversity within fragments, and lower or maintain genetic differentiation among fragments.

Gene flow among fragments is, then, a key element determining the effect of forest fragmentation on the genetic composition of remnant populations. Changes in pollinator or seed disperser behavior due to changes in the physical configuration of biological landscapes could therefore have direct effects on the amount and spatial distribution of genetic variation. The genetically effective size (N_e, which is generally less than the number of reproductive adults) of fragmented populations and the genetic related-ness of the adults within fragments will also affect genetic changes due to genetic drift and inbreeding.

BREEDING STRUCTURE OF NEOTROPICAL DRY-FOREST TREE SPECIES

Recently molecular genetic markers have been used to estimate rates and distances of pollen movement in fragmented tropical landscapes. From these analyses, breeding patterns and pollen movement distances within study sites can be described, and estimates can be made of rates of pollen and seed dispersal into the sites (i.e., gene flow). In the sections that follow we discuss the results of several case studies of the breeding structure of Neotropical dry-forest tree species. The studies involve species that oc-cur in the tropical dry forests of Costa Rica, al-though in some instances the studies were con-ducted elsewhere within the range of the species. Thus, it is possible that some differences might occur between locations owing to differences in the quantity and quality of pollinators or popu-lation densities of the trees.

SPONDIAS MOMBIN L. (ANACARDIACEAE; COMMON NAME, JOBO)

S. mombin, a canopy tree, is pollinated by small diverse insects (including small bees, beetles, flies, wasps, moths, and butterflies; Bawa et al. 1985). In the more mesic parts of its range it is an early successional species, but in the seasonal dry forests of Costa Rica it is a major compo-nent, along with its congener S. radlkoferi, of pri-mary forests (Janzen 1983). Nason and Hamrick (1997) studied pollen flow into two semi-isolated S. mombin populations located in the continuous forests of Barro Colorado Island (BCI), Panama, as well as into several small islands located near BCI in Lake Gatun. In the two continuous forest sites (separated by 100 and 200 m from other S. mombin), total rates of pollen immigration averaged 45 percent (table 3.1). Average rates of pollen flow into small island populations (< 9 individuals) isolated by distances as great as 1,000 m were nearly twice those observed for the larger BCI populations. Fruit set and seed germination were reduced in the small island populations relative to the larger BCI popula-tions, indicating either that fruit production was pollen-limited or that higher rates of inbreeding and subsequent abortion occurred. These re-sults indicate that the small insect pollinators of S. mombin can move large distances across in-hospitable habitat (i.e., water). Although S. mom-bin occurs at higher densities in the tropical dry forests of Palo Verde National Park in Guana-caste Province, Costa Rica, levels of gene flow were generally consistent with the BCI results; study sites in continuous forests experienced less gene flow than sites isolated by several hun-dred meters (J. Hamrick unpubl. data).

ENTEROLOBIUM CYCLOCARPUM (JACQ.) GRISEB. (FABACEAE; MIMOSOIDAE; COMMON NAME, GUANACASTE)

E. cyclocarpum is a large dominant tree of the tropical dry forests of Central America and northern South America. It is pollinated by moths, hawk moths, beetles, and other small nocturnal insects and possibly by diurnal insects such as bees (Janzen 1982; Rocha and Aguilar 2001a; K. Bawa pers. comm.; G. Frankie pers. comm.). Mimosoid legumes such as E. cyclo-carpum have a pollination system that ensures that seeds within individual fruits are usually full-sibs. With mimosoid legumes, a single ball of pollen (a polyad) originating from a single pollen parent is deposited on the stigma. Poly-ads contain more pollen grains than the maxi-mum number of ovules in the ovary (Kendrick and Knox 1989). As a result, the diploid geno-type of the pollen parent can be inferred from the genetic composition of the full-sib progeny array.

Apsit (1998) used standard paternity analysis procedures to describe the breeding structure of

TABLE 3.1
Estimates of Pollen Flow Rates and Minimum Distances of Pollen Immigration for Tropical Dry-Forest Tree Species

SPECIES	LOCATION	RATE OF POLLEN FLOW (%)	DISTANCE(S)	REFERENCE
SPONDIAS MOMBIN				
Continuous forest	BCI, Panama	45	100–200	Nason and Hamrick 1997
Islands		60–100	100–1,000	
ENTEROLOBIUM CYCLOCARPUM				
Paternity analyses	Guanacaste, CR	80–100	120–350	Apsit et al. in review
Full-sib analysis	Guanacaste, CR	70–74	250	Apsit et al. 2001
	Coto Brus, CR	50	500	Hamrick and Aldrich unpubl. data
Cordia alliodora	Turrialba, CR	3	280	Boshier et al. 1995
Cedrela odorata	Coto Brus, CR	100	300	James et al. 1998

Note: BCI = Barro Colorado Island; CR = Costa Rica.

six fragmented populations located in two areas of Guanacaste Province. The six populations each consisted of 3–12 adults. She showed that the dominant pollen parents varied among maternal trees within the same fragment and that there was statistically significant heterogeneity in the genetic composition of the pollen received by various maternal parents. Comparisons between years also indicated significant heterogeneity in the genetic composition of pollen received by individuals. Estimates of pollen flow rates were high (80–100%) over distances ranging from 120 m to 350 m (table 3.1). The paternity analyses also indicated that isolated pasture trees donated pollen to trees within forest fragments.

Apsit et al. (2001) also used full-sib progeny from individual fruits to analyze further the breeding structure of one forest fragment (5 adults) over a three-year period. Estimates of the number of pollen parents per maternal tree ranged from 27 to 83 trees across 5 maternal trees for the 1994 fruit crop and from 15 to 60 trees for the 1995 crop. An average of 70 to 74 percent of the pollen parents came from outside the study area (minimum distance 250 m). Hamrick and Aldrich (unpubl. data) also used

full-sib analyses over a three-year period to study the breeding structure of a cluster of four *E. cyclocarpum* adults and four isolated trees located in a small area of dry forest in southern Costa Rica. In all three years the same tree within the cluster was the dominant pollen parent (approximately 30%) of the other three trees. The four isolated trees tended to receive pollen from a wider array of pollen parents than trees in the fragment. Approximately 50 percent of the effective pollen immigrated into the four-tree cluster from beyond 500 m. Finally, a more extensive study of the breeding structure of *E. cyclocarpum* populations located in habitats ranging from primary forest to highly disturbed agricultural sites in the vicinity of Palo Verde National Park (J. Hamrick unpubl. data) supported these earlier studies and further indicated that the number of pollen donors was largest for single trees located in highly disturbed habitats. These results are consistent with those of Koptur (1984), who demonstrated for seven *Inga* species that pollen often traveled as much as 500 m.

To summarize, it appears that most *E. cyclocarpum* trees in fragments receive pollen from a diverse array of pollen donors and that more than 50 percent of the pollen immigrates from beyond 500 m. Furthermore, trees isolated in pastures or agricultural fields play an important role in the overall breeding dynamics of these populations.

CORDIA ALLIODORA (BORGAINACEAE; COMMON NAME, LAUREL)

C. alliodora, a large hermaphroditic, moth-pollinated tree (Bawa et al. 1985), is widespread on the Atlantic and Pacific coasts of Central America. Boshier et al. (1995) estimated gene flow in a dense, nearly monospecific population located on the Atlantic slope near Pavones, Turrialba, Costa Rica. First, they documented pollen movement with a rare allele that occurred in a single tree within the study site. They also used standard paternity analyses. Both procedures indicated that most of the pollen was dispersed within 75 m of its source but that 3 percent of the pollen movements were beyond 280 m (table 3.1).

CEDRELA ODORATA (MELIACEAE; COMMON NAME, SPANISH CEDAR)

C. odorata is a functionally monoecious canopy tree that is locally abundant in the dry forests of Costa Rica. Its small white flowers are thought to be moth-pollinated (Bawa 1985). James et al. (1998) conducted a study of the mating system of C. ordorata in the highly fragmented dry forests of Coto Brus in southern Costa Rica. C. ordorata is predominantly outcrossing even in very small fragmented populations. One tree isolated in a pasture more than 300 m from the nearest conspecific successfully set outcrossed fruit. Evidently, its small-moth pollinators disperse pollen over several hundred meters of disturbed habitat.

CONCLUSIONS CONCERNING POLLEN MOVEMENT

In each of the studies just described, pollen was often dispersed over a minimum of several hundred meters. These results are in stark contrast to the predictions of early tropical biologists who felt that most tropical tree species were self-compatible and inbred (Corner 1954; Baker 1959; Federov 1966) but are consistent with observations (e.g., Janzen 1971; Stiles 1975; Frankie et al. 1976) that tropical forest pollinators move large distances between conspecific individuals. The high species diversity of tropical forests often produces situations in which conspecifics are separated by a few hundred meters. As a result, their pollinators have evolved the ability to locate and fly between trees separated by several hundred meters. Furthermore, in contrast to the findings of Ghazoul et al. (1998) on *Shorea siamensis* from Thailand, forest fragmentation does not appear to prevent intertree movement by the pollinators of Neotropical dry-forest tree species. Pollinator visitation to single isolated trees indicates that pollinators fly long distances over disturbed habitats to reach flowering individuals. In some cases pollinator movement may have increased, perhaps in response to lower tree densities (Murawski and Hamrick 1991; Stacy et al. 1996). The more limited pollen movement documented by Boshier et al. (1995) for a dense population of *Cordia alliodora* is consistent with such conclusions.

These genetic-marker-based studies do not, however, provide information on whether pollinator visitation rates and fruit set are quantitatively lower for isolated trees. The available evidence indicates that pollinator visitation rates may be, on average, lower for trees in disturbed habitats (e.g., *Andira inermis;* Frankie et al. 1997) and that probably, as a result, fruit set is lower for these trees (e.g., *S. siamensis;* Ghazoul et al. 1998; *E. cyclocarpum;* Rocha and Aguilar 2001b).

CONSERVATION IMPLICATIONS

Estimates of gene flow rates into fragmented populations of tropical dry-forest tree species are quite high. It is therefore tempting to generalize from these results that forest fragmentation has had or will have few adverse effects on the maintenance of genetic diversity in these disturbed landscapes. Such generalizations are unwarranted, however, because the reproductive biology of other species may not be consistent with these results. A case in point is a study by Aldrich and Hamrick (1998) of *Symphonia globulifera* populations located in a fragmented premontane wet forest near San Vito, Coto Brus, in southern Costa Rica. In this area *S. globulifera* is predominantly hummingbird-pollinated and bat-dispersed. Using microsatellite loci to reconstruct genealogies of seedlings established in a 1-ha fragment, Aldrich and Hamrick (1998) demonstrated that more than 50 percent of the gametes within these seedlings originated from two trees located in an adjacent pasture. Similar analyses of seedlings and saplings in nearby undisturbed forests indicated that parentage was more evenly spread among adults in these sites. Evidently, the release from competition of the pasture trees led to increased flower production. The larger floral resource apparently led to the formation of territories by hummingbirds that typically move in a trap-line fashion among several adults in undisturbed forests. Bats concentrate seeds of pasture trees below feeding roosts in the nearby fragment. Thus, for certain tropical tree species, forest fragmentation can change pollinator behavior and adversely affect the genetic composition of subsequent generations. Our generally inadequate knowledge of the natural history and reproductive biology of tropical dry-forest tree species will therefore make generalizations concerning the effects of forest fragmentation on genetic diversity a chancy proposition.

At a scale of several kilometers, outcrossing tropical trees have approximately 95 percent of their total genetic diversity within their populations (Hamrick and Loveless 1989). This result is consistent with direct estimates of high rates of gene movement in undisturbed, continuously distributed forests (table 3.1). Assuming that these populations were in gene flow-drift equilibrium prior to fragmentation, the number of migrants per generation (*Nm*) would be approximately 4.75, well above the level (*Nm* > 1) at which genetic drift would be the predominate factor influencing genetic structure. Superficially it would appear that the high rates of pollen flow observed among fragmented Neotropical dry-

forest tree populations should maintain the genetic structure seen in continuous, relatively undisturbed forests. However, a pollen flow rate of 50 percent represents a gene flow rate of 25 percent (i.e., 50% of the gametes come from local maternal trees, 25% of the gametes are locally produced male gametes, and 25% are immigrant male gametes). In a forest fragment with five adults and an effective population size (N_e) of four (owing to uneven male and female reproductive success) that experiences a 50 percent rate of pollen flow, N_em would equal 1.0 (i.e., 4×0.25). At gene flow-drift equilibrium, 20 percent of the total genetic diversity would reside among populations. Thus, as a result of fragmentation, genetic differentiation among populations might increase fourfold assuming that gene flow rates and effective population sizes are constant. In addition, low-frequency alleles may be lost, and inbreeding may increase. Estimates of *Nm* for fragmented populations of *E. cyclocarpum* are consistent with this example (Apsit 1998). Thus, even the high rates of observed pollen flow may not be adequate to prevent changes in the genetic composition of small, fragmented populations of dry-forest trees.

Isolated individuals appear to play a significant role in the overall breeding populations of tropical trees. Not only are such individuals reservoirs of genetic diversity, but also they contribute pollen and perhaps even seeds to nearby fragments, increasing effective sizes of these populations. Often when management decisions are being made for a region, the primary focus is to preserve large, undisturbed habitats. Isolated trees and small fragments are often regarded as unimportant and are destroyed. If the studies presented earlier are generally applicable, the loss of these lone trees could have significant negative effects on breeding populations. Similarly, destruction or extinction of fragmented populations reduces overall size of a breeding population. Not only will genetic diversity be lost to the metapopulation of fragments, but the active role of isolated individuals or fragment populations in the local breeding populations of the species will also be lost. It is possible that loss of a few key individuals or of whole fragments may produce a domino effect that further decreases effective population sizes of remaining fragments, increasing the influence of genetic drift and inbreeding on their genetic composition.

does not provide the information needed to understand fully and predict the long-term evolutionary and ecological responses of tropical dry-forest trees to the human-modified landscapes they now occupy.

RESEARCH PRIORITIES

The use of genetic markers to describe patterns of mating within populations of Neotropical tree species produces quantitative estimates of selfing and outcrossing rates in viable seeds, of the genetic relatedness of individuals, and of the rates and patterns of gene movement. Availability of such genetic markers allows unprecedented insights into many aspects of the reproductive biology of tropical tree species. However, these analyses provide little or no information on other aspects of the reproductive biology of these species. For example, genetic-marker-based approaches do not provide information on the proportion of flowers receiving pollen, the proportion of flowers that produce mature fruits or viable seeds, or the relative viability of seeds or seedlings produced by trees experiencing different habitat conditions. Nor do genetic-marker-based studies provide insights into the effects of changes in the quantity or quality (or both) of pollinators. Genetic markers allow us to quantify the final results of a number of processes that influence the breeding structure of populations, but they do not provide insights into how these results came about.

To understand more completely the effects of habitat disturbance and population fragmentation on the reproductive biology of species, studies that thoroughly integrate observations of pollinator visitation and pollen deposition with experiments and observations of fruit and seed set are needed. These analyses should be coupled with quantitative estimates of the population genetic parameters (e.g., gene flow) that result. Such integrated studies should be performed on species with varying densities, distributions, pollinators, and the like so that robust comparisons and generalizations can be generated. The largely piecemeal approach of the past

REFERENCES

Aldrich, P. R., and J. L. Hamrick. 1998. Reproductive dominance of pasture trees in a fragmented tropical forest mosaic. *Science* 281:103–5.

Apsit, V. J. 1998. Fragmentation and pollen movement in a Costa Rican dry forest tree species. Ph.D. diss., University of Georgia. 122 pp.

Apsit, V. J., J. L. Hamrick, and J. D. Nason. 2001. Breeding neighborhood size of a Costa Rican dry forest tree species. *Journal of Heredity* 92: 415–20.

Baker, H. G. 1959. Reproductive methods as factors in speciation in flowering plants. *Genetics and Twentieth Century Darwinism: Cold Spring Harbor Symposium on Quantative Biology* (24th), 177–99. Cold Spring Harbor, N.Y.: Cold Spring Harbor Laboratory.

Bawa, K. S. 1974. Breeding systems of tree species in a lowland tropical community. *Evolution* 28: 85–92.

Bawa, K. S., S. H. Bullock, D. R. Perry, R. E. Coville, and M. H. Grayum. 1985. Reproductive biology of tropical lowland rain forest trees. II. Pollination systems. *American Journal of Botany* 72: 346–56.

Bierregaard, R. O. J., T. E. Lovejoy, V. Kopos, A. A. dos Santos, and R. W. Hutchings. 1992. The biological dynamics of tropical rainforest fragments: A prospective comparison of fragments and continuous forest. *BioScience* 42:859–66.

Boshier, D. H., M. R. Chase, and K. S. Bawa. 1995. Population genetics of *Cordia alliodora* (Boraginaceae), a neotropical tree. 3. Gene flow, neighborhood and population structure. *American Journal of Botany* 82:484–90.

Chase, M. R., C. Moller, R. Kessell, and K. S. Bawa. 1996. Distant gene flow in tropical trees. *Nature* 383:398–99.

Corner, E. J. H. 1954. The evolution of tropical forests. In *Evolution as a process*, ed. J. Huxley, A. C. Hardy, and E. B. Ford, 34–46. London: Allen and Unwin.

Federov, A. A. 1966. The structure of the tropical rain forest and speciation in humid tropics. *Journal of Ecology* 54:1–11.

Frankie, G. W., P. A. Opler, and K. S. Bawa. 1976. Foraging behavior of solitary bees: Implications for outcrossing of a neotropical forest tree species. *Journal of Ecology* 64:1049–57.

Frankie, G. W., S. B. Vinson, M. A. Rizzardi, T. L. Griswold, S. O'Keefe, and R. R. Snelling. 1997. Diversity and abundance of bees visiting a mass flowering tree species in disturbed seasonal dry forest, Costa Rica. *Journal of the Kansas Entomological Society* 70:281–96.

Ghazoul, J., K. A. Liston, and T. J. B. Boyle. 1998. Disturbance induced density-dependent seed set in *Shorea siamensis* (Dipterocarpaceae), a tropical forest tree. *Journal of Ecology* 86:462–73.

Hamrick, J. L. 1994. Genetic diversity and conservation in tropical forests. In *Proceedings: International Symposium on Genetic Conservation and Production of Tropical Forest Tree Seed: 14–16 June 1993, Chiang Mai, Thailand,* ed. R. M. Drysdale, S. E. T. John, and A. C. Yopa, 1–9. Muak-Lek, Saraburi, Thailand: ASEAN-Canada Forest Tree Centre.

Hamrick, J. L., and M. D. Loveless. 1989. The genetic structure of tropical tree populations: Association with reproductive biology. In *Plant evolutionary biology,* ed. J. H. Bock and Y. B. Linhart, 131–46. Boulder, Colo.: Westview Press.

Hamrick, J. L., and D. A. Murawski. 1990. The breeding structure of tropical tree populations. *Plant Species Biology* 5:157–65.

Harris, L. D. 1984. *The fragmented forest: Island biogeography theory and the preservation of biotic diversity.* Chicago: University of Chicago Press. 211 pp.

James, T., S. Vege, P. Aldrich, and J. L. Hamrick. 1998. Mating systems of three tropical dry forest tree species. *Biotropica* 30:587–94.

Janzen, D. H. 1971. Euglossine bees as long-distance pollinators of tropical plants. *Science* 171:203–5.

———. 1982. Variation in average seed size and fruit seediness in a fruit crop of a Guanacaste tree (Leguminosae: *Enterolobium cyclocarpum*). *American Journal of Botany* 69:1169–78.

———. 1983. *Costa Rican natural history.* Chicago: University of Chicago Press. 816 pp.

Kendrick, J., and R. B. Knox. 1989. Pollen-pistil interactions in Leguminosae (Mimosoideae).

In *Advances in legume biology,* ed. C. H. Stirton and J. L. Zarucci, 1–31. Monographs in Systematic Botany 29. St. Louis: Missouri Botanical Garden.

Koptur, S. 1984. Outcrossing and pollinator limitation of fruit set: Breeding systems of neotropical Inga trees (Fabaceae: Mimosoideae). *Evolution* 38:1130–43.

Levin, D. A. 1995. Plant outliers: An ecogenetic perspective. *American Naturalist* 145:109–18.

Loveless, M. D. 1992. Isozyme variation in tropical trees: Patterns of genetic organization. *New Forests* 6:67–94.

Murawski, D. A., and J. L. Hamrick. 1991. The effect of density of flowering individuals on the mating systems of nine tropical tree species. *Heredity* 67:167–74.

Nason, J. D., and J. L. Hamrick. 1997. Reproductive and genetic consequences of forest fragmentation: Two case studies of neotropical canopy trees. *Journal of Heredity* 88:264–76.

Opler, P. A., and K. S. Bawa. 1978. Sex ratios in tropical forest trees. *Evolution* 32:812–21.

Rocha, O., and G. Aguilar. 2001a. Variation in the breeding behavior of the dry forest tree, *Enterolobium cyclocarpum* (guanacaste) in Costa Rica. *American Journal of Botany* 88:1600–1606.

———. 2001b. Reproductive biology of the dry forest tree *Enterolobium cyclocarpum* Jacq. (Guanacaste) in Costa Rica: A comparison between trees left in pastures and trees in continuous forest. *American Journal of Botany* 88:1607–14.

Stacy, E. A., J. L. Hamrick, J. D. Nason, S. P. Hubbell, R. B. Foster, and R. Condit. 1996. Pollen dispersal in low-density populations of three neotropical tree species. *American Naturalist* 148:275–98.

Stiles, G. F. 1975. Ecology, flowering phenology, and hummingbird pollination of some Costa Rican *Heliconia* species. *Ecology* 56:285–301.

Young, A., T. Boyle, and T. Brown. 1996. The population genetic consequences of habitat fragmentation for plants. *Trends in Ecology and Evolution* 11:413–18.

CHAPTER 4

Impact of Global Changes on the Reproductive Biology of Trees in Tropical Dry Forests

Kamaljit S. Bawa

THE MOST SPECTACULAR feature of tropical dry forests of Guanacaste is perhaps the mass flowering of many tree species during the dry season. As the dry season begins toward the end of December, a number of species start to bloom, displaying flowers of various shapes, sizes, and colors in the leafless canopy until the end of April (Janzen 1967; Frankie et al. 1974). The seasonal progression of flowering of various species is also mirrored in the daily rhythms, as flowers of various species start opening at dawn, progress through the morning, and then are replaced by nocturnally flowering species at dusk. Since almost all tree species are animal-pollinated, the activity of various pollinators—insects, birds, and mammals—is tied to the phenology of flowers of their host plants, providing a kaleidoscope of plant-pollinator interactions resulting from millions of years of coevolution (Frankie et al. 1983; chapter 2). Flower-pollinator interactions are only one of many interactions involved in the reproductive processes of tropical plants. Before

flowers mature and after fruits initiate development, many insects protect reproductive parts of the plants (Bentley 1977). Following seed and fruit development, a wide variety of animals disperse seeds (Howe and Smallwood 1982). Immature and mature seeds and fruits are subject to predation by a diverse array of invertebrates and vertebrates, and such interactions in turn have profound effects on the structure and diversity of tropical forests (Janzen 1970; Connell 1971).

The complex plant and animal interactions are being affected by global environmental change, resulting principally from deforestation and forest fragmentation, climate change, and invasive species. In particular, mutualistic interactions between plants and animals, so vital to the reproduction and survival of both groups of organisms, are likely to be disrupted with severe consequences on the composition of tropical biota. Here, I focus on the effects of deforestation and forest fragmentation on reproductive processes of forest trees in tropical dry forests of

Costa Rica. I address the following questions: (1) What are the effects of habitat loss and habitat fragmentation on plant-pollinator interactions? (2) What are the consequences of changes in plant-pollinator interactions caused by anthropogenic pressures on the reproductive output and mating systems of plants? (3) What are the cumulative effects of changes in reproductive processes on fitness of plant populations and eventually on species composition of tropical dry forests? I start with a consideration of various threats to tropical forests, then briefly review the reproductive processes, and finally discuss how these processes might be affected by various forces that threaten tropical forests, primarily habitat changes.

THREATS

Tropical dry forests may be among the most threatened of all terrestrial ecosystems. These ecosystems are more suited for agriculture and human settlements than wet evergreen forests because the pronounced dry season can restrain the growth of insect pests and weeds (Janzen 1973). As a result, dry forests throughout the world have disappeared at a rapid rate. In the Western Hemisphere only 0.09 percent of the tropical dry forests that existed when the Spaniards colonized the continent are now under some form of protection, and only 2 percent of the area is sufficiently intact to be of interest to conservationists (Janzen 1988).

Contemporary threats to tropical dry forests have multiple origins. Deforestation and forest fragmentation, caused by a host of social and economic factors (Brown and Pearce 1994; Bawa and Dayanandan 1997 and the references therein) are the main factors. Apart from land-use changes in the form of deforestation and habitat fragmentation, forests are being degraded by extraction of timber and nontimber forest products (Chambers et al. 1989; Vasquez and Gentry 1989; Nepstad et al. 1992; Clay 1997). Anthropogenic effects also include the introduction and spread of exotic invasive species, which can further influence the distribution and

abundance of native species (Mooney and Hobbs 2000). Finally, global climate change is likely to alter forest structure and composition with unknown consequences for the biodiversity and function of dry forests (Bawa and Dayanandan 1998).

REPRODUCTIVE PROCESSES

PHENOLOGY

Flowering phenology of trees in tropical dry forests is strongly seasonal and, as expected, correlates with the phenology of their insect pollinators. A vast majority of dry-forest tree species are pollinated by bees, and the seasonal flowering of many bee-pollinated tree species in the dry months is now well documented in dry forests in different parts of the world (Janzen 1967; Bullock and Solís Magallanes 1980; Frankie et al. 1983; Sivaraj and Krishnamurthy 1989). Flowering of moth-pollinated species is also seasonal. The number of moth-pollinated species increases steadily from April, which marks the beginning of the wet season; it peaks in the wet season and then declines (Haber and Frankie 1989; chapter 2).

Strongly seasonal flowering and associated phenologies of pollinators are products of many years of evolution and are influenced by a variety of biotic and abiotic factors. Abiotic mechanisms mediating flowering are expected to be diverse (Janzen 1967; Frankie et al. 1974; Borchert 1983; Bullock 1995). Nevertheless, water stress in the dry season seems to play an important role in triggering flowering (Borchert 1983, 1998). Thus climate change and habitat alterations that modify rainfall patterns and soil moisture, as discussed later in this chapter, are expected to initiate a cascade of effects on flowering, pollinators, and mating patterns, thereby affecting the fitness of both plant and pollinator populations.

MATING SYSTEMS

Most dry-forest trees are obligately outcrossed. Bawa (1974) showed that in Guanacaste a vast majority of tree species with hermaphroditic flowers (78%) are self-incompatible. Dioecious species characterized by separate male and female plants account for 22 percent of all tree species (Bawa and Opler 1975). Genetic analyses of mating systems have also revealed high levels of outcrossing (Boshier et al. 1995a; James et al. 1998; chapters 3 and 16). Foraging ranges of pollinators (see later in this chapter) and estimation of gene flow suggest that extensive gene exchange occurs over large distances among canopy trees (Boshier et al. 1995a; chapters 3 and 16). Thus habitat alterations can have a marked effect on outcrossing rates and genetic diversity in trees.

POLLINATORS

Dry-forest tree species display a tremendous diversity of pollination mechanisms. Pollinators range from small wasps, less than 1 mm in length, to large bats with a wing span of more than 1 m in the Old World tropics. Many tree species in the dry forests of Guanacaste are pollinated by medium-sized to large bees (Frankie et al. 1983) and many others by moths (Haber and Frankie 1989) and bats (Heithaus et al. 1975) (see also chapter 2). In most species, pollination mechanisms are specialized in the sense that plants are pollinated by a restricted set of vectors, belonging to the same genus or same family (but see Johnson and Steiner 2000). Our inability to distinguish actual pollinators from a wide array of floral visitors to a particular plant species has been a major impediment to determining the extent of specialization. The almost total dependence on animal pollen vectors makes tree species vulnerable to changes affecting the habitats and populations not only of the trees but also of their pollinators, which require a wide array of natural habitats for persistence of their populations.

FORAGING RANGES OF POLLINATORS

There are extensive data on foraging ranges of pollinators of dry-forest species. Janzen (1971) was among the first to suggest that large bees, the major pollinators of most tree species, forage over long distances. Frankie et al. (1976) empirically

demonstrated that certain bee species can move within hours between trees as far away as 0.8 km. Similarly, bats, the principal pollinators of many tree species in the dry forest, are known to forage over distances of several kilometers in a single night (Heithaus et al. 1975). Africanized honeybees have been shown to transport pollen more than 20 km among trees in Amazonia (Dick 2001), though generally their foraging ranges are within a 2 km radius. Studies utilizing genetic markers show that long-distance foraging does result in long-distance gene flow by pollen (Boshier et al. 1995b; Chase et al. 1996; Nason et al. 1998). Genetic analyses of populations also reveal frequent migrations among populations via pollen and seeds (chapter 3).

Apart from extensive foraging ranges of many tropical pollinators, several pollen vectors migrate among habitats that may be spread over vast areas. For example, in Guanacaste, moths that pollinate many tree species in the rainy season migrate to adjacent wet evergreen forests in the dry season (Janzen 1987; chapter 8). There is extensive migration of moths and butterflies across the continental divide at the end of the dry season. Foraging across diverse habitats can also occur on a daily basis. Many moths captured in Monteverde, in montane forests, have been found to carry pollen from trees in the dry forests to surrounding lowlands (chapter 8).

EFFECTS OF DEFORESTATION AND FOREST FRAGMENTATION

In considering the effects of various forces that threaten tropical dry forests, it is important to emphasize a few points at the outset. First, there is a great deal of uncertainty about effects such as global climate change. Models of climate change make predictions of changes in greenhouse gasses, temperature, rainfall, and other parameters at spatial scales much larger than scales typically used for ecological studies. Second, for threats such as invasive species, there are relatively few data on the effects of exotics on the reproductive biology of other species. Third, effects of many threats are similar. For example, deforestation, fragmentation, degradation, and invasive species all are expected to reduce the amount of total habitat for certain species, reduce population sizes of many species, increase the prospect of drift or inbreeding (or both), and alter species composition. Fourth, several factors are likely to interact synergistically with one another, further compounding deleterious effects induced by one or more factors. The discussion that follows pertains largely to effects of deforestation and forest fragmentation.

REPRODUCTIVE OUTPUT

Reproductive output may be reduced as a result of several factors associated with the loss and degradation of dry tropical forests. Reduction could occur owing to effects on flowering, abundance of pollinators, and mating systems. Decreased output may set in motion changes in recruitment patterns, eventually influencing species composition.

Flowering. Global climate change may influence flowering phenology of tropical plant species (Bawa and Dayanandan 1998; Borchert 1998; Corlett and LaFrankie 1998). As mentioned earlier, most tree species in dry forests flower during the dry season. One predicted effect of climate change in Central America is the extension of the dry season (Hulme and Viner 1998). Data also indicate that the amount of rainfall in Guanacaste has steadily decreased over the past 70 years (Borchert 1998: fig. 4). Such a reduction may indirectly lead to an increase in the intensity of the dry season, through a decrease in soil moisture, which is an important determinant of flowering time and duration (Borchert 1983, 1998). Changes in duration, intensity, and the onset of the dry season are likely to affect the phenology of species flowering in the dry months as well as those flowering in the interphase of dry and wet seasons. Alterations may be manifested as changes in the timing, intensity, and duration of flowering.

Long-term phenological data are required to assess effects of climate change. Such data for other tropical forests reveal significant alteration in the reproductive behavior of plants; however,

the trends are not consistent. Wright (1999) observed high levels of fruit production in El Niño years—1969, 1992, 1997—in a wet forest in Panama, but the fruit production declined in 1970, 1993, and 1998, the years following the El Niño years. Wright attributes the high production of fruit to higher amounts of light available during the prolonged drought in the El Niño years. The drought itself is assumed to trigger flowering. Lower levels of fruit production in 1970, 1993, and 1998, according to Wright, may be due to exhaustion of reserves during the preceding years of high fruit production. Effects of fluctuations in fruit size on population dynamics of plants have not been investigated in these forests.

Pollinator Populations. Shifts in timing and duration of flowering could have marked effects on pollinator populations. In 1998, following the El Niño year of 1997, the intensity of flowering was reduced in trees in Guanacaste. Reduction in food resources influenced the abundance of bees almost throughout the dry season (G. Frankie pers. comm.).

Deforestation and forest fragmentation are also likely to result in the decline of pollinator populations, simply owing to loss of food resources and nesting habitats. The decline in pollinator populations may, however, be disproportionate to the loss of forest habitat for three reasons. First, many pollinators require habitat heterogeneity over hundreds of square kilometers for persistence. Thus, for example, if pollinators utilize a range of forest types, population numbers may decrease with the destruction of one or more forest types, even though a given forest type may not suffer any attrition. Second, many factors may act synergistically. Fragmentation, for instance, may increase the probability of fire (Malcolm 1998), which in turn may reduce floral resources without affecting the total forest area. Fires can also affect nesting sites for bees (Frankie et al. 1997). Third, factors responsible for deforestation and forest degradation may have a ripple effect on processes involved in plant-pollinator interactions. Dryness due to fragmentation, increased incidence of fire, or climate change may adversely affect nesting sites, leading to a reduction in pollinator populations, which in turn may eventually lead to reproductive failure of host plants and, in the case of annual plants, fewer floral resources for the next generation of pollinators. Negative feedback loops, once established, can severely reduce numbers of pollinators.

Decline in the abundance of pollinators has been suspected in ecosystems throughout the world (Nabhan 1996; Allen-Wardell et al. 1998). For dry forests of Guanacaste, Frankie and his associates have studied changes in bee populations over many years (Frankie et al. 1997; Vinson et al. 1997). Frankie et al. (1997) compared the number of bee species and their abundance on the same trees in 1972 and 1996. Over the 24-year period, the number of bee species captured declined from 70 to 28, and the average number of individuals sampled per tree decreased from 824 ± 210 to 92 ± 5, or about 90 percent (chapter 6).

Deforestation, habitat fragmentation, increased incidence of fire, and introduction of exotic species (Frankie et al. 1997) have apparently led to a marked reduction in populations of a wide variety of native bees over the 24-year period. The major factor in deforestation has been conversion of forestland to pasture for raising cattle (Frankie et al. 1997). Negative effects of this land-use change on native biota have been compounded by the introduction of the exotic *jaragua* grass, *Hyparrhenia rufa,* which has spread over large areas. As forest fires burn trees and shrubs, the grass invades resulting open areas, increasing fuel loads for future fires. Thus, deforestation, the exotic grass, and fire interact to reduce floral resources. Moreover, fires burn deadwood and important habitat for cavity and ground-nesting bees (Frankie et al. 1997; chapter 6).

Except for bees, populations of pollinators have not been monitored in tropical forests. Pollinators with large foraging ranges are expected to be the most susceptible to decline in the quality and quantity of habits because such pollen vectors depend for their survival on a range of heterogeneous habitats over a large geographi-cal area. As mentioned earlier, nectarivorous bats and hawkmoths in Guanacaste may forage over several kilometers in a single night and require a diverse array of habitats to sustain themselves. Little is known, however, about changes in the abundance of these pollen vectors.

Decline in the abundance of pollinators should be reflected in changes in seed and fruit set of plant species. Although there are no temporal data on alterations in reproductive output, many authors have documented reductions in seed and fruit set in fragmented habitats (Kearns et al. 1998; Paton 2000). In the dry deciduous forests of Guanacaste, Rocha and Aguilar (2001) have compared seed and fruit sets of *Enterolobium cyclocarpum,* and trees in pastures have lower seed and fruit sets than those in contiguous forests.

Apart from quantity, the quality of the seed can also be affected. In a lowland tropical wet forest in the Sarapiqui region of Costa Rica, seed germination in *Pithecellobium elegans* in degraded forests and pastures was lower than in contiguous forests (K. Bawa unpubl. data). Although comparable data from dry forests of Guanacaste are lacking, Rocha and Aguilar (2001) found that seedlings of *Enterolobium cyclocarpum* in pastures have less vigor than those from trees in contiguous forests.

Mating Systems. Effects on seed germination may be a manifestation of changes in mating systems, or the alle effect. Decrease in pollinator abundance by itself may have only limited effect on seed viability. Most tropical tree species are self-incompatible, or dioecious. Self-incompatibility, however, is not absolute. There is a certain proportion of individuals or seeds on the same individuals that result from selfing (Bawa 1974). Although decline in pollinator populations may increase the proportion of seeds that result from selfing and these selfed seeds may have lower germination rates than outcrossed seeds, low viability is likely to result from increased inbreeding.

Inbreeding in forests affected by deforestation, fragmentation, degradation, and invasive species may increase in two ways. First, population size may be considerably reduced in fragmented habitats, and the incidence of mating among neighbors or relatives may increase. Second, in degraded forests, the density of individuals may decrease. Reduction in density may lead to alterations in foraging behavior of pollinators. For example, Franceschinelli and Bawa (2000) found that when density is low, hummingbirds move less frequently among plants than when the density is high. As a result, the progeny arrays show a higher rate of inbreeding than plants in high-density patches.

Thus, change in phenology or pollinator abundances can have a cascade of effects leading to fewer and more inbred seeds than those in contiguous forests. The smaller quantities of seeds that are highly inbred may have a low viability and lead to a decrease in regeneration. Poor regeneration may further decrease the density of adult plants, resulting in ever increasing losses in reproductive output and more inbreeding. Interestingly, although there is a clear relationship between changes in phenology and plant fitness, no study has documented the direct link between changes in reproductive parameters arising from human disturbance of one type and fitness as manifested by a decrease in regeneration or the density of individuals.

GENETIC DIVERSITY

Changes in pollinator abundance and mating systems of plants are also expected to influence genetic diversity of tree populations. Fragmented populations, considerably reduced in size, may lose genetic variation as a result of inbreeding and genetic drift. The rate and extent of loss may be determined by gene flow via pollen and seed among populations. Gene flow via pollen in tropical trees is extensive. In contiguous forests, pollen vectors can transport pollen among conspecific trees over long distances. As a result, interbreeding individuals in a population can cover vast areas of tens of square kilometers, if not more.

The impact of deforestation and other forces threatening tropical forests may be greater on gene flow via seed than on movement of genes via pollen. First, seed dispersal is more limited

than pollen dispersal. Most seeds fall in the vicinity of the parent tree (Howe and Smallwood 1982), and many tree species have no known mechanisms of dispersal (Van der Pijl 1982). Further, a large proportion of tropical trees have wind-dispersed seeds with no mechanism of long-distance dispersal, except during storms and hurricanes. Second, the seeds of many species are dispersed by nonflying mammals that may not readily move across inhospitable habitats separating fragmented forests. Even in contiguous forests, individuals over as large an area as 10 ha may all be derived from a single maternal parent (Hamilton 1999). Thus, forest fragmentation is likely to severely curtail gene flow via seed in many species.

Deforestation and forest fragmentation may also reduce genetic diversity of populations in relatively large contiguous reserves. Although population sizes of tropical trees are not known, it is known that gene flow via pollen is extensive. Trees in fragments surrounding contiguous forests may be a part of the same population and contribute to the maintenance of genetic diversity within contiguous forests. With increasing deforestation, fragments may disappear over time, reducing overall population size.

Extraction, too, can alter genetic diversity of populations. First, extraction can lower population density with a concomitant increase in inbreeding as described earlier. Second, extraction can lead to dysgenic selection of harvested populations if extracted individuals are more vigorous and the degree of vigor is positively correlated with heterozygosity.

CHANGES IN SPECIES COMPOSITION

The deleterious effects of deforestation and forest fragmentation should lead to a decline in the fitness of populations and eventually to the local extinction of tree species. Is there any evidence that species have become locally extinct in tropical dry forests as a result of contemporary anthropogenic pressures? There are two lines of evidence that suggest such extinctions may be common.

First, dioecious species may be more prone to extinction as a result of fragmentation than hermaphroditic species for two reasons. In small fragments, sex ratios may become heavily biased in favor of one sex. Imbalances in sex ratio could reduce effective population size and ultimately fitness. In addition, a greater proportion of dioecious species have fleshy fruits and are animal-dispersed rather than hermaphroditic species (Bawa 1980). Specialized vertebrate frugivores may be absent in small fragments. Indeed, Gillespie (1999) has found that the proportion of dioecious species in a number of Central American forests is positively correlated with fragment size.

Second, Ganeshaiah et al. (1998) compared the proportion of species whose seeds are dispersed by animals and wind in a dry deciduous forest in two locations, one closer to human settlements and the other farther away. They found that forests closer to human settlements have a greater proportion of wind-dispersed tree species than forests farther away from settlements. The implication is that the absence of animal dispersal agents in areas inhabited by humans leads to domination of the flora having an unusually high representation of wind-dispersed species.

Both examples demonstrate that changes in forest composition may be subtle and, in general, may lead to depauperization of biological diversity.

RECOMMENDATIONS

Climate change, fragmentation and degradation of habitats, and invasive species are likely to have profound consequences on biotic interactions involved in the reproduction of trees. I have considered only consequences for plant-pollinator interactions and the concomitant effects on mating patterns and genetic diversity of trees. Undoubtedly there are consequences for many other biological processes and interactions. The cumulative and synergistic effects of global changes in climate, habitats, and the composition of biota due to the introduction of alien species have the potential to influence various aspects of ecosystem structure and function.

The ongoing changes call for two types of responses. First, policy makers need to take appropriate action to stem the pace of global change resulting from climate change, habitat loss, and introduction of invasive species. Vinson et al. (chapter 6) further elaborate on this response. Second, the scientific community needs to undertake appropriate research to reduce uncertainty about effects of changes, accumulate adequate evidence for predicted changes, and present clear options to policy makers for mitigation measures (chapter 24).

Only long-term phenological records can indicate the extent to which climate change has or will affect phenological patterns of plants. Yet there are few, if any, places in the world where well-designed studies that quantify flowering and fruiting on a long-term basis are under way. Ironically, many authors associated with this volume were involved in long-term phenological studies in the 1960s, but the studies were discontinued because of lack of funding and the perception by funding agencies at the time about the value of long-term phenological studies. Now, 25 years later, many funding agencies and others believe that such studies are critical for assessment of possible effects of climate change.

Long-term phenological studies must be accompanied by monitoring of pollinators. Except for medium-sized to large solitary bees in the Neotropics (Frankie et al. 1997), there are no data on long-term trends in the abundance of tropical pollinators. Several questions need to be addressed: Are populations of pollinators declining? Is the reduction in number disproportionate to the reduction in the habitat? Do various classes of pollinators differ in their sensitivity to changes resulting from habitat loss, alterations in climate, and the introduction of alien species?

Other issues relate to possible reduction in pollinator abundance on the fitness of plants. Here we have virtually no data. Roubik (2000) cites studies that show reduction in seed and fruit set in plants in nonforested habitats resulting possibly from displacement of pollinators by Africanized honey bees. However, we also need to document trends in seed and fruit production in plants in natural habitats to assess how natural communities are being affected by an overall decline in pollinators. Furthermore, alterations in mating patterns of plants and the attendant effects on genetic diversity of plant populations due to decline in pollinators remain unexplored.

Clearly an integrated approach is required. First, we need to frame questions regarding the relative and synergistic impact of habitat loss, climate change, and the introduction of alien species, both plants and animals, on pollinators. Second, we need to frame specific hypotheses to examine effects of abundance on plant-pollinator interactions and plant fitness and how changes in interactions and fitness may in turn influence population and community structure. Long-term studies at specific sites on specific groups of pollinators and plants pollinated by these vectors are required. The resolution of scientific issues will be critical to the eventual success of mitigation measures that might be designed to counter losses in populations of pollinators and to preserve the integrity of plant pollinator interactions.

REFERENCES

Allen-Wardell, G., et al. 1998. The potential consequences of pollinator decline on the conservation of biodiversity and stability of food crop yields. *Conservation Biology* 12:8–17.

Bawa, K. S. 1974. Breeding systems of tree species of a lowland tropical community. *Evolution* 28: 85–92.

———. 1980. The evolution of dioecy in flowering plants. *Annual Review of Ecology and Systematics* 11:15–40.

Bawa, K. S., and S. Dayanandan. 1997. Causes of tropical deforestation and institutional constraints to conservation. In *Tropical rain forest: A wider perspective,* ed. B. Goldsmith, 175–98. London: Chapman and Hall.

———. 1998. Climate change and tropical forest genetic resources. *Climate Change* 23:449–66.

Bawa, K. S., and P. A. Opler. 1975. Dioecism in tropical forest trees. *Evolution* 29:167–79.

Bentley, B. 1977. The protection function of ants visiting extrafloral nectarines of *Bxca orellan* L. (Biscaceae). *Journal of Ecology* 65:27–38.

Borchert, R. 1983. Phenology and control of flowering in tropical trees. *Biotropica* 15:81–89.

———. 1998. Responses of tropical trees to rainfall seasonality and its long-term changes. *Climate Change* 39:381–93.

Boshier, D. H., M. R. Chase, and K. S. Bawa. 1995a. Population genetics of *Cordia alliodora* (Boraginaceae), a neotropical tree. 2. Mating system. *American Journal of Botany* 82: 476–83.

Boshier, D. H., M. R. Chase, and K. S. Bawa. 1995b. Population genetics of *Cordia alliodora* (Boraginaceae), a neotropical tree. 3. Gene flow, neighborhood, and population substructure. *American Journal of Botany* 82:484–90.

Brown, K., and D. W. Pearce, eds. 1994. *The causes of tropical deforestation: The economic and statistical analysis of factors giving rise to the loss of the tropical forests.* London: University College Press. 338 pp.

Bullock, S. H. 1995. Plant reproduction in neotropical dry forests. In *Seasonally dry tropical forests,* ed. S. H. Bullock, H. A. Mooney, and E. Medina, 277–303. Cambridge: Cambridge University Press.

Bullock, S. H., and J. A. Solís Magallanes. 1980. Phenology of canopy trees of tropical deciduous forests in Mexico. *Biotropica* 15:292–94.

Chambers, R. C., N. C. Saxena, and T. Shah. 1989. *To the hands of the poor: Water and trees.* Boulder, Colo.: Westview Press. 273 pp.

Chase, M. R., C. Moller, R. Kesseli, and K. Bawa. 1996. Distant gene flow in tropical trees. *Nature* 383:398–99.

Clay, J. 1997. The impact of palm harvest in the Amazon estuary. In *Harvesting wild species: Implications for biodiversity conservation,* ed. C. H. Freese, 283–314. Baltimore: John Hopkins University Press.

Connell, J. H. 1971. On the role of natural enemies in preventing competitive exclusion in some marine mammals and in rain forest trees. In *Dynamics of populations,* ed. P. J. Boer and G. Gradwell, 298–312. Proceedings of the Advanced Study Institute on Dynamics of Numbers in Populations, Oosterbeck, 1970. Wageningen, Netherlands: Center for Agricultural Publishing and Documentation.

Corlett, R. T., and J. V. LaFrankie Jr. 1998. Potential impacts of climate change in tropical Asian forests through an influence on phenology. *Climate Change* 39:439–53.

Curran, L. M., I. Caniago, G. D. Paoli, D. Astianti, M. Kusneti, M. Leighton, C. E. Nirarita, and H. Haeruman. 1999. Impact of El Niño and logging on canopy tree recruitment in Borneo. *Science* 286:2184–88.

Dick, C. 2001. Genetic rescue of remnant tropical trees by an alien pollinator. *Proceedings of the Royal Society of London* B. 268:2391–97.

Franceschinelli, E. V., and K. S. Bawa. 2000. The effect of ecological factors on the mating system of a South American shrub species (*Helicters brevispira*). *Heredity* 84:116–223.

Frankie, G. W., P. A. Opler, and H. G. Baker. 1974. Comparative phenological studies of trees in wet and dry forests in the lowlands of Costa Rica. *Journal of Ecology* 62:881–919.

Frankie, G. W., P. A. Opler, and K. S. Bawa. 1976. Foraging behavior of solitary bees: Implications for outcrossing of a neotropical forest tree species. *Journal of Ecology* 64:1049–57.

Frankie, G. W., W. A. Haber, P. A. Opler, and K. S. Bawa. 1983. Characteristics and organization of the large bee pollination system in the Costa Rican dry forest. In *Handbook of experimental pollination biology*, ed. C. E. Jones and R. J. Little, 411–47. New York: Van Nostrand-Reinhold.

Frankie, G. W., S. B. Vinson, M. A. Rizzardi, T. L. Griswold, S. O'Keefe, and R. R. Snelling. 1997. Diversity and abundance of bees visiting a mass flowering tree species in disturbed seasonal dry forest, Costa Rica. *Journal of the Kansas Entomological Society* 70:281–96.

Ganeshaiah, K. N., R. Uma Shaanker, K. S. Murali, Uma Shankar, and K. S. Bawa. 1998. Extraction of nontimber forest products in the forests of Biligiri Rangan Hills, India. 5. Influence of dispersal mode on species response to anthropogenic pressures. *Economic Botany* 52:316–19.

Gillespie, M. B. 1999. Plant life history characteristics and rarity in tropical dry forest fragments of Central America. *Journal of Tropical Ecology* 15:637–49.

Haber, W. A. 1984. Pollination by deceit in a mass-flowering tropical tree *Plumerica rubra* L. (Apocynaceae). *Biotropica* 16:269–75.

Haber, W. A., and G. W. Frankie. 1989. A tropical hawkmoth community: Costa Rican dry forest Sphingidae. *Biotropica* 21:155–72.

Hamilton, M. B. 1999. Deforestation affects the genetic structure of the surviving forest fragments. *Nature* 401:129–30.

Heithaus, E. R., T. H. Fleming, and P. A. Opler. 1975. Foraging patterns and resource utilization in seven species of bats in a seasonal tropical forest. *Ecology* 56:841–54.

Howe, H. F., and J. Smallwood. 1982. Ecology of seed dispersal. *Annual Review of Ecology and Systematics* 13:201–28.

Hulme, M., and D. Viner. 1998. A climate change scenario for the tropics. *Climate Change* 39:145–70.

James, T., S. Vege, P. Aldrich, and J. L. Hamrick. 1998. Mating systems of three tropical dry forest species. *Biotropica* 30:587–94.

Janzen, D. H. 1967. Synchronization of sexual reproduction of trees within the dry season in Central America. *Evolution* 21:620–37.

———. 1970. Herbivores and the number of tree species in tropical forests. *American Naturalist* 104:501–28.

———. 1971. Euglossine bees as long-distance pollinators of tropical plants. *Science* 171:203–5.

———. 1973. Tropical agroecosystems. *Science* 182:1212–19.

———. 1987. How moths pass the dry season in a Costa Rican dry forest. *Insect Science and Its Application* 8:498–500.

———. 1988. Tropical dry forests, the most endangered major tropical ecosystem. In *Biodiversity*, ed. E. O. Wilson, 130–37. Washington, D.C.: National Academy Press.

Johnson, D., and J. E. Steiner. 2000. Generalization versus specialization in plant pollination systems. *Tree* 15:140–43.

Kearns, C., D. Inouye, and N. Waser. 1998. Endangered mutualisms: The conservation of plant-pollinator interactions. *Annual Review of Ecology and Systematics* 29:83–112.

Malcolm, J. R. 1998. A model of conductive heat flow in forest edges and fragmented landscapes. *Climate Change* 39:487–502.

Mooney, H. A., and R. J. Hobbs, eds. 2000. *Invasive species in a changing world*. Washington, D.C.: Island Press. 457 pp.

Nabhan, G. P. 1996. *Pollinator redbook. Vol. 1: Global list of threatened vertebrate wildlife species serving as pollinators for crops and wild plants*. Tucson: Arizona-Sonora Desert Museum and Forgotten Pollinators Campaign Monographs.

Nason, J. D., E. Allen Herre, and J. L. Hamrick. 1998. The breeding structure of a tropical keystone plant resource. *Nature* 391:685–87.

Nepstad, D. C., F. Brown, L. Luz, A. Alechandra, and V. Viana. 1992. Biotic impoverishment of Amazonian forests by rubber tapers, loggers, and cattle ranchers. In *Non timber products from tropical forests: Evaluation of a conservation and development strategy*, ed. D. C. Nepstad and S. Schwartzman, 1–14. New York: New York Botanical Garden.

Nepstad, D. C., A. Verissimo, A. Alencar, C. Nobre, E. Lima, P. Lefebvre, P. Schlesinger, C. Potter, P. Moutinho, E. Mendoza, M. Cochrane, and V. Brooks. 1999. Large-scale impoverishment of Amazonian forests by logging and fire. *Nature* 398:505–8.

Opler, P. A., G. W. Frankie, and H. G. Baker. 1980. Comparative phenological studies of treelet and shrub species in tropical wet and dry forests in the lowlands of Costa Rica. *Journal of Ecology* 68:167–88.

Paton, D. C. 2000. Disruption of bird pollination systems in southern Australia. *Conservation Biology* 14:1232–34.

Rocha, O. J., and G. Aguilar. 2001. Reproductive biology of the dry forest tree *Enterolobium cyclocarpum* (Guanacaste) in Costa Rica: A comparison between trees left in pastures and trees in continuous forests. *American Journal of Botany* 88:1607–14.

Roubik, D. W. 2000. Pollination system stability in tropical America. *Conservation Biology* 14:1235–36.

Sivaraj, N., and K. V. Krishnamurthy. 1989. Flowering phenology in the vegetation of Shervaroys, South India. *Vegetation* 79:85–88.

Van der Pijl, L. 1982. *Principles of dispersal in higher plants.* Berlin: Springer-Verlag.

Vasquez, R., and A. H. Gentry. 1989. Use and misuse of forest-harvested fruits in the Iquitos area. *Conservation Biology* 3:350–61.

Vinson, S. B., H. J. Williams, G. W. Frankie, and G. Shrum. 1997. Floral lipid chemistry of *Byrsonima crassifolia* (Malpigheaceae) and a use of floral lipids by *Centris* bees (Hymenoptera: Apidae). *Biotropica* 29:76–83.

Wright, S. J. 1999. El Niño events influence plant reproduction in a wet tropical forest. *CTFS News* (Center for Tropical Science, Smithsonian Institution, Washington, D.C.) (Summer 1999): 10.

CHAPTER 5

Tropical Dry-Forest Mammals of Palo Verde

ECOLOGY AND CONSERVATION IN A CHANGING LANDSCAPE

Kathryn E. Stoner and Robert M. Timm

MESOAMERICA CONTAINS some of the world's most diverse forests. It has at least 20 major life zones, based on variations of temperature and precipitation that can be broadly summarized in five tropical forest types—dry forest, wet forest, montane forest, coniferous forest, and mangrove swamp (Holdridge et al. 1971). When the Spaniards arrived in the New World, there were perhaps 550,000 km² of dry forest on the Pacific side of lowland tropical Mesoamerica. This dry forest occupied as much or more of the Mesoamerican lowlands as did wet forests. Unfortunately, no habitat type in Mesoamerica has been more influenced by humans than the tropical dry forest; today less than 1 percent remains intact, with less than 0.01 percent under protection.

In Costa Rica tropical dry forests occur throughout the Pacific lowlands of Guanacaste Province and adjacent Puntarenas Province from sea level to about 500 m. Costa Rica's dry forest is characterized by a five- to six-month dry sea-

son from December through May, an annual precipitation of approximately 1,500 mm, and an average annual temperature higher than 24°C (Maldonado et al. 1995). These dry forests are largely deciduous today and encompass heterogeneous habitats varying in species composition, abundance, rainfall, and soils. These characteristics contribute to creating a harsh and heterogeneous, yet seasonally resource-rich, environment for the native mammals.

Mesoamerica has a diverse mammal fauna that includes elements from both North and South America as well as endemic species. More than 275 species in 28 families are recognized from the region, at least 17.8 percent of which are endemic to Mesoamerica. The mammals of the tropical dry forest are among the most poorly known of any of the bioclimatic life zones. Mammals that inhabit tropical dry-forest areas must be capable of dealing with high temperatures (to 40–41°C), very low precipitation in the dry season, and large fluctuations in the availability of food resources over time. Most mammals of the dry forest can be characterized as resident generalists that shift their diets to utilize seasonally available food resources, as resident specialists that forage on insects, seeds, or fruit and nectar, or as migrants that occupy dry forests only seasonally and migrate to different habitats during periods of low food availability in search of available food sources.

As in all tropical ecosystems, a wide variety of mammals contribute to the maintenance of dry tropical forests through their role in seed dispersal and pollination (Heithaus et al. 1975; Chapman 1989; Helversen 1993; see chapter 13). Bats visit, and presumably pollinate, at least 14 species of flowers in the tropical dry forest of Palo Verde, and 29 species of fruits are consumed by bats, which in turn disperse their seeds (K. Stoner and R. Timm unpubl. data). In Guanacaste there are two peak periods of flowering activity: one during the long dry season and the other during the middle of the rainy season (Frankie et al. 1974). Primates, many rodents, and several generalist carnivores also are important seed dispersers in Costa Rica's tropical dry forests. Thus the preservation of wildlife and its habitats are interrelated challenges, and conservation efforts in Guanacaste's tropical dry forests need to consider both of these issues together.

DIVERSITY, DISTRIBUTION, AND ENDEMISM

At least 207 species of mammals, including 110 species of bats, have been documented within Costa Rica's borders, and more will undoubtedly be discovered (Timm 1994; Rodríguez and Chinchilla 1996; Timm and LaVal 1998; Timm et al. 1999). The majority of mammals found in Costa Rica's tropical dry forest are distributed northward through Mesoamerica (sometimes as far as western Mexico), and many occur southward into South America. Of the approximately 114 species of mammals originally present in Guanacaste's tropical dry forest, perhaps 110 are still found in this habitat. Bats are by far the most diverse group, with more than 66 species, followed by 11 species of rodents, 7 species of marsupials, 6 species in the weasel family, 5 species of cats, 3 species in the raccoon family, 3 species of primates, 3 species of artiodactyls, 2 species of canids, 2 species of xenarthrans (edentates), 1 rabbit (*Sylvilagus floridanus*), and 1 tapir (*Tapirus bairdii*). Species reaching the southern boundary of their distribution in Costa Rica's dry forest include opossum (*Didelphis virginiana*), gray sac-winged bat (*Balantiopteryx plicata*), gray short-tailed bat (*Carollia subrufa*), long-tongued bat (*Glossophaga leachii*), Salvin's spiny pocket mouse (*Liomys salvini*), slender harvest mouse (*Reithrodontomys gracilis*), harvest mouse (*R. paradoxus*), and hooded skunk (*Mephitis macoura*). Raccoons (*Procyon lotor*), coyotes (*Canis latrans*), Mexican porcupines (*Coendou mexicanus*), and Underwood's long-tongued bats (*Hylonycteris underwoodi*) are found as far south as southwestern Panama. No species reaches the northern limit of its distribution in Costa Rica's dry forest.

Dry forests are believed to be less diverse than wet forests because of the harsh seasonal environment. However, in Costa Rica the documented mammal fauna of the Pacific lowlands consists of 114 species, which is only slightly lower than that of lowland rain forest of La Selva in northeastern Costa Rica, with 123 species (Timm 1994; R. Timm unpubl. data). The dry forest has 66 species of bats and La Selva 67 species. The pattern of lower diversity in tropical dry-forest habitats has been observed in Mexico for other groups of vertebrates (Ceballos 1995) as well as for flora (Gentry 1995).

Most of the resident mammal species of the dry forest are generalists that have a broad diet allowing them to survive changes in food abundance. Some of these generalists include mantled howler monkeys (*Alouatta palliata*), white-faced capuchins (*Cebus capucinus*), white-tailed deer (*Odocoileus virginianus*), coyotes, white-nosed coatis (*Nasua narica*), raccoons, opossums, and some frugivorous bats. Although howler monkeys are mainly folivorous and are selective of the leaves they ingest, they can consume more than 60 different species of plants within any one area (Glander 1978), allowing them sufficient flexibility to find food throughout the year. During the driest months, when more than 80 percent of the trees have lost their leaves, howlers may still find edible leaves in some of the evergreen species such as *Cecropia peltata* and the wild cashew *Anacardium excelsum*. White-faced capuchins also fare well in the dry forest even when fruit is scarce at the beginning of the rainy season because they then shift their diet to consume mostly insects (Chapman 1988), which are especially abundant at this time (Janzen and Wilson 1983). Capuchins also consume other sources of protein, such as birds' eggs, young birds, and baby coatis. Although white-tailed deer populations in dry forests experience periodic crashes during particularly harsh years, deer are browsers and consume many species of both herbaceous and woody plants and are thus well adapted to cope with the dry tropical forest environment (Vaughan and Rodríguez 1991). Coyotes consume significant amounts of insects, fruits, and grasses in tropical dry forests, and their diet varies seasonally in Costa Rica (Vaughan and Rodríguez 1986), as it does throughout their range. Coatis, raccoons, and opossums are generalists and consume a wide variety of invertebrates (especially insects), fruits, seeds, and smaller vertebrates such as frogs and snakes. Some frugivorous bats, such as Seba's short-tailed fruit bat (*Carollia perspicillata*), consume more insects during periods in which fruit is not available (Fleming 1988; but see the section "Migratory Species" later in this chapter).

Several dry-forest specialists with specific diets are present throughout the year. These include various species of insectivorous bats (funnel-eared bats [*Natalus stramineus*], leaf-chinned bats [*Pteronotus* spp.]), the smaller rodents, and several carnivores. Seasonal migrants that are more abundant during certain periods of the year when specific food sources are present include spider monkeys (*Ateles geoffroyi*) and some nectarivorous (*Glossophaga* spp.) and frugivorous bats (Stoner 2001).

Costa Rica's mammal fauna includes several species that are endemic to the country, including at least six rodents, two shrews, and one bat; these species are found at mid- and high elevations (Timm 1994). All species that historically were found in the dry forest of Costa Rica also were found in the dry forest of adjacent Nicaragua or farther north; thus Costa Rica has no truly endemic dry-forest mammals. However, one species of harvest mouse (*R. paradoxus*) is a dry-forest endemic restricted to the Pacific lowlands of Costa Rica and Nicaragua. In contrast to Costa Rica, tropical dry forests in western Mexico contain as many as 26 endemic mammal species (Ceballos 1995).

EXTIRPATED SPECIES

It is likely that more than 114 mammal species historically were present in the dry forest of Guanacaste. Although most of these can still be found in some areas of this dry forest, several have been extirpated from the Palo Verde region and throughout much of Costa Rica's Pacific lowlands during the past several decades. These include the water opossum (*Chironectes minimus*), giant anteater (*Myrmecophaga tridactyla*), Hoffmann's two-toed sloth (*Choloepus hoffmanni*), the brown-throated three-toed sloth (*Bradypus variegatus*), grison (*Galictis vittata*), southern river otter (*Lutra longicaudis*), white-lipped peccary (*Tayassu pecari*), and Baird's tapir (*Tapirus bairdii*).

Giant anteaters were once found throughout Costa Rica from the Pacific and Caribbean coasts to nearly the highest elevations (Timm et al. 1989). Populations of giant anteaters have been severely reduced throughout their range in the past several decades as a result of overhunting and habitat destruction. Giant anteaters must be considered extremely rare in Costa Rica and in danger of extinction.

Water opossums and southern river otters, and perhaps grisons, require fresh running streams. River otters are still present in Lomas Barbudal, Hacienda Monteverde, on the Corobicí River, and at Parque Nacional Guanacaste. We have historical reports of otters in the Cañas River near its confluence with the Tempisque River, and we suspect that they were found throughout the Tempisque River Basin. Although we have no specific records of water opossums and grisons in Palo Verde, we strongly suspect that they were present historically, as they were widely distributed in both the Pacific and Caribbean lowlands from sea level to mid-elevations. It is likely that stream contamination and erosion caused by both the sugarcane and rice industries in this region contributed significantly to the disappearance of these aquatic and semiaquatic animals from much of the Pacific lowlands.

There have been no observations of white-lipped peccaries or tapirs reported in the Palo Verde region for several decades. David Stewart informed us that during the 1950s tapirs were found only as far west as the vicinity of the Pan American Highway, and neither species was at Palo Verde. Both tapirs and white-lipped peccaries are still found in the tropical dry forest of Parque Nacional Guanacaste, but they are best considered extirpated from the vast majority of the Guanacaste lowlands.

Although we do not have the historical documentation of how widely distributed two-toed sloths and three-toed sloths were in the tropical dry forest, we suspect that they were much more widely distributed when there were larger expanses of mature forest. Mature stands of tropical dry forest would provide a variety of tree species that would be seasonally available for the folivorous sloths as well as cool, shady habitat. Because sloths have a low metabolic rate, maintain a low body temperature, and are imperfect homeotherms (McNab 1985), they may be physiologically less able to survive in the harsh, hotter, drier habitats created by opening up mature stands of tropical dry forest. It is likely that sloths in the dry forest originally occupied riparian habitats that provided both evergreen trees for them to forage on throughout the year and shade for thermoregulation. Forested areas surrounding riparian habitats throughout the Guanacaste lowlands have been largely destroyed owing to the development of agriculture. Costa Rican law prohibits the destruction of habitat within 15 m of rivers (Law No. 7575, Article No. 33); however, this is not enforced, and in most agricultural areas the crops often run up to the rivers' edge.

With such a diverse group of species having disappeared from Palo Verde, it is informative to ask what traits these taxa share that may account for their extirpation or susceptibility. The species that are extirpated are all either highly prized game species that have been eliminated by over-hunting (white-lipped peccaries and tapirs) or specialists that either feed on specific foods or have very specific habitat requirements. In general, species that first disappear from a region following alterations are those that have a large body size, low initial population density, large territory size, or narrow habitat tolerance.

ENDANGERED SPECIES

Costa Rica recognizes 13 species of mammals as endangered species in the country—the mantled howler monkey, spider monkey, squirrel monkey (*Saimiri oerstedii*), giant anteater, jaguar (*Panthera onca*), puma (*Puma concolor*), ocelot (*Leopardus pardalis*), margay (*Leopardus wiedii*), oncilla (*Leopardus tigrinus*), jaguarundi, West Indian manatee (*Trichechus manatus*), white-lipped peccary, and tapir (MINAE 1999). An additional 14 species of mammals are recognized as being found in reduced populations. Of these, 7 are found within the dry forest of Costa Rica—the great false vampire bat (*Vampyrum spectrum*), white-faced capuchin, Hoffmann's two-toed sloth, Deppe's squirrel (*Sciurus deppei*), Underwood's pocket gopher (*Orthogeomys underwoodi*), grison, and southern river otter. Additionally, several species that are especially sensitive to habitat destruction and forest fragmentation include spider monkeys, felids, and predaceous bats of the family Phyllostomidae, subfamily Phyllostominae. Spider monkeys require a large home range because of their dietary preference for ripe fruits (Chapman 1988, 1989). Habitat fragmentation not only necessitates that they must travel farther to find the required ripe fruit resources but also sometimes eliminates arboreal passages that allow access to resources. Felids also require a large home range based on their carnivorous diet. The need to pass through open areas in a fragmented landscape makes them more vulnerable to illegal hunting. Previous studies on the predaceous phyllostomine bats have shown that they are sensitive to habitat destruction, and some species are rarely found in disturbed environments (Timm 1994; Schulze et al. 2000). Our data on bat populations in the dry forest suggest that a number of species are rare in this habitat and should be considered as endangered (table 5.1).

MIGRATORY SPECIES

Seasonal migrations along elevational gradients have been well documented for several species of tropical birds and butterflies; however, it only recently has been suggested that migrations may occur in Neotropical bats (Timm and LaVal 2000; Stoner 2001, 2002). The abundance of several species of bats at Palo Verde changes significantly over seasons, suggesting that they shift habitats seasonally or migrate into and out of the region (Stoner 2001).

Bats were mist-netted at Palo Verde approximately once every three weeks from January 1994 through July 1997, for a total of 56 nights. A total of 1,245 individuals representing 47 species were captured at one site, the Guayacán waterhole (10°21' N, 85°20' W) (table 5.1). All netting at the waterhole was with ground-level mist nets, which are excellent for sampling most frugivores, nectarivores, and some insectivores but underestimate higher-flying insectivores. Because Palo Verde has a marked dry season, bats are concentrated around waterholes, and sampling there produces a higher number of taxa and greater numbers of individuals than would be expected to be captured at any one site in the surrounding forest. Including our data from netting at Palo Verde, which began in the 1970s and continues to the present, we have captured or observed an additional 12 species in the area, for a total of 59 species.

Significant differences occur in abundances (estimated as bats/m^2FD net × hour) of the most common frugivorous bats over different seasons.

The frugivorous Seba's short-tailed fruit bat and the Jamaican fruit-eating bat (*Artibeus jamaicensis*) account for more than 50 percent of the bats captured at this site. An additional 12 species account for 40 percent of captures, whereas the majority of species (33) account for less than 10 percent of total captures, and most of these were captured on fewer than 5 nights of the 56 nights sampled. Excluding the aerial insectivores, of the 10 species captured only once, there were 4 nectarivores, 3 carnivores, 2 gleaning insectivores, and 1 frugivore. Although mist-net data do not accurately sample the abundance of aerial insectivores, they provide useful data for comparing relative abundance of most other bat species within a community. Our mist-netting efforts at Palo Verde suggest that several of the nectarivorous and predaceous bats are found at very low densities, likely a result of disturbance within Palo Verde (i.e., fire and cattle), lack of mature trees, habitat fragmentation surrounding Palo Verde, and lack of forested corridors within the region.

Patterns of capture for some other species of bats also suggest that abundances vary seasonally. The pygmy fruit-eating bat (*Artibeus phaeotis*) and Thomas' fruit-eating bat (*Artibeus watsoni*) were never captured in March, April, May, July, or August. The wrinkled-faced bat (*Centurio senex*) was captured in December (1995), January (1996), and February (1996, 1997) but rarely in August (one individual was captured in August 1995). The insectivorous orange-throated bat (*Micronycteris brachyotis*) was caught from December through April (and two individuals in July), and the tiny big-eared bat (*Micronycteris minuta*) was caught from January through April (and one was captured in June). Although sample sizes for these species were not sufficient to compare statistically, their abundance over seasons and the fact that the same pattern was observed over several years suggest that most of these species are likely moving in and out of the area on a seasonal basis. These patterns of abundance and absence are not one of source/sink because individually marked animals return after months of absence (Stoner 2001).

TABLE 5.1
Abundance of 47 Species of Bats Captured at the Guayacán Water Hole
in Palo Verde from January 1994 through July 1997

SPECIES	TOTAL NUMBER CAUGHT	PERCENT OF TOTAL BATS CAUGHT	NUMBER OF NIGHTS CAUGHT	PERCENT OF NIGHTS CAUGHT
Carollia perspicillata	472	37.9	47	84
Artibeus jamaicensis	174	13.9	40	71
Sturnira lilium	111	8.9	33	59
Artibeus lituratus	65	5.2	27	48
Rhogeessa tumida	49	3.9	17	30
Pteronotus davyi	47	3.8	17	30
Glossophaga soricina	43	3.4	17	30
Artibeus phaeotis	38	3.0	21	38
Centurio senex	38	3.0	11	20
Micronycteris brachyotis	37	3.0	15	27
Artibeus watsoni	25	2.0	14	25
Pteronotus parnellii	17	1.4	12	21
Natalus stramineus	16	1.3	9	16
Desmodus rotundus	13	1.0	8	14
Pteronotus gymnonotus	11	0.9	9	16
Trachops cirrhosus	10	0.8	8	14
Micronycteris minuta	9	0.7	8	14
Uroderma bilobatum	7	0.6	2	4
Carollia brevicauda	6	0.5	4	7
Noctilio leporinus	6	0.5	4	7
Platyrrhinus helleri	5	0.4	2	4
Micronycteris microtis	5	0.4	5	9
Carollia castanea	4	0.3	4	7
Lasiurus blossevillii	4	0.3	NA	NA
Vampyressa nymphaea	4	0.3	4	7
Micronycteris nicefori	3	0.2	3	5
Micronycteris schmidtorum	3	0.2	3	5
Chrotopterus auritus	2	0.2	2	4
Diphylla ecaudata	2	0.2	2	4
Tonatia brasiliensis	2	0.2	2	4
Glossophaga commissarisi	1	0.08	1	2

TABLE 5.1 *(continued)*

SPECIES	TOTAL NUMBER CAUGHT	PERCENT OF TOTAL BATS CAUGHT	NUMBER OF NIGHTS CAUGHT	PERCENT OF NIGHTS CAUGHT
Glossophaga leachii	1	0.08	1	2
Pteronotus personatus	1	0.08	1	2
Noctilio albiventris	1	0.08	1	2
Macrophyllum macrophyllum	1	0.08	1	2
Phyllostomus discolor	1	0.08	1	2
Vampyrum spectrum	1	0.08	1	2
Hylonycteris underwoodi	1	0.08	1	2
Carollia subrufa	1	0.08	1	2
Lichonycteris obscura	1	0.08	1	2
Micronycteris hirsuta	1	0.08	1	2
Cyttarops alecto	1	0.08	NA	NA
Rhynchonycteris naso	1	0.08	NA	NA
Saccopteryx bilineata	1	0.08	NA	NA
Myotis elegans	1	0.08	NA	NA
Myotis riparius	1	0.08	NA	NA
Molossus molossus	1	0.08	NA	NA
Balantiopteryx plicata[a]				
Saccopteryx leptura[a]				
Diclidurus albus[a]				
Chiroderma villosum[b]				
Peropteryx kappleri[b]				
Peropteryx macrotis[b]				
Myotis albescens[b]				
Myotis nigricans[b]				
Eumops auripendulus[c]				
Molossus ater[c]				
Molossus pretiosus[c]				
Molossus sinaloae[c]				
Micronycteris sylvestris[d]				
Mimon cozumelae[d]				
Mimon crenulatum[d]				
Tonatia bidens[d]				

TABLE 5.1 *(continued)*

SPECIES	TOTAL NUMBER CAUGHT	PERCENT OF TOTAL BATS CAUGHT	NUMBER OF NIGHTS CAUGHT	PERCENT OF NIGHTS CAUGHT
Tonatia silvicola[d]				
Uroderma magnirostrum[d]				
Vampyrodes caraccioli[d]				
Eumops underwoodi[d]				
Total	1,245			

Note: All data presented in this table are based on 56 nights of netting. Species listed as NA (not applicable) refer to aerial insectivores whose abundance is poorly estimated with mist-netting techniques and thus would be underestimated by our sampling method. Twelve additional species that are listed were observed or captured within the area, and eight additional species listed are expected to occur at Palo Verde (see individual notes).
[a]Bats observed roosting within the area.
[b]Bats captured within the dry forest in the Palo Verde region.
[c]Species detected by their echolocation signals (E. Kalko pers. comm.).
[d]Species that are expected to be found in Palo Verde.

At Palo Verde, Peter's tent-making bat (*Uroderma bilobatum*) also exhibits a seasonal pattern in abundance and reproduction (Timm and Lewis 1991 and subsequent observations by Timm through January 2003). During June and July (mid–rainy season) adult males and females as well as juvenile bats are present in a breeding colony. All adult females captured during the mid–rainy season were either pregnant or lactating. During January and February (dry season), only a couple or in most cases no bats were observed. The few bats that were captured during the dry season were males with testes only moderately developed.

Although we have not yet identified where the bats are moving when they are not in the area, we suspect two areas. The first possibility is that during periods of reduced resource availability bats change habitats to riparian areas within the lowland forest of Guanacaste, possibly near the Bebedero River, Piedras River, or Tempisque River. Another possibility is that bats in the lowland tropical dry forest migrate elevationally to higher areas with more abundant resources during certain seasons.

In addition to bats, some arboreal and terrestrial mammals of the tropical dry forest are migratory. Spider monkeys are present in Palo Verde only during the rainy season and appear to migrate out of the area during the dry season. Fruit availability is strongly seasonal here (Frankie et al. 1974), and the migration of spider monkeys is probably related to the lack of abundant fruit resources during the dry season. Large herds of white-lipped peccaries originally were found in the dry forests of Guanacaste and also were migratory (Janzen 1986). We suspect that the peccary herds would have fed heavily on the seasonally abundant acorns (*Quercus oleoides*) and palm fruits such as *Acrocomia vinifera*, *Attalea butyracea* (= *Scheelea rostrata*), *Bactris major*, and *B. minor*.

FACTORS AFFECTING MAMMALS OF THE TROPICAL DRY FOREST

HUNTING

Hunting and deforestation were the first important influences on the recent distribution and density of mammals of the tropical dry forest, as they were in other areas within the Neotropics. All large and some small mammals in tropical dry forests have been subjected to extreme hunting pressures. The Chorotega, the dominant pre-Columbian human inhabitants of the Guanacaste lowlands, hunted a wide variety of mammals (Quesada López-Calleja 1980). The most common mammals hunted today as a source of protein in the lowlands of Guanacaste include white-tailed deer, pacas (*Agouti paca*, known in Costa Rica as *tepezcuintle*), collared peccaries (*Pecari tajacu*), armadillos (*Dasypus novemcinctus*), and opossums. Pacas are highly prized but infrequently obtained because they occur in such low numbers. Hunters with whom we have spoken are opportunistic, taking any of the preferred game animals when they are available.

Poaching continues to be one of the most serious problems that threaten Parque Nacional Palo Verde, and this is largely attributed to the lack of guards to protect this approximately 20,000 ha park (Vaughan et al. 1995). White-tailed deer and collared peccaries are the most common animals poached in the park. Most illegal poaching occurs within protected areas such as Palo Verde because these areas provide the best wildlife habitat and consequently the highest densities of game species. In 1997 in the Area de Conservación Tempisque, of the hunters arrested for poaching, approximately three were released for every one that was actually convicted (MINAE 1998). Poaching likely will continue in national parks and other protected areas until more park personnel are available to monitor these areas and stronger laws are enacted and enforced to protect wildlife.

DEFORESTATION AND CONVERSION OF TROPICAL DRY FOREST

The single factor that has most strongly influenced the current distribution and abundance of mammals in the dry forest is land conversion—the loss of tropical dry forest. Conversion of tropical dry forest in Costa Rica has resulted from various activities, including cattle ranching, the timber industry, agricultural development, and the tourism industry (see chapter 21). Regardless of the reasons for deforestation, the result has been the creation of vast expanses of open pastures, agricultural fields,

fragmented-forested habitats, and extensive areas in various stages of succession. Hence, large areas of land are only marginally inhabitable by most native species. Opening up forest in the harsh, highly seasonal environment of this area has had additional consequences, including a subsequent increase in dryness, higher temperatures, reduced availability of appropriate forest habitat for both food resources and living space for mammals, and erosion of topsoil, which limits nutrients. The few fragments of dry forest that remain in Costa Rica have all been influenced by the surrounding habitat alterations.

Much of the recent conversion is due to agricultural development, especially sugarcane and rice production. Sugarcane fields, not present in the Guanacaste area until the 1960s, accounted for approximately 16 percent of the area in the basin by 1992–93, and rice and other agricultural crops accounted for an additional 13.9 percent. The lower Tempisque Basin is one of the areas that has been designated by the Ministerio de Agricultura y Ganaderia and the Servicio Nacional de Aguas Subterraneas Riego y Avenamiento as a rice production area, and many pastures and small forest fragments are being converted to rice fields. Because of the extensive rice fields between Palo Verde and Lomas Barbudal, the movement of most terrestrial mammals between these two important reserves is no longer possible.

CATTLE, *JARAGUA*, FIRE, CATTAILS, AND LAND MANAGEMENT

It is our intent here to review briefly the history of cattle use and the introduction of African grasses in the region and to assess their impact on native mammals. In recent years, the use of cattle as a habitat management tool in Palo Verde has been the source of considerable controversy (McCoy 1994; McCoy and Rodríguez 1994; Stern et al. 2002; see chapter 21). Cattle ranching has been important in Guanacaste for more than three centuries, and all of what is now Parque Nacional Palo Verde was a working cattle ranch until the creation of the wildlife refuge in 1977. Cattle were slowly removed from the refuge during the period 1978–81 (when it was designated a national park); however, some cattle were reintroduced into Palo Verde in 1987 as part of an active management plan to control cattails (*Typha dominguensis*—locally called *enea*), which had expanded dramatically and quickly in the lagoon, effectively eliminating much of the open water needed by waterfowl. In 1991 more cattle were introduced into Palo Verde as part of a management plan to control fires within the park. During the late 1990s, some 1,500 to 6,000 head of cattle were present in the park, with some 600 head in the Palo Verde lagoon and the rest in forested areas and pastures.

One of the earliest ranches in what is now Costa Rica and adjacent Nicaragua was established at Santa Rosa in the late 1500s (Janzen 1986). By 1800, large ranches were present throughout Guanacaste (Boucher et al. 1983). Cattle were raised in Guanacaste primarily for the hides, which were exported to Europe for use as leather; to a lesser extent lard and dried beef also were exported. The *finqueros* (ranch hands) hunted native mammals, especially peccaries, for food and killed jaguars, pumas, and coyotes because they were a threat to livestock.

The rapid deforestation of Costa Rica's dry forest during the 1950s, 1960s, and 1970s, converting mature forest into pastureland, was encouraged by low-interest loans from the national banks, as well as by support from the Agency for International Development and the World Bank (Parsons 1983). During this rapid expansion of the cattle industry, ranchers experimented with several breeds, progressing from the Spanish criollo to various beef breeds, including Herefords, Angus, and Charolais. Today, zebus and Brahman are found throughout the lower elevations of Costa Rica, as well as throughout the Neotropics, because they are well adapted to the hot climate and extremes of rainy and dry seasons and are highly resistant to bites from ticks, flies, and other arthropods.

Jaragua, or African star grass (*Hyparrhenia rufa*), and other African savanna grasses were introduced into Costa Rica in the 1920s as cattle forage because the native Costa Rican grasses

are not well adapted for large-scale production in open pastures (Sáenz-Maroto 1955; León S. et al. 1982). The *jaragua*, which came to Central America via Brazil, was introduced into the Palo Verde area from Puntarenas in the 1920s (Sáenz-Maroto 1955; Parsons 1972). As in all C_4 grasses, the nutrient levels of growing stems and leaves during the rainy season are high, and the young grasses provide good forage for cattle (McCammon-Feldman 1980); however, the mature plants during the dry season have little nutritional value (Daubenmire 1972) and are not consumed by cattle. This species is native to the plains of Africa, grows to a height of 2 m or more, and is highly adapted to fires. Throughout the Neotropics, regular burning was, and continues to be, a management strategy to remove mature, nondigestible woody stems during the dry season, promoting growth during the succeeding rainy season. This practice has been the source of numerous uncontrolled fires since its introduction into the area. The fuel provided by this non-native grass allows the fires to burn hotter and to be more destructive than they are by the burning of native vegetation.

C_4 grasses such as *jaragua* grow best in warm, dry conditions, and they mature much more quickly than C_3 grasses. Tall C_4 grasses often become so dense that other plant species are unable to compete. Annual burning of dry aboveground vegetation releases nitrogen, enriching the soil for more dominant C_4 grasses, enhancing their growth and allowing them to outcompete other plant species (Collins et al. 1998). Fires also warm the soil, which favors the growth of C_4 grasses. In temperate prairies of the midwestern United States, annually burned watersheds had the lowest plant species richness, as burning increases the dominance of C_4 grasses and reduces plant species diversity (Collins et al. 1998).

In tropical rain forests of the Amazon Basin, fires have been found to create a positive feedback system whereby periodic burning causes an increase in fuel loading, fire intensity, and fire susceptibility (Cochrane et al. 1999). The first fires characteristically kill only the smaller trees, especially those with thin bark. Because of fuel buildup, second fires are faster moving and more intense, often killing larger, thicker-barked trees. The long-term effect of recurrent fires in Brazil is to create an open canopy savanna or scrub habitat. In the Mesoamerican dry forest, several tree species with smooth, photosynthetic bark (especially species such as *Bursera simaruba*) are often killed by the first fires. Although some tree species that have bark of medium thickness, such as *Guazuma ulmifolia, Crescentia alata, Byrsonima crassifolia,* and *Curatella americana,* may survive initial burns, continued exposure to surface fires from adjacent pastures eventually penetrates and eliminates the forest (B. Williamson pers. comm.).

Forest fragments have persisted only where they have been protected by humans or by natural firebreaks such as roads and limestone outcrops. Remnant trees, such as *cenizero* (*Samanea saman*) and *guanacaste* (*Enterolobium cyclocarpum*), can be found in pastures, but usually only as older, isolated individuals. Recruits into pastures are limited to a few species, namely, *Byrsonima crassifolia, Crescentia alata, Curatella americana,* and *Guazuma ulmifolia.* These four species are widespread as tree islands throughout the pastures of Mesoamerica and provide some of the few fruits and roost sites available for wildlife in this anthropogenic landscape (Hartshorn 1983).

The development of large-scale cattle ranching in Guanacaste in the early 1900s, combined with the introduction of *jaragua,* not only reduced the available forested habitats for mammals but also stimulated a series of other changes that dramatically affected the remaining habitat and fauna. Previous studies on cattle document that livestock alter ecosystem processes by reducing the cover of herbaceous plants and litter, disturbing and compacting soils, reducing water infiltration rates, and increasing soil erosion (Belsky and Blumenthal 1997). Furthermore, they suggest that forests subjected to grazing pressure are less resilient to natural disturbances such as fire and diseases.

Other direct effects of cattle include competition with native mammalian herbivores (Janzen and Wilson 1983; Robinson and Bolen 1984) and selective grazing on many native plant species. Cattle directly compete with deer for forage, and inadequate habitat may be available for native wildlife because of intensive cattle grazing. A number of previous studies in other habitats demonstrate that competition with cattle may increase annual deer mortality by as much as 40 percent (Robinson and Bolen 1984). Conklin (1987), in a study of several species of plants that are potential browse for cattle at La Pacifica, found that cattle readily consume a large number of native dry-forest trees and shrubs, eating leaves, stems, fruits, and seeds of a wide number of species. Saplings of native species provide excellent protein, nutrients, and crude fiber for cattle, which are able to digest the leaf tannins in native saplings. Unlike *jaragua,* many browse species retain their nutrient levels fairly constantly throughout both the rainy and dry seasons. In contrast, grasses, especially *jaragua,* show significant reduction in digestibility and nutrient levels during the dry season. Native dry-forest trees and shrubs are both more palatable and more nutritious than *jaragua* for grazing by domestic livestock, and free-ranging cattle shift their foraging to native species during the dry season when given the opportunity. Hartshorn (1983: 131) reported that he was "unable to find seedlings or small saplings of *Brosimum alicastrum*" in the inventory plots at Palo Verde after cattle had grazed in the plots. No native mammals of Costa Rica will feed on the stems or leaves of mature *jaragua,* and it is unlikely that even native grazers such as cotton rats (*Sigmodon hispidus*) and eastern cottontail rabbits feed on anything but the youngest shoots.

Our survey efforts in *jaragua* for small mammals have identified only one species of native mammal that can occupy this grass, cotton rats. Daubenmire (1972: 37), in a year-long study on the ecological consequences of converting dry forest to pasturelands near Cañas, noted the lack of mammals (only two rabbits seen) and other animals in *Hyparrhenia,* stating that "[al]though rodents and insects were present, they were very few in species and numbers and their use of the vegetation [*Hyparrhenia*] was negligible." Cattle also destroy bee nests, especially those of the large, ground-nesting anthophorid bees that are the major pollinators of much of the dry forest (Frankie et al. 1997). We suspect that cattle also will negatively affect the nests of small mammals, as many nests along the periphery of the marsh are at the surface (*Oryzomys* and *Sigmodon* nest at the surface or in aboveground vegetation). The combination of even moderate grazing by cattle and regular burning has an extremely negative impact on rodent populations.

The presence of single-species stands of *jaragua* and of artificially created, open savannalike habitat within the tropical dry forest of Guanacaste has reduced or eliminated the populations of most native dry-forest mammals from those habitats. However, a few species have increased in numbers and distribution with the creation of these grasslands. Cotton rats are much more widespread and abundant in Costa Rica today than they were in the past. Cotton rats are an open-grassland species, and they would have been rare in Guanacaste before the removal of the forests and the introduction of grasses. Other mammals that probably are more common now than before the creation of the open savannalike habitats include opossums, vampire bats, cottontail rabbits, armadillos, coyotes, and gray foxes (*Urocyon cinereoargenteus*).

Controlled cattle grazing potentially may be an effective management tool in reducing the biomass of *jaragua* when cattle are grazed on the growing grass during the rainy season and are then removed. However, the presence of cattle in tropical dry forest will change the structure and composition of that habitat (Stern et al. 2002). Cattle cannot be sustained on *jaragua* throughout the year and must be allowed to forage on other species. Cattle lose weight on a diet consisting solely of *jaragua* during the dry season (D. A. Stewart pers. comm.) because most of the plants' nutrients are stored in the roots and the stems, and leaves are primarily dried cellulose.

Cattle as a management tool for controlling cattails in the Palo Verde marsh have proved ineffective (figs. 5.1–5.3). Although cattle will consume some young, actively growing cattail shoots, they do not consume the mature leaves (D. A. Stewart pers. comm.), and they prefer other species when given the opportunity to feed on them. The explosion of cattails in the marsh began shortly after the transfer of land from a cattle ranch to a national park. At this time, cement gates or weirs that were used in the dry season to maintain water in the lagoon after high tide were abandoned, thus contributing to the flourishing of cattails in the lagoon. Within five years of the change, cattails had eliminated most of the open areas of the marsh, which were critical for waterfowl. Cattle in the marsh primarily feed on floating water hyacinths (*Eichhornia crassipes* and *E. heterosperma*), which are locally called *lirio de agua* or *choreja,* but they will eat a wide variety of species, especially *Pistia stratiotes* (locally called *lechuga*). Cattle will eat young cattails, but they prefer other species. When cattle are allowed to graze in upland areas, they have a significant and detrimental impact on the composition and structure of native forest trees and shrubs. Overgrazing by cattle, the presence of vast areas of *jaragua,* and uncontrolled fires continue to be among the most serious threats to the native flora and fauna in the dry forest of Costa Rica. In recent years, we have observed that in areas where cattle were grazing, most of the smaller saplings had been either consumed or trampled and that there were very few rodents on the forest floor in heavily grazed areas. The use of cattle within Parque Nacional Palo Verde is having a significant negative impact on the regeneration of the forest and on the abundance of native mammals.

PESTICIDE CONTAMINATION

Pesticide contamination is a problem worldwide, and in recent years, with the increase in agricultural development in Guanacaste, it has become

FIGURE 5.1. Laguna Palo Verde in February 1970. The marsh included diverse characteristic aquatic vegetation and open areas between patches of *Parkinsonia aculeata* trees, water hyacinth, water lilies, and bullrush. Large areas of open, shallow water were present. No cattails were visible because they occurred only in small patches along the airstrip (shown in the lower part of photo) near a freshwater spring draining into the marsh. Photograph by Gordon Frankie.

FIGURE 5.2. Laguna Palo Verde in February 1970. A close-up view of the marsh. Photograph by Gordon Frankie.

FIGURE 5.3. Laguna Palo Verde in February 2001. Since the mid-1980s, the diversity of both plants and waterfowl has declined dramatically, and the marsh has become choked with cattails (*Typha dominguensis*, Typhaceae) and two aquatic perennial grasses, *Hymenachne amplexicaulis* and *Paspalidium geminatum* (Araceae). Photograph by Robert Timm.

a serious threat to the fauna in this region. Organophosphates and carbamates, the most common insecticides in use today throughout the world, are known as cholinesterase-inhibiting pesticides because they kill by interfering with the enzyme vital for nerve transmission. Organophosphates and carbamates work well against a wide range of insect pests and are often less expensive than many alternatives, which adds to their popularity. In addition to affecting insects, many are acutely (immediately) toxic to most vertebrates and other invertebrates. Because they break down quickly in soil and water, they often need to be applied to crops more than once during the growing season. Organochlorine insecticides, such as DDT, also are very effective in killing a broad range of insects; however, they are slow to break down, remain toxic for a considerable length of time, and accumulate in body fat. Additionally, the long-lived organic pesticides act as endocrine disrupters, mimicking naturally occurring androgens (estrogens), and may be detrimental to mammalian reproductive cycles—

for example, by lowering sperm count. Die-offs of both birds and mammals occur even when pesticides are applied responsibly because many animals consume the pesticide, either directly or indirectly. Pesticide residues in the stomachs of poisoned mammals and birds are known to kill predators and scavengers.

Cropdusters in Guanacaste (as well as elsewhere in Costa Rica) have customarily dumped into rivers unused pesticides remaining from aerial spraying, and this practice continues. A number of toxic pesticides have been isolated from the Tempisque River, including aldrin, chlordane, DDT, heptachlor, and lindane (Mata and Blanco 1994). These five insecticides are all organochlorine compounds and are known to cause an increase in cancer incidence in humans and to persist in the environment for many years. Aldrin, chlordane, and heptachlor are cyclodienes that are similar to, but more toxic than, DDT. Chlorinated hydrocarbon pesticides are notorious for their severe effects on nontarget organisms, whereas target species, particularly many species of insects, develop resistance (Laws 1993). Thirty pesticides have been identified as commonly used in rice fields in the area adjacent to Palo Verde (Robinson 1993). Some of these pesticides are extremely toxic to wildlife (and humans), and their use is illegal in Costa Rica, but they are still available on the black market and are commonly used (Hilje 1988). High levels of pesticide residuals, including organic chlorides and their metabolites, have been found in eggshells of herons that nest on Isla de Pájaros in Parque Nacional Palo Verde (Hidalgo 1986). The effects of agrochemicals on tropical mammals have yet to be studied.

PREDICTIONS AND RECOMMENDATIONS

RESEARCH PRIORITIES FOR DRY-FOREST MAMMALS

Because little is known about the abundance and distribution of most species of mammals in the tropical dry forest, monitoring populations in its many distinct habitats should be a top research priority. In order to identify critical areas for protection and adopt the best strategies for successful conservation, it is imperative to collect basic information about population densities and changes in densities over time within this life zone. This information will help to identify vulnerable species as such and to concentrate research and conservation efforts. Furthermore, monitoring the abundance of mammals within these various habitats throughout the year will help to identify potential migratory patterns; this information, in turn, will help determine which areas to protect as biological corridors connecting tropical dry forest to other habitats. Finally, coordinated efforts should be established between Latin American countries that still have tropical dry forest in order to accumulate information on the distribution and abundance of tropical dry forest mammal species over their entire range.

In addition to documenting the distribution and abundance of dry-forest mammals, it is important to identify ecologically significant species for management and monitoring. Researchers have recognized three categories of species whose interactions in ecosystems are important for providing information about the quality of the habitat: (1) keystone species: species whose disappearance results in the disappearance of several other species; (2) indicator species: species whose population changes are thought to indicate the effects of management activities; and (3) mobile link species: species who are important links to more than one food chain, plant-animal association, or ecosystem (Soulé 1989). Research efforts on mammals in tropical dry forest should concentrate on species that fall into these categories with the goal of conserving both fauna and flora of dry forest regions.

TRAINING AND EDUCATION PROGRAMS FOR PARK PERSONNEL

The implementation of long-term programs for the monitoring and conservation of dry-forest mammals in Costa Rica requires trained professionals working in the national parks. The limited budget that currently supports protected areas in Costa Rica, however, is not sufficient to employ specialized professionals, and most park personnel have no formal training in biology. Creative proposals to increase the budget of national parks should be evaluated, including imposing a tourist tax on hotels with the funds going directly to protected areas (see chapter 21). The goal should be to have at least one specialized, professionally trained biologist working within a protected area to initiate monitoring and conservation programs and train park personnel in fieldwork.

ECONOMIC ALTERNATIVES AND SUSTAINABLE DEVELOPMENT

Although the consensus among conservation biologists is to protect as much land as possible as quickly as possible, the human factor of population expansion and economic needs cannot be easily ignored. Unless conservation programs take into account the needs of human societies, it is unlikely that the goals of long-term conservation will be achieved. Sound economic alternatives need to be provided to rural Costa Ricans in areas of tropical dry forest if we are to conserve this fragile ecosystem and the mammal fauna that it supports. Alternative means of generating economic benefits beyond the traditional use of the land for timber, agricultural crops, and cattle grazing should be evaluated and encouraged by the Costa Rican government. One possibility is to provide the highest economic incentives for reforestation programs that provide total protection. Under the current forestry policy, programs in which land is devoted to reforestation with plantations and selective logging programs receive larger economic incentives than programs providing total protection (see chapter 21).

It is of utmost importance to encourage research on the sustainable development of ecosystems and to evaluate potential alternative means of land and water exploitation that will have a minimum impact on ecosystems. In particular, in the dry-forest region of Guanacaste, studies evaluating the effects of forest fragmentation, large-scale irrigation projects, and rice cultivation on local mammals should be undertaken. Before sustainable development programs are implemented within or surrounding protected areas, feasibility studies should be conducted in order to estimate not only the economic benefit of the new activity but also the ecological cost to the area. For example, the management plan implemented in Palo Verde using cows within the park was part of a sustainable development plan; unfortunately this activity was implemented without first evaluating the economic benefits or the ecological costs. The economic benefits are at best minimal and the ecological costs high (Mozo 1995; see chapter 21).

PROTECTION, REGENERATION, AND BUFFER AREAS

If the native mammals of Costa Rica's tropical dry forest are to be conserved, additional efforts must be made to protect the forest that remains and allow natural succession to regenerate mature stands of dry forest. Although increased forest regeneration is a positive development, young, regenerating forests do not provide the same environmental benefits for mammalian communities as do old-growth forests. Combined with projects that foster regeneration of degraded areas, continued efforts need to focus on conserving old-growth forests, as many native mammals may be found only in this habitat.

Since dry forests in Costa Rica are largely restricted to protected areas, the habitats immediately surrounding these areas should be evaluated before any type of development is carried out. Buffer areas surrounding national parks and other protected areas theoretically exist in Costa Rica, but little has been done to evaluate or restrict activities in these areas. For example, the agricultural development of rice fields bordering Palo Verde and Lomas Barbudal destroyed the biological corridor that connected them. The potential effect that agricultural development on the borders of the national parks has on native mammal fauna needs to be evaluated more fully.

CONCLUSIONS

No habitat type in Costa Rica (and throughout Mesoamerica) has been more affected by humans than the tropical dry forest. Open pastureland and grazed forested tracts are common habitats within this region today. In recent years rice, sugarcane, and hay fields have replaced natural habitats throughout the Guanacaste region. Palo Verde has lost at least eight species of native mammals to date, and it is likely that more mammals in this habitat will become extinct if efforts are not made to reduce the effects of humans on this ecosystem. Some species of mammals are still abundant at Palo Verde, and a few species (those that live in the savanna) are undoubtedly more abundant today than they were prior to settlement; however, the long-term effects that the fragmented landscape will have on populations of native mammals are still unknown. Because there is no simple solution to guarantee the successful conservation of any particular species or group of species, we suggest a combined effort that includes (1) research; (2) education and training; (3) economic alternatives and evaluation of alternative uses of land

and water; and (4) protection and regeneration of habitats. We believe that such a multifaceted approach will be the most successful way to protect dry-forest mammals and their habitat.

ACKNOWLEDGMENTS

We thank the Ministerio del Ambiente y Energía and Sistema Nacional de Areas de Conservación, especially Javier Guevara Sequeira, for giving us the opportunity to work at Parque Nacional Palo Verde. Gordon Frankie, Eric Fuchs, Doug Gill, Richard LaVal, Melissa Panger, Mauricio Quesada, and Bruce Williamson unselfishly shared with us original observations they have made. David A. Stewart generously provided us with a history of the Stewart Ranch, details of cattle ranching, and historical information on wildlife in the area. Gordon Frankie, Doug Gill, Marion Klaus, Richard LaVal, Deedra McClearn, Mauricio Quesada, and Heather York offered editorial comments on earlier drafts of this chapter, significantly improving it.

REFERENCES

Belsky, A. J., and D. M. Blumenthal. 1997. Effects of livestock grazing on stand dynamics and soils in upland forests of the Interior West. *Conservation Biology* 11:315–27.

Boucher, D. H., M. Hanson, S. Risch, and J. H. Vandermeer. 1983. Agriculture: Introduction. In *Costa Rican natural history*, ed. D. H. Janzen, 66–73. Chicago: University of Chicago Press.

Ceballos, G. 1995. Vertebrate diversity, ecology, and conservation in neotropical dry forests. In *Seasonally dry tropical forests*, ed. S. H. Bullock, H. A. Mooney, and E. Medina, 195–220. Cambridge: Cambridge University Press.

Chapman, C. A. 1988. Patterns of foraging and range use by three species of Neotropical primates. *Primates* 29:177–94.

———. 1989. Primate seed dispersal: The fate of dispersed seeds. *Biotropica* 21:148–54.

Cochrane, M. A., A. Alencar, M. D. Schulze, C. M. Souza Jr., D. C. Nepstad, P. Lefebure, and E. A. Davidson. 1999. Positive feedbacks in the fire dynamics of closed canopy tropical forests. *Science* 284:1832–35.

Collins, S. L., A. K. Knapp, J. M. Briggs, J. M. Blair, and E. M. Steinauer. 1998. Modulation of di-versity by grazing and mowing in native tall-grass prairie. *Science* 280:745–47.

Conklin, N. L. 1987. The potential nutritional value to cattle of some tropical browse species from Guanacaste, Costa Rica. Ph.D. diss., Cornell University, Ithaca, N.Y. 329 pp.

Daubenmire, R. 1972. Some ecologic consequences of converting forest to savanna in northwestern Costa Rica. *Tropical Ecology* 13:31–51.

Fleming, T. H. 1988. *The short-tailed fruit bat: A study in plant-animal interactions*. Chicago: University of Chicago Press. 365 pp.

Frankie, G. W., H. G. Baker, and P. A. Opler. 1974. Comparative phenological studies of trees in tropical wet and dry forest in the lowlands of Costa Rica. *Journal of Ecology* 62:881–919.

Frankie, G. W., S. B. Vinson, M. A. Rizzardi, T. L. Griswold, S. O'Keefe, and R. R. Snelling. 1997. Diversity and abundance of bees visiting a mass flowering tree species in disturbed seasonal dry forest, Costa Rica. *Journal of the Kansas Entomological Society* 70:281–96.

Gentry, A. H. 1995. Diversity and floristic composition of neotropical dry forests. In *Seasonally dry tropical forests*, ed. S. H. Bullock, H. A. Mooney, and E. Medina, 146–94. Cambridge: Cambridge University Press.

Glander, K. E. 1978. Howling monkey feeding behavior and plant secondary compounds: A study of strategies. In *The ecology of arboreal folivores*, ed. G. G. Montgomery, 561–74. Washington, D.C.: Smithsonian Institution Press.

Hartshorn, G. S. 1983. Plants: Introduction. In *Costa Rican natural history*, ed. D. H. Janzen, 118–57. Chicago: University of Chicago Press.

Heithaus, E. R., T. H. Fleming, and P. A. Opler. 1975. Foraging patterns and resource utilization in seven species of bats in a seasonal tropical forest. *Ecology* 56:841–54.

Helversen, O. von. 1993. Adaptations of flowers to the pollination by glossophagine bats. In *Animal-plant interactions in tropical environments*, ed. W. Barthlott, C. M. Naumann, K. Schmidt-Loske, and K.-L. Schuchmann, 41–59. Bonn, Germany: Zoologisches Forschungsinstitut und Museum Alexander Koenig.

Hidalgo, C. C. 1986. Determinación de residuos de plaguicidas organoclorados en huevos de ocho especies de aves acuáticas, colectados durante 1983–1984 en la Isla Pájaros, Guanacaste, Costa Rica. Tesis de Grado, Escuela de Biología, Universidad de Costa Rica, San José.

Hilje, L. 1988. *El uso de los plaguicidas en Costa Rica*. San José: Editorial Universidad Estatal a Distancia.

Holdridge, L. R., W. C. Grenke, W. H. Hatheway, T. Liang, and J. A. Tosi Jr. 1971. *Forest environments in tropical life zones: A pilot study.* Oxford: Pergamon Press. 747 pp.

Janzen, D. H. 1986. *Guanacaste National Park: Tropical ecological and cultural restoration.* San José: Editorial Universidad Estatal a Distancia. 103 pp.

Janzen, D. H., and D. E. Wilson. 1983. Mammals: Introduction. In *Costa Rican natural history,* ed. D. H. Janzen, 426–42. Chicago: University of Chicago Press.

Laws, E. A. 1993. *Aquatic pollution: An introductory text.* 2d ed. New York: John Wiley and Sons. 611 pp.

León S., J., C. Barboza V., and J. Aguilar F. 1982. *Desarrollo tecnológico en la ganadería de carne.* San José: Consejo Nacional de Investigaciones Científicas y Tecnológicas.

Maldonado U., T., J. Bravo, G. Castro S., Q. Jiménez M., O. Saborío, and L. Paniagua C. 1995. *Evaluación ecológica rápida región del Tempisque Guanacaste, Costa Rica.* San José: Fundación Neotrópica, Centro de Estudios Ambientales y Políticas. 104 pp. + 8 appendixes.

Mata, A., and O. Blanco. 1994. *La cuenca del Golfo de Nicoya: Un reto al desarrollo sostenible.* San José: Editorial de la Universidad de Costa Rica. 235 pp.

McCammon-Feldman, B. 1980. A critical analysis of tropical savanna forage consumption and utilization by goats. Ph.D. diss., University of Illinois, Urbana.

McCoy, M. B. 1994. Seasonal, freshwater marshes in the tropics: A case in which cattle grazing is not detrimental. In *Principles of conservation biology,* ed. G. K. Meffe and C. R. Carroll, 352–53. Sunderland, Mass.: Sinauer Associates.

McCoy, M. B., and J. M. Rodríguez. 1994. Cattail (*Typha dominguensis*) eradication methods in the restoration of a tropical, seasonal, freshwater marsh. In *Global wetlands: Old World and New,* ed. W. J. Mitsch, 469–82. New York: Elsevier.

McNab, B. K. 1985. Energetics, population biology, and distribution of xenarthrans, living and extinct. In *The evolution and ecology of armadillos, sloths, and vermilinguas,* ed. G. G. Montgomery, 219–32. Washington, D.C.: Smithsonian Institution Press.

MINAE (Ministerio de Ambiente y Energía). 1998. *Un recuento de los logros del Área de Conservación Tempisque, 1997.* San José: Ministerio del Ambiente y Energía, Sistema Nacional de Áreas de Conservación, Área de Conservación Tempisque. 30 pp.

———. 1999. Lista oficial de la República de Costa Rica: Lista de especies de fauna silvestre con poblaciones reducidas y en peligro de extinción para Costa Rica. Decreto 26435-MINAE. In *Lista de fauna de importancia para la conservación en Centroamérica y México: Listas rojas, listas oficiales y especies en apéndices CITES,* ed. V. Solís Rivera, A. Jiménez Elizondo, O. Brenes, and L. Vilnitzky Strusberg, 127–40. Sistema de Integración Centroamericana. Direccion Ambiental, con el apoyo técnico de UICN–ORMA y WWF Centroamérica. San José: WWF, UICN, SICA.

Mozo, E. T. 1995. *Pastoreo con ganado vacuno, una alternativa del ACT para prevención de incendios forestales, recuperación de humedales y restauración del bosque tropical seco.* Bagaces, Costa Rica: Convenio MIRENEM–Opción Colombia, Universidad Sergio Arboleda. 56 pp.

Parsons, J. J. 1972. Spread of African pasture grasses to the American tropics. *Journal of Range Management* 25:12–17.

———. 1983. Beef cattle (ganado). In *Costa Rican natural history,* ed. D. H. Janzen, 77–79. Chicago: University of Chicago Press.

Pepper, I. L., C. P. Gerba, and M. L. Brusseau, eds. 1996. *Pollution science.* New York: Academic Press. 397 pp.

Quesada López-Calleja, R. 1980. *Costa Rica: La frontera sur de Mesoamérica.* 2d ed. Madrid: Instituto Costarricense de Turismo. 288 pp.

Robinson, T. H. 1993. Fate and transport of agricultural contaminants from rice paddies: Impact sampling strategies and the potential environmental degradation to dry tropical coastal wetlands—Guanacaste, Costa Rica. Master's thesis, University of California, Santa Barbara. 47 pp.

Robinson, W. L., and E. G. Bolen. 1984. *Wildlife ecology and management.* New York: Macmillan. 478 pp.

Rodríguez, F. J., and F. A. Chinchilla. 1996. Lista de mamíferos de Costa Rica. *Revista de Biología Tropical* 44:877–90.

Sáenz-Maroto, A. 1955. *Los forrajes de Costa Rica.* San José: Editorial Universitaria, Universidad de Costa Rica.

Schulze, M. D., N. E. Seavy, and D. F. Whitacre. 2000. A comparison of the phyllostomid bat assemblages in undisturbed Neotropical forest and in forest fragments of a slash-and-burn farming mosaic in Petén, Guatemala. *Biotropica* 32:174–84.

Soulé, M. E. 1989. Conservation biology in the twenty-first century: Summary and outlook. In *Conservation for the twenty-first century,* ed.

D. Western and M. Pearl, 297–303. New York: Oxford University Press.

Stern, M., M. Quesada, and K. E. Stoner. 2002. Changes in composition and structure of a tropical dry forest following intermittent cattle grazing. *Revista de Biología Tropical* 50:1021–34.

Stoner, K. E. 2001. Differential habitat use and reproductive patterns of frugivorous bats in tropical dry forest of northwestern Costa Rica. *Canadian Journal of Zoology* 79:1626–33.

———. 2002. Murciélagos nectarívoros y frugívoros del bosque caducifolio de la Reserva de la Biosfera Chamela-Cuixmala. In *Historia natural del bosque caducifolia de Chamela*, ed. F. A. Noguera, M. Quesada, J. Vega, and A. Garcia-Aldrete, 379–95. Mexico City: Instituto de Biología, Universidad Nacional Autónoma de México.

Timm, R. M. 1994. The mammal fauna. In *La Selva: Ecology and natural history of a Neotropical rain forest*, ed. L. A. McDade, K. S. Bawa, H. A. Hespenheide, and G. S. Hartshorn, 229–37, 394–98. Chicago: University of Chicago Press.

Timm, R. M., and R. K. LaVal. 1998. A field key to the bats of Costa Rica. *Occasional Publication Series, Center of Latin American Studies, University of Kansas* 22:1–30.

———. 2000. Mammals. In *Monteverde: Ecology and conservation of a tropical cloud forest*, ed. N. M. Nadkarni and N. T. Wheelwright, 223–44, 553–60. New York: Oxford University Press.

Timm, R. M., and S. E. Lewis. 1991. Tent construction and use by *Uroderma bilobatum* in coconut palms (*Cocos nucifera*) in Costa Rica. *Bulletin of the American Museum of Natural History* 206: 251–60.

Timm, R. M., D. E. Wilson, B. L. Clauson, R. K. LaVal, and C. S. Vaughan. 1989. Mammals of the La Selva–Braulio Carrillo complex, Costa Rica. *North American Fauna* 75:1–162.

Timm, R. M., R. K. LaVal, and B. Rodríguez-Herrera. 1999. Clave de campo para los murciélagos de Costa Rica. *Brenesia* (Museo Nacional de Costa Rica) 52:1–32.

Vaughan, C., and M. Rodríguez. 1986. Comparación de los hábitos alimentarios del coyote (*Canis latrans*) en dos localidades en Costa Rica. *Vida Silvestre Neotropical* 1:6–11.

———. 1991. White-tailed deer management in Costa Rica. In *Neotropical wildlife use and conservation*, ed. J. G. Robinson and K. H. Redford, 288–99. Chicago: University of Chicago Press.

Vaughan, C., M. McCoy, J. Fallas, H. Cháves, G. Barboza, G. Wong, M. Carbonell, J. Rau, and M. Carranza. 1995. *Plan de manejo y desarrollo del Parque Nacional Palo Verde y Reserva Biológica Lomas Barbudal*. Heredia, Costa Rica: Universidad Nacional. 206 pp.

CHAPTER 6

The Conservation Values of Bees and Ants in the Costa Rican Dry Forest

S. Bradleigh Vinson, Sean T. O'Keefe, and Gordon W. Frankie

OVER THE PAST 30 YEARS of solitary-bee studies in the Costa Rican dry forest we have observed a steady decline in native solitary-bee populations. In 1972 bee diversity was surveyed from a small population of the fabaceous tree *Andira inermis,* at a site just south of the town limits of Liberia (see maps in chapter 1). At that time about 70 species were collected (Frankie et al. 1976). In 1989 we casually sampled bees again from several *A. inermis* trees in the vicinity of Liberia and found only 37 species (Vinson et al. 1993). Another sampling at the original Liberia site in 1996, during a year of robust *A. inermis* flowering, revealed that diversity had declined from a high of 70 species in 1972 to only 28 species. Further, overall numbers of bees had declined by slightly more than 90 percent (Frankie et al. 1997).

What brought on this decline? Our data suggest four major factors. The first is habitat destruction, caused primarily by agricultural development and urbanization, between the towns of Liberia and Cañas (see maps in chapter 1). The second factor is the introduction of *jaragua* grass, *Hyparrhenia rufa,* from Africa. The third factor, often linked to the second, is human-caused fire. *Jaragua* grows 2–3 m higher than the short native grasses, becomes highly flammable during the dry season, and burns very hot. *Jaragua* is also fire-adapted and readily resurges after a fire. It is fanned by dry-season trade winds that allow fire to burn well inside the dry-forest edge, which opens the forest to further *jaragua* invasion. Besides slowly converting forest to grassland, fires sometimes invade deep into the forest, resulting in loss of deadwood that is used by nesting anthophorid bees including some *Centris* (Frankie et al. 1988) and several *Xylocopa* species. Deadwood-nesting species were rare in the 1996 captures (Frankie et al. 1997). Fire also leads to other problems for bees. Important resource trees such as three *Tabebuia* species, *Dalbergia retusa, Caesalpinia eriostachys,* and *Cochlospermum vitifolium* are resistant to "cool" native-grass fires, but not the hot-burning *jaragua* that results in tree loss following one or two fires (Frankie et al. 1997). Fire also removes ground cover, increasing vulnerability of ground-nesting bees to predation (S. Vinson pers. obs.) and increasing solar radiation, which alters microclimate and solitary-bee nesting success (Frankie et al. 1988). The fourth factor is introduction of ornamental flowering plants and reforestation using exotic tree species that do not supply proper bee requisites. Intensive studies on the relationship of Africanized honeybees to native bees from 1996 to 2001 in this area revealed little evidence that this exotic bee is having an impact on the native bee fauna (Frankie et al. 2002).

It is clear that over the past 30 years, as the dry forest declined, solitary bees also declined. Despite the establishment of reserves and national parks, factors such as fire, exotic invaders, and human encroachment threaten the Costa Rican dry forest (Frankie et al. 1997; chapters 7, 9, 12, 13, 21–24). Further, habitat fragmentation and isolation continues (chapter 3). To protect remaining forests and their diversity we must first identify threatened areas. This requires long-term monitoring of habitats with consistently applied, quantitative methods that can detect changes in organism populations and their habitats and at the same time recognize new problems. Developing methods and procedures for monitoring the health of protected areas becomes critical. Here we propose using both bees and ants as bioindicators.

MONITORING ECOSYSTEM HEALTH

Although there are many approaches to monitoring and assessing ecosystem health, the most practical and widely implemented includes the use of indicator organisms. Originally, this approach was used to assess the effects of pollutants on selected organisms—for example, lichens to monitor for air pollution (Richardson 1992). Indicator organisms are also used for broader ecological monitoring, such as measuring effects of management practices on ecosystems (Christensen et al. 1996), especially aquatic ecosystems (Loeb and Spacie 1994).

One major dilemma of this approach is determining which groups of organisms are the best indicators. Pearson (1994) offered seven criteria that should be met by indicator groups: (1) the group is taxonomically well known, (2) their biology and general life history are understood, (3) their populations can be surveyed and manipulated, (4) some species of the group occupy a breadth of habitats with a broad geographical range, (5) some populations should be specialized, (6) observed patterns in the indicator group are reflected in other related and unrelated taxa, and (7) the group is of potential economic importance. These criteria suggest the use of species from different trophic levels, but Williams and Gaston (1994) advocated using only higher taxonomic groups, Oliver and Beattie (1996) suggested using selected morphospecies, and Lambeck (1997) suggested using an umbrella species, a single species that may indicate areas for conservation. Birds and mammals are commonly used for monitoring because they are well known, often easier to identify, have larger habitat requirements, and are not so numerous as to overwhelm a study. Further, their numbers and frequency of occurrence are influenced by environmental disturbance. Sea turtles, for example, can be used as "flagship" organisms because they generate sympathy from financial donors (see chapter 15). In addition, many bird assemblages have a loyal human following, the bird watchers.

Although birds and mammals are useful in monitoring large landscapes, they are not useful for monitoring small unique habitat fragments embedded within larger conserved areas or smaller isolated fragments remaining on private lands (both referred to in this chapter as "habitat fragments"). This is because different groups of organisms operate at different scales in order to live and reproduce and thus differ in the ways they can be used as indicators. Scale is extremely important, and organisms that depend on diversity and derive their requisite needs within the scale in question must be selected. For such habitat fragments, specific insect groups (Hammond 1994), such as aquatic insects (Loeb and Spacie 1994) and ants (Agosti et al. 2000), have been frequently used. But should we be concerned about habitat fragments? Habitat fragments may provide resources, act as stepping-stones to other areas, or serve as refuges or sinks. They may harbor unique organisms, have strong populations of species that are less common or threatened in other areas, or contain different species or genotypes (chapter 16). In addition, habitat fragments may contain the only remnants of original habitat, which may include representative species on which restoration projects could draw. Unfortunately, habitat fragments and investment in their preservation are largely ignored, either because they are considered safe within larger protected areas or because they are considered too small or of low value.

We suggest that Hymenoptera are an ideal indicator group for habitat fragments and focus on bee and ant taxa that access different habitat attributes. Bees are dependent on a number of specific requisite plant species and nesting conditions distributed in several microhabitats. Because bees depend on several microhabitats, they can provide information on more than the health of the location in which they are recorded. In contrast, ants are more sessile and dependent on local microclimate and availability of local resources. In this chapter we discuss the diversity and ecological relationships of these two taxa and argue why they may be good bioindicators. We then discuss how they may be monitored and how the data may be interpreted and used to effect change.

DIVERSITY OF BEES AND ANTS

In any monitoring effort it is important to identify the species encountered. Hanson and Gauld (1995) provide an excellent review of the taxonomy and biology of Costa Rican Hymenoptera. Bees are classified as a single family, the Apidae (Michener 2000). Worldwide, there are 25,000 to 30,000 species representing more than 400 genera, and Costa Rica alone has at least 785 species and 98 genera (Griswold et al. 2000). The bee fauna in Costa Rica appears to be rich on a per-area basis, as there are more than 129 species/10^4 sq km in Costa Rica, compared with 8 in Mexico and 4.8 in the United States. In other words, in Costa Rica there are 16 times as many bee species per area as in Mexico and 27 times as many as in the United States (Hanson and Gauld 1995). The major bee groups are the Halictinae (195 spp.), Anthophorinae (143 spp.), Megachilinae (96 spp.), Euglossinae (58 spp.), Meliponinae (48 spp.), and Xylopinae (37 spp.) (Hanson and Gauld 1995). In the dry forest, Meliponines along with *Centris, Epicharis, Xylocopa,* and introduced honeybees are common. The Tempisque dry-forest region of Costa Rica alone has more than 250 bee species (chapter 2). Michener (2000) provides modern keys to identify bee genera and subgenera, but there is no single source for identification to species, and many smaller species await description.

Worldwide there are about 300 genera of ants (Formicidae) with some 8,800 species (Hölldobler and Wilson 1990). Ants of Costa Rica are better known than those of any other New World region south of the United States. Longino and Hanson (1995) recorded 81 genera and 620 species in Costa Rica, and many more await description, particularly the smaller, cryptic forms. Most ant genera are known, and many are found in the dry forest, but genera new to Costa Rica are still being found (O'Keefe and Agosti 1998). Bolton (1994) has provided a thorough key to identify ants to genus. Identification to species is more problematic because there is no synthetic treatment of all species (MacKay and Vinson 1989).

ECOLOGICAL RELATIONSHIPS OF BEES AND ANTS AND THEIR REQUISITE NEEDS

BEES

Bees and ants have numerous ecological functions in the Costa Rican dry forest, and understanding these specific interactions is necessary if these taxa are to be used in monitoring. Bees require a number of resources and conditions, referred to as their biological and ecological requisites. Many bee species are specialists in their requisite needs, requiring particular resources and conditions to survive. As some requisite needs are fulfilled, select plants are pollinated. Plants have also evolved specializations that influence the species of bees that visit. Pollen-producing specialists include trees such as *Cochlospermum vitifolium*, numerous *Cassia* and *Senna* species, *Curatella americana*, and *Byrsonima crassifolia* (Vinson et al. 1993). Some plants, such as *C. vitifolium* and the shrub *Cassia biflora*, contain their small, dry pollen in tubular anthers, which bees collect with a behavior called "buzz-collecting" (Thorp 1979). Bees of several genera perform buzz pollination, such as those of *Xylocopa, Centris, Epicharis, Gaesischia, Exomalopsis, Melipona*, and *Bombus* (Buchmann 1985); the introduced honeybee or stingless bees of the tribe Trigonini cannot.

A primary energy source for all adult bees is nectar, which also serves as an important provisioned resource. Important nectar plants include *Tabebuia* species, *Gliricidia sepium, Caesalpinia eriostachys, Andira inermis, Myrospermum frutescens, Pterocarpus michelianus*, and *Dalbergia retusa* (Vinson et al. 1993).

Centris species are an important pollinator group in the Costa Rican dry forest (Frankie et al. 1976). In addition to pollen and nectar, they need floral oils as provisioned larval food or for nest construction (or both) (Vinson et al. 1997). The major oil resource plants are the tree *Byrsonima crassifolia* (Malpighiaceae) and, to a lesser extent, several malpighiaceous vines (Vinson et al. 1993). Resource accessibility also influences a bee's impact on plant pollination as well as its ability to fulfill its requisites. Small bees are more effective in servicing smaller flowers that they can manipulate (Gottsberger 1986), but large bees can gain access to large flowers and can move pollen over long distances (Frankie et al. 1976; Michener and Brooks 1984).

In addition to nutrition, bees require specific substrates for nest construction. For example,

some species (*Centris flavifrons*) nest in the ground and prefer soil, others (*C. flavofasciata*) prefer sand, and still others (*C. bicornuta*) nest in preexisting wood cavities (Coville et al. 1983 in Vinson et al. 1993). Bees construct nests consisting of a series of cells using secretions and resources from the surrounding environment, such as sand, wood borings (sawdust), spider webs, plant leaves, petals, waxes, saps, and resins (Eickwort et al. 1981). Further, most solitary bees seal the nest entrance with a plug often composed of other materials that are found in the local environment (Roubik 1989). Nests must be located in appropriate habitats. For example, we found that some bee species produce fewer cells per nest in recently burned over or rocky soil or fail to complete development when their nests were located in exposed, hot areas (see Frankie et al. 1988, and Vinson and Frankie 1988 in Vinson et al. 1993).

ANTS

Ants are even more dependent than bees on specific habitats. The two major ant guilds are those associated with plants and those that are predators. Ant-plant associations include ant-plant mutualisms, seed dispersal, and herbivory. Two well-studied ant-plant mutualisms include relationships between *Azteca* ants and *Cecropia* plants and those between *Pseudomyrmex* ants and *Acacia* plants, each involving several species of ants and plants (Huxley and Cutler 1991). Seed-dispersing ants, ecologically important in many arid regions, include only *Solenopsis* and *Pheidole* in Costa Rica (Longino and Hanson 1995). Ants belonging to the genera *Atta* and *Acromyrmex* (known as leaf-cutters and grass-cutters) are dominant herbivores in the Neotropics, consuming far more vegetation than any other animal group (Stradling 1991).

Predatory ants in Costa Rica can be divided into four subguilds: roaming army ants, large predatory ponerines, cryptic soil-litter ants, and generalist predators. Army ants have a major impact on tropical ecosystems (Gotwald 1995). *Eciton burchelli* form fronts 3–15 m wide, feeding mainly on other arthropods, including other ants (Franks 1982a). Other species of army ants raid in columns and are insect prey specialists. Ponerines, which have a powerful sting, are generalist predators that form small colonies but represent a significant portion of the dry-forest ant fauna (Longino and Hanson 1995). The rarely seen soil-litter ants are mostly generalist predators, feeding on whatever they can catch, with a few specialist predator species. This fauna relies on a deep and established litter layer, in which as many as 30–35 genera can be encountered. The last group consists of the generalist predators and scavengers such as *Crematogaster* and *Solenopsis*. Ants of this last group feed on almost any insect they can subdue but will also feed on carrion, seeds, select plant parts, or honeydew from homopterans (Vinson 1997). Further details of predatory ants can be found in Hölldobler and Wilson (1990).

Ants influence their ecosystem in many ways, such as modifying habitat near their nests through translocation of large amounts of organic material into deeper soil layers. As a result, soil pH is altered, soil water-holding capacity is increased, and salts are increased—all of which are important to plant root health (Pętal 1978). Ants are a major soil-turnover group that rival or surpass termites and earthworms (Wilson 1990). Ants are also an important food resource for many vertebrates (Hölldobler and Wilson 1990), particularly birds. Willis and Oniki (1978) listed 50 bird species that depend on and consume a great number of arthropods fleeing army ant raids (Franks 1982b).

BEES AND ANTS ARE GOOD CANDIDATES AS BIOINDICATORS OF ENVIRONMENTAL CHANGE

Members of the order Hymenoptera are abundant in most ecosystems and are involved in many interactions with other taxa (LaSalle and Gauld 1993a,b). Hymenoptera fit the indicator group criteria discussed by Pearson (1994), and, compared with vertebrates, they rapidly respond in numbers to environmental change because of their high reproductive capacity and short life span. Species diversity, ranges of sociality, numbers of individuals, diverse requisite needs, and numerous ecological roles are factors that make this order ideal for evaluating forest fragments. Scale is important (Lawton et al. 1998), and bees and ants are sensitive to, but differ in their responses to, the scale of environmental disturbances, such as wildfires, invasion by exotic organisms, or the loss of critical requisite resources.

There is much to justify the use of bees and ants as indicators of ecosystem health. Bees can move between several resources present in one or more habitats and thus may be dependent on several different nearby habitat fragments (Banaszak 1996). Bees have not been used extensively to monitor, although this situation is changing as more information is gathered (Kearns and Inouye 1997; Frankie et al. 1998, 2002; Kevan 2001). In contrast, because native ant colonies persist over time, have limited ranges, and require an extensive but local foraging area, they are less susceptible to fragmentation than vertebrates or even bees. Thus they are dependent on resources that are in specific habitats in which they reside (Andersen 1990). Their disappearance is an early sign of local stresses in an ecosystem. However, several ant species are good invaders of disturbed habitats, and their presence is a warning of detrimental changes occurring in the habitat. Some ant genera and species are widespread and thus provide comparative data. Other ant genera have high species diversity with many specialist species. Finally, ants occupy higher trophic levels, are easily sampled, are relatively easy to identify to genus, and are responsive to changing environmental conditions (Majer 1983). Great species diversity, filling numerous ecological roles, and sensitivity to disturbance make ants an important ecological indicator group (Alonso 2000).

DOCUMENTING CHANGES IN ORGANISMS USED FOR MONITORING

New (1999) reviewed aspects of conducting invertebrate surveys for conservation that included ants and wasps but not bees. Through the use of trap nests (Strickler et al. 1996; Frankie et al. 1998) or sweep netting (Gess and Gess 1993; Kevan et al. 1997), populations of bees can now be surveyed in specific habitats (Kevan 2001). In addition, a relatively noninvasive monitoring technique, involving floral visitation counts, has been developed to assess relative floral attraction, diversity, and abundance of bees in an area (Frankie et al. 2002).

In contrast, ants have been extensively sampled by numerous methods, such as pitfall or bait traps, leaf litter sampling, beating or canopy fogging, and observation (see review by Bestelmeyer et al. 2000). Many of these methods sample different ecological groups with little species overlap. For example, bait traps placed on vegetation sample canopy-foraging species, whereas the same trap placed in holes in the ground collect only subterranean-foraging species.

USING BEES AND ANTS AS BIOINDICATORS

Bees have been rarely used as a monitoring tool, although honeybees (Bromenshenk et al. 1985) and solitary bees (Kevan et al. 1997) have been used to detect and monitor for pollutants. One reason that they have rarely been used is the lack of simple nondestructive monitoring methods. Another is the high variation in diversity (Williams et al. 2001) and population numbers (Frankie et al. 1998; Roubik 2001) of the native bee fauna from one place and time to another. The development of floral visitation counts (Frankie et al. 2002) and grouping of bees into functional groups, as suggested in table 6.1, should provide new opportunities for the use of bees in biological monitoring.

Ant monitoring has been used for fire management, pesticide contamination, habitat disturbance, and reserve design (Andersen 1990). Majer (1983) listed seven parameters for using ants as indicators: species richness, species density, Shannon's diversity index, Eveness index, Mountford's similarity index, indicator species, and indicator groups. In addition to Majer's

parameters, ant diversity can be examined by ecological roles if the ant genera are first organized into functional groups to reduce complexity (Greenslade 1985; Andersen 1986). Andersen (1991) described seven Australian ant-fauna functional groups based on their relative dominance within the ant community, resource needs, foraging preferences, and environmental preferences. He included opportunists, which are characteristic of disturbed habitats and share several attributes (i.e., generalized habits, omnivorous diets, flexible foraging times, poor competitors, easily displaced from food resources, most abundant at sites where dominant ants are least abundant), because their increase is an indicator of habitat disturbance. The occurrence of highly invasive (tramp) ants (Passera 1994) is of concern, and Saks and Carroll (1980) showed that tramp ants could become abundant in disturbed areas while remaining uncommon in nearby undisturbed forests. Exotic tramp ant species have been found to produce major changes in abundance and diversity of invertebrate species in other regions (Lubin 1984; Zenner-Polania 1994). Tennant (1994) found, however, that the tramp *Wasmannia auropunctata* was not a pest in its native Costa Rica. Kaspari and Majer (2000) give a more thorough discussion of using ants to monitor environmental changes.

CHANGES THAT ARE IMPORTANT TO BEES AND ANTS

Bees require a consistent supply of diverse, critical resources that are available in an intact dry forest. Changes in one or two plant resource species that provide either nesting or food materials can result in a void that can be detrimental. As forest fragments become smaller and more isolated, the loss of critical resources increases. For example, fewer nest sites can result in increased nest site competition and usurpation (Vinson and Frankie 2000) and an increase in mortality due to disease, parasites, and predator activity. As the population declines, abundant resources, such as nectar, may be under-

TABLE 6.1
Functional Groups of the More Common Bees in Costa Rica Based on Foraging and Nest Habits

FUNCTIONAL GROUPS	(SUBFAMILY) *GENUS*
Large to medium flower pollinators—deadwood nesters	(Xylocopinae) *Xylocopa*, (Apinae) *Centris*
Large to medium flower pollinators—ground nesters	(Apinae) *Centris, Epicharis*
Oil flower pollinators	(Apinae) *Centris, Paratetrapedia, Tetrapedia*
Moderate to small flower specialist pollinators	(Panurginae), (Apinae) *Ancyloscelis, Melitoma, Peponapis, Xenoglossa,* (Megachilinae) *Lithurgus*
Moderate to small flower generalists—cavity nesters	(Apinae) *Melipona*
Moderate to small flower generalists—ground nesters	(Colletinae), *Colletes*
Moderate to small flower generalists—leaf collectors	(Megachilinae) *Osmia, Anthidium, Megachile*
Moderate to small flower generalists—resin collectors	(Megachilinae), (Apinae) *Melipona*
Moderate to large flower specialists—fragrance collectors	(Apinae)
Nocturnal foragers	(Halictinae) *Megalopta*
Dawn foragers	(Apinae) *Peponapis, Xenoglossa*
Cleptoparasitic	(Megachilinae) *Coelioxys, Dolichostelis,* (Nomadinae) *Nomada,* (Apinae) *Mesoplia*
Buzz pollen collectors	(Diphaglossinae) *Ptiloglossa,* (Halictinae) *Megalopta,* (Apinae) *Centris, Epicharis; Gaesischia, Exomalopsis, Thygater,* (Xylocopinae) *Xylocopa*
Social generalist pollinators	(Apinae) *Apis, Melipona*

utilized, causing nectar-producing plant species to receive limited pollination (Frankie et al. 1997). If a resource within a fragment is lost, even temporarily, causing the extinction of the consumer, consumers from other habitat fragments may be unable to locate or reach to recolonize the fragment.

As forests are reduced or altered (or both), challenges to their health increase. Local environmental changes can also alter timing of important biological events, disrupting seasonal synchronizations. For example, the premature emergence of an important pollinator or premature flowering of a resource could have serious reproductive consequences for both (see chapter 4). Another serious problem for bees is the introduction of nonpreferred floral resource plants, planting of exotic flowers, and reforestation with non-native trees (Frankie et al. 1997, 1998). For ants these same plants may provide new prey or opportunities for invasive species. As a result, there is a change in the balance of biological interactions that can release some species from their controls or increase the susceptibility of an area to invasion.

CONSIDERATIONS IN MONITORING CHANGES IN BEE AND ANT POPULATIONS

Although recommendations regarding conservation of large areas and corridors (see chapters 3, 4, 9, 21, and 23) are essential, preserving diversity of habitat fragments is also important to maintain the region's overall diversity (see chapter 16). To use Hymenoptera as a conservation tool, monitoring techniques need to be implemented and parameters for evaluation developed. Parameters that target specific focus or functional groups (e.g., army ants or oil-collecting bees) that include the bee or ant fauna (i.e., number of genera or functional groups present) must be considered. Bees or ants can then be surveyed and monitored in an undisturbed area to establish baseline data. These data are essential as a comparison with disturbed areas or other areas of concern. Parameters already known to be useful include the presence or absence of certain focus or functional groups, such as army or tramp ant species or buzz-pollen or nectar-collecting bee species, and a survey of total numbers of genera present.

For example, the Costa Rican dry-forest ant fauna could be organized—in a manner similar to Andersen's (1991) organization—to include *Atta, Pseudomyrmex, Azteca, Eciton,* and *Labidus* as dominates; *Solenopsis, Camponotus, Gnamptogenys,* and *Pheidole* as subordinates; and *Crematogaster, Leptothorax,* and *Monomorium* as the generalist predators. The cryptic leaf-litter fauna include ponerine and myrmecine genera; opportunists include *Solenopsis, Wasmannia,* and *Pheidole;* and *Pachycondyla* and *Ectatomma* would round out the list as the large solitary foragers.

Although 67 percent of the world's flowering plants depend on insects for pollination (Tepedino 1979) with bees predominating (see chapter 2), to our knowledge no one has developed or

used bee functional groups as a survey or monitoring tool. As Stebbins (1979) noted, as habitats are fragmented, remnant plant populations become isolated, resulting in "ecological traps." Resident pollinators may be unable to locate required resources at the right time and thus may suffer declines (Jennersten 1988; Cane 2001). But such problems are not specific to habitat fragments. Janzen et al. (1982) reported that different habitats even in a conserved region differed dramatically in bee diversity. Some bees, such as euglossines, travel great distances, whereas others, such as *Centris flavofasciata*, are more local (Vinson et al. 1987). Further, a particular bee species may nest in one habitat type and travel to another for nest construction resources and then to a third or fourth for provisions. Thus, changes in bee species composition should be revealing, considered from a functional group standpoint.

With regard to establishing threshold levels for ants or bees in Costa Rica, there are no data for ants and only some for bees (Frankie et al. 2002). However, some preliminary suggestions can be offered. To establish upper threshold levels—levels at which the fauna can be considered "healthy"—climax-growth habitats and specialized embedded habitats in areas already protected should be surveyed. The establishment of lower threshold levels is more problematic. Future research lies in establishing quantitative measures of functional groups, determining lower threshold levels of target groups, and implementing warning systems for habitats in peril.

One method for measuring ecosystems' health would be to create a scale by establishing an upper threshold level for the number of ant genera or species present in a healthy habitat and comparing it, and the species composition, with the same information from habitats with various levels of disturbance. The upper threshold of genera present in a pristine area may be 50–60 genera, whereas in very disturbed areas, at least 5–8 genera largely composed of tramp ants should still be found. With ant functional groups as a parameter, intact, healthy habitat patches should have all six functional ant groups present, whereas highly disturbed areas may have only opportunistic species.

Bees could be dealt with similarly, but at the species level. For example, a decrease in the number of wood-nesting *Centris* and *Xylocopa* species would suggest a loss of deadwood nest resources, whereas an overall decrease in *Centris* but not other bee species would suggest a loss of oil resources. In the case of bees, another factor to consider is resource utilization in terms of flower visitation counts (Frankie et al. 2002). A decline in *Centris* at both nectar and oil resource trees in which the nectar is not completely removed but the oil resource is would suggest that the oil resource was limiting. As a result, restoring more oil-producing *B. crassifolia* trees to an area would be of more benefit to *Centris* than planting nectar-producing trees.

In summary, upper and lower threshold levels can be determined by surveying healthy, unaffected habitats, habitats of various sizes, and habitats with various levels of disturbance. Once thresholds are established, habitat patches can be monitored, and these results can be compared to assess levels of impact or disturbance or success of restoration efforts. Historical collections from undisturbed habitats are useful for long-term comparisons (Frankie et al. 1997).

IDENTIFICATION AND RESTORATION OF SPECIFIC HABITATS AND CRITICAL RESOURCES

First, various habitats should be characterized according to the bee and ant species present, including associated plants, animals, and environmental requirements. Second, bee and ant service or functional groups should be defined for each habitat type (table 6.1). Third, once bee and ant species and their various associations are known, a monitoring program can be initiated. This program should include abundance, distribution, species' composition, and occurrence of their requisite needs. Finally, the value of monitoring is in identifying habitats with problems and then attempting restoration to some desired level. For bees, this may involve planting missing preferred plant species or providing nest sites (see chapter 2). Ant restoration may require selective removal of tramp ant species, restoring certain associated plants, or providing other requisite resources.

RECOMMENDATIONS

Biologists involved in habitat or wildlife management, field ecology, or pest management should become involved in monitoring both native and exotic insects, including bees and ants, using mostly nondestructive methods. Monitoring should be scheduled for several distinct seasons, over a broad area, and ideally at several key times of day.

The most essential component to any conservation program is education. This requires development of educational materials that emphasize importance and value of insects such as bees and ants. In many cases it will be up to biologists to develop outreach materials for different audiences such as children, farmers, ranchers, and rural communities. Information is needed regarding the importance of bee diversity for efficient pollination of plants in conserved areas and many crops and the importance of native ants in managing pest outbreaks in natural and managed systems. Also needed is an increased awareness of invader species and ways in which they gain access to an area. Most landowners and stewards could also use this information to learn about the value of setting aside land for conservation and for being vigilant against invader organisms.

Attitudes toward natural resource use and exploitation must be changed, and governmental policy should play a role in implementing some of the outlined recommendations. The government could provide incentives to landholders to restore marginal or nonproductive agricultural land. Government policy could encourage and support biologists who interpret data collected in monitoring programs in public lands and in other conserved areas. Advisory groups should be established in selected regions that consist of several biologists (botanists, zoologists, and conservation-oriented specialists) and people from the agricultural community, tourist industry, municipal government, and educational community who can provide advice and suggestions to higher-level governmental agencies (see chapters 18 and 19).

ACKNOWLEDGMENTS

The authors thank Ronald Weeks, Peter Kevan, and Stan Schneider for manuscript suggestions.

REFERENCES

Agosti, D., J. D. Majer, L. E. Alonso, and T. R. Schultz, eds. 2000. *Ants: Standard methods for measuring and monitoring biodiversity.* Washington, D.C.: Smithsonian Institution Press. 299 pp.

Alonso, L. E. 2000. Ants as indicators of diversity. In *Ants: Standard methods for measuring and monitoring biodiversity,* ed. D. Agosti, J. D. Majer, L. E. Alonso, and T. R. Schultz, 80–88. Washington, D.C.: Smithsonian Institution Press.

Andersen, A. N. 1986. Patterns of ant community organization in mesic southeastern Australia. *Australian Journal of Ecology* 11:87–97.

———. 1990. The use of ant communities to evaluate change in Australian terrestrial ecosystems: A review and a recipe. *Proceedings of the Ecological Society of Australia* 16:347–57.

———. 1991. Parallels between ants and plants: Implications for community ecology. In *Ant-plant interactions,* ed. C. R. Huxley and D. F. Cutler, 539–58. Oxford: Oxford University Press.

———. 1997. Using ants as bioindicators: Multi-scale issues in ant community ecology. *Conservation Ecology* 1(1):8. [On-line] URL: http://www.consecol.org/vol1/iss1/art8

Banaszak, J. 1996. Ecological basis of conservation of wild bees. In *The conservation of bees,* ed. A. Mattheson, S. L. Buchmann, C. O'Toole, P. Westrich, and I. H. Williams, 55–62. Linnean Society Symposium Series 18. London: Academic Press.

Bestelmeyer, B. T., and Wiens. 1996. The effects of land use on the structure of ground-foraging ant communities in the Argentine Chaco. *Ecological Applications* 6:1225–40.

Bestelmeyer, B. T., D. Agosti, L. E. Alonso, C. R. F. Brandão, W. L. Brown, J. H. C. Delabie, and R. Silvestre. 2000. Field techniques for the study of ground-dwelling ants: An overview, description, and evaluation. In *Ants: Standard methods for measuring and monitoring biodiversity,* ed. D. Agosti, J. D. Majer, L. E. Alonso, and T. R. Schultz, 122–44. Washington, D.C.: Smithsonian Institution Press.

Bolton, B. 1994. *Identification guide to the ant genera of the world.* Cambridge, Mass.: Harvard University Press. 224 pp.

Bromenshenk, J. J., S. R. Carlson, J. C. Simpson, and M. J. Thomas. 1985. Pollution monitoring of Puget Sound with honey bees. *Science* 227: 632–34.

Buchmann, S. L. 1985. Bees use vibration to aid pollen collection from non-poricidal flowers. *Journal of the Kansas Entomological Society* 58:517–25.

Buchmann, S. L., and G. P. Nabhan. 1996. *The forgotten pollinators.* Covelo, Calif.: Island Press. 292 pp.

Cane, J. H. 2001. Habitat fragmentation and native bees: A premature verdict? *Conservation Ecology* 5(1):3. [On-line] URL: http://www.consecol.org/vol5/iss1/art3

Cherrett, J. M. 1989. Leaf-cutting ants. In *Ecosystems of the world.* 14B. *Tropical rain forest ecosystems,* ed. H. Lieth and M. J. A. Werger, 473–88. Biogeographical and Ecological Studies. Amsterdam: Elsevier.

Christensen, N. L., A. M. Bartuska, J. H. Brown, S. Carpenter, C. D'Antonio, R. Francis, J. F. Franklin, J. A. MacMahon, R. F. Noss, D. J. Parson, C. H. Petersen, M. G. Turner, and R. G. Woodmansee. 1996. The report of the Ecological Society of America Committee on the scientific basis for ecosystem management. *Ecological Applications* 6:665–91.

Eickwort, G. C., R. W. Matthews, and J. Carpenter. 1981. Observations on the nesting behavior of *Megachile rubi* and *M. texana* with a discussion of the significance of soil nesting in the evolution of Megachilid bees. *Journal of the Kansas Entomological Society* 54:557–70.

Frankie, G. W., and S. B. Vinson. 2001. Diversity, structure, and variations in pollination systems of the seasonal dry forest of Costa Rica. In *Tropical ecosystems: Structure, diversity and human welfare.* Proceedings of the International Conference on Tropical Ecosystems, ed. K. N. Ganeshaiah, R. Uma Shaanker, and K. S. Bawa, 202–3. New Delhi: Oxford-IBH.

Frankie, G. W., P. A. Opler, and K. S. Bawa. 1976. Foraging behavior of solitary bees: Implications for outcrossing of a neotropical forest tree species. *Journal of Ecology* 64:1049–57.

Frankie, G. W., S. B. Vinson, L. Newstrom, and J. F. Barthell. 1988. Nest site and habitat preferences of *Centris* bees in the Costa Rican dry forest. *Biotropica* 20:301–10.

Frankie, G. W., S. B. Vinson, M. A. Rizzardi, T. L. Griswold, S. O'Keefe, and R. R. Snelling. 1997. Diversity and abundance of bees visiting a mass flowering tree species in disturbed seasonal dry forest, Costa Rica. *Journal of the Kansas Entomological Society* 70:281–96.

Frankie, G. W., R. W. Thorp, L. E. Newstrom-Lloyd, M. A. Rizzardi, J. F. Barthell, T. L. Griswold, J.-Y. Kim, and S. Kappagoda. 1998. Monitoring solitary bees in modified wildland habitats: Implications for bee ecology and conservation. *Environmental Entomology* 27: 1137–48.

Frankie, G. W., S. B. Vinson, S. O'Keefe, and M. A. Rizzardi. 2000. Assessing impacts of Africanized honey bees in Costa Rica and California: A progress report. In *Proceedings of the Sixth International Conference on Apiculture in Tropical Climates*, 157–61. Cardiff, Wales: International Bee Research Association.

Frankie, G. W., S. B. Vinson, R. W. Thorp, M. A. Rizzardi, N. Zamora, and P. S. Ronchi. 2002. Coexistence of Africanized honey bees and native bees in the Costa Rican seasonal dry forest. In *Proceedings of the Second International Conference on Africanized Honeybees and Their Mites*, ed. E. H. Erickson et al., 327–39. Medina, Ohio: A. I. Root Co.

Franks, N. A. 1982a. Ecology and population regulation in the army ant *Eciton burchelli*. In *The ecology of a tropical forest: Seasonal rhythms and long-term changes*, ed. E. G. Leigh, A. S. Rand, and D. M. Windsor, 389–95. Washington, D.C.: Smithsonian Institution Press.

———. 1982b. A new method for censussing animal populations: The number of *Eciton burchelli* army ant colonies on Barro Colorado Island, Panama. *Oecologia* 52:266–68.

Gess, F. W., and S. K. Gess. 1993. Aculate wasps and bees in semi-arid areas of Southern Africa. In *Hymenoptera and biodiversity*, ed. J. LaSalle and I. D. Gauld, 83–114. Wallingford, England: CAB International.

Gottsberger, G. 1986. Some pollination strategies in neotropical savannas forests. *Plant Systematics and Evolution* 152:29–45.

Gotwald, W. H. 1995. *Army ants: The biology of social predation*. Ithaca, N.Y.: Cornell University Press. 302 pp.

Greenslade, P. J. M. 1985. Some effects of season and geographic aspect on ants (Hymenoptera: Formicidae) in the Mt. Lofty Ranges, South Australia. *Transactions of the Royal Society of South Australia* 109:17–23.

Griswold, T., F. D. Parker, and P. E. Hanson. 2000. An inventory of the bees of Costa Rica: The myth of the depauperate tropics. In *Proceedings of the Sixth International Conference on Apiculture in Tropical Climates, 152–56*. Cardiff, Wales: International Bee Research Association.

Hammond, P. M. 1994. Practical approaches to the estimation of the extent of biodiversity in speciose groups. *Philosophical Transactions of the Royal Society of London*, ser. B, 345:119–36.

Hanson, P. E., and I. D. Gauld. 1995. *The Hymenoptera of Costa Rica*. Oxford: Oxford University Press. 914 pp.

Hölldobler, B., and E. O. Wilson. 1990. *The Ants*. Cambridge: Belknap Press, Harvard University Press. 732 pp.

Huryn, V. M. B. 1997. Ecological impacts of introduced honeybees. *Quarterly Review of Biology* 72:275–97.

Huxley, C. R., and D. F. Cutler, eds. 1991. *Ant-plant interactions*. Oxford: Oxford University Press. 601 pp.

Janzen, D. H., P. J. DeVries, M. L. Higgins, and L. S. Kimsey. 1982. Seasonal and site variation in Costa Rican euglossine bees at chemical baits in lowland deciduous and evergreen forests. *Ecology* 63:66–74.

Jennersten, O. 1988. Pollination in *Dianthus deltoides* (Caryophyllaceae): Effects of habitat fragmentation on visitation and seed set. *Conservation Biology* 2:359–66.

Kaspari, M., and J. D. Majer. 2000. Using ants to monitor environmental change. In *Ants: Standard methods for measuring and monitoring biodiversity*, ed. D. Agosti, J. D. Majer, L. E. Alonso, and T. R. Schultz, 89–98. Washington, D.C.: Smithsonian Institution Press.

Kearns, C. A., and D. W. Inouye. 1993. *Techniques for pollination biologists*. Niwot: University Press of Colorado. 583 pp.

———. 1997. Pollinators, flowering plants, and conservation biology. *BioScience* 47:279–307.

Kevan, P. G. 2001. Pollinators as sensitive bioindicators of environmental conditions: Ecological and practical concerns. In *Tropical ecosystems: Structure, diversity and human welfare*. Proceedings of the International Conference on Tropical Ecosystems, ed. K. N. Ganeshaiah, R. Uma Shaanker, and K. S. Bawa, 198–99. New Delhi: Oxford-IBH.

Kevan, P. G., C. F. Greco, and S. Belaoussoff. 1997. Log-normality of biodiversity and abundance in diagnosis and measuring of ecosystemic health: Pesticide stress on pollinators on blueberry heaths. *Journal of Applied Ecology* 34: 1122–36.

Kruess, A., and T. Tscharntke. 1994. Habitat fragmentation, species loss, and biological control. *Science* 264:1581–84.

Lambeck, R. J. 1997. Focal species: A multi-species umbrella for nature conservation. *Conservation Biology* 11:849–56.

LaSalle, J., and I. D. Gauld. 1993a. Hymenoptera: Their diversity, and their impact on the diversity of other organisms. In *Hymenoptera and biodiversity*, ed. J. LaSalle and I. D. Gauld, 1–26. Wallingford, England: CAB International.

———, eds. 1993b. *Hymenoptera and biodiversity*. Wallingford, England: CAB International. 348 pp.

Lawton, J. H., D. E. Bignel, B. Boulton, G. F. Bloemers, P. Eggleton, P. M. Hammond, M. Hodda, R. D. Holt, T. B. Larsen, N. A. Mawdsley, and N. E. Stork. 1998. Biodiversity inventories, indicator taxa and effects of habitat modification in tropical forest. *Nature* (London) 391:72–76.

Loeb, S. L., and A. Spacie, eds. 1994. *Biological monitoring of aquatic systems*. Ann Arbor, Mich.: CRC Press. 381 pp.

Longino, J. T., and P. E. Hanson. 1995. The ants (Formicidae). In *The Hymenoptera of Costa Rica*, ed. P. E. Hanson and I. D. Gauld, 588–620. Oxford: Oxford University Press.

Lubin, Y. D. 1984. Changes in the native fauna of the Galapagos Islands following invasion by the little red fire ant, *Wasmannia auropunctata*. *Biological Journal of the Linnean Society* 21:229–42.

MacKay, W. P., and S. B. Vinson. 1989. A guide to the species identification of New World ants (Hymenoptera: Formicidae). *Sociobiology* 16:3–47.

Majer, J. D. 1983. Ants: Bio-indicators of minesite rehabilitation, land-use, and land conservation. *Environmental Management* 7:375–83.

Michener, C. D. 2000. *The bees of the world*. Baltimore: Johns Hopkins University Press. 872 pp.

Michener, C. D., and R. W. Brooks. 1984. Comparative study of the glossae of bees. *Contributions of the American Entomology Institute, Ann Arbor* 22:1–73.

New, R. T. 1999. Limits to species focusing in insect conservation. *Annals of the Entomological Society of America* 92:853–60.

O'Keefe, S. T., and D. Agosti. 1998. A new species of *Probolomyrmex* (Hymenoptera: Formicidae) from Guanacaste, Costa Rica. *Journal of the New York Entomological Society* 105:190–92.

Oliver, J., and A. J. Beattie. 1996. Designing a cost-effective invertebrate survey: A test of methods for rapid assessment of biodiversity. *Ecological Applications* 6:594–607.

Passera, L. 1994. Characteristics of tramp species. In *Exotic ants: Biology, impact, and control of introduced species*, ed. D. F. Williams, 23–43. San Francisco: Westview Press.

Pearson, D. L. 1994. Selecting indicator taxa for the quantitative assessment of biodiversity. *Philosophical Transactions of the Royal Society of London* B 345:75–79.

Pętal, J. 1978. The role of ants in ecosystems. In *Production ecology of ants and termites*, ed. M. V. Brian, 293–325. Cambridge: Cambridge University Press.

Richardson, D. H. S. 1992. *Pollution monitoring with lichens*. Naturalists' Handbooks 19. Slough, England: Richmond Publishing Co. 92 pp.

Roubik, D. W. 1989. *Ecology and natural history of tropical bees*. New York: Cambridge University Press. 514 pp.

———. 1996. African honeybees as exotic pollinators in French Guiana. In *The conservation of bees*, ed. A. Matheson, S. L. Buchmann, C. O'Toole, P. Westrich, and I. H. Williams, 73–182. London: Academic Press.

———. 2001. Ups and downs in pollinator populations: When is there a decline? *Conservation Ecology* 5(1):2. [On-line] URL: http://www.consecol.org/vol5/iss1/art2

Saks, M., and C. R. Carroll. 1980. Ant foraging activity in tropical agro-ecosystems. *Agro-Ecosystems* 6:177–88.

Samways, M. J. 1994. *Insect conservation biology*. London: Chapman and Hall. 358 pp.

Stebbins, G. L. 1979. Rare species as examples of plant evolution. In *Great Basin Naturalist Memoirs*, no. 3: *The Endangered Species: A Symposium; 7–8 Dec. 1978*, 113–18. Provo, Utah: Brigham Young University.

Stradling, D. J. 1991. An introduction to the fungus-growing ants, Attini. In *Ant-plant interactions*, ed. C. R. Huxley and D. F. Cutler, 5–18. Oxford: Oxford University Press.

Strickler, K., V. L. Scott, and R. L. Fisher. 1996. Comparative nesting ecology of two sympatric leafcutting bees that differ in body size (Hymenoptera: Megachilidae). *Journal of the Kansas Entomological Society* 69:26–44.

Sugden, E. A., R. W. Thorp, and S. L. Buchmann. 1995. Honeybee–native bee competition in Australia: Focal point for environmental change and apicultural response. *Bee World* 77:26–44.

Tennant, L. E. 1994. The ecology of *Wasmannia auropunctata* in primary tropical rainforest in Costa Rica and Panama. In *Exotic ants: Biology, impact, and control of introduced species,* ed. D. F. Williams, 80–90. San Francisco: Westview Press.

Tepedino, V. J. 1979. The importance of bees and other insect pollinators in maintaining floral species composition. In *Great Basin Naturalist Memoirs,* no. 3: *The Endangered Species: A Symposium; 7–8 Dec. 1978,* 39–150. Provo, Utah: Brigham Young University.

Thorp, R. W. 1979. Structural, behavioral and physiological adaptations of bees for collecting pollen. *Annals of the Missouri Botanical Garden* 66:788–813.

Tscharntke, T., A. Gathmann, and I. Steffan-Dewenter. 1998. Bioindication using trap-nesting bees and wasps and their natural enemies: Community structure and interactions. *Journal of Applied Ecology* 35:708–19.

Unruh, T. R., and R. H. Messing. 1993. Interspecific biodiversity in Hymenoptera: Implications for conservation and biological control. In *Hymenoptera and biodiversity,* ed. J. LaSalle and I. D. Gauld, 27–52. Wallingford, England: CAB International.

Vinson, S. B. 1997. Invasion of the red imported fire ant (Hymenoptera: Formicidae): Spread, biology and impact. *American Entomologist* 43: 23–39.

Vinson, S. B., and G. W. Frankie. 2000. Nest selection, usurpation, and a function for the nest entrance plug of *Centris bicornuta* (Hymenoptera: Apidae). *Annals of the Entomological Society of America* 93:254–60.

Vinson, S. B., G. W. Frankie, and R. E. Coville. 1987. Nesting habits of *Centris flavofasciata* (Hymenoptera: Apoidea: Anthophoridae) in Costa Rica. *Journal of the Kansas Entomological Society* 60:249–63.

Vinson, S. B., G. W. Frankie, and J. Barthell. 1993. Threats to the diversity of solitary bees in a neotropical dry forest in Central America. In *Hymenoptera and biodiversity,* ed. J. LaSalle and I. D. Gauld, 53–81. Wallingford, England: CAB International.

Vinson, S. B., H. J. Williams, G. W. Frankie, and G. Shrum. 1997. Floral lipid chemistry of *Byrsonima crassifolia* (Malpigheaceae) and a use of floral lipids by *Centris* bees (Hymenoptera: Apidae). *Biotropica* 29:76–83.

Wcislo, W. T. 1987. The roles of seasonality, host synchrony, and behaviour in the evolutions and distributions of nest parasites in Hymenoptera, with special reference to bees. *Biological Reviews. Cambridge Philosophical Society* 62:515–43.

Williams, D. F., ed. 1994. *Exotic ants: Biology, impact, and control of introduced species.* San Francisco: Westview Press. 332 pp.

Williams, N. M., R. L. Minckley, and F. A. Silvera. 2001. Variation in native bee faunas and its implications for detecting community changes. *Conservation Ecology* 5(1):7. [On-line] URL: http://www.consecol.org/vol5/iss1/art7

Williams, P. H., and K. J. Gaston. 1994. Measuring more biodiversity: Can higher-taxon richness predict wholesale species richness? *Biological Conservation* 67:211–17.

Willis, E. O., and Y. Oniki. 1978. Birds and army ants. *Annual Review of Ecology and Systematics* 9:243–63.

Wilson, E. O. 1990. *Success and dominance in ecosystems: The case of the social insects.* Oldendorf/Luhe, Germany: Ecology Institute. 104 pp.

Zenner-Polania, I. 1994. Impact of *Paratrechina fulva* on other ant species. In *Exotic ants: Biology, impact, and control of introduced species,* ed. D. F. Williams, 121–32. San Francisco: Westview Press.

CHAPTER 7

Ecology of Dry-Forest Wildland Insects in the Area de Conservación Guanacaste

Daniel H. Janzen

TROPICAL DRY FOREST (Murphy and Lugo 1986; Bullock et al. 1995) once occupied at least 60 percent of the forested tropics. Today, it is largely eliminated (Janzen 1988a). Where present, it is almost entirely in some complex state of incomplete and iterative secondary succession (e.g., Janzen 1974a, 1986a,b, 1988b,c, 1990, 2002; Holl 1999; Holl and Kappelle 1999; Toh et al. 1999). The elimination of tropical dry forest is largely due to its ease of removal and perturbation by timber mining and human-facilitated fire and its comparative ease of occupation by humans engaged in agriculture and their domesticated animals and plants, as compared with lowland tropical rain forest and deserts (Janzen 1988a). Contemporary anthropogenic drying and heating trends are accentuating the process in dry forest and also rendering former cloud forest and rain forest habitats more "dry forest-like" (e.g., Cochrane et al. 1999; Goldammer 1999; Nepstad et al. 1999; Pounds et al. 1999; Still et al. 1999). Although the restoration of tropical dry forest is still possible, humanity will not give the globe back to its wildland denizens, and old-growth tropical dry forest will never again cover large areas.

The ecology of wildland tropical dry-forest insects is therefore largely that of populations and individuals persisting in successional forests on the agroscape or in conserved wildlands that are "being restored." The latter are ecological islands that will forever be under the influence of human-generated biotic and climatological forces sweeping through the agroscape (e.g., Janzen 1983d, 1986b, 1988a–d), forces that the comparatively small patches of conserved wildlands cannot escape. As the few conserved wildlands in tropical dry forests are gradually restored over the centuries into whatever ecosystems are able to persist on their sites, future generations may be able to view a somewhat more "old-growth" version of what once existed. The larger the conserved area and the less perturbed it was before restoration began, the closer it will be to the original. But it will still be substantially distorted from the prehuman state, owing to permanently altered circumstances for insects as well as for all the other organisms and their ecosystems.

Ironically, this permanently changed state may not be as significant as an academic generation of evolutionary ecologists and conservationists have wanted to believe. At least on continental mainlands, the great majority of species in any specific contemporary habitat did not evolve in that particular place with that habitat's particular interactants (e.g., Janzen 1986d); rather, they evolved within some ecological island or under other isolational circumstances elsewhere and then immigrated to their place and current habitat.

A wildland habitat is a collection of species that persisted on their arrival and thus colonized the habitat, and their interactions from that point on are largely a product of the combination of the traits they had on arrival and which species were present when they arrived (Janzen 1985a, 1986d). When humans make massive and widespread changes in a habitat, it becomes a new habitat or ecosystem. In effect, every species is yet again an immigrant by virtue of being thrust into new ecological circumstances and biological relationships. Almost all the tropical dry forest and its denizens studied today are in this state. As a result, some species disappear, and others become more common, but those that remain adjust to a new habitat ecologically and largely with the traits they had before changes were introduced, just as each of these species adjusted in the past as it spread from its place of origin. In designating certain areas "conserved wildlands," humans are, in effect, creating ecological island ecosystems. The species that eventually populate these islands are those that are inherently able to survive in the new habitat; for some species, however, the isolation of the conserved wildlands produces the circumstances for further evolution. The new forms will adjust evolutionarily to the conserved wildland as well as fit into it ecologically. The time frame of this process clearly varies among species: the process affects jaguars differently than it affects

bacteria. But if the island is small enough and the selection intense enough, the rate of the evolutionary adjustment process may even begin to approximate that of the ecological adjustment process (e.g., Agrawal et al. 1999; Haukioja 1999). Permanent habitat fragmentation by humanity has the potential to generate speciation and impoverishment on a massive scale, as though the world were abruptly converted into thousands of archipelagoes rich in small islands. Insect population structures and evolutionary dynamics are such that they should be strongly affected by such a restructuring of the world.

In the past three decades, the scientific community has learned much more about the insect ecology of tropical dry forest. However, these new insights do not add substantially to what is already generally understood about insects and their interactions with the biotic and abiotic world. Rather, they reveal that the insect ecology of tropical dry forest is a matter of proportionality with respect to the multitude of ways that sets of species do things. And if these years of peering intently at one kind of tropical dry forest— the lowland Mesoamerican coastal plain from Veracruz, Mexico, to Pacific Panama—while glancing briefly at insects in other tropical sites (e.g., Janzen 1972, 1974b,c, 1976a, 1988d) have taught me anything, it is that one needs to focus on one place in order to understand this proportionality. Place-based ecological understanding is, however, very often subordinated in the pursuit of broadly applicable scientific principles. However, a local vision is essential to understanding how and why organisms do what they do. Furthermore, place-based understanding serves as a critical informational infrastructure for the very pragmatic process of integrating any specific conserved wildland with its resident, national, and international society, an integration that must sustain and develop with the conserved wildland if it is to be permanent (e.g., Janzen 1998a,b, 1999a,b, 2000a,b, 2001a,b).

What follows is a brief comment on a few aspects of the insect ecology of the tropical dry forest in the Area de Conservación Guanacaste (ACG) in northwestern Costa Rica. I focus on

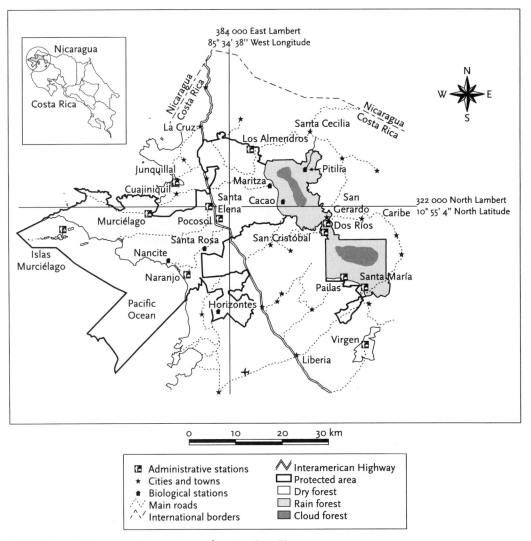

0   10   20   30 km

▣ Administrative stations	∧ Interamerican Highway
★ Cities and towns	▢ Protected area
▪ Biological stations	▢ Dry forest
⟋ Main roads	▨ Rain forest
⌒ International borders	▨ Cloud forest

MAP 7.1. Area de Conservación Guanacaste, northwestern Costa Rica.

the physical setting, the beginning of the rainy season, and seasonal movements, and I largely refrain from redescribing what I have already published on ACG dry-forest insect ecology per se (e.g., Janzen 1967a,b, 1973a,b, 1976b, 1978, 1979, 1980, 1981a, 1982a–d, 1983a–c, 1984a–c, 1986a–d, 1987a–c, 1988e,f, 1989, 1993; Janzen and Schoener 1968; Janzen et al. 1980a; Janzen et al. 1982; Janzen and Waterman 1984; Sharkey and Janzen 1995; Woodley and Janzen 1995; Janzen and Gauld 1997; Miller et al. 1997; Janzen et al. 1998; Hunt et al. 1999). This is not meant to be a review of these topics.

THE PHYSICAL SETTING

The 153,000-ha ACG (see http://www.acguana-caste.ac.cr) (map 7.1) begins out in the Pacific Ocean, and its 60,000 ha of dry forests extend inland eastward across 15–40 km of lowland coastal plain, mesas, and hills to the western lower slopes of Volcán Orosí, Volcán Cacao, and Volcán Rincón de la Vieja. Here, these extremely seasonal forests merge with the midelevation wetter forests leading into upper-elevation cloud forest (1,000–2,000 m) and thence down into the Caribbean rain forest (400–600 m) in the northern and eastern portions of the ACG. The ACG is bounded on the north, south, and east by agroscape. This 85-km-long conserved transect contains the three widespread Neotropical vegetation types—dry forest, cloud forest, and rain forest—and many intergrades (it contains nine Holdridge Life Zones and a plethora of transitions). The underlying physical substrate ranges from 85-million-year-old serpentine barrens to marine limestone and volcanic deposits from tens of millions of years to only a few days old.

The ACG dry-forest ecosystem contained between the volcanic slope evergreen forests and the coastal mangroves is meteorologically characterized by five to seven continuously rain-free months (roughly December to mid-May), a total rainfall of about 800–2,800 mm (contemporary 15-year average of about 1,500 mm), and a short (zero- to six-week) dry season (the Spanish-language *veranillo*, July–August) in the middle of the rainy season. The ACG dry-forest meteorology is that of a rain shadow in the western lee of the volcanoes, affected by the rainy season brought by the twice-annual passage of the thermal equator (the ACG is about 10° N latitude). The heating from the thermal equator pulls in moist air from the Pacific, air that rises and cools/condenses to create afternoon and evening thunderstorms. This moist air is occasionally overlain by masses of moist air pushed in from hurricanes over the Caribbean, mostly in the rainy season. Nocturnal temperatures in this dry forest generally range between 18°C and 22°C, with the lowest values on cloudless nights in the dry season. The diurnal temperatures range between 26°C and 36°C, the hottest days occurring during the relatively wind-free last two months of the dry season and the coldest days during the second half of the rainy season (October–November), when heavy rains produced by hurricanes affect the area. The most abrupt temperature change is the sudden cooling that comes with the first rains at the end of the long dry season (fig. 7.1) (Janzen 1984a, 1993; and see detailed weather records at http://www.acguana-caste.ac.cr/1999/indice_bases_datos/index.htm).

The dry season is relatively cloud-free; the rainy season alternates between heavy cloud cover and frequent clear mornings. This meteorological pattern is also affected by strong trade winds from the east-northeast for the first half of the dry season, bringing cooler air from the volcanoes to the northeast. Hurricanes have generally lost much of their windy force, but not their rain, by the time they arrive from the Caribbean and the Pacific.

The dry-forest ecosystem of the ACG was once continuous, stretching all the way north to the foothills of the mountains west of Mazatlán, Mexico (e.g., Martin et al. 1998), and south at least to the Canal Zone, broken by rain forest in the Golfo Dulce region of southern Pacific Costa Rica and Pacific coastal Guatemala, a desert break at the Balsas River Basin in western Mexico, and dry-forest extensions to the coastal lowlands of the Gulf of Mexico (Tampico to Yucatán and eastern Guatemala).

Some physical characteristics of the ACG that are key for insect ecology are that

- its dry forest lies within a few tens of kilometers of both (cooler) high-elevation cloud forests and (wetter) low-elevation rain forests and its margins intergrade with these other ecosystems;

- the dry season is severe enough to create deciduous and semideciduous forest types coupled with very strong seasonal phenology in plant growth and reproduction;

- the internal rain-fed aquatic systems are severely dried out by the long (and hot) rain-free season but the adjacent volcanoes create ever-flowing rivers that cross some of the dry forest as linear seasonal oases on their way to both the Atlantic and Pacific;

- the diverse ages and chemistries of the ACG rock and soil substrates, combined with complex meteorological conditions, sustain a complex array of plant species, phenologies, and life forms as food and shelter for insects;

- all fires in this forest are caused by humans and are therefore not part of the "natural"

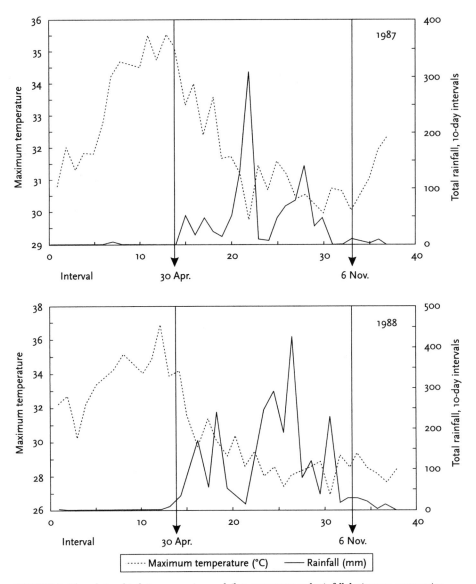

FIGURE 7.1. The relationship between maximum daily temperature and rainfall during two consecutive years at the weather station in the administration area, Sector Santa Rosa, Area de Conservación Guanacaste.

events that the insect community has experienced in the dry season prior to human entry; and,

· despite four centuries of European-style agriculture and ranching and millennia of indigenous use, the relatively low-quality soils and long sociopolitical distances from Costa Rican and Nicaraguan social centers have protected the general area from having

been thoroughly cleaned of its vegetation and hence much of its insect fauna.

The ACG old-growth forest remnants range from several thousand hectares of dwarf forest on serpentine on the western tip of the Santa Elena Peninsula to patches of a few tens of - hectares on volcanic soils; the rest of the remnants are highly complex mosaics of secondary successional stages that did not begin the long transformation to old-growth status until the fires were eliminated or controlled in the mid-1980s.

WHAT HAPPENS AT THE BEGINNING OF THE RAINY SEASON

The beginning of the rainy season, between late April and late May, is the most conspicuous aspect of ACG dry-forest insect ecology. The topics discussed later in this chapter—migration/movements, seasonal effects, dry/wet contrasts—all relate in some way to this meteorological event and its cascading biological consequences. Humans have long marked the beginning of the ACG rainy season entomologically by the masses of adult moths and beetles congregating at lights, the conspicuous defoliation by caterpillars and beetles, and the nesting of insectivorous birds. Other indications are the huge numbers of *Photinus* fireflies on the first dead-calm nights, the inescapable mating swarms of termites cued by the first rains, and, more poetically, the sensation of a world "crawling with insects."

The massive "appearance" of large numbers of species and individuals of adult phytophagous insects in the few days before and the month following the first heavy rains is in fact an extremely complex phenomenon. Some arrive by migration from distant cloud forests and rain forests (see the section "Migration and Other Movements" later in this chapter), others are simply now-active adults that have been hiding throughout the dry season in more moist habitats and microhabitats within the dry forest, and still others are newly eclosed from dormant prepupae and pupae in cocoons or the soil/litter (e.g., Janzen 1983a, 1987a,c, 1988e,f, 1993; see also chapter 8). Strikingly, almost none of the resultant juveniles, except for those of Orthoptera, are from eggs that passed the dry season in a dormant state (see Janzen 1984b for the exception by a saturniid moth, *Hylesia lineata*).

The "beginning of the rains," as indicated by the increased amount of rainfall and the concomitant drop in temperature (fig. 7.1), does not correlate exactly with the pulse of phytophagous insects in May. Many dormant pupae are somehow able to perceive the oncoming rains, and they initiate pupal development to the adult form, or even actually eclose, before the days of the first rains. When there is a single cohort of sib pupae, even sequestered in the monotonous ambient-air temperature of an ACG laboratory, the rainy season initiation does not bring them to eclose on a single day. Rather, their eclosion is spread over one to several weeks, a phenomenon that creates overlapping distributions of abundance (e.g., Janzen 1984a, 1993).

All this phenology varies within the year and between years. Even within a group of taxonomically and ecologically related species, such as the Saturniidae, each species perceives and reacts to the beginning of the rainy season somewhat differently, creating noncongruent peaks of adult species densities, followed by yet more variation in the peaks of caterpillar densities (Janzen 1993). In addition, each of the species' phenologies is affected somewhat differently by gradients in intensity and the timing of the onset of the rains, causing each year's "beginning of the rainy season" to be somewhat different from that of other years (fig. 7.1; see also Braby 1995; Nijhout 1999; Roskam and Brakefield 1999). In some species with short-lived adults, there are even color morphs that match the specific background colors characteristic of a few days before the rains begin and a few days after, respectively. For example, *Rothschildia lebeau* eclosing during the weeks before the rains are a rust red (which matches well the dry fallen leaves in the sun), whereas their sibs eclosing during the weeks after the rains are dark chocolate brown (which matches well the moist moldy fallen leaves in the shade of new leaf crops) (e.g., Janzen 1984a).

Many univoltine species remain hidden as dormant prepupae and pupae from the second month of the rainy season through the remaining four wet (and very leafy) months and the following six-month dry season (see nearly year-long prepupal and pupal duration records in Janzen and Hallwachs 2003 for select Ichneumonidae,

Braconidae, Tachinidae, Saturniidae, Sphingidae, Noctuidae, Geometridae, Notodontidae, Pyralidae, Lymantriidae, and Papilionidae). These species are displaying a biology structured much like that of classic univoltine extratropical and desert insects. By remaining dormant during this part of the rainy season, they are apparently avoiding what would otherwise be a carnivore-rich season generated by their own cadavers (Janzen 1987c, 1988e, 1993). Their lack of on-site reproduction is not due to more unpalatable or toxic foliage (Janzen and Waterman 1984). They do not attempt to reproduce during the long dry season because of the physical challenges and the scarcity of foliage. Most species that pass this long dormancy as prepupae do so in extremely tough and desiccation-proof cocoons (often underground, as well), and those that are dormant as pupae (in the litter or cocoons) have notably tough, thick, and presumably desiccation-resistant pupal cuticles. Some examples of the former are *Thyreodon* and *Enicospilus* (Ichneumonidae), *Microplitis* (Braconidae), *Sylepta belialis* (Pyralidae), *Ethmia* spp. (Ethmiidae), and many Limacodidae and Megalopygidae. Examples with notably tough pupal cuticles are *Xylophanes turbata*, *Manduca lefeburii* and *M. dilucida* (Sphingidae), *Schausiella santarosensis* (Saturniidae), *Goacampa variabilis* (Notodontidae), *Holochroa* (Geometridae), *Euscirrhopterus poeyi* (Noctuidae), *Eurytides epidaus* and *E. philolaus* (Papilionidae), and *Metavoria* (Tachinidae). The univoltine (or facultatively bivoltine) species that pass most or all the intervening months as reproductively inactive adults (e.g., *Eulepidotis, Melipotis, Letis, Coenipita*, and many other Noctuidae) are particularly confusing because collectors can find them in the daytime or at night in almost any season (they may appear at lights on virtually any night of the year) and therefore label them incorrectly as "multivoltine."

Insect species of tropical dry forest have evolved a plethora of forms of multivoltinism. In some species, phytophagous and carnivorous species alike, there are second to fourth generations in the rainy season while some members of the first generation remain dormant as prepupae or pupae, others are active nonreproductive adults, and yet others even migrate (e.g., *Xylophanes lefeburii* and *X. juanita* in the Sphingidae; *Epargyreus* in the Hesperiidae) to rain forest. Other species are reproductively active in the rainy season and either become dormant in the long dry season or leave (or are locally extinguished). Some species are extremely synchronized within the population, having virtually no overlap of rainy season generations, whereas others have natural histories such that sometimes by the second, and definitely by the fourth, generation virtually all life stages may be found in the habitat at the same time (though not in equal proportions). In general, the multivoltine species with nonfeeding adults (e.g., bombycoid Lepidoptera) maintain better synchrony of broods in the rainy season than do those with feeding adults. It is particularily commonplace for Hesperiidae (skipper butterflies) to have broadly overlapping generations during the rainy season and no or few caterpillars in the dry season, leaving the parasitoids of the caterpillars to survive the dry season as equally reproductively inactive adults (e.g., Janzen et al. 1998). The ease of finding hesperiid caterpillars in their conspicuous resting shelters greatly facilitates the tracking of this seasonal demography and interaction.

Many species that are full-time residents of dry forest have only one generation of insects when the rains begin, and they then live as nonreproductive adults for most of the year; this trait creates havoc with classic attempts to map the phenology of their natural history by ordinary collecting processes. The huge number of moths at lights during the first week following the first rain, for example, has long been intuitively interpreted as "emergence following the rains" when in fact it is initially made up mostly of a combination of incoming migrants and newly active adults that have been present for 6–11 months but hiding in the foliage and in locally moist areas. The groups of moths at lights for the next several weeks are made up largely of individuals newly eclosed from dormant pre-pupae or pupae.

During the first three months of the ACG rainy season in dry forest, then, there is a massive pulse of reproductive activity by phytophagous insects and their carnivores, followed by an extremely variable interannual second, and greatly reduced, "breeding period" during the second half of the rainy season. This is followed by a near absence of breeding insect populations during the long dry season, except for a few examples (e.g., bees, bruchid beetles) discussed later in this chapter. Understanding the phenologies of decomposers (e.g., Janzen 1983b), pollinator systems (e.g., Janzen 1967b; Janzen et al. 1980b, 1982), food for breeding birds (Janzen and Joyce, unpubl. data), and other major insect interactions needs to take this entomophenological process into account. These systems all reinforce and detract from one another on both ecological and evolutionary time scales.

Although there is a great burst of new foliage at the beginning of the rainy season, individual plants may refoliate as much as a month before to a month after, depending on the species of plant and even the specific age/ecological circumstances of the individual (e.g., young plants often leaf out earlier than do adults, plants on ridges often have quite different leaf phenologies than do conspecifics in valley bottoms). Since many species of dry-forest herbivores are host-specific to one or a few species of plants and often are even leaf-age specific (e.g., Janzen 1979, 1984b,c, 1985b; Janzen and Hallwachs 2003), the interspecific phenological differences are important and may be reflected in the details of abundance of a given insect species within and between years.

The great bulk of the carnivores in the ACG dry forest are also quite specific in their needs: the species of prey/hosts, the ecological circumstances in which they occur, or both (e.g., Janzen and Pond 1975; Janzen 1981b; Gauld et al. 1992; Janzen and Gauld 1997; Janzen et al. 1998). Not only does the general beginning of the rains

create food phenology, but the different reactions to the rains by various species that are food for others affect food availability. For a bird that brings only sphinx and saturniid moth caterpillars to its nestlings (Janzen and Joyce unpubl. data), a year in which there are tons of noctuid caterpillars per hectare may be a year of nestling starvation.

Being large diurnal mammals, most humans do not appreciate the microgeographical variation in tropical dry forest that is largely generated by the subtleties of differential drying of slopes, soil types, and wind exposures. However, insects are very sensitive to these place-based variations in their food, heat, and moisture. The anticipation of the rainy season by adult insects that are newly active, newly eclosed, and in-migrating begins near the ACG coast and spreads inland to the base of the volcanoes over a several-week period. A riparian tree that leafs out a week before its conspecifics on dry ridge soil may receive the great bulk of the egg load of the population of a univoltine noctuid that has its only generation on new leaves "at the beginning of the rains." The plants on a dry ridge that become totally deciduous in the long dry season may have quite different herbivore loads than those of a slightly more moist site that contains a few evergreen (shady tree) sites ideal for estivation (Janzen 1973a, 1976b). The cooler, shady understory of more evergreen riparian vegetation (e.g., Janzen 1976c) is an excellent habitat for insects during the dry season but a poor one during the rainy season (owing to the lack of photosynthesis), while a ridge a few meters away provides the opposite circumstance.

MIGRATION AND OTHER MOVEMENTS

Three types of migration occur in the ACG. The first consists of extremely complex local movements within the dry forest. Local seasonal movements by dry-forest insects between sun and shade, moist and dry areas, warm and cool areas, and food-abundant and food-poor areas are anticipated and obvious. The ACG is somewhat atypical as a dry forest in this context because in addition to its seasonal rain-fed temporary watercourses and pools, it has rivers flowing through portions of it from the cloud forest volcanoes to both oceans (northern ACG rivers flow into Lake Nicaragua and thence the Atlantic). These rivers offer more moist and more permanent dry-season refugia (and more shady photosynthate-free habitats) than do the temporary watercourses and also are wet corridors that connect many kinds of dry forest.

However, in addition to the local seasonal ebb and flow of insect populations, there are two striking and generally unappreciated other local insect movements. First, and as yet poorly documented, is what may be termed a "rolling seasonal invasion" from the more evergreen and wetter forests to the east. These are insects of the rain forest and wetter intergrade forests whose resident populations fly into the adjacent newly green dry forest at the beginning of the rainy season and produce their first-generation larvae. The second generation of these species then moves farther into the dry forest (toward the Pacific Ocean). The third and fourth generations, if any, move yet farther. By the end of a long and wet rainy season they may have invaded the entire ACG dry forest wherever their host plants (or prey) occur. The long dry season then results in the local extinction of all (an unknown number of individuals retreat all the way back to the volcanoes). If there is a run of relatively dry rainy seasons, many of these species are not encountered as "dry-forest species." However, if there is a run of relatively wet (and, in particular, long) rainy seasons, these species appear in visiting scientists' inventories as normal dry-forest species.

The relevance of this phenomenon depends on the proximity of dry forest to wetter forests, but the entire ACG dry forest is well within its range. This phenomenon has its obvious parallels in the annual variable degree of summer invasion of southern U.S. species into more northern latitudes and invasion of arid Mexico from the Gulf Coast (e.g., Powell and Brown 1990). Interestingly, a phenomenon of this na-

ture probably gave rise to classic monarch butterfly migration between highland Mexico and the United States, and the local resident ACG population of monarch butterflies is one of the rolling seasonal invaders of the ACG dry forest.

The third type of migration is the movement of many species of ACG insects between the ACG dry forest and more distant (but national) ecosystems (also see chapter 8). (The appearance of adults from dormant prepupae and pupae a few millimeters to centimeters below the soil is a very short distance variation on this theme.) There are at least two types of these migrants.

One type appears to migrate out to another ecosystem to be dormant there, to wait for the next year's rains. Social wasps such as *Polistes variabilis* (Vespidae) illustrate this well (Hunt et al. 1999), as do many other carnivores, such as tachinid flies, parasitic wasps, and dragonflies. In the last half of the rainy season, most but not all *P. variabilis* wasps abandon their small nests in the dry forest in the ACG lowlands (in which caterpillar prey is sparse) and fly up into the cold cloud forests on the volcano tops. There several thousands (mostly female) of dormant individuals sequester themselves in masses in hollow trees. When the rains come, they descend to the dry-forest lowlands and establish many new (small) nests scattered throughout the dry forest. The relatedness of the individuals in these new nests is unknown. A skipper butterfly, *Aguna asander* (Hesperiidae), whose caterpillars feed on *Bauhinia ungulata* (Fabaceae) leaves in the rainy season in the dry-forest lowlands, does the same but roosts individually in the cold cloud forest understory.

The much more conspicuous kind of distant migration is displayed by the many species of butterflies and moths that arrive with the first rains, have one generation on ACG dry foliage, eclose from their pupae within several weeks, and leave to have other generations in rain forest (in a small set of species, some individuals remain and generate a second or third generation, which in turn leave at the end of the rainy season) (Janzen 1987c, 1988e, 1993; Powell and

Brown 1990; chapter 8). Many of their parasitoids leave with them and may well have other generations in the rain forest ecosystems to which the adults migrate. It is likely that only part of the adults from the rain forest generations return to the dry forest at the beginning of the next rainy season. The numbers of individual migrants of a given species appearing each year in the ACG dry forest vary dramatically from virtually none to so many that the caterpillars thoroughly defoliate their food plants (e.g., Janzen 1985b, 1988f). Many but not all of these species have caterpillars that specialize on leaves only a few days to weeks old, and virtually all are species that feed as adults.

The Lepidoptera species that participate in the east-west (wet-dry) seasonal migration are species with very large geographical distributions (from tropical Mexico to lower tropical South America). The migrating moth species can occur in huge numbers at lights in passes at 600 to 2500 m elevation in Costa Rica's mountain ranges that separate the rain forests from the dry forests (and see Powell and Brown 1990). It is very striking that there is roughly a 50:50 sex ratio in these migrants arriving at lights (presumably used for orientation), in contrast to the extremely heavy bias in favor of males arriving at lights in the lowland breeding areas (where the light is used as part of the males' orientation during search for females; Janzen 1983a).

Since the adults seem incapable of surviving the dry season in the dry forest (and the immatures by and large do not remain dormant during this time), they might be best thought of as rain forest species that seasonally perform long-distance invasion of the dry forest during the first half of its relatively carnivore-free rainy season. Later, rather than stay for another generation in the second half of the rainy season, they flee from the (rapidly burgeoning) carnivore community, generated by the larvae of their generation and the larvae of residents (Janzen 1987c). In this sense they are analogous to the many birds that migrate into extratropical latitudes to have a single generation and then leave. It would be only a short step for these moths and butter-

flies to evolve such that they do not even have a generation on the rain forest side of Costa Rica. However, their relatively low capacity for full-year life spans as nonreproductive adult insects suggests that the evolution of univoltinism would require the evolution of pupal dormancy as displayed by some dry-forest nonmigrants.

It is unknown in which species of migrants the entire population moves back to the dry forest and in which species only a portion of the population returns. In the ACG, each year of caterpillar inventory (http://janzen.sas.upenn.edu) has located additional species of Lepidoptera with a very low density of caterpillars on the rain forest side throughout the year and a large number of caterpillars in the first half of the rainy season in dry forest (e.g., *Manduca occulta*, *M. sexta*, *Xylophanes pluto*, *X. chiron*, *Unzela japix*, *Enyo ocypete*, *Pachylioides resumens*, *Pachylia ficus*, *Neococytius cluentis*, *Cocytius anteus*, *Eupyrrhoglossum sagra*, *Aellopos titan*, all in the Sphingidae; many species of Noctuidae, Nymphalidae, Hesperiidae, and Papilionidae). Equally, every season of rearing parasitoids in the rain forest locates more "dry forest" parasitoids that have a large generation in the first half of the rainy season but are also breeding at other times of the year in the lowland rain forest on the eastern (Atlantic) side of the ACG (e.g., many species of *Belvosia*, *Drino*, *Blepharipa*, *Hyphantrophaga*, *Siphosturmia*, *Chetogena*, *Patelloa*, and *Atacta* in the Tachinidae).

It is likely that other insects are doing the same thing as the Lepidoptera and their parasitoids, but to date the only truly spectacular example is the millions of dragonflies (Odonata) that move from the ACG dry forest to the Atlantic rain forests in August and January, using the same low-elevation passes that the migrant moths and butterflies use. Their return, if they return, is not conspicuous.

When one considers the dry season's violent winds, dry soil and air, burning sun, leafless trees, lack of breeding birds and insects, and other seasonal "difficulties," there is a strong tendency to label the rainy season as "good" for insects and the long dry season as "bad" (thereby equating the dry season with the northern winter). However, as with the other dry-forest life forms of organisms, it all depends on natural history. If food is present in the dry season, then that may well be the good time of year.

For *Liomys salvini* hispid pocket mice (Heteromyidae), which are major predators on ACG dry-forest seeds and moth pupae in the litter (Janzen 1986e), the rainy season becomes progressively more food-impoverished as the seeds germinate and the first-generation crop of moth pupae ecloses or is harvested. Seeds for food are not abundant again until the following dry season. For bruchid beetles (Bruchidae), which have their one or two generations on these same seeds in the dry season (Janzen 1975, 1980), the last half of the dry season and the entire rainy season are periods of population decline, and the reproductively dormant adults hide in rolled leaves to avoid carnivores. Seed-eating weevils (Curculionidae) have to wait one and sometimes two years as hidden and reproductively dormant adults between (dry-season) fruit crops (e.g., Janzen 1974a, 1976d, 1978, 1982c,d, 1989). For many species of bees and other flower visitors, some portion of the dry season is the reproductive time of year (e.g., Frankie et al. 1997), and, as for bruchid beetles, the rainy season is something to be tolerated in some form of dormancy. This is even reflected in the beekeepers' general need to feed domestic *Apis mellifera* bees during the first half of the rainy season in Guanacaste Province, the same bees from which a honey surplus can be harvested in the dry season. Even leaf-cutter ants (*Atta*) may actually be harvesting higher-quality food in the dry season (e.g., Wirth et al. 1997), though the dry-season air is too dry to permit foraging in the daytime.

Each season brings some very specialized kinds of habitats. The strong winds of the first two months of the dry season break living branches, and the exposed wounds are ideal oviposition sites for cerambycid beetles and Cossidae moths, reflected in a peak in numbers of adult species and individuals at the lights in January. Drying streams have small puddles filled with apparently reproductively dormant adult aquatic beetles and bugs that will fly out across the newly wet landscape six months later in search of temporary swamps rich in decomposing vegetation and associated microbiota. The end of the short period of dry weather that occurs during the middle of the rainy season can deceive pupae into behaving as if it is the end of the long dry season, and consequently the newly eclosed adults (and their offspring) are thrust into the carnivore-rich second half of the rainy season. The first half of the rainy season is the time when densities of insect-eating carnivores are at their annual minimum because of the relative absence of insects as food during the long dry season, and in the second half of the rainy season they should be at their maximum (unless they migrate).

Newly fallen crops of dry-season fruits, rich in proteins and sugars for (extinct) large vertebrates (Janzen and Martin 1982), offer a non-rotting food for generations of pyralid moth larvae (e.g., *Anypsipyla univitella*), which are then deprived of these foods by fungi with the onset of the first rains (e.g., Janzen 1982a, 1983c). The distribution of ant-lion nests in the dry season (everywhere) and in the rainy season (only under rain-free overhangs) is illustrative. The life-giving rain that falls in the forest canopy also distributes lethal viruses, fungi, and bacteria among the leaves eaten by caterpillars. Many caterpillars may eat the foliage at the very beginning of leaf flush because of its microbiological cleanliness as much as for some specific nutrient content or lack of internal chemical defenses.

In contrast to what many have believed or wanted to believe, however, once the foliage has become several weeks old, it is basically the same food throughout the rainy season (Janzen et al. 1980a; Janzen and Waterman 1984). This is even more so for the leaves of the evergreen species sprinkled through the dry forest (e.g., *Hymenaea courbaril*, *Swietenia macrophylla*, *Manilkara chicle*, *Swartzia cubensis*, *Inga vera*, *Hirtella racemosa*, *Ocotea veraguensis*, *Ouratea lucens*, *Sloanea terniflora*, *Andira inermis*, *Licania arborea*).

What is "good" habitat for an insect also shifts dramatically in microlocation with the seasons. For example, in the long dry season, the cool and shady deep forest understory in riparian habitats and under individual evergreen tree species (and in relatively evergreen old-growth forest as opposed to more deciduous secondary succession) is a highly favored place for those species of insects that pass the dry season as adults in reproductive dormancy. When the rains come, the photosynthate-poor, heavily shaded forest understory is quickly vacated in search of insolated canopies at all levels. Likewise, the friendly moist soil and litter of riparian sites in the dry season may become an anaerobic swamp in the full rainy season.

CONCLUSION

The ACG's insect biodiversity, as is the case with other taxa, has been affected by humanity in four irreversible ways. Its actions continue to have an impact even though the ACG is now being allowed to return to old-growth status over its entire 110,000 terrestrial hectares of dry forest, rain forest, cloud forest, and intergrades.

First, the ACG will always be an ecological island of this size, with the attendant characteristics of an island that was sliced off a mainland (as opposed to an oceanic island whose biota arrives only by long-distance immigration and on-site evolution). It is unclear as to what equilibrium level its species density and community structure will move. The dry-forest side of the ACG appears to be large enough to sustain a major portion of its original dry-forest biodiversity, though the destruction of complementary wetter areas outside the ACG—homes for seasonal migrants—will take its toll. The volcano cloud forest ecosystems are currently about the same size they originally were, but climate change is shrinking them (Pounds et al. 1999). The rain forest in the eastern ACG, now just a small fragment, was once thousands of times larger in an eastern direction. This rain forest fragment is destined to go the way of all small islands with one exception: it has the peculiar characteristic of being a haven for both dry-forest migrants and wet-forest elevational migrants.

Second, because the ACG will always be an ecological island surrounded by a large and complex agroscape, it will always be influenced by distinctive edge effects generated by that agroscape, such as local climate change, invasive biological control agents, and introduced species (e.g., Janzen 1986b; Estrada et al. 1998; Williams-Linera et al. 1998). Converting some portion of this neighboring agroscape to various kinds of permanent secondary succession, such as semiwild timber plantations or hunting areas, will offer suitable habitat for many secondary successional species at high densities. However, these in turn create a huge biotic edge effect penetrating kilometers into the (regenerating) old-growth forest; the secondary successional species invade the old growth at a density that would never be generated by the old growth itself (Janzen 1983d). Ironically, it may well be better for the ACG to be surrounded by a polished and economically viable agroscape than by a so-called buffer zone of permanent secondary succession and economically disadvantaged subsistence agrarians.

Third, no matter how high the quality attained by the ACG's regenerating old-growth dry forest, it will never again receive the large number of migrants that it once received from the huge area of lowland rain forest to the east, and hence it will also never generate the large numbers of migrants that it once did. There is no way to know which of these two processes will be more strongly affected. It will depend a great deal on which species are affected most severely by converting old-growth rain forest to patchy secondary succession. Similarly, the dry forest can never again generate and receive the same numbers of migrants to and from the cloud forest (even if climate change is reversed and the cloud forests regain their territory).

Fourth, the oncoming climate changes (drying and warming for the ACG) will create massive changes in species' distributions and interactions, both directly and through tiny shifts in species' natural histories, as are now being documented outside the tropics (e.g., Petersen 1998; Brown et al. 1999).

These four permanent changes and aspects, however, do not create an ecosystem that falls outside "naturally" occurring circumstances for large old-growth dry forests that once occurred elsewhere in the Neotropics. In other words, there are dry-forest areas far from rain forest (and cloud forest) generators and receivers of migrants and dry forests with no rain forests or cloud forests on their margins. There are dry-forest islands and peninsulas surrounded by deserts, oceans, and other unfavorable habitats. Invasion by new biological entities, species that have arrived (by whatever means) and eventually become part of what is old growth, has been part of the normal construction process for mainland ecosystems as long as they have existed. Future generations will have at least some idea of what once was the ACG's dry forest.

In the end, the ACG will be what it will be, as long as we can cause it to be viewed as sufficiently useful and important to society that it is accepted as a member with full rights (Janzen 1998a,b, 1999a,b, 2000a,b, 2001a,b). If we fail in this challenge, a challenge as much sociological as scientific, neither the ACG nor its dry-forest ecosystem will survive.

ACKNOWLEDGMENTS

This chapter, and the caterpillar/host/parasitoid inventory that provided some of the information for it, has been supported by NSF grants BSR 90-24770, DEB 93-06296, DEB-94-00829, DEB-97-05072, and DEB-00-72730, as well as by financial, administrative, and logistic support from INBio, the government of Costa Rica, the Area de Conservación Guanacaste, CONICIT of Costa Rica, Keidanren of Japan, the Children's Rainforest Japan, the Children's Rainforest Sweden, and the Children's Rainforest UK. Many individuals have supported the development of the project in a multitude of ways. I especially thank W. Hallwachs, A. Masis, R. Robbins, J. M. Burns, D. Harvey, A. Solis, C. Lemaire, R. Poole, J.-M. Cadiou, J. Miller, J. Franclemont, J. Rawlins, P. Gentili, E. Munroe, R. Hodges, J. A. Powell, M. Epstein, J. Corrales, D. Whitehead, J. King-solver, P. J. DeVries, M. Scoble, L. Pitkin, M. Schauff, M. Sharkey, I. Gauld, S. Ward, N. Zamora, R. Liesner, M. M. Chavarria, R. Espinoza, M. Wood, N. Woodley, S. Shaw, J. Whitfield, D. Quicke, S. Shaw, C. Darling, and D. Carmean for identifications, and for caterpillar and parasitoid hunting and husbandry, R. Moraga, G. Sihezar, G. Pereira, L. Rios, M. Pereira, O. Espinosa, E. Cantillano, M. Pereira, R. Franco, H. Ramirez, F. Chavarria, M. M. Chavarria, E. Olson, C. Moraga, P. Rios, C. Cano, D. Garcia, F. Quesada, E. Araya, E. Guadamuz, R. Espinosa, R. Blanco, A. Guadamuz, D. Perez, R. Blanco, F. Chavarria, C. Camargo, H. Kidono, A. Masis, W. Haber, and W. Hallwachs.

REFERENCES

Agrawal, A. A., C. Laforsch, and J. Tollrian. 1999. Transgenerational induction of defences in animals and plants. *Nature* 401:60–62.

Braby, M. F. 1995. Reproductive seasonality in tropical satyrine butterflies: Strategies for the dry season. *Ecological Entomology* 20:5–17.

Brown, J. L., S.-H. Li, and N. Bhagabati. 1999. Long-term trend toward earlier breeding in an American bird: A response to global warming. *Proceedings of the National Academy of Sciences* 96:5565–69.

Bullock, S. H., H. A. Mooney, and E. Medina. 1995. *Seaonally dry tropical forests.* Cambridge: Cambridge University Press. 450 pp.

Cochrane, M. A., A. Alencar, M. D. Schulze, C. M. Souza Jr., D. C. Nepstad, P. Lefebvre, and E. A. Davidson. 1999. Positive feedbacks in the fire dynamics of closed canopy tropical forests. *Science* 284:1832–35.

Estrada, A., R. Coates-Estrada, D. A. Anzures, and P. Cammarano. 1998. Dung and carrion beetles in tropical rain forest fragments and agricultural habitats at Los Tuxtlas, Mexico. *Journal of Tropical Ecology* 14:577–93.

Frankie, G. W., S. B. Vinson, M. A. Rizzardi, T. L. Griswold, S. O'Keefe, and R. R. Snelling. 1997. Diversity and abundance of bees visiting a mass flowering tree species in disturbed seasonal dry forest, Costa Rica. *Journal of the Kansas Entomological Society* 70:281–96.

Gauld, I. D., K. J. Gaston, and D. H. Janzen. 1992. Plant allelochemicals, tritrophic interactions and the anomalous diversity of tropical parasitoids: The "nasty" host hypothesis. *Oikos* 65:353–57.

Goldammer, J. G. 1999. Forests on fire. *Science* 284:1782–83.

Harvey, C. A., and W. A. Haber. 1999. Remnant trees and the conservation of biodiversity in Costa Rican pastures. *Agroforestry Systems* 44: 37–68.

Haukioja, E. 1999. Bite the mother, fight the daughter. *Nature* 401:22–23.

Holl, K. 1999. Factors limiting tropical rain forest regeneration in abandoned pasture: Seed rain, seed germination, microclimate and soil. *Biotropica* 31:229–42.

Holl, K., and M. Kappelle. 1999. Tropical forest recovery and restoration. *Tree* 14:378–79.

Hunt, J. H., R. J. Brodie, T. P. Carithers, P. Z. Goldstein, and D. H. Janzen. 1999. Dry season migration by Costa Rican lowland paper wasps to high elevation cold dormancy sites. *Biotropica* 31:192–96.

Janzen, D. H. 1967a. Fire, vegetation structure, and the ant × acacia interaction in Central America. *Ecology* 48:26–35.

———. 1967b. Synchronization of sexual reproduction of trees with the dry season in Central America. *Evolution* 21:620–37.

———. 1972. Protection of *Barteria* (Passifloraceae) by *Pachysima* ants (Pseudomyrmecinae) in a Nigerian rain forest. *Ecology* 53:885–92.

———. 1973a. Sweep samples of tropical foliage insects: Effects of seasons, vegetation types, elevation, time of day, and insularity. *Ecology* 54:687–708.

———. 1973b. Evolution of polygynous obligate acacia-ants in western Mexico. *Journal of Animal Ecology* 42:727–50.

———. 1974a. The deflowering of Central America. *Natural History* 83:48–53.

———. 1974b. Tropical blackwater rivers, animals, and mast fruiting by the Dipterocarpaceae. *Biotropica* 6:69–103.

———. 1974c. Epiphytic myrmecophytes in Sarawak: Mutualism through the feeding of plants by ants. *Biotropica* 6:237–59.

———. 1975. Interactions of seeds and their insect predators/parasitoids in a tropical deciduous forest. In *Evolutionary strategies of parasitic insects and mites*, ed. P. W. Price, 154–86. New York: Plenum Press.

———. 1976a. The depression of reptile biomass by large herbivores. *American Naturalist* 110: 371–400.

———. 1976b. Sweep samples of tropical deciduous forest foliage-inhabiting insects: Seasonal changes and inter-field differences in adult bugs and beetles. *Revista de Biología Tropical* 24:149–61.

———. 1976c. The microclimate differences between a deciduous forest and adjacent riparian forest in Guanacaste Province, Costa Rica. *Brenesia* 8:29–33.

———. 1976d. Two patterns of pre-dispersal seed predation by insects on Central American deciduous forest trees. In *Tropical trees: Variation, breeding and conservation*, ed. J. Burley and B. T. Styles, 179–88. London: Academic Press.

———. 1978. Seeding patterns of tropical trees. In *Tropical trees as living systems*, ed. P. B. Tomlinson and M. H. Zimmerman, 83–128. New York: Cambridge University Press.

———. 1979. Natural history of *Phelypera distigma* (Boheman), Curculionidae, a Costa Rican defoliator of *Guazuma ulmifolia* Lam. (Sterculiaceae). *Brenesia* 16:213–19.

———. 1980. Specificity of seed-attacking beetles in a Costa Rican deciduous forest. *Journal of Ecology* 68:929–52.

———. 1981a. Patterns of herbivory in a tropical deciduous forest. *Biotropica* 13:271–82.

———. 1981b. The peak in North American ichneumonid species richness lies between 38 and 42 degrees north latitude. *Ecology* 62:532–37.

———. 1982a. Cenízero tree (Leguminosae: *Pithecellobium saman*) delayed fruit development in Costa Rican deciduous forests. *American Journal of Botany* 69:1269–76.

———. 1982b. Natural history of guacimo fruits (Sterculiaceae: *Guazuma ulmifolia*) with respect to consumption by large mammals. *American Journal of Botany* 69:1240–50.

———. 1982c. *Cleogonus* weevil seed predation on *Andira* can be predicted by fruit punctures. *Brenesia* 19/20:591–93.

———. 1982d. Simulation of *Andira* fruit pulp removal by bats reduces seed predation by *Cleogonus* weevils. *Brenesia* 19/20:165–70.

———. 1983a. Insects. In *Costa Rican natural history*, ed. D. H. Janzen, 619–45. Chicago: University of Chicago Press.

———. 1983b. Seasonal change in abundance of large nocturnal dung beetles (Scarabaeidae) in a Costa Rican deciduous forest and adjacent horse pasture. *Oikos* 41:274–83.

———. 1983c. Larval biology of *Ectomyelois muriscis* (Pyralidae: Phycitinae), a Costa Rican fruit parasite of *Hymenaea courbaril* (Leguminosae: Caesalpinioideae). *Brenesia* 21:387–93.

———. 1983d. No park is an island: Increase in interference from outside as park size decreases. *Oikos* 41:402–10.

———. 1984a. Weather-related color polymorphism of *Rothschildia lebeau* (Saturniidae). *Bulletin of the Entomological Society of America* 30 (2):16–20.

———. 1984b. Natural History of *Hylesia lineata* (Saturniidae: Hemileucinae) in Santa Rosa National Park, Costa Rica. *Journal of the Kansas Entomological Society* 57:490–514.

———. 1984c. Two ways to be a tropical big moth: Santa Rosa saturniids and sphingids. *Oxford Surveys in Evolutionary Biology* 1:85–140.

———. 1985a. On ecological fitting. *Oikos* 45: 308–10.

———. 1985b. A host plant is more than its chemistry. *Illinois Natural History Bulletin* 33:141–74.

———. 1986a. The future of tropical ecology. *Annual Review of Ecology and Systematics* 17: 305–24.

———. 1986b. The eternal external threat. In *Conservation biology: The science of scarcity and diversity*, ed. M. E. Soule, 286–303. Sunderland, Mass.: Sinauer Associates.

———. 1986c. Disruption and recovery of intra-crown fruiting synchrony in a *Cassia grandis* (Leguminosae) tree. *Brenesia* 25/26:179–85.

———. 1986d. Biogeography of an unexceptional place: What determines the saturniid and sphingid moth fauna of Santa Rosa National Park, Costa Rica, and what does it mean to conservation biology? *Brenesia* 25/26:51–87.

———. 1986e. Mice, big mammals, and seeds: It matters who defecates what where. In *Frugivores and seed dispersal*, ed. A. Estrada and T. H. Fleming, 251–71. Dordrecht, Holland: Dr. W. Junk Publishers.

———. 1987a. How moths pass the dry season in a Costa Rican dry forest. *Insect Science and Its Application* 8:489–500.

———. 1987b. Insect diversity of a Costa Rican dry forest: Why keep it, and how? *Biological Journal of the Linnean Society* 30:343–56.

———. 1987c. When, and when not to leave. *Oikos* 49:241–43.

———. 1988a. Tropical dry forests: The most endangered major tropical ecosystem. In *Biodiversity*, ed. E. O. Wilson, 130–37. Washington, D.C.: National Academy Press.

———. 1988b. Management of habitat fragments in a tropical dry forest: Growth. *Annals of the Missouri Botanical Garden* 75:105–16.

———. 1988c. Tropical ecological and biocultural restoration. *Science* 239:243–44.

———. 1988d. Complexity is in the eye of the beholder. In *Tropical rainforests: Diversity and conservation*, ed. F. Almeda and C. M. Pringle, 29–51. San Francisco: California Academy of Science and AAAS.

———. 1988e. The migrant moths of Guanacaste. *Orion Nature Quarterly* 7:38–41.

———. 1988f. Ecological characterization of a Costa Rican dry forest caterpillar fauna. *Biotropica* 20:120–35.

———. 1989. Natural history of a wind-pollinated Central American dry forest legume tree (*Ateleia herbert-smithii* Pittier). *Monographs in Systematic Botany from the Missouri Botanical Garden* 29:293–376.

———. 1990. An abandoned field is not a tree fall gap. *Vida Silvestre Neotropical* 2:64–67.

———. 1993. Caterpillar seasonality in a Costa Rican dry forest. In *Caterpillars: Ecological and evolutionary constraints on foraging*, ed. N. E. Stamp and T. M. Casey, 448–77. New York: Chapman and Hall.

———. 1998a. Gardenification of wildland nature and the human footprint. *Science* 279:1312–13.

———. 1998b. How to grow a wildland: The gardenification of nature. *Insect Science and Application* 17:269–76.

———. 1999a. Gardenification of tropical conserved wildlands: Multitasking, multicropping, and multiusers. *Proceedings of the National Academy of Sciences* 96:5987–94.

———. 1999b. La sobrevivencia de las areas silvestres de Costa Rica por medio de su jardinificación. *Ciencias Ambientales*, no. 16:8–18.

———. 2000a. Costa Rica's Area de Conservacion Guanacaste: A long march to survival through non-damaging biodevelopment. *Biodiversity* 1 (2):7–20.

———. 2000b. Wildlands as gardens. *National Parks Magazine* 74(11–12):50–51.

———. 2001a. Latent extinctions—the living dead. In *Encyclopedia of biodiversity*, ed. S. A. Levin, 3:689–99. New York: Academic Press.

———. 2001b. Good fences make good neighbors. *Parks* 11(2):41–49.

———. 2002. Tropical dry forest: Area de Conservación Guanacaste, northwestern Costa Rica. In *Handbook of ecological restoration*, vol. 2, *Restoration in practice*, ed. M. R. Perrow and A. J. Davy, 559–83. Cambridge: Cambridge University Press.

Janzen, D. H., and I. D. Gauld. 1997. Patterns of use of large moth caterpillars (Lepidoptera: Saturniidae and Sphingidae) by ichneumonid parasitoids (Hymenoptera) in Costa Rican dry forest. In *Forests and insects,* ed. A. D. Watt, N. E. Stork, and M. D. Hunter, 251–71. London: Chapman and Hall.

Janzen, D. H., and W. Hallwachs. 2003. Philosophy, navigation and use of a dynamic database ("ACG Caterpillars SRNP") for an inventory of the macrocaterpillar fauna, and its food plants and parasitoids, of the Area de Conservación Guanacaste (ACG), northwestern Costa Rica. http://janzen.sas.upenn.edu.

Janzen, D. H., and P. S. Martin. 1982. Neotropical anachronisms: The fruits the gomphotheres ate. *Science* 215:19–27.

Janzen, D. H., and C. M. Pond. 1975. A comparison, by sweep sampling, of the arthropod fauna of secondary vegetation in Michigan, England and Costa Rica. *Transactions of the Royal Entomological Society of London* 127:33–50.

Janzen, D. H., and T. W. Schoener. 1968. Differences in insect abundance and diversity between wetter and drier sites during a tropical dry season. *Ecology* 49:96–110.

Janzen, D. H., and P. G. Waterman. 1984. A seasonal census of phenolics, fibre and alkaloids in foliage of forest trees in Costa Rica: Some factors influencing their distribution and relation to host selection by Sphingidae and Saturniidae. *Biological Journal of the Linnean Society* 21:439–54.

Janzen, D. H., S. T. Doerner, and E. E. Conn. 1980a. Seasonal constancy of intra-population variation of HCN content of Costa Rican *Acacia farnesiana* foliage. *Phytochemistry* 19:2022–23.

Janzen, D. H., P. DeVries, D. E. Gladstone, M. L. Higgins, and T. M. Lewinson. 1980b. Self- and cross-pollination of *Encyclia cordigera* (Orchidaceae) in Santa Rosa National Park, Costa Rica. *Biotropica* 12:72–74.

Janzen, D. H., P. J. DeVries, M. L. Higgins, and L. S. Kimsey. 1982. Seasonal and site variation in Costa Rican euglossine bees at chemical baits in lowland deciduous and evergreen forests. *Ecology* 63:66–74.

Janzen, D. H., M. J. Sharkey, and J. M. Burns. 1998. Parasitization biology of a new species of Braconidae (Hymenoptera) feeding on larvae of Costa Rican dry forest skippers (Lepidoptera: Hesperiidae: Pyrginae). *Tropical Lepidoptera* 9 (suppl.):33–41.

Martin, P. S., D. Yetman, T. R. Van Devender, P. Jenkins, M. Fishbein, and R. Wilson, eds. 1998. *Gentry's Rio Mayo plants: The tropical deciduous forest and environs of northwest Mexico.* Tucson: University of Arizona Press. 381 pp.

Miller, J. S., D. H. Janzen, and J. G. Franclemont. 1997. New species of *Euhapigioides,* new genus, and *Hapigiodes* in Hapigiini, new tribe, from Costa Rica, with notes on their life history and immatures (Lepidoptera: Notodontidae). *Tropical Lepidoptera* 8(2):81–99.

Murphy, P. G., and A. Lugo. 1986. Ecology of tropical dry forest. *Annual Review of Ecology and Systematics* 17:67–88.

Nepstad, D. C., A. Verissimo, A. Alencar, C. Nobre, E. Lima, P. Lefebvre, P. Schlesinger, C. Potter, P. Moutinho, E. Mendoza, M. Cochrane, and V. Brooks. 1999. Large-scale impoverishment of Amazonian forests by logging and fire. *Nature* 398:505–8.

Nijhout, H. F. 1999. Control mechanisms of polyphenic development in insects. *BioScience* 49:181–92.

Petersen, J. S. 1998. Notes on the effect of the El Niño phenomenon and forest fires on Lepidoptera populations of Palawan, the Philippines, during 1997–1998. *Lepidoptera News,* no. 3:4.

Pounds, J. A., M. P. L. Fodgen, and J. H. Campbell. 1999. Biological response to climate change on a tropical mountain. *Nature* 398:611–15.

Powell, J. A., and J. W. Brown. 1990. Concentrations of lowland sphingid and noctuid moths at high mountain passes in eastern Mexico. *Biotropica* 22:316–19.

Roskam, J. C., and P. M. Brakefield. 1999. Seasonal polyphenism in *Bicyclus* (Lepidoptera: Satyridae) butterflies: Different climates need different clues. *Biological Journal of the Linnean Society* 66:345–56.

Sharkey, M. J., and D. H. Janzen. 1995. Review of the world species of *Sigalaphus* (Hymenoptera: Braconidae: Sigalaphinae) and biology of *Sigalaphus romeroi,* new species. *Journal of Hymenoptera Research* 4:99–109.

Still, C. J., P. N. Foster, and S. H. Schneider. 1999. Simulating the effects of climate change on tropical montane cloud forests. *Nature* 398: 608–10.

Toh, I., M. Gillespie, and D. Lamb. 1999. The role of isolated trees in facilitating tree seedling recruitment at a degraded sub-tropical rainforest site. *Restoration Ecology* 7:288–97.

Williams-Linera, G., V. Dominguez-Gastelu, and M. E. Garcia-Zurita. 1998. Microenvironment and floristics of different edges in a fragmented tropical rainforest. *Conservation Biology* 12:1091–1102.

Wirth, R., W. Beyschlag, R. J. Ryel, and B. Holldobler. 1997. Annual foraging of the leaf-cutting ant *Atta colombica* in a semideciduous rain forest in Panama. *Journal of Tropical Ecology* 13:741–57.

Woodley, N. E., and D. H. Janzen. 1995. A new species of *Melanagromyza* (Diptera: Agromyzi-dae) mining leaves of *Bromelia pinguin* (Bromeliaceae) in a dry forest in Costa Rica. *Journal of Natural History* 29:1329–37.

*Section B. Biotic Relationships with
Other Costa Rican Forests*

CHAPTER 8

Diversity, Migration, and Conservation of Butterflies in Northern Costa Rica

William A. Haber and Robert D. Stevenson

MIGRATION CAN BE simply defined as a sustained, directional movement by an animal that takes it out of one habitat and into another (Dingle 1996), and this is the definition used here. It distinguishes migrating behavior from local movements within an animal's home range that tend to be nonlinear, of short duration, and confined to a single habitat (Dingle 1996). Seasonal migration typically involves a two-way trip between habitats, exemplified by the annual back-and-forth flights of Neotropical migrant songbirds between the North Temperate Zone and the tropics (Levey 1994; Martin and Finch 1995). Two-way migration by individual butterflies occurs in some longer-lived species such as the monarch in North America (Brower 1991, 1996) and the common Costa Rican migrant *Manataria maculata* (Satyrinae; Stevenson and Haber 2000a). However, the migration of most insects, relatively short-lived compared with vertebrates, is a one-way trip for a given individual, and members of a succeeding generation make the return trip (Haber 1993; Dingle 1996; chapter 7).

Migration behavior has been recognized in butterflies for centuries (Williams 1930; Johnson 1969; Baker 1978; Dingle 1996), although it has been studied in detail for only a few species, such as the monarch (*Danaus plexippus*) (Brower 1991, 1996) and the painted lady (*Vanessa cardui*) (Hansen 1997). Among butterflies, migrating individuals are generally easy to distinguish from nonmigrants. Migrants fly in a relatively straight line, usually 1–2 m above the ground, and rise over objects in their path, such as houses or forest patches, rather than flying around them. In contrast, active butterflies that are not migrating fly a crooked route, alighting often to bask or feed. Females stop frequently to check potential host plants, and males perch to watch for passing females. Their directed flights rarely take them more than 20 to 30 m in a given direction.

Most migration is a response to seasonal changes in the environmental resources that affect the probability of reproductive success. Butterflies of the North Temperate Zone that migrate do so for the same reason that birds do—to take advantage of the short-term abundance of food that becomes available in early summer and to escape a harsh winter when food is limited and reproduction becomes impossible (Levey 1994; Dingle 1996). Most species migrate to the south in late summer or autumn and return northward in summer (Walker 1978, 1980). Often, movements over several generations are required for a population to reach the northernmost limits of its distribution during the summer (Walker 1978, 1980; Brower 1996).

In the tropics, where a cold winter season is lacking, it is less obvious why animals migrate (Loiselle and Blake 1991; Levey and Stiles 1992; Powell and Bjork, 1995). Migrations have been most commonly observed to pass between seasonally very dry habitats and less seasonal wet habitats—for example, between the dry forest of Costa Rica's northwest and the evergreen forest of the Atlantic plain (Janzen 1984, 1987a–c; Haber 1993; Stevenson and Haber 2000a,b). Migrations are usually associated with seasonal changes, and climatic factors apparently serve as proximate cues for initiating migrating behavior (Dingle 1996). Ultimate selective causes responsible for migration probably include a variety of factors among different species, such as poor quality of host-plant leaves, an increase in predators and parasitoids, severe weather, and limited availability of adult food resources (Janzen 1984, 1987a–c, 1988; Haber 1993; Dingle 1996).

The Costa Rican dry forest is characterized by strong seasonality, with a six-month dry season (mid-November to mid-May) creating the most obvious seasonal pattern (Janzen 1983; chapter 7). Seasonal rainfall results in a semideciduous forest that is shady in the wet season and open in the dry season with much higher temperatures and lower humidity (Janzen 1983). These changes in climate result in seasonal shifts in the quality and availability of most

resources used by both immature and adult butterflies. A consequence of this pronounced climatic seasonality is the migration behavior so characteristic of the Costa Rican dry-forest fauna.

Migration among Costa Rican Lepidoptera has been studied relatively little. DeVries (1983, 1987, 1997) recorded many observations of apparent migration. In several papers Janzen (1984, 1987a–c, 1988) discussed migration by moths in relation to seasonality and the biology of caterpillars in the dry forest of Parque Nacional Santa Rosa. Opler (1989) described a pattern of migration and diapause in *Eurema daira* (Pieridae). Haber (1993) and Stevenson and Haber (2000b) studied butterfly migration in the Monteverde region, particularly censusing seasonal movements of many species across the mountains between the dry Pacific slope and the wet Atlantic slope. Stevenson and Haber (2000a) described the natural history of *M. maculata*, a long-lived species that makes a two-way, elevational migration between the dry forest and the cloud forest at Monteverde.

In this chapter, we compare the butterfly faunas of the Costa Rican dry forest, the cloud forest of the neighboring mountains, and wet forest on the adjacent Atlantic slope. We identify the most conspicuous migrating taxa and describe the main patterns of migratory behavior of dry-forest butterflies that we have observed and relate these responses to dry-forest seasonality. We also point out some gaps in research knowledge and make recommendations relevant to conservation issues involving migrating butterflies and their adaptation to a changing seasonal environment.

STUDY AREA AND METHODS

STUDY AREAS

The area discussed in this chapter centers on the Cordillera de Tilarán in northern Costa Rica and the adjacent Pacific and Atlantic slopes and lowlands (map 8.1). On the Pacific slope, the study area includes northern Puntarenas Province and southern Guanacaste Province east to the Conti-

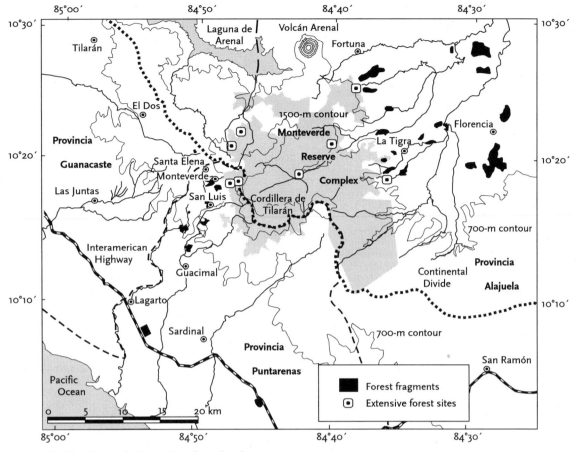

MAP 8.1. Monteverde Reserve Complex and study sites.

nental Divide at Monteverde. Although the vegetation of the lowlands in this area is popularly referred to as dry forest, it actually consists of a mosaic of different life zones (Tropical dry forest, Tropical moist forest, and Premontane moist forest; Holdridge 1967; Bolaños and Watson 1993). All these vegetation types include deciduous tree species, but the proportion of canopy that goes leafless in the dry season can vary from close to nothing to almost 100 percent depending on the drainage, disturbance history, local climate, and proximity to streams (Hartshorn 1983; Haber 2000). Most research on the lower Pacific slope was conducted in forest fragments within the Tropical moist forest life zone be-

tween the villages of Cuatro Cruces, Lagarto, and San Luis, ranging from 50 to 700 m in elevation (map 8.1).

In the montane region near Monteverde, where counts of migrating butterflies as well as forest censuses were carried out, we worked in Premontane wet forest, Lower montane wet forest, and Lower montane rain forest life zones (all are evergreen forests from 700 to 1,800 m elevation). The two Lower montane zones are popularly known as cloud forest (Hartshorn 1983; Haber 2000). The Pacific lowlands in the study area receive 1,500 to 2,000 mm of rainfall annually (mostly between May and November); rainfall increases to 2,500 mm (also with a strong seasonal distribution) on the upper Pacific slope at Monteverde, at 1,200–1,500 m elevation. With added moisture from cloud interception, the cloud forest (1,500–1,850 m) receives more than 3,000 mm of rain per year.

On the Atlantic slope, research was concentrated in the foothills of the Cordillera de Tilarán and the adjacent plains near Fortuna, La Tigra, and Florencia, ranging from 70 to 850 m. The vegetation of this area consists of a complex mix of Tropical moist forest, Tropical wet forest, Premontane wet forest, and Premontane rain forest life zons and transition zone types (Bolaños and Watson 1993). These forest types can be characterized generally as rain forest, and they receive 3,000–7,000 mm of rainfall annually (Instituto Meteorológico de Costa Rica; Clark et al. 2000; Michael Fogden unpubl. data). The dry season (January–April) is milder and much more irregular on the Atlantic side than on the Pacific side.

CENSUS OF BUTTERFLIES IN FOREST SITES

Adult butterflies were censused monthly in forest fragments and at sites within extensive forest of the Monteverde reserve complex along a northeasterly trajectory from the Pacific lowlands, through the cloud forest at Monteverde, and down to the adjacent Atlantic lowlands. A total of 45 sites were sampled over a three-year period from 1994 to 1997. Each sample consisted of the total individuals and species of butterflies identified during a one-hour walk (approximately 0.6 km) along a trail or transect exclusively either through forest interior or along the outer forest edge. Butterflies within 5 m on either side of the transect were recorded. The same transects were sampled each month. These sites consisted mostly of primary forest, although virtually all lowland sites were disturbed by the removal of some timber trees and most included some secondary areas. The personnel conducting the censuses included D. Brenes, C. Guindon, N. Obando, M. Ramírez, R. Rojas, M. Wainwright, and W. Haber, who trained the others in censusing techniques.

COUNTS OF MIGRATING BUTTERFLIES

Butterflies were systematically counted as they passed through a roadcut that crosses a ridge near the entrance to the Monteverde Cloud Forest Preserve at Monteverde. At this site, known as Windy Corner because it is exposed to the northeast trade winds, butterflies crossed the ridge close to the ground where the road cuts through forest. Counts were made during sunny weather between 0900 and 1200 hr CST (= local time).

IDENTIFICATION RESOURCES

Identification resources included publications (DeVries 1983, 1987, 1997), museum collections, and determinations by specialists. Within Costa Rica, we used collections at the Museo Nacional de Costa Rica and the Instituto Nacional de Biodiversidad. Identifications were also provided by Isidro Chacón, German Vega, Philip DeVries, Daniel Janzen, Paul Opler, Robert Robbins, and Andrew Warren.

RESULTS

BUTTERFLY DIVERSITY

Regional Species Richness. Excluding skippers (Hesperiidae), about 1,036 butterfly species are currently known from Costa Rica (table 8.1). A species list in progress for skippers currently includes more than 500 species (A. Warren pers. comm.), compared with 431 species listed by DeVries (1983). Estimating from the numbers of skippers known at Monteverde and Santa Rosa, we (W. Haber and D. Janzen) expect a total number of skippers for the country to be 600–800 species. Estimating from known species and ranges of species that overlap Costa Rica, 274 lycaenid species are expected to occur in the country (R. Robbins pers. comm.). This provides a total of Costa Rican butterfly species ranging from a conservative 1,576 to a liberal 1,900.

Although the total number in the Costa Rican dry forest is also not precisely known, collections from several northwestern sites provide

TABLE 8.1
Species Richness of Butterflies in Three Costa Rican Faunal Regions

FAMILY	SANTA ROSA	MONTEVERDE	LA SELVA	COSTA RICA
Papilionidae	13	22	21	42
Pieridae	21	51	20	67
Nymphalidae	89	197	165	438
Riodinidae	32	24	84	255
Lycaenidae (estimated)	ca. 50 (ca. 80)	85 (ca. 100)	79 (ca. 110)	234 (274)
Hesperiidae (estimated)	281 ca. 300	157 ca. 200	175 ca. 300	500 (ca. 700)
Total (estimated)	486 (ca. 535)	536 (594)	544 (700)	1,536 (ca. 1,776)

Sources: DeVries (1983, 1987, 1997); D. Janzen (1988, 2002, pers. comm.); W. Haber (1993 and unpubl. data); P. Opler (pers. comm.); R. Robbins (pers. comm.).

Note: The three faunal areas were lowland dry forest (Santa Rosa National Park), montane wet forest (Monteverde, above 1,200 m), and lowland wet forest (La Selva Biological Station).

an estimate of about 535 species, or one-third of the country's fauna (table 8.1), with 32 percent recorded at Santa Rosa National Park. In comparison, 35 percent of the known species have been recorded in the wet montane area at Monteverde and from the Atlantic lowland rain forest at La Selva Biological Station.

Species Richness in Life Zones along an Elevational Gradient. The census of butterflies along an elevational gradient from the Pacific lowlands across the mountains at Monteverde to the Atlantic lowlands showed species numbers increasing from the Pacific lowlands to midelevation forest at Monteverde but decreasing from the Atlantic lowlands to the mountaintop (table 8.2). In addition, the Tropical wet forest of the Atlantic lowlands (380 species) was much richer than the Tropical moist forest life zone of the Pacific lowlands (265 species). In contrast, Pacific slope (leeward) cloud forest at Monteverde (>1,500 m) had about twice as many species (161 species) as Atlantic slope (windward) cloud forest (85 species).

Dry-Forest Endemics. None of the butterflies that live in dry forest are endemic to Costa Rica (DeVries 1987, 1997; R. Robbins pers. comm.). Although many of the rarest Costa Rican butterflies belong to the Riodinidae (DeVries 1997), most of the 32 species known from the dry forest have broad distributions, ranging from Mexico to Costa Rica or extending into South America (DeVries 1997). Only six of these are restricted to the dry forest (DeVries 1997); the others also occur in moister habitats. Some of these species are extremely rare in Costa Rica, such as *Pandemos godmanii*, Riodinidae (collected only once in Costa Rica, near Cañas), but are not rare everywhere in their range (DeVries 1997; P. Opler pers. comm.).

Although we know of no endemic dry-forest butterflies, it seems probable that some species that were rare or periodic colonists from Atlantic slope wet forest are now missing from the dry forest. Some of these species show up as rare individuals (seemingly strays) from time to time (DeVries 1987; W. Haber pers. obs.; D. Janzen

TABLE 8.2

Species Richness of Butterflies at Sites along an Elevational Gradient from
the Pacific Lowlands through Monteverde to the Atlantic Lowlands

	PACIFIC SLOPE			ATLANTIC SLOPE		
	0–600 M	600–1,200 M	1,200–1,800 M	0–600 M	600–1,200 M	1,200–1,800 M
Papilionidae	19	15	22	14	4	3
Pieridae	29	30	51	17	19	21
Nymphalidae	116	135	197	162	126	82
Riodinidae	19	21	24	31	49	4
Lycaenidae	8	25	85	30	23	2
Hesperiidae	74	59	157	126	63	18
Total	265	285	536	380	284	130

Note: Numbers include both census data and collateral records.

pers. comm.). Many species known from the general region of our study sites were apparently absent from the small forest patches studied and are presumed to be locally extinct (DeVries 1983, 1987, 1997). More extensive forest tracts in Guanacaste could presumably support some species that are now restricted to wet forest on the Atlantic slope (see also chapter 7).

SEASONALITY OF THE FAUNA

Decrease in Species Richness during the Dry Season. The number of butterfly species in the Pacific lowlands significantly decreases during the dry season. In censuses of forest fragments in the lowlands below Monteverde, butterfly species richness declined by 40–50 percent (fig. 8.1). The difference between wet and dry season numbers decreased with elevation, as do the length and severity of the dry season. Montane sites above 1,200 m on the Pacific slope had a reduction in species during the dry season, but the decrease was less pronounced (20–30%). The upper Atlantic slope was similar to the Pacific side. However, on the mid- and lower Atlantic slope (below 1,200 m), species numbers substantially increased during the dry season. At a site in the center of the extensive Monteverde reserve complex at 800 m, the species richness increased by about 20 percent during the dry season, whereas it almost doubled in some lowland fragments (fig. 8.1). The decrease in species numbers in the dry forest during the dry season, at least in part, results from the migration of butterflies out of the Pacific lowlands to less seasonal habitats on the upper Pacific slope and on the Atlantic slope (see the section "Migration Patterns" later in this chapter).

Some butterflies (e.g., *Eurema dina* and *Phoebis sennae*, Pieridae) that remained in the lowlands through the dry season continued to reproduce, whereas others ceased reproductive activity and entered diapause (see the next section, "Reproductive Diapause"). Among these are some species of open areas (pasture and second growth) that moved into the forest in the dry season, taking advantage of cool, humid conditions there, especially in shaded ravines along streams and rivers. For example, many skippers rest in the deep shade of overhanging stream banks, where they are virtually invisible until they ex-

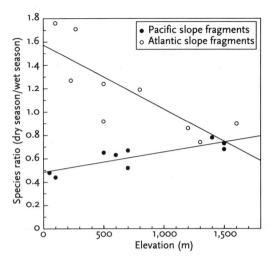

FIGURE 8.1. Comparison of butterfly species during the dry season and wet season at sites along a transect from the Pacific lowlands through Monteverde to the Atlantic lowlands. Species numbers in the middle of the dry season (February–March) are divided by numbers in the early wet season (June–July). $P < .01$ for Pacific slope ($r = .84$) and Atlantic slope ($r = .80$).

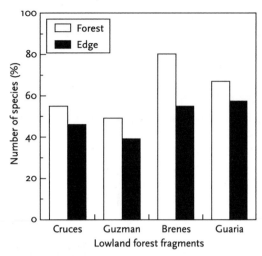

FIGURE 8.2. Differences between wet season and dry season in species numbers in forest and edge censuses from four forest fragments in the Pacific lowlands; dry season species numbers are expressed as a percentage of the wet season totals. At each site the dry edge species were depressed more than the forest species (mean = 13.5% fewer species).

plode into flight when approached. In the middle of the dry season (February–March) in the four Pacific lowland sites, the forest edge censuses averaged 13 percent lower in species numbers than the forest interior censuses, supporting our observations that some open-area butterflies (e.g., *Eurema daira,* Pieridae; *Urbanus dorantes,* Hesperiidae) moved into forest habitat during the dry season (fig. 8.2).

Reproductive Diapause. Reproductive diapause is a common strategy characteristic of butterflies in highly seasonal habitats (Haber 1993; Braby 1995; Dingle 1996). Many butterflies that do not emigrate from the Costa Rican dry forest in the dry season enter a state of reproductive diapause that physiologically halts mating, egg maturation, and oviposition during part of the dry season (DeVries 1987; Opler 1989; Haber 1993, unpubl. data). By dissecting females collected during the dry season, we documented 63 species that enter reproductive diapause (38 nymphalids, 14 pierids, 9 hesperiids, and 2 riodinids). Diapausing butterflies remained quiescent for long

periods, interrupted only by periodic feeding activity.

For some of these species, such as *Mechanitis polymnia* (Ithomiinae), diapause occurred sporadically during the dry season, with some individuals diapausing while others were reproductive concurrently at the same site. The dry-season diapause for most species began in December at the start of dry season and ended in May with the onset of the first wet season showers. Some individuals of *M. polymnia* broke diapause and became reproductive following an isolated shower in one of the fragments in January 1995. Some species displayed a high degree of plasticity, including both migrating and diapausing individuals (e.g., *E. daira*). Some butterflies that remained reproductive throughout the dry season include *Itaballia demophile* and *E. dina* (Pieridae), *Cissia renata* (Satyrinae), *Papilio thoas* and *Parides iphidamus* (Papilionidae). Yet individuals of these same species were also occasionally recorded while migrating through Monteverde—well above their reproductive ranges. It is not yet clear whether migration and diapause were alternative strategies that occurred at the same site.

Diapausing butterflies were also found occasionally in other areas that are both wetter and less seasonal in rainfall than the Pacific lowland sites. Diapausing individuals of seven species (two pierids, five ithomiines) were found in the Atlantic lowlands during the exceptionally pronounced dry season of 1994 near La Fortuna, Provincia Alajuela. Nineteen diapausing species were detected at Monteverde during the dry season in various years in Premontane wet forest at 1,400 m. These species included both cross-country migrants that apparently suppress egg maturation during migration and elevational migrants from the Pacific slope and lowlands that spend the dry season in moister habitats in the mountains (see the section "Elevational Migration" later in this chapter).

MIGRATION PATTERNS

We have identified three distinct patterns of migration among dry-forest butterflies. The pattern encompassing most species is a back-and-forth migration between the Pacific and Atlantic sides of the country over the central mountain chain and Continental Divide (cross-country migration). A smaller number of dry-forest species migrate to cool, moist habitats in the nearby mountains during the dry season (elevational migration). In a third pattern, butterflies migrate from the dry forest southeast along the Pacific coast to lowland wet forest in the southern Pacific region (coastal migration).

Cross-Country Migration. Migrating butterflies are especially visible as they pass over deforested ridges (flyways) near the Continental Divide at Monteverde, where the strong northeast trade winds force them to fly near the ground (Haber 1993). These migrants originate in all the different habitats along the gradient from lowland dry forest to the cloud forest. Even species (e.g., *Actinote leucomelas* [Acraeinae] and several ithomiines) that breed in cloud forest on the upper Pacific slope above 1,500 m migrate seasonally to the Atlantic side of the mountain range. For most individual butterflies, the migration is a one-way trip with reproduction occurring after migration. It is the offspring produced one or more generations in the future that make the return trip. We recorded more than 300 butterfly species at the migration sampling sites in Monteverde, most during the eastward leg of the migration (see also Haber 1993).

The migration of any given species is distinctly seasonal and more or less predictable from year to year, although annual variation in climate greatly affected the numbers and timing of migrants (e.g., rates of eastward migration were very low in El Niño years). However, different species each have their own life history pattern, so that at any time of year a subset of species may be migrating. Peaks in eastward migration occurred late in the wet season to early in the dry season (October–January) and during the *veranillo* or "little dry season" (late June through mid-August). Westward migration (from Atlantic to Pacific slope) occurred in April–May, during the transition from the dry to the wet season.

Cross-country migration of alternating generations involves a substantial seasonal interchange among the butterfly faunas of the Pacific and Atlantic slopes that results in a spectacular annual increase in butterfly numbers in the dry forest. Depending on the site, 40 to 75 percent of the Pacific slope species migrate to the Atlantic slope. Offspring of eastward migrants return to the Pacific side, usually preceding or coinciding with the start of the wet season, and they begin reproducing as soon as they arrive. Reproduction by this influx of westward migrants, along with the breaking of diapause in nonmigrants, results in a large flush of first generation butterflies in late June and July. Many of these newly emerged butterflies (e.g., *Marpesia petreus* and *Smyrna blomfildia* [Nymphalinae], *Aphrissa statira* [Pieridae], and *Manataria maculata* [Satyrinae]) migrate back to the Atlantic side during the *veranillo*, while the others stay to reproduce on the Pacific side, completing one or more generations before the dry season arrives. Butterflies that reach the Atlantic slope continue to reproduce there. With very few exceptions (see the section "Reproductive Diapause" earlier in this chapter), butterflies sampled during migration through Monteverde and on the Atlantic slope during the dry season were reproductively active (see also Haber 1993).

Elevational Migration. Elevational migration is defined here as the seasonal movement of butterflies uphill from their breeding range to a different life zone or habitat type at a higher elevation. Comparatively few species of elevational migrants have been observed compared with cross-country migrants. Some of these species, such as *Greta oto* (Ithomiinae), *M. maculata,* and *Siproeta stelenes,* entered reproductive diapause in the high-elevation refuge sites where they passed the dry season in a manner very similar to that of *Polistes instabilis* (Vespidae) (Hunt et al. 1999; Stevenson and Haber 2000a,b). After producing a single generation of offspring on the Pacific slope below Monteverde (at 50 to 800 m), the emerging adults of *M. maculata* (June through August) immediately migrate upslope to cloud forest sites (at 1,400–1,600 m). In the montane forest, they spend 8–11 months as virgin adults in reproductive diapause, returning to their breeding sites during the following April to May, cued by the first heavy shower of the wet season (Stevenson and Haber 2000a). A few other species, such as *D. plexippus* (Danainae), *Anartia fatima,* and *Siproeta epaphus* (Nymphalinae), continue to reproduce during the dry season as they move upslope to moister, evergreen areas at midelevation, where effects of the dry season arrive later and are less pronounced.

Coastal Migration. A small number of butterfly species were observed repeatedly at several points along the Pacific coast from Puntarenas to Uvita, migrating in a southeasterly direction closely following the coastline or crossing the ocean from the Peninsula de Nicoya to the mainland. These butterflies were apparently moving from dry forest in Guanacaste and northern Puntarenas Provinces to less seasonal, tropical wet forest in the southern Pacific region. The most common species were the nymphalids *A. fatima, Euptoieta hegesia,* and *S. stelenes,* the danaids

Danaus gilippus and *eresimus,* the heliconiids *Agraulis vanillae* and *Dryas iulia,* and the pierids *Anteos clorinde, Aphrissa statira, Ascia monuste,* and *P. sennae.* All these species were also observed migrating through Monteverde. We observed this southeasterly migration along the Pacific coast during most years between 1992 and the present at Puntarenas, Jacó, Dominical, and Punta Uvita at various times, but most noticeably during August. At Puerto Caldera we observed butterflies coming to shore across the Golfo de Nicoya, apparently having crossed the gulf from the southern end of the Peninsula de Nicoya. The behavior of these butterflies differed sharply from that of the cross-country migrants. They held a bearing of about 90 degrees to the northeast trade winds and maintained their southeasterly flight direction even as the sea breeze arose from the west during the day. In contrast, the flight path of cross-country migrants was directly into the trade winds. Nielsen and Nielsen (1950) described a similar coastal migration of one of these same species, *A. monuste,* in response to changes in its host plant along the eastern coast of Florida.

Proportion of Fauna That Migrates. About 60 percent of the species found in the lowland and intermediate sites up to 1,200 m on the Pacific slope were also observed to migrate through Monteverde (fig. 8.3). Only 46 percent of the species that are known or suspected to breed at the upper elevation sites (1,200–1,800 m) also migrated seasonally. In sharp contrast, 74 percent of the species at sites above 1,200 m on the Atlantic slope migrate. The highest site on the Atlantic slope (1,600 m) had 87 percent migrants. This proportion decreased to 41 percent at intermediate elevation sites and to 51 percent at lowland sites on the Atlantic side. In general, the proportion of migrant species was about the same in lowland sites on each side but became increasingly disparate at higher elevations.

About three-quarters of the 536 butterfly species recorded from the upper Pacific slope at Monteverde migrate to some extent, with migrating species from lower elevations contributing substantially to species richness of the

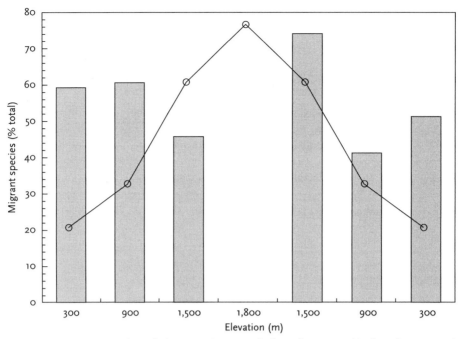

FIGURE 8.3. Proportions of migrant species among the butterflies censused in forest fragments and extensive forest from the Pacific lowlands through Monteverde to the Atlantic lowlands (bars). The sites are grouped into three elevational blocks (0–600 m, 600–1,200 m, 1,200–1,800 m) on each slope shown diagrammatically (open circles).

montane area. Many of these butterflies (e.g., *Aguna asander* [Hesperiidae], *Adelpha iphiclus*, *Marpesia petreus, S. stelenes* [Nymphalinae], *Aphrissa* spp., *Eurema* spp. [Pieridae], and *Eurybia elvina* [Riodinidae]) appear in Monteverde only during their passage between the lowland habitats on either slope and do not reproduce there. However, they contribute to the ecology of the region while feeding along the way, and they often spend days or weeks in the area below the cloud forest waiting for favorable weather in order to cross the divide.

DISCUSSION

DRY-FOREST CONNECTIONS

As one of the most important herbivore taxa in tropical forests, Lepidoptera form a key component in the food chain as selective agents on plants and as prey for parasitoids and predators, such as tachinid flies, many families of para-sitoid wasps, and birds. Moths are also major players in the pollination of dry-forest plants (Haber and Frankie 1988; chapter 2). In addition, with their diurnal behavior, sometimes massive numbers, and colorful aspect, migrating butterflies offer one of the more spectacular natural history phenomena observable in Costa Rica. However, butterflies are actually just the tip of the iceberg. They are diurnal and highly visible compared with the largely unnoticed thousands of species of moths, flies, wasps, bugs, beetles, and dragonflies that also migrate seasonally (Haber 1993, unpubl. data; D. Janzen pers. comm.). Lay people often notice migrating butterflies in Costa Rica, but, with the exception of the most spectacular migrations, they seldom recognize migrating behavior and often think that these butterflies are just unusually abundant (W. A. Haber pers. obs.).

These migrating species form broad ecological and geographical connections among the main biological regions of Costa Rica. Our studies of butterflies and moths (see chapter 7) can identify indicators for the conservation status of other insect groups and point to habitat needing protection. Indeed, the realization that a major portion of the dry-forest moth fauna in the Area de Conservación Guanacaste (ACG) seasonally migrates to the wet forests to the east was a major rationale in the mid-1980s for expanding the original dry forest of Parque Nacional Santa Rosa into the much larger ACG to include rain forest and cloud forest (D. Janzen pers. comm.). In addition, our emerging understanding of intra-tropical migrating behavior of butterflies, sphingid moths, and birds within the Monteverde region provided motivation for increasing the reserve complex at Monteverde from 4,500 ha to 25,000 ha during the same period.

HOW MUCH WE KNOW

Our knowledge of butterfly distribution, abundance, and natural history may be too poor to determine whether dry-forest butterfly species have become extinct or even to know if any are currently in danger of extinction. Although fairly complete species lists exist for several research sites (Monteverde, La Selva, Santa Rosa), we do not have a thorough knowledge of the butterfly fauna of any research station or protected area in Costa Rica. All these sites have a profusion of species that were observed only once or a few times. The ecological and conservation status of such rare or transient species is essentially unknown without data on larval host plants, seasonality, annual fluctuations, and migration behavior. Moreover, species may be recorded as breeding at a site and then become extinct locally. They may be recorded on a species list for a site but are actually accidental visitors appearing there only during periods of unusual climate, such as El Niño years. An example is the influx of hundreds of *Heliconius sara* into Monteverde during August 1998. Although this lowland species found no suitable host plants (*Passiflora auriculata;* DeVries 1987) and soon died out, it will remain on the Monteverde checklist forever.

Some species are judged to be rare because they are known from only a few individuals, often at widely separated sites, such as an undescribed riodinid known from a total of three individuals at three widely separated sites in Costa Rica (P. J. DeVries, W. A. Haber, and I. Chacon unpubl. data). A species that seems rare may be abundant in the canopy, where observation is difficult except by specialized methods such as fruit trapping (DeVries 1988). In some cases, rare species may represent periodic colonists or strays from neighboring habitats where they are more abundant and maintain resident populations. More detailed information is needed about most rare species before we can assign them a conservation status.

Long-term monitoring can provide data needed to assess the conservation status of rare species and their habitats. Monitoring programs have been conducted in various places in the world (Murphy and Weiss 1988; Pinheiro and Ortiz 1992; Blair and Launer 1997), but the most notable long-term monitoring efforts have been in Great Britain (Pollard et al. 1995) and Europe (van Swaay 1990), where amateur and professional butterfly enthusiasts have surveyed butterflies in a systematic way for many years (New et al. 1995). These studies were able to detect annual changes in population size and distribution as well as immigration events. Periodic censuses of butterflies were also used successfully in the Amazonian forest fragment study (Brown and Hutchings 1997) to follow changes after fragmentation created small forest patches.

Systematic, long-term monitoring programs for butterflies are nonexistent in Costa Rica, although Dan Janzen's caterpillar-rearing program is producing extremely valuable data on the breeding biology of Lepidoptera of the ACG (see chapter 7). We carried out a sampling program for three years at Monteverde, but this was an intensive and costly effort involving four people. The data have been used in setting conservation priorities at the regional level, for defining research goals, and in mapping areas for protection, as well as in applied efforts such as reforestation by the Monteverde Conservation

League and the Monteverde Cloud Forest Preserve. Haber continues to monitor migrant butterflies with a permanent flight trap at Monteverde. Despite previous intensive inventories, this low-key effort has added about 20 species to the regional checklist.

Our experience suggests that the diversity at most Costa Rican sites is too high for a casual monitoring effort to census the butterfly fauna adequately. Often, the most interesting species from a conservation standpoint are undescribed or taxonomically confusing, so that they do not appear in field guides or are recognizable only by specialists (W. Haber pers. obs.; D. Janzen, P. Opler, A. Warren, R. Robbins pers. comm.). In addition, census results are too dependent on weather and observer expertise to make butterflies as a group the best choice for monitoring. Taxa that can be trapped with baits or attracted to scents by standardized methods may be preferable as practical indicators.

POTENTIAL CAUSES OF EXTINCTION

The most likely cause of butterfly extinction in the dry forest is loss of habitat, particularly mature forest—perhaps exacerbated by fire and pesticides. Frankie et al. (1998) suggested that agricultural pesticides have contributed to the decreased abundance and diversity of solitary bees in Guanacaste Province. However, no comparable data are available for butterflies. In Jamaica, Emmel and Garraway (1990) and Garraway et al. (1993) implicated both habitat loss and pesticides as significant factors in reducing diversity and contracting the range of the endemic *Papilio homerus* (Papilionidae). Acting together, they are possibly much more serious.

Fragmented habitats leave populations with highly reduced ranges, existing as small relicts, and often these habitat patches have been degraded by timber removal, fire, and cattle grazing. These isolated populations tend to become extinct through annual population fluctuations (Hanski and Thomas 1994; Hanski et al. 1994, 1995; New et al. 1995; Brown and Hutchings 1997) and from loss of host plants. Pesticides especially threaten small populations in forest fragments isolated within agricultural landscapes. Species of mature forest are likely to be those most sensitive to extinction because their habitat tends to decrease with any kind of human disturbance and recovers slowly (Brown and Hutchings 1997). Even high grading can result in the loss of deep forest butterflies, presumably through increased canopy opening. In Indonesia, Hill et al. (1995) noted that six species of endemic or narrowly distributed forest butterflies were present in undisturbed forest but absent from adjacent high-graded forest. Unfortunately, we have no data to compare dry-forest butterflies before and after disturbance. Studies comparing the butterfly populations of mature and secondary habitats with varying size and disturbance regimes would show what resources are needed to support different species.

For some species migration can function as a hedge against regional extinctions as migrants colonize habitat fragments where small populations have died out. Reservoir populations on the Atlantic side of the country that can inject a new wave of immigrants into the Pacific lowlands each season create a mosaic of extinction and recolonization over time, forming metapopulations at the regional level (Pollard and Yates 1992; Hanski et al. 1994, 1995; Neve et al. 1996). However, as forest fragments are lost on both Atlantic and Pacific slopes, the migration system will break down, leaving a higher proportion of open-area species as forest butterflies gradually drop out of the fauna. For this reason, a regional approach to conservation planning seems essential, which means integrating information and action across habitat boundaries, as has been the case in conservation of the Three-wattled Bellbird and Resplendent Quetzal (Powell and Bjork 1995).

Superimposed on these human threats is the pattern of extreme climate fluctuations experienced in Costa Rica over the past decade (Pounds et al. 1999; Lawton et al. 2001). With populations reduced in size by habitat fragmentation, a severe drought year, such as several recent El Niño years, could wipe out species that maintain only a marginal residence in the dry forest. As an apparent result, during strong El Niño years, cross-country migration through Monteverde almost disappears (W. Haber pers. obs.). Each of our Pacific lowland forest fragments supported only a fraction of the species known from similar habitat on a regional scale. Thus, most deep forest species already have highly contracted ranges within the dry forest.

BIODIVERSITY LAW AND COMMERCIAL THREATS

Costa Rica's biodiversity law (Ley de Conservación de la Vida Silvestre, No. 7317, 1992) claims all biodiversity as property of the state. Anyone interested in collecting, farming, or conducting research on Lepidoptera must apply for a permit from the Ministry of Environment and Energy (MINAE). In practice, the law is strictly applied only in national parks. In addition, a permit is required for exporting specimens. Illegal collecting of Lepidoptera in Costa Rica is not perceived as a problem as it has been in some sites such as Jamaica, where targeted, commercial collecting threatens a relict population of the swallowtail *Papilio homerus* (Emmel and Garraway 1990). No Costa Rican insects are listed by CITES. Costa Rica is at the point where observing, monitoring, and collecting Lepidoptera should be encouraged in the cause of generating information useful for conservation planning.

RECOMMENDATIONS FOR RESEARCH AND PUBLIC INVOLVEMENT

Any kind of inventory work, especially observations of host-plant use by butterflies, is worth recording. A sample of the host plant should always be pressed and dried for identification by an expert. Researchers interested in butterflies should be encouraged to make this a part of ongoing work and education activities in their study areas. An Internet-based site where field data could be posted and collated would stimulate the capture of distribution and life history records and make it feasible to share them across the research and amateur communities. We are currently developing an electronic field guide with the potential for anyone to record

natural history observations in a database on the Internet using common Web browsers (Morris and Stevenson 2002; Stevenson et al. 2002).

Encouraging an interest in butterflies among amateurs has had a great effect in generating distribution data in the United States, Great Britain, and Europe. Initiating annual butterfly counts (such as the July Butterfly Count conducted in the United States) at major research sites in Costa Rica would stimulate interest in butterfly observation and also serve as a training workshop for local guides and amateurs with a natural history interest. The annual Christmas bird counts based at Monteverde and the La Selva Biological Station demonstrate the value of these group activities in building enthusiasm as well as for accruing long-term data. Organizing both a Christmas and July butterfly count would be ideal for taking a snapshot of butterfly populations in both the dry and the wet seasons.

Our current limited knowledge of how thousands of species of seasonally migrating invertebrates and dozens of vertebrate species (particularly birds and bats) connect the ecology and conservation of dry forest, cloud forest, and rain forest in Costa Rica is beginning to reach the consciousness of biologists, natural resource managers, and even the general public. Promoting a wider understanding of these connections will also motivate public support for biodiversity conservation.

ACKNOWLEDGMENTS

We thank the Monteverde Cloud Forest Preserve, the Monteverde Conservation League, and many landowners for permission to work on their property, as well as the Instituto Nacional de Biodiversidad and Museo Nacional de Costa Rica for providing access to their collections. We also thank R. Rojas, N. Obando, D. Brenes, C. Guindon, M. Ramírez, and M. Wainwright for assistance in the field; P. DeVries, D. Janzen, P. Opler, R. Robbins, D. Wagner, and A. Warren for sharing unpublished data; I. Chacón, P. DeVries, D. Janzen, R. Robbins, G. Vega, and A. Warren for help with butterfly identifications; and

G. Frankie, D. Janzen, P. Opler, and J. Powell for reviewing the manuscript. The study was supported by NSF grant A9400011 to R. Stevenson and NSF DBI-9808462 to R. Stevenson and R. Morris, as well as the National Fish and Wildlife Foundation, the National Geographic Society, and the Missouri Botanical Garden.

REFERENCES

Baker, R. R. 1978. *The evolutionary ecology of animal migrations*. New York: Holmes and Meier. 1012 pp.

Blair, R. B., and A. E. Launer. 1997. Butterfly diversity and human land use: Species assemblages along an urban gradient. *Biological Conservation* 80:113–25.

Bolaños, R. A., and V. Watson. 1993. *Mapa ecológico de Costa Rica*. San José: Centro Científico Tropical.

Braby, M. F. 1995. Reproductive seasonality in tropical satyrine butterflies: Strategies for the dry season. *Ecological Entomology* 20:5–17.

Brower, L. P. 1991. Animal migrations: Endangered phenomena. *American Zoologist* 31:265–76.

———. 1996. Monarch butterfly orientation: Missing pieces of a magnificent puzzle. *Journal of Experimental Biology* 199:93–103.

Brown, K. S., and R. W. Hutchings. 1997. Disturbance, fragmentation, and the dynamics of diversity. In *Tropical forest remnants: Ecology, management, and conservation of fragmented communities*, ed. W. F. Laurance and R. O. Bierregaard Jr., 91–110. Chicago: University of Chicago Press.

Clark, K. L., R. O. Lawton, and P. R. Butler. 2000. The physical environment. In *Monteverde: Ecology and conservation of a tropical cloud forest*, ed. N. Nadkarni and N. Wheelwright, 15–38. New York: Oxford University Press.

DeVries, P. J. 1983. Checklist of butterflies. In *Costa Rican natural history*, ed. D. H. Janzen, 654–78. Chicago: University of Chicago Press.

———. 1987. *The butterflies of Costa Rica and their natural history*. Vol. 1, *Papilionidae, Pieridae, Nymphalidae*. Princeton, N.J.: Princeton University Press. 327 pp.

———. 1988. Stratification of fruit-feeding nymphalid butterflies in a Costa Rican rainforest. *Journal of Research on the Lepidoptera* 26:98–108.

———. 1997. *The butterflies of Costa Rica and their natural history*. Vol. 2, *Riodinidae*. Princeton, N.J.: Princeton University Press. 288 pp.

Dingle, H. 1996. *Migration, the biology of life on the move*. New York: Oxford University Press. 474 pp.

Emmel, T. C., and E. Garraway. 1990. Ecology and conservation biology of the Homerus Swallowtail in Jamaica. *Tropical Lepidoptera* 1:63–76.

Frankie, G. W., S. B. Vinson, M. A. Rizzardi, T. L. Griswold, S. O'Keefe, and R. R. Snelling. 1998. Diversity and abundance of bees visiting a mass flowering tree species in disturbed seasonal dry forest, Costa Rica. *Journal of the Kansas Entomological Society* 70:281–96.

Garraway, E., A. J. A. Bailey, and T. C. Emmel. 1993. Contribution to the ecology and conservation biology of the endangered *Papilio homerus* (Lepidoptera: Papilionidae). *Tropical Lepidoptera* 4:83–91.

Haber, W. A. 1993. Seasonal migration of monarchs and other butterflies in Costa Rica. In *Biology and conservation of the monarch butterfly*, ed. S. B. Malcolm and M. Zalucki, 201–7. Los Angeles: Los Angeles County Museum of Natural History.

———. 2000. Plants and vegetation. In *Monteverde: Ecology and conservation of a tropical cloud forest*, ed. N. Nadkarni and N. Wheelwright, 39–94. New York: Oxford University Press.

Haber, W. A., and G. W. Frankie. 1988. A tropical hawkmoth community: Costa Rican dry forest Sphingidae. *Biotropica* 21:155–72.

Hansen, M. D. D. 1997. Observations on the migrations of the Painted Lady (*Vanessa cardui* (L.)) in Denmark in 1996 (Lepidoptera: Nymphalidae). *Entomologiske Meddelelser* 65: 165–73.

Hanski, I., and C. D. Thomas. 1994. Metapopulation dynamics and conservation: A spatially explicit model applied to butterflies. *Biological Conservation* 68:167–80.

Hanski, I., M. Kuussaari, and M. Nieminen. 1994. Metapopulation structure and migration in the butterfly *Melitaea cinxia*. *Ecology* 75:747–62.

Hanski, I., T. Pakkala, M. Kuussaari, and G. Lei. 1995. Metapopulation persistence of an endangered butterfly in a fragmented landscape. *Oikos* 72:21–28.

Hartshorn, G. S. 1983. Plants: Introduction. In *Costa Rican natural history*, ed. D. H. Janzen, 118–57. Chicago: University of Chicago Press.

Hill, J. K., K. C. Hamer, L. A. Lace, and W. M. Banham. 1995. Effects of selective logging on tropical forest butterflies on Buru, Indonesia. *Journal of Applied Ecology* 32:754–60.

Holdridge, L. R. 1967. *Life zone ecology*. Rev. ed. San José: Tropical Science Center.

Hunt, J. H., R. J. Brodie, T. P. Carithers, P. Z. Goldstein, and D. H. Janzen. 1999. Dry season
migration by Costa Rican lowland paper wasps
to high elevation cold dormancy sites. *Biotropica* 31:192–96.

Janzen, D. H. 1984. Two ways to be a tropical big
moth: Santa Rosa saturniids and sphingids. *Oxford Surveys in Evolutionary Biology* 1:85–140.

———. 1987a. Biogeography of an unexceptional
place: What determines the saturniid and sphingid moth fauna of Santa Rosa National Park,
Costa Rica, and what does it mean to conservation biology. *Brenesia* 25/26:51–87.

———. 1987b. How moths pass the dry season in
a Costa Rican dry forest. *Insect Science and Its
Application* 8:489–500.

———. 1987c. When, and when not to leave. *Oikos*
49:241–43.

———. 1988. Ecological characterization of a
Costa Rican dry forest caterpillar fauna. *Biotropica* 20:120–35.

———. 2002. Caterpillar rearing voucher databases for the Area de Conservación (ACG) in
northwestern Costa Rica (http://janzen.sas.
upenn.edu/caterpillars/database.htm).

———, ed. 1983. *Costa Rican natural history.* Chicago: University of Chicago Press. 816 pp.

Johnson, C. G. 1969. *Migration and dispersal of
insects by flight.* London: Methuen. 763 pp.

Lawton, R. O., U. S. Nair, R. A. Pielke, and R. M.
Welch. 2001. Climatic impact of tropical lowland deforestation on nearby montane cloud
forests. *Science* 294:584–87.

Levey, D. J. 1994. Why we should adopt a broader
view of neotropical migrants. *Auk* 111:233–36.

Levey, D. J., and F. G. Stiles. 1992. Evolutionary
precursors of long-distance migration: Resource
availability and movement patterns in neotropical landbirds. *American Naturalist* 140:447–76.

Loiselle, B. A., and J. G. Blake. 1991. Temporal
variation in birds and fruits along an elevational
gradient in Costa Rica. *Ecology* 72:180–93.

Martin, T. E., and D. M. Finch, eds. 1995. *Ecology
and management of Neotropical migratory birds.*
New York: Oxford University Press. 489 pp.

Morris, R. A., and R. D. Stevenson. 2002. Electronic field guide: An object oriented WWW
database to identify species and record ecological observations (http://www.cs.umb.edu/efg/).

Murphy, D. D., and S. B. Weiss. 1988. A long-term
monitoring plan for a threatened butterfly. *Conservation Biology* 2:367–74.

Neve, G., B. Barascud, R. Hughs, J. Aubert, H. De-
scimon, P. Lebrun, and M. Baguette. 1996. Dispersal, colonization power and metapopulation

structure in the vulnerable butterfly *Proclossiana
eunomia* (Lepidoptera: Nymphalidae). *Journal
of Applied Ecology* 33:14–22.

New, T. R., R. M. Pyle, J. A. Thomas, C. D. Thomas,
and P. C. Hammond. 1995. Butterfly conservation management. *Annual Review of Entomology*
40:57–83.

Nielsen, E. T., and A. T. Nielsen. 1950. Contributions toward the knowledge of the migration
of butterflies. *American Museum Novitates* 1471:
1–29.

Opler, P. A. 1989. Ecological and behavioral aspects of seasonal polyphenism in *Eurema daira*
(Pieridae, Lepidoptera). In *The evolutionary ecology of plants*, ed. J. H. Brock and Y. B. Linhart,
515–33. Boulder, Colo.: Westview Press.

Pinheiro, C. E. G., and J. V. C. Ortiz. 1992. Communities of fruit-feeding butterflies along a
vegetation gradient in central Brazil. *Journal of
Biogeography* 19:505–511.

Pollard, E., and T. J. Yates. 1992. The extinction
and foundation of local butterfly populations
in relation to population variability and other
factors. *Ecological Entomology* 17:249–54.

Pollard, E., D. Moss, and T. J. Yates. 1995. Population
trends of common British butterflies at monitored sites. *Journal of Applied Ecology* 32:9–16.

Pounds, J. A., M. P. Fogden, and J. H. Campbell.
1999. Biological response to climate change on
a tropical mountain. *Nature* 398:611–15.

Powell, G. V. N., and R. Bjork. 1995. Implications
of intra-tropical migration on reserve design: A
case study using *Pharomachrus mocinno*. *Conservation Biology* 9:354–62.

Stevenson, R. D., and W. A. Haber. 2000a. *Manataria maculata* (Nymphalidae: Satyrinae). In
*Monteverde: Ecology and conservation of a tropical
cloud forest*, ed. N. Nadkarni and N. Wheelwright,
119–20. New York: Oxford University Press.

———. 2000b. Migration of butterflies through
Monteverde. In *Monteverde: Ecology and conservation of a tropical cloud forest*, ed. N. Nadkarni
and N. Wheelwright, 118–19. New York: Oxford
University Press.

Stevenson, R. D., W. A. Haber, and R. A. Morris.
2002. Electronic field guides and user communities in the eco-informatics revolution. *Conservation Ecology* 7(1). [On-line] URL: http://www.
consecol.org/vol7/iss1/art3

van Swaay, C. A. M. 1990. An assessment of the
changes in butterfly abundance in the Netherlands during the 20th century. *Biological Conservation* 52:287–302.

Walker, T. J. 1978. Migration and re-migration
of butterflies through north peninsular Florida:

Quantification with malaise traps. *Journal of the Lepidopterists' Society* 32:178–190.

———. 1980. Migrating Lepidoptera: Are butterflies better than moths? *Florida Entomology* 63: 81–98.

Williams, C. B. 1930. *The migration of butterflies.* London: Oliver and Boyd. 473 pp.

CHAPTER 9

Watershed Ecology and Conservation

HYDROLOGICAL RESOURCES IN THE NORTHWEST OF COSTA RICA

Alfonso Mata

AQUATIC RESOURCES represent one of the most valuable and sought-after natural treasures, although in many areas of the planet they are deteriorating. Playing a key role in climatic, ecological, and biogeochemical processes, the terrestrial water cycle is being destroyed at alarming rates (Vörösmarty and Sahagian 2000). Human populations have already appropriated half of the accessible global freshwater runoff, and this share will continue to rise to as much as 70 percent by the year 2025 if these populations continue to grow as expected (Postel et al. 1996; Pringle 2000). In Costa Rica these resources are still abundant in regions such as the Atlantic and southern basins but are scarce in others owing to overuse or overpopulation, as in the Central Valley of San José. This apparent abundance has allowed this country to neglect important precautionary measures (strategic planning and conservation) to protect and develop these resources as a fundamental element of sustainable development and biodiversity protection (Quesada 1990). Perhaps the most critical area is Guanacaste, the Costa Rican northwest, where the dry season lasts six months. It is in this area that the largest extant territory of dry forest in Mesoamerica is protected (Boza 1999).

The existing hydrological connection between the different terrestrial, fluvial, and estuarine systems in that region obviously involves habitats drained by the river web as well as all their ecologically related species (birds, bats, butterflies, bees, mammals, fish, and humans, to name a few). However, biological and ecological studies on the biota of dry-forest watersheds and connecting uplands are scarce. Specific information on the flora and fauna of riparian habitats is usually limited and widely scattered in the literature. With the Guanacaste region as a frame, this chapter analyzes the importance of the stream corridors, current human affects, river research and studies needed, and the actions that are being or could be implemented to reduce or avoid major or irreversible damages.

THE ECOLOGICAL
IMPORTANCE OF RIVERS

"The biological diversity sustained by the fluvio-riparian system is a critical step in the whole natural food web of which human beings form a part" (Doppelt et al. 1993: 10). The fluvio-riparian habitat, also called a stream corridor, is one of the most productive ecosystems. It is composed of a complex aquatic biological continuum nourished by the bank and floodplain forest and the entire watershed. It provides nutrients reaching the river food web (Riley 1998: 97; Pringle and Scatena 1999: 112) from the headwaters to the estuary and ocean. Even under extreme conditions, the surface and subsoil riparian water discharges (epirrhoeic and hyporrhoeic flow, respectively) always sustain prosperous vegetation and favor the associated fauna (see chapter 12). In general, these ecosystems have the following properties:

1. Protection and stabilization of soil that is infiltrated by water, or the saturation zone. This area is located upland on one or both sides of the riverbank; it is a transitional land edge between the river and surrounding landscape or floodplain. This area is most vulnerable to high surface runoff and nutrient leaching.

2. The system works with multidimensional dynamics: longitudinal (displacement of aquatic species, with and against the flow); to the lateral directions in the alluvial terraces (movement of water and species toward the floodplains and wetlands); and with vertical direction (groundwater current and river channel current zone).

3. Retention of sediments, organic matter, and pollutants that reach the river from surrounding areas in mulch and underbrush vegetation.

4. Source of nutrients and species for other rivers (down the watershed), lagoons, lakes, estuaries, and the ocean.

5. Control of water temperature of creeks, favoring aquatic life and increasing dissolved oxygen retention capacity. Forest shade plays an important role.

6. Biodiversity conservation: biological corridor and wildlife species refuge in the dry and migratory seasons (Riley 1998: 96; chapter 12).

Other benefits are derived from aesthetic qualities, shade, industrial and commercial transport, water provision for agriculture, and space for outdoor sports, industry, and homes. Stream corridors are also important connections between larger areas of natural habitats at different elevational levels. They must be protected in and outside preserved areas (such as national parks and refuges), from the headwaters to the seashore.

RIVERS OF THE NICOYA PENINSULA
AND TEMPISQUE RIVER BASIN

Characteristics of the northwest region of Costa Rica are described in chapter 1. Map 1.1 shows the hydrological region of Guanacaste, featuring at the center the estuarine, littoral, and terrestrial systems and watersheds that are all connected by the fluvial system. Rivers of the region can be grouped in two well-defined sectors: rivers of the northwestern coastal strip and those of the Gulf of Nicoya Basin (GNB). There are a few others flowing to Lake Nicaragua (see also chapter 1).

RIVERS OF THE NORTHWESTERN
COASTAL STRIP

There are low coastal mountains (50–250 m above sea level) in the northwestern area of Guanacaste in which many creeks and a few small rivers originate, their microbasins emptying directly into the Pacific Ocean. The region presents the driest life zones of the country, such as the tropical dry forest, the moist forest, and the premontane moist forest (chapter 1). These rivers remain waterless during the six-month dry season, but they rapidly flood with the persistent precipitation of the rainy season. The local orography and winds from the south are crucial in the establishment of heavier rainy conditions, which make the Nicoya Peninsula more humid. The Nosara River and Bongo River, the largest ones in the coastal strip, maintain a perceptible base flow from March to May.

RIVERS THAT FLOW TO THE GULF OF NICOYA

The GNB is an ample territory connected with a net of rivers that have the gulf as their common destiny (chapter 1). It covers around 12,000 km², almost half of the Pacific Ocean versant of Costa Rica. It is important not only because it covers almost 25 percent of the national territory (Mata and Blanco 1994) but also because it contains almost all the life zones occurring in Costa Rica, with a wide variety of terrestrial and aquatic ecosystems.

The Tempisque River Basin. The most extensive hydrological subregion in Guanacaste Province, the Tempisque River Basin (TRB), located in the center of this region, has an average annual flow of 308 m³/s and has most of the seasonal dry forest and related transitions in the country. It consists of the watersheds of the Tempisque and Bebedero Rivers. Variation in river flow is high, reflecting wide seasonal climatic extremes with the potential for flooding as well as water scarcity (Ramirez and Jimenez 1998). Various habitats are crossed and drained by the stream network. The following are noteworthy: collections of hills and mountains (coastal mountains and the Guanacaste Volcanic Mountain Range), small natural reservoirs, wetlands (such as the floodplains of the middle watershed of the Tempisque River and the mouth of the Bebedero River), and mangroves. This entire lowland region covers approximately 1,300 km². Eighty percent of it can be considered a wetland, though the majority of the area is traversed by agricultural activities (sugarcane, melon, rice). This river should have top national priority in any decision regarding ecological protection.

The TRB has an area of 5,454 km², equivalent to 54 percent of Guanacaste Province and 10 percent of the national territory. It has primarily a humid tropical climate, with assorted geological formations of enormous beauty and tourist po-

tential. The area has witnessed development of large agro-industries and hotels with good communication networks. Its ethnographic and archaeological contributions are among the most relevant of the country. It is one of the main areas of Costa Rica, second in economic importance only to the Central Valley (Mata and Blanco 1994). The watershed of the Tempisque River, with an area of 3,407.8 km², constitutes the western part of the TRB. Its principal cities are Liberia, capital of the province of Guanacaste; Filadelfia; and Santa Cruz. The Bebedero watershed has an area of 2,052.4 km², and its principal cities are Bagaces, Cañas, and Tilarán.

Extensive agricultural areas, devoted primarily to grains, sugarcane and, more recently, melon and livestock, dominate the physical and economic landscape. The TRB hosts virtually half of the production of rice and sugarcane and a high percentage of the cattle ranching in Costa Rica. Other activities with impact on a national level are melon production and forestry plantations. Nevertheless, all these activities carry an environmental cost in terms of contamination, soil erosion, and decrease in water quality and quantity. Clearly, the economic and natural systems are intimately linked, and it is necessary to use the limited resources in a way that maximizes benefits to society. Three zones of the National System of Conservation Areas (SINAC) have influence in this basin. Established by the Ministry of Environment and Energy (MINAE) for the protection and conservation of natural resources, these areas are Area de Conservación Guanacaste, Area de Conservación Tempisque, and Area de Conservación Arenal.

Other Basins and Subbasins. Other important subbasins are that of the Abangares, Lagartos, Guacimal, and Barranca Rivers, which empty into the Gulf of Nicoya. They have also suffered extensive deforestation. The Lake Arenal subbasin (which includes Cote and Arenal Lakes and Chiquito River) originally emptied into the Caribbean Sea through the San Juan River. However, it was incorporated into the Pacific watershed after the Arenal River was dammed, causing its volume to grow considerably and the lake area to increase to 84 km². This artificial connection, which supplies about 90 m³/s, established the largest hydrological installation ever assembled in the country, which is also called the Arenal-Tempisque Hydropower-Irrigation System. Hydroelectricity is produced through three cascading power plants (Arenal, Corobici, and Sandillal), and irrigation from three principal channels supply the low flatlands of the Bebedero River subbasin in the TRB.

GROUNDWATER

Groundwater has been very important in Guanacaste, especially in the most isolated regions, where there has not been a municipal network of drinking water distribution, and because of the six-month dry period. Even during the rainy season, wells are a necessity because of the irregularity of precipitation. The Zapandi area, on the right side of the Tempisque River, has the potential to supply water for use in the intensive agricultural months of summer, to some extent paralleling the irrigation system on the left side of this river, under the authority of the National Irrigation and Drainage Service.

STREAM CORRIDOR BIOTA AND THE DRY FOREST

Except for a few general documents, biological and ecological studies on the biota of dry-forest watersheds and connecting uplands are scarce. Information on the flora and fauna of riparian habitats within watersheds is available for some species, but it is usually limited and widely scattered in the literature. Surveys in 1969–70 along several permanent watercourses in the lowland dry forest indicated that tree species are about twice as diverse as compared with adjacent dry deciduous forest (Frankie et al. 1974). More recent surveys indicate that a species-rich plant understory forms a regular part of most riparian habitats. A wide variety of resident bird species are known to use riparian areas, and, as the dry season advances, resident as well as migratory species seek riparian areas for food and cover

(chapter 12). Amphibians, reptiles, and mammals also make extensive use of riparian habitats (chapters 5 and 12). Riparian areas are required by several dry-forest bee species for nesting (Frankie et al. 1988, 1993), and larval host plants of butterflies and moths are commonly found in this habitat (chapters 7 and 8).

Nearly 15 percent of the 130 freshwater fish species found in Costa Rica dwell in the fresh aquatic environment of Guanacaste rivers (Bussing 1998). Some fish of lowland dry-forest rivers (e.g., free-ranging convict cichclids) have received considerable study (Wisenden and Keenleyside 1994, 1995) over a period of several years. An important survey (Bussing and Lopez 1977) of fish associated with the interbasin transfer of the Arenal hydropower system was made before the diversion of waters from the Caribbean to the Pacific slope, but it has not been followed up.

Finally, studies on aquatic invertebrates are rare, but it is believed that a relatively rich fauna exists in many rivers that have not been subject to extensive human disturbance. Overall, it is safe to say that riparian zones and stream corridors need much more biological and ecological study, especially in relation to associated human activities (Pringle et al. 2000a).

SYSTEM INTERACTION

The area of the TRB, largest in the northwestern sector of the country (also known as the Chorotega region), contains various aquatic and terrestrial ecosystems. They can be found in diverse environments, such as estuaries, mangroves, floodplains, lagoons, prairies, and forests, and all of them are located in different life zones that characterize the region. The wetland ecosystems, rich in flora and fauna, are located in the floodplains and are characterized by their geographical location and type of water (stagnant or flowing, fresh or brackish) that reaches them. According to the World Conservation Union classification for wetlands, the following can be found there (World Conservation Union 1992: 14): freshwater swamps, floodplains, estuaries, coastal lagoons, and artificial wetlands (chapter 11). The six principal life zones that occur on land indicate a variety of elevational ranges, even though the most important one corresponds to the tropical dry forest with its transition to moist environments (see the section "Life Zones" in chapter 1). This life zone covers 10,400 km², representing roughly 10 percent of the national territory. It exists nowhere else in Costa Rica.

The amount of water that reaches the plains during the dry season depends entirely on the base flow of headwaters in the highlands, created by the groundwater recharge during the rainy months. The larger rivers (Tempisque, Bolson, Bebedero, and a few of their principal tributaries) are perennial streams. The principal emptying stream is the estuary of the Tempisque River, where the main interaction between fresh water and the Gulf of Nicoya saline water occurs. The gulf is the most important estuary in Costa Rica and one of the most attractive in tropical America. It penetrates the northwestern part of the country, forming the Nicoya Peninsula (see map 1.1 in chapter 1), with an area of approximately 1,530 km². It arches from the Pacific Ocean toward the northwest, extending about 85 km to the mouth of the Tempisque River (see chapter 10).

During the past 60 years, several agricultural (monocultures) and industrial activities have been developed throughout the GNB, which together have produced structural distortions in economic, social, and cultural activities. These activities have had dramatic environmental effects on the basin water, which has led to rapid repercussions downstream, all the way to the estuary.

The Guanacaste Conservation Area and Tempisque Conservation Area, which currently include six national parks, five wildlife refuges, two biological corridors, three wetlands, and a number of forestry reserves, would be better integrated ecologically if the fluvial-riparian zones (stream corridors) were restored and expanded. This territory is extremely important because it protects a large part of the most extensive tropical-dry-forest zone that remains in Central America (Boza 1999: 54; Vargas 1999: 95). It must be noted that the driest regions of Central America, which coincide with Pacific watersheds,

are densely populated and have historically suffered from strong human intervention (Vargas 1999: 88). In the case of the TRB and neighboring areas, there are important population centers, such as Nicoya, Santa Cruz, Filadelfia, Cañas, Bagaces, Tilarán, and Liberia, that produce wastes. Others have been growing rapidly and are creating problems that require prompt solutions, such as Cobano, Nandayure, Paquera, El Coco, Santa Cruz, and Las Juntas.

HUMAN IMPACT ON HYDROLOGICAL RESOURCES

Human effects on the environment, which lead to general ecological simplification of the rivers, occur in various ways (Doppelt et al. 1993; Federal Interagency Stream Restoration Working Group 1998; Vörösmarty and Sahagian 2000). The main river ecological problems in the region are related to extensive land use, fragmentation and alteration of stream corridors, fluvial contamination, and recent new efforts to construct levees in the floodplains. The final destinations of many pollutants from populated areas are the Tempisque estuary and the Gulf of Nicoya.

WATER EXTRACTION

The most relevant water consumers in the basin region are sugar industries, the Arenal-Tempisque Irrigation System, fruit packaging plants (melon), aquaculture of tilapia, cities and towns, and, to a minor degree, the coffee factories of Tilarán. The Taboga, CATSA, and El Viejo sugar mills tap the Cañas, Liberia, and Tempisque Rivers, respectively. These mills extract volumes varying from 5 to 10 m³/s just for industrial use, requiring another large quantity for irrigation. Since most of the harvest occurs during the dry season, water consumption dramatically alters the volume of the Tempisque River and some tributaries, which have already been depleted upstream.

MODIFICATION OF THE NATURAL CHANNEL

The slow expansion of sugarcane and watermelon cultivation needs more territories in the form of reclamation works, channels, levees, and fluvial detours. These alterations in the environment require strict regulation, especially considering the vulnerability that these activities introduce. Over the past few years, the time it takes floodwater to withdraw has increased, a condition attributable in part to the presence of levees that hinder waters from returning to their normal course. So far, the main intervention consists of a 4-km channel and levees (built in 1983 by the National Service for Irrigation and Drainage) circumventing 12 km of the Tempisque River that had supplied water to wetlands in this area. No riparian forests in the channel have been restored after these developments. In fact, the service has plans to dam the river and to continue dredging and canalization. Measures should be considered in order to preserve river corridors, from the headwaters all the way to the receiving water body (lake, estuary, or sea). "Adopt a River" public action projects, similar to those implemented in Puerto Viejo, Sarapiquí, in the northern Caribbean slope of Costa Rica, will become increasingly important (Pringle et al. 2000b).

FRAGMENTATION OF THE RIPARIAN SYSTEM

The riparian and fluvial continuum (the stream corridor) is essential to the maintenance of biodiversity in terrestrial ecosystems. The fragmentation and ecological discontinuity produced by human activities result in a visible impact on the riparian and stream systems. These damages are apparent in a large part of Guanacaste's rivers and in Costa Rica's rivers in general. Each bridge, road, or agricultural activity that is developed at or near the river results in varying degrees of riparian fragmentation. In many cases, these could be prevented by protecting the stream corridors by means of appropriate construction design as well as enforcement of current laws (chapters 22 and 23).

Rivers of the Tempisque lower basin have also suffered great damages from the sugarcane fields. When one passes through Liberia, Cañas, Filadelfia, and Santa Cruz, the devastating effect of the urban presence on the banks is evident,

indicating an absence of urban planning. These alterations have almost reached the shores of the rivers as they flow through the cities, where another component is added: contamination from organic wastes and trash. Several smaller rivers or creeks have only a few spaced trees with no understory vegetation.

During the 1940s several laws established the prohibition of tree cutting near banks of the country's rivers and springs. Water Law No. 276 of 1942 banned the cutting of trees within 50 m of the riverbanks, sometimes corresponding with the transitional upland fringe. The Forestry Law of 1996, No. 75757, indicates that a protection area of 100 m around the springs must be respected. Furthermore, cutting is prohibited within 15 m of each side of the rivers and creeks in rural areas. In urban areas, a 10-m strip on each side is protected if the terrain is flat, and 50 horizontal meters are protected if the terrain is inclined. The old Costa Rican farmer has generally respected these ordinances, although it is common to see domestic animals devastating rich understory vegetation. Some authors (Watson et al. 1998) consider the riparian forest to be a common element in the scenery across the country, but not everyone has complied with the established measures, particularly the large monoculture industries such as pineapple, sugarcane, rice, and bananas. In many cases, their lands have been deforested all the way to the river edge, with the excuse that the canopies obstruct aerial fumigation operations. This outdated practice has slowly been changing, and some industries have taken measures to restore these forests.

It is evident that 10 or 15 m of protection are too few for a flat land and even less for an inclined terrain. The appropriate measurement should be determined by practical and scientific observations of the stream's conditions: its role in local ecological processes, the amount of biodiversity it contains, stream dynamics, and the equilibrium of related ecosystems. Appropriate limits are extremely important because in reality landowners will cut to that limit or more, in detriment to the stream corridor.

Protection of these areas must be considered immediately, as there are still rivers in the northwestern coastal strip (see map 1.1 in chapter 1) and important tracts of the thin Zapandi Riparian Protected Zone of the TRB (ca. 400 ha) that contain segments in very good condition, some with trees that in nearby regions have been extirpated or are becoming extinct in Guanacaste. In fact, it is not too late to consider restoring the entire Tempisque River corridor.

CONTAMINATION FROM RESIDUAL WATERS

Many pristine streams can still be found, but some streams suffer the impact of urban and agricultural wastes. Rivers of the Pacific coast are clean during the rainy season, but only when storms and persistent rainfall are absent. When these events occur, rivers are loaded with sediments resulting from land use in their basins. Further, owing to lack of regulation or enforcement of a corresponding law, it is common to observe small settlements or clusters of houses and shacks where roads and bridges cross streams, which plays a role in polluting the streams. Once rivers begin to pass through the cities, they become contaminated. Even so, their waters are exploited in great volumes downstream by the sugar industry. Dissolved oxygen contents are at near normal levels in most of the Tempisque River course and tributaries, with the exception of tracts flowing through and after main cities.

Sewage. The treatment system for domestic wastewaters in the main cities of Guanacaste, installed 25 years ago, initially covered 70 percent of the urban areas. However, expansion of sewage service has not kept pace with population growth, and wastewater treatment now covers only 33 percent of urban zones (Echeverría et al. 1998). Furthermore, this growth means a larger production of organic matter that the environment will have to absorb, whether from oxidation in septic tanks or by direct dumping into surface currents. As a result, surface contamination of rivers passing through cities will increase noticeably in the coming years. A large investment is necessary to expand treatment systems, not only to maintain initial coverage but also to increase it and, it is hoped, reach total coverage.

Population Growth and Urban Planning. Although the waste treatment plant of Liberia was built in an unpopulated area near the western sector of the Pan American Highway following the basin's slope, its southern and eastern perimeters have now been reached by heavily populated housing settlements. Another problem is flooding of the lowest sectors of the fast-growing town of Filadelfia, which are closest to the Tempisque River and some of its tributaries (such as Palmas River). When flooding occurs, latrines and septic tanks overflow, and their fermented content is dispersed, creating severe fecal pollution. There is a lack of authority and coordination among governing offices to give the respective permits or to produce plans for appropriate urban development.

NUTRIENTS AND PESTICIDES

Liquid wastes from a large part of the industrial sugarcane process should end up in the field as irrigation or in large aeration lagoons. However, if there are periods when there is no concerted coordination of clearing, plowing, and irrigation of the field, the principal channel carrying wastewaters will empty into streams or associated wetlands. There have been reports of river fish kills, due to depletion of normal dissolved oxygen of the stream, when oxidation pond contents are released.

A three-year monitoring of waters from the drainage channels of the extensive irrigation system, including the Bagatzi channel, near the Palo Verde National Park, indicates that the water coming out of rice fields that have a high input of fertilizers, although reflecting the integration of the inputs on the system, shows low to moderate nutrient contents, such as nitrate (Rodríguez-Ulloa 1997). There is no soil pollution or appreciable changes in soil fertility (Cabalceta 1997). With respect to pesticide content in waterfowl and fish, studies (Rodríguez-Brenes 1997) showed very low levels of organochlorine compounds and other substances

(Lindane, Aldrin, Dieldrin, β-BHC, Heptachlor, α- and γ-chlordane, chlorpirifos, malathion, etc.). These residues are much lower than those encountered a decade ago in Isla Pajaros, in the lower Tempisque River (Hidalgo 1986). None of these chemicals exceed the drinking water standards. Heavy metals in birds showed contents similar to natural levels.

SOLID WASTES

Nowhere in the basin are wastes being treated appropriately (Echeverría et al. 1998). Despite some efforts made by the government, this problem applies to the rest of the country as well. It is estimated that, at the municipal level, there are no political measures to coordinate the conservation of the environment regionally, and there is a significant lack of environmental education in all strata of society. Lack of financing, insufficient technical assistance, and an inadequate database are also common problems.

THREATS TO THE GULF OF NICOYA

Since the biological production of this estuary is so important to the country, much attention should be paid to the large burden of contaminants being poured into the Tempisque River. However, because the population of Guanacaste influencing the gulf directly represents only 10 percent of the national population (4 million), it is necessary to consider the effects of the Tárcoles River middle basin, where a million and a half inhabitants are concentrated in the San José Valley (see chapter 10 for discussion). Several efforts have been carried out by universities (Marine Science Center/University of Costa Rica; Environmental Pollution Research Center/University of Costa Rica; Marine Sciences Laboratory/Universidad Nacional de Costa Rica) in order to establish levels of pollution in the gulf. There is evidence that this contamination is more significant in the upper gulf and at the mouth of the Tempisque River. The largest concentration of contaminants is located in the Puntarenas estuary, but they are extensively diluted by daily tidal currents from the gulf (Mata and Blanco 1994).

Changes in the estuary's water conditions are highly dynamic in the upper sector. Water-mixing processes are generally effective because of important geographical barriers, such as Toro Island at the mouth of the Tempisque River, Chira Island in the middle part of the upper gulf, and other islands. Furthermore, the estuary is fairly shallow, with an average depth of 4 m in the upper sector and 30 m in the outer gulf (Mata and Blanco 1994). The established tidal cycles, winds, net surface and bottom currents system, stratification, mixing processes, and bottom roughness efficiently mix the entire water body (Voorhis et al. 1983). However, its capacity for diluting and alleviating contamination could be surpassed by the intensity of future inputs. Chapter 10 discusses these subjects.

PRIORITIZING ENVIRONMENTAL CONSERVATION MEASURES

There is currently no strategy in Costa Rica to initiate restoration and appropriate conservation of its fluvial systems. No study has yet been done to determine which rivers nationwide are in pristine condition, from their birth to their receiving body (river, lake, estuary, or sea). As a result, no program can use this missing information for their special protection. This analysis is needed to connect the conservation needs of the fluvial-riparian ecosystems with state policies and with conservationist, governmental, academic, and private activities. Urgent needs, priorities, and proper actions related to the conservation of these extremely valuable ecosystems must be defined. There are plenty of viable possibilities for conservation, restoration, and urban planning. Such actions will not only preserve Costa Rica's valuable resources for future generations but, in the more immediate future, will decrease vulnerability to natural disasters triggered by natural hydrological phenomena. The following recommendations are offered for safeguarding hydrological resources and their associated biodiversity in Guanacaste:

1. Implementing protection zones for sources of drinking water from wells and springs.

Only half of these, administered by the Aqueducts and Sewage Institute, are subject to adequate bacteriological control of water quality. The rest, managed by rural administration groups, have no integral protection policies or strict regulations.

2. Selection of representative rivers and their corridors for protection as depositories of biodiversity and connectors of preserved ecosystems or watersheds from the mountains to receiving water systems (lagoon, estuary, or ocean).

3. Reinforcement of protection laws for stream corridors (perennial, intermittent, and ephemeral currents). Although forestry law requires protection of certain zones on rivers' edges, it is not rigorously applied because most of these strips continue to be private property. The actual protection strip width is not sufficient, and it seems that the importance of this ecosystem is not a priority for municipal and governmental authorities. The whole Tempisque River corridor should be declared of national interest, extending the protected strips of wetlands, Zapandi Riparian Protected Zone.

4. Effective protection for aquifer recharges and soil conservation areas, which correspond to the upper basins of rivers and creeks. Their protection would mitigate aquifer contamination and would diminish flood threats in the lowlands.

5. Strict regulations and enforcement of existing legal measures that limit coastal zone groundwater extraction.

6. Extension and improvement of sewers, an increase in wastewater treatment capacity for the principal urban centers of the region (see the section "Population Growth and Urban Planning" earlier in the chapter), and better industrial wastewater control (mainly sugar mills and aquaculture).

7. New sanitary landfills, rehabilitation of controlled solid waste dump sites, and establishment of integrated waste management systems, at least for the main cities and tourism centers.

8. Strict control of, and restrictions on, channeling and construction of levees and a clear environmental policy for the Institute for Irrigation and Drainage.

9. Development of environmental awareness among citizens, students, nongovernmental organizations, and political leaders through educational methods and other strategies (see chapters 19 and 20). Educational programs can lead to local projects for stream corridor protection and restoration (slogan for the communities: Adopt a River; see Pringle et al. 2000b).

10. Better selection and training of committed personnel in the institutions in charge of conserving resources. Although there are good programs and dedicated public servants, there is a lack of conservationist leadership and commitment at the highest levels of the administration and, in general, a weak and inefficient bureaucracy in the Park Service (see chapters 7, 12, 15, 19, 21, 22, and 23).

11. Sponsorship of more stream corridor biological studies, especially in relation to fish and riparian overstory and understory vegetation.

REFERENCES

Boza, M. 1999. Biodiversity conservation in Mesoamerica. In *Managed ecosystems: The Mesoamerican experience*, ed. L. Hupton Hatch and M. E. Swisher, 51–60. New York: Oxford University Press.

Bussing, W. 1998. *Peces de las aguas continentales de Costa Rica (Fresh water fishes of Costa Rica)*. 2d ed. San José: Editorial University of Costa Rica. 468 pp.

Bussing, W., and M. Lopez. 1977. Distribución y aspectos ecológicos de los peces de las cuencas hidrográficas de Arenal, Bebedero y Tempisque, Costa Rica. *Revista de Biología Tropical* 25(1): 13–37.

Cabalceta, G. 1997. *Presencia de residuos de especies químicas clave en los suelos. Proyecto de Riego*

Arenal-Tempisque. Final Report. San José: Environmental Pollution Research Center/University of Costa Rica. 99 pp.

de la Rosa, C. 1999. Conservation and sustainable use of streams and rivers in Central America. In *Managed ecosystems: The Mesoamerican experience,* ed. L. Hupton Hatch and M. E. Swisher, 122–32. New York: Oxford University Press.

Doppelt, B., M. Scurlock, C. Frissell, and J. Karr. 1993. *Entering the watershed: A new approach to save America's river ecosystems.* Washington, D.C.: Island Press. 463 pp.

Echeverría, J., A. Echeverría, and A. Mata. 1998. *Plan de acción para la Cuenca del Río Tempisque: Antecedentes del estudio y resumen ejecutivo.* San José: Centro Científico Tropical/Asociación para el Manejo de la Cuenca del Tempisque. 39 pp.

Federal Interagency Stream Restoration Working Group. 1998. Stream corridor restoration: Principles, processes and practices. Washington, D.C.: Federal Interagency Stream Restoration Working Group. 568 pp (CD).

Frankie, G. W., H. G. Baker, and P. A. Opler. 1974. Comparative phenological studies of trees in tropical wet and dry forests in the lowlands of Costa Rica. *Journal of Ecology* 62:881–919.

Frankie, G. W., S. B. Vinson, L. Newstrom, and J. F. Barthell. 1988. Nest site and habitat preferences of *Centris* bees in the Costa Rican dry forest. *Biotropica* 20:301–10.

Frankie, G. W., L. Newstrom, S. B. Vinson, and J. F. Barthell. 1993. Nesting-habitat preferences of selected *Centris* bee species in Costa Rican dry forest. *Biotropica* 25:322–33.

Hidalgo, C. 1986. Determinación de residuos de plaguicidas organoclorados en huevos de ocho especies de aves acuáticas que anidan en la Isla Pájaros, Guanacaste, Costa Rica. Graduate thesis, Postgraduate Studies System, University of Costa Rica. 89 pp.

Mata, A., and O. Blanco. 1994. La Cuenca del Golfo de Nicoya: Reto al desarrollo sostenible. San José: Editorial de la Universidad de Costa Rica. 235 pp.

Postel, S. L., G. C. Daily, and P. R. Ehrlich. 1996. Human appropriation of renewable freshwater. *Science* 271:785–88.

Pringle, C. M. 2000. Threats to U.S. public lands from cumulative hydrologic alterations outside of their boundaries. *Ecological Applications* 10 (4):971–89.

Pringle, C. M., and F. Scatena. 1999. Aquatic ecosystem deterioration in Latin America and the Caribbean. In *Managed ecosystems: The Mesoamerican experience,* ed. L. Hupton Hatch and M. E. Swisher, 104–13. New York: Oxford University Press.

Pringle, C. M., M. C. Freeman, and B. J. Freeman. 2000a. Regional effects of hydrological alterations on riverine macrobiota in the New World: Tropical-temperate comparisons. *BioScience* 50: 807–23.

Pringle, C. M., F. N. Scatena, P. Paaby, and M. Nuñez-Ferrera. 2000b. River conservation in Latin America and the Caribbean. In *Global perspectives on river conservation: Science, policy and practice,* ed. P. J. Boon, B. R. Davies, and G. N. Petts, 41–47. New York: John Wiley and Sons.

Quesada, C., ed. 1990. *Estrategia de conservación para el desarrollo sostenible.* San José: Servicios Litograficos. 180 pp.

Ramirez, G., and J. Jimenez. 1998. *Diagnóstico de la situación actual de los recursos hídricos en la Provincia de Guanacaste, Costa Rica.* San José: Instituto Costarricense de Acueductos y Alcantarillado. 19 pp.

Riley, Ann L. 1998. *Restoring streams in cities.* Washington, D.C.: Island Press. 426 pp.

Rodríguez-Brenes, O. M. 1997. Residuos de plaguicidas en la zona de influencia del Proyecto de Riego Arenal-Tempisque. Final Report. San José: Environmental Pollution Research Center/University of Costa Rica. 85 pp.

Rodríguez-Ulloa, A. 1997. Vigilancia de la calidad de las aguas superficiales en la zona de influencia del Proyecto de Riego Arenal-Tempisque. Final Report. San José: Environmental Pollution Research Center/University of Costa Rica. 85 pp.

Vargas, G. 1999. The geography of dry land plant formations in Central America. In *Managed ecosystems: The Mesoamerican experience,* ed. L. Hupton Hatch and M. E. Swisher, 88–97. New York: Oxford University Press.

Voorhis, A., C. Epifanio, C. Maurer, A. Dittel, and J. A. Vargas. 1983. The estuarine character of the Gulf of Nicoya, an embayment on the Pacific coast of Central America. *Hydrobiologia* 99: 225–37.

Vörösmarty, C. J., and D. Sahagian. 2000. Anthropogenic disturbance of the terrestrial water cycle. *BioScience* 50:753–65.

Watson, V., S. Cervantes, C. Castro, L. Mora, M. Solís, I. Porras, and B. Conejo. 1998. *Making space for better forestry.* Series 6, *Policy that works for forests and people.* Edited by J. Mayers. International Institute for Environment and Development. Nottingham, England: Russell Press. 110 pp.

Wisenden, B. D., and M. H. A. Keenleyside. 1994. The dilution effect and differential predation following brood adoption in free-ranging convict cichlids (*Cichlasoma nigrofasciatum*). *Ethology* 96:203–12.

———. 1995. Brood size and economy of brood defence: Examining Lack's hypothesis in a biparental cichlid fish. *Environmental Biology of Fishes* 43:145–51.

World Conservation Union. 1992. Conservación de humedales. Edited by P. J. Dugan. Paris: Imprimerie Sadag. 100 pp.

CHAPTER 10

Where the Dry Forest Feeds the Sea

THE GULF OF NICOYA ESTUARY

José A. Vargas and Alfonso Mata

THE GULF OF NICOYA (GN) is an estuary located in the northwestern part of the Pacific coast of Costa Rica (10° N, 85° W). The extensive hydrological connection between the GN and watersheds draining into it gives rise to one of the most prominent ecological and geographical systems of Costa Rica (maps 1.1 and 1.2 in chapter 1; chapter 9). Half of this large estuarine-terrestrial basin consists of the Tempisque River Basin (TRB), with a variety of ecological, cultural, and socioeconomic resources, some of them conflicting. If the Tárcoles River watershed, which drains the lower sector of the GN, is included, the whole area represents about 25 percent of the country. It has become clear over the past decades that deforestation of the watershed has led to a reduction in average flow of the Tempisque River (TR) in the dry season and to an increase in the magnitude of floods during the rainy season (Lizano 1998). The dry-forest–TR–GN system can no longer be considered as composed of separate units because what occurs in the dry-forest watershed has effects on the estuary via the rivers. This chapter focuses on the main physical, chemical, and biological features of the estuary, as well as the main human activities that endanger its sustainable development.

HYDROLOGICAL REGIME OF THE GN BASIN

The GN receives waters collected by a group of watersheds associated mainly with the TRB in the upper sector of the gulf and the Tárcoles River watershed (from the Western Central Valley), together with other minor areas in the lower sector of the GN (see map 1.1 in chapter 1). Half of the entire drainage system corresponds to the Tempisque Valley, with a total surface area of 5,965 km². Input from the Caribbean versant through the Arenal reservoir discharges nearly 90 m³/s of fresh water from the Arenal-Tempisque hydroelectric generating system. Part of this flow is used during the dry season for irrigation of floodplains. Properties of this hydrological system are discussed in chapter 9.

DEFINITION OF THE GN AS AN ESTUARY

The GN is a shallow system (around 20 m) in its upper reaches, but it deepens steadily to nearly 500 m at its mouth. Its estuarine character is provided mainly by the freshwater input from the Tempisque, Bebedero, and Tárcoles Rivers. The most important of these is the TR, whose watershed irrigates most of the dry-forest land of Guanacaste. This river is also important in defining strong horizontal and vertical salinity gradients in the middle of the upper gulf, a region characterized by mangrove forests, sand and mudflats, sandy beaches, and islands.

MAIN FEATURES OF THE GN AS AN ESTUARY

The GN is the country's main fishing ground for finfish, penaeid shrimp, and shellfish. The decline of these resources, together with the lack of ecological information to aid in policy making, prompted several institutions, including the University of Costa Rica, National University, and the Costarrican Institute of Fishing and Aquaculture, to develop research programs in the GN region. Some miscellaneous studies were also conducted by the Costarrican Institute of Waterworks and Sewage and by nongovernmental organizations such as the Tropical Science Center and the Organization for Tropical Studies. The University of Costa Rica established the Gulf of Nicoya Ecological Evaluation Research Program (GNEEP) in 1979 at its Center for Research in Marine Science and Limnology (CIMAR), and more than 100 scientific papers on the ecology and oceanography of the estuary have been published, making the GN the best-known tropical estuary in the world. Cooperative research between local and foreign scientists allowed the development of complex sampling programs aboard research vessels, the most recent of which was the expedition of the German research vessel *Victor Hensen*. Results have been published in the *Revista de Biología Tropical* (vol. 44, Suppl. 3, 1996; vol. 46, Suppl. 6, 1998). Because the GNEEP was developed after several centuries of land use that resulted in the conversion of dry forests into pasturelands, it is unknown whether the effects observed in the biota in recent years started years before commercial exploitation of the resource (in the 1950s) and were later enhanced by increased fishing that reached its peak in the 1970s and 1980s.

According to Voorhis et al. (1983), fresh water discharged in the upper GN by the TR (and its large tributary Bebedero) and other rivers results in a southward flow through the constriction between San Lucas Island and the Puntarenas Peninsula in the middle section of the estuary. This flow is compensated for by a northward flow of more saline water into the upper estuary along the bottom, which is termed estuarine circulation. Flushing time (amount of time required to replace all existing fresh water at a rate equal to the runoff discharge) was estimated at one to two months, a key figure in pollution studies. Looking at the GN from a chemical oceanography perspective, Epifanio et al. (1983) showed that the GN is similar to other tropical estuaries because it is subject to extreme seasonal variations in riverine flow. Recent work by Chaves and Birkicht (1996) on the *Victor Hensen* provided additional information on offshore sources of nitrogen for the GN, in addition to that entering from rivers, which has yet to be measured. Using a simple box model, Lizano (1998) illustrated the relationship between freshwater input from the TR and other rivers and the estuary's salinity. The model shows that the more freshwater input into the system, the farther upstream the estuarine bottom salinity flow moves. Deforestation of watersheds during the past centuries (see chapters 1 and 9) and more recent use of river water for irrigation increased floods during heavy rains and may have altered the average flow of the TR.

BIOTA OF THE GN

A great deal of work under CIMAR's GNEEP was focused on studying the GN from the biological oceanography point of view. A list of relevant publications prior to 1994 is included in Vargas (1995). Among these, Bartels et al. (1983, 1984) provided a description of finfish populations, and others focused on fauna living in (Maurer and Vargas 1984) or on sediments (Maurer et al. 1984, 1987). A total of 214 fish species were identified, many of which were already under heavy exploitation by fishers, such as corvinas (sea trout), snappers, groupers, sea-catfish, snooks, and sharks. An update on fish biodiversity in the GN is presented in Bussing (1994) and Wolff (1996). The recent description of a new species of stingray (*Urotrygon cimar*) by López and Bussing (1998) indicates that there is still work to be done on the GN's fish diversity, particularly in its rocky shores and intertidal areas.

Sediment faunal surveys yielded about 100 species collected in trawl samples. Decapod crustaceans were the dominant taxon, with 54 species. Recent updates on this fauna are provided by Dean (1996, 1998, 2001a,b), Vargas et al. (1996), and Cruz (1996) for marine worms (Polychaeta), crustaceans, and mollusks, respectively. Among crustaceans, particular attention was given to the blue crab *Callinectes arcuatus,* a species of potential commercial importance (Epifanio and Dittel 1982; DeVries et al. 1983; Dittel and Epifanio 1984; Dittel et al. 1985). All these studies also emphasized that the GN is an ecosystem rich in species composition. Voucher specimens from most species that were identified were deposited in the Museum of Zoology of the University of Costa Rica. Despite significant attempts to identify all specimens collected, many of these remain unidentified or undescribed to date because of lack of expertise or updated taxonomic keys, or both.

Study of the GN's marine biodiversity continues at CIMAR and includes the work of Vargas (1987, 1988, 1989), Szelistowski (1990), Dittel (1991), Mielke (1992), Berman and Brooks (1994), Marques et al. (1995), Morales and Vargas (1995), Vargas (1996), and Dean (1996, 1998, 2001a,b). The first report on the presence of phylum Kinorhyncha in the GN was made by De la Cruz and Vargas (1986), and species of

phyla Brachiopoda, Sipuncula, Chaetognatha, and Echiura were reported for the first time by Emig and Vargas (1990), Cutler et al. (1992), Hossfeld (1996), and Dean and Cutler (1998), respectively. New flatworm species parasitic in stingrays have been described by Marques et al. (1995).

Ecological studies in the GN that have been conducted as part of the GNEEP include those on the impact of shrimp trawling (Campos et al. 1984; Rostad and Hansen 1999); trophic dynamics (Campos and Corrales 1986; Dittel 1993; Dittel et al. 1997); fish biology (Lai et al. 1993; Duncan and Szelistowski 1998); fish larval ecology (López 1983; López and Arias, 1987; Ramírez et al. 1989, 1990; Molina-Ureña 1996); artificial reefs (Campos and Gamboa 1989; Thorne et al. 1989); and the ecology of mangroves (Gocke et al. 1981; Villalobos et al. 1985; Perry 1988; Soto 1988; Borjesson and Szelistowski 1989; Wehrtmann and Dittel 1990; Koch and Wolff 1996).

The first reports on primary production in the GN waters come from Gocke et al. (1990) and Córdoba-Muñoz (1998). They establish the GN as one of the most productive (in terms of organic carbon fixed by primary producers) estuaries in the world. Only recently has there been an effort (Wolff et al. 1998) to integrate most of the available environmental information into a holistic ecological model of the GN. The resulting model represents a steady-state approach in which biomass production of—and imports to—the system compartments are balanced by consumption and exports. According to the model, shrimp and demersal fish are the most prominent benthic groups in terms of biomass, whereas plankton, small pelagic fish, carangids, and squids dominate the pelagic biomass. The key role of mangroves is emphasized, as these forests contribute more than 75 percent of the system's biomass (but only about 1 percent of the primary production). The model shows that shrimp occupy a central role in the GN's trophic dynamics as converters of much of the system's detritus and other bentho-pelagic matter into food biomass. Overexploitation of shrimp populations means a significant reduction of food stock for some predators. Some key topics still need to be considered to improve the predictive power of the model, such as accounting for intra-annual changes associated with seasonal conditions (dry versus rainy) in the gulf; quantifying the sediment-nutrient-detritus input from rivers; the relative contribution of microorganisms, phytoplankton, and phytobenthos to the system's productivity; and an evaluation of the microbial loop. These data will provide a better picture of the GN as a system for development of a management plan of the estuary and its watershed (Wolff et al. 1998). An improved model will depend on these data and will further emphasize the strong link between the GN and the drainage basin of its rivers, particularly the TR. A similar model is also available for Golfo Dulce, a fjordlike embayment also in the Pacific coast of Costa Rica (Wolff et al. 1996).

IMPACTS ON THE GN

A pioneer study in environmental economics showed a clear decline of the GN's fishing resources (Solórzano et al. 1991). Since 1983 there has been a significant and steady decline in total fish capture in the GN, with a concomitant increase in fishing efforts necessary to obtain the same capture.

TR DISCHARGES

Most of the population of Guanacaste Province lives in the Tempisque Valley, concentrated in the cities of Cañas, Bagaces, Liberia (capital), Filadelfia, and Santa Cruz, as well as in many towns (see maps in chapter 1). Old sewage treatment plants of larger cities were built about 30 years ago, and actual coverage is only around 30 percent of the cities' needs (see chapter 1). The rest of the towns use septic tanks and latrines. Massive deaths of shrimp and fish (e.g., sea bass) in this river are observed every year. This mortality rate is associated with the presence of xenobiotic substances (Szelistowski and Garita 1989), pollutants introduced by washings and land erosion from agricultural activity around

the gulf (De la Cruz 1989; Robinson 1993), and the presence of organic wastes from the sugarcane industry, which also depletes the water's oxygen content (see chapter 9). Sugar factories have recently improved their antipollution measures, but the fast-growing aquaculture of tilapia fish in artificial ponds poses new and large demands for water and the disposal of residues.

The presence of organochlorine pesticides in eggs of eight species of aquatic birds at Isla Pajaros, near the mouth of the TR, has been described by Hidalgo (1986). Sum of the residues of DDT detected was around 10 µg/g of dry sample; the heavy elements also showed very low levels. Mercury was found in normal background concentrations (De la Cruz 1989). All these studies are not conclusive; no systematic sampling was conducted, including water and animal tissue samples. Rice production is growing in lowland areas, and the entire situation calls for urgent and thorough research on the biota and limnological characteristics of the TR, particularly in the dynamic zone where the river meets the estuary.

The problem of urban garbage management has not been solved yet, mainly because of uncontrolled urban development, lack of public awareness and education, and poor governmental assistance for appropriate waste management (see chapter 9). An ambitious project ("Let's Save the Estuary") was recently launched by the government, and results thus far have been acceptable. The concern now is whether government support will continue.

THE PUNTARENAS ESTUARY: A CASE STUDY

This estuary, located in the central eastern part of the GN, is a small-scale model of the gulf. Liquid wastes reach this estuary from the densely populated port area of Puntarenas. Metabolic activity of this enclosed body of water permits absorption of a large amount of organic matter. Biochemical oxygen demand from effluents emitted by the sugar industry was greater at the head of the estuary but was rapidly reduced toward its mouth (Mata and Blanco 1994), where dissolved oxygen values increase, approaching acceptable levels for aquatic wildlife. There is an important mixing of waters from inland with those from the GN, with different patterns of vertical homogeneity and partial mixing along the estuary (Acuña et al. 1998). These waters show measurable stratification and a definite biodegradation of organic wastes.

DISCHARGES OF THE WESTERN CENTRAL VALLEY

The Great Metropolitan Area (GMA) of Costa Rica is located in the Central Valley at an elevation of around 1,000 m. The GMA has no sewage treatment, and as of today a significant part of these waters are left to natural river self-purification. The coliform concentrations vary from several dozens of thousands per 100 ml outside the GMA (Pacheco 1987) to millions in several creeks and rivers of the densely populated central zone. Most of the nutrient inorganic load, sediments and resilient organic matter, enters, via the Tárcoles River, the lower sector of the GN, which is a much deeper water body in which dynamic mixing and strong tidal current conditions favor dilution of this load. However, an effective and definitive solution to these urban and industrial wastewaters is long overdue.

Until a few years ago, coffee and sugar mills produced organic pollution in the Central Valley equivalent to 4.2 million inhabitants (Ramírez 1999). However, with new processes and the installation of waste treatment plants, pollution loads have dropped by more than 50 percent, and another 50 percent improvement is expected during the next five years. Population growth continues at a fast pace, however, and no municipal treatment is visible on the horizon.

Although heavy metals (Cr, Cu, Pb) are found at very low concentrations in running waters (Ramírez 1987), in view of current industrial growth it will be necessary to monitor possible increases of metal waste discharges. Heavy metal contents in sediments are more significant. For example, chromium from leather industries in the Central Valley is 83 times higher in fine sediments of the Virilla-Tárcoles river system than in those of the GN estuary (Dean et al. 1986; Fuller et al. 1990). The sediment load coming out of the highlands, which is due to destructive agricultural practices and land movement for construction of buildings and roads, also has to be considered.

Although solid waste recycling and landfills may have improved over the past decade, there is still much to do. At the beginning of 1999 the municipal service collected around 90 tons of garbage per day from the streets of San José. It was also estimated that careless people threw about 250 tons per day in rivers. The impact on the GN has diminished very recently with the reconstruction of the Brazil Dam on the Virilla River. Cost for the extraction of 200 tons of garbage per day (mainly wood and plastic objects) was $200,000 in 1999; when hours lost to cleaning generators are added, total cost for that year was $360,000. This means that cost of the lack of education was at least $30,000 per month, without taking into account damage to the river biota and its habitats.

EFFECTS OF POPULATION GROWTH

The natural inertia of the demographic growth of Costa Rica is a well manifested urban all-directional growth factor. Cities located in the watersheds of the GN greater basin are growing with doubling periods as short as 20 years. Despite recent advances in the coffee industry and garbage management, the number of waste treatment plant systems available for the GMA is still unacceptable. The fast pace of urban growth in the Central Valley volcanic slopes on the outskirts of the GMA is resulting in the loss of options for development or conservation (or both) of the area's extant resources. The National Strategy of Conservation for Sustainable Development (Quesada 1990) proposed a general plan for conservation of watersheds and urban development that should have been developed by the beginning of the present century. Although positive results have been less than expected, interest in the rescue of this beautiful valley is still alive (Echeverría et al. 1998).

THE IMPACT OF CONTROL INITIATIVES

In order to protect and promote the rational use of resources, several important and well-coordinated steps must be taken into account. Needed actions include

1. the more efficient implementation and reinforcement of various standing laws, including strict application of management plans for protected areas (chapters 21–24);

2. improvement of laws and bylaws for the rational use and protection of resources;

3. strict compliance with international agreements and conventions;

4. increased interinstitutional coordination and collaboration;

5. support for environmental education (especially in fishing communities and schools and among consumers);

6. reduction of unnecessary habitat destruction;

7. control of coastal and inland pollution sources (input by rivers);

8. enlargement and updating of the sewage treatment capacity of the Guanacaste region, particularly the Western Central Valley;

9. support for marine and fish catch research; and

10. support for ecological research on the TR and at the dynamic zone where the river meets the estuary.

The following are some actions that are being implemented:

1. "Let's Save the Estuary," a program created by decree (Gaceta Oficial 23/10/95) and coordinated by the Costarrican Institute of Fishing and Aquaculture, with the participation of various governmental institutions, municipalities, and community members. The Gulf of Nicoya Contingency Plan is a strategy being designed and implemented by this institute with the help of two public universities.

2. Reinforcement of selected laws and regulations to protect fishing grounds from overexploitation, along with measures such as fishing bans, fines, and net impoundment.

3. Implementation of coffee, sugar mill, and pig-farming industrial agreements for pollution abatement, particularly in the TR and Tárcoles River Basins.

4. Various actions for the recovery and recycling of solid wastes, mainly in the GMA.

However, something missing in the whole scenario of actions is an integral management plan of the GN and the TR and Tárcoles River Basins. This plan would be multidisciplinary and would represent a great opportunity for terrestrial ecologists, limnologists, oceanographers, and planners to come together and find appropriate mechanisms for the sustainable use of this invaluable area of the country.

FINAL COMMENTS

In recent years there has been a trend among some economists to leave territorial ordering to the laws of supply and demand. It is clear that this approach benefits only those rich sectors of society who could profit from opportunism and reflects the lack of formal courses in environmental economics in most training programs that prepare professionals at undergraduate and graduate levels. If problems associated with the dry forest and the GN are to be approached from the point of view of sustainable development, an integral management plan, organized by the principles of Integrated Coastal Management (ICM) (GESAMP 1996), for the entire region is urgently needed. It should involve (a) public participation such that the values, concerns, and aspirations of affected communities are discussed and future directions are negotiated for appropriate guidance of community-based development; (b) steps by which relevant policies, legislation, and institutional arrangements can be developed and implemented to meet local needs and circumstances while recognizing national priorities; and (c) collaboration between managers and scientists in all stages of developing management policy and programs (see chapter 18), especially in the design, conduction, interpretation, and application of research and monitoring.

In the case of the GN and its dry-forest watershed, development of an ICM plan should first bring to the table representatives from the main governmental sectors involved, including the Ministry of the Environment, the Costarrican Institute of Tourism, and the Costarrican Institute of Fishing and Aquaculture. A crucial role has to be played by municipal governments, which are the main actors in the granting of permits for land use. To gain experience in this process, the design of an ICM plan for the estuary of Puntarenas and its relatively small watershed should be the first priority. It can then be used as a reference model for the more complex GN estuary. Finally, it is well known that world fish production is stagnated (Ludicello et al. 1999) and is showing signs of decline, as is the case of the GN (Solórzano et al. 1991). It has also been estimated that world fishing fleets are 30 percent larger than necessary to catch maximum sustainable yield of global fish stocks (McGuinn 1998). These findings have created an uncertain atmosphere in conservation and governmental sectors of the country, and it is urgent to understand the causal factors.

The GN's production capacity has a theoretical limit (Wolff et al. 1998) supported by an important input of nutrients from the ocean by bottom currents and from the mainland via the rivers. High rates of dispersion and absorption of biodegradable pollutants are characteristics of this estuary; however, more quantitative studies are needed about pollution and its possible effects on the marine biota. Studies are still needed to determine the fishery and aquacultural potential of the GN's 215 identified fish species (Bartels et al. 1983). Considering that fisheries in the GN have reached their capacity, fishing prohibitions and enforcement are insufficient, the existing fishing capacity is larger than necessary, and the population is growing relentlessly forcing the government to meet short-term needs, a well-coordinated effort of all agencies dealing directly or indirectly with the GN estuary in the country is absolutely necessary.

REFERENCES

Acuña, J., V. García, and J. Mondragon. 1998. Comparación de algunos aspectos físico-químicos y calidad sanitaria del Estero de Puntarenas, Costa Rica. *Revista de Biología Tropical* 46(Suppl. 6): 1–10.

Baltz, C., and J. Campos. 1996. Hydrophone identification and characterization of *Cynoscion squamipinnis* (Perciformes: Scianidae) spawning sites in the Gulf of Nicoya, Costa Rica. *Revista de Biología Tropical* 44:743–51.

Bartels, C., K. Price, M. López, and W. Bussing. 1983. Occurrence, distribution, abundance and diversity of fishes in the Gulf of Nicoya, Costa Rica. *Revista de Biología Tropical* 31:75–101.

———. 1984. Ecological assessment of finfish as indicators of habitats in the Gulf of Nicoya, Costa Rica. *Hydrobiologia* 112:197–207.

Berman, R., and D. Brooks. 1994. *Escherbothrium molinae* n. gen. et n. sp. (Eucestoda: Tetraphyllidae: Triloculaiidae) in *Urotrygon chilensis* (Chondrichthyes: Myliobatiformes: Urolophidae) from the Gulf of Nicoya, Costa Rica. *Journal of Parasitology* 80(5): 775–80.

Borjesson, D. L., and W. A. Szelistowski. 1989. Shell selection, utilization, and predation in the hermit crab *Clibanarius panamensis* Stimpson in a tropical mangrove estuary. *Journal of Experimental Marine Biology and Ecology* 133:213–28.

Bussing, W. 1994. Demersal and pelagic inshore fishes of the Pacific coast of lower Central America. Special publication, *Revista de Biología Tropical*. 163 pp.

Cameron, W. M., and D. W. Pritchard. 1963. Estuaries. In *The Sea*, ed. M. N. Hill, 2:306–24. New York: Wiley Interscience.

Campos, J., and A. Corrales. 1986. Preliminary results of the trophic dynamics of the Gulf of Nicoya, Costa Rica. *Anales del Instituto de Ciencias del Mar y Limnología* (Universidad Nacional Autonoma de México) 13:329–34.

Campos, J., and C. Gamboa. 1989. An artificial tire reef in a tropical marine system: A management tool. *Bulletin of Marine Science* 44:757–66.

Campos, J., B. Burgos, and C. Gamboa. 1984. Effect of shrimp trawling on the commercial ichthyofauna of the Gulf of Nicoya, Costa Rica. *Revista de Biología Tropical* 32:203–7.

Chaves, J., and M. Birkicht. 1996. Equatorial subsurface water and the nutrient seasonality distribution of the Gulf of Nicoya, Costa Rica. *Revista de Biología Tropical* 44(Suppl. 3):41–47.

Córdoba-Muñoz, R. 1998. Primary productivity in the water column of Estero Morales, a mangrove system in the Gulf of Nicoya. *Revista de Biología Tropical* 46(Suppl. 6):257–62.

Cruz, R. A. 1996. Annotated list of marine mollusks collected during the R.V. Victor Hensen Costa Rica Expedition, 1993–1994. *Revista de Biología Tropical* 44(Suppl. 3):59–67.

Cutler, N., E. Cutler, and J. A. Vargas. 1992. Peanut worms (Phylum Sipuncula) from Costa Rica. *Revista de Biología Tropical* 40:153–58.

Dean, H. K. 1996. Subtidal benthic polychaetes (Annelida) of the Gulf of Nicoya, Costa Rica. *Revista de Biología Tropical* 44(Suppl. 3):69–80.

———. 1998. The Pilargidae (Polychaeta) of the Pacific Coast of Costa Rica. *Revista de Biología Tropical* 46(Suppl. 6):47–62.

———. 2001a. Some Nereididae (Annelida: Polychaeta) from the Pacific coast of Costa Rica. *Revista de Biología Tropical* 49(Suppl. 2):37–67.

———2001b. Capitellidae (Annelida: Polychaeta) from the Pacific coast of Costa Rica. *Revista de Biología Tropical* 49(Suppl. 2):69–84.

Dean, H. K., and E. B. Cutler. 1998. Range extension of *Nephasoma pellucidum*, and new records of *Apionsoma (Edmonsius) pectinatum*, Sipuncula and *Thalassema steinbecki* (Echiura) from the Pacific of Costa Rica. *Revista de Biología Tropical* 46(Suppl. 6):279–80.

Dean, H. K., D. Maurer, J. A. Vargas, and C. H. Tinsman. 1986. Trace metal concentrations in sediment and invertebrates from the Gulf of Nicoya, Costa Rica. *Marine Pollution Bulletin* 17:128–31.

De la Cruz, E. 1989. Organochlorine and total mercury in the *Anadara tuberculosa* bivalve and other species from the Nicoya Gulf, Costa Rica. Master's thesis, Free University of Brussels, Belgium. 58 pp.

De la Cruz, E., and J. A. Vargas. 1986. Estudio preliminar de la meiofauna de la playa fangosa de Punta Morales, Golfo de Nicoya, Costa Rica. *Brenesia* 25–26:89–97.

DeVries, M., C. E. Epifanio, and A. Dittel. 1983. Reproductive periodicity of the tropical crab *Callinectes arcuatus* Ordway in the Gulf of Nicoya, Costa Rica. *Estuarine, Coastal, and Shelf Science* 17:709–16.

Dittel, A. 1991. Distribution, abundance and sexual composition of stomatopod Crustacea in the Gulf of Nicoya, Costa Rica. *Journal of Crustacean Biology* 11:269–76.

———. 1993. Cambios en los hábitos alimentarios de *Callinectes arcuatus* (Crustacea: Decapoda) en el Golfo de Nicoya, Costa Rica. *Revista de Biología Tropical* 41:639–46.

Dittel, A., and C. Epifanio. 1984. Growth and development of the portunid crab *Callinectes arcuatus* Ordway: Zoeae, megalopae and juveniles. *Journal of Crustacean Biology* 4:491–94.

Dittel, A., C. E. Epifanio, and J. B. Chavarría. 1985. Population biology of the portunid crab *Callinectes arcuatus* Ordway in the Gulf of Nicoya, Costa Rica; Central America. *Estuarine, Coastal, and Shelf Science* 20:593–602.

Dittel, A., C. E. Epifanio, L. A. Cifuentes, and D. Kirchman. 1997. Carbon and nitrogen sources from shrimp postlarvae fed natural diets from a tropical mangrove system. *Estuarine, Coastal, and Shelf Science* 45:629–37.

Duncan, R. S., and W. A. Szelistowski. 1998. Influence of puffer predation on vertical distribution of mangrove littorinids in the Gulf of Nicoya, Costa Rica. *Oecologia* 117:433–42.

Echeverría, J., A. Echeverría, and A. Mata. 1998. *Plan de acción para la Cuenca del Río Tempisque: Antecedentes del estudio y resumen ejecutivo.* San José: Tropical Science Center/Association for the Tempisque River Management. 39 pp.

Emig, C., and J. A. Vargas. 1990. *Glottidia audebarti* (Broderip) (Brachiopoda, Lingulidae) from the Gulf of Nicoya, Costa Rica. *Revista de Biología Tropical* 38:251–58.

Epifanio, C. E., and A. Dittel. 1982. Comparison of dispersal of crab larvae in Delaware Bay (USA) and Gulf of Nicoya (Central America). In *Estuarine comparisons*, ed. V. Kennedy, 447–87. New York: Academic Press.

Epifanio, C. E., D. Maurer, and A. I. Dittel. 1983. Seasonal changes in nutrients and dissolved oxygen in the Gulf of Nicoya, a tropical estuary on the Pacific coast of Central America. *Hydrobiologia* 101:231–328

Fuller, C. C., J. A. Davis, D. J. Cain, P. J. Lamothe, T. L. Fries, G. Fernandez, J. A.Vargas, and M. M. Murillo. 1990. Distribution and transport of sediment bound metal contaminants in the Río Grande de Tárcoles, Costa Rica. *Water Research* 24:805–12.

GESAMP (IMO/FAO/UNESCO-IOC/WMO/WHO/IAEA/UN/UNEP Joint Group of Experts on the Scientific Aspects of Marine Environmental Protection). 1996. *The contributions of science to coastal zone management.* Rep. Stud. GESAMP 61. 66 pp.

Gocke, K., M. Vitola, and G. Rojas. 1981. Oxygen consumption patterns in a mangrove swamp on the Pacific coast of Costa Rica. *Revista de Biología Tropical* 29:143–54.

Gocke, K., J. Cortes, and C. Villalobos. 1990. Effects of red tides on oxygen concentration and distribution in the Gulf of Nicoya, Costa Rica. *Revista de Biología Tropical* 38:401–7.

Hidalgo, C. C. 1986. Determinación de residuos de plaguicidas organoclorados en huevos de ocho especies de aves acuáticas, colectados durante 1983–1984 en la Isla Pájaros, Guanacaste, Costa Rica. Master of Science thesis, Universidad de Costa Rica, Costa Rica. 120 pp.

Hossfeld, B. 1996. Distribution and biomass of arrow worms (Chaetognatha) in the Golfo de Nicoya and Golfo Dulce, Costa Rica. *Revista de Biología Tropical* 44(Suppl. 3):157–72.

Koch, V., and M. Wolff. 1996. The mangrove snail *Thais kioskiformis* (Duclos): A case of life history adaptation to an extreme environment. *Journal of Shellfish Research* 15:421–32.

Lai, H. L., M. Mug-Villanueva, and V. F. Gallucci. 1993. Management strategies for the tropical corvina reina, *Cynoscion albus*, in a multi-mesh size gillnet artisanal fishery. In *Proceedings of the International Symposium on Management Strategies for Exploited Fish Populations*, 21–38. Alaska Sea Grant College Program, AK-SG-93-02.

Lizano, O. 1998. Dinámica de las aguas en la parte interna del Golfo de Nicoya ante las descargas del Río Tempisque. *Revista de Biología Tropical* 46(Suppl. 6):11–20.

López, M. 1983. *Lycodontis verrilli* (Pisces: Muraenidae) descripción de su larva leptocéfala del Golfo de Nicoya, Costa Rica. *Revista de Biología Tropical* 31:343–44.

López, M., and C. Arias. 1987. Distribución temporal y espacial del ictioplancton en el estuario de Pochote, Bahía Ballena, Pacífico de Costa Rica. *Revista de Biología Tropical* 35:121–26.

López, M., and W. Bussing. 1998. *Urotrygon cimar*, a new eastern Pacific stingray (Pisces: Urolophidae). *Revista de Biología Tropical* 46(Suppl. 6): 371–77.

Ludicello, Z., M. Weber, and R. Wieland. 1999. *Fish, markets, and fishermen: The economics of overfishing.* Washington, D.C.: Island Press. 193 pp.

Marques, F., D. R. Brooks, and S. Monks. 1995. Five new species of *Acanthobothrium* van Beneden, 1849 (Eucestoda: Tetraphylidea: Onchobothiidae) in stingrays from the Gulf of Nicoya, Costa Rica. *Journal of Parasitology* 81:942–51.

Mata, A., and O. Blanco. 1994. *La Cuenca del Golfo de Nicoya: Reto al desarrollo sostenible.* San José: Editorial de la Universidad de Costa Rica. 235 pp.

Maurer, D., and J. A. Vargas. 1984. Diversity of soft-bottom benthos in a tropical estuary: Gulf of Nicoya, Costa Rica. *Marine Biology* 81:97–106.

Maurer, D., C. E. Epifanio, H. K. Dean, S. Howe, J. A. Vargas, A. Dittel, and M. Murillo. 1984. Benthic invertebrates of a tropical estuary: Gulf of Nicoya, Costa Rica. *Journal of Natural History* 18:47–61.

Maurer, D., H. K. Dean, and J. A. Vargas. 1987. Soft bottom invertebrate communities from the Gulf of Nicoya, Costa Rica. *Memorias del V Simposio de Biología Marina*, Universidad Autonoma de Baja California, Sur: 107–12.

McGuinn, A. P. 1998. *Rocking the boat: Conserving fisheries and protecting jobs.* Worldwatch Paper No. 142. Washington, D.C.: Worldwatch Institute.

Mielke, W. 1992. Six representatives of the Tetragonicipitidae (Copepoda) from Costa Rica. *Microfauna Marina* 7:101–46.

Molina-Ureña, H. 1996. Ichthyoplankton assemblages in the Gulf of Nicoya and Golfo Dulce embayments, Pacific coast of Costa Rica. *Revista de Biología Tropical* 44(Suppl. 3):173–82.

Morales, R. A., and J. A. Vargas. 1995. Especies comunes de copepodos (Crustacea: Copepoda) pelágicos del Golfo de Nicoya. *Revista de Biología Tropical* 43:207–18.

Pacheco, A. V. 1987. Evaluación preliminar del Río Tiribí, 1981–82. *Tecnología en Marcha* (Costa Rica) 2–3:5–10.

Perry, D. 1988. Effects of associated fauna on growth and productivity in the red mangrove. *Ecology* 69:1064–75.

Peterson, C. L. 1960. The physical oceanography of the Gulf of Nicoya, Costa Rica, a tropical estuary. *Bulletin of the Interamerican Tropical Tuna Commission* 4:139–216.

Quesada, C., ed. 1990. *Estrategia de conservación para el desarrollo sostenible de Costa Rica.* Ministerio de Recursos Naturales Energía y Minas (MIRENEM). San José: Servicios Litográficos. 163 pp.

Ramírez, A. R., W. A. Szelistowski, and M. López. 1989. Spawning pattern and larval recruitment in Gulf of Nicoya anchovies (Pisces: Engraulidae). *Revista de Biología Tropical* 37:55–62.

Ramírez, A. R., M. López, and W. A. Szelistowski. 1990. Composition and abundance of ichthyoplankton in a Gulf of Nicoya mangrove estuary. *Revista de Biología Tropical* 38:463–66.

Ramírez, J. M. 1987. Metales pesados en los ríos Virilla y Grande de Tárcoles. *Ingeniería y Ciencia Química* 11(2–3):57–59.

———. 1999. Contaminación de ríos en la Cuenca Virilla-Tárcoles. In *San José: Gloria, ocaso y recate*, ed. E. Flores, 50–59. Memoria de la Academia Nacional de Ciencias, vol. 3. San José: Academia Nacional de Ciencias.

Robinson, T. 1993. *Fate and transport of agricultural contaminants from rice paddies, Guanacaste, Costa Rica*. Servicio Nacional de Riego y Avenamiento, Costa Rica. Santa Barbara: University of California. 48 pp.

Rostad, T., and K. L. Hansen. 1999. The effects of trawling on the benthic fauna of the Gulf of Nicoya, Costa Rica. *Revista de Biología Tropical* 49(Suppl. 2):91–95.

Solórzano, R., R. de Camino, R. Woodward, J. Tosi, V. Watson, A. Vazquez, C. Villalobos, J. Jimenez, R. Repetto, and W. Cruz. 1991. *Accounts overdue: Natural resource depreciation in Costa Rica*. San Pedro and Washington, D.C.: Centro Científico Tropical and World Resources Institute. 110 pp.

Soto, R. 1988. Geometry, biomass allocation and leaf demography of *Avicennia germinans* (L.) L. (Avicenniaceae) along a salinity gradient in Salinas, Puntarenas, Costa Rica. *Revista de Biología Tropical* 36:309–23.

Szelistowski, W. A. 1990. A new clingfish (Teleostei: Gobiesocidae) from mangroves of Costa Rica, with notes on its ecology and early development. *Copeia* 1990:500–507.

Szelistowski, W. A., and J. Garita. 1989. Mass mortality of sciaenid fishes in the Gulf of Nicoya, Costa Rica. *Fishery Bulletin* 87:363–65.

Thorne, R. E., J. B. Hedgepeth, and J. Campos. 1989. Hydroacoustic observations of fish and behavior around an artificial reef in Costa Rica. *Bulletin of Marine Science* 44:1058–64.

Vargas, J. A. 1987. The benthic community of an intertidal mud flat in the Gulf of Nicoya, Costa Rica: Description of the community. *Revista de Biología Tropical* 35:229–316.

———. 1988. A survey of the meiofauna of an eastern tropical Pacific intertidal mud flat. *Revista de Biología Tropical* 36:541–44.

———. 1989. Seasonal abundance of *Coricuma nicoyensis* (Crustacea: Cumacea) on an intertidal mud flat in the Gulf of Nicoya, Costa Rica. *Revista de Biología Tropical* 37:207–11.

———. 1995. The Gulf of Nicoya estuary, Costa Rica: Past, present and future cooperative research. *Helgoländer Meeresunters* 49:821–28.

———. 1996. Ecological dynamics of a tropical intertidal mudflat community. In *Estuarine shores: Evolution, environments and human alterations*, ed. K. F. Nordstrom and C. T. Roman, 355–71. London: John Wiley and Sons.

Vargas, R. C., S. Jesse, and M. Castro. 1996. Checklist of crustaceans (Decapoda and Stomatopoda) collected during the Victor Hensen Expedition (1993/1994). *Revista de Biología Tropical* 44 (Suppl. 3):97–102.

Villalobos, C., G. Cruz, and R. A. Cruz. 1985. Notas sobre la biología de *Sphaeroma terebrans* Bate 1966 (Sphaeromatidae, Isopoda) en el manglar de Pochote, Provincia de Puntarenas, Costa Rica. *Brenesia* 24:287–96.

Voorhis, A., C. E. Epifanio, D. Maurer, A. I. Dittel, and J. A. Vargas. 1983. The estuarine character of Gulf of Nicoya, an embayment on the Pacific Coast of Central America. *Hydrobiologia* 99:225–37.

Wehrtmann, I., and A. Dittel. 1990. Utilization of floating mangrove leaves as a transport mechanism of estuarine organisms, with emphasis on Decapod Crustacea. *Marine Ecology Progress Series* 60:67–73.

Wolff, M. 1996. Demersal fish assemblages along the Pacific coast of Costa Rica: A quantitative and multivariate assessment based on the Victor Hensen Costa Rica Expedition (1993–1994). *Revista de Biología Tropical* 44(Suppl. 3):187–214.

Wolff, M., H. J. Hartmann, and V. Koch. 1996. A pilot trophic model for Golfo Dulce, a fjord-like tropical embayment, Costa Rica. *Revista de Biología Tropical* 44(Suppl. 3):215–231.

Wolff, M., J. B. Chavarría, V. Koch, and J. A. Vargas. 1998. A trophic flow model of the Golfo de Nicoya, Costa Rica. *Revista de Biología Tropical* 46(Suppl. 6):63–79.

CHAPTER 11

Mangrove Forests under Dry Seasonal Climates in Costa Rica

Jorge A. Jiménez

ALONG THE 6,600-KM coastline of Central America, mangrove forests are a distinctive element in the landscape. More than 340,000 ha of mangroves exist along the Pacific coast, and 225,000 ha are found on the Caribbean coast of the isthmus. These forests represent around 7 percent of Central America's natural forest coverage and 8 percent of the world's mangroves (CCAD 1998).

More than 20 percent of the human population of Central America lives near coastal areas, and more than 200,000 people directly depend on coastal fishery industries in Central America (CCAD 1998). Mangrove forests have, therefore, high socioeconomic relevance in the region.

In Costa Rica, mangrove forests are almost exclusively located on the Pacific coast of the country. The Caribbean coastline, lacking inlets, bays, and other wave-protected areas, does not provide suitable habitats for mangrove development. In addition, a tidal range of only 30 cm

further reduces the amount of appropriate habitats. As a result, mangrove areas on this coast are limited to small isolated patches in some river mouths and coastal lagoons.

This chapter summarizes available information on biological characteristics and conservation issues associated with mangrove forests under dry seasonal climates in Costa Rica. I emphasize the impact that dry seasonal climates have on diversity patterns and the structural and functional attributes of these ecosystems. I also discuss the strong dependence of these forests and their associated fauna on the surrounding ecosystems. Finally, I offer recommendations on key areas needing research and integrative approaches to coastline management.

MANGROVES ON THE PACIFIC COAST OF COSTA RICA

Within the Pacific region, current climatic patterns have produced two different associations:

mangroves growing under rainy, less seasonal climates and mangroves growing under dry seasonal climates (Jiménez 1994). Mangrove forests in and north of the Gulf of Nicoya are influenced by strongly seasonal precipitation averaging between 1,500 and 2,000 mm per year, whereas those south of the gulf receive between 2,500 and 4,000 mm per year in a less seasonal pattern. Floristic differentiation of these two associations is evident at the internal edge of the forests. Here floral elements are more diverse under rainy climates. Differences in floristic diversity are also the result of climatic influence on hydrological regimes within mangrove forests. Surface water running into mangroves (runoff) and subsurface water infiltrating mangrove soils (seepage) modify interstitial salinity patterns. During dry months, runoff and seepage are reduced, resulting in an increase in soil salinity that is due to salt concentration, which in turn is a result of evapotranspiration processes. During rainy months soil salinity is reduced when salt is washed away by higher runoff and seepage. Species diversity (especially in the interior of mangrove forests) is higher where fresh water is abundant and constant.

PLANT SPECIES DISTRIBUTION

About 46 percent (19,000 ha) of the mangrove forests in Costa Rica are growing under dry seasonal climates. The dominant floristic elements in these forests are the trees: *Rhizophora racemosa, R. mangle, Laguncularia racemosa, Avicennia germinans,* and *A. bicolor.*

Some floristic elements are restricted to mangroves under dry seasonal climates. *A. bicolor* is limited to these mangroves, where it can be a dominant forest component. *Clerodendrum pittieri* and *Sesuvium portulacastrum* are herbs also restricted to this type of mangrove, but neither is a dominant element in the forest. Some plant species (*Caparis odoratissima, Heliotropium curassavicum,* and *Philoxerus vermicularis*) associated with the internal zone of the forest are also restricted to dry seasonal mangrove sites (Jiménez and Soto 1985).

In the internal zone of the forest, runoff and seepage are absent for six to eight months of the year. Soil salinity therefore tends to increase after the rainy season and with distance away from the tidal channels. Such spatial gradients can vary from 35 parts per thousand (ppt) close to the tidal channel to 163 ppt in the innermost areas of the forest (Soto and Corrales 1987). The innermost sections are not only the ones with the highest soil salinities during the dry season but also the ones with highest variations in soil salinity between dry and wet seasons. When soil salinity reaches above 100 ppt, vegetation disappears, giving way to salt flats; some of these are quite extensive, such as the 583 ha of salt flats at the Gulf of Nicoya (Solórzano et al. 1991).

STRUCTURAL ATTRIBUTES

As with species diversity, structural attributes exhibit the largest variations along the internal zone. Under dry seasonal climates most structural attributes (such as height, diameter, basal area, wood volume, and bark volume) show a reduction with distance away from the channel. For *Rhizophora* species it is not uncommon to find reductions in wood volume (from 95 m³/ha to 20 m³/ha) and in bark volumes (from 8 m³/ha to 2 m³/ha) in the first 100 m away from the channel (Jiménez 1994). As soil salinity increases landward, plants need to lock more amino acids and other organic compounds into their cytoplasm to achieve proper osmotic balance (Tomlinson 1986). These compounds are therefore not utilized in tissue growth, which results in lower structural development of the forest (Scholander et al. 1965).

In areas where the internal zone receives abundant runoff and seepage, the structural development is higher, particularly in the *A. bicolor* stands, located in the landward edge. Basal areas of around 40 m²/ha can be found in these stands (Jiménez 1990; Jiménez and Sauter 1991).

FAUNAL ELEMENTS

Because they constitute an ecotone between terrestrial and coastal ecosystems, mangrove forests show faunal elements from both systems. In mangrove forests, the avian community is less diverse than in other forest types. Nevertheless, more than 200 species of birds are associated with mangrove forests in Costa Rica (Jiménez 1994). In highly seasonal mangroves, however, bird diversity is lower; about 90 species use these forests. Mudflats and salt evaporation ponds at the external edge of mangroves are used as feeding grounds by more than 35 species of birds that feed on benthic invertebrates (Alvarado-Quesada and Moreno 1997). Around 64 bird species (mainly insectivores) use *Avicennia* stands (*A. germinans* and *A. bicolor* alike) at the internal edge of the forest (Warkentin and Hernández 1995).

Migratory species are an important component of mangroves. Of the 64 bird species reported only in *Avicennia* stands, 31 percent are Nearctic migrants. This percentage is higher than the 24 percent for migrants present in the total avifauna of Costa Rica. Migratory species can account for 64 percent of the bird individuals found in a mangrove forest (Warkentin and Hernández 1995). The high proportion of migrants emphasizes the value of mangrove forests as stopover habitats for migrating birds. They use this habitat largely as foraging areas or as night-time roosts during their annual migrations (chapter 12).

Local species of high relevance to conservation are also associated with mangrove habitats. Some are permanent residents, whereas others are only seasonal or occasional visitors. The Scarlet Macao (*Ara macao*) at the Carara Biological Reserve roosts at night in the Guacalillo mangrove forest while feeding during the day in the nearby rain forest (Vaughan et al. 1991). The Yellow-naped Parrot (*Amazona ochrocephala*), an endangered species, uses hollow trunks of *Avicennia* forests during the nesting season and spends the rest of the year outside the mangrove forest.

No endemic bird species is reported for dry seasonal mangroves in Costa Rica, although the hummingbird *Amazilia boucardii* is endemic to the rainy nonseasonal mangroves of southern Costa Rica, where it is common in *Pelliciera rhizophorae* stands. *Dendroica erithacorides,* an insectivore warbler, and the Mangrove Vireo (*Vireo pallens*) are restricted to mangrove habitats both in rainy and dry climates and can be found throughout the eastern Pacific mangroves.

Insects in mangrove forests have received little study. The moth *Lygropia erythrobathrum* (Pyralidae) eats the mesophyl of *Avicennia* leaves, leaving only the translucent cuticle in many of the tree crowns. *Avicennia* seedlings are eaten by massive groups of *Junonia evarete* (Nymphalidae; Turner and Parnell 1985). In *A. germinans* leaf galls are induced by three different species of flies (Cecidomyiidae), by *Telmapsylla minuta* (Homoptera: Psylloidea), and by an unidentified mite (P. Hanson pers. comm.). Interestingly, galls seem to be restricted to *A. germinans* individuals, whereas *A. bicolor* adjacent plants are gall-free. In *Laguncularia racemosa* leaf galls are produced by *Limbopsylla lagunculariae* (Homoptera: Psylloidea).

Mammals in dry seasonal mangrove forests, although not present in large populations, include frequently observed species such as the collared anteater (*Tamandua mexicana*), the white-faced monkey (*Cebus capuchinus*), the water opossum (*Chironectes minimus*), and the northern raccoon (*Procyon lotor*). Occasionally, large mammals such as the white-tailed deer (*Odocoileus virginianus*) and the jaguarundi (*Felis jaguarundi*) are observed within *Avicennia* forests.

Crustaceans, mollusks, and fishes dominate the estuarine component of the mangrove macrofauna. More than 50 species of crabs are found throughout the mangrove forest (Jiménez 1994). Several species, such as *Callinectes arcuatus* and *C. toxotes,* extend their distribution into adjacent estuarine environments, where their swimming capabilities allow them to thrive. Others crab species are ground-dwellers (e.g., *Sesarma sulcatum*) restricted to the forest floor and decomposing trunks. Land crabs (e.g., *Cardisoma crassum* and *Gecarcinus quadratus*) have developed physiological and anatomical properties that allow them to thrive in more terrestrial environments away from water bodies. Massive migration between adjacent dry forests and mangrove areas is part of their reproductive cycle. Other crabs are highly specialized for arboreal life, such as *Aratus pisonii*, which leave mangrove trees and move into coastal waters during the mating season.

Regarding mollusks, 78 species of bivalves and 46 species of gastropods are reported in mangroves of the Pacific coast of Central America (Cruz and Jiménez 1994). Several, such as *Grandiarca grandis, Anadara tuberculosa, Chione subrugosa, Protothaca asperrima,* and *Mytella guyanensis,* have high commercial value. Many species are restricted to specific habitats. Some gastropods, such as *Detracia graminea* and *Ellobium stagnalis,* are restricted to decomposing trunks. Other species, such as the gastropods *Marinula concinna* and *Cerithidea pulchra,* are associated with decomposing litterfall in areas dominated by *Rhizophora* species. More than 125 species of fish have been reported from mangrove areas in Costa Rica (Szelistowski 1990; Jiménez 1994). Estuarine fish families such as Gerreidae, Engraulidae, Tetraodontidae, Atherinidae, Ariidae, and Centropomidae dominate the ichthyofauna. The often cited migration of fish species in early stages of development between coastal waters and mangrove areas holds for most fish species in the Gulf of Nicoya mangroves, underscoring the ecological connection between mangroves and coastal waters. A large percentage of these fish species support artisanal and subsistence fisheries within the gulf and adjacent coastal waters. Faunal elements within mangrove forest are clearly associated with specific zones along the flooding gradient. Bivalves such as *Melongena patula, Natica cheminitzii,* and *Chione subrugosa,* most fish species, and crabs such as Xanthidae or Portunidae species are largely limited to the seaward areas of the forest in close contact with estuarine environments under daily tidal influence. Mollusk species such as *A. tuberculosa, Polymesoda inflata, Littoraria zebra, Cerithium stercusmuscarum,* and *Cerithidea montagnei* are restricted to the external edge of the forest among prop roots of *Rhizophora* trees. In interior sections of the forest, other groups of species, such as the gastropods *Theodoxus luteofasciatus* and *Melampus carolianus,* as well as several *Uca* crab species are associated with the pneumatophores of *Avicennia* species.

SEASONAL PATTERNS

Sharp seasonality in water availability in dry seasonal mangrove forests regulates many of its functional attributes. Growth patterns are clearly seasonal in these forests. Height and diameter increase during June–October, when groundwater recharge is highest and soil salinities lowest. This growth seasonality results in lower annual growth rates than those exhibited by trees under more rainy climates (Jiménez 1988, 1990).

Leaf fall increases at the beginning of the dry season (December–January), followed by a second leaf drop event at the onset of the rainy season (May), just before a flush of new leaves occurs. Herbivorous populations closely follow this seasonal pattern. The moth *Junonia evarete* exhibits high densities around September, which is closely linked to the seasonal establishment of a new cohort of *Avicennia* in the seedling bank. Moth density declines by November.

Flowering in *A. bicolor* forests starts in December and extends to late January, during the onset of dry conditions. The hummingbird (*Amazilia boucardii*) populations visiting and (supposedly) pollinating *Pelliciera rhizophorae* may have seasonal visitation patterns, since *P. rhizophorae* flowering is clearly seasonal. Climatic anomalies such as El Niño result in significant alterations of phenological cycles. Massive flower abortion has been associated with severe drought conditions (Jiménez 1990).

When runoff from the onset of the rains starts in May–June, fruit development sharply increases, reaching maturity in mid-August, when water levels in the forest are highest. Propagule crops in *Avicennia bicolor* vary dramatically from year to year, from 83 to 380 propagules per square meter (Jiménez 1990). Crab populations feeding on propagules seem to follow these seasonal patterns of propagule production.

Seedling establishment for *Avicennia* species occurs within two weeks after propagule drop. Established seedlings show a clear seasonal pattern of mortality, with about 35 percent of a cohort dying during the following dry season. Both establishment and mortality levels vary along the flooding gradient. The more severe conditions in the innermost edge of the forest result in higher mortality levels during the dry season. Drought seasonality along the flooding gradient also regulates differential survival of *Avicennia* and *Rhizophora* seedlings, reinforcing zonation patterns within the forest (Jiménez and Sauter 1991).

The seasonal nature of mangrove forests is also reflected in the faunal communities. Many species, especially in the internal edge of the forest, sharply reduce their densities during the dry season, when the ground becomes drier and saltier owing to a decrease in runoff and rainfall. The gastropod *Theodoxus luteofasciatus* reduces its population densities from more than 300 individuals per square meter to fewer than 1 individual per square meter. Similar crashes in population density are observed in gastropods such as *Melampus carolianus* and many fiddler-crab species (*Uca* spp.). Because tidal inundation is reduced in accordance with a reduction in river flow during the dry season, large sections of the mangrove floor become drier, even in the external edge of the forest. Ground-dweller mollusks such as *Cerithidea pulchra*, *Littoraria zebra*, and the bivalve *Polymesoda inflata* also reduce their numbers. With the onset of the wet season, insect populations and ground-dweller mollusks (e.g., *T. luteofasciatus*) and crustaceans (e.g., *Sesarma* spp.) rapidly colonize the forest again. Mating and nesting of canopy birds such as *Dendroica erithacorides* and *Amazona ochrocephala* coincide with the start of the rainy season when food availability is higher (Barrantes 1998).

Seasonal faunal movements between mangroves and surrounding environments are common. Some mangrove crabs (*Gecarcinus quadratus*, *Cardisoma crassum*, *Ucides occidentalis*) show seasonal migrations between mangroves and nearby land forests for mating purposes. In the canopy, migratory bird species escaping the boreal winter become abundant during the dry season, sometimes surpassing local residents in number, whereas the white-faced monkeys migrate to areas of the forest adjacent to freshwater courses. In water channels fish and crustaceans show seasonal migration patterns between mangroves and adjacent coastal areas (Szelistowski 1990). These relationships highlight the close dependency that mangroves have on adjacent habitats.

CONSERVATION STATUS

Mangrove forests in Costa Rica have been protected under legislation such as the Coastal-Maritime Law (1977), the Wildlife Law (1992), and more recently the Environment Law (1995). A series of executive decrees during the past three decades have also regulated specific aspects of mangrove conservation and management.

This legal framework has proved effective in preventing mangrove destruction in most areas. However, reclamation has occurred at specific sites where pressure for land or resources is high and enforcement has been limited. The Gulf of Nicoya mangroves (around 14,000 ha) have been the most affected; around 7 percent of the gulf's original coverage has been lost as a result of shrimp cultivation ponds (630 ha) and salt evaporation ponds (350 ha). This reclamation has occurred mainly at the expense of *Avicennia germinans* stands in the internal zone of the forests (Solórzano et al. 1991). The shrimp operations at Chomes and salt evaporation ponds around Jicaral are responsible for the greatest impact.

Small areas (1–6 ha each) have been developed for hotel and marina sites in the Nicoya Peninsula in a piecemeal fashion. Landfilling of mangroves in Samara, Conchal, and Playa Grande for hotel construction is an example of this destructive process. In these cases, however, the total number of hectares destroyed has been relatively low (20–30).

Although total area destroyed is comparatively low, mangrove forests, water quality, and associated faunal communities have been more extensively degraded. Existing legislation provides little support to prevent this environmental degradation. Socioeconomic processes are closely associated with this problem. Economical recession and armed conflicts in a neighboring country have resulted in heavy human immigration to the mangrove areas during the past two decades. A higher number of people living at subsistence levels seek mangrove areas as sources of firewood, poles, charcoal, shellfish, crustaceans, and other products.

The slower growth rates of mangrove forests in dry seasonal climates make their conservation harder in areas of increasing demand for wood resources. Areas such as Estero Pitahaya, Costa de Pajaros, and Puerto Thiel exhibit forest degradation as a result of wood extraction for poles, firewood, and charcoal. Overexploitation of faunal resources is notorious and widespread. A species of mangrove cockle (*Grandiarca grandis*) is listed as endangered as a result of overexploitation and has almost disappeared within the Gulf of Nicoya. Around 8 million individuals of another seacockle species (*Anadara tuberculosa*) are harvested yearly from mangroves in the Gulf of Nicoya (Solórzano et al. 1991). A historical reduction in the average size of captures indicates overexploitation of the resource. Shrimp species (such as *Penaeus stylirostris*) also show a reduction in the average size of captured individuals (Palacios et al. 1996). Although legislation forbids the use of gill nets within mangrove areas, illegal fishing is widespread, despite analysis showing overexploitation of fish populations. Artisanal fisheries within the Gulf of Nicoya have been reduced by 40 percent, and the number of fishing boats has doubled (Foer and Olsen 1992).

The close linkage between dry seasonal mangroves and associated river basins as sources of freshwater discharges poses a major conservation challenge. No programs are, however, being implemented to achieve integrated management. The Tempisque River, with its 3,700 ha of associated mangroves, is literally dried out during the dry season. Pumping stations extract water for sugarcane irrigation in the lower watershed. Ecological consequences of these alterations are largely unknown.

The quality of freshwater discharges is also severely deteriorated in most river basins. Sediment-bound metal contaminants such as chromium, originating from leather tanneries in the Central Valley, find their way into mangrove sediments at the Gulf of Nicoya via the Grande de Tárcoles River (or Tárcoles River) (Fuller et al. 1990). Coliforms from untreated sewage disposals also are affecting areas such as the Guacalillo and Chacarita mangroves (see chapters 9 and 10). Large amounts of solid waste (especially plastic debris) are transported by the Tárcoles River and distributed by longshore drift currents into nearby Guacalillo, Tivives, and Bajamar mangrove areas.

Agroindustrial processes in the associated basins are also a main source of pollution. Sugarcane processing has resulted in strong seasonal variations in water quality within the Chacarita estuary. Dissolved oxygen can drop to zero during harvest season, resulting in massive mortality of fish, crustaceans, and other associated fauna in the mangrove estuary (Blanco and Mata 1994). The quality of some faunal resources (such as bivalves, crabs, and fishes) extracted from mangrove areas for human consumption is likely affected. The absence of long-term monitoring programs on water quality is lamentable.

RECOMMENDATIONS

Interactions between mangroves and surrounding environments highlight the need for further analysis of the processes regulating these interactions. Little is understood about the dependence of mangrove organisms on surrounding environments. Several elements of the avian community (such as the Mangrove Hummingbird and the Mangrove Warbler) seem to depend on adjacent forests for seasonal foraging. Endangered species (such as *Ara macao* and *Amazona ocrocephala*) may have a strong dependence on mangrove areas. How alterations in the surrounding landscape affect mangrove avian populations is in need of immediate study. Mangrove areas seem to function as refuges for fauna displaced from deforested coastal plains. Some bird species of Dendrocolapidae, the silk anteater (*Cyclopes dydactilus*), and the tree anteater (*Tamandua mexicana*), among others, seem to have increased their use of mangrove areas (J. Jiménez pers. obs). More research is needed to elucidate the processes that regulate mammal use of mangroves and movements between coastal plain ecosystems and mangroves. Seasonal rhythms followed by insect, crab, and mollusk populations have been studied only superficially. The strong seasonality in dry seasonal mangrove areas highlights the dependence of many of their communities on freshwater supply. Alteration of hydrological and climatic regimes might have a severe impact on these seasonal patterns. Pollination processes (in *Avicennia, Laguncular a,* and *Pelliciera*) are unknown. Besides massive flower abortions, what is the impact of El Niño/La Niña phenomena on pollinators and propagule-feeding crabs? Bottom-dwelling mollusks have a close dependence on runoff regimes, but no information is available on the impact of water diversion on this seasonal fauna.

In addition to more information on ecological interactions, there is a need for long-term programs that monitor water flows and water quality reaching mangrove forests. This type of information will allow a better understanding of the linkages between mangrove areas and upstream ecosystems and processes. The impact of changes in patterns and quality of freshwater discharges on the aquatic and benthic fauna within mangrove forests is also largely unknown.

Mangrove reclamation by tourism infrastructure, salt evaporation ponds, shrimp farms, and urban development is a threat in many mangrove areas of northwestern Costa Rica. However, deterioration of forest resources, alteration of water quality, overexploitation of faunal resources, and the diversion of freshwater discharges seem to be more relevant menaces to the conservation of dry-seasonal mangrove forests.

A more integral approach to mangrove management is required in light of the close dependence of these systems to biophysical processes in surrounding systems. Closer coordination among different isolated government agencies and regional NGOs is urgently needed. The involvement of local communities and the agro-industrial sector in decision-making processes and management plans is insufficient. The weak enforcement of existing legislation needs to be strengthened. These deficiencies have until now prevented an integrated management of mangrove areas.

REFERENCES

Alvarado-Quesada, G. M., and L. I. Moreno. 1997. Use of salt evaporation ponds by aquatic birds and bird abundance. In *Proceedings of the ATB-OTS Symposium: Tropical Biodiversity: Origins and Maintenance,* 35. San José: Organization for Tropical Studies.

Barrantes, G. 1998. Biologia y comportamiento de *Dendroica petechia xanthotera. Brenesia* 49–50: 61–69.

Blanco, O., and A. Mata. 1994. *La Cuenca del Golfo de Nicoya: Reto al desarrollo sostenible.* San José: Editorial de la Universidad de Costa Rica. 336 pp.

CCAD (Comisión Centroamericana de Ambiente y Desarrollo). 1998. *Estado del ambiente y los recursos naturales en Centroamerica.* San José: Comisión Centroamericana de Abiente y Desarrollo. 179 pp.

Cruz, R. A., and J. A. Jiménez. 1994. *Moluscos asociados a las áreas de manglar de la costa Pacífica de América Central.* Heredia, Costa Rica: Editorial Fundación UNA. 182 pp.

Delgado, P., J. A. Jiménez, and D. Justic. 1999. Population dynamics of mangrove *Avicennia bicolor* on the Pacific coast of Costa Rica. *Wetlands Ecology and Management* 7:113–20.

Ellison, A. M., E. J. Farnsworth, and R. E. Merkt. 1999. Origins of mangrove ecosystems and the mangrove biodiversity anomaly. *Global Ecology and Biogeography* 8(2):95–115.

Foer, G., and S. Olsen. 1992. *Las costas de CentroAmerica.* Washington, D.C.: U.S. Agency for International Development. 290 pp.

Fuller, C. C., J. A. Davis, D. J. Cain, T. L. Fries, G. Fernández, J. A. Vargas, and M. M. Murillo.

1990. Distribution and transport of sediment-bound metal contaminants in the Río Grande de Tárcoles, Costa Rica. *Water Research* 24:805–12.

Graham, A. 1995. Diversification of gulf/Caribbean mangrove communities through Cenozoic time. *Biotropica* 27:20–27.

Jiménez, J. A. 1984. A hypothesis to explain the reduced distribution of the mangrove *Pelliciera rhizophorae* Tr. & Pl. *Biotropica* 16:304–8.

———. 1988. The dynamics of *Rhizophora racemosa* forests on the Pacific coast of Costa Rica. *Brenesia* 30:1–12.

———. 1990. The structure and function of dry weather mangroves on the Pacific coast of Central America, with emphasis in *Avicennia bicolor* forests. *Estuaries* 13(2):182–92.

———. 1994. *Los manglares del Pacífico Centroamericano.* Heredia, Costa Rica: Editorial FUNA. 336 pp.

Jiménez, J. A., and K. M. Sauter. 1991. Structure and dynamics of mangrove forests along a flooding gradient. *Estuaries* 14(1):49–56.

Jiménez, J. A., and R. Soto. 1985. Patrones regionales en la estructura y composición florística de los manglares de la costa Pacífica de Costa Rica. *Revista de Biología Tropical* 33:25–37.

Palacios, J. A., R. Angulo, and J. A. Rodríguez. 1996. La pesqueria de *Penaeus stylirostris* en el Golfo de Nicoya. *Revista de Biología Tropical* 44:225–31.

Ramírez, A. R., M. I. López-Sánchez, and W. A. Szelistowski. 1990. Composition and abundance of ichthyoplankton in a Gulf of Nicoya mangrove estuary. *Revista de Biología Tropical* 38:463–66.

Roth, L. C., and A. Grijalva. 1991. New record of the mangrove *Pelliciera rhizophorae* (Theaceae) on the Caribbean coast of Nicaragua. *Rhodora* 93:183–86.

Scholander, P. F., H. T. Ha, E. E. Bradstreet, and E. A. Hemmingsen. 1965. Sap pressure in vascular plants. *Science* 148:339–45.

Solórzano, R., R. de Camino, R. Woodward, J. Tosi, V. Watson, A. Vasquez, C. Villalobos, R. Repetto, and W. Cruz. 1991. *Accounts overdue: Natural resource depreciation in Costa Rica.* Washington, D.C.: World Resources Institute. 111 pp.

Soto, R., and L. F. Corrales. 1987. Variación de algunas características foliares de *Avicennia germinans* en un grdiente climático y de salinidad. *Revista de Biología Tropical* 35:245–56.

Szelistowski, W. A. 1990. Importance of mangrove plant litter in fish food webs and as temporary, floating habitat in the Gulf of Nicoya, Costa Rica. Ph.D. diss., University of Southern California. 78 pp.

Tomlinson, P. B. 1986. *The botany of mangroves.* Cambridge Tropical Biology Series. Cambridge: Cambridge University Press. 419 pp.

Turner, T. W., and J. R. Parnell. 1985. The identification of two species of *Junonia* Hubner (Lepidoptera: Nymphalidae): *J. evarete* and *J. genoveva* in Jamaica. *Journal of Research on the Lepidoptera* 24:142–53.

Vaughan, C., M. McCoy, and M. B. Liske. 1991. Scarlet macaw (Ara macao) ecology and management perspectives in Carara Biological Reserve, Costa Rica. *Miscellaneous Publications from the Center for Study of Tropical Birds* 1:23–34.

Warkentin, I. G., and D. Hernández. 1995. Avifaunal composition of a Costa Rican mangrove forest during the boreal winter. *Vida Silvestre Neotropical* 4(2):140–43.

Section C. Biotic Relationships with Other Geographical Areas

Geographical Distribution, Ecology, and Conservation Status of Costa Rican Dry-Forest Avifauna

Gilbert Barrantes and Julio E. Sánchez

I N COSTA RICA the dry forest covers the Santa Elena Peninsula and adjacent areas and some small areas around the Gulf of Nicoya (Slud 1980; Gómez 1986; see maps in chapter 1). Large tracts of semideciduous forest also occur below 500 m in the northwest of Costa Rica. For the purpose of this chapter, we consider deciduous, semideciduous, and other associated habitats as the dry-forest ecosystem. The ecosystem includes both terrestrial and aquatic habitats. Deciduous and riparian forests and savanna are the most extensive terrestrial habitats, and mangroves, mudflats, lagoons, and swamps are the most common aquatic habitats. Mangroves and mudflats cover large areas in the Gulf of Nicoya, and lagoons and swamps are part of the complex hydrological system that occurs at the lower basin of the Tempisque River. We excluded more humid areas of the Nicoya Peninsula (e.g., Reserva Absoluta Cabo Blanco; Gómez 1986).

The average temperature of the region is 27.6°C ± 0.7°C and the annual precipitation 1,619 mm (Gómez 1986). Temperature varies little throughout year. Precipitation, however, fluctuates dramatically, with a well-defined dry season from December to May (some years to June) (see chapter 1). Seasonality in the dry-forest ecosystem largely influences species composition, food resource availability, habitat use, and, to a large extent, mutualistic interactions that occur in this life zone.

SOURCES OF INFORMATION

Most of this chapter's information on avian species richness, migratory status, habitat use, and reproduction comes from years of fieldwork by the authors. We complemented our data on some aspects of the reproduction of some species with information from Slud (1964) and Stiles and Skutch (1989). We also used part of the

TABLE 12.1
Number of Dry-Forest Species (Residents, Migrants, and Species with
Populations of Both) Using Aquatic and Terrestrial Habitats

	NUMBER OF SPECIES PER HABITAT		
	AQUATIC	TERRESTRIAL	TOTAL (%)
Residents	37	163	200 (58)
Migrants	58	66	124 (36)
Resident/migratory	13	8	21 (6)
Total	108	237	345

Note: Resident species may or may not reproduce in dry forest.

information recorded and compiled by Stotz et al. (1996), which helped to limit the Costa Rican dry-forest avifauna to a more regional scale and identify the endemic species.

We also used information on the phenological patterns of dry-forest plants (Frankie et al. 1974; Opler et al. 1980; see chapter 2) and changes in insect abundance (Janzen 1973) as a baseline to explain the response of dry-forest birds to seasonal changes in food abundance. Such information provided a general pattern of fluctuation of insects and flower and fruit abundance.

GENERAL ASPECTS OF COSTA RICAN DRY-FOREST AVIFAUNA

The dry-forest avifauna of Costa Rica includes 345 species. Of this total, 58 percent of the species are resident, 36 percent are latitudinal migrants, and about 6 percent have resident and migratory populations (table 12.1). A large percentage of dry-forest species (31%) are associated with aquatic environments. Yet the proportion of aquatic birds varies substantially between migrants and residents (table 12.1). About 50 percent of the latitudinal migrants are aquatic species, whereas only 19 percent of the resident species use aquatic habitats (table 12.1).

There are five main aquatic environments in the Costa Rican dry-forest ecosystem: mudflats, mangroves, lagoons, seasonal marshes, and rivers. Large extensions of mudflats become exposed during low tides within the Gulf of Nicoya (Barrantes and Pereira 1992). These muddy extensions are important stopover and wintering grounds for a large group of migratory aquatic birds, particularly shorebirds and their relatives. Invertebrates present in these substrates are the food source for thousands of these birds, which, having different prey preferences and using different foraging strategies, coexist in the Gulf of Nicoya for several months every year (Barrantes and Pereira 1992).

Mangrove forests cover relatively large areas along the coast within the Gulf of Nicoya and particularly at the mouth of large rivers (e.g., Barranca, Tempisque). This seashore forest, despite its low plant species richness (Jiménez and Soto 1985), is used by a relatively large number of aquatic birds (Barrantes 1998). Herons, egrets, ibises, and some large shorebirds are common users of mangroves. This forest is the most important habitat for foraging, roosting, and reproduction of several herons (e.g., Black-crowned Night Heron, Yellow-crowned Night Heron, Boat-billed Heron). Other species, although not as closely associated with mangroves as night herons or the Boat-billed Heron, rely largely on it to reproduce (e.g., Green-backed Heron) and/or roost (e.g., Cattle Egret, Little Blue Heron, White Ibis).

Freshwater habitats (i.e., lagoons, seasonal marshes, rivers) are also of great importance for numerous resident and migratory aquatic species. Lagoons and seasonal marshes serve as foraging and breeding habitat for some resident species. Some aquatic species, such as the Pinnated Bittern and Least Bittern, breed and feed exclusively in lagoons and seasonal marshes in the Costa Rican dry forest. Many other resident birds (e.g., Bared-throated Tiger Heron, Wood Stork, Jabiru, Northern Jacana, Black-bellied Whistling Duck) use these freshwater environments intensively as their foraging areas. Such sites are especially important during the breeding season, as they become primary sources of food for the birds' offspring. These two freshwater habitats are also heavily used as foraging and resting areas by latitudinal migrants (e.g., some shorebirds, egrets, herons), especially ducks (e.g., Blue-winged Teal). Few species, either migratory or resident, use rivers as their primary habitat.

The most extensive habitats for terrestrial birds in the dry forest are savanna and riparian, deciduous, and mangrove forests. Savanna combines pasturelands and some extensions that are in different early successional stages as a result of deforestation, cattle ranching, and a variety of agricultural systems (e.g., sorghum, sugarcane, rice plantations) (Hartshorn 1983; Janzen 1988). The majority of birds present in this habitat are resident, and all of them are also present in adjacent forests. Raptors (e.g., Roadside Hawk, Bay-winged Hawk), granivores (e.g., White-collared Seedeater, Inca Dove), and insectivores (e.g., Lesser Ground Cuckoo, Tropical Kingbird) are common species in the savanna.

Deciduous forest, although greatly destroyed and fragmented by human activities (chapter 1), still covers relatively large areas in the northwestern region of Costa Rica, particularly on hills and calcareous soils (Janzen 1988). Riparian forest, however, is naturally restricted to small tracts along seasonal and perennial watercourses (Hartshorn 1983). The majority of terrestrial resident and migratory species occur in both riparian and deciduous forests. Thus, very few

species may be considered exclusive to either one (table 12.2). A larger trophic diversity is also found in these forests (table 12.2). For instance, nectar feeders (e.g., Blue-throated Goldentail, Streaked-backed Oriole), frugivores (e.g., Long-tailed Manakin), raptors (e.g., Collared Forest Falcon, Spectacle Owl), and seed eaters (e.g., Yellow-naped Parrot) are all well represented in both forests.

Mangrove forest has lower bird species richness in comparison with deciduous and riparian forests. This is partially explained by the low abundance of fleshy fruits and bird-pollinated plants in mangroves (Tomlinson 1986). Consequently, nectar- and fruit-feeding birds are poorly represented. Insectivores are the group of terrestrial birds best represented in mangroves. This habitat is intensively used by a large group of insectivorous migrants, particularly warblers, which in some areas surpass the resident birds in abundance (G. Barrantes pers. obs.)

ORIGIN AND DISTINCTIVENESS OF DRY-FOREST AVIFAUNA OF COSTA RICA

The avifauna of the Pacific Arid Slope of Mesoamerica (PAS) consists of a group of species with different origins that share the capacity to cope with the environmental conditions of the dry-forest ecosystem. In Costa Rica, of 345 bird species that have been recorded in the dry forest (J. E. Sánchez unpubl. data), 87 have South American affinity, 38 North American, 26 Central American, 13 pantropical, 37 Old World, and 144 with unknown origin (following Karr 1976). A large proportion of this avifauna involves either species with broad distributions (e.g., Northern Jacana), which are also present in tropical rain forests, or seasonal (e.g., Black-hooded Antshrike) and occasional visitors (e.g., Ornate Hawk-Eagle) that enter into dry forest during the rainy season (G. Barrantes and J. E. Sánchez pers. obs.). Yet, even when more typical dry-forest birds are considered, the broad biogeographical origin still remains as an emergent characteristic of the Costa Rican dry-forest avifauna and, in general, of the avifauna of the entire PAS region.

TABLE 12.2
Distribution, Habitat, and Forest Dependence of Dry-Forest Bird Species in Costa Rica

	DISTRIBUTION	HABITAT	FOREST DEPENDENCE
Agelaius phoeniceus	U.S.–Costa Rica	lag	None
Aimophila botterii	U.S.–Costa Rica	sav/dec	None
A. ruficauda	Mexico–Costa Rica	sav/dec	None
Amazilia rutila	Mexico–Costa Rica	dec	Low
Amazona albifrons	Mexico–Costa Rica	sav/rip/dec/man	Moderate
A. auropalliata	Mexico–Costa Rica	sav/rip/dec/man	Moderate
Ammodramus savannarum	Canada–Ecuador	sav	None
Aratinga canicularis	Mexico–Costa Rica	sav/rip/dec/man	None
Arremonops rufivirgatus	Mexico–Costa Rica	sav/dec	None
Asturina nitida plagiada	U.S.–Costa Rica	sav/rip/dec	Low
Burhinus bistriatus	Mexico–Brazil	sav	None
Buteo albicaudatus	U.S.–Argentina	sav	None
B. albonotatus	U.S.–Argentina	sav	Low
Buteogallus subtilis	Mexico–Peru	man	Moderate
Calocitta formosa	Mexico–Costa Rica	sav/rip/dec/man	Low
Camptostoma imberbe	U.S.–Costa Rica	dec	Low
Campylorhynchus rufinucha	Mexico–Costa Rica	sav/rip/dec/man	Low
Caracara plancus	U.S.–Argentina	sav/rip/dec	None
Chiroxiphia linearis	Mexico–Costa Rica	rip/dec	Moderate
Colinus cristatus leucopogon	Guatemala–Costa Rica	sav/dec	None
Columbina inca	U.S.–Costa Rica	sav/dec/man	None
Crypturellus cinnamomeus	Mexico–Costa Rica	rip/dec	Moderate
Dendroica petechia xanthotera	Guatemala–Costa Rica	man	Moderate
Eumomota superciliosa	Mexico–Costa Rica	rip/dec/man	Low
Euphonia affinis	Mexico–Costa Rica	sav/dec	Low
Glaucidium brasilianum	U.S.–Argentina	sav/rip/dec	Low
Guiraca caerulea[a]	U.S.–Costa Rica	sav/dec	None
Heliomaster constantii	Mexico–Brazil	sav/dec	Low
Icterus pectoralis	Mexico–Costa Rica	dec/man	Low
I. pustulatus	Mexico–Costa Rica	dec/rip	Low
Laterallus ruber	Mexico–Costa Rica	lag	None
Melanerpes hoffmannii	Honduras–Costa Rica	sav/rip/dec/man	Low

TABLE 12.2 *(continued)*

	DISTRIBUTION	HABITAT	FOREST DEPENDENCE
Morococcyx erythropygius	Mexico–Costa Rica	sav/dec	Low
Myiarchus nuttingi	Mexico–Costa Rica	rip	Moderate
M. tyrannulus brachyurus	Nicaragua–Costa Rica	sav/rip/dec/man	Low
Myiodynastes maculatus[a]	Mexico–Brazil	rip/dec/man	Moderate
Ortalis vetula	U.S.–Costa Rica	rip/dec	High
Otus cooperi	Mexico–Costa Rica	dec/man	Moderate
Pachyramphus aglaiae	U.S.–Costa Rica	sav/rip/dec	Low
Parabuteo unicinctus	U.S.–Argentina	sav	Low
Passerina ciris[b]	U.S.–Panama	sav/dec	Low
Platyrinchus cancrominus	Mexico–Costa Rica	rip/dec	Very high
Plegadis falcinellus	U.S.–Costa Rica	rip/man	Moderate
Polioptila albiloris	Mexico–Costa Rica	dec/man	Low
Quiscalus mexicanus	U.S.–Venezuela	sav/man	None
Rosthramus sociabilis	U.S.–Argentina	lag	None
Salpinctes obsoletus	Canada–Costa Rica	sav	None
Sporophila torqueola	U.S.–Panama	sav/dec	None
Sublegatus arenarum arenarum	Costa Rica–Panama	man	Moderate
Thryothorus pleurostictus	Mexico–Costa Rica	rip/dec	Moderate
T. rufalbus	Mexico–Colombia	rip	High
Trogon elegans	U.S.–Costa Rica	rip	High
T. melanocephalus	Mexico–Costa Rica	dec	Low
Tyrannus forficatus	U.S.–Costa Rica	sav/man	None
Vireo pallens	Mexico–Costa Rica	man	Moderate
Xiphorhynchus flavigaster	Mexico–Costa Rica	rip/dec	Moderate
Zenaida asiatica[a]	U.S.–Panama	rip/dec/man	None
Z. macroura[a]	Canada–Panama	rip/dec/man	None

Note: Only species exclusive to the Mesoamerican dry-forest region or typical of Costa Rican dry forest are included. Habitat: rip = riparian forest; dec = deciduous forest; sav = savanna; man = mangrove; lag = lagoon.
[a] Species with migratory and resident populations.
[b] Migratory species.

Two components of the dry-forest avifauna, the Mesoamerican and North American, may be considered autochthonous to the PAS. These species may have become adapted to climatic and physiognomic conditions of the dry forest along with the historical climatic changes that have occurred in this region since the Tertiary (Haffer 1974). South American species (or ancestors), however, likely arrived in Mesoamerica during the Pleistocene, after formation of the first bridge that connected South America with North America (Haffer 1974; Webb and Rancy 1996). Thus, historical events, such as climatic changes and geological events, have likely shaped the current composition of the avifauna of Mesoamerica's dry forest, the third most diverse dry-forest region of the Neotropics (Stotz et al. 1996).

Species richness in the PAS increases slightly from Costa Rica to Mexico (Stiles 1983). This increment in species number with latitude may be explained by the larger area of dry forest in Mexico and northern Central America (Murphy and Lugo 1995). Of all the bird species that inhabit the Pacific Mesoamerican region, only 32 out of the 71 (typical) deciduous forest species are shared with the Yucatán Peninsula region (separated from the PAS by some hundreds of kilometers) and 12 with the northern South American dry-forest region (Stotz et al. 1996). This indicates that large tracts of more humid forests that surround dry-forest areas may function as efficient barriers for many dry-forest species.

In Costa Rica the northern Pacific region (NPR), which is a small area that constitutes the southernmost segment of the PAS, contains more than half (58 species) of the Pacific Mesoamerican typical dry-forest birds (table 12.2). The small differences in species composition throughout the PAS region indicate the absence of geographical barriers and lack of habitat specialization in dry-forest birds. Lack of specialization in dry-forest birds may have originated from adaptation to the contrasting conditions (e.g., flower and fruit production) that occur in dry forests between rainy and dry seasons (Frankie et al. 1974; Opler et al. 1980; chapter 2). Thus, the low degree of habitat specialization

may allow movements of individuals between distant localities.

ENDEMISM

Endemism in dry-forest and arid scrub regions is as high as (or higher than) that in lowland humid forests (Stotz et al. 1996). Endemism in the PAS region, and in all dry-forest regions in general, is more common in terrestrial than in aquatic birds. The PAS embraces seven endemic species, four of which are present in the Costa Rican dry forest (Lesser Ground Cuckoo, Pacific Screech Owl, Long-tailed Manakin, and White-throated Magpie-Jay). None of these species are restricted to Costa Rica, although all four are abundant in the NPR.

REPRODUCTIVE ACTIVITY

Reproductive activity of dry-forest birds occurs year-round (fig. 12.1), with a peak between March and July (reproductive information is given for 183 species that are known to breed in the NPR). Breeding periods differ between terrestrial and aquatic species and within and between some taxonomic and/or ecological groups in both categories, as well. Reproduction of terrestrial species is concentrated in the period from March to July (Barrantes 1998). In a large number of small terrestrial birds (e.g., wrens, woodcreepers, warblers, and most flycatchers and their relatives), this activity begins at the onset of the rainy season (April–May) and extends to the end of June/beginning of July. Insects, particularly larvae, are present in great numbers after the first heavy rains, and this abundance is exploited by terrestrial birds in rearing their offspring at this time (Janzen 1973; see also chapters 7 and 8).

Raptors (i.e., Falconiformes and Strigiformes), some hummingbirds, and a few other species, however, reproduce during the dry season. Greater prey availability (e.g., mice) during this season is perhaps the most important factor in determining the reproductive period for birds of prey (Janzen and Stiles 1983). Furthermore, leafless vegetation in the dry season makes ro-

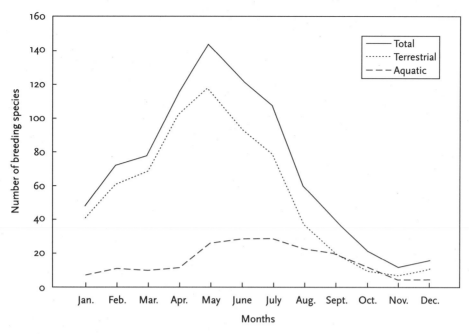

FIGURE 12.1. Number of breeding species per month for terrestrial, aquatic, and total species in Costa Rican dry forest. The 183 species for which reproduction information is available are included.

dents and other prey much more conspicuous, and this greater detectability of prey probably influences time of reproduction in raptors, as well. Likewise, reproduction of dry-forest hummingbirds is largely determined by nectar availability. Large numbers of plants bloom, including those used by hummingbirds (e.g., *Combretum farinosum, Aphelandra* spp.), during the dry season (Frankie et al. 1974; chapters 1 and 2) and at the beginning of rainy season (Opler et al. 1976). Hence, this resource seems to be an important factor in timing the reproduction of these birds. It is possible that the dry and windy conditions prevalent in this period may increase reproductive success of hummingbirds because insect parasites and vectors of blood parasites decrease during this season (Ricklefs 1992).

The reproduction of parrots, trogons, woodpeckers, and other cavity nesters also occurs during the dry season (Stiles 1983). Timing in these species may be determined by the relatively high abundance of fruits and seeds during the second half of the dry season (Frankie et al. 1974). Yet Stiles (1983) proposed that micro-climate inside nests is responsible for determining the reproduction timing in these birds. Cavity nests maintain constant temperature (about 20°C) and low (but not extremely low) relative humidity, even during the driest and hottest periods of the dry season, thereby creating an appropriate microclimate that protects embryos and nestlings from desiccation and pathogens (Stiles 1983; Collias and Collias 1984).

The reproduction of waterbirds begins toward the second half of the year. The majority of aquatic birds reproduce during the rainy season, between April and October (fig. 12.1). Food availability (e.g., fish, tadpoles, frogs, snails, aquatic insects) increases dramatically when water levels in lagoons and seasonal swamps are high. Numerous groups of birds, such as herons, ducks, rails, cranes, jacanas, and some hawks, benefit from the increasing availability of food resources to raise their progeny. A small group of aquatic birds (e.g., Ciconiidae, Threskiornithidae) breed outside the rainy season. These species feed mostly on fish, crustaceans, and other invertebrates trapped in small shallow ponds. These prey become more available when water levels begin to decline after the rainy season.

DIET AND HABITAT USE: COPING WITH SEASONALITY

LAND BIRDS

Diet and the habitat used by birds are greatly influenced by environmental changes. Tropical dry forests are sharply seasonal as a consequence of changes in rainfall, temperature, and wind pattern. These changes affect habitat conditions (e.g., foliage cover) and food abundance (Karr 1976). Consequently, resident birds in tropical dry forest need to adjust to these changes in order to meet the energy needs, not only for their growth and maintenance but also for molting and reproduction (King 1973). Seasonal variation in food resources poses a challenge to birds, which are likely "adapted" to respond to limitation of food in different ways (e.g., changing habitats, shifting diet).

Insect composition and abundance (Janzen 1973, 1985), as well as plant resources (Frankie et al. 1974; Borchert 1983), change drastically on a seasonal basis in Costa Rican dry forests. Yet because dry forest consists of a mosaic of different habitats, with deciduous and evergreen forests dominating, the magnitude and direction of such changes vary with the particular conditions in each habitat (e.g., insect abundance varies from one forest to another). Consequently, birds may use different strategies to cope with such changes:

1. Movements to localities with milder environmental conditions and/or higher resource abundance. Presence and abundance of numerous dry-forest birds depend, to a large extent, on availability of food resources. Thus, abundance and spatial distribution of species such as Long-tailed Manakins, tityras, and some flycatchers are largely determined by abundance of the food resource. In periods of scarcity, abun-

dance of these species decreases greatly, as expected. Other species seem to be affected not only by food availability but also by extreme conditions of the dry season. For example, populations of Elegant Trogon decrease notably during the driest periods in riparian forests (J. E. Sánchez pers. obs.). It is likely that this species moves between different locations to avoid extreme conditions. This behavior differs from that of the Black-headed Trogon, despite the similarity in their diets. The Black-headed Trogon is a common inhabitant of deciduous forest year-round. This suggests that severity in environmental conditions, more than food availability, defines the pattern of movement for the Elegant Trogon. Field observations suggest that some species might move either to middle and high elevations on the cordilleras de Guanacaste and Tilarán (following the riparian corridors) or to evergreen forests of the Nicoya Península.

2. Changes in forest type. The large number of phytophagous insects decreases dramatically as foliage availability declines with progression of the dry season (Janzen 1973). Some groups of insects migrate, but many others enter into reproductive diapause. Consequently, during this season insect larvae are practically absent, and adults concentrate in riparian forests. With the onset of the rainy season many plants sprout leaves, and insects, particularly moth and butterfly larvae, increase dramatically in deciduous forests (Janzen 1973; chapters 7 and 8). Seasonal changes in abundance and distribution of arthropods force some insectivorous birds (e.g., Northern-barred Woodcreeper, Streaked-headed Woodcreeper, Banded Wren) to follow these fluctuations to fulfill their energy requirements.

3. Shifting diet on a seasonal basis. Like arthropods, blooming and fruiting are also

seasonal in dry forests. A large proportion of trees flower during the dry season and produce their fruits between the second half of this season and beginning of the rainy season (Frankie et al. 1974; Opler et al. 1976). As a consequence of this phenological pattern, fruits and bird-pollinated flowers may become scarce during part of the year. Such fluctuations in food resource availability may influence some species (e.g., Rose-throated Becard, Masked Tityra, Bright-rumped Attila, Streak-backed Oriole) to change their diet on a seasonal basis.

A direct consequence of dry-forest seasonality on the avifauna composition is the absence of frugivores and specialized insectivorous groups. For example, families with a predominance of frugivorous species (e.g., Ramphastidae, Cotingidae, Tharupidae) are poorly represented (or absent) in dry forests. Similarly, specialized groups of insectivores, such as furnarids, that feed mostly in moss, vines, and tangles of vegetation and formicarids, the army ant followers, are practically absent in dry forests (table 12.2).

AQUATIC BIRDS

Some aquatic habitats, such as lagoons and swamps, are seasonal in Costa Rican dry forests and practically disappear after two or three months of drought. Consequently, the majority of birds that require these habitats must migrate to avoid food shortages. Thus, presence of waterbirds in the dry-forest region is largely determined by availability of their habitats and food resources. Dependence of aquatic birds on specific habitats increases because very few species are inherently able to shift habitats or diet (or both) when drought makes these habitats unsuitable. Hence, the relatively low flexibility in habitat use and diet of aquatic birds makes a large proportion of these species more susceptible to even slight environmental disturbances than terrestrial species in terms of their reproduction and survival.

HABITAT DETERIORATION AND CONSERVATION OF THE DRY-FOREST AVIFAUNA

Destruction of natural habitats in Costa Rica caused by expansion of the agricultural frontier, cattle raising, and logging activities has been devastating (Janzen 1986; Sader and Joyce 1988; chapters 1, 21, and 23). Forest management strategies that have been recently implemented by the Costa Rican government have done little to reduce the high rate of deforestation in the country (Barrantes et al. 1999). Lack of knowledge in basic reproductive biology of tropical trees (e.g., phenology, sex ratio, pollination, seed dispersal, germination) makes forest management unsustainable in Costa Rica. Despite this situation, during the past several decades, the combination of cattle ranching, expansion of agricultural lands (e.g., rice, sugarcane), and lumbering activities has greatly reduced this ecosystem, the most threatened in Costa Rica (Janzen 1988), to small patches surrounded by second-growth areas and large extensions of pastureland. The establishment of national reserves such as Parque Nacional Santa Rosa, Parque Nacional Palo Verde, and Parque Nacional Guanacaste has, however, gradually permitted some regeneration, at least in these protected areas.

The massive destruction of this ecosystem has obviously affected populations of many bird species in the region and has already caused local extinction of at least one species (the White-faced Whistling Duck [*Dendrocygna viduata*]; table 12.3). A total of 26 species show a notable decline in population size (the population of most of these species has decreased along their whole distribution, but we refer to Costa Rican dry forest in particular) (Rodríguez-Ramírez and Hernández-Benavidez 1999). Both aquatic and terrestrial species are affected by human alteration of natural habitats, although the effect of such changes is proportionally higher on waterbirds (table 12.3). More terrestrial species can overcome the alteration of primary habitats and subsist in altered or areas in regeneration

TABLE 12.3

Conservation Status, Habitat, and Possible Causes for Changes in Population Size and Survivorship of Dry-Forest Birds

	CONSERVATION STATUS	HABITAT	POSSIBLE CAUSES
ARDEIDAE (HERONS, EGRETS)			
Botaurus pinnatus	T	a	Habitat destruction
Ixobrychus exilis	T	a	Habitat destruction
THRESKIORNITHIDAE (IBISES, SPOONBILLS)			
Ajaia ajaja	ID	a	Habitat destruction, nesting predation?, water pollution?
CICONIIDAE (STORKS)			
Jabiru mycteria	ID	a	Habitat destruction
Sarcoramphus papa	ID	t	Habitat destruction
ANATIDAE (DUCKS)			
*Dendrocygna viduata**	E	a	Unknown, habitat destruction?
Cairina moschata	T	a	Hunting, habitat destruction
Nomonyx dominicus	T	a	Habitat destruction, hunting
ACCIPITRIDAE (HAWKS, EAGLES)			
*Pandion haliaetus**	T	a	Habitat destruction (mainly in breeding areas)
*Leptodon cayanensis**	T	t	Habitat destruction (mainly in breeding areas)
Chondrohierax uncinatus	T	t	Habitat destruction
Rostrhamus sociabilis	T	a	Habitat destruction
Busarellus nigricollis	T	a	Habitat destruction, water pollution?
*Circus cyaneus**	T	a	Habitat destruction (breeding and wintering areas)
Geranospiza caerulescens	T	t	Habitat destruction
Buteogallus urubitinga	T	t	Habitat destruction
*Parabuteo unicinctus**	ID	t	Unknown, habitat destruction?
Buteo albicaudatus	T	t	Habitat destruction
Spizaetus ornatus	T	t	Habitat destruction
FALCONIDAE (FALCONS, CARACARAS)			
Micrastur semitorquatus	T	t	Habitat destruction
Falco peregrinus	ID	t	Habitat destruction, water pollution (breeding and wintering areas)

TABLE 12.3 *(continued)*

	CONSERVATION STATUS	HABITAT	POSSIBLE CAUSES
PSITTACIDAE (PARROTS)			
Aratinga canicularis	T	t	Habitat destruction, poaching
Ara macao	ID	t	Habitat destruction, poaching
*Amazona auropalliata**	ID	t	Habitat destruction, poaching
TROCHILIDAE (HUMMINGBIRDS)			
Amazilia boucardi	T	t	Habitat destruction
VIREONIDAE (VIREOS, GREENLETS)			
*Vireo pallens**	T	t	Habitat destruction
ICTERIDAE (ORIOLES, BLACKBIRDS)			
*Icterus pectoralis**	T	t	Unknown, poaching?, habitat destruction?

Source: Following Rodríguez-Ramírez and Hernández-Benavidez (1999).

Note: Conservation status: T = threatened; ID = in danger; E = locally extinct. Habitat: a = aquatic; t = terrestrial. * = Redefined status based on our observations.

than aquatic birds. As expected, destruction of natural environments is the main factor that affects population size and increases risk of extinction in many species (Table 12.3). Yet other factors, such as water pollution, hunting, and poaching, also affect the survival of birds. Unfortunately, the available habitat for many threatened or endangered species seems insufficient for their populations to recover. Therefore, if an intensive program of restoration in unprotected areas is not implemented in the near future, local extinction will be the most likely fate for several of these species, as in the case of the White-faced Whistling Duck.

RECOMMENDATIONS FOR THE CONSERVATION OF DRY-FOREST BIRDS

The extinction of a large number of dry-forest birds seems imminent if current practices in land development and use continue without appropriate measures to conserve all wildlife in the region. Thus, to reverse or at least lessen this trend, it is necessary to take several actions:

1. Protection of aquatic habitats. Despite international agreements and treaties, many swamps and seasonal lagoons in the northwestern region of Costa Rica are illegally being drained and transformed into rice fields. This clearly reflects the passive attitude of Costa Rican government authorities toward this issue and their unwillingness to deal with it. To solve this problem, national laws and international treaties need to be enforced immediately (chapters 21–23).

2. Connection between dry-forest patches. The majority of dry-forest tracts, including some protected areas (e.g., Parque Nacional Palo Verde), are interspersed within a deforested area. It is extremely important to connect these patches to lessen the loss of diversity caused by isolation. The first step is to consolidate the system of conservation areas in northwestern Costa Rica; the Tempisque Conservation Area, in particular, would benefit from a change in the way these conservation areas are administered. Since its creation, this area has been ruled

more by political interests than by the biological interest of preserving its unique natural ecosystem. Unfortunately, the solution to this problem also depends on decisions of the government, whose interest in the conservation of natural ecosystems has steadily decreased over the past several years. We consider it important for national and international nongovernmental organizations interested in the conservation of dry forests to assume more leadership in the future and have a positive influence on decision makers in the Costa Rican government.

3. Elimination of fire. Annually, thousands of hectares of dry forest are destroyed by fires that are caused by humans (chapters 19 and 21). In addition to resulting in the deaths of many individual birds, fires affect most (if not all) species indirectly because food resource and reproductive substrates decrease drastically. Thus, a very aggressive campaign and environmental education program are imperative to eliminate fires in the dry forest (chapter 19). In the Guanacaste Conservation Area, a program of environmental education with a focus on local primary schools has been in progress for more than ten years. Similar programs for children and adults need to be implemented in the whole region if positive results in the conservation and protection of dry forests are expected.

Other activities, such as deforestation, hunting, poaching, and chemical contamination in rivers, also increase the risk of local extinction of many aquatic and terrestrial dry-forest birds. Unfortunately, these problems also receive little attention from the Costa Rican government, particularly the Ministry of Environment and Energy (MINAE).

REFERENCES

Barrantes, G. 1998. Reproductive activity of birds in a mangrove swamp in northwest Costa Rica. *Revista de Biología Tropical* 46:1163–66.

Barrantes, G., and A. Pereira. 1992. Abundancia y fluctuaciones de aves limnícolas (Charadriiformes) en una playa fangosa de Chomes, Costa Rica. *Revista de Biología Tropical* 40:303–8.

Barrantes, G., Q. Jiménez, J. Lobo, T. Maldonado, M. Quesada, and R. Quesada. 1999. Evaluación de los planes de manejo forestal autorizados en el periodo 1997–1999 en la Península de Osa. Cumplimiento de normas técnicas ambientales e impacto sobre el bosque natural. Unpublished report. Funcación Cecropia. 96 pp.

Borchert, R. 1983. Phenology and control flowering in tropical trees. *Biotropica* 15:81–89.

Collias, N. E., and E. C. Collias. 1984. *Nest building and bird behavior.* Princeton, N.J.: Princeton University Press.

Frankie, G. W., H. G. Baker, and P. A. Opler. 1974. Comparative phenological studies in tropical wet and dry forests in the lowlands of Costa Rica. *Journal of Ecology* 62:881–919.

Gómez, L. D. 1986. *Vegetación de Costa Rica. Apuntes para una biogeografía costarricense.* San José: Editorial Universidad Estatal a Distancia. 327 pp.

Haffer, J. 1974. *Avian speciation in tropical South America.* Publications of the Nuttall Ornithological Club, No. 14. Cambridge, Mass.: Nuttall Ornithological Club. 390 pp.

Hartshorn, G. S. 1983. Plants: Introduction. In *Costa Rican natural history,* ed. D. H. Janzen, 118–57. Chicago: University of Chicago Press.

Janzen, D. H. 1973. Sweep samples of tropical foliage insects: Effects of seasons, vegetation types, elevation, time of day, and insularity. *Ecology* 54: 687–708.

———. 1985. Heterogeneity of potential food abundance for tropical small landbirds. In *Migrant birds in the Neotropics: Ecology, behavior, distribution, and conservation,* ed. A. Keast and E. S. Morton, 545–52. Washington, D.C.: Smithsonian Institution Press.

———. 1986. *Guanacaste National Park: Tropical ecological and cultural restoration.* San José: Editorial Universidad Estatal a Distancia. 103 pp.

———. 1988. Management of habitat fragmentation in a tropical dry forest: Growth. *Annals of the Missouri Botanical Garden* 75:105–16.

Janzen, D. H., and F. G. Stiles. 1983. *Buteo magnirostris* (gavilán chapulinero, roadside hawk). In *Costa Rican natural history,* ed. D. H. Janzen, 551–52. Chicago: University of Chicago Press.

Jiménez, J. A., and R. Soto. 1985. Patrones regionales en la estructura y composición florística de los manglares de la costa pacífica de Costa Rica. *Revista de Biología Tropical* 33:25–37.

Karr, J. R. 1976. Birds of Panama: Biogeography and ecological dynamics. In *The botany and natural history of Panamá*, ed. W. G. D'Arcy and M. Correa, 77–93. Monograph Systematics in Botany 10. St. Louis: Missouri Botanical Garden.

King, J. R. 1973. Energetics of reproduction in birds. In *Breeding biology of birds*, ed. D. S. Farner, 78–107. Washington, D.C.: National Academy of Sciences.

Murphy, P. G., and A. E. Lugo. 1995. Dry forests of Central America and the Caribbean. In *Seasonally dry tropical forests*, ed. S. H. Bullock, H. A. Mooney, and E. Medina, 9–34. Cambridge: Cambridge University Press.

Opler, P. A., G. W. Frankie, and H. G. Baker. 1976. Rainfall as a factor in the release, timing, and synchronization of anthesis by tropical trees and shrubs. *Journal of Biogeography* 3:231–36.

———. 1980. Comparative phenological studies of treelet and shrub species in tropical wet and dry forests in the lowlands of Costa Rica. *Journal of Ecology* 68:167–88.

Ricklefs, R. E. 1992. Embryonic development period and the prevalence of avian blood parasites. *Proceedings of the National Academy of Sciences* 89:4722–25.

Rodríguez-Ramírez, J., and J. Hernández-Benavidez. 1999. Especies de flora y fauna silvestre con poblaciones reducidas y en peligro de extinción. Unpublished report. Ministerio del Ambiente y Energía y Sistema de Areas de Conservación. 28 pp.

Sader, A., and A. T. Joyce. 1988. Deforestation rates and trends in Costa Rica, 1940 to 1983. *Biotropica* 20:11–19.

Slud, P. 1964. The birds of Costa Rica: Distribution and ecology. *Bulletin of the American Museum of Natural History* 128:1–430.

———. 1980. The birds of Hacienda Palo Verde, Guanacaste, Costa Rica. *Smithsonian Contributions to Zoology* 292:1–92.

Stiles, F. G. 1983. Birds: Introduction. In *Costa Rican natural history*, ed. D. H. Janzen, 502–30. Chicago: University of Chicago Press.

Stiles, F. G., and A. F. Skutch. 1989. *A guide to the birds of Costa Rica*. Ithaca, N.Y.: Cornell University Press. 511 pp.

Stotz, D. F., J. W. Fitzpatrick, T. A. Parker III, and D. K. Moskovits. 1996. *Neotropical birds: Ecology and conservation*. Chicago: University of Chicago Press. 478 pp.

Tomlinson, P. B. 1986. *The botany of mangroves*. Cambridge Tropical Biology Series. New York: Cambridge University Press. 413 pp.

Webb, S. D., and A. Rancy. 1996. Late Cenozoic evolution of the Neotropical mammal fauna. In *Evolution and environment in tropical America*, ed. J. B. C. Jackson, A. F. Budd, and A. G. Coates, 335–58. Chicago: University of Chicago Press.

CHAPTER 13

An Ultrasonically Silent Night

THE TROPICAL DRY FOREST WITHOUT BATS

Richard K. LaVal

WITHOUT BATS, in their varied roles as pollinators of commercially important trees, seed dispersers critical for forest succession, and consummate predators of nocturnal insects, the tropical dry-forest life zone would be a vastly different place. Despite the unquestioned importance of these common mammals, few scientific papers have dealt specifically with bat conservation until very recently. Fenton (1997) has clarified the relationship between recent advances in bat biology and bat conservation, and a book edited by Kunz and Racey (1998) addresses bat conservation issues worldwide. Ceballos (1995) discusses vertebrate conservation in the dry forest, with special emphasis on the importance of bats.

For the purposes of this chapter, "dry forest" refers to a deciduous-forested life zone that extends at low elevations along the entire Pacific coast from west-central Mexico to northwestern Costa Rica, with rainfall mostly less than 1,500 mm. Much of this forest has been con-verted to nonforest land uses, primarily agricultural (Janzen 1988). Although a large portion of the land area included would be classified as tropical dry forest under the Holdridge Life Zone System (Holdridge 1967), there are areas of moist forest (to the south) and very dry forest (to the north) that I include in the dry-forest life zone because of floral and faunal similarities.

DIVERSITY AND ABUNDANCE OF BATS IN THE DRY FOREST

Ninety-two bat species occur in the dry forest as defined in the previous paragraph (based primarily on maps in Hall 1981). Of these, 15 are endemic to the dry forest or nearly so. Sixteen are restricted to Mexico, 67 occur in both Mexico and Central America, and 9 are found only in Central America. Most Central American species also occur in South America. In comparison, there are 93 species in the tropical wet forest of the Caribbean lowlands, extending from east-

TABLE 13.1
Conservation Priorities for Dry-Forest Bats Based on Distribution and Abundance

PRIORITY	CATEGORY	NUMBER OF SPECIES
1	Locally scarce, with restricted distribution	12
2	Locally abundant, with restricted distribution	5
3	Locally scarce, with widespread distribution	53
4	Locally abundant, with widespread distribution	22

central Mexico to Costa Rica. Only 3 of these are endemic. If, as noted by Arita and Ortega (1998), there are a total of 166 bat species in Mesoamerica (Mexico plus Central America), then more than half of those occur in the dry forest.

In Costa Rica, where detailed surveys of bat faunas have been carried out at several sites, an interesting comparison of species numbers in dry forest, wet forest, and premontane wet forest/lower montane wet forest can be made. Studies in Guanacaste Province at Santa Rosa National Park, Lomas Barbudal Biological Reserve, and Hacienda La Pacifica (Fleming et al. 1972; LaVal and Fitch 1977; Wilson 1983; Fleming 1988) have documented a total of 55 dry-forest species. In the wet forest of La Selva 68 species have been captured (Timm and LaVal 1998). As expected, fewer species (46) are known in the premontane and lower montane forests of Monteverde (Timm and LaVal 2000). In summary, dry forest in Costa Rica is only slightly less diverse than the wet forest (see maps in chapter 1).

Although actual bat abundance is difficult to estimate, it is possible at least to compare mist-net capture rates. One such comparison can be made using selected data from LaVal and Fitch (1977) and Fleming (1988): bats were caught at a rate of 1.05 bats per net-hour at La Selva in wet forest and 1.41 per net-hour at Santa Rosa in dry forest. Over a period of one year, I mist-netted 1,208 bats at La Selva, and over a ten-year period, Fleming (1988) netted 11,627 at Santa Rosa. Clearly, these are abundant animals, which, because of the ecological roles they play, strongly affect the dry-forest ecosystem.

CONSERVATION ISSUES FOR DRY-FOREST BATS

SPECIES OF SPECIAL CONSERVATION CONCERN

Using a scheme proposed by Marinho-Filho and Sazima (1998) for illustrating the relative rarity of bats for conservation purposes, I categorized the 92 species of Mesoamerican dry-forest bats as shown in table 13.1. Assignment to these categories was by necessity rather subjective because data on abundance or distribution (or both) are sparse or lacking for many dry-forest species. However, to the extent that the focus in conservation efforts reflects concerns for individual species, the species in categories 1 and 2 (table 13.1) should be given the most attention. This includes most of the 15 species that are endemic (or mostly endemic) to North American dry forest. The most seriously threatened species are those that have the most restricted distribution. These include *Musonycteris harrisoni, Myotis findleyi, M. carteri,* and *Rhogeessa mira,* all of which seem to be uncommon and restricted to very small areas of western Mexico. *Artibeus inopinatus* is in the same category but is restricted to a small portion of western Central America. Other scarce dry-forest species with restricted distributions include *Micronycteris schmidtorum, Choeronycteris mexicana, Rhogeessa genowaysi, R. alleni, Nyctinomops femorosaccus, N. macrotis,* and *Eumops underwoodi.* Five additional species have restricted distributions but are relatively abundant, including *Balantiopteryx plicata, Glossophaga alticola, G. morenoi, Artibeus hirsutus,* and *Rhogeessa parvula*. The others are somewhat buffered from local extinction events by having a larger distributional area.

Using a different set of criteria, Wilson (1996: app. 9.1, pp. 172–77) listed 14 dry-forest species as being endangered, vulnerable, or potentially vulnerable. "Endangered" means that "the taxon is in danger of extinction, and its survival is unlikely if the causal factors continue operating." "Vulnerable" signifies "that the taxon likely will be relisted under the endangered category in the near future, if causal factors do not change." "Potentially vulnerable" indicates that "the taxon has small world populations, occupies only a small percentage of its preferred habitat, or occupies a very specific, limited habitat, thus is faced with present or foreseeable pressures that could lead to its becoming vulnerable." Of the 14 listed dry-forest species, he considered only *Myotis velifer* as endangered (*M. velifer* is a common species in some parts of its range, for example, in western Texas; further, it does not occur in dry forest as it is defined herein). *Leptonycteris curasoae*, *L. nivilis*, and *Eumops glaucinus* were classified as vulnerable, and the rest (*Noctilio leporinus*, *Mormoops megalophyla*, *Chrotopterus auritus*, *Lonchorhina aurita*, *Micronycteris minuta*, *M. sylvestris*, *Vampyrum spectrum*, *Choeronycteris mexicana*, *Musonycteris harrisoni*, and *Rhogeessa mira*) are potentially vulnerable.

Using yet another set of criteria, Arita and Ortega (1998) listed ten species of dry-forest bats as being of critical or special concern. The critical species are scarce with restricted distribution and are dry-forest endemics. Bats of special concern have traits that make them important for conservation or have habitats susceptible to perturbation. Included in this category are species that are endemic or quasi-endemic to Mesoamerica (as defined earlier) and that show one or more of the following characteristics: (1) widespread, but with very low population levels; (2) habitat specialists; (3) ecological specialists; (4) migratory; (5) potential keystone species; and/or (6) roost in caves used by vampire bats. Among those Arita and Ortega (1998) considered of critical status were *Artibeus inopinatus*,

Musonycteris harrisoni, *Myotis findleyi*, and *Rhogeessa mira*. Those of special concern included *Artibeus hirsutus*, *Choeronycteris mexicana*, *Hylonycteris underwoodi*, *Leptonycteris nivalis*, *Myotis elegans*, and *Rhogeessa alleni* (*H. underwoodi* and *M. elegans* are not dry-forest species as here defined). In a subsequent report Arita and Santos-del-Prado (1999) pointed out that 11 species of Mexican nectar-feeding bats occur mostly in dry forest and are particularly at risk because of their specialized diets.

It is clear that, irrespective of the different criteria used to compile the three lists, many species appear on all three, some on two, and a few only on one. Unless new data show that some of these species have large, relatively safe populations, it would be prudent to consider all listed species as subject to some level of threat and therefore deserving of special conservation efforts.

MIGRATION

Although long-distance migration of certain species, most notably *Leptonycteris curasoae* and *Tadarida brasiliensis*, has been well documented (Cockrum 1969, 1991; Fleming 1991, 1997; Rojas-Martinez et al. 1999) and must be carefully considered in any conservation strategy, short-range seasonal movements into and out of the dry-forest zone have been little studied. These seasonal movements could be primarily elevational migrations, as have been amply documented for birds (in Costa Rica by Stiles 1988) and butterflies (also in Costa Rica; see chapter 8). In western Mexico, Alvarez and González-Quintero (1970) and Herrera-Montalvo (1997) presented convincing evidence that glossophagine bats displayed elevational movements. Timm and LaVal (2000) demonstrated that two common dry-forest species (*Sturnira lilium* and *Artibeus lituratus*) are seasonally absent from Monteverde (premontane wet forest) and probably migrate elevationally in search of preferred fruiting plants. Stoner (1997) and Stoner and Timm (chapter 5) suggested, based on data from Palo Verde National Park (Tempisque Conservation Area), that several frugivorous and nectariv-

TABLE 13.2

Numbers of Bat-Serviced Trees and Shrubs in the Dry Forest (Santa Rosa National Park), the Wet Forest of La Selva, and the Premontane Wet and Lower Montane Rain Forests of Monteverde

	DRY FOREST	WET FOREST	PREMONTANE AND LOWER MONTANE FORESTS
Number pollinated	23	21[a]	14
Number seed-dispersed	32	>60	59
Total bar-serviced	57	>81	73
Percentage of total species	21.9	>13.3	8.4
Total species of trees and shrubs	260	608	874

[a]Includes all growth forms, not just trees and shrubs.

orous species migrate out of the dry forest seasonally. In western Mexico, Iñiguez (1997) noted that the most common species in his cloud forest study area, *Sturnira ludovici,* migrated out of the area seasonally. He believes that they migrate into the dry forest (pers. comm), and indeed, that species is known in dry forest in western Mexico south to El Salvador (Ramírez-Pulido et al. 1977). There is reason to believe that future studies will document extensive movement of bats into and out of the dry forest.

From a conservation perspective this means that some species will not be adequately protected until all habitats used within their migratory pathways are safeguarded. In the case of long-distance migrants, habitat protection at both ends of the migratory route is crucial but is made more difficult for *Leptonycteris* and *Tadarida,* as noted earlier, because they cross international boundaries. Fortunately, both Mexico and the United States have recently taken initial steps toward protecting migratory bats ("Binational partnership" 1994; Walker 1995).

BATS AS DISPERSERS OF SEEDS AND POLLEN: THE MAINTENANCE OF FOREST DIVERSITY

Bats are commonly regarded as among the most important of all dispersers. In a recent study, conducted in Chiapas, Mexico (Medellín and Gaona 1999: 478), the authors stated, "Since bats dispersed more seeds than birds (primarily to disturbed areas and consisting primarily of pioneer species), they are likely to play an important role in successional and restoration processes among habitats as structurally and vegetationally different as cornfields, old fields, cacao plantations, and forest."

Detailed lists of dispersers have been compiled only for certain localities in Costa Rica's dry forest. In Santa Rosa National Park about 23 tree and shrub species are bat-pollinated, and another 32 species have bat-dispersed fruits (Heithaus et al. 1975; Fleming 1988; W. A. Haber pers. comm.). Thus, about 55 of a total of 260 species (B. Hammel and N. Zamora pers. comm.) of trees and shrubs are currently known to be serviced by bats (table 13.2). Among these are both common primary forest trees and successional trees and shrubs that are often among the first colonists following human disturbances such as fire or agricultural clearing. Commercially important dry-forest trees, such as *Pochota quinata* (Bombacaceae), are also bat-pollinated. At Chamela Biological Station (Estación de Investigación, Experimentación, y Difusión "Chamela," Jalisco, Mexico), perhaps 25 to 35 species have seeds that are bat-dispersed (A. Pérez pers. comm.), suggesting that bats are important seed dispersers throughout the Mesoamerican dry-forest zone. Because phyllostomid fruit bats

FIGURE 13.1. *Sturnira ludovici* (Stenoderminae: Phyllostomidae) about to pick a fruit of *Solanum umbellatum* (Solanaceae), a widespread pioneer species with small seeds that are ingested and later defecated by the bat.

often defecate in flight, they are more likely than birds (which habitually defecate while perched) to drop seeds into deforested areas.

In the tropical wet forest of La Selva, which has much higher plant diversity, fewer species (21 trees, shrubs, and epiphytes) are known to be bat-pollinated (M. Tschapka pers. comm.). An unknown number have seeds that are bat-dispersed, but it must be a fairly large number (>60 and perhaps >75), considering that most species of *Piper* have seeds that are bat-dispersed and 44 species occur at La Selva and also that 17 species of *Ficus* (whose seeds are often bat-dispersed) are found at La Selva. López (1996), examining bat fecal samples at La Selva, found seeds from 42 species of plants during the period January–August 1995. His count is likely an underestimate, as he would have missed species fruiting later in the year as well as species with large seeds that are dropped without being passed through the digestive tract. In the premontane wet and lower montane rain forests of Monteverde, also with much higher plant diversity than dry forest, only 14 trees and shrubs are

bat-pollinated, but 59 have seeds that are dispersed by bats (Murray et al. 2000). As evident from table 13.2, a higher percentage of trees and shrubs are bat-serviced in the dry forest. Bats not only service many kinds of plants but also handle/visit a vast number of fruits/flowers. For example, Kalko (1997a) calculated that fruit bats on 15-km² Barro Colorado Island, Panama, dispersed seeds of 16 million to 32 million fruits per year. Disappearance of bats would likely precipitate major changes in the structure of the dry-forest community.

Two widespread groups of dry-forest plants largely pollinated by bats deserve special mention. The columnar cacti are composed of various genera, and many species occur conspicuously throughout the dry forest. The highest rates of species diversity and abundance are found in the drier portions of western Mexico. In fact, in many areas these are the dominant plants, reaching abundance levels of 1,650 plants per hectare, with 70 species in Mexico alone. Two-thirds of these species show characteristic adaptations for bat pollination, and several spe-

FIGURE 13.2. *Glossophaga commissarisi* (Glossophaginae: Phyllostomidae) pollinating the flowers of a common tropical forest liana, *Mucuna urens* (Fabaceae). Apparently, only bats can open the flowers and successfully pollinate this plant.

cies studied in western Mexico depend entirely or primarily on bats as pollinators (Valiente-Banuet et al. 1996). Another abundant group of dry-forest plants (occurring in other life zones, as well) pollinated by bats are *Agave* species, some of which are widely cultivated commercially for fiber and for distilling tequila, especially in Mexico. Arita and Wilson (1987) reported that seed set in agaves drops by a factor of 3,000 if not pollinated by bats. Bats responsible for pollination of columnar cacti and agaves may well be regarded as keystone species in many parts of the dry forest.

BATS AS A BIOLOGICAL CONTROL OF INSECT PESTS

Aerial insectivores feed on a large variety of flying insects, but in most species studied to date, lepidopterans and coleopterans predominate in bats' diets. Dipterans (and sometimes other orders) are also important to some species (for examples, see Black 1974; Gardner 1977; Humphrey et al. 1983; Willig et al. 1993). Members of these insect orders include those insects most damaging to crops and human health.

Although few dietary studies exist for Neotropical insectivores, several have appeared for *T. brasiliensis,* which is common in parts of the dry forest and in the southern United States. *T. brasiliensis* in central Texas averaged nightly feeding rates of 39 percent to 73 percent of the bats' body weight (Kunz et al. 1995). These bats have a mean weight of 11.5 g. Because they live in cave colonies of millions, they must have a significant impact on insect populations, as was suggested by McCracken (1996). In a large colony of mormoopid bats (as many as 800,000) in western Mexico, a quantity estimated as high as 3,805 kg of insects per night was consumed (Bateman and Vaughan 1974). Kalko (1997a) calculated that one of 28 species of insectivorous bats on Barro Colorado Island, Panama, might eat 1.3 million large insects per year. One species of *Rhogeessa,* a genus that reaches maximum species diversity in the dry forest of Mexico, was recently studied by Sosa et al. (1996) in

Venezuela. They found that the diet of *R. minutilla*, in what is probably very dry forest, was composed of 42.5 percent Diptera, 13.3 percent Lepidoptera, 10.9 percent Coleoptera, and 18.2 percent Hymenoptera.

Because many species of insectivorous bats tend to be environmentally stratified, having preferred foraging spaces that often differ from those of other species (Fenton 1982, 1997; Findley 1993), the impact of foraging insectivorous bats is felt in almost all dry-forest microhabitats accessible to volant mammals. Since in-flight defecation is common, insectivorous bats may be important in nutrient transfer in ecosystems, acting as "nutrient pepper shakers" (Pierson 1998).

EFFECTS OF LARGE-SCALE HABITAT ALTERATION

As pointed out by Janzen (1988), only about 2 percent of the original Central American dry forest remains, and only about 0.1 percent has protected status (Maass 1995). According to Ceballos and García (1995), the largest remaining dry forests north of the equator are in western Mexico, although no specific figures are given. However, these authors give a deforestation rate of 300,000 ha per year, or 2 percent of total surviving Mexican dry forest per year. Although this is an appalling rate of deforestation, their data also imply that millions of hectares remain. Protected and otherwise undisturbed patches of dry forest are widely separated by a mosaic of disturbed habitats, mainly agricultural. These disturbed habitats vary widely in their usefulness to bats. In a study carried out in tropical wet/rain forest in southern Veracruz, sampling sites varied from those supporting essentially no bats (pastures) to mixed agricultural habitats (coffee, cocoa, citrus, and banana) whose species richness and abundance were only slightly less than that of nearby small patches of primary forest. About 80 percent of bat species known from large tracts of undisturbed forest in the region were captured in the study, with highest species diversity in primary forest patches (Estrada et al. 1993).

In another relevant investigation in French Guiana, a dam project resulted in the creation of fragments of land ranging in size from less than 5 ha to 40 ha (Granjon et al. 1996; Cosson et al. 1999). Bats were sampled in the fragments before the reservoir filled, and one year after the fragments became islands. The data demonstrated that the islands, even though separated from the "mainland" by relatively short distances, contained a significantly less diverse bat community, with a concomitant decrease in bat abundance. From this study, it appears that bats are less inclined to cross a barrier of water than a barrier composed of disturbed terrestrial habitats.

Although no equivalent studies have been done in dry forest, I suggest that a habitat mosaic similar to that described by Estrada et al. (1993), but in dry forest, may support a large percentage of the original bat species. Much depends on how the habitat has been modified. If most of it has been converted to pasture, only edges, steep ravines, and riparian strips remain to serve as bat habitat, and species richness and abundance will be low. Often, however, patches of clear-cut forest are allowed to regenerate, at least temporarily. Parklands often contain sizable areas of secondary forest in various stages of regeneration. For example, in Guanacaste Conservation Area in Costa Rica (104,000 ha), most of the protected area is regenerating dry forest, much of it having been pasture ten years ago. Because the conservation area contains patches of primary forest and older secondary forest, conservationists hope that most of the species diversity has been preserved.

Nevertheless, results of several studies suggest a significant change in the structure of bat faunas in disturbed versus primary forest, including the disappearance of certain groups of bats in deforested areas (LaVal and Fitch 1977; Fenton et al. 1992; Brosset et al. 1996; Kalko 1998; Simmons and Voss 1998; Wilson et al. 1998; Ochoa 2000). Notable is that in these studies populations and species diversity in the subfamily Phyllostominae were greatly reduced in disturbed habitats, making this a potential indicator group for measuring the degree of disturbance.

As pointed out by Brosset et al. (1996), habitats disturbed by humans often offer bats an abundance of bat-dispersed fruits, such as species of *Piper*, *Solanum*, *Cecropia*, and *Vismia*, which occur in early stage successional forest in most Neotropical life zones. The first three of these plant genera are widespread in dry forest, but *Piper* and *Cecropia* seem to be restricted to mesic habitats such as riparian strips in western Mexico, according to Lott (1993) and Alfredo Pérez (pers. comm.). They found bats to be much more abundant in these disturbed areas, with capture rates of 1.68 to 3.6 bats per net-hour, as contrasted with 0.16 to 0.45 per net-hour in undisturbed primary forest. Their data show that higher capture rates of a few species of fruit bats (Stenoderminae), especially of the genera *Artibeus*, *Carollia*, and *Sturnira*, were responsible for the increase in capture rates in disturbed habitats.

Studies in various areas, including dry forest, support these conclusions (Fleming et al. 1972; Heithaus et al. 1975; LaVal and Fitch 1977; Ramírez-Pulido and Armella 1987; Estrada et al. 1993; Ochoa 2000). In general these studies reported relatively low numbers and diversity of aerial insectivores, owing to the inadequacy of prevailing mist-net capture techniques. However, Kalko et al. (1996) and Kalko (1997b), using acoustic monitoring in Panama (tropical moist forest), demonstrated that insectivorous bats can be both common and diverse. My preliminary data from acoustic monitoring in Guanacaste suggest that insectivorous bats are also abundant there.

Species that roost in human habitations are frequently abundant in urban areas. This is evident in almost any town in the dry forest, where roosts of molossids in buildings can be easily located by odor, vocalizations, or exit flight observations. Insectivorous bats, however, may be affected in either a positive or negative manner by human constructs. For example, in Europe a study demonstrated that "some species of bats avoid open habitats for foraging, and these species may be negatively affected by patchiness or habitat fragmentation" (de Jong 1995: 246).

In another European study, *Eptesicus serotinus* were observed following corridors of woodland from their colonies to foraging areas, which were increasingly fragmented, resulting in higher commuting costs to bats (Robinson and Stebbings 1997).

Bats, being small mammals, can probably maintain adequate populations in smaller habitat patches than can larger mammals. However, rare bats, of which there are many species in the tropics, may require sizable protected areas to survive. This problem certainly deserves investigation. Without becoming embroiled in issues of minimum patch sizes required to protect viable ecosystems of organisms, it is clear that the destruction of most Central American dry forest, and the concomitant survival of only small isolated parcels, bode ill for the survival of dry-forest endemic and rare bat species.

GENERAL CONSERVATION ISSUES RELATING TO NEOTROPICAL BATS

THE VAMPIRE BAT AND RABIES PROBLEMS

In the past two decades a gradual improvement in the public image of bats, and thus increased public support for bat conservation, have occurred in Europe, the United States, and Canada. This is primarily due to the leadership of organizations such as Bat Conservation International (BCI) of Austin, Texas. However, fear and dislike of bats continue to be a major problem for conservation in Latin America and other parts of the world.

Rural Latin Americans tend to be very tolerant of wild animals as long as they have no effect that local people interpret as negative. Thus, most bats would be ignored and left in peace (even odoriferous roost colonies are rarely molested) if not for the common vampire, *Desmodus rotundus*. Because livestock, mainly cattle, are kept in large numbers throughout the Neotropics, vampires have multiplied and become abundant in most disturbed areas. They are regarded as pests because they can transmit the rabies virus to cattle during epidemics. An unchecked rabies epidemic may cause 30–50 percent herd mortality

(Constantine 1970). Vampire bats also may transmit rabies to humans, although normally few humans are bitten. However, in some areas, significant numbers of human rabies cases are attributed to vampire bats. During the period 1931–90, a total of 330 cases were documented as being bat-transmitted, mainly in Peru, Trinidad, Brazil, and Mexico (Schneider and Santos-Burgoa 1995).

Even where rabies is rare or unknown, cattle farmers dislike vampires because they inflict wounds that sometimes attract damaging screwworms or bacteria. (The recent depression of screwworm [*Cochliomyia hominivora*] populations by the sterile male release technique may actually have a beneficial effect on the reputation of vampires by reducing or eliminating this problem.) It is also widely believed that vampires weaken cattle by extracting large amounts of blood. A vampire may consume more than 20 ml nightly, and if an individual cow was attacked each night by multiple vampires, the animal might be significantly weakened (Lord 1988). However, a single bite resulting in a 20-ml blood loss would hardly be noticeable to such a large mammal. Effective control measures are now available, although they are neither simple nor inexpensive. The commonly used method involves applying "vampiricide" (an anticoagulant) to the fur of captured vampires. They are then released, and, on returning to their home colony, they are groomed by fellow colony members, thus ensuring their demise. This method has the advantage of causing little or no harm to other bat species (Lord 1988), assuming workers can recognize vampires so that other species are not treated with the toxic salve. Unfortunately, this is often not the case. For example, in Venezuela government technicians implementing a vampire control program were reported to apply the paste to all bats captured, including an endangered species (Ochoa 1992).

Regrettably, most rural Latin Americans are poorly informed about bats. A widely held belief is that all bats are vampires. The Spanish word for vampire (*vampiro*) is commonly used interchangeably with the word for bat (*murciélago*).

Thus, when a vampire problem exists, especially if rabies is involved, the usual reaction is to destroy any bats that can be found. The most easily located roosting bats are in caves and hollow trees, sites also used by vampires. Unfortunately, bats commonly found in such situations tend to be highly beneficial insectivores, frugivores, and nectarivores, which then become the object of extermination efforts. As stated by Lord (1988: 217), "For many years vampire bats have been destroyed by burning, gassing, and even dynamiting their roosts. Clearly, all bats, not just vampires, were killed." In recent decades government campaigns to eradicate vampires have resulted in the slaughter of countless thousands of harmless beneficial bats, yet vampires have remained common (Tuttle 1988). The answer is better environmental education among Latin Americans, especially in rural areas, with the help of international and national conservation organizations.

THREATS TO PREFERRED ROOST SITES

Nearly three decades ago Humphrey (1975: 321) pointed out that "the distribution and abundance of colonial Nearctic bats is determined largely by the availability of suitable roosts." He further emphasized that "the importance of roosts indicates that roosts should be managed as a key feature of the habitat of bats whose populations are in need of protection." It seems likely that a similar situation prevails in the Neotropics. However, although certain kinds of roost sites (caves, most obviously) are probably limiting for populations of some bat species, other types of roost sites (for example, among twigs and leaves of trees) are unlikely to be limiting. Findley (1993) provides a concise discussion of resource limitation. In some cases the availability of adequate foraging habitat may be the important limiting factor (Pierson 1998). Fortunately for those cases in which roost sites are especially important to a bat species, conservation efforts may be focused on these more easily and with less conservation investment than would be required to protect large areas of foraging habitat. As pointed out by McCracken (1988), roost site losses account for the most serious threats to bat populations. Sheffield et al. (1992) have provided a valuable set of guidelines for the protection of bat roosts. The impact of bat roost disturbance depends on three factors: the type of roost, the bats' fidelity to that roost, and the bats' propensity to exploit new roosts (Fenton and Rautenbach 1998). Clearly, without adequate biological knowledge of a species it is difficult to determine how its roost sites should best be protected or even if it is possible or practical to do so.

Caves. Arita (1993) demonstrated that 60 species (more than half) of Mexican bats used cave roosts. Of these, 29 used caves as their main roost; the remaining species used caves as alternate roosts. The author also noted that individual caves are used by as many as 13 species. Although caves are widespread and locally abundant, many parts of Central America and western Mexico have few or no caves because of tectonic and igneous development of mountain ranges. In some areas, such as Costa Rica's Nicoya Peninsula, interiors of caves are so inaccessible that bats have apparently been little disturbed. Fortunately, most of those caves are within a national park. However, in a survey of Mexican caves used or formerly used by *T. brasiliensis,* more than half of the ten most important overwintering caves have lost 95 to 100 percent of their bats ("Binational partnership" 1994). Some of these caves have been rendered unsuitable for future use by bats.

Arita (1993: 697) suggested that "an effective plan for the conservation of Mexican cave bats would require a double strategy: the protection of caves with unusually high diversity and multispecies populations and the management of cave bats of special concern (fragile, vulnerable, and endemic species)." As demonstrated in the United States, organizations of cave explorers working in conjunction with government agencies can cooperate to provide protection for important bat caves (Thorne 1990; McCabe 1995). Joint U.S.-Mexican efforts to protect remaining *T. brasiliensis* caves in Mexico have involved various government agencies in both countries, Mexican caving organizations, and bat biologists

("Binational partnership" 1994; Walker 1995). But hundreds of caves deserving protection have received little or no attention (in Mexico alone there are at least 215 in which bats are known to live, according to Arita [1993]), including most caves in Central America. Abandoned mines as bat habitat may be more common or important (or both) than caves in some areas to some species. Most such mines have yet to receive conservation attention in Mesoamerica, although a movement to protect mines used by bats has gained momentum in North America (Tuttle and Taylor 1998).

Crevices. Crevices in rocks and cliffs provide shelter for many bats, especially in the insectivorous family Molossidae (Kunz 1982). One direct threat to these colonies is rock-quarrying operations, which are often short-lived and may still provide roosting habitat when abandoned. Only a much higher conservation awareness than now exists could provide protection to these bats; fortunately, many are situated in inaccessible sites that provide excellent natural protection.

Tree Cavities. Hollow spaces within tree trunks are used by many species of bats, especially those in the common and diverse Neotropical family Phyllostomidae. At least 28 species in this family roost in tree cavities (Tuttle 1976). In extensive areas of primary forest, tree cavities may be the only available sites for bats that require this type of roosting habitat. Only primary forest provides trees of adequate size and age. Thus, both clear-cutting and selective logging tend to destroy most roost trees. Even in protected areas with mature trees, fires, a serious dry-forest problem, can result in death for those trees (pers. obs.). Few protected areas in the dry forest have adequate fire control programs, and fires burning into protected areas from adjoining private land during the dry season will gradually eliminate trees that provide cavity roosts for many bat species. A significant exception is the Guanacaste Conservation Area in Costa Rica, which uses firebreaks, firefighting teams, and local environmental education to reduce fire damage (G. Frankie pers. comm.). Because deforestation is so widespread in the dry forest, any forest patch or riparian strip with mature trees provides important habitat to cavity-roosting bats and should be protected. It is likely that cavity roost space is limiting to many dry-forest bat species.

Foliage, Tree Limbs, and Similar Roosts. Many species of Neotropical bats roost on the bark of limbs and trunks, as well as within dense vegetation, rolled leaves, or tents constructed from leaves by the bats themselves (Kunz 1982). Adequate roost sites can often be found in secondary forest or even in mixed agricultural habitats. These species are the least threatened from the standpoint of roosting habitat loss.

Anthropogenic Roosts. Humans have created a myriad of structures for many uses. These usually occupy space that was once available as bat foraging or roosting habitat. Nevertheless, in many of these structures new types of roosting spaces become available to bats, especially cave-, crevice-, and cavity-roosting species (Kunz 1982). In North America *Eptesicus fuscus, Myotis lucifugus,* and *M. yumanensis* are found almost entirely in buildings during the summer (Kunz 1982), and several dry-forest species, especially in the genus *Molossus,* are usually found in spaces under metal roofs. Tunnels, culverts, mines, and similar structures are frequently used by cave bats (Kunz 1982). Finally, introduced plants have frequently proved to be suitable roost sites for foliage- and surface-roosting bats.

Thus, human activity has unwittingly provided roost sites to replace many of those that have disappeared with forest clearing and disturbance of caves. Unfortunately, appropriate foraging resources may not exist in proximity to these potential roost sites, especially for more specialized species. As noted, species diversity seems to decrease rapidly as levels of disturbance increase. Further, bats are often considered unwelcome guests, notwithstanding that many of the reasons for their poor reputation are invalid. Pierson (1998) opined that negative effects of human alterations, in general, outweigh positive effects.

As people have finally begun to realize that bats are worthwhile neighbors, mainly in North America and Europe, they have designed artificial roost structures ("bat houses"), of which thousands have now been erected. In one North American campaign, occupancy rates of up to 50 percent have been reported (Tuttle and Hensley 1993). A recent news note in *Bats* magazine (April 1999: 14) mentions occupancy rates of 75 percent. When these bat houses are placed in sites where roosting space is limiting, they could be a boon for some species. However, bat houses as currently designed may not help those species with the most restrictive roost requirements, and there has been little or no experimentation with artificial roost structures in the dry forest or elsewhere in the Neotropics. Still, the potential exists for the implementation of successful designs.

OTHER ANTHROPOGENIC EFFECTS ON BAT HABITAT

Habitat Destruction. Perhaps the most serious problem to be addressed is the replacement of natural habitats with disturbed habitats. It is almost certain that the dry-forest zone of Mesoamerica was covered with forest when Europeans first arrived (about 500 years ago), even though small areas have been cleared for agriculture for at least 5,000 years (Murphy and Lugo 1995). Today approximately 2 percent of Central American dry forest remains in pristine condition (Janzen 1988). A much larger but unquantified area remains in western Mexico (Ceballos and García 1995). Surviving forest is a patchwork of small tracts separated by various kinds of disturbed habitat. Much of this disturbed habitat supports an abundance of bats of low diversity. Species that are largely absent from disturbed areas may all be considered at risk, especially if most of the remaining Central American dry forest is to be cut. Relatively small protected zones in parks and reserves, mostly in the Guanacaste Conservation Area and the Chamela-Cuixmala, Manantlán, and La Sepultura Biosphere Reserves, already exist, but there is potential to protect much more (Ceballos and García 1995, 1996). If *only* these areas are protected in the long run, those "at risk" species that do not occur in one of the protected zones will likely become extinct, unless they are also found in large protected tracts in other life zones.

With approximately 2,700 km separating western Mexico and Guanacaste, and dry-forest patches in general being small and widely separated, there is little chance of establishing protected corridors between patches. As stated by Janzen (1983) and documented for bats by Estrada et al. (1993) in Mexico, primary forest patches have lower diversity than large tracts of undisturbed forest, and the smaller the patch, the lower the diversity. Because Mesoamerican dry forest extends through six relatively poor third world countries, each with differing conservation priorities and resources, the outlook for any broadly based program to protect, much less to increase, dry forest is dim.

Toxic Chemicals. A clear but hardly documented threat to Neotropical bats is the poorly controlled use of agricultural and other toxic chemicals. It is generally believed that control of these chemicals is more lax in Latin America than in North America and Europe. However, this kind of information is rarely published, and in the opinion of two biologists (D. R. Clark and M. Mora pers. comm.) who study effects of pesticides on wildlife, there is no firm evidence that this is true. On the contrary, the total amount of pesticides applied per hectare has been and remains much greater in the southwestern United States (where migratory bats are found) than in Latin America, according to Clark and Mora. Clark's analyses of *T. brasiliensis* (a migratory species) from Carlsbad Caverns, New Mexico, indicates that bats accumulate more DDE during their summer stay in the United States than during their winter in Mexico. Clark and Mora also pointed out that many studies of migratory birds (with the exception of one study of peregrine falcons) have failed to demonstrate that birds accumulate more pesticide residues while in Latin America than in the United States. Finally, they note an almost complete lack of scientific studies of the effect of pesticide applications on wildlife in Latin America.

Pesticides have sometimes been connected with bat mortality in the United States, although such studies have been relatively few. One example is the destruction of a cave colony of endangered *Myotis grisescens* in Missouri by toxic levels of pesticide residues (Clark et al. 1978; Clark et al. 1983). Residues of toxic compounds were taken from tissues of 23 species of bats by Clark (1981). Samples of bat guano from nine major bat caves in Mexico all showed residues of dangerous pesticides, but they were not yet at toxic levels (Clark et al. 1995). It is safe to say that few dead and dying bats are found and taken to laboratories for testing of toxic chemical residues. Therefore, although the extent of this threat remains unknown, I suggest that extensive spraying of toxic chemicals for agricultural purposes must have locally serious effects on bat populations in the dry-forest zone, if for no other reason than the destruction of the bats' prey. A ray of hope is that current progress in the use of biological controls in place of chemicals may eventually lead to reduced mortality from this cause.

Human Population Growth. The overriding threat to the dry forest and its biota is human population pressure, which tends to exacerbate all other negative effects of human activity on bats. Murphy and Lugo (1995) emphasized that the population density of humans in the dry-forest zone of Guatemala, Honduras, Nicaragua, and Costa Rica was more than twice that of moist forest and 6.6 times as dense as in the wet forest. There is no evidence that population growth in this part of the world will be halted in the near future. Fortunately for bats as a group, disturbed habitats will probably continue to provide refuge for many species, some of which will remain abundant.

POTENTIAL EFFECTS OF GLOBAL CLIMATE CHANGE

To date, most known effects of global warming are physical changes, indicated mainly by temperature records. Biologically it can be predicted that under warming conditions species whose distribution is limited by latitude and elevation will move northward and to higher elevations, with loss of range at lower elevations and latitudes

(Parmesan 1996). By looking at a long-studied species of butterfly found in the western United States, Canada, and Baja California, Parmesan (1996) was able to document these predicted movements. Although comparable data do not yet exist for bats, Scheel et al. (1996) constructed a model to predict the effect of global warming on the habitat of all 27 bat species in Texas. Although they predicted no extinctions within the state due to global warming, they did predict major shifts in distribution and abundance, mainly because the model predicts major changes in vegetation types in the state. Cave- and crevice-roosting bats may have enhanced or decreased foraging potential around areas where these roost sites are available, thus affecting their populations. Scheel et al. also predicted that some species of tropical Mexican bats would be added to the Texas bat fauna.

Although no similar studies have yet been published for Mesoamerican bats, there is evidence that changes in temperature, rainfall patterns, and vegetation types affect bat populations (LaVal in press), as has been documented for birds, lizards, and frogs at Monteverde, Costa Rica (Pounds et al. 1999). For example, some life zones on mountaintops and ridgetops may cease to exist, thus eliminating habitat for species that occur only in those life zones. Studies at Monteverde (LaVal in press) demonstrate that the relative abundance of the two most common bat species has changed drastically over a 27-year period and that in general species from lower elevations are increasingly common. However, with respect to the dry forest, this life zone will likely occur at increasingly higher elevations under global warming conditions, possibly augmenting the habitat available to dry-forest bats (see also chapter 4).

APPROPRIATE ENVIRONMENTAL EDUCATION

As pointed out earlier, increased levels of bat awareness in North America have led to greater interest in conservation. Wider and more positive media coverage of bats, books for children and the general public, videos, slide shows, and museum exhibits, often sponsored by organiza-

tions such as BCI, have gradually improved the public image of bats (as chronicled in *Bats* magazine over the past decade).

Similar positive developments are being initiated in Mesoamerica. BCI distributes brochures, videos, and slide shows in Spanish throughout the region, although relatively few people have been reached so far, especially in Central America. In Mexico impressive progress has been made. An organization called Programa para la Conservacíon de Murciélagos Migratorios (PCMM), a binational coalition of BCI, government agencies, museums, universities, and professional organizations, has been formed to protect bats that migrate between the United States and Mexico. A major goal of PCMM is to educate children and adults in communities near major bat caves, and substantial progress has been reported (Navarro et al. 1996). Recently PCMM received a large grant for bat conservation from the Mexican Nature Conservation Fund (Walker 1997). If this program proves to be a success (as suggested by preliminary analysis of results; L. Navarro and J. Arroyo pers. comm.), it could serve as a model for similar environmental education programs in Central America. Another BCI program, an interactive museum exhibit called "Masters of the Night," has just toured Mexico after a successful tour of U.S. and Canadian museums (Keleher 1996).

Another avenue of education in bat conservation is to take advantage of scientific studies of trained bat biologists, both foreign and local. In Mesoamerica, only Mexico has a significant number of local bat researchers, although there are also several in Costa Rica. In these two countries there has been substantial research on bats, often carried out by foreign biologists. These researchers are a priceless resource and should be involved in conservation efforts by local organizations and agencies. For example, in March 1997 Bernal Rodríguez, a Costa Rican bat specialist, and I organized and taught a workshop on bat biology and conservation for employees of Guanacaste and other conservation areas throughout the northern half of the country (mostly from dry-forest parks). Subsequently

Rodríguez constructed and installed an excellent interactive bat exhibit, including a bat cave with live bats, at the National Museum of Costa Rica. Thousands of Costa Ricans, especially large groups of school children, responded with great enthusiasm to the exhibit, which lasted for two months and resulted in very favorable press coverage.

In early 2001 a new program, called the Programa para la Conservación de Murciélagos de Costa Rica, was initiated with the help of BCI and PCMM. The focus of this program was educating school children living in or near the conservation areas of Guanacaste about the benefits of bats. A set of original children's books in Spanish and other excellent teaching materials have been provided by PCMM for use in the Costa Rican program. Over the course of several years, I have given more than a hundred slide lectures on bats to groups of students and adults, usually followed by hands-on experience in mist-netting bats (stressing conservation) in Monteverde and Lomas Barbudal. No doubt other biologists have carried out similar activities, and more should be encouraged to do so. Particular emphasis should be given to including government employees charged with controlling vampires or interpreting park wildlife to the public.

ACKNOWLEDGMENTS

The following people sent me literature, materials, and useful contacts with E-mail addresses; answered my questions about their research; and in many cases allowed me to cite unpublished data: Gordon Frankie, Jeff Cosson, Alejandro Estrada, Hector Arita, Marco Tschapka, Alfredo Pérez, Gerardo Ceballos, Manuel Maass, Roger Blanco, Barry Hammel, Nelson Zamora, Don Clark, and Miguel Mora. Book editors Tom Kunz, Paul Racey, Nalini Nadkarni, and Nat Wheelwright gave me access to manuscripts of chapters in books not yet published as I was writing this chapter. Barbara French of BCI was especially helpful in supplying me with information, names of publications, E-mail addresses, and facsimile copies of relevant papers. Bob Timm read and commented on an early draft, and Dixie Pierson critically read and improved a later draft. I thank my wife, Margaret, as well as Bernal Rodríguez for being continuous sources of inspiration.

REFERENCES

Alvarez, T., and L. González-Quintero. 1970. Análisis polínico del contenido gástrico de murciélagos Glossophaginae de México. *Anales Escuela Nacional de Ciencias Biológicas, México* 18:137–165.

Arita, H. T. 1993. Conservation biology of the cave bats of Mexico. *Journal of Mammalogy* 74:693–702.

Arita, H. T., and J. Ortega. 1998. The middle-American bat fauna: Conservation in the Neotropical-Nearctic border. In *Bat biology and conservation*, ed. T. H. Kunz and P. A. Racey, 295–308. Washington, D.C.: Smithsonian Institution Press.

Arita, H. T., and K. Santos-del-Prado. 1999. Conservation biology of nectar-feeding bats in Mexico. *Journal of Mammalogy* 80:31–41.

Arita, H. T., and D. E. Wilson. 1987. Long-nosed bats and agaves: The tequila connection. *Bats* 5(4):3–5.

Bateman, G. C., and T. A. Vaughan. 1974. Nightly activities of mormoopid bats. *Journal of Mammalogy* 55:45–65.

A binational partnership to protect Mexican free-tailed bats. 1994. *Bats* 12(4):6–7.

Black, H. L. 1974. A north temperate bat community: Structure and prey populations. *Journal of Mammalogy* 55:138–57.

Brosset, A., P. Charles-Dominique, A. Cockle, J.-F. Cosson, and D. Masson. 1996. Bat communities and deforestation in French Guiana. *Canadian Journal of Zoology* 74:1974–82.

Ceballos, G. 1995. Vertebrate diversity, ecology, and conservation in Neotropical dry forests. In *Seasonally dry tropical forests*, ed. S. H. Bullock, H. A. Mooney, and E. Medina, 195–220. Cambridge: Cambridge University Press.

Ceballos, G., and A. García. 1995. Conserving Neotropical biodiversity: The role of dry forests in western Mexico. *Conservation Biology* 9:1349–53.

———. 1996. La selva baja: Biodiversidad única en peligro. *Ocelotl* 5:4–9.

Clark, D. R., Jr. 1981. *Bats and environmental contaminants: A review*. Special Science Report—

Wildlife No. 235. Washington, D.C.: U.S. Department of the Interior, Fish and Wildlife Service. 27 pp.

Clark, D. R., Jr., R. K. LaVal, and D. M. Swineford. 1978. Dieldrin-induced mortality in an endangered species, the gray bat (Myotis grisescens). Science 199:1357–59.

Clark, D. R., Jr., C. M. Bunck, E. Cromartie, and R. K. LaVal. 1983. Year and age effects on residues of dieldrin and heptachlor in dead gray bats, Franklin County, Missouri—1976, 1977, and 1978. Environmental Toxicology and Chemistry 2:387–93.

Clark, D. R., Jr., A. Moreno-Valdez, and M. A. Mora. 1995. Organochlorine residues in bat guano from nine Mexican caves, 1991. Ecotoxicology 4: 258–65.

Cockrum, E. L. 1969. Migration in the guano bat, Tadarida brasiliensis. University of Kansas Museum of Natural History Miscellaneous Publications 31:303–36.

———. 1991. Seasonal distribution of northwestern populations of the long nosed bats, Leptonycteris sanborni Family Phyllostomidae. Anales Instituto de Biología Universidad Nacional Autónomo México. 62:181–202.

Constantine, D. G. 1970. Bats in relation to the health, welfare, and economy of man. In Biology of bats, ed. W. A. Wimsatt, 2:320–449. New York: Academic Press.

Cosson, J. F., J.-M. Pons, and D. Masson. 1999. Effects of forest fragmentation on frugivorous and nectarivorous bats in French Guiana. Journal of Tropical Ecology 15:515–34.

de Jong, J. 1995. Habitat use and species richness of bats in a patchy landscape. Acta Theriologica 40:237–48.

Estrada, A., R. Coates-Estrada, and D. Merritt Jr. 1993. Bat species richness and abundance in tropical rainforest fragments and in agricultural habitats at Los Tuxtlas, Mexico. Ecography 16:309–18.

Fenton, M. B. 1982. Echolocation, insect hearing, and feeding ecology of insectivorous bats. In Ecology of bats, ed. T. H. Kunz, 261–80. New York: Plenum Press.

———. 1997. Science and the conservation of bats. Journal of Mammalogy 78:1–14.

Fenton, M. B., and I. L. Rautenbach. 1998. The impacts of ignorance and human and elephant populations on the conservation of bats in African woodlands. In Bat biology and conservation, ed. T. H. Kunz and P. A. Racey, 261–81. Washington, D.C.: Smithsonian Institution Press.

Fenton, M. B., L. Acharya, D. Audet, M. B. C. Hickey, C. Merriman, M. K. Obrist, and D. M. Syme. 1992. Phyllostomid bats (Chiroptera: Phyllostomidae) as indicators of habitat disruption in the Neotropics. Biotropica 24:440–46.

Findley, J. S. 1993. Bats: A community perspective. Cambridge: Cambridge University Press. 167 pp.

Fleming, T. H. 1988. The short-tailed fruit bat: A study in plant-animal interactions. Chicago: University of Chicago Press. 365 pp.

———. 1991. Following the nectar trail. Bats 9(4): 4–7.

———. 1997. The long and short of it: Comparative ecology of two plant-visiting phyllostomid bats. Abstract from the annual meeting of the Association for Tropical Biology. Bat Research News 39(2):40.

Fleming, T. H., E. T. Hooper, and D. E. Wilson. 1972. Three Central American bat communities: Structure, reproductive cycles, and movement patterns. Ecology 53:555–69.

Gardner, A. L. 1977. Feeding habits. In Biology of bats of the New World family Phyllostomatidae, pt. 2, ed. R. J. Baker, J. K. Jones Jr., and D. C. Carter, 293–350. Lubbock: Texas Tech Press.

Granjon, L., J. F. Cosson, J. Judas, and S. Ringuet. 1996. Influence of tropical rainforest fragmentation on mammal communities in French Guiana: Short-term effects. Acta Oecologica 17: 673–84.

Hall, E. R. 1981. The mammals of North America. 2 vols. New York: John Wiley and Sons. 1,181 pp.

Heithaus, E. R., T. H. Fleming, and P. A. Opler. 1975. Foraging patterns and resource utilization in seven species of bats in a seasonal tropical forest. Ecology 56:841–54.

Herrera-Montalvo, L. G. 1997. Evidence of altitudinal movements of Leptonycteris curasoae (Chiroptera: Phyllostomidae) in Central Mexico. Revista Mexicana de Mastozoología 2:116–18.

Holdridge, L. R. 1967. Life zone ecology. San José: Tropical Science Center. 206 pp.

Humphrey, S. R. 1975. Nursery roosts and community diversity of Nearctic bats. Journal of Mammalogy 56:321–46.

Humphrey, S. R., F. J. Bonaccorso, and T. L. Zinn. 1983. Guild structure of surface-gleaning bats in Panamá. Ecology 64:284–94.

Iñiguez, L. I. 1997. Ecology of Sturnira ludovici in the Sierra de Manatlan, Jalisco, Mexico. Abstract from the annual meeting of the Association for Tropical Biology. Bat Research News 38(2):39.

Janzen, D. H. 1983. No park is an island: Increase in interference from outside as park size decreases. Oikos 41:402–10.

———. 1988. Tropical dry forests: The most endangered major tropical ecosystem. In *Biodiversity*, ed. E. O. Wilson, 130–37. Washington, D.C.: National Academy Press.

Kalko, E. K. V. 1997a. Diversity in tropical bats. In *Tropical biodiversity and systematics: Proceedings of the International Symposium on Biodiversity and Systematics in Tropical Ecosystems*, ed. H. Ulrich, 13–43. Bonn: Zoologisches Forschungsinstitut und Museum Alexander Koenig.

———. 1997b. Conservation of Neotropical bats: Monitoring techniques, community comparisons, and long-term studies. Abstract from the annual meeting of the Association for Tropical Biology. *Bat Research News* 39(2):40.

———. 1998. Organisation and diversity of tropical bat communities through space and time. *Zoology* 101:281–97.

Kalko, E. K. V., C. O. Handley Jr., and D. Handley. 1996. Organization, diversity, and long-term dynamics of a Neotropical bat community. In *Long-term studies of vertebrate communities*, ed. M. L. Cody and J. A. Smallwood, 503–53. New York: Academic Press.

Keleher, S. 1996. The Masters of the Night Exhibit: A winner for bats. *Bats* 14(2):3–6.

Kunz, T. H. 1982. Roosting ecology of bats. In *Ecology of bats*, ed. T. H. Kunz, 1–55. New York: Plenum Press.

Kunz, T. H., and P. A. Racey, eds. 1998. *Bat biology and conservation*. Washington, D.C.: Smithsonian Institution Press.

Kunz, T. H., J. O. Whitaker Jr., and M. D. Wadanoli. 1995. Dietary energetics of the insectivorous Mexican free-tailed bat (*Tadarida brasiliensis*) during pregnancy and lactation. *Oecologia* 101: 407–15.

LaVal, R. K. In press. Impact of global warming and locally changing climate on tropical cloud forest bats. *Journal of Mammalogy*.

LaVal, R. K., and H. S. Fitch. 1977. Structure, movements and reproduction in three Costa Rican bat communities. *Occasional Papers of the Museum of Natural History, University of Kansas* 69:1–28.

López, J. 1996. Habitos alimentarios de murciélagos frugívoros y su participación en la dispersión de semillas, en bosques secundarias húmedos de Costa Rica. Thesis. Programa Regional en Manejo de Vida Silvestre para Mesoamerica y el Caribe—Universidad Nacional, Heredia, Costa Rica. 73 pp.

Lord, R. D. 1988. Control of vampire bats. In *Natural history of vampire bats*, ed. A. M. Greenhall and U. Schmidt, 216–26. Boca Raton, Fla.: CRC Press.

Lott, E. J. 1993. Annotated checklist of the vascular flora of the Chamela Bay Region, Jalisco, Mexico. *Occasional Papers of the California Academy of Science* 148:1–60.

Maass, J. M. 1995. Conversion of tropical dry forest to pasture and agriculture. In *Seasonally dry tropical forests*, ed. S. H. Bullock, H. A. Mooney, and E. Medina, 399–418. Cambridge: Cambridge University Press.

Marinho-Filho, J., and I. Sazima. 1998. Brazilian bats and conservation biology: A first survey. In *Bat biology and conservation*, ed. T. H. Kunz and P. A. Racey, 282–94. Washington, D.C.: Smithsonian Institution Press.

McCabe, S. 1995. Bob Currie: The quiet conservationist. *Bats* 13(3):12–15.

McCracken, G. F. 1988. Who's endangered and what can we do? *Bats* 6(3):5–9.

———. 1996. Bats aloft: A study of high-altitude feeding. *Bats* 14(3):7–10.

Medellín, R. A., and O. Gaona. 1999. Seed dispersal by bats and birds in forest and disturbed habitats in Chiapas, México. *Biotropica* 31: 478–85.

Murphy, P. G., and A. E. Lugo. 1995. Dry forests of Central America and the Caribbean. In *Seasonally dry tropical forests*, ed. S. H. Bullock, H. A. Mooney, and E. Medina, 9–34. Cambridge: Cambridge University Press.

Murray, K. G., S. Kinsman, and J. L. Bronstein. 2000. Plant-animal interactions. In *Monteverde: Ecology and conservation of a tropical cloud forest*, ed. N. M. Nadkarni and N. T. Wheelwright, 245–302. New York: Oxford University Press.

Navarro, L., J. Arroyo, and R. Medellín. 1996. Bat awareness in Mexico begins with children. *Bats* 14(3):3–7.

Ochoa, J. 1992. Venezuela's bats: A case for conservation. *Bats* 10(3):10–13.

———. 2000. Efectos de la extracción de maderas sobre la diversidad de mamíferos pequeños en bosques de tierras bajas de la Guayana Venezolana. *Biotropica* 32:146–64.

Parmesan, C. 1996. Climate and species range. *Nature* 382:765–66.

Pierson, E. D. 1998. Tall trees, deep holes, and scarred landscapes: Conservation biology of North American bats. In *Bat biology and conservation*, ed. T. H. Kunz and P. A. Racey, 309–25. Washington, D.C.: Smithsonian Institution Press.

Pierson, E. D., and P. A. Racey. 1998. Introduction to pt. 4, Conservation biology. In *Bat biology and conservation*, ed. T. H. Kunz and P. A. Racey,

247–48. Washington, D.C.: Smithsonian Institution Press.

Pounds, J. A., M. P. L. Fogden, and J. H. Campbell. 1999. Biological response to climate change on a tropical mountain. *Nature* 398:611–15.

Ramírez-Pulido, J., and M. A. Armella. 1987. Activity patterns of Neotropical bats (Chiroptera: Phyllostomidae) in Guerrero, Mexico. *Southwestern Naturalist* 32:363–70.

Ramírez-Pulido, J., A. Martínez, and G. Urbano. 1977. Mamíferos de la Costa Grande de Guerrero, México. *Anales Instituto de Biología Universidad Nacional Autónomo México* 48:243–92.

Robinson, M. F., and R. E. Stebbings. 1997. Home range and habitat use by the serotine bat, *Eptesicus serotinus*, in England. *Journal of Zoology, London* 243:117–36.

Rojas-Martinez, A., A. Valiente-Banuet, M. del Coro Arizmendi, A. Alcántara-Eguren, and H. T. Arita. 1999. Seasonal distribution of the long-nosed bat (*Leptonycteris curasoae*) in North America: Does a generalized migration pattern really exist? *Journal of Biogeography* 26:1065–77.

Scheel, D., T. L. S. Vincent, and G. N. Cameron. 1996. Global warming and the species richness of bats in Texas. *Conservation Biology* 10:452–64.

Schneider, M. C., and C. Santos-Burgoa. 1995. Algunas consideraciones sobre la rabia humana transmitida por murciélago. *Salud Pública México* 37:354–62.

Sheffield, S. R., J. H. Shaw, G. A. Heidt, and L. R. McClenaghan. 1992. Guidelines for the protection of bat roosts. *Journal of Mammalogy* 73:707–10.

Simmons, N. B., and R. S. Voss. 1998. The mammals of Paracou, French Guiana: A Neotropical lowland rainforest fauna. Pt. 1, Bats. *Bulletin of the American Museum of Natural History* 237:1–219.

Sosa, M., A. De Ascençào, and P. J. Soriano. 1996. Dieta y patrón reproductivo de *Rhogeessa minutila* (Chiroptera: Vespertilionidae) en una zona árida de Los Andes de Venezuela. *Revista de Biología Tropical* 44:867–75.

Stiles, F. G. 1988. Altitudinal movements of birds on the Caribbean slope of Costa Rica: Implications for conservation. In *Tropical rainforests: Diversity and conservation*, ed. F. Almeda and C. M. Pringle, 243–58. San Francisco: California Academy of Science and American Association for the Advancement of Science.

Stoner, K. E. 1997. Changes of abundance and sex ratio of frugivorous and nectarivorous bats in tropical dry forest and their implications for seasonal migration. Abstract from the annual meeting of the Association for Tropical Biology. *Bat Research News* 38(2):39.

Thorne, J. 1990. Bats and cavers. *Bats* 8(1):10–14.

Timm, R. M. 1994. The mammal fauna. In *La Selva: Ecology and natural history of a Neotropical rain forest*, ed. L. A. McDade, K. S. Bawa, H. A. Hespenheide, and G. S. Hartshorn, 229–37. Chicago: University of Chicago Press.

Timm, R. M., and R. K. LaVal. 1998. A field key to the bats of Costa Rica. *Occasional Publications Series, Center for Latin American Studies, University of Kansas* 22:1–30.

———. 2000. Mammals. In *Monteverde: Ecology and conservation of a tropical cloud forest*, ed. N. M. Nadkarni and N. T. Wheelwright, 223–44. New York: Oxford University Press.

Tuttle, M. D. 1976. Collecting techniques. In *Biology of bats of the New World family Phyllostomatidae*, pt. 1, ed. R. J. Baker, J. K. Jones Jr., and D. C. Carter, 71–88. Lubbock: Texas Tech Press.

———. 1988. Introduction to the natural history of vampire bats. In *Natural history of vampire bats*, ed. A. M. Greenhall and U. Schmidt, 1–6. Boca Raton, Fla.: CRC Press.

Tuttle, M. D., and D. Hensley. 1993. Bat houses: The secrets of success. *Bats* 11(1):3–14.

Tuttle, M. D., and D. A. R. Taylor. 1998. Bats and mines. *Bat Conservation International, Resource Publications* 3:1–50.

Valiente-Banuet, A., M.del C. Arizmendi, A. Rojas-Martínez, and L. Domínguez-Canseco. 1996. Ecological relationships between columnar cacti and nectar-feeding bats in Mexico. *Journal of Tropical Ecology* 12:103–19.

Walker, S. 1995. Mexico-U.S. partnership makes gains for migratory bats. *Bats* 13(3):3–5.

———. 1997. Murciélagos de Nuevo León. *Bats* 15(1):16.

Willig, M. R., G. R. Camilo, and S. J. Noble. 1993. Dietary overlap in frugivorous and insectivorous bats from edaphic cerrado habitats of Brazil. *Journal of Mammalogy* 74:117–28.

Wilson, D. E. 1983. Checklist of mammals. In *Costa Rican natural history*, ed. D. H. Janzen, 443–47. Chicago: University of Chicago Press.

———. 1996. Neotropical bats: A checklist with conservation status. In *Neotropical biodiversity and conservation*, ed. A. C. Gibson, 167–77. Los Angeles: Mildred E. Mathias Botanical Garden, University of California, Los Angeles.

Wilson, D. E., C. F. Ascorra, and S. Solari. 1998. Bats as indicators of habitat disturbance. In *Manu: The biodiversity of southeastern Peru*, ed. D. E. Wilson and A. Sandoval, 613–26. Washington: Smithsonian Institution Press.

CHAPTER 14

Biodiversity and Conservation of Mesoamerican Dry-Forest Herpetofauna

Mahmood Sasa and Federico Bolaños

THE HERPETOFAUNA of Mesoamerica (defined as the region running south from about central Mexico through Panama) is undoubtedly one of the richest and most complex vertebrate faunas of the New World. It involves more than 210 genera, comprising approximately 693 species of reptiles and 598 species of amphibians. Such high diversity results from the divergence of species that evolved *in situ* in Mesoamerica, as well as from the interchange of species between North and South America (Duellman 1966; Savage 1966).

Based on the distribution of reptiles and amphibians in Mesoamerica, Duellman (1966) recognized five major ecological assemblages: humid tropical, humid mountain, high mountain, arid mountain, and arid tropical. This last ecological unit, the tropical arid assemblage, includes species distributed in subhumid lowlands covered by scrub forest, savannas, and deciduous vegetation and is the primary focus of this chapter. We based our account on preliminary studies of the amphibians and reptiles of northwestern Costa Rica (Sasa and Solórzano 1995) and on extensive material recently collected from the dry forests of Mexico (Oaxaca, Chiapas), Guatemala, Honduras, and Nicaragua. We begin by summarizing biodiversity and biogeographical aspects of reptiles and amphibians associated with dry environments in Mesoamerica. We then describe general patterns of resource use of dry-forest reptiles and amphibians and their adaptation to arid conditions, emphasizing the roles that some species have in the community and the threat that human activities might pose to them. Finally, we discuss the importance of conservation of this herpetofaunal assemblage in terms of area selection and conservation.

THE DRY-FOREST ENVIRONMENTS OF MESOAMERICA

Approximately 26 percent of the surface of Mesoamerica is seasonally dry, covered by different

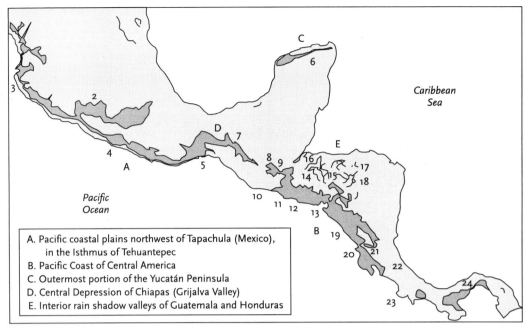

MAP 14.1. Lowland tropical dry forest in Mesoamerica. Numbers refer to the localities listed in table 14.1; locality 1 is out of the range of the map. Modified from Wilson and McCranie (1998).

xerophytic and deciduous vegetation types (Ceballos 1995; Murphy and Lugo, 1995). These vegetation associations occur in five geographical regions: (1) the Pacific coastal plains and foothills northwest of Tapachula (Mexico), in the Isthmus of Tehuantepec, (2) the Pacific Coast of Central America, (3) the lowlands of the outermost portion of the Yucatán Peninsula, (4) the Central Depression of Chiapas, and (5) the series of interior rain shadow valleys of Guatemala and Honduras (map 14.1). A disjunct dry-forest area also occurs in the Azuero Peninsula, Panama (Holdridge and Budowski 1959; Murphy and Lugo, 1995), but has been poorly studied.

SPECIES COMPOSITION AND RICHNESS

Species accounts for amphibians and reptiles are available for several localities in Mesoamerican arid regions. Localities that have been surveyed include Jalisco (García and Ceballos 1994; Ramírez-Bautista 1994), Michoacán (Duellman 1961, 1965b), the Isthmus of Tehuantepec (Hart-weg and Oliver 1940; Duellman 1960), northwestern nuclear Central America (Johnson 1989), the Yucatán and dry savannas in Petén (Stuart 1935; Duellman 1965a; Lee 1996; Campbell 1998), and interior dry valleys (Schmidt and Stuart 1941; Stuart 1954a; Campbell and Vannini 1988; Wilson and McCranie 1998). Also see Mertens (1952), Stuart (1954b), Rand (1957), Savage and Villa (1986), Campbell and Vannini (1989), Sasa and Solórzano (1995), and Stafford (1998) for data on the herpetological communities along the Pacific versant from southern Guatemala to Costa Rica.

Overall, 266 species of amphibians and reptiles are known to occur in Mesoamerica's arid environments. The total number of species includes 2 caecilians, 5 salamanders, 50 anurans, 13 turtles, 3 crocodilians, 76 lizards, and 117 snakes.

Species compositions for 20 tropical dry-forest localities of Mesoamerica are presented in table 14.1. We also include data from three wet-forest localities (La Selva, Osa Peninsula, and Barro Colorado Island), as well as a list for Sonora, located in extratropical Mexico. We quantified the number of species of amphibians, turtles, crocodilians, saurians, and snakes relative to the total number of species at each locality and then compared the resulting proportion of species per locality. No differences were observed in the proportion of species inhabiting tropical dry localities (table 14.1, G-statistic = 49.8, d.f. = 69, P = 0.961). However, the proportion of species of each taxonomical category differs between dry and wet localities (G-statistic = 120.1, d.f. = 3, P < 0.001). Furthermore, the mean number of species in dry localities is 69, whereas localities in wet lowland forest have a mean of 123 species. The most visible difference in species composition between dry and wet-forest localities is in amphibian richness. For the 20 dry-forest sites, amphibians represent merely 26.2 percent of the total number of species (percentage range: 14.1–28.0), whereas in wet-forest sites they account for 39 percent (percentage range: 37.1–39.4).

COSTA RICAN DRY-FOREST HERPETOFAUNA

Costa Rica is a country with a well-known herpetofauna composed of a total of 397 species, 174 amphibians and 223 reptiles (table 14.2). The dry forest contains 21 percent of the country's total number of species. With one caecilian, no salamanders, and few species of frogs and toads, the dry forest differs greatly in amphibian composition from the country as a whole. The proportion of reptiles, on the other hand, is similar for both Costa Rica as a whole and areas of dry forest (table 14.2, G-statistic = 5.733, d.f. = 3, P = 0.126), varying from 4 species of turtles to 34 species of snakes.

RESOURCE USE

To our knowledge, a quantitative study of the relative abundance of species in an arid herpetofauna community has never been performed.

Likewise, general aspects of ecology and natural history of the majority of dry-forest reptile and amphibian species are poorly known or are restricted primarily to the rainy season.

DIEL ACTIVITY

Activity patterns within a species can vary depending on locality and season, but generalizations can be offered regarding reptiles and amphibians of dry forests. Duellman (1965b) recognized two patterns of diel activity in Michoacán: diurnal (51.1% of reported species) and nocturnal (48.9% of species). In Sector Santa Rosa (Guanacaste Conservation Area, Costa Rica), 37 percent of the species can be considered diurnal, in particular lizards and their snake predators, whereas 34 percent of the species (almost all geckos, all frogs, and most of their snake predators) are nocturnal (Sasa and Solórzano 1995). The remaining percentage includes species with unknown patterns or that are active during both night and day.

MICROHABITAT USE

As in other ecosystems, reptiles and amphibians that inhabit seasonal dry forests use a variety of microhabitats, depending on species and season. Amphibians are usually observed above ground only during the rainy season, and we assume that most species enter a state of estivation and burrow in the ground during the arid months (see section "Adaptations to Highly Seasonal Climate" later in this chapter). Dry-forest frogs, lizards, and snakes are found in five generally exclusive microhabitats (table 14.3). Overall, 18 percent of the species are fossorial or live under the leaf-litter, 29 percent are found exclusively on the ground, 7 percent are associated with rivers and ponds, 14 percent inhabit bushes and tree trunks, and the remaining 30 percent are likely to be found both on the ground and in bushes. The majority of anurans and snakes in dry forests are ground dwellers, whereas lizards tend to use more bushes and tree trunks. This pattern differs from the patterns in other ecosystems. In extratropical arid regions, almost a

TABLE 14.1
Comparison of Herpetofaunas at 24 Mesoamerican Localities

LOCALITY	CAECILIANS AND SALAMANDERS	ANURANS (FROGS/TOADS)	TURTLES AND CROCODILIANS	SAURIA (LIZARDS)	SERPENTES (SNAKES)	TOTAL
MEXICO						
1. Sonora	2	26	9	89	61	187
2. Michoacán	0	20	4	28	28	80
3. Jalisco	0	19	4	21	37	81
4. Guerrero	1	19	7	24	47	98
5. Tehuantepec	1	22	9	27	46	105
6. Yucatán	1	15	7	21	47	91
7. Grijalva Valley	1	19	3	27	36	86
GUATEMALA						
8. Río Negro	0	13	0	10	15	38
9. Motagua Valley	1	12	3	15	22	53
10. Pacific Guatemala	2	15	6	18	27	68
EL SALVADOR						
11. Pacific El Salvador	2	17	5	21	34	79
HONDURAS						
12. Pacific Honduras	2	10	3	13	21	49
13. Choluteca Valley	1	13	2	16	23	55
14. Comayagua Valley	0	11	2	8	15	36
15. Otoro Valley	0	11	1	8	3	23

Locality						
16. Sula Plain	3	15	7	20	45	90
17. Aguán Valley	1	10	0	15	11	37
18. Guaype Valley	1	16	5	14	14	50
NICARAGUA						
19. Pacific Nicaragua	2	18	5	20	35	80
COSTA RICA						
20. North Pacific Costa Rica	1	19	5	17	34	76
21. Cañas	1	22	6	16	34	79
22. La Selva	4	41	6	23	45	119
23. Osa Peninsula	6	40	5	22	44	117
PANAMA						
24. Barro Colorado	3	50	7	26	47	133
Total	17	124	27	193	210	571

Note: Locality 1 is extratropical, localities 2–21 correspond to tropical dry forest, and localities 22–24 correspond to lowland wet forest in isthmian Central America.

TABLE 14.2
Number of Species of Amphibians and Reptiles in Costa Rica and in the Costa Rican Dry Forest

	COSTA RICA	DRY FOREST
AMPHIBIANS		
Cecilians	4	1
Salamanders	37	—
Frogs and toads	133	24
REPTILES		
Lizards	73	17
Snakes	134	34
Turtles	14	4
Crocodiles	2	2
Total	397	81

third of the snake species are fossorial, whereas most lizards are ground dwellers (table 14.3). Conversely, in more mesic forest, a significantly higher number of reptiles and amphibians live in the canopy and tree trunks (Guyer 1990; table 14.3). The lack of canopy dwellers in dry forest might be related to the great proportion (close to 100% in nonriparian habitats) of trees that are deciduous and to differences in density, height, and productivity of dry-forest associations (Gentry 1995).

FEEDING ECOLOGY

Diet analyses for the majority of amphibians and reptiles inhabiting dry regions of Mesoamerica are scarce, and valuable information on prey types, foraging behavior, and temporal and spatial feeding activity for most species is still lacking. In general, a predator can follow two major feeding strategies: (1) diet specialization toward one (or a few) prey items, or (2) an increase in the variety of diet items accepted. These two modes should be considered as ex-

TABLE 14.3
Percentage of Species of Anurans, Lizards, and Snakes Found in Five Microhabitats in Three Mesoamerican Ecosystems

	AQUATIC	ARBOREAL	GROUND (EXCLUSIVE)	FOSSORIAL AND LEAF LITTER	GROUND AND BUSHES
TROPICAL DRY FOREST					
Anurans	10.46	7.38	48.70	9.86	23.51
Lizards	0.00	38.10	28.34	4.29	28.27
Snakes	2.52	9.99	47.40	17.66	22.40
EXTRATROPICAL DRY FOREST					
Anurans	16.67	8.33	58.33	12.51	4.16
Lizards	0.00	25.00	65.00	3.33	6.67
Snakes	1.81	1.81	50.90	30.90	14.54
TROPICAL WET FOREST					
Anurans	15.15	33.33	38.63	3.03	23.48
Lizards	0.00	53.12	26.56	12.50	7.81
Snakes	0.77	17.05	45.73	16.27	20.15

tremes in a continuum of possible feeding strategies. Pianka (1986) indicates that in circumstances of scant food supply, mean search time per item encountered is long, and therefore the rate of prey encounter is low. In a tropical dry forest, food abundance varies both in space and time. Most anurans seem to have generalist diets, preying on insects and other invertebrates, but some are specialists (i.e., *Hypopachus variolosus* and *Rhynophrynus dorsalis*, which prey on termites). Lizards also feed on small invertebrates, with some exceptions being the herbivorous green iguana (*Iguana iguana*), the omnivorous black iguana (*Ctenosaura*), and basilisk lizard (*Basiliscus*). In contrast to amphibians and lizards, snakes are dietary specialists. Sasa and Solórzano (1995) recognized three foraging modes in Santa Rosa National Park's dry forest (Costa Rica):

1. Absolute specialist: snakes with a low number of prey species. This category is composed of 31 percent of the species with known diets for that locality and includes, among others, *Leptotyphlops goudotii*, which feeds on termites; *Scolecophis atrocinctus*, which preys on myriapods; and *Sibon anthracops*, which feeds on slugs and snails.

2. Specialists on morpho-types (40%): species that restrict themselves to prey of the same type but whose prey comprises several species (e.g., ophiophagous *Micrurus nigrocinctus* and the spider eater *Stenorrhina freminvilli*).

3. Generalists (29%): species whose diets include a variety of species of diverse types (e.g., *Drymarchon corais, Boa constrictor, Conophis lineatus*).

The majority of snakes inhabiting dry forest in Santa Rosa are stenophagous (categories 1 and 2), which may represent an adaptation to reduce competition. High food partitioning has also been observed in other snake communities (Vitt 1987). In the rain forests of Izabal (eastern Guatemala), Smith (1994) found that snake diets do not overlap much among species. Interest-

ingly, prey types from this wet-forest community do not differ substantially from those observed in Santa Rosa by Sasa and Solórzano (1995). However, with a less seasonal regimen, anurans and slugs are the most common prey items of snakes. At Izabal, 30 percent of the snake species prey on frogs, whereas in Santa Rosa only 12 percent of the snake fauna feeds on them.

REPRODUCTION

In dry forest, the majority of species have a marked breeding season. In lizards and snakes, mating starts early in the year, during the middle of the dry season. In some snakes (e.g., *Crotalus durissus;* Solórzano and Cerdas 1988) females are reproductively active during the beginning of the rainy season (May to October). It is not clear what factor or factors trigger reproductive activity; however, some indirect evidence suggests that seasonal changes in precipitation have an effect on reproductive cycles of the lizards *Norops sagrei* (Brown and Sexton 1973) and *N. cupreus* (Fleming and Hooker 1975).

Reproductive aspects of amphibians are highly diverse, and some reproductive modes and life cycles found in dry forest are obvious adaptations to subhumid conditions. In anurans, reproduction is highly synchronized and depends on water availability and relative humidity. Several burrowing frogs (e.g., *Rhynophrynus dorsalis, Hypopachus variolosus*) are explosive breeders, and their reproduction is restricted to a few days at the beginning of the rainy season. In 1993, for example, only during three nights were *R. dorsalis* heard calling in Santa Rosa National Park.

Five reproductive modes can be found in amphibians inhabiting dry forest: (1) viviparity, (2) direct development, (3) eggs deposited in water, (4) eggs deposited in vegetation, and (5) foam nest. The first mode is found only in caecilians and thus is the least common strategy. Among amphibians that lay eggs, direct development is also a rare mode in dry forests, found only in Plethodontid salamanders and the frog genus *Eleutherodactylus*. This strategy usually involves large eggs that take a long period to develop, hence increasing the risk of desiccation. Direct development has been mentioned as an adaptation for dry conditions in Australian desert species (Tyler 1994), but in the dry forest of Mesoamerica, direct development occurs only in peripheral species whose closest relatives inhabit wet forests. The great majority of species (58%) deposit their eggs in water, usually in shallow places (temporal or permanent ponds) where predators are scarce. In those species, eggs and all stages of metamorphosis occur in the water. Other species, in particular some leptodactylids (*Leptodactylus labialis, L. melanonotus,* and *Physalaemus pustulosus*), construct foam nests to avoid desiccation of eggs and larvae. In this reproductive mode, early stages of metamorphosis might occur in the foam, but the larvae finish their development in water. Thus, the foam nest is an adaptation to dry environments that allow the use of temporal bodies of water. Finally, few frogs (*Agalychnis callidryas, Hyla ebraccata*) lay their eggs in the vegetation, but the larvae develop in water. As in the case of species with direct development, these species face the problem of desiccation of the egg mass.

There are remarkable differences between the reproductive modes used by dry-forest and wet-forest amphibians. In wet forest, a great proportion (54%) of amphibians lay their eggs out of water (direct development and eggs deposited in vegetation), and there are relatively fewer foam-nest anurans. Furthermore, in wet forest a sixth reproductive strategy can be identified: eggs deposited on land and larvae transported to water (frog family Dendrobatidae), a mode that is absent in dry forests.

ADAPTATIONS TO HIGHLY SEASONAL CLIMATE

Like many other animals living in arid areas, amphibians and reptiles in Mesoamerican dry forests must be able to tolerate high temperatures, low precipitation, and low relative humidity. In addition, resource availability is highly seasonal in tropical dry forests (Janzen and Schoener 1968), which affects ecological aspects of the species. In general, adaptations to drought include seasonal reproductive cycles (discussed previously), seasonal changes in niche and behavior, and estivation.

Seasonal changes in diet, habitat, and activity are evident in the lizard *Norops cupreus* when niche overlap is greater during the dry season (especially for perch sites) than during the rainy season (Fleming and Hooker 1975). This species also exhibits variation in the mean prey size consumed by males and females, a feature that might reduce intersexual competition for food during the dry season (Fleming and Hooker 1975). Seasonal diet shifts have also been reported for *Basiliscus basiliscus* (Van Devender 1983).

Behavioral responses are among the most important means for dealing with hot, dry seasons. Reptiles and amphibians can restrict their activity to the cooler parts of the day, move to shaded areas for protection, or seek shelter and become inactive during periods of hot, dry weather. Turtles and crocodilians cool down in water during the hottest hours of the day. In Jalisco and the Yucatán, frogs of the genus *Triprion* plug the openings of their tree holes with their head, a behavior that may prevent predators from capturing them (Duellman 1960). This behavior, termed phragmosis, may also help in preventing desiccation.

In arid regions, weight loss and an increase in electrolytes in the plasma have been reported for several reptiles and amphibians (Ruibal et al. 1969; Minnich 1977). In those cases, feeding may cease, apparently to prevent further increase in plasma electrolytes when there is insufficient water to excrete them (Gregory 1982). Under these conditions, animals become inactive and enter estivation, a physiological state that parallels hibernation. Factors stimulating onset of estivation are unknown, although high temperature, drought, and dehydration of food have been mentioned. Estivation can be obligate or facultative depending on the species and area. For dry-forest reptiles, estivation has been reported for *Heloderma horridum* (Bogert and Martín del Campo 1993).

Amphibians also avoid periods of dehydration by burrowing into a moist substrate and entering a state of dormancy. The permeability of amphibian skin to water—a characteristic that always has been viewed as a disadvantage for their distribution in arid environments—actually might be an adaptive advantage because it allows effective absorption of water from the soil (Ruibal et al. 1969). Secretions of the skin are also important adaptations. For example, in the hylid *Phrynohyas venulosa,* the skin glands become more developed during the dry season (Duellman 1956; McDiarmid 1968). These glands secrete a mucous excretion that might confer some protection against desiccation. Other species of frogs, including desert dwellers (Lee and Mercer 1967) and the dry-forest-inhabiting *Smilisca baudinii* (McDiarmid and Foster 1987) and *Pternohyla fodiens* (Ruibal and Hillman 1981), form estivation cocoons. These cocoons are formed from numerous layers of the epidermal *stratum corneum* separated by subcorneal spaces filled with mucuslike secretions (Ruibal and Hillman 1981). McDiarmid and Foster (1987) suggest that cocoon-forming frogs might burrow near the surface and thus are stimulated by the start of the wet season's first rains. In this way, they become active earlier than more deeply burrowing species.

Frogs that do not form cocoons have other strategies. In *Bufo marinus,* shallow burrows are created and the nares are usually exposed to the surface, enabling the toad to avoid periods of unfavorable conditions on the surface. In a hydrated *B. marinus,* most carbon dioxide of respiration is eliminated by cutaneous diffusion. When the toad has burrowed (and when the cutaneous moisture is low), skin gas exchange is reduced, and the toad responds with a reduction in breathing rate (Boutilier et al. 1979). Codeco (1999) found that breathing frequency in *B. marinus* could be reduced to enter long periods of apnea, lasting up to eight hours. This long period of apnea, together with torpidity, suggests that metabolism is reduced during burrowing. All of these mechanisms lower the risk of death from overheating and desiccation by reducing body temperatures or keeping an adequate moisture level in the body during dry season.

THREATENED AND EXTINCT SPECIES

Information on population biology for most species inhabiting arid regions of Mesoamerica is almost nonexistent. This precludes a direct analysis of the status of those populations, and therefore an examination of the human impact over the species must be accounted for indirectly. There is still considerable debate about the quality of natural ecosystems in arid regions of Mesoamerica. Moreover, it is not yet clear if the reduced forest in northwestern Costa Rica constitutes an example of the magnificent forest that once extended from south Guatemala to Costa Rica or if the savannas in arid regions of nuclear Central America are natural or the result of human activities (Johnson 1989). It is clear, however, that human activities have substantially modified the biotic and abiotic composition of arid areas. The process might have started 3,000–3,500 years ago, when the distinctive cultures and civilizations of Mesoamerica emerged (Willey et al. 1964). There are two direct threats to the herpetofauna of the region: hunting pressures and habitat loss (or its modification). In general, reptiles and amphibians are considered by most modern locals as dangerous and dirty animals, some of them (snakes) dramatically so. However, in the past (as well as in the present) some species have played an important role in tradition, medicine, and diet. Thus, it is necessary to address the relationship of the local herpetofauna with human societies from a historical perspective. A comprehensive account on ethnoherpetology of Mesoamerican civilizations is beyond the scope of this chapter, but the role that some species of reptiles and amphibians have played in the Mayan-Nahual societies is addressed in J. C. Lee's (1996) chapter on the ethnoherpetology of the Yucatán and in Gutiérrez-González's (1993) account on the vertebrate remains at Nacascole (Nicoya, Costa Rica).

Mayan civilization extended from the Isthmus of Tehuantepec to the western part of Honduras and El Salvador and was characterized by a great architectural development in Petén and the Yucatán Peninsula. To the south, a Nahual cultural region extended along the Pacific coast of Honduras, Nicaragua, and northern Costa Rica. From these two cultures, it is common to find representations of amphibians and reptiles in archaeological artifacts, especially in monuments, paintings, stelae, and ceramics (Ferrero 1987). According to Lee (1996), increasing demand for crop production would have reduced populations of game animals, thus increasing consumption of animals such as amphibians and reptiles. In support of this idea, there are massive remains of reptiles in archaeological sites throughout the lowland Mayan area, from Cozumel to Lubaantun. Common remains include bones of freshwater turtles (*Rhinoclemmys areolata, Trachemys scripta, Kinosternon* sp., *Dermatemys mawii*), marine turtles (*Chelonia mydas*), lizards (*Ctenosaura similis, Iguana iguana*), and crocodiles (*Crocodylus moreletii*). The iguanas *Ctenosaura similis* and *I. iguana* were also extensively consumed along the Pacific coast of Nicaragua and the Nicoya Peninsula (Gutiérrez-González 1993). Another list of uses reflects medicinal and religious beliefs. The fat bodies of *Iguana* and *Ctenosaura* were, and still are, commonly used as remedies for a list long of illnesses. Some toads and frogs (*Bufo marinus, Rhinophrynus dorsalis*) were used to disinfect wounds or in ceremonies. Snakes played a very important role in the mythological tradition of Mayas and Nahuals, in particular the vipers *Crotalus durissus, Bothrops asper,* and *Agkistrodon bilineatus*. These snakes are also common in the artistic tradition of these people.

Hunting pressure for some reptiles and amphibians prevails today. The green and black iguanas (*I. iguana, Ctenosaura similis*), and the basilisk lizards (*Basiliscus* spp.) are still an important source of protein in arid environments. Throughout the dry forest, residents hunt *C. similis* for entertainment, for important dietary supplements, and to feed dogs and other domestic animals. Turtles are also hunted for their meat in several localities. Eggs of marine turtles con-

stitute a major source of protein for many human populations along coastal areas (see chapter 15). Snakes are usually considered dangerous animals, and although most people know that not all snakes are venomous, they are commonly killed. This "just in case" attitude derives from the lack of information on how to discriminate between venomous and harmless snakes. One species, the rattlesnake *Crotalus durissus*, is as important in popular medicine of modern culture as it was in the Mayan-Nahual tradition. This species is hunted for its putative curative properties, for it is a common Mesoamerican belief that the dry carcass of a rattlesnake, once pulverized, is a potent supplement to the diet. The powder of rattlesnake is also considered to be effective against any type of cancer and anemia (Campbell 1998), a belief that is deeply rooted in rural communities along Central America.

In recent years, several species of reptiles and amphibians in tropical Mesoamerica have been hunted for the pet trade. There is increasing interest in domestically keeping tropical amphibians and reptiles, especially in North America, Europe, and some Asiatic countries. Breeding amphibians and reptiles in captivity has yielded information about their reproduction and other aspects of their biology, as well as created some renewable resources. Although less quantifiable, another positive aspect of the pet trade is the exposure of reptiles and amphibians to the general public, allowing a positive attitude toward conservation to be nurtured. However, the pet trade has also produced some undesirable consequences, such as the high rate of mortality during transportation. The effect of this trade on populations (if any) is unknown. Furthermore, in an attempt to regulate the trade, governments and conservation agencies have restricted permits to study and collect specimens for scientific purposes (Campbell and Frost 1993).

Without a doubt, habitat destruction is the most important factor affecting the herpetofauna of dry forests. Archaeological evidence, and the fact that in some areas extensive crops were established, might suggest that pre-Columbian societies had a tremendous impact on the environment and local herpetofauna. However, a substantial modification has occurred in the past 500 years, with the opening of forest for cattle production. By the beginning of the previous century, extensive cattle ranches were firmly established in most dry areas of Mesoamerica (chapter 5), leading to decreased herpetofauna habitat.

Habitat destruction in Mesoamerican dry environments includes extensive deforestation, the creation of grasslands for cattle breeding, change to ponds and rivers for soil irrigation, contamination, and fires to open areas. Each of these aspects affects a particular group of organisms in a specific way.

Human-caused fires are common during the dry season, and their effects on amphibian and reptile populations are not clear. Seasonal burning has modified the ecosystem throughout most of tropical Mesoamerica, resulting in a reduction of critical habitat for some amphibians and reptiles. Species that are slow moving or that cannot burrow deep enough during fires are particularly susceptible. Acuña (1990) studied the mortality of mud turtles (*Kinosternon scorpioides*) during a dry season in Laguna de Palo Verde (northwestern Costa Rica). Of a total of 164 observed casualties, 140 were attributed to the effect of a three-day fire, 38 percent of them adult females.

Loss of tropical dry forest by logging is a crucial problem along the Pacific coast of Central America. Species that are associated with gallery forests and secondary growth are clearly more susceptible to logging and clearance of dry forest than those inhabiting open areas. Amphibians such as *Bolitoglossa mexicana, Oedipina taylori, Eleutherodactylus stejnegerianus,* and *E. rhodopis* only occur in riparian forest. Other species such as *Gymnopis multiplicata, Ctenosaura palearis, C. quinquecarinata, Norops pentaprion, Sibon* spp., and *Agkistrodon bilineatus* are strongly associated with deciduous and semideciduous forest. The iguana *C. palearis* has a restricted distribution in few interior dry valleys of Guatemala and

Honduras and inhabits only dense forest. When examining the effects of land-use changes, the case of the cantil *Agkistrodon bilineatus* deserves further consideration. This pit viper occurs in dry forests along the Pacific coast and foothills from southern Sonora (Mexico) southward to Nicaragua and northwestern Costa Rica (Campbell and Lamar 1989). Despite recent efforts to locate *A. bilineatus* in many parts of its range, only in Sector Santa Rosa (Guanacaste Conservation Area) are specimens easily found (Solórzano et al. 1999). The cantil seems to be associated with mature forest, and given strong deforestation throughout most of its range, we suspect that over much of its distribution *A. bilineatus* is probably extinct.

Amphibians provide the most dramatic example of threatened populations and local disappearances. Throughout tropical Mesoamerica there are several documented cases of declining populations or population and species extinction, or both; the most notorious are the golden toad (*Bufo periglenes*) and harlequin frog (*Atelopus varius*) of Monteverde, Costa Rica (Pounds and Crump 1994). Other species have also disappeared mysteriously in that area (Pounds et al. 1997). The extinction of an *A. varius* population in the Osa Peninsula (South Pacific) has been hypothesized in recent years, providing the first Costa Rican example of a lowland population in decline (F. Bolaños unpubl. data). We are not aware of any reports on amphibian declines in lowland dry forests of Mesoamerica. Therefore, an effort to monitor such populations is crucial, not only to detect possible declines but, more important, to produce adequate information to be used as a reference for comparative studies in the future.

PROBLEMS OF CONSERVATION

Perhaps the greatest concern related to the conservation of amphibians and reptiles is the lack of baseline information. Although we have a good idea of which species are distributed in the dry forest of Mesoamerica, we are still ignorant about important aspects of behavior, ecology, population dynamics, population genetics, home ranges, and mobility for the majority of species. To help alleviate this information gap, governments and conservation agencies should collaborate with researchers, acting as facilitators for studies in natural areas. Permits for research and scientific collection should be accessible to both national and international scientists, a situation that, unfortunately, is not common at present. In Costa Rica, for example, research fees in national parks are very high for local biologists and students, a situation that has forced many study sites to be moved to private protected reserves.

Conservation efforts on a species-specific basis will be costly, if not impossible, and a good representation of the overall community might not be assured. Alternatively, we can focus on the protection of areas and ecosystems, thus maintaining a multitude of species and their habitats. However, these efforts may be of little help if the home range and mobility of those species that we aim to protect are unknown.

Obviously, it is not possible to preserve the entire dry forest of Mesoamerica. We can, however, protect a portion of that ecosystem, thus attempting to save some species as ecologically functional members of the community. To this day, protection of dry forests and associated ecosystems in Mesoamerica occurs only in 15 reserves scattered in the Yucatán and along the Pacific coast of Mexico and Costa Rica (table 14.4). In contrast, the efforts to preserve natural areas in the humid Caribbean coast have resulted in the creation of a Mesoamerican biological corridor that connects several reserves from the Yucatán to Panama (Rodríguez and Montero 1999). Envisioning a similar effort to protect dry forests along the Pacific coast of Mesoamerica implies the creation of new protected areas in Guatemala, El Salvador, Honduras, and Nicaragua. This indeed requires a serious commitment from the governments and conservationists of those countries.

To evaluate whether the reserves listed in table 14.4 give some measure of assurance for

the protection of dry-forest herpetofauna, focus must be brought to bear on two aspects: location of the reserves and their size.

LOCATION OF RESERVES

At least five major geographical regions are evident from a biogeographical analysis of the herpetofauna of Mesoamerica's dry environments (fig. 14.1): (a) Mexico's western (Pacific) coast (Jalisco/Michoacán), (b) Tehuantepec Plains, (c) Yucatán Peninsula, (d) Central America's Pacific coast (plus the Motagua Valley), and (e) interior dry valleys of Honduras. Furthermore, several snake populations distributed in these regions are genetically distinct (M. Sasa unpubl. data). Hence, these dry regions contain much of the genetic diversity and evolutionary differentiation of the herpetofauna populations under protection. In an effort to create reserves with an adequate representation of reptiles and amphibians (and their genetic diversity) occurring in arid Mesoamerica, it can be argued that these conservation areas should at least be located in each biogeographical region. When the current dry-forest reserves in Mesoamerica (table 14.4) are compared with these biogeographical regions, however, the areas are not found to overlap.

AREA OF RESERVES

The next heuristic step is to investigate if the current reserves are large enough to sustain viable populations of the dry-forest herpetofauna. One could approach this question by estimating the area necessary to maintain predetermined numbers of individuals of the larger predators in the herpetofaunal community. Large predators are likely to require more space than other species and therefore may serve as "umbrella" species for other vertebrates. Unfortunately, we do not have direct estimates of population densities of the largest reptilian predators in tropical dry forests: crocodilians and the snakes *Crotalus durissus, Boa constrictor,* and *Drymarchon corais.* Based on minimum viable population (MVP) of 500 individuals, a reasonable size given theoretical and empirical considerations, Jorge

TABLE 14.4
Federal and State Reserves That Protect Dry-Forest Herpetofauna in Mesoamerica

RESERVE	STATE	COUNTRY	AREA (HA)	VEGETATION TYPES
Chamela, Chísmala	Jalisco	Mexico	13,142	Lowland deciduous forest, spiny shrub
Sierra de Manantlán[a]	Jalisco, Colima	Mexico	139,570	Savanna, pine-oak forest
El Veladero	Guerrero	Mexico	3,159	Lowland deciduous forest
Laguna de Chacahua[a]	Oaxaca	Mexico	14,187	Mangrove, evergreen forest
Benito Juarez[a]	Oaxaca	Mexico	2,737	Pine-oak forest, lowland deciduous forest
La Encrucijada[a]	Chiapas	Mexico	144,868	Mangrove
La Sepultura	Chiapas	Mexico	167,309	Lowland deciduous forest, spiny shrub
Río Lagartos	Yucatán	Mexico	47,840	Lowland deciduous forest, mangrove
Dzibilchaltun	Yucatán	Mexico	533	Lowland deciduous forest
Isla Contoy	Quintana Roo	Mexico	176	Coastal vegetation, mangrove
Sian Ka'an	Quintana Roo	Mexico	528,147	Savanna
Tulum[a]	Quintana Roo	Mexico	664	Coastal vegetation, mangrove
Sierra Gorda[a]	Queretaro	Mexico	383,567	Deciduous forest, evergreen forest
El Cimatario[a]	Queretaro	Mexico	2,447	Xerophytic vegetation, savanna
Guanacaste	Guanacaste	Costa Rica	110,000	Lowland deciduous forest
Tempisque	Guanacaste	Costa Rica	20,500	Riparian forest, lowland deciduous forest

Source: Unidad Coordinadora de Areas Naturales Protegidas (Mexico) and Sistema Nacional de Areas de Conservación (Costa Rica).

[a]Reserves that also include ecosystems other than dry forest.

da Silva and Sites (1995) assessed the potential of Brazilian reserves for the conservation of three large snake species. They suggest that in order to sustain that MVP for large snakes, reserves should range between 19,700 and 162,700 ha. If we adopt a similar range, only 53 percent of the reserves currently established (table 14.4) have areas big enough to maintain large herpetofaunal species. Furthermore, prob-ably only El Veladero, La Sepultura, Río Lagartos, and Guanacaste Conservation Area have areas of dry forest as large as recommended by Jorge da Silva and Sites (1995).

From these data, it is clear that protected areas should be established in the Yucatán and on the Pacific coast of northern Central America. Moreover, some taxa—in particular those distributed in dry valleys of Guatemala and

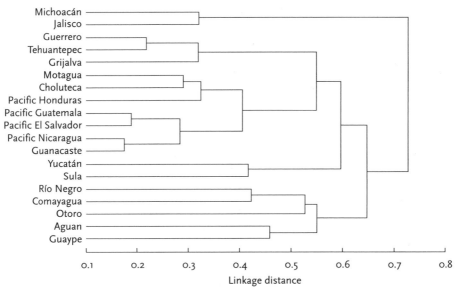

FIGURE 14.1. Herpetofaunal similarities among 19 arid localities in Mesoamerica. Pairwise similarities estimated using Dice (1945) coefficient. Amalgamation rule is unweighted pair group average (UPGA).

Honduras—are not currently included in any protected areas (e.g., *Ctenosaura palearis*, *Heloderma horridum charlesbogartii*), and unless some efforts are made, they will probably perish as habitat modification proceeds.

RECOMMENDATIONS

Although the preservation of dry-forest herpetofauna is not an easy task, we believe that positive results can be achieved through increased research, land conservation, and, most important, educational outreach.

Even though species diversity and geographical distributions of the herpetofauna of Mesoamerican dry forests are well known, little information is currently available on the ecology, behavior, and natural history of most species. We recommend that more studies be conducted immediately on representative species of the various herpetofauna groups. The urgency is related, in part, to the enormous habitat disturbances that are in progress throughout the Mesoamerican region. This research is especially important in the case of amphibians, as species in this group are being lost with little understanding of the causes of extinction.

It is also recommended that biologists work more closely with public and private conservationists to conserve more habitat for herpetofauna. This will require proposal writing and collaboration. In the case of public land in Costa Rica, we recommend that the two large dry-forest conservation areas, Guanacaste Conservation Area and Tempisque Conservation Area, be expanded to include more herpetofauna habitat. This may be achieved through new land acquisitions or possibly through private conservation easements.

Parallel to the efforts in area conservation, an intense environmental education campaign should be established in the region. Education should occur not only on a university level but administratively, as well. In order to study the herpetofauna, permits must often be secured, and this process can be cumbersome. We recommend that more knowledgeable and better educated government personnel be assigned to issue permits to study high-risk organisms such as some reptiles. Also needed are responsible land managers, public and private, who can receive and use the results to improve on the protection of herpetofauna, which will require that biologists invest some of their research time in a variety of outreach efforts (see chapter 19).

Educating people about the important roles of reptiles and amphibians in the ecosystem is particularly significant given the poor reputation that some species (particularly snakes) have among humans. The challenge for herpetologists is to support teachers and update environmental education programs with current information on the biology and conservation of local herpetofauna. It is necessary to direct more efforts to the education and information of the general population, especially children, through the integration of scientific authorities and conservation programs. Some interesting efforts have been conducted in Costa Rica, through an extensive program at the Instituto Clodomiro Picado (Universidad de Costa Rica). Since 1985, biologists of this institute, led by Rodrigo Aymerich, have been giving speeches to a wide variety of audiences, lecturing on the biology of venomous snakes and prevention of snakebites. Although conservation has not been its major goal, this program has helped to demystify snakes as evil creatures, and a new generation of teachers and students have acquired more positive attitudes toward snakes. The achievements of this program have never been quantified, but it is obvious that in Costa Rica more people (especially young people) are currently more interested in the topic than few decades ago. The reinforcement of this and similar programs and the incorporation of biodiversity conservation as a formal topic in the school curriculum are necessary components if we want to create awareness to preserve a good sample of the rich herpetofauna of the region.

It is easy for most people to appreciate charismatic animals such as birds, mammals, sea turtles, butterflies, or flashy beetles. For one reason or another, it is not as easy to appreciate snakes, salamanders, lizards, and frogs. In summary, the only way these often overlooked groups can gain improved status in Mesoamerica is through appropriate environmental education. More aggressive, larger campaigns must be initiated to improve the understanding of the ecological services that herpetofauna provide for nature, as well as humans. In order to reach this goal, biologists must invest a greater amount of their time in outreach projects.

ACKNOWLEDGMENTS

We are grateful for the valuable revisions to this chapter made by Jonathan Campbell, Paul T. Chippindale, Lisa Patrick, William W. Lamar, and Gerardo Chaves. This is a contribution from the Museo de Zoología, Escuela de Biología, Universidad de Costa Rica. Gustavo Serrano drew map 14.1. Fieldwork for this chapter was financed partially through a grant from the Vicerrectoría de Investigación (Universidad de Costa Rica) and through National Science Foundation Grant 003656001 to J. A. Campbell.

REFERENCES

Acuña, R. A. 1990. El impacto del fuego y la sequía sobre la estructura de la población de *Kinosternon scorpioides* (Testudines: Kirnosternidae) en Palo Verde, Guanacaste, Costa Rica. *Brenesia* 33:85–97.

Baroni-Urbani, C., and M. W. Buser. 1976. Similarity of binary data. *Systematic Zoology* 25: 251–59.

Bogert, C. M., and R. Martín del Campo. 1993. *The Gila monster and its allies*. 2d ed. Oxford, Ohio: Society for the Study of Amphibians and Reptiles. 262 pp.

Boutilier, R. G., D. J. Randall, G. Shelton, and D. P. Towens. 1979. Acid-base relationships in the blood of the toad *Bufo marinus*. III. The effects of burrowing. *Journal of Experimental Biololgy* 82:357–65.

Brown, C. M., and O. J. Sexton. 1973. Stimulation of reproductive activity of females *Anolis sagrei* by moisture. *Physiological Zoology* 46:168–172.

Campbell, J. A. 1998. *Amphibians and reptiles of northern Guatemala, the Yucatán, and Belize*. Norman: University of Oklahoma Press. 400 pp.

Campbell, J. A., and D. R. Frost. 1993. Anguide lizards of the genus *Abronia:* Revisionary notes, description of four new species, a phylogenetic analysis, and key. *Bulletin of the Museum of Natural History* 216:1–121.

Campbell, J. A., and W. W. Lamar. 1989. *The venomous reptiles of Latin America*. Ithaca, N.Y.: Cornell University Press. 425 pp.

Campbell, J. A., and J. P. Vannini. 1988. A new subspecies of beaded lizard *Heloderma horridum*, from the Motagua Valley of Guatemala. *Journal of Herpetology* 22:457–68.

———. 1989. Distribution of amphibians and reptiles in Guatemala and Belize. *Proceedings of the Western Foundation of Vertebrate Zoology* 4:1–21.

Ceballos, G. 1995. Vertebrate diversity, ecology, and conservation in neotropical dry forests. In *Seasonally dry tropical forests*, ed. S. H. Bullock, H. A. Mooney, and E. Medina, 195–220. New York: Cambridge University Press.

Codeco, F. 1999. Afferent signal oscillations and the control of breathing in *Bufo marinus*. Ph.D. diss., University of Texas. 96 pp.

Dice, L. R. 1945. Measures of the amount of ecological association between species. *Ecology* 26: 297–302.

Duellman, W. E. 1956. The frogs of the hylid genus *Phrynohyas* Fitzinger, 1843. *Miscellaneous Publications of the Museum of Zoology, University of Michigan* 96:1–47.

———. 1960. A distributional study of the amphibians of the Isthmus of Tehuantepec. *University of Kansas Publications of the Museum of Natural History* 13:19–72.

———. 1961. The amphibians and reptiles of Michoacán, Mexico. *University of Kansas Publications of the Museum of Natural History* 15:1–148.

———. 1965a. Amphibians and reptiles from the Yucatán Peninsula, Mexico. *University of Kansas Publications of the Museum of Natural History* 15: 577–614.

———. 1965b. A biogeographic account of the herpetofauna of Michoacán, Mexico. *University of Kansas Publications of the Museum of Natural History* 15:627–709.

———. 1966. The Central American herpetofauna: An ecological perspective. *Copeia* 1966:700–719.

Ferrero, L. 1987. *Costa Rica Precolombina*. San José: Editorial Costa Rica. 89 pp.

Fleming, T. H., and R. S. Hooker. 1975. *Anolis cupreus*: The response of a lizard to tropical seasonality. *Ecology* 56:1243–61.

García, A., and G. Ceballos. 1994. *Guía de campo de los anfibios de la costa de Jalisco, México*. Mexico City: Fundación Ecológica de Cuixmala. 184 pp.

Gentry, A. H. 1995. Diversity and floristic composition of Neotropical dry forest. In *Seasonally dry tropical forests*, ed. S. H. Bullock, H. A. Mooney, and E. Medina, 46–194. New York: Cambridge University Press.

Gregory, P. T. 1982. Reptilian hibernation. In *Biology of the Reptilia*, ed. C. Gans and F. H. Pough,

vol. 13, *Physiological ecology*, 53–154. New York: Academic Press.

Gutiérrez-González, M. 1993. El aprovechamiento de la fauna en el sitio arqueológico Nacascole, Bahía Culebra, Guanacaste. Tesis de Licenciatura, Universidad de Costa Rica.

Guyer, C. 1990. The herpetofauna of La Selva, Costa Rica. In *Four Neotropical rainforests*, ed. A. H. Gentry, 371–85. New Haven: Yale University Press.

Hartweg, N., and J. A. Oliver. 1940. A contribution to the herpetology of the Isthmus of Tehuantepec. IV. An annotated list of the amphibians and reptiles collected on the Pacific slope during the summer of 1936. *Miscellaneous Publications of the Museum of Zoology, University of Michigan* 47:1–29.

Holdridge, L. R., and G. Budowski. 1959. Mapa ecológico de Panamá. Instituto Interamericano de Ciencias Agrícolas (IICA), San José, Costa Rica.

Janzen, D. H., and T. W. Schoener. 1968. Differences in insect abundance and diversity between wetter and drier sites during a tropical dry season. *Ecology* 49:96–110.

Johnson, J. D. 1989. A biogeographic analysis of the herpetofauna of northwestern Central America. *Contributions in Biology and Geology Milwaukee Public Museum* 76:1–66.

Jorge da Silva, N., and J. W. Sites. 1995. Patterns of diversity of Neotropical squamate reptile species with emphasis on the Brazilian Amazon and the conservation potential of indigenous reserves. *Conservation Biology* 9:873–901.

Lee, A. K., and E. H. Mercer. 1967. Cocoon surrounding desert-dwelling frogs. *Science* 157: 87–88.

Lee, J. C. 1996. *The amphibians and reptiles of the Yucatán Peninsula*. Ithaca, N.Y.: Cornell University Press. 512 pp.

McDiarmid, R. W. 1968. Population variation in the frog genus *Phrynohyas* in Middle America. *Contributions in Science Natural History Museum of Los Angeles County* 134:1–25.

McDiarmid, R. W., and M. S. Foster. 1987. Cocoon formation in another hylid frog, *Smilisca baudinii*. *Journal of Herpetology* 21:352–55.

Mertens, R. 1952. Die amphibien und reptilien von El Salvador. *Abhandlungen der Senckenbergischen Naturforschenden Gesellschaft* 487:1–120.

Minnich, J. E. 1977. Adaptive responses in water and electrolyte budgets of native and captive desert tortoises, *Gopherus agassizii*, to chronic drought. In *Desert Tortoise Council, Proceedings* of 1977 Symposium, ed. M. Trotter and C. G. Jackson Jr., 102–29. San Diego: Desert Tortoise Council.

Murphy, P. G., and A. E. Lugo. 1995. Dry forest of Central America and the Caribbean Islands. In *Seasonally dry tropical forests*, ed. S. H. Bullock, H. A. Mooney, and E. Medina, 9–34. New York: Cambridge University Press.

Pianka, E. R. 1986. *Ecology and natural history of desert lizards: Analyses of the ecological niche and community structure*. Princeton: Princeton University Press. 222 pp.

Pounds, J. A., and M. L. Crump. 1994. Amphibian declines and climate disturbance: The case of the golden toad and the harlequin frog. *Conservation Biology* 8:72–85.

Pounds, J. A., M. L. Fogden, J. M. Savage, and G. C. Gorman. 1997. Test of null models for amphibian declines on a tropical mountain. *Conservation Biology* 11:1307–22.

Ramírez-Bautista, A. 1994. *Manual y claves ilustradas de los anfibios y reptiles de la región de Chamela, Jalisco, México*. Mexico DF: Instituto de Biología, Universidad Autónoma de México. 127 pp.

Rand, A. S. 1957. *Notes on amphibians and reptiles from El Salvador. Fieldiana: Zoology* 34:505–34.

Rodríguez, E., and V. V. Montero. 1999. *Corredor biológico mesoamericano: Sección Costa Rica*. San José: Ministerio de Ambiente y Energía.

Ruibal, R., and S. Hillman. 1981. Cocoon structure and function in the burrowing hylid frog *Pternohyla fodiens. Journal of Herpetology* 15: 403–8.

Ruibal, R., L. Tevis Jr., and V. Roig. 1969. The terrestrial ecology of the spadefoot toad *Scaphiopus hammondii. Copeia* 1969:571–84.

Sasa, M., and A. Solórzano. 1995. The reptiles and amphibians of Santa Rosa National Park, Costa Rica, with comments about the herpetofauna of xerophytic areas. *Herpetological Natural History* 3:113–26.

Savage, J. M. 1966. The origins and history of the Central America herpetofauna. *Copeia* 1966: 719–66.

Savage, J. M., and J. R. Villa 1986. Introduction to the Herpetofauna of Costa Rica. *Society for the Study of Amphibians and Reptiles Contributions in Herpetology* 3:1–207.

Schmidt, K. P., and L. C. Stuart. 1941. The herpetological fauna of the Salama Basin, Baja Verapaz, Guatemala. *Field Museum of Natural History, Zoology Series*. 24:233–47.

Smith, E. N. 1994. Biology of the snake fauna of the Caribbean rainforest of Guatemala. Master's thesis, University of Texas.

Solórzano, A., and L. Cerdas. 1988. Biología reproductiva de la cascabel Centroamericana *Crotalus durissus durissus* (Serpentes: Viperidae) in Costa Rica. *Revista de Biología Tropical* 36:221–26.

Solórzano, A., M. Romero, J. M. Gutiérrez, and M. Sasa. 1999. Natural history and venom composition of the cantil *Agkistrodon bilineatus howardgloydi* (Serpentes: Viperidae): Venom composition and diet. *Southwestern Naturalist* 44(4):478–83.

Stafford, P. J. 1998. Amphibians and reptiles of the Cordillera de Guanacaste, Costa Rica: A field list with notes on color patterns and other observations. *British Herpetology Society Bulletin* 62:9–19.

Stuart, L. C. 1935. A contribution to the knowledge of the herpetology of a portion of the savanna region of central Peten, Guatemala. *Miscellaneous Publications of the Museum of Zoology, University of Michigan* 29:1–59.

———. 1954a. A description of a subhumid corridor across northern Central America, with comments on its herpetofaunal indicators. *Contributions of the Laboratory of Vertebrate Biology, University of Michigan* 65:1–26.

———. 1954b. Herpetofauna of the southeastern highlands of Guatemala. *Contributions of the Laboratory of Vertebrate Biology, University of Michigan* 69:1–65.

Tyler, M. J. 1994. *Australian frogs: A natural history*. 2d ed. Auckland, New Zealand: Reed Books. 192 pp.

Van Devender, R. W. 1983. *Basiliscus basiliscus*. In *Costa Rican natural history*, ed. D. H. Janzen, 379–80. Chicago: University of Chicago Press.

Vitt, L. J. 1987. Communities. In *Snakes: Ecology and evolutionary biology*, ed. R. S. Seigel, J. T. Collins, and S. S. Novak, 335–65. New York: Macmillan. 529 pp.

Willey, G. R., G. F. Ekholm, and R. F. Millon. 1964. The patterns of farming life and civilization. In *Natural environment and early cultures*, ed. R. C. West and R. Waunchope, 446–98. Austin: University of Texas Press.

Wilson, L. D., and J. R. McCranie. 1998. The biogeography of the herpetofauna of the subhumid forest of Middle America (Isthmus of Tehuantepec to northwestern Costa Rica). *Royal Ontario Museum, Life Science Contributions* 163:1–50.

CHAPTER 15

Parque Marino Las Baulas

CONSERVATION LESSONS FROM A NEW NATIONAL PARK AND FROM

45 YEARS OF CONSERVATION OF SEA TURTLES IN COSTA RICA

James R. Spotila and Frank V. Paladino

THE EDGE OF THE SEA marks one boundary of the tropical dry forest in Costa Rica. Just as the ocean draws Costa Ricans and foreigners to vacation spots along the Pacific coast in the summer, the beaches are a magnet for biologists, conservationists, developers, and politicians. This is because the beaches are critical habitat for all these people and a focal point for one of the greatest dramas in conservation at the beginning of the twenty-first century. Biologists come to study sea turtles and other exotic flora and fauna, conservationists come to save species from extinction, developers come with international financing to foster coastal development as an economic boom, and politicians chant the mantra of "sustainable development" to justify the uncontrolled spread of tourist and residential facilities along the coast. In one sense, all these people interact in a play that will determine the future of this ecotone between the forest and the marine ecosystems. Local residents are on stage as minor characters, and exotic species

make occasional cameo appearances to attract the attention of tourists and potential buyers of land and houses before disappearing from the scene. It is not at all clear that this play will have a happy ending.

The star of this play is the flagship species for this ecotone, the sea turtle. Unfortunately for the star and its ecosystem, it is not clear whether in the future we will look back on this play as high drama, a comedy of errors, or a tragedy. The stage is one of the newest parks in the Costa Rican system of natural areas, Parque Marino Las Baulas. The park is situated along the Guanacaste coast and protects the largest surviving nesting population of leatherback turtles in the Pacific Ocean.

In this chapter we focus on the biology of sea turtles that nest on tropical dry forest beaches of Costa Rica; give the history of conservation efforts for these species in Costa Rica; discuss local, national, and international aspects of this conservation activity; present the status of Parque Marino Las Baulas; detail the process that led to its formation; consider flaws and limitations of the human and turtle actors; and present recommendations for the future.

BIOLOGY OF SEA TURTLES

Four species of sea turtles nest on the Pacific coast of Costa Rica. Leatherback turtles, *Dermochelys coriacea,* nest primarily in Guanacaste Province. Olive ridley turtles, *Lepidochelys olivacea,* nest in large flotillas or *arribadas* at Playa Nancite in the Santa Rosa Sector of Parque Nacional Guanacaste and at Ostional on the Nicoya Peninsula and singly on other beaches. Black turtles, *Chelonia mydas agassizii,* nest in small numbers at several beaches from Parque Nacional Guanacaste to the Osa Peninsula, including Playa Naranjo, Playa Cabuyal, and Playa Naranjo in Guanacaste and Playa Carate and Playa Río Oro in Osa. Hawksbill turtles, *Eretmochelys imbricata,* nest on Playa Carate and Playa Río Oro on the Osa Peninsula (Drake 1996).

LEATHERBACK TURTLE

The leatherback turtle is the largest sea turtle, reaching a length of 2.8 m from head to tail and a mass of 916 kg. The carapace (upper shell) is 130 to 190 cm long and elongate with seven sharply peaked longitudinal ridges. It tapers to a point in the rear called the pygal process. The thin, leathery skin is black with white spots, and the head is large with an irregular pink spot above the pineal gland. On the Pacific coast leatherbacks nest primarily from October to February, whereas on the Caribbean coast they nest from March to June. This coincides with the dry season on each coast. Between 70 and 90 percent of leatherbacks on the Pacific coast of Costa Rica nest at Parque Marino Las Baulas.

OLIVE RIDLEY TURTLE

The olive ridley is the smallest sea turtle, with an adult size of 36 kg and length of 76 cm. It has a hard shell and is olive drab in color. It nests in large *arribadas* at Playa Nancite and Playa Ostional and as solitary individuals at these and other beaches on the Pacific coast of Costa Rica during most months of the year, but especially from August to February. There are no ridley turtles on the Caribbean coast of Costa Rica.

BLACK TURTLE

The black turtle is a subspecies of the green turtle and is 100 cm long, compared with 120 cm for the green. Eastern Pacific Chelonia populations are distinct but are not taxonomically distinct at the species level (Karl and Bowen 1999). On the Pacific coast black turtles nest primarily from August to February, although some nesting occurs throughout the year. On the Caribbean coast green turtles nest from June to September.

HAWKSBILL TURTLE

Hawksbill turtles are rare on the Pacific coast of Costa Rica. They are 90 cm long and are distinguished by their birdlike beak and beautiful "tortoise shell"–covered carapace. In general, hawksbill populations are only a small fraction of their presettlement numbers throughout their range (Bjorndal 1999). They are now seen primarily as solitary nesters, but in areas where they are protected, such as Buck Island Reef National Monument in the U.S. Virgin Islands and Jumby Bay Island off Antigua, they nest in groups just like green and black turtles (Meylan 1999). They probably did so in the past before they were hunted to near extinction for their shells. There is little scientific information about their biology in Costa Rica, but hawksbills are in the Golfo Dulce and nest on the beaches of the Osa Peninsula (Drake 1996). Hawksbills also nest along the Caribbean coast of Costa Rica.

REGIONAL AND GLOBAL CONTEXT

Sea turtles are an excellent example of the need for conservation efforts to focus on local, national, and international levels in order to establish effective protection plans and policies. Because these species travel great distances in the ocean, they live in waters controlled by many nations and in international waters, as well.

Hundreds of leatherback turtles nest on the Caribbean coast of Costa Rica and Panama. Protection is provided in Tortuguero National Park, where the Caribbean Conservation Corporation (CCC) has an ongoing study. Farther south, John Denham's Pacuare Reserve protects 6 km of beach where in some years 100–200 leatherbacks nest. His rangers patrol the beach and face poachers who are armed with weapons ranging from machetes to automatic weapons. The aggressive program of patrolling and arrests deters poachers and keeps nest loss to a minimum. Denham's rangers also use hatcheries to protect nests from more remote portions of the beach. South of Limón, Didier Chacón and his volunteers of Asociación ANAI protect beaches in the Refugio Nacional de Fauna Silvestre Gandoca-Manzanillo near the Panamanian border. In Panama leatherbacks are unprotected, and poachers kill adults to get their eggs in addition to digging up nests in the Bocas del Torro region. John Denham and Clara Padilla of the Wildlife Conservation Society began a protection program there in cooperation with Panamanian authorities in 2002.

There are other major nesting beaches for leatherbacks in Mexico. The Mexican population was 70,000 females in 1980 (Pritchard 1982) but declined to fewer than 200 in 1999 (Spotila et al. 1996; L. Sarti and D. Dutton pers. comm.). Although biologists monitor many beaches and provide protection at Mexiquillo in Michoacán, there is no protection on beaches to the south such as Tierra Colorado in Guerrero and Bahía Chacahua and Barra de la Cruz in Oaxaca. Poachers take essentially all the eggs on these beaches and kill some adults (E. Possardt pers. comm.). In 1998 and 1999 Georgita Ruiz's federal rangers in Oaxaca confiscated trailer truck loads of turtle eggs from middlemen who purchased eggs from poachers. These included tens of thousands of eggs from olive ridley, black, and leatherback turtles. A few leatherbacks also nest in Nicaragua.

The leatherback turtle is declining in numbers at a catastrophic rate in the Pacific Ocean, and if current trends continue, it will disappear from these waters within the next few years (Spotila et al. 1996, 2000). The decline is due primarily to the incidental catch of turtles in longline, gill net, and trawl fisheries. Harvesting of eggs from nesting beaches and some killing of adults on nesting beaches and at sea by indigenous peoples for food and medicinal oils and ointments also all have an impact.

Olive ridley turtles that nest in Costa Rica traverse great distances in the eastern Pacific (Plotkin et al. 1995, 1996). In contrast to leatherbacks (Morreale et al. 1996), olive ridleys do not follow migration corridors but rather swim in diverse patterns in waters ranging from Mexico to Peru and the Galápagos. These turtles live in waters under the jurisdiction of many countries and in international waters. Any successful conservation plan must address the problem of interactions of sea turtles with the fishing industry of the Americas and Asia, as well.

In addition to the two *arribada* beaches in Costa Rica, olive ridleys nest at one *arribada* beach in Pacific Mexico and two *arribada* beaches in India. Other *arribada* beaches in Mexico were destroyed by the 1980s through extensive killing of adult females for the leather trade. There are some minor *arribada* beaches on the Pacific coast of Nicaragua and Guatemala and scattered nesting along Pacific Mesoamerica.

Black turtles nest in Nicaragua, El Salvador, Guatemala, and Mexico, as well as Costa Rica. Conservation takes place at many beaches in these countries, but the poaching of eggs takes place on most beaches and is a serious problem for survival of this species. In Nicaragua conservationists working with members of local communities protect the main beaches of Chococente and La Flor. Soldiers provide protection for the beaches, and hatcheries protect some nests. Development threatens these beaches. In Guatemala the Asociación de Rescate y Conservación de Vida Silvestre (ARCAS) protects several small beaches and places eggs in hatcheries. Local people are paid in flour, corn, and other foods in return for ten eggs from every nest of eggs that they take. That means that only 10 percent of the eggs at most are being saved. Although

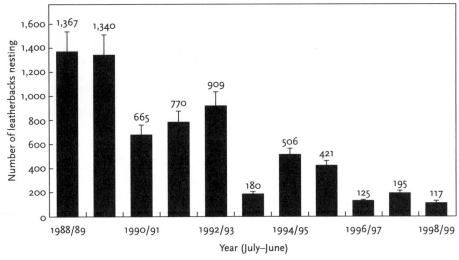

FIGURE 15.1. Numbers of leatherback turtles nesting on Playa Grande from the 1988/89 nesting season to the 1998/99 nesting season. Data from 1988 to 1992/93 are based on counts of the number of nests and assume a clutch frequency of 7. Numbers from 1993/94 to 1998/99 are based on Passive Integrated Transponder (PIT) tag identification of individual nesting female turtles. The population has undergone an exponential decline during this period.

this is a noble effort, it is doomed to failure. Studies on freshwater turtles (Congdon et al. 1994) and modeling of life history characteristics of sea turtles (Spotila et al. 1996) demonstrate that this level of predation on nests cannot be sustained by a turtle population. Owing to the high rate of mortality of the few turtle hatchlings released into the ocean, insufficient animals are being produced to ensure a return of adults when this cohort would be maturing and returning to nest.

In Mexico considerable effort is being made to monitor black turtle beaches in Michoacán. In addition, Mexican marines have provided protection for biologists, turtles, and their nests. However, poaching is still rampant, and despite efforts with local communities, these populations are still being heavily exploited.

EXTINCTION OF LEATHERBACK TURTLES?

In 1996 (Spotila et al. 1996) we estimated the number of leatherbacks nesting on 28 beaches around the world from the literature and from communications with investigators studying those beaches. In 1995 there were about 34,500

adult female leatherbacks, compared with about 115,000 in 1980 (Pritchard 1982). The greatest declines occurred in Malaysia and the Pacific coast of Mexico. Both of these colonies experienced an exponential decline. We are now seeing an exponential decline at the beaches of Las Baulas National Park, as well (fig. 15.1). The eastern Pacific population is now about 1,750, and the world population is about 27,600 (table 15.1).

Stable leatherback populations cannot withstand an increase in adult mortality above natural background levels without decreasing. However, protection of eggs and hatchlings during the first day of life can have a significant effect on overall stability of leatherback populations with a moderate increase in adult mortality (5%). Leatherback populations in the Pacific and Indian Oceans cannot survive the current levels of adult mortality from fisheries in these oceans. Atlantic populations are also being exploited at a rate that cannot be sustained. Thus, leatherbacks are on the verge of extinction (Spotila et al. 1996, 2000).

If our models are right and protection of nests and hatchlings can offset moderate levels of adult mortality, then perhaps an all-out

TABLE 15.1
Regional Population Estimates for
Nesting Leatherback Turtles, Dermochelys coriacea

REGION	ESTIMATED NUMBER OF NESTING FEMALES
Western Atlantic	15,000
Eastern Atlantic	4,700
Caribbean	4,000
Eastern Pacific	1,750
Western Pacific	1,700
Indian Ocean	450
Total	27,600

Source: Numbers are based on data reported in Spotila et al. (1996) and recent information from nesting beaches.

conservation effort in Costa Rica may save the leatherback in the Pacific Ocean. Certainly nesting beaches must be preserved and nests protected or there will be no "next generation." However, this effort will not be sufficient in the face of large-scale mortality in the fishery.

PARQUE MARINO LAS BAULAS

Parque Marino Las Baulas (map 15.1) on the Guanacaste coast includes the Bahía de Tamarindo, adjacent beaches, and mangrove estuaries. The park has three beaches that are used by leatherbacks as nesting sites, Playa Ventanas, Playa Grande, and Playa Langosta.

Playa Grande is a crescent-shaped white sand beach composed of finely broken shell rubble and sand and is regarded as one of the world's finest surfing areas. The other beaches are of similar composition but smaller in length. Eighty to 90 percent of leatherbacks nest on Playa Grande. There is increasing development along all three beaches just outside the 50-m public zone. The Estero Tamarindo is the largest estuary in dry Pacific Central America and hosts many species of plants and animals. Flagship species include the red, white, black, buttonwood, and tea mangroves, American crocodile, Roseate

Spoonbill, White Ibis, Boatbill Heron, Wood Stork, Great Blue Heron, egrets, howler monkeys, kinkajous, jaguars, and raccoons.

The town of Tamarindo is built behind what once was a leatherback nesting beach. Only rarely does a leatherback come ashore to nest in Tamarindo now. This area is not in the park. Lights of the town are a major problem for both adult and hatchling leatherbacks because the animals are attracted to the lights. Adults get entangled in boat lines in the anchorage off the town, and hatchlings wash ashore after swimming to the light sources. There is no law prohibiting lights from shining onto a turtle beach. Thus, unchecked development undermines protection of the park because of the lack of a lighting ordinance.

Just offshore from Tamarindo the Isla Capitan provides habitat for many marine birds. Tamarindo Bay is filled with fish and shellfish, but there has not been a scientific survey of the species living there. Although this is a protected zone of the park and turtles are protected by law within Costa Rican waters, commercial trawlers ply the bay at will, since the park does not have a large patrol boat.

The Estero San Francisco is another large estuary with mangrove forests and abundant bird life; it isolates Playa Langosta from Tamarindo. The beach is set aside as a biological reserve and is not open to tourism or visitation of nesting leatherbacks. Behind the beach and estuary is Finca Pinilla, which is being developed with homes, a golf course, and hotels. A new hotel on the rocky shore north of Playa Langosta and the estuary poses a threat to this nesting beach from its lights, noise, and activity. Workers filled in part of the estuary near the hotel site. Despite the filing of a legal action (denuncio) against the hotel by park officials, the estuary has not been restored as of 2003. The hotel now blocks access to Playa Langosta and uses the beach and estuary as a private location for guests despite their reserve status. Again, another denuncio has had no effect on this activity.

In the 1988/89 season, 1,367 leatherbacks nested on Playa Grande. In contrast, during the

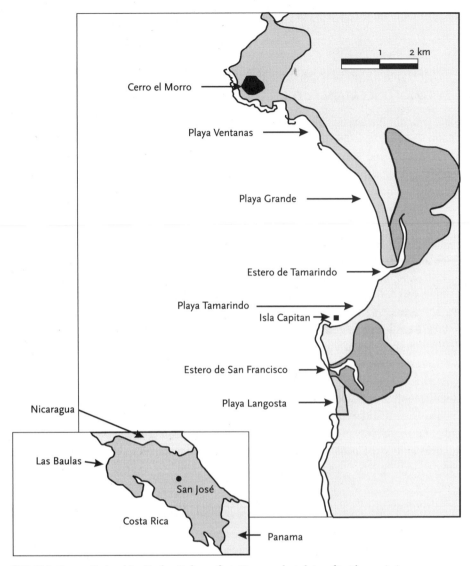

MAP 15.1. Parque Nacional Las Baulas. Redrawn from Steyermark et al. (1996) with permission.

1998/99 season only 117 leatherbacks nested there (fig. 15.1). Average annual mortality at sea for these turtles is 28 percent. In a given year 75 percent of leatherbacks are first-time nesters, and 25 percent are repeat migrants. Most sea turtle populations have a smaller percentage of repeat migrants than do freshwater turtles (Congdon et al. 1993, 1994) owing to some level of exploitation by humans. However, these percentages are especially low for the Las Baulas population.

Leatherbacks are long-lived like other large marine organisms. Populations of long-lived organisms cannot withstand heavy human exploitation (Congdon et al. 1994; Crouse 1999; Heppell et al. 1999; Musick 1999). The short lives of leatherbacks that we observe at Las Baulas today are not normal and reflect intense fishing pressure imposed on them. Thousands of leatherbacks died each year in oceanic longline and gill net fisheries in the 1980s and 1990s (Frazier and Brito Montero 1990; Nishimura and

Nakahigashi 1990; Wetherall et al. 1993; Eckert and Sarti 1997).

THE MAKING OF A PARK: THE LONG JOURNEY TO AN UNCERTAIN FUTURE

Parque Marino Las Baulas exists primarily because of the efforts of Maria Teresa Koberg, Mario Boza, Clara Padilla, and Peter Pritchard. Much has been written in the popular press, magazines, and books about this park, and much is incorrect. We worked at Las Baulas since 1990 and participated in or observed most of the activity surrounding the park. We were involved in research and conservation efforts at the park and worked with officials of the Ministry of Environment and Energy (MINAE) and its National Park Service (SPN) in efforts to consolidate the park. Between 1990 and 1999 we raised more than $788,000 in grants and donations to support these efforts from ten organizations (including Earthwatch, the U.S. National Science Foundation, the National Geographic Society, Drexel University, World Wildlife Fund, Guinness, Ltd., and the U.S. National Marine Fisheries Service) and many individuals. Here we relate the history of the park as we participated in it.

In the late 1980s the Estero de Tamarindo and Playa Grande were designated as the Tamarindo Wildlife Refuge, a Refugio Nacional de Vida Silvestre, and the estuary was protected as a wetland under the RAMSAR Convention on wetlands. The beach was protected up to 50 m above the high-tide mark. However, the refuge designation did not improve on the nationwide legal protection given to mangroves, ocean beaches, and turtles.

Under its refuge status Playa Grande was the scene of uncontrolled poaching, tourism, and beachfront development. The beach was bright with camera flashes during the height of the nesting season, and many people rode on the backs of leatherbacks as they crawled up and down the beach. Poachers stole almost every egg laid. One person built a hotel along the northern portion of the beach without any environmental assessment or permits. Another person built a hotel at the southern end of the beach by cutting mangroves and filling in part of the Tamarindo estuary. Plans also existed for a major development of 250 houses behind Playa Grande and more than 50 behind Playa Ventanas. A major luxury resort for 5,000 with a casino, nightclub, hotel, condominiums, and a yacht club was planned for Playa Grande.

Maria Teresa Koberg led the early efforts to obtain protection for the leatherbacks and was a pioneer in converting poachers to guides and rangers. Her most famous convert was Esperanza Rodríguez, the matriarch of a family that was long the major source of poaching on Playa Grande. From 1988 to 1996 Rodríguez made daily nest counts on Playa Grande while riding the beach at sunrise on her horse. These data were critical to our understanding of the population trends of leatherbacks there. Koberg, not Wilson and Pastor (Honey 1999), mounted a program of education and protection. She brought in Boy Scouts from Costa Rica and Minnesota. They patrolled the beach and protected nests and turtles by persuasion. She obtained national media attention and promoted the idea of a park.

In 1990 a report by Pritchard and members of the local community (Pritchard et al. 1990) recommended the formation of a park. In 1991 President Rafael Angel Calderón issued a decree that established the park as Las Baulas de Guanacaste (Executive Decree No. 20518, 5 June 1991). Even though the limit to the park was only 125 m inland from the high tide, it did protect the ocean offshore to 19.2 km.

Koberg was the first director of the park and established a protection program involving leaders and members of the Playa Grande and Tamarindo communities. She brought in a young biologist, Randall Arauz, who began a program of education in nearby villages. In 1992 he became the second director of the park and carried out a vigorous program of research and conservation on Playa Grande (Arauz and Naranjo 1994). Gradually residents began to accept the park as they became turtle guides and realized that their concerns were being heard (Naranjo and Arauz 1994).

In 1991–92 we raised funds for rural guards and obtained grant support for Anny Chaves, who, with her students, conducted a study of the nesting ecology on nearby Playa Langosta and a program of environmental education in local villages (Chaves et al. 1996). On Playa Grande a 1,300-m restricted zone that tourists could not enter provided a haven for nesting leatherbacks (Herzog 1992). Significant progress was made with local residents through a cooperative program with the Fundación la Gran Chorotega, a local nongovernmental organization that promoted preservation of local cultural and biological resources of Guanacaste.

During the 1992/93 nesting season we moved our research to Playa Grande to assist in conservation efforts, population data collection, and other research in the main portion of the park. Earthwatch volunteers and students and faculty from Drexel and Indiana-Purdue University at Fort Wayne tagged turtles and controlled ecotourists. Paladino taught guides in Spanish about turtles and control of ecotourists. In addition, we helped park rangers construct the first house for the park that served as the headquarters and a home for the director and his family. We also conducted botanical surveys and produced guidebooks for the estuary and dry forest.

In the 1993/94 season we began to tag permanently all leatherbacks on the beach and continued studying their nesting ecology and physiological ecology (Steyermark et al. 1996). A cooperative agreement between MINAE and Drexel University provided English-language training to several ministry employees involved in developing the park. The park, under director José Quiros, continued to offer training courses for local guides, and we continued our meetings and education efforts, as well. We also met with many of delegates of the National Assembly to educate them about turtles and the need for a national law to formalize the park.

From 1994/95 to 1997/98 Sergio Obando was director and did an excellent job in beginning the consolidation of the park. Outreach in local villages increased, and we established a program of conservation education in the Playa Grande community and Matapalo school. In 1995 the National Assembly finally passed a law making the park a permanent entity. Unfortunately, an apparent "clerical error" established the park as 125 m under the sea instead of 125 m inland from high tide. As of 2002 this error has not been corrected.

During the Obando period more funds came to the park. With the help of Earthwatch Europe we obtained a grant from the Guinness Corporation's "Water of Life" program to provide a building fund for the park. This grant allowed the construction of a large dormitory building for park volunteers. We also funded and mentored students from the Universidad Nacional in Heredia, who carried out tagging and nesting ecology studies on Playa Langosta. They controlled poaching and when necessary brought park rangers to that beach to maintain order. The park closed Playa Langosta to tourists so that it was a refuge for leatherbacks.

In the 1998/99 season one of our Universidad Nacional students became the director of the park after graduation. Rotney Piedra brought to the position not only enthusiasm but also training in sea turtle biology. By 1999, residents generally accepted the park. Tourists could only go on the beach with a guide, group size was officially limited to ten, and park rangers were more diligent about their duties. English-language and conservation training at Drexel improved Piedra's ability to manage the park. He increased controls on the beach and worked with local landowners to improve protection of the turtles. By 2001 Piedra's rangers were effective, and guides cooperated with researchers.

As of 2002 there were still many problems. The park law needed to be fixed to establish boundaries properly along the land behind the beaches. Agreements were needed with landowners behind Playa Grande to support the park.

A lighting law was needed to protect adults and hatchlings from lights behind the beaches and from Tamarindo. The urbanization plan for the area needed to be completed, and park consolidation was still ongoing. Development was the dominant factor threatening the park. Completion of the hotel in Tamarindo overlooking Playa Langosta created a new threat to that beach. Conservation at Las Baulas is thus still a work in progress. To assist in this effort we formed a nongovernmental organization, the Leatherback Trust, and registered it in Costa Rica as Fideocomiso Baulas. Funds from the Leatherback Trust support a biologist, two rangers, development of a management plan, and other initiatives toward park consolidation. In 2003 we raised another $325,000 for this effort.

45 YEARS OF SEA TURTLE CONSERVATION IN COSTA RICA

Conservation biologist Archie Carr began sea turtle conservation in Costa Rica in 1954 when he visited Tortuguero with Costa Rican businessman Guillermo "Billy" Cruz. In 1955 he started the green turtle tagging project that continues to this day (Bjorndal et al. 1999). In 1959 U.S. businessman Joshua Powers formed the Brotherhood of the Turtle after reading *The Windward Road* (Carr 1955). This later became the Caribbean Conservation Corporation (CCC), which ensured continued funding for the green turtle project at Tortuguero. The original goal of the CCC was "to save the green turtle from destruction, to give it a chance to renew its numbers, and to redistribute it to all beaches where it was once common" (Godfrey 1999: 1). The approach was one of scientific research, conservation, and restoration.

Along the way Archie Carr worked with leading citizens of Costa Rica to convince them to protect turtles. In 1963 President Francisco Orlich signed the first executive decree regulating hunting of sea turtles and collection of their eggs. Also in 1963 the first guards came to Tortuguero to protect turtles. In 1970 Costa Rica prohibited all turtle hunting and egg collection and established Tortuguero as a national park,

thus protecting the 48-km nesting beach. In 1973 Costa Rica signed the Convention on International Trade in Endangered Species (CITES), making international trade in sea turtles and other endangered species illegal. In 1975 the government expanded Tortuguero National Park to include the nearby hills and lowlands.

Throughout this time Carr continued his green turtle studies at Tortuguero and established an ethic in Tortuguero that respected and protected turtles. By employing villagers at the Casa Verde field station and doing turtle nest counts in the park, Carr had a significant impact on the local economy, and this formed an economic basis for the development of turtle conservation in the village. He linked economic progress of the local community with conservation long before anyone made up terms such as "grassroots community-based conservation, parks for people, sustainable development and use, and conservation for development" (Brandon et al. 1998: 1). This later laid the groundwork for ecotourism there. Carr's students carried out numerous pioneering studies on the hearing and orientation of hatchlings. Scientific research was always a key part of the conservation effort at Tortuguero (Spotila 1988). There was little interest in research and conservation at Tortuguero among Costa Rican universities during this period. The Escuela de Biología was just beginning at the University of Costa Rica. In addition, Limón Province was far removed from the Central Valley in travel time and mind-set.

In 1978 a major scientific expedition sailed to Tortuguero on the *Alpha Helix,* and several key physiological studies took place. It was here that Standora et al. (1982) accomplished the first successful radio and sonic telemetry of sea turtles. In 1980 Morreale et al. (1982) demonstrated the importance of temperature-dependent sex determination to the conservation of sea turtles. Throughout this period there was a continued harvest of 500 adult green turtles a year for slaughter in Limón. In 1982 local pressure led to an increase in the regulated harvest to 1,800 green turtles per year. By the mid-1980s an ecotourism boom started in Tortuguero, and the nighttime population of the village jumped from about 100 to 500 with the addition of several hotels and cabinas. The turtle ethic began to break down as more people came to Tortuguero from other areas and money flowed into the community from illegal arms traffic to Nicaragua during the Contra war. The paving of the runway, development of the area inland from Tortuguero, and finally construction of an illegal road to Tortuguero in 1996 ended its isolation.

Throughout this period the CCC increased its conservation efforts. It erected an information kiosk in 1985, initiated a comprehensive conservation and development plan in 1989, and obtained approval of a maritime terrestrial zone for Tortuguero in 1993. Despite the untimely death of Archie Carr in 1987, his family, students, and the CCC staff, energized by Cindy Taft, redoubled their efforts to preserve green turtles and expand conservation efforts in Nicaragua and into the leatherback nesting season. We began physiological and nesting ecology studies on leatherbacks at Tortuguero in 1989 (Paladino et al. 1990) and included education and conservation as a central part of our program.

Talks in the schools, visits with community leaders, employment of local residents, and encouragement of the park guards brought visibility to the leatherbacks and gave them a status and level of protection approaching those of green turtles. Our rule of thumb became "no scientists, no protection," and we expanded our project to the entire leatherback nesting season. That extended protection on the beach to include both the leatherback and green turtle seasons, March through September. This developed into an annual tagging program (Campbell et al. 1996) and nicely complemented the CCC conservation efforts in Tortuguero and Nicaragua. In 1994 the CCC completed its new field station and visitor center in Tortuguero, and in 1998 Costa Rica and Panama signed an agreement for the collaborative management of sea turtles in the Caribbean.

More green turtles arrived to lay eggs in 1998 than ever before. The nesting beach was protected. Thousands of people had their first mystical encounter with a green turtle in the dark and silence of the night. They did so under the watchful eye of a local conservationist/guide trained and certified by the CCC. The guides were well informed, friendly, and staunch defenders of turtles. Protection of the beach was increasing.

Meanwhile, on the Pacific coast, olive ridleys, along with leatherbacks at Las Baulas, dominate the nesting beaches of Pacific Costa Rica. Hughes and Richard (1974) were the first to document the large number of sea turtles that nested on many beaches there and the mass nesting of olive ridleys at Playas Nancite and Ostional. Steve Cornelius, a Peace Corps volunteer, documented the nesting of turtles on Playa Naranjo. Through the 1970s and 1980s he and Douglas Robinson of the University of Costa Rica carried out a series of studies on sea turtles along the Pacific coast (Cornelius 1976, 1986). Robinson and his university students began serious study of sea turtles on most of these beaches.

Robinson came to the University of Costa Rica in 1966 from Texas A&M University for a brief stay and spent the rest of his life there. He established the Museum of Zoology at the University and the Programa de Tortugas Marinas, which served as a focal point for education of Costa Rican and foreign students in sea turtle biology and conservation. He directed the thesis studies of several students and established the first computer database for flipper tag returns from turtles along the Pacific coast of Central America. He also played a key advisory role in the development of conservation policies and laws in Costa Rica. The program continued at the university after his death in 1991 but, lacking a director with his mature leadership and scientific training, was floundering by the mid-1990s, and the university ended it. Fortunately, a vigorous program directed by Claudette Mo remained at nearby Universidad Nacional. In addition, a cadre of former students remained from the Robinson group at the University of Costa Rica, and Mario Alvarado, Randall Arauz, Jorge Ballestero, Juan Carlos Castro, Anny Chaves, and Isabel Naranjo continued to be active in sea turtle biology and conservation. Unfortunately only Roldan Valverde continued on to receive a Ph.D.

Perhaps the most ambitious project started by Robinson was the experiment with a controlled harvest of olive ridley eggs at Ostional. In 1980 he saw that the little village situated on one of the most important sea turtle nesting beaches in the world would play a critical role in the future of sea turtle conservation. Even though harvesting of sea turtle eggs had been illegal in Costa Rica since 1966, it still took place at night at Ostional and elsewhere. Robinson established the Ostional turtle station of the University of Costa Rica to study the *arribada* phenomenon and began to involve villagers in the protection of the *arribada*. The concept evolved that villagers could take the eggs from the first 24 hours of the *arribada*, since they would be destroyed anyway, and protect them from the later portion of the event. This led to the current controlled harvest. From 1977, when Robinson first proposed the idea, until 1987, when the Costa Rican Congress reformed the Wildlife Conservation Law, which prohibited egg harvesting, to allow a controlled harvest at Ostional, a vigorous debate within Costa Rica and worldwide among sea turtle biologists considered all aspects of the plan. The final arrangement saw the Ostional community form an economic development association, Asociación de Desarrollo Integral de Ostional (ADIO), to manage the harvest and the University of Costa Rica entrusted with legal responsibility for carrying out scientific studies needed to sustain the population.

The Ostional experiment is a qualified success and has been the subject of numerous articles worldwide (e.g., Baker 1994). The village has a new school, a new clinic, a new Guardia Rural office, and a new sense of civic pride in what the members of the community have accomplished. Local wardens patrol the beach, villagers help to count the turtles, and the egg harvest is conducted in a regular and fairly well managed way (Ballestero et al. 1996).

Many problems remain, however. The Ostional project has not diminished the illegal egg trade, which still occurs on both coasts of Costa Rica and invades national parks whenever rangers or scientists let their guard down. Away from the beaches enforcement is severely lacking or nonexistent. In addition, since the loss of Robinson, efforts of biologists have lacked the guidance needed to maintain the scientific integrity of the project. The *arribadas* have decreased in numbers of turtles during the late 1990s. It is not clear how much of this decline is due to the long-term egg harvest and how much is due to the mortality of olive ridleys in the net and longline fisheries in the Pacific. Development in Nosara, 12 km south, has forced land values out of the reach of local people, just as at Las Baulas. Developers are buying land surrounding Ostional and planning to build tourist facilities. It would be premature to term this experiment a success and a major mistake to take it as a model for sustainable development of other communities near sea turtle nesting beaches. This is an unfinished experiment, one in great need of more vigorous management by MINAE, in concert with more vigorous enforcement of laws for sea turtle protection throughout Costa Rica.

LESSONS AND RECOMMENDATIONS FOR THE FUTURE

Many lessons can be learned from the story of sea turtles in Costa Rica. In 1964 Archie Carr wrote the following about conservation in Africa: "But the saving of wild beings from obliteration cannot be expected to pay for itself in more than a sprinkling of special cases. For most of the wild things on earth, the future must depend upon the conscience of mankind. . . . The welfare of the wildlife will have to be reckoned against the rights of multiplying African man" (172–73). In 1993 Bonner echoed these sentiments when he stated that if Africa's wildlife is to be saved it will require radical policies and changes in attitudes. Certainly both of these sentiments apply to the saving of sea turtles in Costa Rica. The central lesson of the past 45 years is that there has to be a radical change in the approach of Costa Ricans and their government if they are to succeed in preserving sea turtles on their beaches and in the oceans.

SUCCESS IN SOME ASPECTS

A dedicated cadre of conservationists have succeeded in establishing and maintaining a wonderful park system in Costa Rica. Mario Boza, Alvaro Ugalde, Pedro León, Sigfredo Marín, and their colleagues have worked vigorously and effectively for the parks. At the same time they have been helped by many North American biologists who have provided a scientific basis for management of the parks. From the beginning foreigners have played an essential role in the national park system (Wallace 1992). In general, parks have had the support of most of the people of Costa Rica. Sea turtles are viewed as charismatic creatures, and certainly people of the Central Valley believe that Costa Rica is defending these animals.

THE FUNDAMENTAL PROBLEM

The consensus is that it is on the beaches and among local people where problems arise. This is a convenient alibi that masks a more fundamental problem in the Costa Rican approach to sea turtle protection and wildlife conservation in general: the "power elite"—the ruling class that controls the political and economic power in a country—of Costa Rica sees economic development and profit as more important than conservation of natural resources, development of a modern park system, and protection of wildlife, including sea turtles. This is a familiar problem in all countries. It is always a matter of balancing budget priorities in government and of raising private funds for conservation organizations. However, in Costa Rica conservation is losing, and whereas in the United States and Europe the "civil society" is committed to conservation, this is not true in Costa Rica. There is a fundamental lack of philanthropy on the part of wealthy Costa Ricans. They expect foreigners and their conservation organizations to continue to provide monetary support for the park system. Although many young Costa Ricans and middle-class adults have volunteered their time and donated modest amounts of money (from $5 to $10,000) to support sea turtle and other conservation projects, wealthy Costa Ricans, in general, have not provided substantial amounts to support the park system. In addition, there is little support in the government for the park system. This is most obvious in the lack of commitment of funds to the parks. Despite ecotourism being the number one source of foreign revenue, inadequate funding hinders development of park infrastructure, training of park personnel, and protection. Even more damaging is the subservience of the park system and environmental protection to development and tourism interests. When there is a choice between demands of protection of turtles on the beach at Las Baulas and access to turtles by guides and tourists, the latter wins because of the power of the tourism agency, Instituto Costarricense de Turismo (ICT), to overrule MINAE. There is a tax on tourists entering and leaving the country, but this money goes to support ICT, not the parks. Although Costa Rica is seen as a leader in ecotourism and parks (Terborgh 1999), it is essentially mining its parks for tourist dollars and putting few resources back into parks to sustain them. Finally, laws to prevent poaching, protect beaches, regulate fishing, and defend wildlife are weakly enforced (see chapters 22 and 23).

There is a lack of leadership at the highest levels in MINAE and the government and an entrenched, inefficient bureaucracy in MINAE and the Park Service. The low priority the government gives to protection leads to institutional weakness. The political leadership fails to demand successful conservation and fails to provide adequate training and motivation to MINAE and Park Service staffs. Most personnel of the park system and MINAE lack formal training in how to develop a park, build infrastructure, interact with tourists, and defend the parks. They spend their time ensuring their own welfare in the bureaucracy rather than the welfare of the natural resources they are supposed to protect. Most rangers are poorly educated, poorly paid, and little motivated to do their jobs. In fact, they do not know exactly what a park ranger is supposed to do. As in other countries (Terborgh 1999), most guards are not empowered, and so they occupy themselves with controlling tourists and scientists while closing their eyes to the more serious challenge of evicting squatters and controlling developers. Although it is true that Costa Rica has a much more organized park system than most other tropical countries (Terborgh 1999), it is also true that its parks sustain a much greater number of ecotourists and a much greater rate of development along their borders than parks in those countries.

Costa Rica is caught in the same trap as many other nations. With an expanding population, a declining resource base, and a large foreign debt, there seems to be little hope for securing the resources needed to ensure protection of the established national parks, let alone new ones such as Las Baulas. Without sustainable development the future will be grim, and our play about sea turtles will indeed end as a tragedy. However, no nation has captured or is close to reaching the golden egg of sustainable development, and there is no guarantee that sustainable development will lead to harmony between humans and nature (Frazier 1997).

NEED FOR RADICAL CHANGE

Costa Ricans will have to outgrow their laissez-faire attitude toward environmental protection and establish strong, clear laws to control development and protect the parks and natural resources contained in them on land and sea. They also will have to reform the legal system to provide vigorous enforcement of these laws. We agree with Terborgh (1999) that there is no substitute for enforcement. Without it all is lost.

Next the park system will have to be revitalized. It can no longer operate as a biodiversity welfare system dependent on donations from foreign governments and conservation organizations. Plenty of resources are available in the form of ecotourism dollars and biodiversity royalties. If Costa Ricans want to preserve their biodiversity, their parks, and, most important for this story, their sea turtles, they will have to use some of those resources to fund their conservation infrastructure adequately. Personnel need to be adequately trained, led, and paid in order for them to do their jobs effectively. Professionals with university and advanced degrees need to be hired. Perhaps an exchange program with park systems in nations such as the United States and Canada, not based on a welfare program but on a work program, would be effective. Rangers from those nations could be given release time to come to Costa Rica to train rangers on-site and to learn about the biodiversity in Costa Rica firsthand, and rangers from Costa Rica could take their place in the home country and learn how an effective park system functions by working in it.

If more progress is not made, it may be necessary to internationalize the parks in order to save them (Boza 1993). Sea turtles are international resources. Leatherbacks at Las Baulas are an international treasure, and the beaches there must be vigorously protected or leatherbacks will become extinct in the Pacific Ocean. If the people of Costa Rica cannot protect the nesting beaches, pressure will increase for the international community to step in and carry out that function. Certainly the precedent has been established that the international community has the right to intervene in a country to protect human rights, as in Bosnia and Kosovo. It will not be too long in the future before the international community establishes the precedent that it has the right to intervene in a country to protect nature and biodiversity vital to the future well-being of the global community. This is one basis of the evolving theory of environmental security. This theory arose from the concept of preventive defense (Carter and Perry 1999), which seeks to prevent wars before they occur. Environmental security goes a step further and states that environmental problems such as overpopulation, lack of resources, and environmental degradation can be the causes of conflict and will become the predominant causes of conflict in the decades to come (Myers 1993).

Because Costa Rica has so much biodiversity and the most critical sea turtle nesting beaches in the Pacific, it has the obligation to protect them by making changes in its conservation strategy so that its parks accomplish their stated purpose. If it does not, it can expect that other nations will become increasingly involved.

This play does not have to end as a tragedy. Costa Rica has the basis for success in sea turtle conservation and in reforming its park system and environmental ministry. It has a democratically elected government that enjoys the support of the people. Most of its population appreciates the intrinsic value of nature, and most of its people are educated. There is already a large area of land set aside in parks and a cadre of senior conservationists who can lead a revitalized park system, and the youth of the nation are committed to the protection of plants and animals. There is no nation in the tropics better positioned to take the next step into real nature conservation. All that is needed is the political will on the part of the power elite to change their priorities and make conservation an ethical imperative (Oates 1999) instead of an advertising initiative.

REFERENCES

Arauz, R. M., and I. Naranjo. 1994. Hatching success of leatherback turtles (*Dermochelys coriacea*) in the leatherbacks of Guanacaste Marine National Park, Costa Rica. Proceedings of the 13th Annual Workshop on Sea Turtle Biology and Conservation (NOAA technical memorandum NMFS-SEFC-278), 11–14.

Baker, C. P. 1994. Hatching their eggs and eating them, too. *Pacific Discovery* (Summer): 10–18.

Ballestero, J., G. Ordonez, and J. Gomez. 1996. Potential threats for the survival of sea turtles in the Ostional Wildlife Refuge, Santa Cruz, Guanacaste, Costa Rica. Proceedings of the 15th Annual Workshop on Sea Turtle Biology and Conservation (NOAA technical memorandum NMFS-SEFC-278), 31–34.

Bjorndal, K. A. 1999. Conservation of hawksbill sea turtles: Perceptions and realities. *Chelonian Conservation and Biology* 3:174–76.

Bjorndal, K. A., J. A. Wetherall, A. Bolten, and J. A. Mortimer. 1999. Twenty-six years of green turtle nesting at Tortuguero, Costa Rica: An encouraging trend. *Conservation Biology* 13:126–34.

Bonner, R. 1993. *At the hand of man, peril and hope for Africa's wildlife.* New York: Knopf. 322 pp.

Boza, M. A. 1993. Conservation in action: Past, present, and future of the National Park System in Costa Rica. *Conservation Biology* 7:239–47.

Brandon, K., K. H. Redford, and S. E. Sanderson. 1998. *Parks in peril: People, politics, and protected areas.* Washington, D.C.: Island Press.

Campbell, C. L., C. J. Lagueux, and J. A. Mortimer. 1996. Leatherback turtle, *Dermochelys coriacea*, nesting at Tortuguero, Costa Rica, in 1995. *Chelonian Conservation and Biology* 2:169–72.

Carr, A. 1955. *The windward road: Adventures of a naturalist on remote Caribbean shores.* New York: Knopf. 266 pp.

———. 1964. *The land and wildlife of Africa.* New York: Time. 200 pp.

Carter, A. B., and W. J. Perry. 1999. *Preventive defense: A new security strategy for America.* Washington, D.C.: Brookings Institution Press. 243 pp.

Chaves, A., G. Serrano, G. Marín, E. Arguedas, A. Jimenez, and J. R. Spotila. 1996. Biology and conservation of leatherback turtles, *Dermochelys coriacea*, at Playa Langosta, Costa Rica. *Chelonian Conservation and Biology* 2:184–89.

Congdon, J. D., A. E. Dunham, and R. C. van Loben Sels. 1993. Delayed sexual maturity and demographics of Blanding's turtle (*Emydoidea blandingii*): Implications for conservation and management of long-lived organisms. *Conservation Biology* 7:826–33.

Congdon, J. D., A. E. Dunham, and R. C. van Loben Sels. 1994. Demographics of common snapping turtles (*Chelydra serpentina*): Implications for conservation and management of long-lived organisms. *American Zoologist* 34: 397–408.

Cornelius, S. E. 1976. Marine turtle nesting activity at Playa Naranjo, Costa Rica. *Brenesia* 8:1–27.

———. 1986. *The sea turtles of Santa Rosa National Park.* Madrid: Hermanos Ramos. 64 pp.

Crouse, D. T. 1999. The consequences of delayed maturity in a human-dominated world. In *Life in the slow lane: Ecology and conservation of long-lived marine animals*, ed. J. A. Musick, 195–202. Bethesda, Md.: American Fisheries Society.

Drake, D. L. 1996. Marine turtle nesting, nest predation, hatch frequency, and nesting seasonality on the Osa Peninsula, Costa Rica. *Chelonian Conservation and Biology* 2:89–92.

Eckert, S. A., and L. Sarti. 1997. Distant fisheries implicated in the loss of the world's largest leatherback nesting population. *Marine Turtle Newsletter* 78:2–7.

Frazier, J. G. 1997. Sustainable development: Modern elixir or sack dress? *Environmental Conservation* 24:182–93.

Frazier, J. G., and J. L. Brito Montero. 1990. Incidental capture of marine turtles by the swordfish fishery at San Antonia, Chile. *Marine Turtle Newsletter* 49:8–13.

Godfrey, D. 1999. CCC celebrates 40 years of sea turtle conservation. *Veladon, Caribbean Conservation Corporation Newsletter* (Winter 1999): 1–2.

Heppell, L., B. Crowder, and T. R. Menzel. 1999. Life table analysis of long-lived marine species with implications for conservation and management. In *Life in the slow lane: Ecology and conservation of long-lived marine animals*, ed. J. A. Musick, 137–48. Bethesda, Md.: American Fisheries Society.

Herzog, P. 1992. An assessment of ecotourism and its impact on leatherback sea turtles at Playa Grande, Costa Rica. Programa Regional en Manejo de Vida Silvestre, Universidad Nacional, Heredia, Costa Rica. Unpublished report.

Honey, M. 1999. *Ecotourism and sustainable development: Who owns paradise?* Washington, D.C.: Island Press. 405 pp.

Hughes, D. A., and J. D. Richard. 1974. The nesting of the Pacific ridley turtle *Lepidochelys olivacea* on Playa Nancite, Costa Rica. *Marine Biology* 24:97–107.

Karl, S. A., and B. W. Bowen. 1999. Evolutionary significant units versus geopolitical taxonomy: Molecular systematics of an endangered sea turtle (genus *Chelonia*). *Conservation Biology* 13: 990–99.

Leslie, A. J., D. N. Penick, J. R. Spotila, and F. V. Paladino. 1996. Leatherback turtle, *Dermochelys coriacea*, nesting and nest success at Tortuguero, Costa Rica, in 1990–1991. *Chelonian Conservation and Biology* 2:159–68.

Meylan, A. B. 1999. Status of the hawksbill turtle (*Eretmochelys imbricata*) in the Caribbean region. *Chelonian Conservation and Biology* 3: 177–84.

Morreale, S. J., G. J. Ruiz, J. R. Spotila, and E. A. Standora. 1982. Temperature dependent sex determination: Current practices threaten conservation of sea turtles. *Science* 216:1245–47.

Morreale, S. J., E. A. Standora, J. R. Spotila, and F. V. Paladino. 1996. Migration corridor for sea turtles. *Nature* 384:319–20.

Musick, J. A. 1999. Ecology and conservation of long-lived marine animals. In *Life in the slow lane: Ecology and conservation of long-lived marine animals*, ed. J. A. Musick, 1–10. Bethesda, Md: American Fisheries Society.

Myers, N. 1993. *Ultimate security: The environmental basis of political stability.* New York: Norton. 308 pp.

Naranjo, I., and R. Arauz. 1994. Local guides in the Leatherbacks of Guanacaste Marine National Park: Sustained development and sea turtle conservation. Proceedings of the 13th Annual Workshop on Sea Turtle Biology and Conservation (NOAA technical memorandum NMFS-SEFC-278), 124–26.

Nishimura, W., and S. Nakahigashi. 1990. Incidental capture of sea turtles by Japanese research and training vessels: Results of a questionnaire. *Marine Turtle Newsletter* 51:1–4.

Oates, J. F. 1999. *Myth and reality in the rain forest: How conservation strategies are failing in West Africa.* Berkeley: University of California Press. 310 pp.

Paladino, F. V., M. P. O'Connor, and J. R. Spotila. 1990. Metabolism of leatherback turtles, gigantothermy, and thermoregulation of dinosaurs. *Nature* 344:858–60.

Plotkin, P. T., R. A. Byles, D. C. Rostal, and D. W. Owens. 1995. Independent versus socially facilitated oceanic migration of the olive ridley, *Lepidochelys olivacea. Marine Biology* 122:137–43.

Plotkin, P. T., D. W. Owens, R. A. Byles, and R. Patterson. 1996. Departure of male olive ridley turtles (*Lepidochelys olivacea*) from a nearshore breeding area. *Herpetologica* 52:1–7.

Pritchard, P. C. H. 1982. Nesting of the leatherback turtle, *Dermochelys coriacea*, in Pacific Mexico, with a new estimate of the world population status. *Copeia* 1982:741–47.

Pritchard, P. C. H., H. Elizondo, C. Rodríguez, N. Guadamuz, E. Rodríguez, G. Rosales, and Q. Jiménez. 1990. Las Baulas de Guanacaste, a new national park for Costa Rica. Report to Ministerio de Recursos Naturales, Energía, y Minas, Programa de Rescate de Tortugas Marinas, San José, Costa Rica. 82 pp.

Spotila, J. R. 1988. Archie Carr: To the edge of hope, 1909–1987. *Herpetologica* 44:128–32.

Spotila, J. R., A. E. Dunham, A. J. Leslie, A. C. Steyermark, P. T. Plotkin, and F. V. Paladino. 1996. Worldwide population decline of *Dermochelys coriacea*: Are leatherback turtles going extinct? *Chelonian Conservation and Biology* 2:209–22.

Spotila, J. R., R. D. Reina, A. C. Steyermark, P. T. Plotkin, and F. V. Paladino. 2000. Pacific leatherback turtles face extinction. *Nature* 405: 529–30.

Standora, E. A., J. R. Spotila, and R. E. Foley. 1982. Regional endothermy in the sea turtle, *Chelonia mydas. Journal of Thermal Biology* 7:159–65.

Steyermark, A. C., K. Williams, J. R. Spotila, F. V. Paladino, D. C. Rostal, S. J. Morreale, M. T. Koberg, and R. Arauz. 1996. Nesting leatherback turtles at Las Baulas National Park, Costa Rica. *Chelonian Conservation and Biology* 2: 173–83.

Terborgh, J. 1999. *Requiem for nature*. Washington, D.C.: Island Press. 234 pp.

Wallace, D. R. 1992. *The Quetzal and the macaw: The story of Costa Rica's national parks*. San Francisco: Sierra Club Books. 222 pp.

Wetherall, J. A., G. H. Balazs, R. A. Tokunga, and M. Y. Y. Yong. 1993. Bycatch of marine turtles in North Pacific high-seas driftnet fisheries and impacts on the stocks. *North Pacific Fisheries Commission Bulletin* 53:519–38.

CHAPTER 16

Prospects for *Circa Situm*
Tree Conservation in Mesoamerican
Dry-Forest Agro-Ecosystems

David H. Boshier, James E. Gordon, and Adrian J. Barrance

RY FOREST ONCE STRETCHED almost continuously along the Mesoamerican (Central American/Mexican) Pacific coast, from Sonora in Mexico to Guanacaste in Costa Rica (area of 550,000 km²). Conditions suitable for dry forest also exist on the Yucatán Peninsula, the coast of the Mexican states of Puebla and Tamaulipas, with significant inland areas in dry valleys (e.g., Motagua Valley, Guatemala) throughout the region (see Graham and Dilcher 1995 and Murphy and Lugo 1995 for the distribution and origins of this forest type). Human preference for the seasonally dry tropical environment (Murphy and Lugo 1995) and the ease of clearing its vegetation have, however, led to the destruction and fragmentation of much of its forest. Janzen (1988: 130) estimated that less than 2 percent of the original forest is in a state "sufficiently intact to attract the attention of the traditional conservationist," with only 0.09 percent having official reserve status. Only on the Pacific Mexican coast are there significant areas of mature, possibly primary, dry forest. Even in these areas it is rare to find a forest with no evidence of occasional timber and firewood extraction, extensive livestock browsing, or hunting. In Central America the dry-forest zone is reduced to a patchwork of various types of agricultural land and small forests of secondary origin. Unregulated selective felling of economically important tree species continues, resulting in the commercial extinction of timber species in some areas (e.g., *Astronium graveolens* Jacq., *Guaiacum sanctum* L.). Reserve selection is often opportunistic, determined more by political, social, and economic constraints than by optimal biological criteria. Consequently the location of reserves may bias floristic composition (at species and gene pool levels), limiting their overall value for biodiversity conservation (Ledig 1988).

Any conservation initiative requires consideration of the extent and value of and threat to the resource to be targeted. Tropical dry forests are species-rich in comparison with most of the world's forest types (Gentry 1995). Biodiversity can, however, be measured at a variety of levels, and species numbers alone are an insufficient and poor measure of the conservation importance of any ecosystem. Consideration must also be given to the biota's uniqueness, as well as the importance of interactions with other ecosystems. At the species level, Mesoamerican dry forests contain a woody flora that is distinct from that of Mesoamerican wet forests (Gentry 1995). Even for tree species that occur in both wet and dry forests, the dry-forest populations have typically been shown to be genetically distinct from wet forest populations (e.g., *Cordia alliodora* [R. et P.] Oken, Chase et al. 1995; *Cedrela odorata* L., Gillies et al. 1997). Mesoamerican dry forests are also host, depending on the season, to many migratory species, including species from the wet tropics (chapters 7 and 8), such that its conservation is important in protecting more than just its own biota.

Interest in the conservation of these species and their habitat is not confined to biologists. Mesoamerican dry forests are the natural habitat of a disproportionately high number of species commonly used in tropical agriculture and forestry for a variety of goods and services, such as *Gliricidia sepium* (Jacq.) Steudel, *Leucaena* spp., *Prosopis juliflora* (Swartz) D.C., and *Samanea saman* (Jacq.) Merrill. These species are now propagated over much broader climatic and geographical ranges than their natural distributions and have considerable socioeconomic importance (e.g., Stewart et al. 1992). Continued use and improvement of such species depend to some extent on the maintenance of genetic variation within and between natural and seminatural populations.

OPTIONS FOR CONSERVATION

IN SITU CONSERVATION

Conservation faces a problem. Mesoamerican dry forest is diverse and distinctive, containing many socioeconomically important species; however, existing reserves cover a very small fraction of the original forest, and few intact dry forests are left to conserve. The degree to which *in situ* reserves are appropriate for conservation depends on a variety of factors, such as forest size, the extent of fragmentation, and the prevailing socioeconomic context. Those forests that do remain are usually small (e.g., 1–500 ha), below the size that might be considered viable, and highly intervened, such that the ideal of maintaining a single large reserve is often irrelevant (as in the "single large or several small" debate; see Soulé 1987). Consideration must therefore be given to the biological and social feasibility of managing networks of small patches within the current land-use mosaic. Conservation initiatives for dry forest must examine approaches that depart from the traditional *in situ* conservation paradigm, involving protected "wilderness areas," and focus as well on ways in which the species of an already highly altered forest type can be conserved.

ECOLOGICAL RESTORATION

Ecological restoration has been proposed as a tool to redress the inadequacies of current reserves (e.g., Janzen 1986a), and extensive areas are currently under restoration management of various types in both the Guanacaste and Tempisque Conservation Areas in Costa Rica. Such restoration is facilitated by the very presence of existing *in situ* reserves, but in practice it is rarely feasible elsewhere given the socioeconomic conditions prevalent in large parts of Mesoamerica. Even, for example, the establishment of Guanacaste National Park required the displacement of a human population living in, or farming, the area, with smaller farmers and squatters faring relatively poorly in the purchase and compensation process (Utting 1993). Nonetheless, in this case, sufficient national and international interest has probably been generated for the long-term maintenance of such management. Guanacaste, along with parts of Pacific lowland Mexico and the Yucatán Peninsula, however, represents the better end of the spectrum in terms of the size and quality of remnant dry-forest patches. Although, at a smaller scale, restoration ecology may have great relevance in the creation of biological corridors between more or less intact areas of forest, it and traditional *in situ* conservation will be inappropriate for much of the rest of the Mesoamerican dry-forest life zone, given the highly degraded and patchy nature of the forest resource and prevailing socioeconomic conditions.

EX SITU CONSERVATION

Similarly, *ex situ* methods (e.g., seed banks, seed stands, botanic gardens) offer limited long-term potential for most tropical tree species. This is clear from the small number of tree taxa (some 100 worldwide, mainly of economic importance; National Research Council 1991) subject to effective *ex situ* conservation; the scientific, technical, and resource limitations that constrain *ex situ* programs (National Research Council 1991); and inherent deficiencies of *ex situ* populations as conservation gene pools (Brown et al. 1989).

CIRCA SITUM CONSERVATION

The limitations of both *in situ* and *ex situ* approaches, and the recognition that farmers maintain a large array of plant biodiversity in some traditional farming systems, have led to a reexamination of the potential role of "conservation through use" on farms (e.g., Maxted et al. 1997). The term *circa situm* (also *"circa situ,"* "farmer-based conservation," "conservation *in hortus*"; Hughes 1998) has been used to distinguish the very different circumstances of conservation within altered agricultural landscapes (e.g., agroforestry systems, home gardens) outside natural habitats but within a species' native geographical range. Tree species have long been maintained, and hence conserved, in Mesoamerican agro-ecosystems. Hughes (1998) attributes the relative abundance of a wide range of *Leucaena* species in Mesoamerica, despite the loss of forest cover in most areas, to their management for several centuries by local communities and farmers in various ways and for various products and services. Indeed, he suggests that *L. salvadorensis* has been saved from extinction only because of its maintenance on farms, and there is also evidence for maintenance of

genetic diversity within these on-farm populations (Chamberlain et al. 1996). Other examples of traditional management systems that maintain tree species are given for the dry-forest zone of Central America (Kass et al. 1993) and the Mixtec region of Guerrero, Mexico (Casas and Caballero 1996). Only recently, however, have tree conservation strategies sought to capitalize on such practices (e.g., Halladay and Gilmour 1995), and consequently there is much to learn if we are to realize the potential of *circa situm* strategies and appreciate their limitations. In essence, *circa situm* conservation requires identification of compatibility between natural resource management systems found in native ranges of priority species (in this case trees) and conservation objectives. Human inhabitants within such areas are thus recognized as agents of conservation. *Circa situm* conservation aims to integrate conservation with prevailing socioeconomic trends, whereas the *in situ* and *ex situ* types of conservation aim to remove areas and species from the influence of those trends.

FOCUS OF THIS CHAPTER

The focus of this chapter is to question the assumption that trees in scattered tropical agroecosystems have no long-term viability and therefore no role in conservation. We discuss the role *circa situm* approaches could play in conserving the tree species of the Mesoamerican dry forest. We are concerned here with the prospects for such an approach rather than the precise prescriptions that will need to be formulated independently for each species and situation. We do not propose that *circa situm* conservation can replace *in situ* conservation. Rather, we argue that for highly threatened, disturbed, and fragmented vegetation types, it could have an important complementary role. This may be through the conservation of particular species and genes not conserved *in situ* and/or the provision of additional habitat and the facilitation of gene flow between existing reserves. The potential gain is great if the many tree species that exist in such disturbed vegetation can be shown to be conservable there through existing land-use practices, thus freeing scarce resources for the conservation of more critically threatened species that require more conventional, resource-intensive approaches. Provision of effective *circa situm* options requires multidisciplinary research to establish the general potential for the integration of conservation and development and more specifically which species are, or could be, sustainably conserved in such systems, from both biological and human management perspectives. The utility of particular species will not guarantee their long-term conservation if, for example, genetic diversity and regeneration within critical populations are compromised. Conversely, maintenance of genetic diversity and adaptive capacity is irrelevant if current management drastically alters population persistence. We examine results from our ecological, genetic, and socioeconomic research conducted within dry forests of Costa Rica, Honduras, and Mexico, which overlap principally within southern Honduras. In particular, we consider results for two timber species, *Bombacopsis quinata* (Jacq.) Dugand, Bombacaceae, and *Swietenia humilis* Zucc., Meliaceae, both of local socioeconomic importance, with superficially similar ecology and considered of conservation concern (see the section "The Case Study Species" later in this chapter). We consider general principles that may influence under what conditions and for what species *circa situm* conservation will prove effective and how it might be implemented. Finally we highlight research and training needs to explore further the feasibility and implementation of this approach.

RESEARCH IN SOUTHERN HONDURAS

Our research has had a common focus in southern Honduras (taken here as the lowlands and foothills of the departments of Choluteca and Valle), an area within the dry subtropical life zone (Holdridge 1987) with a distinct dry season from October to May. The southern Honduran lowlands are mainly occupied by cattle pasture and export agriculture (cantaloupe, watermelon,

sugarcane). The foothills show a fluctuating mosaic of land uses, with a predominance of basic grain production (*milpas*), alternating with fallows, some low-density cattle raising and, in more humid areas, low-intensity coffee production. The lack of mechanized tillage and the control of livestock movement typically allow natural regeneration of a highly variable range of tree species from seed banks, stumps, and newly arrived seed. From these species many farmers actively protect a subset of those most valued for a range of products (e.g., firewood and timber), reflecting a desire to optimize the use of available resources. Thus some trees reach, and remain in, reproductive maturity in *milpas* or pasture. Another subset of species remains as stumps and resprouts (up to 17,000 per hectare) simply because the removal cost is not perceived to produce adequate benefits (Barrance et al. in review). Many of these trees reach reproductive maturity during fallow periods. The area therefore presents suitable conditions in terms of forest patchiness, the surrounding forest-agriculture interface, and socioeconomic circumstances to allow the synthesis of results across research disciplines.

THE CASE STUDY SPECIES

Bombacopsis quinata is a medium- to large-size deciduous tree from Central America, Colombia, and Venezuela. It is hermaphroditic, largely self-incompatible (Sandiford 1998), and pollinated principally by the bat *Glossophaga soricina*. Its seeds are loosely attached to kapok, which facilitates their wind dispersal. Its timber is much in demand and has led to investment in large plantations, as well as planting by farmers within Central America. This species can be propagated by stakes and is used for living fences in parts of its range. Because of selective felling, deforestation, and destructive agricultural practices, this once common species is largely limited to isolated forest remnants. It is considered as endangered at the level of some populations (FAO 1986; Oldfield et al. 1998).

Swietenia humilis is a monoecious, medium-sized deciduous tree found along the Pacific watershed of Central America and Mexico. It is pollinated by small butterflies, bees, and other insects, and its fruits contain large wind-dispersed seeds. Under controlled pollination it is self-incompatible (D. Boshier unpubl. data). Its sawn timber is highly valued, but commercial reforestation within its native range is hindered by the high incidence of attack by the shoot borer *Hypsipyla grandella*. Where populations of *S. humilis* and *S. macrophylla* are sympatric, hybridization is known, and their distinctness as species has been questioned (Styles 1981). Populations over much of the species' range have been reduced and fragmented, leading to its listing in 1973 in appendix II of the Convention on International Trade in Endangered Species of Wild Fauna and Flora (CITES) and classification as "vulnerable" by the International Union for Conservation of Nature and Natural Resources (IUCN) (Oldfield et al. 1998).

GENETIC DIVERSITY AND ITS MAINTENANCE

Evidence to date shows that a high proportion of tropical tree species are naturally outcrossing (e.g., Bawa et al. 1985), with associated risks from inbreeding such as reduced fertility, growth, and susceptibility to pests or diseases (e.g., Griffin 1990). Maintenance of genetic diversity is therefore vital for the long-term viability and adaptability of populations of many tree species. Reproductive biology, levels of genetic diversity and gene flow, and extent of localized adaptation have been studied within the native range of both *B. quinata* and *S. humilis* (see Sandiford 1998; White 1998; Billingham 1999; White et al. 1999; Boshier and Billingham 2000; and White and Boshier 2000 for methodologies and results). Remnant stands of secondary dry forest, confined principally to hillsides and remnant trees in pastures in the Punta Ratón region of the Honduran Pacific alluvial coastal plains, near Choluteca, were used, along with control plots in more continuous forest in both Honduras and Guanacaste, Costa Rica. The fragments varied in size (7–150 trees) and degree of spatial isolation (1–4.5 km). For both species, genetic markers (allozymes or microsatellites)

showed that, at the degree of isolation studied, fragmentation did not impose a genetic barrier between remnants, direct measures of current mating patterns giving altered and proportionately higher levels of interfragment pollen flow over longer distances. Common to both controls and fragments for both species was a predominance of near neighbor mating (<300 m of the maternal tree). A large proportion of pollen donors were, however, from outside each fragment across the sampled area, indicating an extensive network of gene exchange at this spatial scale (16 km²). So in two fragments (22 and 44 *S. humilis* trees), 62 percent and 53 percent, respectively, of pollen donors were from within the fragment, whereas 24 percent and 34 percent were from distances greater than 1.5 km and 3.6 km, respectively. There was no evidence for increased inbreeding in fragments, with both species continuing to show high levels of outcrossing even in the smallest fragments. Indeed, an *S. humilis* tree, "isolated" by 1.2 km from the nearest flowering trees, showed 100 percent external pollen sources, with more than 70 percent from trees in the main area of forest (>4.5 km), in accord with the species' self-incompatibility and in contrast to predictions that spatially isolated trees are more likely to deviate from random mating and receive pollen from fewer donors (Murawski and Hamrick 1991).

Such enhanced levels of long-distance gene flow into smaller fragments, also seen in *Spondias mombin* L. (Nason and Hamrick 1997), will potentially restore or maintain genetic variation in populations of these species within the modified environment. This contrasts with traditional views of the genetic effects of fragmenting populations whereby increases in spatial isolation and population size reduction have been considered to reduce gene flow between fragments (e.g., Saunders et al. 1991). Although the genetic effects of fragmentation are complex, for some tree species under fragmentation, pollination may occur over much greater distances than previously considered. The distance given here for *S. humilis* is more than ten times greater than that considered as distant by Chase et al.

(1996) and more in accord with distances previously identified by zoologists (e.g., Janzen 1971; Frankie et al. 1976). There will, however, be a distance beyond which genetic isolation will occur, with associated problems for population viability and adaptation (see Young et al. 1996). Although determination is experimentally problematic, thresholds will vary between species depending on pollinator characteristics, availability, the specificity of the tree-pollinator relationship, and the presence and strength of any self-incompatibility mechanism. Self-compatible species that normally show some level of outcrossing (e.g., Murawski and Hamrick 1992) are likely to show increased levels of inbreeding at much shorter distances of separation (lower thresholds) than self-incompatible species.

PATTERNS OF DISTRIBUTION AT THE SPECIES LEVEL IN SOUTHERN HONDURAS

Two rapid botanical surveys (RBS) were undertaken to determine the tree and shrub species composition of the southern Honduras agroecosystem. The RBS technique follows the plotless or "unmeasured" sampling described by Hawthorne and Abu-Juam (1995), with minor modifications. A first, village-level survey consisted of species inventories in four rural communities selected nonrandomly to reflect regional variation across socioeconomic and environmental gradients. Within each community 20 households were selected along a socioeconomic gradient and a random subset of land units selected for inventory from those farmed by these families. Land unit categories followed definitions given by householders. In each land unit species were scored as present or absent, a species being considered present if it could be identified as a woody individual, such that live stumps were included. A second, forest-level survey inventoried tree diversity in a subset of forest patches in southern Honduras. Forests were selected nonrandomly to maximize geographical spread and biased toward the few remaining relatively large forest areas (i.e., >50 ha). All forests appeared to be largely, if not completely, composed of secondary regeneration of varying ages. Primary dry forest apparently no longer exists in southern Honduras, although it is probable that some older trees are remnants of much older forests (White et al. 1999). The forest cover that does remain is composed of stands of trees of as little as 2 ha in area and rarely greater than 20 ha, areas usually considered too small to be of value to conservation practitioners.

The two species differ in terms of where they occur. *S. humilis*, one of the most commonly encountered species (only 7 of more than 250 woody species identified were found more often), was found as frequently in farmland as in forests (table 16.1). In contrast, *B. quinata* was found less than *S. humilis*, but much more often in forests than on farmland. Both species were more common in fallows, fields, and pastures (table 16.1), which are typified as naturally regenerating management systems, than in home gardens and orchards, where planting is more typical. Both species also showed considerable variation in occurrence between the four communities (table 16.1), probably owing to a combination of biological and anthropogenic factors, although in southern Honduras a lack of undisturbed dry forest where the two species are sympatric makes it difficult to distinguish the principal factors. Two of the larger forests in Choluteca suggest that both species may show similar levels of occurrence in mature forest. In relatively undisturbed semievergreen forest on Cerro Guanacaure, *B. quinata* is common, as is *S. humilis* (J. Gordon pers. obs.). On Cerro Las Tablas, one of the most mature secondary forests in the area, many mature trees of *B. quinata* and *S. humilis* occur (densities up to 17.0 and 9.6 per ha, respectively). In Costa Rica both species occur at similar levels in more undisturbed areas of protected dry forest (e.g., Lomas Barbudal, Playa Nancite mature forest area; table 16.2). Thus, we have grounds to speculate that in southern Honduras the relatively low occurrence of *B. quinata* on farms results, at least in part, from unfavorable management practices (further discussed later in this chapter) rather than a natural tendency toward low densities.

TABLE 16.1

Occurrence of Bombacopsis quinata *and* Swietenia humilis *by Land Use and Community in Southern Honduras, 1999*

LAND USE	TOTAL NUMBER OF SAMPLES	PERCENTAGE CONTAINING *B. QUINATA*	PERCENTAGE CONTAINING *S. HUMILIS*
Forest	48	27	52
Farm	105	11	56
Fallow, field, and pasture	58	16	67
Home garden and orchard	47	4	36
COMMUNITY/DEPARTMENT			
San Juan Arriba, Choluteca	25	12	4
Agua Zarca, Valle	38	5	74
San José de las Conchas, Choluteca	24	17	46
Los Coyotes, Choluteca	25	16	64

The common on-farm occurrence of *S. humilis* cannot be explained simply by farmer preference (see the section "Patterns of Management of *B. quinata* and *S. humilis* in Southern Honduras" later in this chapter), given that natural regeneration has to occur before farmers can aid its recruitment. *S. humilis*, like its close relative *S. macrophylla* King, undoubtedly thrives in regimes of heavy disturbance (Snook 1996) as provided by traditional agriculture in southern Honduras. Once established, it can survive for decades in the closed forests that may form when fallows are abandoned. Gerhardt (1994) showed that germination of *S. macrophylla* in Guanacaste was not affected by differences in light levels and could establish equally well in pasture and young secondary forest. A study of localized adaptation in both Costa Rica and Honduras, with seedlings in pasture and secondary and mature forest, showed zero survival of *B. quinata* at three years of age in any of these land uses, compared with 15–60 percent for *S. humilis* (M. R. Billingham and D. H. Boshier unpubl. data). This is borne out at Playa Nancite (Santa Rosa National Park), where *S. humilis* regeneration in adjoining areas of abandoned degraded pasture (table 16.2) is abundant and that of *B. quinata* nonexistent. In contrast to other predictions and some studies (e.g., Ghazoul et al. 1998), seed production of *S. humilis* (table 16.3) was also more reliable and higher in disturbed environments than in closed forest, whereas that of *B. quinata* showed no differences by forest type, except at Playa Nancite, where it was low in all four fruiting seasons. During this period 13 percent of the *B. quinata* trees at Playa Nancite died from apparent old age/creepers/wind. Given the lack of any regeneration, the future of *B. quinata* at this site, although it is within a protected area, seems insecure. Indeed, fires and tree felling evident over four years (table 16.2) confirm threats to both species, even within "protected" areas.

We can conclude that species are likely to be scattered nonrandomly in the various land-use types and communities of an agro-ecosystem and that these distribution patterns must be known for *circa situm* conservation options to be assessed and for strategies to be devised and implemented. The fact that 76 percent of the species identified in the surveys were found in

TABLE 16.2

Mortality of Bombacopsis quinata *and* Swietenia humilis *Trees over a Four-Year Period at Sites in Costa Rica and Honduras*

SPECIES	SITE	COUNTRY	SITE TYPE	AREA STUDIED (HA)	NO. OF TREES	MEAN DBH IN CM (S.D.)	PERCENTAGE OF TREES CUT/DEAD
B. quinata	Lomas Barbudal Biological Reserve	Costa Rica	Protected area	25	61	69.2 (25.5)	0/6.6[a]
	Playa Nancite, Santa Rosa National Park	Costa Rica	Protected area/ mature	28	62	71.6 (42.8)	0/12.9
	Playa Nancite, Santa Rosa National Park	Costa Rica	Protected area/ regeneration	3	0		
	Punta Ratón, Choluteca	Honduras	Private forest/ farm	240	172	54.2 (20.9)	8.1/5.8[a]
S. humilis	Lomas Barbudal Biological Reserve[b]	Costa Rica	Protected area	25	57	47.4 (17.0)	0/14.0[a]
	Playa Nancite, Santa Rosa National Park	Costa Rica	Protected area/ mature	28	156	46.7 (16.0)	0/5.8
	Playa Nancite, Santa Rosa National Park	Costa Rica	Protected area/ regeneration	3	23	20.3 (3.7)	0/0
	Cerro Las Tablas, Choluteca	Honduras	Private forest/ farm	68	105	41.9 (14.0)	25.7/1.9
	Punta Ratón, Choluteca	Honduras	Private forest/ farm	240	75	37.9 (14.1)	5.3/5.3

Note: Mortality occurred through either natural causes or human intervention. dbh = Diameter at breast height.
[a]Killed by 1994 fire.
[b]Possibly *S. macrophylla* or *S. macrophylla × S. humilis.*

TABLE 16.3

Percentage of Bombacopsis quinata *and* Swietenia humilis *Trees per Year with*
Moderate to Heavy Seed Production at Various Sites

SPECIES	SITE[a]	SAMPLE SIZE[b]	1994 (%)	1995 (%)	1996 (%)	1997 (%)	1998 (%)
B. quinata	Lomas Barbudal	>45	70.6	66.7		68.9	
	Playa Nancite	>30	61.5	56.4	55.2	31.5	
	Punta Ratón	>105	76.4	61.9	73.3	90.1	
S. humilis	Lomas Barbudal	>46		12.1	0.0	16.3	20.8
	Playa Nancite	>143		32.9	11.0	18.4	17.2
	Cerro Las Tablas	>61		48.7	12.6	29.5	44.6
	Punta Ratón	>45	28.0	36.1	42.2	49.1	33.3
	Comayagua	30	66.7		60.0	83.3	76.7

Note: Moderate to heavy seed production for *B. quinata* is more than 20 seed capsules; for *S. humilis*, more than 10 seed capsules.
[a] Sites are ranked for increasing degree of disturbance: Lomas Barbudal, relatively undisturbed area within a reserve; Playa Nancite, area of the Santa Rosa National Park with disturbance; Cerro Las Tablas, forest with remnant trees and secondary regeneration; Punta Ratón, remnant trees and secondary regeneration in small fragments and pasture; Comayagua, planted trees by roadside.
[b] Sample size varies from year to year owing to mortality.

agro-ecosystems (i.e., not limited to forest) emphasizes the potential for on-farm trees to make a contribution to conservation strategies. This is borne out by Harvey and Haber (1999), who found 190 tree species in 237 ha of upland pasture near Monteverde Reserve in Costa Rica. Assuming that greater occurrence means greater conservation potential, the potential for different sites to be the foci of successful *circa situm* conservation will vary. For example, taking the distribution evidence in isolation, the Agua Zarca community has a high potential for conservation of *S. humilis* but very little for *B. quinata* (table 16.1). *S. humilis* appears ecologically suited to *circa situm* conservation "through use" on these farms, where tillage is minimal, livestock movement controlled, and fallows sporadically allowed. *B. quinata,* however, appears less suited, being much more susceptible to reductions in forest cover, although even for such species that appear to be predominantly "forest species," the relatively few individuals on farms may be important for gene flow between forests (see the section

"Genetic Diversity and Its Maintenance" earlier in this chapter). Evidently conservation strategies for these two species need to be very different.

PATTERNS OF MANAGEMENT OF *B. QUINATA* AND *S. HUMILIS* IN SOUTHERN HONDURAS

A study in the same small farmer communities where village-level species inventories were taken (see previous section) shows that, in addition to differences in reproductive biology, ecology, and local distribution, *B. quinata* and *S. humilis* differ in management by local people. In general, within these communities, people mentioned that many of the same tree species under active protection are also used for timber, although there was a marked contrast between the frequency of active protection for *S. humilis* (second only to *Cordia alliodora*) and that of *B. quinata* (table 16.4).

A focal group meeting in Los Coyotes, where species were rated for present and past use, also revealed marked differences between the two species in terms of their past and present socio-

TABLE 16.4

Principal Tree Species Mentioned as Used for Timber or Actively Protected within Agricultural Areas as Sources of Timber or Posts in Four Communities in Southern Honduras in 1998

SPECIES USED	PERCENTAGE OF INTERVIEWEES[a]	SPECIES PROTECTED	PERCENTAGE OF INTERVIEWEES[a]
Cordia alliodora	84.8	Cordia alliodora	38.0
Bombacopsis quinata	20.3	Swietenia humilis	22.8
Enterolobium cyclocarpum	19.0	Lysiloma spp.	20.3
Albizia saman	16.5	Enterolobium cyclocarpum	10.1
Lysiloma spp.	16.5	Albizia saman	10.1
Swietenia humilis	16.5	42 other tree species, including Bombacopsis quinata	1.3–6.3 each
Calycophyllum candidissimum	15.2		
Cedrela odorata	15.2		
Conocarpus/Rhizopora spp. (mangrove)	15.2		
Simarouba glauca	11.4		

Note: The four communities were San Juan Arriba, Agua Zarca, San José de las Conchas, and Los Coyotes.
[a]Figures given as a percentage of 79 interviewees.

economic niches. Previously ("in the time of their grandfathers") *B. quinata* was almost the only species used for timber; however, its exploitation to supply furniture workshops in the nearby town of El Triunfo led to a large decrease in its numbers in the area. Farmers now use a broad range of previously little-used species, including *S. humilis,* others of which (e.g., *Guazuma ulmifolia* Lam) have far inferior timber value. Farmers also contrasted previous management during field clearance, whereby many valuable timber trees were felled and burned on-site or used for firewood, with current practices, whereby valued trees are protected and only timber offcuts used as firewood.

Apparently because of a scarcity of off-field tree resources, resulting from high human population densities and growth rates, many farmers, by favoring certain species during clearance, protect and manage valued trees within their fields to meet their subsistence needs and as a naturally regenerated cash crop. Furthermore, stumps and seeds survive regardless of felling, as stump removal is difficult and mechanical tillage is rarely practiced owing to topographical constraints. Farmers are also adept at controlling grazing, a prerequisite of successful maize cultivation, so that livestock does not necessarily prevent regeneration and indeed may facilitate it (Janzen 1986a). Patches of fallow and forest within the mosaic continue, despite their small size, to be propagule sources of many of the species found in these fields. Up to certain limits the benefits of maintaining trees outweigh negative effects (e.g., shade) that farmers perceive the trees to have on crops (Barrance et al. in review). This form of management represents a rational response to resource scarcity rather than a desire to conserve biological diversity per se.

The relatively low frequency of protection of *B. quinata* in fields (tables 16.1, 16.4) does not appear to result from its being less valued than *S. humilis* or from differences in farmers' perceptions of tree/crop interactions (no important negative interactions were reported by farmers between either species and crops). A more probable explanation is the relative scarcity and patchy distribution of *B. quinata* natural regeneration, particularly in fields. Farmers protect it where they find it but find it much less frequently than *S. humilis*. The current scarcity of *B. quinata* appears to stem, at least in part, from its past overexploitation, prior to the self-imposition of tree management controls by farmers as a response to scarcity and its ecological characteristics. *S. humilis* differs in that it appears to have been rather less valued than *B. quinata* and as a result largely escaped overexploitation. It now benefits from the current practice of active protection of the remaining valued species and its ease of regeneration. However, despite farmers' clear preference for both species and their promotion by extension agencies, neither species is commonly planted. This probably reflects the cost of planted trees, compared with "free" natural regeneration and possibly the greater risks to planted trees from cattle that are periodically introduced into *milpas* to eat crop residues.

Both *B. quinata* and *S. humilis* also occur in forest patches and pastures within larger estates (e.g., Cerro Las Tablas), although the management systems and socioeconomic conditions are very different from those found in the small farmer communities. In both pasture and forest remnants on these estates there appears to be a continued decline due to piecemeal felling (table 16.2), possibly as the landowners do not face the same conditions of overall resource scarcity that motivate small farmers to nurture natural regeneration. In addition, conditions in many pastures (they are normally destumped on clearing and then periodically burned to encourage grass development) are less propitious to tree regeneration than those on steeper land under subsistence production systems.

CONCLUSIONS

In situ conservation of the remaining areas of mature Mesoamerican dry forest is likely to be the most effective and efficient means of safeguarding a substantial part of the threatened specific and subspecific tree diversity of this forest type. However, many species and populations of concern are not well or not at all represented in such areas and require a different approach. Habitat restoration may also have a role, but the socioeconomic conditions that make this a possibility are uncommon, and costs may be prohibitive. *Circa situm* conservation has much to offer in these situations but also significant limitations; for it to be effective, its application must be guided by information from multidisciplinary research of the type discussed in this chapter. As the contrasting examples of *B. quinata* and *S. humilis* show, we cannot permit ourselves the luxury of assuming that all species are likely to persist in an agricultural mosaic until this is proved otherwise. However, on the basis of such evidence, neither should we underestimate the capability of many species to persist in large numbers in these agro-ecosystems under current practices, as this could lead to the misdirection of limited conservation resources toward species not under threat. *Circa situm* conservation of tree diversity is already occurring, albeit as a side effect of resource-poor farmer practices. Given apparently similar conditions across large parts of the dry zone foothills of El Salvador, Guatemala, and Nicaragua, *circa situm* populations may represent a considerable conservation resource. If conservation planners were to take this resource into consideration, how many species currently assumed to be threatened by habitat loss might prove to be thriving (Vandermeer and Perfecto 1997)?

An enhanced future role for *circa situm* conservation in the dry tropics of Mesoamerica will depend principally on the existence of species of conservation importance in the agro-ecosystems and forests in question. Species of widespread occurrence whose status does not appear about to change and species well represented in adequately protected areas should not attract more of the scarce resources available for conservation. Are agro-ecosystems likely to contain the types of species we wish to conserve? To answer this question we offer the following generalizations. Agro-ecosystems are highly disturbed in comparison with the original vegetation, and the dominant species are likely to be either "preadapted" to disturbance (i.e., weedy, pioneer, and/or coppicing) or positively selected by farmers (or both). The long-distance dispersal propagules of these typically pioneer type species, coupled with ever increasing disturbance, ensure that they will generally not be conservation priorities. One priority must therefore be the relatively few species with much narrower distributions, endemic to areas now completely converted to agro-ecosystems (e.g., *Leucaena salvadorensis;* Hellin and Hughes 1993). For these species *in situ* is de facto, not a conservation option. A second priority would be those species and species assemblages whose continued *in situ* conservation would be enhanced by their conservation *circa situm*. Here conservation in agro-ecosystems between reserves increases habitat area, connectivity, and population sizes.

Knowledge of which tree species occur where says nothing about the species' viability within an agro-ecosystem. The effects of fragmentation and the regeneration of secondary forest patches are likely to be dynamic, and to ensure that we deal with populations with a long-term future, we must carefully consider the reproductive and regenerative capacities of priority species and the perpetuation of management practices that allow natural or artificial regeneration. Yet knowledge of the effects of human interventions (e.g., logging, fragmentation) on tree gene pools is relatively poor. We do not know at what stage forest fragments become genetically isolated; nor do we understand the consequences of gene flow between managed and remnant natural populations. Selection pressures exerted by farmers, intentionally or unintentionally, at species, population, and within-population levels are also

little understood, and their compatibility with conservation objectives are unclear.

For the species studied here and others elsewhere (e.g., chapter 3), it appears that descriptions of remnant trees and forest patches as "isolated" or "living dead" (Janzen 1986b), with little or no conservation value, may be misleading and more human perception than a true reflection of actual gene flow and any biological reality. It is more realistic to view remnant forests not as islands but rather as existing within a mosaic of land uses that differ in their capacity to provide habitat or permit movement for any organism. In this sense it is important to recognize the complementary habitat role that maintenance of trees on farms is already playing to *in situ* dry-forest conservation. With adequate gene flow and seed production, some remnant forest patches and trees may be important contributors to connectivity and conservation, both *in situ* and *circa situm*, more generally. The capacity of some pollinators to move long distances has been shown, although the potential to move between patches will depend on their behavioral response to such a mosaic. Some bat species move preferentially down forest tracks and pathways (e.g., Estrada et al. 1993). Whereas some bee species are generally restricted in their movements (Powell and Powell 1987), most show some long-distance movements, and some will move more than 4 km across agro-ecosystems between forest patches (e.g., Frankie et al. 1976; Raw 1989). With a range of nonspecialist pollinators, pollen flow dynamics in *S. humilis* are probably far less susceptible to habitat disturbance than tree species with more specialist pollinators, although *Ficus* species, with species-specific wasp pollinators, may form extensive metapopulations in fragmented landscapes (Nason et al. 1998). Changes in pollinator assemblages in fragmented landscapes may strongly affect patterns of gene flow and reproduction in remnant tree populations. Concerns that declines in pollinator populations in such agro-ecosystems may eventually limit tree reproduction require monitoring of numbers, as well as evidence for pollinator limitation (Allen-Wardell et al. 1998).

Active tree protection by farmers is strongly dependent on their perceptions of the trees' potential value to them and on other community members' recognition of their ownership rights to the trees. However, the *B. quinata* case clearly demonstrates that even if a species is valued its conservation is not guaranteed (Gordon et al. 2003). In fact, *use value* may lead to a species' decline until a threshold is reached whereby farmers are obliged to modify their practices if they wish to ensure a continued supply. It appears that at this point the rate of decline of many species tends to level out as mature individuals are managed on a more rational basis and removals replaced by natural regeneration that receives active protection by farmers. However, if regeneration is poor in agro-ecosystems, as appears to be so for *B. quinata,* it may continue to decline and disappear. Alternatively farmers may switch much of their demand for a particular product to another species.

Hughes (1998) suggests that *circa situm* conservation is probably limited to species that tolerate disturbance and are actively used and preferred by farmers. However, although it indeed favors disturbance-tolerant species, the examples from southern Honduras and those of Kass et al. (1993) suggest its applicability to a broader range of species than just the actively preferred ones. However, survival of nonpreferred species may to a large extent depend on the technology level of land management practices; for example, a larger number of stumps of nonvalued coppicing species is allowed to persist in low-intensity swidden agriculture of southern Honduran hillsides than in ploughed fields of the central valleys of Oaxaca, Mexico. It would be unfair to promote conservation initiatives at a landscape scale across the Mesoamerican dry zone that prevent poor farmers from adopting more profitable practices, although in many parts there are significant biophysical constraints (e.g., topography, resource availability) to those seeking to intensify production. At least in southern Honduras there appears to be little immediate risk of agricultural

intensification leading to massive extinctions (cf. Janzen 1986b). *Circa situm* conservation strategies are more likely to be effective when planned on a species-by-species basis, within the farming systems context of a particular area, with resources focused on target species so as to minimize negative socioeconomic effects. The "area" or "management unit" over which such strategies would operate would be measured in numbers of participating households or land units in which target species conservation is successfully incorporated into existing, or acceptable, farm management practices.

The prospects for *circa situm* conservation for *S. humilis* appear good, but less so for *B. quinata,* and it is ironic that of these two species the former is the one afforded more protection by international convention (appendix II of CITES). However, for it or similar species, some monitoring may be advisable to ensure that its niche in the farming system is maintained in the face of changing socioeconomic trends. Current trends, at least in some areas, involve an iterative process of property subdivision and elimination of forest and fallow areas, with a corresponding increase in numbers of trees in grain fields and pastures. It is possible that farm size will eventually reach a threshold beyond which farmers are unwilling to divide their property further among their heirs, and increased dependence on off-farm income sources will divert pressure from land and tree resources, leading to a stable situation. However, it is unclear at what point a threshold will be reached, to what degree this will be influenced by available off-farm income, and whether farm size reductions will lead farmers to increase tree densities on farms to satisfy tree product needs or reduce them to increase basic grain yields. The challenge offered by *circa situm* conservation is to adapt to these changes over a relatively wide geographical area rather than seek to halt such processes within a confined area such as a reserve. To this end there is a need to raise awareness among development professionals of the value of natural regeneration as both conservation and socioeconomic resources. Efforts to promote planting and the use of multipurpose or exotic tree species (or both) at the expense of natural regeneration may have deleterious effects not only on conservation but also on farmer welfare. This would be evident through a reduction in the range of forest products normally available to farmers from natural regeneration and an increased cost of tree establishment.

RECOMMENDATIONS FOR RESEARCH AND TRAINING

The data requirements to answer the questions raised in this chapter are considerable, and realization of the potential of *circa situm* conservation requires a range of actions. For *circa situm* conservation to have anything but a minor role in the conservation of tropical forest resources, priorities among species and forest types will need to be set and shortcuts found. We end this chapter by listing recommendations for research and dissemination priorities for the further development of *circa situm* conservation. The list is neither prescriptive nor exhaustive and reflects primarily the situation as we understand it in southern Honduras. It is presented to illustrate the types of information demands that *circa situm* prescriptions will make. However, overriding such specificity is the need for conservation planners, more accustomed to *in situ* methods, to consider the possibility that populations of trees found outside protected areas have a role in the conservation of biodiversity. This in turn will require the direct involvement of development organizations in biodiversity conservation and an effective two-way communication between them and "traditional" conservation organizations to ensure both conservation and development benefits.

- Species distribution patterns need to be established not only at a broad level, to identify species that are rare and therefore a conservation priority, but also at a finer scale, to identify which species are not conserved *in situ* and which land uses within an agro-ecosystem are most appropriate for each species.

- Targeted tree populations need to be described in terms of size class distributions with respect to reproductive maturity. We cannot assume that a *circa situm* population contains the same proportion of reproductively active individuals as an *in situ* population.

- Fragmentation thresholds for gene flow need to be determined and the possible selection pressures exerted by farmers further elucidated.

- Species of conservation concern within agro-ecosystems need to be understood and classified in terms of farmers' perceptions of their value. Species guilds need to be defined, combining biological and socioeconomic variables to reduce, by extrapolation, the information demands of *circa situm* conservation.

- Education and training curricula need to be broadened so that more conservation biologists recognize the potential role of on-farm conservation and more rural development practitioners recognize their role in biodiversity conservation.

- The complementary habitat benefits of different agro-ecosystems for conservation need to be evaluated, recognized, and promoted.

- Rapid rural appraisal techniques (see Chambers and Guijt 1995) need adapting and testing for their ability to provide adequate and cost-effective information for *circa situm* management.

- Strategies need to be explored on a species-by-species basis to ensure effective use of resources and minimum disruption to farming practices.

- The costs/benefits to farmers of actively promoting conservation through a *circa situm* approach need to be carefully balanced and, if necessary, forms of compensation considered.

- Effective systems for long-term monitoring of the biological (e.g., pollinator levels, regeneration levels) and socioeconomic dynamics (e.g., management practice changes) of conservation need to be established.

ACKNOWLEDGMENTS

This chapter is an output from projects funded through the Forestry Research Programme of the United Kingdom Department for International Development (DFID) for the benefit of developing countries. The views expressed are not necessarily those of DFID. Projects R5729, R6516, and R6913 of the Forestry Research Programme.

REFERENCES

Allen-Wardell, G., et al. 1998. The potential consequences of pollinator declines on the conservation of biodiversity and stability of food crop yields. *Conservation Biology* 12:8–17.

Barrance, A. J., L. Flores, E. Padilla, J. E. Gordon, and K. Schreckenberg. In review. Trees and farming in the Honduran dry zone of southern Honduras 1: Campesino tree husbandry practices.

Bawa, K. S., D. R. Perry, and J. H. Beach. 1985. Reproductive biology of tropical lowland rainforest trees 1. Sexual systems and incompatibility mechanisms. *American Journal of Botany* 72:331–45.

Billingham, M. R. 1999. Genetic structure, localised adaptation and optimal outcrossing distance in two neotropical tree species. D.Phil. thesis, University of Oxford. 177 pp.

Boshier, D. H., and M. R. Billingham. 2000. Genetic variation and adaptation in tree populations. In *Ecological consequences of habitat heterogeneity*, ed. M. J. Hutchings, E. A. John, and A. J. A. Stewart, 267–89. Oxford: Blackwell Science.

Brown, A. H. D., O. H. Frankel, D. R. Marshall, and J. T. Williams, eds. 1989. *The use of plant genetic resources*. Cambridge: Cambridge University Press. 382 pp.

Casas, A., and J. Caballero. 1996. Traditional management and morphological variation in *Leucaena esculenta* (Fabaceae: Mimosoideae) in the Mixtec region of Guerrero, Mexico. *Economic Botany* 50:167–81.

Chamberlain, J. R., C. E. Hughes, and N. W. Galwey. 1996. Patterns of variation in the *Leucaena shannonii* alliance (Leguminosae: Mimosoideae). *Silvae Genetica* 45:1–7.

Chambers, R., and I. Guijt. 1995. PRA—five years later: Where are we now? *Forests, Trees and People Newsletter* 26/27:4–14.

Chase, M. R., D. H. Boshier, and K. S. Bawa. 1995. Population genetics of *Cordia alliodora* (Boraginaceae), a neotropical tree: 1. Genetic variation in natural populations. *American Journal of Botany* 82:468–75.

Chase, M. R., C. Moller, R. Kesseli, and K. S. Bawa. 1996. Distant gene flow in tropical trees. *Nature* 383:398–99.

Estrada, A., R. Coates-Estrada, D. Meritt Jr., S. Montiel, and D. Curiel. 1993. Patterns of frugivore species richness and abundance in forest islands and in agricultural habitats at Los Tuxtlas, Mexico. *Vegetatio* 107/108:245–57.

FAO (Food and Agriculture Organization of the United Nations). 1986. *Databook on endangered tree and shrub species and provenances*. Rome: FAO. 524 pp.

Frankie, G. W., P. A. Opler, and K. S. Bawa. 1976. Foraging behaviour of solitary bees: Implications for outcrossing of a neotropical forest tree species. *Journal of Ecology* 64:1049–57.

Gentry, A. H. 1995. Diversity and floristic composition of neotropical dry forests. In *Seasonally dry tropical forests*, ed. S. H. Bullock, H. A. Mooney, and E. Medina, 146–94. Cambridge: Cambridge University Press.

Gerhardt, K. 1994. Seedling development of four tree species in secondary tropical dry forest in Gunanacaste, Costa Rica. Ph.D. diss., University of Uppsala, Sweden.

Ghazoul, J., K. A. Liston, and T. J. B. Boyle. 1998. Disturbance induced density-dependent seed set in *Shorea siamensis* (Dipterocapaceae), a tropical forest tree. *Journal of Ecology* 86:462–73.

Gillies, A. C. M., et al. 1997. Genetic variation in Costa Rican populations of the tropical timber species *Cedrela odorata* L., assessed using RAPDs. *Molecular Ecology* 6:1133–45.

Gordon, J. E., A. J. Barrance, and K. Schreckenberg. 2003. Are rare species useful species? Obstacles to the conservation of tree diversity in the dry forest zone agro-ecosystems of Mesoamerica. *Global Ecology and Biogeography* 12:13–19.

Graham, A., and D. Dilcher. 1995. The Cenozoic record of tropical dry forest in northern Latin America and the southern United States. In *Seasonally dry tropical forests*, ed. S. H. Bullock, H. A. Mooney, and E. Medina, 124–45. Cambridge: Cambridge University Press.

Griffin, A. R. 1990. Effects of inbreeding on growth of forest trees and implications for management of seed supplies for plantation programmes. In *Reproductive ecology of tropical forest plants,* ed. K. S. Bawa and M. Hadley, 355–74. Man and the Biosphere Series, vol. 7. Carnforth, England: Parthenon Publishing Group.

Halladay, P., and D. A. Gilmour, eds. 1995. *Conserving biodiversity outside protected areas: The role of traditional agro-ecosystems.* Gland, Switzerland: IUCN. 229 pp.

Harvey, C. A., and W. A. Haber. 1999. Remnant trees and the conservation of biodiversity in Costa Rican pastures. *Agroforestry Systems* 44: 37–68.

Hawthorne, W. D., and M. Abu-Juam. 1995. *Forest protection in Ghana.* Gland, Switzerland: IUCN. 202 pp.

Hellin, J. J., and C. E. Hughes. 1993. *Leucaena salvadorensis: Conservation and utilization in Central America.* Serie Miscelanea CONSEFORH, No. 39-21/93. Comayagua, Honduras: CONSEFORH. 41 pp.

Holdridge, L. R. 1987. *Ecología basada en zonas de vida.* San José: IICA. 216 pp.

Hughes, C. E. 1998. *Leucaena:* A genetic resources handbook. Tropical Forestry Paper 37, Oxford Forestry Institute. 274 pp.

Janzen, D. H. 1971. Euglossine bees as long distance pollinators of tropical plants. *Science* 171: 204–5.

———. 1986a. *Guanacaste National Park: Tropical ecological and cultural restoration.* San José: UNED. 103 pp.

———. 1986b. Blurry catastrophes. *Oikos* 47:1–2.

———. 1988. Tropical dry forests: The most endangered major tropical ecosystem. In *Biodiversity,* ed. E. O. Wilson, 130–37. Washington, D.C.: National Academy Press.

Kass, D. C. L., C. Foletti, L. T. Szott, R. Landaverde, and R. Nolasco. 1993. Traditional fallow systems of the Americas. *Agroforestry Systems* 23:207–18.

Ledig, F. T. 1988. The conservation of genetic diversity in forest trees. *BioScience* 38:471–79.

Maxted, N., B. V. Ford-Lloyd, and J. G. Hawkes, eds. 1997. *Plant conservation: The in situ approach.* London: Chapman and Hall. 446 pp.

Murawski, D. A., and J. L. Hamrick. 1991. The effects of the density of flowering individuals on the mating systems of nine tropical tree species. *Heredity* 67:167–74.

———. 1992. The mating system of *Cavanillesia platanifolia* under extremes of flowering tree density: A test of predictions. *Biotropica* 24:99–101.

Murphy, P. G., and A. E. Lugo. 1995. Dry forests of Central America and the Caribbean. In *Seasonally dry tropical forests,* ed. S. H. Bullock, H. A. Mooney, and E. Medina, 9–34. Cambridge: Cambridge University Press.

Murray, M. G., M. J. Green, G. C. Bunting, and J. R. Paine. 1995. Biodiversity conservation in the tropics: Gaps in habitat protection and funding priorities. Unpublished report. World Conservation Monitoring Centre, Cambridge, England.

Nason, J. D., and J. L. Hamrick. 1997. Reproductive and genetic consequences of forest fragmentation: Two case studies of neotropical canopy trees. *Journal of Heredity* 88:264–76.

Nason, J. D., E. A. Herre, and J. L. Hamrick. 1998. The breeding structure of a tropical keystone plant resource. *Nature* 391:685–87.

National Research Council. 1991. *Managing global genetic resources—forest trees.* Washington, D.C.: National Academy Press. 228 pp.

Oldfield, S., C. Lusty, and A. MacKinven. 1998. *The world list of threatened trees.* Cambridge: World Conservation Press. 650 pp.

Powell, A. H., and G. V. N. Powell. 1987. Population dynamics of male euglossine bees in Amazonian forest fragments. *Biotropica* 19:176–79.

Raw, A. 1989. The dispersal of euglossine bees between isolated patches of eastern Brazilian wet forest (Hymenoptera, Apidae). *Revista Brasileira de Entomologia* 33:103–7.

Sandiford, M. 1998. A study of the reproductive biology of *Bombacopsis quinata.* D.Phil. thesis, University of Oxford. 200 pp.

Saunders, D. A., R. J. Hobbs, and C. R. Margules. 1991. Biological consequences of ecosystem fragmentation: A review. *Biological Conservation* 5:18–32.

Snook, L. K. 1996. Catastrophic disturbance, logging and the ecology of mahogany (*Swietenia macrophylla* King): Grounds for listing a major tropical timber species in CITES. *Botanical Journal of the Linnean Society* 122:35–46.

Soulé, M. E. 1987. *Viable populations for conservation.* Cambridge: Cambridge University Press. 189 pp.

Stewart, J. L., J. J. Hellin, and C. E. Hughes. 1992. Biomass production of Central American semi-arid zone species. Tropical Forestry Paper 26, Oxford Forestry Institute. 83 pp.

Styles, B. T. 1981. Swietenioideae. In *Meliaceae,* Flora Neotropica Monograph No. 28, ed. T. D. Pennington, B. T. Styles, and D. A. H. Taylor, 359–418. New York: New York Botanical Garden.

Utting, P. 1993. *Trees, people and power: Social dimensions of deforestation and forest protection in Central America.* London: Earthscan Publications. 206 pp.

Vandermeer, J., and I. Perfecto. 1997. The agroecosystem: A need for the conservation biologist's lens. *Conservation Biology* 11:591–92.

White, G. M. 1998. A study of the population genetics of *Swietenia humilis* Zucc. in fragmented forest. Ph.D. thesis, University of Dundee, Scotland. 154 pp.

White, G. M., and D. H. Boshier. 2000. Fragmentation in Central American dry forests: Genetic impacts on *Swietenia humilis*. In *Genetics, demography and the viability of fragmented popula-*

tions, ed. A. G. Young and G. Clarke, 293–311. Cambridge: Cambridge University Press.

White, G. M., D. H. Boshier, and W. Powell. 1999. Genetic variation within a fragmented population of *Swietenia humilis* Zucc. *Molecular Ecology* 8:1899–1910.

Young, A. G., T. Boyle, and T. Brown. 1996. The population genetic consequences of habitat fragmentation for plants. *Trends in Ecology and Evolution* 11:413–18.

PART TWO

Transferring Biodiversity Knowledge into Action

The Record

CHAPTER 17

Biodiversity Inventories in Costa Rica and Their Application to Conservation

Paul Hanson

BIODIVERSITY INVENTORYING and monitoring provide essential information used by many basic scientific disciplines as well as many applied sciences such as biotechnology, agriculture, fisheries, and conservation. Most inventorying and monitoring have involved organisms that are relatively well known taxonomically—for example, vertebrates and vascular plants. Yet the poorly known groups of organisms, such as invertebrates and fungi, constitute the majority of the species. Conservation decisions based on data for a limited range of organisms having relatively few species can be misleading (Prendergast et al. 1993). Moreover, poorly known groups of organisms tend to be smaller in size and to have shorter generation times, which means that they respond more rapidly to environmental changes (Brown 1991). Thus, taxonomically difficult organisms are often good indicators of environmental change and can help us to realize that a problem exists before the plants and vertebrates are affected. However, basic taxonomic research is needed before these poorly known groups of organisms can be used in monitoring and other conservation activities.

The problem is that there are too few taxonomists working on the most species-rich groups of organisms (Gaston and May 1992; Hawksworth and Ritchie 1993; Hammond 1995). Worse yet, taxonomists who have a lifetime's experience are retiring, and the knowledge they possess (much of it unpublished) is not being recovered through firsthand transfer to young recruits (Cotterill 1995). In recent years developed countries have begun reducing government expenditures, and thus funding of national museums has diminished markedly in real terms. Increasingly such institutions are expected to become more self-sufficient. This means that traditional taxonomic research now has to compete with more attractive proposals in evolutionary biology, the latter often addressing species/population level questions in taxa that are already well known. Not surprisingly, job opportunities for taxonomists have fallen drastically, and graduate students choose financially more promising fields of research.

Because the majority of species do not yet have scientific names and the process of describing new species is generally slow, an attractive alternative is a rapid biodiversity assessment of taxonomically well-known groups (Oliver and Beattie 1996). When such rapid assessments do include poorly known taxa, they must rely on the separation of morphospecies. Although time is saved by not having to obtain names for the species, if the sorting of morphospecies is done by a nonspecialist, it is prone to serious errors (for example, many insects can be separated only by dissecting male genitalia). Although rapid biodiversity assessments are relatively inexpensive, they are no substitute for the more costly systematic inventories. Moreover, species names are required for determining which sites harbor phylogenetically isolated species and for serving a wider community of users interested in environmental education, bioprospecting, and the like.

In recent years a considerable amount of taxonomic inventory work has been carried out in Costa Rica in general and in dry forests in particular. Because the work done in the dry forests has occurred in a national context, and because the problems facing inventories do not differ fundamentally between terrestrial ecosystems, this chapter treats the broader national process. It thus differs from other chapters in this book by not focusing specifically on dry forests. This chapter briefly evaluates inventory work in Costa Rica by considering what some of the problems have been and how future inventories might be improved. Three aspects of the inventory process are discussed here: (1) the field operation of collecting specimens, (2) the resource base for biodiversity assessment, especially the biological collections and human resources available in the country, and (3) the information that is derived from the inventory, especially as it applies to conservation.

COSTA RICAN INVENTORIES: THE FIELD OPERATION

As in most countries, the early inventories in Costa Rica were quite sporadic (see Gómez and Savage 1983 for a brief history). Subsequent inventories, primarily by staff of the National Museum and the University of Costa Rica, have been primarily museum-based and driven by the motivation of a few individuals. With the creation of the National Biodiversity Institute (INBio) in 1989 there was for the first time a coordinated and institutionalized effort to survey the species present in the country. INBio is a private, nonprofit organization whose mission is to promote a greater consciousness of the value of biodiversity in order to conserve it and hence improve the quality of human life. INBio is not intended to be an institution dedicated to taxonomy as an end in itself, and the term *museum* has been carefully shunned. From the beginning it was felt that neither the time nor the economic resources were available to train Costa Rican taxonomists in foreign universities (Gámez 1999). Instead, foreign taxonomists have been encouraged to visit INBio in order to help identify specimens collected and curated by INBio staff and to train the collectors and curators. The primary emphasis has been on vascular plants and insects, although fungi, mollusks, and nematodes have been added.

At the front end of INBio's inventory are the "parataxonomists"—rural people who grew up in areas surrounding protected wild lands and are trained to collect and mount specimens. After being mounted at the field stations, specimens are brought to INBio, where they are labeled, bar-coded, and classified by technicians and curators (Janzen et al. 1993). How well have the parataxonomists performed with respect to the biodiversity inventory? On the positive side they have amassed the largest collection of insects in Central America in a very short period of time. Because insects were collected primarily by hand-netting and at lights, the inventory has been most successful in those taxa that are readily collected by these methods. Many species are represented by long series from various localities, thus providing information on geographical distribution and intraspecific variation within the country. In general the parataxonomists who have been most motivated have been the most successful. For example, the team of parataxonomists in the Guanacaste Conservation Area have produced more specimen-based information on host ranges of parasitoids than was previously known from all of tropical America (I. Gauld pers. comm.).

Although the use of parataxonomists has proved to be a very effective means to jump-start a collection, in the long run it becomes ever more challenging to employ them efficiently. Without sufficient feedback from curators or taxonomists, overzealous collecting eventually yields vast quantities of the common species, a problem that INBio is now beginning to address. Meanwhile, the minute insects are generally missed by hand-collecting, and the few that are encountered are often poorly mounted, since the mounting is done in the field. To be fair, no human being could possibly do a first-rate job of collecting and mounting all types of insects; that is one of the reasons that entomologists specialize in particular taxa. Recently INBio has trained parataxonomists who specialize in just one order of insects, but there are still certain taxa that are most efficiently collected by the taxonomists themselves.

In order to improve the collection of smaller-sized taxa, INBio has begun placing more emphasis on trapping methods. However, there are still not enough laboratory technicians to handle these mass samples, perhaps because of the institute's legacy of being predominantly field-oriented. For example, a parataxonomist needs only about an hour per month to maintain a Malaise trap, but a laboratory technician will require a minimum of 20 to 30 hours to separate the focal taxa from this same sample. Thus, when it comes to processing bulk trap samples, INBio continues to invest a disproportionate amount of human resources in a task that requires only

a small fraction of the total time. Parataxonomists can, of course, be refocused in their collecting methods—for example, to obtain more biological information (which is being done), but this still does not address the shortage of human resources for separating bulk samples.

To decide on a set of methods for a particular taxon, we need to establish criteria for measuring the performance of different collecting strategies. The number of specimens collected and processed, although widely cited in annual reports, is a poor indicator of performance because it reveals nothing about how many species were collected or the quality of the processed specimens. In cases in which a specialist is actively working with the collection, a much better indicator of performance is the number of new species collected and how much it cost to obtain them.

THE RESOURCE BASE FOR BIODIVERSITY ASSESSMENT

Most inventories result in a collection of specimens, which usually consist of both identified (voucher) specimens and unidentified specimens of taxa for which no specialists are currently available. Voucher collections are essential for the verification of field data and to provide a permanent historical record. Biological reference collections in general, with their associated libraries and staff, are a vital source of baseline data for future inventorying and monitoring (Cotterill 1995).

Biological collections are not mere warehouses for specimens. At the very minimum they require constant vigilance to prevent the ravages of fungal and arthropod pests, which can rapidly destroy specimens. However, a collection whose staff does nothing more than ensure its physical well-being is effectively a dead collection. An active and useful collection requires a constant input of labor for sending and receiving loans of specimens, organizing (curating) specimens so that individual taxa are readily accessible to taxonomists, and similar tasks. Because the continuing cost of maintaining such collections is frequently viewed with suspicion by auditors, it is essential to publicize the importance of biological collections as research facilities, every bit as valuable as their more dazzling counterparts in nuclear physics facilities.

In Costa Rica the oldest biological collection is that of the National Museum. This collection was mismanaged in the late 1940s and did not recover until the 1970s. Despite some unexplained disappearances of type specimens in the past, the National Museum currently houses one of the best vascular plant collections in Central America. Its insect collection is primarily restricted to the butterflies. At the University of Costa Rica the Herbarium was initiated in the 1940s and the Zoology Museum and Insect Museum in the 1960s. Unlike other large herbaria in Central America, that of the university includes a considerable number of nonvascular plants and fungi. The Zoology Museum has substantial collections of marine invertebrates, arachnids, aquatic insects, and especially vertebrates. The Insect Museum has focused on bees, certain families of beetles, and parasitic wasps. The university's biological collections would be impressive if their contents were better documented. The preservation and growth of these biological collections have been assured primarily by motivated individuals working from shoestring budgets, although recently the university has taken a greater interest in them.

The collections at INBio have been an institutional priority since the inception of the institute. The combination of a large, well-curated collection and enthusiastic staff has acted as a magnet for many foreign taxonomists. Perhaps for the first time in the history of Costa Rica, at least some insect taxonomists are coming not primarily to collect but rather to work with the existing collection in INBio. As with the other collections in the country, the staff of INBio has been quite enlightened about loaning specimens to the international taxonomic community.

Besides collections, two other vital resources for carrying out biodiversity assessment are access to scientific literature and people with experience in identifying particular taxa. Libraries in Costa Rica cannot afford subscriptions to most of the necessary scientific journals, which is not surprising because even libraries in developed countries are reducing their subscriptions to these journals. Moreover, despite much recent pontificating, the nuts and bolts of taxonomic literature are still unavailable on the Internet and show no sign of becoming available anytime soon. Thus, budding taxonomists in Costa Rica, like those in other developing countries, have to obtain the necessary literature through their own efforts and those of foreign collaborators.

With respect to human resources, most of the curators at INBio have received firsthand training under the guidance of foreign taxonomists, and some are utilizing this training to publish descriptions of new species. On the other hand, only a few of the curators have had graduate-level courses in systematics, genetics, or evolution, which would greatly facilitate separating the species, understanding species distributions, and providing advice on conservation-related issues. This deficiency is especially ironic because courses in these subjects are taught at the University of Costa Rica.

DATA AND INFORMATION MANAGEMENT AND COMMUNICATION

A general problem among many institutions worldwide is launching a database without clearly defining its intended use, thus forgetting that data management is a tool rather than an end in itself. Although developing one's own software for data management may be superficially attractive, it is usually difficult for a local institution do this in a cost-effective way (Olivieri et al. 1995). INBio has invested heavily in developing its own software, and it would be interesting to analyze whether this effort has been cost-effective. Nonetheless, there has been an institutional commitment to data management (see Zeledón 2000: 100), which allows upgrading as new technology arrives. In contrast, data management in other collections in Costa Rica has generally relied on individual commitment, which often results in disconnected and potentially incompatible databases.

Very little of the inventory effort in Costa Rica has entailed quantitative sampling, which can provide valuable data on the relative abundance of different species and what proportion of the biota remains to be collected. The notable exception is the Arthropods of La Selva project (Longino and Colwell 1997). Yet it is difficult to fault the rest of the inventory work for being non-quantitative because most tropical organisms do not even have names and merely addressing this essential first step is an enormous task. Different taxa require different sampling methods (New 1998), and for a particular taxon there is often uncertainty as to how efficient one method is in comparison with others (Hammond 1994; Samways 1994). Not surprisingly, we must often rely on the taxonomists' intuition.

Although further biological data are usually beyond the scope of most inventories, various field biologists have been carrying out research in Costa Rica for many years, and this information is being compiled by the Organization for Tropical Studies (BINABITROP, or National Bibliography on Tropical Biology, currently comprising 12,000 references). In the future more emphasis needs to be placed on gathering ecological information during the inventory, as is currently being done with macrolepidopteran caterpillars in the Guanacaste Conservation Area (http://Janzen.sas.upenn.edu:591/rearingdb.htm) and the ants of Costa Rica project (www.evergreen.edu/ants).

The information obtained from inventories has to be made available for a variety of uses, notably scientific advancement, environmental education, and conservation management. Toward these ends the National Museum, the public universities, and INBio have all been actively producing a variety of publications (both scientific and popular), although a perennial problem in Latin America in general is the distribution of these publications. Both INBio and the Arthropods of La Selva project are actively producing

species Web pages, which has the potential to disseminate natural history information much more widely than traditional publications.

Finally, how is the inventory information being used in making decisions about conserving biodiversity? In general the staff of the conservation areas has been concerned with how to protect rather than how to manage. The most frequent requests coming from both the conservation areas and the private reserves are for lists of species and field guides, which are useful for environmental education and ecotourism, but less so for management and decision making. Information on rare and endangered plant species was used in planning the Osa and "Paso de la Danta" corridors and in planning a nature trail in Corcovado National Park, but such examples are rare (R. García pers. comm.). Conservation decisions often rely more on ecological information (e.g., mammal migrations) than on raw taxonomic information, yet the latter provides the foundation for the former. Therefore, the sequence of information transfer that needs to occur is systematics → ecology → conservation, although systematics can occasionally provide information directly to conservation (e.g., phylogenetically isolated taxa).

CONCLUSIONS

We obviously cannot afford to delay conservation efforts until all taxa have been fully inventoried. The urgency of the current situation requires us to select areas that need protection on the basis of existing information and rapid biodiversity assessments of taxonomically well-known organisms. At the same time, however, it is prudent to continue the inventories of lesser-known taxa such as microorganisms, fungi, and invertebrates. These taxa constitute the majority of the world's species, and many of them are critical to ecosystem functioning. Moreover, certain species-rich areas would probably be overlooked in conservation planning if we totally ignored the species-rich taxa.

Inventories in Costa Rica have been very patchy in their coverage of the country. Inventory work by the universities has been done primarily outside the national parks, whereas INBio's inventory has been restricted to protected areas. Some areas (e.g., Guanacaste and the Osa Peninsula) have received more emphasis than others (e.g., Braulio Carillo National Park). Very little inventory work has been carried out in the private reserves, which are potentially quite important in conservation (Herzog and Vaughan 1998). A national inventory that includes both protected and nonprotected areas would provide information on the identity and geographical distribution of the species occurring within the country as a whole. This is essential for determining what proportion of the species are not in protected areas and consequently which nonprotected areas are in greatest need of protection.

Inventories are also needed after lands have been acquired for conservation. These lands need to be managed and monitored, but typically only vascular plants and vertebrates have been inventoried. In fact, Costa Rican law requires only that trees and vertebrates be included in environmental impact studies. Yet inventory work in the country has advanced to the point where other taxa could and should be included. The laws are especially outdated in the case of freshwater ecosystems, where environmental impact studies are required only to measure physical and chemical parameters (M. Springer pers. comm.), which recover from dumping events (e.g., pulp from coffee berries) more quickly than do populations of aquatic invertebrates.

National biodiversity inventories have several functions, three of which have been highlighted here: (1) building local taxonomic expertise and biological collections, which are the basis for future scientific studies and conservation efforts, (2) providing basic information that can be used in environmental education, and (3) supplying the information needed in developing management plans for conservation. In general, inventories in Costa Rica have succeeded much better in the first two than in the third. There are many good references treating the types of information needed in conservation (e.g., Noss and Cooperrider 1994), and so the problem is not in deciding what type of information is needed but rather in providing it in an accessible format, disseminating it, and utilizing it. A great deal of the information already exists, some of it readily available but much of it requiring synthesis and dissemination. Perhaps the most serious problem is the final step—applying the information. Too often inventory information is viewed as an end in itself, and even when the information reaches the decision makers, it is often exiled to the file cabinet.

Based on the biodiversity inventory work that has been done in Costa Rica, we can draw on certain facts to make suggestions for future biological inventories:

· *Fact:* Although collecting is obviously an essential first step in the taxonomic process and parataxonmists have been useful in this process, the rate-limiting step in inventory work is the description of new species. This can be done only by taxonomic experts, but they should not have to undertake all the tasks themselves as they have traditionally done. *Suggestion:* Develop more and varied human resources to support monographic taxonomy. For example, the concept of a parataxonomist could be broadened to include people who assist taxonomists in describing new species. After the taxonomist has separated the species and written a preliminary key, these individuals could do some of the more routine tasks (e.g., recording locality data from labels and measuring specimens). Quality control should be maintained by the taxonomist, and the usual peer review processes should be continued.

· *Fact:* There are not enough international taxonomic resources to support an INBio clone in the majority of tropical countries. INBio has benefited greatly from being one of the first such institutions to appear. For example, British taxpayers have invested approximately a million dollars in the Costa Rican inventory through salaries paid to staff of the Natural History Museum who have participated in this inventory (I. Gauld pers. comm.).

Global taxonomic resources are simply not large enough to duplicate such support in most other tropical countries. *Suggestion:* Promote greater regional interinstitutional collaboration and increase employment opportunities for taxonomists. It is worth remembering that no country will ever be self-sufficient with respect to taxonomic expertise. Even the United States and Canada had to import taxonomic expertise in order to produce keys to the genera of Chalcidoidea of North America (Gibson et al. 1997).

· *Fact:* Globally, taxonomy is primarily funded through science research budgets and is subject to changes in science priority. The user community wants taxonomists to produce the tools by which organisms can be identified, but the research required to produce such tools is not currently viewed by the research community as a priority undertaking. *Suggestion:* Potential user communities should identify specific taxonomic needs (e.g., an identification manual for the Neotropical genera of Chalcidoidea), and funding agencies should invite tenders to produce these products rather than invest in more nebulous "capacity building." Funding opportunities for specific products would stimulate organizations to collaborate in formulating competitive bids, which in turn would create jobs for young taxonomists, particularly in developing countries with comparatively low overheads.

Costa Rica has received international accolades for its efforts in conservation and inventory. How well it lives up to this reputation in the future depends on a continued commitment to these interrelated activities. The often repeated phrase "learning occurs through doing" is appropriate, and for other tropical countries that have barely begun doing it, the Costa Rican experience can provide several take-home lessons.

ACKNOWLEDGMENTS

I especially thank Ian Gauld for numerous thought-provoking discussions that provided several important ideas for this chapter. I also thank the following persons for providing useful comments on previous versions of the chapter: Zaidett Barrantes, Wills Flowers, Gordon Frankie, Randall Garcia, Jorge Gómez Laurito, Luis Diego Gómez, Barry Hammel, Jack Longino, Julian Monge, and Rodrigo Zeledón.

REFERENCES

Brown, K. S. 1991. Conservation of neotropical environments: Insects as indicators. In *The conservation of insects and their habitats,* ed. N. M. Collins and J. A. Thomas, 350–404. London: Academic Press.

Colwell, R. K., and J. A. Coddington. 1994. Estimating terrestrial biodiversity through extrapolation. *Philosophical Transactions of the Royal Society of London* B 345:101–18.

Cotterill, F. P. D. 1995. Systematics, biological knowledge and environmental conservation. *Biodiversity and Conservation* 4:183–205.

Gámez, R. 1999. *De biodiversidad, gentes y utopías: Reflexiones en los 10 años del INBio.* Santo Domingo de Heredia: Instituto Nacional de Biodiversidad. 144 pp.

Gaston, K. J., and R. M. May. 1992. The taxonomy of taxonomists. *Nature* 356:281–82.

Gibson, G. A. P., J. T. Huber, and J. B. Woolley, eds. 1997. *Annotated keys to the genera of Nearctic Chalcidoidea (Hymenoptera).* Ottawa: National Research Council Research Press. 794 pp.

Gómez, L. D., and J. M. Savage. 1983. Searchers on that rich coast: Costa Rican field biology, 1400–1980. In *Costa Rican natural history,* ed. D. H. Janzen, 1–11. Chicago: University of Chicago Press.

Hammond, P. M. 1994. Practical approaches to the estimation of the extent of biodiversity in speciose groups. *Philosophical Transactions of the Royal Society London* B 345:119–36.

———. 1995. The current magnitude of biodiversity. In *Global biodiversity assessment,* ed. V. H. Heywood and R. T. Watson, 113–38. Cambridge: Cambridge University Press.

Hawksworth, D. L., and J. M. Ritchie, eds. 1993. *Biodiversity and biosystematic priorities: Microorganisms and invertebrates.* Wallingford, England: CAB International.

Herzog, P., and C. Vaughan. 1998. Conserving biological diversity in the tropics: The role of private nature reserves in Costa Rica. *Revista de Biología Tropical* 46:183–90.

Janzen, D. H., W. Hallwachs, J. Jiménez, and R. Gámez. 1993. The role of the parataxonomists, inventory managers, and taxonomists in Costa Rica's national biodiversity inventory. In *Biodiversity prospecting: Using genetic resources for sustainable development*, ed. W. V. Reid et al., 223–54. Baltimore: World Resources Institute.

Longino, J. T., and R. K. Colwell. 1997. Biodiversity assessment using structured inventory: Capturing the ant fauna of a tropical rain forest. *Ecological Applications* 7:1263–77.

New, T. R. 1998. *Invertebrate surveys for conservation.* Oxford: Oxford University Press. 240 pp.

Noss, R. F., and A. Y. Cooperrider. 1994. *Saving nature's legacy: Protecting and restoring biodiversity.* Washington, D.C.: Island Press. 416 pp.

Oliver, I., and A. J. Beattie. 1996. Designing a cost-effective invertebrate survey: A test of methods for rapid assessment of biodiversity. *Ecological Applications* 6:594–607.

Olivieri, S. T., J. Harrison, and J. R. Busby. 1995. Data and information management and communication. In *Global biodiversity assessment,* ed. V. H. Heywood and R. T. Watson, 607–70. Cambridge: Cambridge University Press.

Prendergast, J. R., R. M. Quinn, J. H. Lawton, B. C. Eversham, and D. W. Gibbons. 1993. Rare species, the coincidence of diversity hotspots and conservation stategies. *Nature* 365:335–37.

Rossman, A. Y., R. E. Tulloss, T. E. O'Dell, and R. G. Thorn. 1998. *Protocols for an all taxa biodiversity inventory of fungi in a Costa Rican conservation area.* Boone, N.C.: Parkway Publishers. 195 pp.

Samways, M. J. 1994. *Insect conservation biology.* London: Chapman and Hall. 358 pp.

Zeledón, R. 2000. *10 años del INBio: De una utopia a una realidad.* Santo Domingo de Heredia: Instituto Nacional de Biodiversidad. 144 pp.

CHAPTER 18

Conflict Resolution

RECOGNIZING AND MANAGING DISCORD IN RESOURCE PROTECTION

Gregory A. Giusti

Editors' note: *This chapter represents the only contribution from an author who has not worked directly in Costa Rica. The topic presented here pertains to collaboration, which is of great importance in implementing any conservation project. As editors, we wanted to include a model for collaboration that could be used universally in cases in which there was sufficient societal infrastructure. Greg Giusti's model fits our need perfectly. It is based on years of work as a practicing cooperative extension specialist and collaboration moderator for the University of California.*

THERE CAN BE no greater accomplishment for a resource professional than to bring together a divergent group of individuals and interests to forge a comprehensive plan for biological conservation. Inherent in this proclamation is the recognition that multiple variables of economic, environmental, and social prejudices will play a role in the dynamics of any group brought together to develop such a plan. Indi-

viduals participating in such a discussion will undoubtedly bring with them biased points of view to suit their particular needs and may have little or no regard for opposing perspectives. In order for a resource professional to assist in resolving resource management conflicts he or she must (1) recognize that such myopic viewpoints exist and (2) develop a *process* that enables a wide-ranging discussion allowing inclusion of multiple viewpoints (Lee 1991). Schindler and Cheek (1999) expand on Lee's approach by identifying six criteria important to the success of citizen-agency interactions. They suggest that the process is most effective when (1) it is open and inclusive; (2) it is built on skilled leadership and interactive forums; (3) it includes innovative and flexible methods; (4) involvement is early and continuous; (5) efforts result in action; and (6) the process seeks to build trust among participants. Simply stated, resource professionals must recognize and accept that natural resource conflict resolution is an exercise in social tutelage, directing and motivating participants in a process of progressive instruction with the ultimate goal of actions that lead to resource conservation.

This chapter provides guidance for those who have been trained in the art and science of biology (or some other scientific discipline) but have never been taught how to deliver their disciplinary expertise to a generally naive citizenry. This new style of resource management (Wondolleck and Yaffee 2000) has important implications for both resource sustainability and professional credibility (see also chapter 20).

PEOPLE AND NATURE: MAKING THE CONNECTION

Most practicing biologists are aware that the primary cause for the loss of biological diversity throughout the world is the alteration of habitats through a variety of human-induced land-use practices (Soulé 1995; USGS 2001). Unfortunately, in today's tumultuous world, few people have the luxury to contemplate abstract and complex theories of biological diversity, ecosystem integrity, or the relationship between *Homo sapiens* and their natural environment. Yet there are those who have repeatedly warned of the consequences of ignoring the protection of the natural systems and the potential impact on human societies (Erlich 1986). Fortunately, if people (and communities) are provided with the information, and if they make the effort, they can begin to understand the basic tenets of evolution, ecological structures, and biological relationships— ecological principles that are the result of millions of years of environmental factors. In order to direct efforts aimed at developing programs that promote sustainable environments, people must be provided with an opportunity to understand how these environments function and recognize how humanity plays an integral part in altering the natural workings of ecological systems. A necessary and important step in establishing a process of helping people assimilate the connection between environmental degradation and human effects is creating a forum that provides the time people need to receive,

consider, and discuss complex biological concepts and ecological relationships (Giusti et al. 1991). Even then, conflict between divergent viewpoints may remain poignant and perhaps bitter.

The realization that broad public participation and community involvement are needed in conservation planning is becoming more accepted even by institutions that have historically been reluctant to involve external participation in planning exercises, such as the United States Forest Service. It is important to remember that many of these institutions were not necessarily designed to consider community issues or cooperative landowner programs when developing regional conservation plans. To help address some of the institutional limitations to community resource conflict resolution, the 1993 report of the President's Council on Environmental Quality (PCEQ) recommended four broad goals aimed at directing participants toward conservation strategies: (1) maintain the viability of native plants and animals; (2) encourage restoration of viable plant and animal populations; (3) complement regional and global biodiversity conservation efforts; and (4) educate employees, community leaders, and the public about biodiversity conservation.

Clearly, this report recognizes the importance of providing information to people in an inclusive manner if they are expected to make decisions that will ultimately protect biological diversity. This approach inherently recognizes that both individuals and communities are integral components to any conservation strategy. However, the report falls short in helping resource managers understand the mechanisms necessary to teach involved individuals *how* to accomplish these goals. In simple terms, it is relatively easy to tell resource managers to educate employees, community leaders, and the public about biodiversity conservation. It is much more difficult to deliver effectively a comprehensive program aimed at people who may feel threatened by the whole process.

A major obstacle to the conservation of biological diversity in today's world is that environmental protection is often at odds with many deeply entrenched social practices, a situation that frequently results in protracted conflict, such as that concerning the protection of salmonids and timber harvest practices in the Pacific Northwest. In many instances, these entrenched practices limit people's ability to visualize and accept new and innovative approaches necessary to address economic viability while providing a greater degree of environmental protection. An example of this type of ingrained narrow view is a scenario in which someone who is confronted with an *ecological* problem provides an *economic* answer. Such a response reveals that the person may not fully understand the ecological implications of the problem being presented. It is then important for the resource professional to determine whether the person failed to, or chose not to, understand the problem being presented and is merely *reacting* to the situation out of fear. In order to manage resource conflicts effectively and ensure an atmosphere for productive communication, all participants in a discussion must be given the opportunity to comprehend fully the complexities of the argument. In the absence of this type of clear, concise communication, the dialogue most likely will not advance.

LAND USE AND ENVIRONMENTAL CONFLICT

Several authors have cited land-use practices as having significant effects on both habitats and dependent species across broad geographical regions, including the Pacific northwest of North America (Franklin 1988; Moyle 1994) and the tropical dry forests of the Western Hemisphere, Australia, Southeast Asia, and Africa (Janzen 1988). Increasingly, local and regional land-use practices and their effects on biological diversity are becoming more prevalent in the scientific literature (Brown et al. 1994; Noss and Cooperrider 1994; Walter 1998).

Walter (1998) provides an overview of the factors he has identified that are driving the land-use conflicts now widespread throughout California: "Most of the current land use con-

flicts are caused and energized by the rapid population growth of California" (p. 112). He further lists the ultimate factors in this dispute: "1) . . . population growth and settlement patterns; 2) absence of sustainable ecosystem planning; 3) new technologies; 4) transformation of rural economies; 5) popularity of outdoor recreational activities and, 6) point and diffuse sources of anthropogenic pollution" (p. 112). In his discussion he uses these factors to defend his position that "explosive population growth and land development have been accompanied by a plethora of environmental problems from air pollution to hazardous wastes and—most of all—large scale landscape transformation and degradation that have reduced some ecosystem types such as wetlands and riparian systems to less than 10% of their spatial expanse in less than 100 years" (p. 112).

The legacy of these past land-use practices, in combination with continuing practices that further degrade existing habitats, is responsible for creating a political and social environment that is often highly charged and emotional as both individuals and communities clash over remnants of these highly modified habitats.

The economic and social costs associated with the litigious actions of divergent interests are enormous and often result in conflicts that go beyond the warring individuals, ultimately spreading and encompassing entire communities. In many cases, though contentious, the competing interests may both be publicly stating that they share similar goals, such as providing a sustainable economic base for the community, promoting tourism, or promoting the natural beauty of the area. However, though competing interests may use similar words to describe their views, they often may have very different viewpoints and meanings. For example, to a timber company the statement "providing a sustainable economic base for a community" could mean maintaining a sustainable timber supply, but to a tourism-based entity it could mean maintaining a sustainable fishing industry. The two are not necessarily compatible activities and may reflect conflicting goals and most likely differing options on land-use practices. It is becoming more apparent that resource professionals must be capable of dissecting the meaning behind the statements of competing interests if scientific-based approaches are to be offered as a solution and ultimately provide a resolution to an existing conflict.

ADDRESSING SOCIAL AND CULTURAL VALUES

Resource professionals, then, need to provide information in an ongoing argument; merely providing information, however, usually will not be sufficient to overcome the underlying value systems that may be the basis for the conflict (Keller 1994). Often, these values are based on social, cultural, and economic systems (or personal needs) having little to do with the biological criteria being addressed. Unfortunately, these anthropocentric assertions can serve as major impediments to conservation programs, distracting and directing the discussion. Further complicating the matter is that most resource professionals are not properly trained to facilitate what are often highly charged, emotional arguments and debates (Wondolleck et al. 1994). One approach to managing social and cultural difference in resource conflict resolution is recognizing the importance of providing a process in which these inherent disparities can be accommodated. Paying attention to the need for providing a structured process is vital to the success of any effort aimed at developing a conservation strategy when working with divergent interests. Failure to address adequately the importance of process can lead to participants feeling that they have no ownership in the decision, thereby limiting their support of the outcome. Wondolleck et al. (1994) provide some basic steps that should be considered when developing an inclusive process aimed at conservation:

1. Participants must view one another as equals. This does not imply that all parties must always agree, rather, it recognizes the need for all parties to work together in order to address the problem successfully.

2. No individual party can impose its will on the other. Participants must not be "forced" to accept any decision.

3. Representatives of stakeholder groups must be in a position to commit themselves and their constituencies to support any decision that is agreed to by the group.

4. All parties must share a sense of urgency to resolve the conflict.

Although this list represents a simplified view of the complex nature of the conflict resolution process, it does guide the resource professional on how to proceed. Ensuring adequate process is not an easy task, particularly when the discussion may be between individuals with strong emotional attachments to a subject or topic.

DEVELOPING A PROCESS FOR RESOURCE CONFLICT RESOLUTION

It is not uncommon for a resource professional to be called on as the resident expert to assist in developing conservation plans (Chess et al. 1990; Magill 1991; Geisler et al. 1994). However, conveying that expertise articulately to a wide spectrum of lay people is a formidable task, and it becomes more difficult in an antagonistic setting. Resource professionals directing a progressive discussion in an attempt to develop a conservation strategy should be aware of the following:

· Interest groups involved in the development of a conservation plan will be vying and lobbying for language that suits their particular need(s).

· It is important for all parties to understand that when developing a *plan* that may eventually become *policy*, the group may not be the final authority in accepting and implementing the conservation strategy.

· A well-articulated, science-based conservation *plan* may be further refined through a political process prior to becoming a conservation *policy*.

Authority/responsibility: Board of supervisors   Resource conservation districts   State/federal resource agency

Significance level:	Species	Community	Landscape	Ecosystem	Scope
Goals:	Short term		Moderate term		Long term
Evaluation:					Monitoring timelines
Objectives:	One-year		Five-year		Ten-year

Process: Consensus ————————————————————————→ Majority rule   Action

Advisory inputs:	Resource professionals	Business interests	Environmental interests
	Forestry	Commodity representatives	State/regional conservation groups
	Planning	Agriculture political advocates	National groups (local representation)
	Wildlife	Real estate	Audubon Society
	Fisheries	Tourism	Sierra Club
	Water quality	Development/construction interests	Special districts
	Air quality	Resource extraction interests	Land trust
	Soil conservation		"Friends of. . ." groups

Tools:	Incentives	Education	Regulation	Mechanisms
	Cost-share programs	Meetings	Policy	
	Stewardship programs	Field trips	Standards	
	Community recognition	Town hall gatherings	Ordinance	
	Coordinated resource	Workshops	California Environmental Quality Act	
	management programs	Literature	Timber Harvest Plans	
	Public purchase	Conferences	National Environmental Quality Act	
	Public hearings			

FIGURE 18.1. An illustrative model to help guide conservation discussions.

I have developed a conceptual model (Giusti 1994) to help guide resource professionals when developing a process to assist various interest groups trying to develop a conservation plan or strategy (fig. 18.1).

IDENTIFYING AUTHORITY: WHO'S IN CHARGE?

A number of factors must be identified before a resolution can be attained through an inclusive process. The first question involves identifying the authority to which the plan will be directed.

Addressing this question early in the process will ensure that all parties understand who will have the final authority in implementing any strategy or plan. This step is crucial even if the process is intended to develop voluntary strategies (i.e., cost-share programs) requiring a willingness on the part of the landowner to work with the jurisdictional authority that will ultimately be administering the program.

Identifying the proper authority can sometimes be complicated, as exemplified by the ex-perience of the Quincy Library Group (QLG) (1996), which had to address the many nuances of identifying authority within a divergent group of people charged with a regional planning process. This group charted a five-year management plan on federal lands in the northern Sierra Nevada of California. In this case, the ultimate authority was the U.S. Congress, which would have the jurisdictional powers to implement the plan. However, at the local level, the discussion needed to include three distinct national forests encompassing eight counties. If the group was to develop and advance a successful plan, it was not enough for the QLG to view all three forests as one entity under the title of "Forest Service" or each county as a single jurisdictional authority as "local government." In this case, for the QLG to develop an inclusive process, it had to recognize the autonomous authority of the individual forests and counties.

In most cases, identifying authority will not be as complex as the QLG example. Often, conservation-planning efforts are conducted at the local level involving a single jurisdiction, such as the local board of supervisors or commissioners, resource conservation districts, regional boards, or commissions. In larger, regional-scale planning efforts the responsible authority may be a resource agency at the state or federal level. Regardless of what the authority may be, it is fundamentally important to identify and include the responsible jurisdiction early in the discussion in order to provide an opportunity for it to assume some ownership in the process and, ultimately, the final outcome. Often, this can result in an invaluable allegiance and institutional support once a final proposal is submitted for consideration.

ADDRESSING THE SCOPE OF A PROJECT

Most "-ologists" are trained to articulate the inherent attributes of spatial analysis at the genetic, species, community, landscape, or ecosystem levels when engaging in ecological deliberations. Although a number of academic questions dealing with genetic integrity are of the highest importance in a global sense, most field biologists are dealing with conservation issues at the species level and beyond. Increasingly, conservation strategies are focusing on protecting biological communities at the landscape and ecosystem levels as a way to ensure population viability. The reality of this approach is that the discussion often involves multiple ownerships and jurisdictions, making for complex group discussions. It is imperative that people involved in the discussion are provided with the necessary information to understand the scope of the effects that are being proposed. Do not assume that everyone knows what you know. Biologists are generally a professional minority in modern society. Few people will have had similar training and experiences from which to make their decisions (chapters 20 and 24).

MANAGEMENT OPTIONS
AND ASSESSMENTS

All too often, inherent conflicts that exist between the scientific disciplines used by land-use managers are not thoroughly discussed. Examples of such conflicts are (1) road construction engineering standards that may not be sensitive to providing upstream migration corridors for migratory fish, (2) even-age forest management and the inherent limitations of providing suitable habitats to sustain viable populations of late seral dependent species, or (3) agricultural pest management practices that may disrupt habitat quality for nontarget species. In many cases, the lack of attention to these conflicts has resulted in negative effects from modern technological advances on biological diversity (Walter 1998).

It is imperative that resource professionals take the time to evaluate and then articulate how the various land-use management disciplines can have counterproductive results at the landscape or ecosystem levels. It is not uncommon to have fierce disagreements between resource professionals who may feel adversarial toward each other (e.g., biologists and foresters; engineers and ecologists); in these cases, personal emotions can impede fruitful discussions.

GOALS AND OBJECTIVES

Undoubtedly, most people will agree on the importance of establishing goals and objectives in order to conserve natural resources. The challenge is to motivate a divergent group to agree on a common set of goals and objectives that can be addressed in realistic time frames and budgets. Reaching such an agreement first requires taking the time to explore the group's needs and desires; one way to begin this discussion is a brainstorming session to get a sense of the group's interests. The next step should be to try to capture some of the points or concepts that seem to have broad acceptance. Next, an attempt should be made to begin the process of developing a *draft* goal(s) statement.

Points to consider when engaged in an exercise to develop a goal statement should include: (1) Goals should be realistic yet comprehensive. (2) Goals are often described in lofty terms to motivate people in a particular direction. (3) Goals should help people visualize what the group is trying to accomplish. (4) Synonyms for *goal* are *aim, intent, purpose,* and *end.* These terms should be considered when developing a stated set of goals.

Examples of a goal statement: (1) The goal of the (*name of the organization*) is to provide a sustainable timber-based economy while ensuring the protection of other, nontimber resources. (2) Our goal is to develop a comprehensive approach to the protection of aquatic habitats while recognizing human needs associated with those habitats.

Although different than a vision statement, a goal statement should help a reader understand the purpose of the conservation effort under way. The purpose of establishing a goal statement is to facilitate the development of objectives as a means of achieving the goal. Objectives should be viewed as a set of actions necessary to achieve the goal. Unlike goals, objectives (1) are described in simple, straightforward terms; (2) should help people understand the tasks necessary to achieve the goal; (3) can be described using short-term, moderate-term, and long-term qualifying language; and (4) should be articulated in a way that allows their success to be evaluated fully.

Examples of short-, moderate-, and long-term objectives: (1) This year, our organization will convene an educational workshop on managing habitat for endangered species (short-term objective). (2) In the next five years, our organization will secure financial support necessary to implement riparian habitat restoration activities along five miles of stream (moderate term). (3) In ten years, our organization will have a fully funded conservation center, staffed by one paid administrator and a cadre of docents who will maintain a continuous educational and restorative program aimed at riparian ecology (long term).

The science of understanding and facilitating group process takes many years to master (Jacobson 1999). Although it is not the responsibility of resource professionals to mediate all conflicts, it is incumbent on them to recognize when mediation can create a forum that will result in a positive progression toward resource protection. Once such a forum is convened, a fundamental issue to be addressed is the process by which the group will decide how best to choose its actions or recommendations.

Paramount to the success of any decision-making process is the selection of the method for deciding on actions—that is, by consensus or majority rule. There are inherent pitfalls in either procedure. Obviously, the risk associated with majority rule is that any decision will have winners and losers. The risk associated with the consensus-driven process is the recognition that every individual involved in the discussion is afforded veto power over the group. Facilitating the group process when participants are contentious should sometimes be left to someone who has formal training in facilitation skills. It may fall to the resource professional to recognize when it would be timely to involve an external facilitator.

The crux of most natural resources conflicts is the anxiety and mistrust that exist between competing interests. It is these elements that make it necessary to improve communications between stakeholders as a means of addressing the conflict. It is important to try to achieve some level of balance when attempting to develop an inclusive process involving competing interests. I have provided a basic list of potential stakeholders (Giusti 1994) that should be considered when trying to identify competing interests (fig. 18.1). Although not complete, the list is meant to serve as a guide to identifying special interest groups that may want to be actively involved in developing a solution to a particular environmental problem.

RECOGNIZING THE TOOLS AVAILABLE TO ACHIEVE POSITIVE CHANGE

What motivates people to action when it comes to conserving natural resources? The answer to this question is highly variable and transitory. Initially, motivation can be caused by either the real or perceived threat of financial loss to an individual (or individuals) or a community, perceived effects from land-use practices (erosion from agricultural operations) that affect a person's or group's sense of stability, or any land-use practice or policy that creates economic, environmental, or social uncertainty.

Often the first response in a resource conflict is for one group or individual to lay blame on the perceived perpetrator of the problem. The resultant claims and counterclaims can often limit the ability of the divergent views to focus on the problem. Wondolleck and Yaffee (2000) stress the need to get opposing viewpoints to focus on finding successful solutions to the problem but not be distracted by prolonged arguments that focus on personalities or past events.

Once everyone's views have been heard, the next step is to guide participants toward realizing what choices they have to address the problem. Generally, there are three broad categories (menus) from which to choose when trying to identify solutions. These menus form the basis from which all decisions are ultimately derived.

MENU 1: INCENTIVES

Incentives are those programs or actions that promote a positive response. Often referred to as the "carrot," they are used to entice a positive action. Incentives can take on many forms. Their principal purpose is to stimulate positive motivation to achieve a desired outcome. Most incentive programs provide one or more of the following benefits: (1) financial gain, (2) improved self-esteem or position in the community, (3) public recognition, (4) financial support. Some common forms of incentives include cost-share programs, cost-deferred tax/zoning laws, public recognition programs, and public purchase programs.

MENU 2: EDUCATION

All too often special interest groups misuse the concept of education in order to promote their particular point of view. We commonly hear groups state the need "to educate the public" as a means of promoting understanding. Usually, this approach simply implies that a campaign is needed to persuade a particular political constituency to support an advocacy position.

Education programs should be used as a forum to increase awareness and understanding of natural resource management complexity. The purpose of an educational approach should be to provide objective, science-based information in order to allow all participants to understand the scope and complexity of the issues.

In order to educate, resource professionals must be willing to remain objective in their delivery of information. Objectivity should not be confused with neutrality. Neutrality implies that a professional does not care what happens to the resource. Objectivity suggests that we take the time to provide the information necessary for an audience to understand the positive and negative consequences of a management decision.

One should consider the scope and the level of complexity of the issue that is being addressed and develop the educational program accordingly. In some instances, it may be necessary to develop a conservation strategy over an extended series of educational meetings in order to allow participants to gather, digest, and understand the issue.

Education programs should not be considered the end product of any conservation scheme. They should be viewed as a vehicle by which people are provided with the information necessary to begin building the scheme. Different types of education forums include workshops, field trips, publications and mass media, and working groups (chapter 20).

MENU 3: REGULATIONS

Regulations are often considered the "stick" component of the "carrot and stick" approach to motivational mechanisms. Although necessary to curb human behaviors, regulations alone have not been proved to be fully successful in resource protection.

One recurring flaw in many regulatory approaches is the lack of monitoring necessary to evaluate effectiveness. This problem is most evident in many forest-related environments where the regulatory focus is often at the stand level and may not be effective in evaluating the cumulative effects of stand management across a watershed or landscapes. Even stringent, pre-scriptive regulations often fail to address adequately the cumulative effects of past and present activities across the landscape, not to mention the effects of these activities on large geographical areas, such as ecosystems.

Another shortcoming of relying purely on a regulatory approach to resource protection is that regulations are the product of a political process, not a scientific process. The inherent unpredictability in this approach often results in a compromised position that may not always be in the best interests of the resource and may favor one special interest group over another.

Regulatory approaches can take many forms and can involve punitive actions against a violator. Some of the most common types associated with land use include zoning requirements, prescriptive land-use regulations, environmental review programs, and performance standards. Although often necessary to address the most egregious situations or to establish a minimal threshold of expected performance, regulations should be viewed in the context of a much larger, comprehensive approach to resource management.

PROFESSIONAL CHALLENGE IN THE FACE OF MOUNTING RESOURCE CONFLICT

Resource scientists, educators, and managers are faced with tremendous social challenges in today's fast-paced world. They are charged with protecting the world's natural wealth in the face of ever increasing demands placed on these resources by the very people who entrust them with this responsibility. Just as these professionals view the various biological components of the systems in which they work as intricate and complex, they must recognize the intricate and complex human element in their managerial approaches. One of those approaches must consider providing a forum for open and honest dialogue that affords all interested groups access to sound, science-based information. Resource professionals must further recognize that many decisions that affect natural resources are the

product of a political and social process and not necessarily a scientific one. That said, it is in the best interest of those resources that these professionals work in an environment that recognizes the political and social realities of our world and that they engage in open and straightforward dialogues aimed at directing people in a positive move toward resource protection.

REFERENCES

Brown, L. R., P. B. Moyle, and R. M. Yoshiyama. 1994. Historical decline and current status of coho salmon in California. *North American Journal of Fisheries Management* 14:237–61.

Chess, C., B. Hance, and P. Sandman. 1990. *Improving dialogue with communities: A short guide for government risk communication*. New Brunswick, N.J.: New Jersey Agricultural Experiment Station. 30 pp.

Erlich, P. R. 1986. *The machinery of nature: The living world around us and how it works*. New York: Simon and Schuster. 320 pp.

Franklin, J. F. 1988. Structural and functional diversity in temperate forests. In *Biodiversity*, ed. E. O. Wilson, 166–75. Washington, D.C.: National Academy Press.

Geisler, M., P. Glover, E. Zieroth, and G. Payton. 1994. Citizen participation in natural resource management. In *Expanding horizons of forest ecosystem management: Proceedings of the Third Habitat Futures Workshop, Oct. 1992*, ed. M. Huff et al., 87–100. USDA General Technical Report PNW-GTR-336. Portland, Ore.: U.S. Department of Agriculture, Forest Service, Pacific Northwest Station, 100 pp.

Giusti, G. A. 1994. Partnerships across ownerships. In *Foresters together: Meeting tomorrow's challenges*, 42–52. Indianapolis, Ind.: Society of American Foresters.

Giusti, G. A., K. R. Churches, and R. H. Schmidt. 1991. Sustainability: A challenge through public education and outreach programs. In *Proceedings of the Symposia on Oak Woodlands and Hardwood Rangeland Management; Oct. 31–Nov, 2, 1990; Davis, Calif.*, R. Standiford, technical coordinator, 246–249. General Technical Report, PSW 126. Berkeley, Calif.: PSW Research Station, USDA-FS.

Jacobson, S. K.1999. *Communication skills for conservation professionals*. Washington, D.C.: Island Press. 351 pp.

Janzen, D. H. 1988. Tropical dry forests: The most endangered major tropical ecosystem. In

Biodiversity, ed. E. O. Wilson, 130–37. Washington, D.C.: National Academy Press.

Keller, S. R. 1994. A sociological perspective: Valuation, socioeconomic and organizational factors. In *Endangered species recovery: Finding the lessons, improving the process*, eds. T. W. Clark, R. P. Reading, and A. L. Clark, 371–90. Washington, D.C.: Island Press.

Lee, R. L. 1991. Four myths of interface communities. *Journal of Forestry* 89(6):35–38.

Magill, A. W. 1991. Barriers to effective public interaction. *Journal of Forestry* 89 (10):16–18.

Moyle, P. B. 1994. The decline of anadromous fishes in California. *Conservation Biology* 8:869–70.

Noss, R. F., and A. Cooperrider. 1994. *Saving nature's legacy: Protecting and restoring biodiversity*. Washington, D.C.: Defenders of Wildlife and Island Press.

Quincy Library Group [on-line]. 1996. http://www.r5.pswfs.gov/robriefings/briefingssept96/9609qlg.html

Schindler, B., and K. Aldred Cheek. 1999. Integrating citizens in adaptive management: A propositional analysis. *Conservation Ecology* 3(1):9. [On-line] URL: http://www.consecol.org/vol3/iss1/art9

Soulé, M. E. 1995. Biodiversity indicators in California: Taking nature's temperature. *California Agriculture* 49(6):40–44.

United States Geological Survey (USGS): National Biological Information Infrastructure. 2001. http://www.nbii.gov/issues/biodiversity/

Walter, H. S. 1998. Land use conflicts in California. *Ecological Studies* 136:107–26.

Wondolleck, J. M., and S. L. Yaffee. 2000. *Making collaboration work: Lessons from innovation in natural resource management*. Washington, D.C.: Island Press. 277 pp.

Wondolleck, J. M., S. L. Yaffee, and J. E. Crowfoot. 1994. A conflict management perspective: Applying the principles of alternate dispute resolution. In *Endangered species recovery: Finding the lessons, improving the process*, ed. Clark et al., 305–26. Washington, D.C.: Island Press.

CHAPTER 19

Conservation and Environmental Education in Rural Northwestern Costa Rica

LEARNING THE LESSONS OF A NONGOVERNMENTAL ORGANIZATION

Gordon W. Frankie and S. Bradleigh Vinson

IT ALL STARTED WITH FIRE! In the late 1970s members of our dry-forest research team were aware that wildfires were becoming common in our general study area between Cañas and Liberia and southwesterly to the Tempisque River in Guanacaste Province, Costa Rica (see maps 1.1 and 1.2 in chapter 1). We also had reason to believe that the risk of fire would increase through time and endanger the remaining plants and wildlife throughout the area. Reasons for our concern included the following. Fire was not a natural phenomenon in the dry forest, and the biota was not adapted to cope with it. Thus, the flora and fauna were extremely vulnerable to fire damage (Frankie et al. 1997) (Our research group had worked in the Tempisque region since 1968, when fires were infrequent and small). Wildfires received their greatest combustible fuel from a fire-adapted exotic African grass, *Hyparrhenia rufa*, and repeated fires in an area usually led to substantially increased fuel loads of *H. rufa*, thereby increasing the risk of future and more

damaging fires. Moreover, all wildfires were human-caused, and the human population in the region was increasing. Fire was commonly used to "clean" fields and roadsides by local people, and "cleaning" fires often escaped and burned their way into forests, including protected areas. Indifference to escaped fires by most local people and authorities was the rule.

We were also aware that these fires could probably be managed with traditional, time-proven methods of prevention and suppression. This view was based on fire experience by one of us (GF), who had previously worked on fire crews for the U.S. Forest Service in several pine forests of northern California.

To deal with these fire concerns, a group of five biologists/naturalists (G. Frankie, J. Frankie, L. D. Gomez, W. Haber, and S. B. Vinson) and the National Parks Foundation of Costa Rica began working together in late 1979 to develop a proposal to protect a seasonal dry-forest site, Lomas Barbudal, having unique biological characteristics, which was being threatened by these fires (see map 1.3 in chapter 1). After six years of work, the 2,400-ha site was decreed a biological reserve of the National Park System on 23 January 1986. At that time we had come to believe that our work was finished and that the National Park Service would assume full responsibility for the new addition to the park system. Such was not the case. In fact, local park service officials informed all who had worked on the project that there was neither "interest nor resources" to care for Lomas Barbudal.

Based on this surprising response, three of the reserve founders (GF, JF, and SV) consulted with the National Parks Foundation (private) and quickly reached an agreement to assume responsibility for managing Lomas Barbudal for an indefinite period (not an uncommon practice at that time for individuals or small groups to manage protected government land). Thus, by 1 February 1986 we began our role as land stewards, biodiversity conservationists, promoters, and fund-raisers for the Lomas Barbudal Biological Reserve of the National Park System. We also quickly became environmental educators on behalf of the reserve.

In this chapter we focus on environmental education (EE) associated with our work at the reserve and vicinity, which lasted from 1986 through 1997. During this 12-year period we developed a nongovernmental organization (NGO) and a wide variety of outreach programs for several different audiences. The goals of this chapter are to

1. describe the main outreach programs and intended audiences;

2. describe major lessons learned from interactions with different audiences and from environmental educators;

3. use selected historical events of our organization and guiding principles of EE from a 1977 UNESCO conference to evaluate the education program we developed; and

4. provide recommendations for future EE programs in rural communities.

DEFINITION OF EE

In this chapter we use the following definition of EE, which evolved over the period of years from 1969 to 1993 (EPA 1993: 1): "Environmental education is . . . the interdisciplinary process of developing a citizenry that is knowledgeable about the total environment—including both its natural and built aspects—and that has the capacity and the commitment to engage in inquiry, problem-solving, decision-making, and action that will assure environmental quality." This definition reflects the kind of broad knowledge that we had as professional biologists; the desire to outreach to a citizenry that consisted of several different audiences; the fact that humans were considered an integral part of the dry-forest environment; and the fact that some of our programs were designed for proactive involvement.

OUTREACH PROGRAMS

Our center of operation was the town of Bagaces and vicinity in Guanacaste Province, where we lived and worked (and still do). Bagaces is an old town that has been in existence for more than 300 years. It has approximately 4,000 inhabitants and an economic base in agriculture, mostly rice and cattle currently. Town leaders are protective of excessive development and modernization, and thus the town has remained small and somewhat provincial in character. With regard to wildlands, the location of the town, which is adjacent to the Pan American Highway, serves as a "gateway" to several nearby protected areas of Guanacaste. The most relevant one for our work was Palo Verde National Park, of which the Lomas Barbudal Reserve is a part (see map 1.3 in chapter 1).

At the beginning of our EE work in 1986 we established a small conservation organization, Amigos de Lomas Barbudal, in Bagaces. Shortly thereafter we legally registered the Friends of Lomas Barbudal in California as a nonprofit conservation organization for the purpose of raising tax-deductible funds for projects of Amigos de

Lomas Barbudal in Costa Rica. Finally, in the early 1990s we registered Amigos de Lomas Barbudal in Costa Rica as a nonprofit NGO. With this action we also established a small board of directors of 12 local professionals.

FIRE PROGRAM

Our EE work began in February 1986 as one of us (GF) trained a group of ten local residents in selected modern fire-fighting techniques that could be applied locally. Working closely with this group produced positive results over a four-year period from 1986 to 1989. During the first start-up year, Lomas Barbudal had almost 50 percent of its 2,400-ha area burned (light to moderate burns). As resources were increased from private donors and as everyone became more familiar with the landscape, access routes, seasonal wind patterns, high fire risk areas, and neighbors from 1987 through 1989, the percentage of the burned area decreased progressively each year to a low of 15 percent in 1989. As an NGO, we removed ourselves as land stewards of the reserve in early 1990, but we continued with EE work at the reserve and in Bagaces. The park service had by then agreed to assume stewardship responsibilities after our departure.

The successful training and development of local firefighters at Lomas Barbudal led to a series of one- to three-day workshops on regional fire management from 1989 to the early 1990s. The workshops, which were organized by Amigos de Lomas Barbudal, involved larger audiences that included many local residents and park service personnel. Professional firefighters (volunteers) from the U.S. Forest Service in California, Idaho, and Oregon regularly assisted in these workshops, and they were well received.

During the early years, our organization recognized the need for education and development of preventative measures as part of the overall fire management program. Thus, an increasing amount of our time was invested in educational activities and projects that promoted fire prevention and alternatives to burning. At the same time local volunteer organizations were emerging in the Bagaces community to help with fire suppression. These groups currently work with the park service as volunteer firefighters and have become an important part of the fire suppression program (Loaiza 2000).

HIGH SCHOOL PROGRAM

During Easter week in 1988 we enlisted the volunteer help of 54 Bagaces High School students to work on a variety of projects at Lomas Barbudal for eight consecutive days. Results of this work were so positive that we decided to develop a year-round EE program with the high schoolers. We began by hiring a teacher (with bachelor's degree in biology) from San José to coordinate the program. She, in turn, helped to organize a high school club with a focus on assisting Lomas Barbudal.

An important lesson learned about this audience of students was their high energy and need to do hands-on work. As we had done during Easter 1988, we engaged them in field projects that ranged from trail building and sign painting to patrolling the reserve and fire fighting in and around Lomas Barbudal. Students were also instrumental in raising funds, planting trees at the reserve, and building benches and developing a picnic area for visitors at Lomas Barbudal. Further, they helped to develop interpretive displays for the reserve visitor center by collecting a variety of natural forest materials such as fruits and seeds (see later in this chapter). Several students also did oil paintings of animals on large waste disposal cans at the reserve and in Bagaces. The program for this audience lasted for two years and was phased out when most students graduated from high school. Toward the program's end our focus began to shift toward another audience—primary school children.

OUTREACH TO OUTLYING SCHOOLS

In the early 1990s we established an EE outreach program in 23 primary schools throughout the Bagaces vicinity—some of which were in remote villages accessible only by a four-wheel-drive vehicle. With the permission of teachers, our education coordinator visited half of the schools every month (the other half were visited less frequently) and presented two-hour talks and activities associated with some topic on conservation or the environment (or both). This educational visit was always well received, as indicated by the children's responses and the teachers' regular invitations to return. Once the program was fully operative, we calculated that slightly more than 1,000 children were receiving our presentations. We also gave weekly talks to a group of local children at our Center for the Conservation of Nature in Bagaces (see the next section).

CENTER FOR THE CONSERVATION OF NATURE IN BAGACES

From 1988 to 1990 we conducted meetings and gave presentations to a wide variety of audiences in several people's homes in Bagaces. Realizing the need for better-quality space, we rented a relatively large house in Bagaces in the early 1990s that became our official headquarters. The house, or "Centro para la Conservación de la Naturaleza," served many EE needs that were previously impossible to accommodate. For example, the center had space for a full-time secretary, a library of almost 900 books and documents, shelves for nature displays, space for a large freshwater fish tank, and ample storage space for equipment and supplies. It also had room for work tables and regular meetings with the children of Bagaces.

Once the Bagaces center was established, a formal program of weekly presentations was developed for Bagaces children of ages 9–12. Topics for presentations were highly variable and often pertained to relevant conservation and environmental issues. Presenters ranged from our immediate staff of professional biologists, to local experts, to professionals from San José. In addition, the center was open every weekday, all day, for children in our program to check out library books and to work on special nature projects, including field trips, using the organization's resources.

Many other functions and activities were carried out at the center. For example, once local residents, teachers, and students from surrounding schools (including the University of Costa Rica in Liberia) learned about the library and other offerings, it became a source of new information for the community. It was also policy to secure requested new information if it could be located. At times, the requests challenged us to make site visits to gather new field data directly. Finally, the center occasionally served as a meeting place for adult groups wanting to discuss local environmental problems and issues such as the Mula Corridor conservation campaign (see the section "Evaluating the EE Program" later in this chapter).

VISITOR CENTER AT LOMAS BARBUDAL

In 1989, we constructed a relatively large visitor and interpretive conservation center at Lomas Barbudal's northwestern boundary. The center, which is actually on the property of the Institute of Agrarian Development (IDA, a large governmental agency), was designed for several functions, two of which were to make ecological and environmental information available to reserve visitors and to provide employment for local residents in the directly adjacent community of San Ramon. Other functions included providing space for EE projects ranging from fire workshops to natural history classes for local schools. One unexpected function was to create a sense of new civic order and structure for the small San Ramon community and IDA. Volunteer donations were solicited from visitors who used the center and nearby trail, picnic area, and river for recreation. We employed local residents to operate the center on a daily basis during the dry season and part of the wet season. We also employed local people to maintain the nearby trail and picnic area. Volunteers from Bagaces also helped in this work.

In 1994, we donated the center and its resources to a small women's association of the community of San Ramon. Despite offers by our organization to assist it, the association attempted to operate the center independently, which did not work very well. Part of the problem could be traced to lack of transportation, electricity, and telecommunications in the community and the fact that many women in the association were illiterate. Another part could be related to expectations of collecting sizeable donations from visitors (which has never happened). Eventually, the association began accepting a small amount of assistance from students at the University of Costa Rica and the park service. As of this writing, however, the future of the center is uncertain. One fact is clear from this comparative experience. Small, community-based ecotourism projects need regular outside assistance in order to maintain even a modest visitor center.

LESSONS LEARNED

We learned numerous lessons during our 12 years of work. These lessons fall into four main categories, which are described in the following sections.

ABOUT THE NGO:
"FRIENDS OF LOMAS BARBUDAL"

It is necessary to legally and physically establish and maintain an organization that is highly visible, interactive with the community, and highly professional in conducting its activities and business affairs. It is critical to develop short (yearly) and long-term goals (five to ten years) and eventually to expect institutionalized status (and its implications) for the organization.

KNOW LOCAL CULTURE

It is important to establish and maintain a variety of working and friendly relationships with cooperators and local leaders. It is equally important to be aware of agendas of groups involved directly or indirectly with conservation. Get involved in community activities related to the environment, but be selective and avoid overextension of time and resources (see chapter 18). Learn patience.

OUTREACH AND KNOWING YOUR AUDIENCE

It is critical to know about the needs, expectations, and limitations of each audience (Jacob-son 1999). This often requires extra time to become familiar with the audience and to develop a sense of good will and trust. It may also require taking a few calculated risks such as experimenting with new approaches. Take audiences into the field to observe conservation/environmental issues directly. Be aware of the wide variety of teaching tools for communicating information (Ham 1992) and environmental teaching philosophies such as Project Wild and Project Learning Tree (PW 2000; PLT 1994).

AVOID POTENTIAL PROBLEMS

Despite our constant vigilance and awareness of potential problem areas, there were always surprises and new challenges. One of our biggest challenges was trying to keep current on frequent replacements of local park service directors and their ever changing agendas. These directors almost always promoted monopolization of any matter that pertained to conservation or the environment, whether or not they had the expertise to do so. A second problem area was local gossip. Most was benign and harmless; often it was humorous. On occasion, however, it was clearly divisive, mean spirited, and designed to attack the credibility and integrity of individuals or, more commonly, organizations such as our NGO. The easiest way for an individual or an organization to cause harm was to claim that there was mismanagement of funds and personal pocketing of money. It made no difference whether an organization such as ours had a certified public accountant who kept records on all incoming and outgoing money. The gossip came regardless. Fortunately, most of it could be dispelled if the source was known and could be vigorously pursued.

The small size of the "Friends" organization worked against us in the long term as logical extensions of ongoing work required more resources and support. Despite an active and successful program in the early and mid-1990s, our organization lacked the basic ingredient of long-term support from a major consistent donor(s) or an endowed fund. Eventually, the lack of sufficient funds and depletion of personal energy led to the closure of our EE program in 1997.

EVALUATING THE EE PROGRAM

During our 12 years of EE work in Bagaces and vicinity, we had ample opportunity to make assessments as biologists and teachers as to whether our work was locally accepted and effective in this rural community. We also had an understanding among the founders that we would develop and pursue EE projects only if we deemed them successful and if we continued to receive positive feedback from local residents. We present here a qualitative evaluation of the EE program in the sense of Jacobson (1999). See also Jacobson and McDuff (1998).

Our best initial indication of acceptance was realized through help and encouragement that we received in 1986 from the mayor of Bagaces, who volunteered municipality assistance for us to begin our work at Lomas Barbudal and vicinity. Help from the mayor came primarily in the form of building materials for construction of the visitor center at Lomas Barbudal. He also assisted by arranging for introductions to leaders in Bagaces. During Easter week in 1988, we received volunteer assistance from the Bagaces High School students through a collaboration with the mayor and school principal. Fifty-four students helped with a variety of field projects during this holiday period.

From 1989 to 1994 we designed and offered several workshops on fire management, which were collaborative efforts between our professional volunteers, park service personnel, and local townspeople. They were always well attended, and the feedback was positive. Eventually some of our local trainees formed or joined local volunteer fire crews. Two of these individuals were recently singled out as fire crew leaders in Bagaces (Loaiza 2000).

Once the center for EE was established in Bagaces, primary school children were readily attracted to the variety of programs offered. There was never a need to solicit the town's children; word of our educational offerings spread rapidly among this audience. Further, we always had the volunteer support of local mothers for field excursions. From 1990 to 1996, when our center was fully operative, we estimated that about 350 children took advantage of our program. Group size at weekly presentations at the center was 15–35 children. The length of time that a youngster spent in our program varied greatly, from about 2 months to 2 years.

In the early 1990s a local civic association in Bagaces solicited help from our organization to stop a planned clear-cut in a forest corridor, La Mula, between Palo Verde National Park and Lomas Barbudal. The corridor was considered to be the last effective biological connection between these two protected areas. The IDA had proposed cutting the Mula on the basis of needed development for local people (note: timber sales of the cut were estimated to be around U.S. $2 million). The challenge was to quickly develop a document demonstrating why this action was not in the best long-term interests of the region and country. Our organization gathered together 35 biologists and over a three-month period produced a document of 126 pages that spoke strongly against the cut (Frankie et al. 1994). We were also aided by environmental journalists, especially Gilda Aburto, and by leaders at that time from the Institute of Biodiversity (INBio) in Heredia. These efforts, which are described in more detail by Aburto (chapter 20), were successful in canceling the government deforestation plan. The Mula Corridor was subsequently protected through its annexation to Palo Verde National Park.

In addition to our positive historical experiences as an NGO, we assessed our program in relation to 12 guiding principles of EE, developed and agreed on at a UNESCO conference in 1977 at Tbilisi, Georgia (in the former USSR) (UNESCO 1978, 1980), which follow. We were able to relate our overall programs in positive ways to all principles except number 2. In this case, the lifelong process was beyond our scope.

1. Consider the environment in its totality—natural and built, technological and social

(economic, political, cultural-historical, moral, aesthetic);

2. Be a continuous lifelong process, beginning at the preschool level and continuing through all formal and non-formal stages;

3. Be interdisciplinary in its approach, drawing on the specific content of each discipline in making possible a holistic and balanced perspective;

4. Examine major environmental issues from local, national, regional, and international points of view so that students receive insights into environmental conditions in other geographic areas;

5. Focus on current and potential environmental situations, while taking into account the historical perspective;

6. Promote the value and necessity of local, national, and international co-operation in the prevention and solution of environmental problems;

7. Explicitly consider environmental aspects in plans for development and growth;

8. Enable learners to have a role in planning their learning experiences and provide an opportunity for making decisions and accepting their consequences;

9. Relate environmental sensitivity, knowledge, problem-solving skills, and values clarification to every age, but with special emphasis on environmental sensitivity to the learner's own community in early years;

10. Help learners discover the symptoms and real causes of environmental problems;

11. Emphasize the complexity of environmental problems and thus the need to develop critical thinking and problem-solving skills;

12. Utilize diverse learning environments and a broad array of educational approaches to teaching/learning about and from the environment, with due stress on practical activities and first-hand experience.

DISCUSSION

To the best of our knowledge, NGOs dedicated specifically to the conservation of biodiversity began to emerge in Costa Rica around the mid-1980s. Our organization also began its first outreach efforts at that time. Each of these organizations has remained characteristically small and localized. A very few of the organizations, such as the National Museum in San José, developed a mobile EE program that outreached to primary schools throughout Costa Rica. One small conservation NGO in San José, FECON, developed a consortium of some 20 small NGOs, which regularly sent representatives to make site visits to conservation projects or environmental problem areas. FECON, in turn, communicated its findings and interpretations to its member organizations and the media. FECON also represented conservation interests at the national level through the Legislative Assembly. Despite its small size, FECON has been one of the most prominent NGO voices for biodiversity conservation in the country.

In our Bagaces work, we used a variety of approaches and teaching tools in our various outreach activities/projects and conservation campaigns (see examples in Ham 1992; Jacobson 1999). Most of these worked well, especially with regard to primary school children and high schoolers. We regularly used the following topic avenues to reach these two audiences: familiar wildlife, common plant species, clean water, healthy watersheds, art, music, public health, and recreation. We had a more cautious and guarded response from adult groups. We assessed audiences and their possible responses, as far as possible, prior to any of the implemented activities. These early assessments greatly aided the execution of our programs (Jacobson 1999).

During the course of 12 years of EE work in the canton of Bagaces, we developed numerous contacts with a wide variety of individuals. Some contacts were made through direct cooperation and collaboration as partners in projects. In many cases, neighbors (including cattle ranchers and rice growers) and other local residents, who took the time to learn about our activities, served as spokespersons on our behalf. Our board of directors (12 individuals) provided support and council, and others, such as environmental journalists and lawyers, also helped. It was clear that as a small NGO we regularly needed and depended on cooperators, neighbors, friends, and other professionals to conduct our various projects (see also chapter 18).

There was only one small local group with whom we continually had problems. This group consisted of middle-management park service officials. At first we all seemed to be speaking the "same conservation and education language." After about five years of trying to cooperate, however, it became clear that cooperation and partnerships were usually not possible. The difficulties were not with the projects, regular park service personnel, or most of the higher-ranking park officials in the capital city, San José. Rather, it came down to a strong sense of territory and monopolization on the part of middle-management individuals.

Based on 20 continual years of observations on wildfires in the canton of Bagaces, there are at least three important conclusions one can reach, and all of these are related to EE. First, forest wildfires are a relatively new phenomenon in this region, and all are human-caused. Damaging effects of fire increase in a forest area if little or no responsible prevention and suppression are undertaken (Frankie et al. 1994, 1997; G. Frankie pers. obs.). Second, once forest habitats are destroyed and the exotic *H. rufa* grass invades, the risk of fire increases dramatically for adjacent forestlands. Third, many fires can be prevented or suppressed using time-proven, traditional fire management techniques. With regard to prevention, EE is one important component. Our fire workshops demonstrated the ease and interest by which local residents could become knowledgeable about fire ecology and trained in traditional fire suppression techniques. Eventually, journalists (newspaper and television) also helped greatly to spread the word about the destruction that fires were causing to forests, agricultural lands, and even private living

and work structures. This antifire campaign was in turn promoted through billboard advertisements and pamphlets by several large government agencies in the country. Volunteer fire crews of private citizens have become more commonplace in the Guanacaste region (Loaiza 2000). All these developments in fire awareness and management have occurred since the late 1980s, and EE programs implemented by a wide variety of individuals have greatly contributed to the success of the antiwildfire campaign. Raising awareness, however, is only the first part of the education process. Continued vigilance to reinforce awareness is also necessary.

RECOMMENDATIONS

Many recommendations can be offered based on our 12 years of experience. Some of these recommendations are implied in the "Lessons Learned" section (earlier in this chapter), especially with regard to establishing and maintaining a conservation NGO. It is important to mention again the need to develop a financially solvent NGO. High energy, numerous opportunities, and soaring expectations for transferring meaningful environmental information must be matched with corresponding support funds.

Is EE needed to conserve biodiversity in Costa Rica? Based on our work and the experiences of colleagues in other parts of the country, EE is a necessity if the system of natural areas is to be conserved and protected for the future. There is both ignorance to dispel and the need for new information by technically competent professionals. EE should also be focused on protected natural areas where rural people live, and they should be the main target audience, as they are likely to have the greatest long-term impact on biodiversity through their traditional use of natural resources. Rural people also have great potential to become allies and extenders of environmental information. The most appropriate type of EE program for rural communities is one that has at least a ten-year life span to ensure enough time to become institutionalized and to observe and work with a generation of new citizens from ages 9 to 18. In contrast, there is also the need for short-term interpretive information for visitors to the protected areas.

EE is best done by well-educated and trained professionals. The natural environment is a complex issue to explain in an appropriate manner. Adding people to the environment makes it even more complex. We recommend that a master's-level person be the target type of individual for leading an EE program. This person should have a degree and some research experience in biology, ecology, and/or natural resource management. The person also needs training in rural sociology, economics, and policy. A course in leadership training is also recommended, as environmental educators must be leaders.

Qualified environmental educators should work in conservation NGOs and also within the Ministry of Natural Resources, and both must be better supported by the government. The situation to date in Costa Rica is that most EE comes from the private sector and a few institutions such as the National Museum in San José and INBio in Heredia. Very little government investment in EE has been made within the ministry (G. Frankie pers. obs.). The government should also hire more educated and better-trained field directors in the park service. At the present time, most field park service personnel have little or no college experience (see chapters 5 and 21).

EE needs to extend beyond the usual audiences mentioned here. It also needs to reach large and small rural landowners, as there is still much biodiversity in rural areas (see chapter 17), and this will require new creative efforts by educators. In our biological work on private ranches and farms, it is clear that many landowners have a strong love for their land and many of the wild organisms that live there. They also think about their children who will one day inherit the land and its wildlife. This recognition provides fertile ground for creative environmental educators. In this regard, conservation easements, which are used to buy future development rights, could become more commonly used in rural Costa Rica, as they are in several places in the United States (Gustanski and Squires 2000).

Well-trained and experienced educators should be encouraged to conduct workshops to train local teachers to provide at least some EE to their pupils. In our experience, the effectiveness of these new extenders will be quite variable, but there will always be some teachers who will embrace environmental information, and these individuals should be targeted for more training and resources.

There is a need for more professional biologists to become involved in the process of transferring their biodiversity and conservation knowledge to audiences other than their own colleagues. They have much information to share, and oftentimes they are in the very best position to influence policy and decision makers (see chapters 18 and 20). This has not been a common role for professional biologists in the past, but times are changing globally. Applying and extending knowledge are becoming attractive to some biologists who have a sense of urgency to protect the environment and who want to play a proactive role in conserving biodiversity (see O'Brien 1993; Meffe 1998; Brown 2000; Kaiser 2000).

To conclude, EE is in its infancy as it relates to conserving and protecting biodiversity in rural areas. There is much to be done, and a large part of the effort will be private. However, the government needs to play a more active role in supporting the general concept and programs of EE, be they private or governmental. Government leaders must make substantial financial investments in EE!

ACKNOWLEDGMENTS

We thank the following individuals for their support during our 12 years of EE work in the canton of Bagaces: Gilda Aburto, Ramon Aguilar, Max Aragón, David Boshier, Mario Boza, Julio Bustos, Jorge Camacho, Magda Campos, Bob Carlson, Alfredo and Paulina Chacón, Dale Cuyler, Marvin Duarte, Jim Duzak, Maria Flexer, Jack and Maribell Fraser, Luis Diego Gómez, George Hagnauer, Verena Hagnauer, Lynn Hartshorn, Tony Hartshorn, Stephen Hopkins, Tony

Leigh, Linda Newstrom-Lloyd, Lilliam Lopez, Alfonso Mata, Emily Miggins, Beatriz Mosquiera, Pedro Ordoñez, Marianella Pastor, Susan Perry, Clara Padilla, Peter Ronchi, Susana Salas, Hilda Sandoval, Valeria Solano, the Stewart family of Comelco, Jennifer Weber, Lewis Wilson, and Brian Wissenden. Don Dahlsten, Stephen Hopkins, Genesis Humphrey, Alfonso Mata, and Mary Schindler kindly read a first draft of this chapter.

We thank the following institutions and organizations for their support: Consultoria Agroeconomica, Cañas, Guanacaste; World Wildlife Fund, Washington, D.C.; Municipality of Bagaces; California Agricultural Experiment Station, Berkeley; Texas Agricultural Experiment Station, College Station; Partners of the Americas, Oregon chapter; Finca La Pacifica, Cañas; U.S. Forest Service; Fundación de Parques Nacionales, San José; Museo National, San José; Rincon Corobici, Cañas; Finca Las Pumas, Cañas; Cederena, San José; FECON, San José; Dutch Embassy, San José; Canadian Embassy, San José; British Embassy, San José; Del Monte Corp., San José; BICSA bank, San José; and Cheeseman's Safaris, California.

REFERENCES

Brown, K. S. 2000. A new breed of scientist-advocates emerges. *Science* 287:1192–95.

EPA. 1993. *First report of the National Advisory Council on Environmental Education.* Washington, D.C.: U.S. Environmental Protection Agency.

Frankie, G. W., V. Solano, and M. McCoy. 1994. *Una evaluación técnica del Corredor La Mula entre La Reseva Biológica Lomas Barbudal y El Parque Nacional Palo Verde.* Bagaces: Amigos de Lomas Barbudal; Berkeley: University of California; and Heredia, Costa Rica: Universidad Nacional de Heredia. 126 pp. Contact frankie@nature.berkeley.edu for copies.

Frankie, G. W., S. B. Vinson, M. A. Rizzardi, T. L. Griswold, S. O'Keefe, and R. R. Snelling. 1997. Diversity and abundance of bees visiting a mass flowering tree species in disturbed seasonal dry forest, Costa Rica. *Journal of the Kansas Entomological Society* 70:281–96.

Gustanski, J. A., and R. H. Squires, eds. 2000. *Protecting the land: Conservation easements past, present, and future.* Covelo, Calif.: Island Press. 566 pp.

Ham, S. H. 1992. *Environmental interpretation: A practical guide for people with big ideas and small budgets.* Golden, Colo.: North American Press. 456 pp.

Jacobson, S. K. 1999. *Communication skills for conservation professionals.* Covelo, Calif.: Island Press. 351 pp.

Jacobson, S. K., and M. D. McDuff. 1998. Conservation education. In *Conservation science and action,* ed. W. J. Sutherland, 237–55. Oxford, England: Blackwell Science.

Kaiser, J. 2000. Ecologists on a mission to save the world. *Science* 287:1188–92.

Loaiza, V. 2000. Ceden los incendios forestales. *La Nación* (national Costa Rican newspaper), 27 February.

Meffe, G. K. 1998. Conservation biology: Into the millennium. In *Conservation Biology* 12:1–3.

O'Brien, M. H. 1993. The professional biologist: Being a scientist means taking sides. *BioScience* 43:706–8.

PLT (Project Learning Tree). 1994. *Project Learning Tree: Environmental education activity guide.* Washington, D.C.: American Forestry Foundation. 402 pp.

PW (Project Wild). 2000. *Project Wild: Activity guide.* Gaithersburg, Md.: Project Wild. 526 pp.

UNESCO. 1978. *Twelve guiding principles to define and guide the development of environmental education.* Final report, intergovernmental conference on environmental education, organized and published by UNESCO in cooperation with UNEP, Tbilisi (Georgia), USSR, 14–26 October 1977.

———. 1980. *Environmental education in the light of the 1977 Tbilisi Conference.* Paris: UNESCO. 25 pp.

CHAPTER 20

The Media and Biodiversity Conservation

Gilda Aburto

FOR HUNDREDS OF YEARS, humans have been in constant battle over natural resources, some for their exploitation and others for their protection and preservation for the future. One of the first people in North America—if not the first—to raise their voice in favor of defending wildlife territories was the legendary John Muir (Tolan 1990), known as the "Father of the National Parks." For years he traveled through the impressive valleys and mountains of the United States, the forests and glaciers of Alaska, identifying species and marveling at the natural beauty of these wildlands. He also observed how these territories were being threatened by the growing population that was rapidly expanding westward, tearing down forests to establish settlements and raise livestock.

A passionate lover of nature, Muir found that it was not enough to be a passive scholar of nature, classifying species of plants and trees that were rapidly being lost to the logging industry, sheep ranchers, and the accelerated population growth that demanded more and more resources. In his attempt to protect these wildlands, Muir also found that there was a tremendous difference between delivering a seminar to a few people and publishing an article in a journal. Published articles could transmit the impressive beauty of these wildlife areas, the forests that he called the "temples of God," to a much wider audience. It was his passionate articles, published in newspapers and magazines, that transported the urban populations to these wild areas, where they would admire them so much that they were moved to protect them.

Biologist Rachel Carson strengthened the environmentalist movement with the publication of her book *Silent Spring* (1962), in which she warned of the dangers of agricultural chemicals. She was especially concerned with the "miraculous insecticide" DDT, which was gravely contaminating the environment, killing wildlife, and poisoning humans. Once again it was the use of a major media resource that alerted the public and raised the voices of protest; until then people had been unaware of the dangers to which they were being exposed.

The struggle continues today. Whereas yesterday pen and paper were sufficient to battle the ax, today chainsaws and tractors have given an advantage to the destroyers. Entire forests fall overnight—before we can even begin to call attention to problems (Soulé 1986; Noss and Cooperrider 1994). Enormous stretches of tropical rain forest disappear before we can discover what animal and plant species they held. It is continuously more difficult for scientists to obtain funding for investigations into diverse natural habitats, yet large transnational corporations easily acquire logging and mining concessions, with outrageous economic advantages, in the impoverished countries of Latin America. Biologists alone cannot stop this destruction. They need the general public to donate money necessary to carry out conservation projects, to write letters to politicians, and to join the voices of protest against the imminent danger to nature. Thus, although the problems involve biological themes, it is the people who not only often create these problems but who also hold the solution in their hands. Only through communication can biologists transmit their much-needed knowledge to the public, empowering it to act.

Scientists have an ally that can help them reach those who will make crucial decisions for the environment. That ally is the media. By means of radio and television, information can literally circle the globe and reach millions in a very short time.

This chapter explores a set of guidelines for establishing effective communication between biologists and the media for raising environmental awareness of the general populace. The guidelines are based on cumulative experiences of journalists working with biologists in Costa Rica and elsewhere in Central America.

Help from the public in creating an effective conservation campaign is absolutely essential, as campaigns initiated by an isolated biologist will have slim chances of success. It is difficult, if not impossible, to visit the numerous government offices, lawmakers, politicians, citizen associations, and international entities required to effect policy, initiate campaigns, or raise funds for environmentally oriented projects. Such a dedicated biologist would have to forgo much of his or her research to pursue this path of action because large amounts of time and economic resources would have to be invested. Moreover, positive results would rarely be obtained. This path is too slow for our quickly changing world. It often happens that, by the time the goal is reached, the threats to the environment on which the campaign was based are already resolved.

Biologists who have traveled this road know that it is unpaved, steep, and rough, like the forests they traverse. However, the often closed doors of the decision makers open miraculously as a result of an effective media campaign. Experience has repeatedly shown that journalists can be very effective and, above all, swift when communicating important information presented to them by biologists. Publications in the press can be very useful to the scientist requesting funds from an international organization, since journal clippings can be affixed to proposals, giving them more weight. More important, this information, widely disseminated by the media, has the potential to recruit thousands of willing and dedicated citizens who can successfully pressure the authorities in ways an isolated biologist simply cannot do (Jacobson 1999).

Contact with the media is an absolutely crucial step because, although there are many informed citizens who are concerned about the damages being done, few have the detailed information needed to act on these concerns. Many more people know nothing at all about the environment, the damage and destruction it faces, or what consequences this damage might have on their own well-being. These people are so immersed in their fast-paced urban world, hurrying to work, hypnotized with sports, concerned with problems of everyday life, that they seldom stop and think about the natural resources that provide the water that runs their in faucets, toilets, and showers. They rarely notice when trucks stacked with huge logs drive by and thus do not even think about where they come from or if their extraction will affect their lives.

Likewise, journalists often do not realize what goes on in the field of biologists. They need scientists to inform them and to provide the necessary information to draft a news report. Patience, above all, is needed to educate journalists so that they can see the need to include the environment in their media agenda. Even if biologists are not, at first, fully understood or if published information does not contain all the data desired, contact with the media is an essential first step in informing the public (Jukofsky and Wille 1993).

Unfortunately, many investigators often act like the animals they study: shy, fleeing, and unwilling to approach people. They fear that they will not be understood or perhaps will be criticized by their peers and prefer to remain hidden in the depths of the forest. Initiating press campaigns also threatens to take up valuable time from their research. Yet biologists must alert the population to the damage being done to nature or risk losing the same forests in which they work.

One route for the biologist who does not wish to speak directly to the media is to use a politician as a go-between. Politicians love the press, benefit from being on television and newspapers as often as possible, and rarely miss an opportunity to make an appearance if there is a good reason to do so. Not only do they enjoy and benefit from press attention, but politicians often have the charisma and power to reach the media. If scientists can gain their attention, they can become valuable allies in environmental media campaigns.

Another avenue for "shy" scientists, if their organizations have the budget, is to hire a journalist or a public relations representative to be in charge of establishing contact with the media and organizing press conferences. These representatives also draft "translated" press bulletins—reports written in plain, simple, and entertaining language free of hard-to-understand scientific terminology—making scientific information accessible to a diverse audience (Jacobson 1999).

Whatever path they choose to reach the media, scientists must establish and maintain their credibility. A scientist that has studied a specific habitat for years has the knowledge and understanding to pinpoint the immediate and potential dangers to this ecosystem. He or she can therefore effectively illustrate and defend his or her arguments (O'Brien 1993).

However, writing for the media is not the same as writing a paper for a scientific journal. One tool required to reach the public ear lies in "humanizing the story" as much as possible. The media, as well as the public, will definitely be more interested if an ecological problem affects not only wild species but humans, as well.

Scientists must also be careful not to write lengthy horror stories or send extensive and complicated bulletins to the media. Many biologists often wait until the last minute, when disaster is imminent, to report their findings to the public. Although such reports are sometimes necessary, people cannot be continually bombarded with disheartening news; otherwise, they will feel desperate and helpless to act meaningfully. To motivate people to act, biologists should make it a point to update the public periodically about their work so that people can begin to feel a connection with the biologist's area of study. Moreover, these updates must include positive news, such as the discovery of new plant and animal species, the development of effective conservation projects, and the detection of a species once thought to be extinct. Finally, these reports should be short, clearly and concisely written, and objective, abandoning overly technical language. To learn and appreciate the biologist's message, the public must first be able to read it (Jacobson 1999).

LA MULA CREEK

In 1993, the Costa Rican Institute of Agrarian Development (IDA) provoked a commotion about a forest known as La Mula Creek in the Tempisque region of Guanacaste Province (see map 1.3 in chapter 1). Located between the Lomas de Barbudal Biological Reserve and Palo Verde National Park, La Mula Creek is largely a pochote (*Bombacopsis quinata*) forest whose timber, valued at $2 million, covers about 350 ha. Intending to donate the lots to local farmers who presumably owned no land, the IDA planned to clear-cut La Mula Creek and divide it into 33 parcels. The institute would then turn it over to the individual farmers, who were to plant rice on the "cleared" land.

The town of Bagatzí, which was adjacent to the pochote forest, protested this decision. It argued that the forest protected the townspeople from strong summer winds, that nearby rice plantations would poison their water resources, and that the fumigation planes would spray them with toxic chemicals. Local biologists and conservationists joined the residents of Bagatzí and emphatically opposed the cutting of the forest. Focusing more on the biological aspects of the forest, they maintained that it was the last haven of higher genetic quality pochote in the country, perhaps in all of Central America (where pochote forests have been mostly eliminated for cattle production), and that it was a refuge for wildlife species that were ecologically connected to the neighboring Palo Verde National Park. Moreover, they argued, during the winter, large currents of water flowed through La Mula Creek and reached La Bocana Lagoon, located inside the Palo Verde National Park. If rice was planted where the pochote forest was, precipitation would wash chemicals used on these crops into the lagoon, poisoning its waters. They pointed out that the government is obligated to protect the lagoon, since it is included in the international RAMSAR Treaty (for migratory waterfowl) signed by Costa Rica years earlier.

Between January and April 1994, Gordon Frankie (a coeditor of this volume), who had studied the ecology of the region for 30 years, asked 35 national and international biologists to carry out a rapid biodiversity assessment of the flora and fauna of La Mula Creek. Specialists in many different fields, from botany to ornithol-

ogy, traveled through the forest for several days and nights, observing and collecting data on diurnal and nocturnal species. Their results were surprising in that the species discovered were far more numerous than what was expected from the area. Hundreds of species, ranging from bats, small rodents, and marsupials to felines (including a jaguar), monkeys, and rabbits, were found in the forest. In addition, 144 species of birds, both native and migratory, and 101 tree species were identified in the small forest of La Mula—a considerable diversity for such a small area (Frankie et al. 1994).

After all the information was collected, it was presented in a report that included aerial and ground-level photographs showing the existing vegetation density. The report was sent to all authorities who had an influence on the decisions concerning the future of the forest. These authorities included the executive president of the IDA, Defensoría de los Habitantes, the minister of natural resources, officials at the Interamerican Development Bank that were to finance a system of irrigation canals throughout the area, and some journalists.

Meanwhile, inhabitants of Bagatzí, as well as those from Bagaces, a nearby town in the same region, joined forces with biologists and conservationists in more direct action to protect the threatened environmental resources. Some were constantly watching over the forest to avoid clandestine cutting, especially during weekends, while others established contacts with the media, inviting journalists to visit the problem area and even providing transportation to take journalists to the forest. There, they were led on guided tours by members of the local organization, the Voice of the People. This organization also contributed to the campaign by writing letters to authorities, making calls to the media to keep them informed of developing events, and traveling to San José to visit lawyers who could instruct them in the law and guide them to the courts to stop the cutting of the forest.

The efforts of these diverse organizations and individuals were dramatically successful.

The journalists who visited the area published several reports on the importance of the forest and the desire of the inhabitants to preserve it. They spoke extensively of the damage that would occur with the destruction of the forest and exerted constant pressure on corresponding authorities to revoke the decision to cut it down (in the latter phase, the Institute of Biodiversity in Heredia also spoke out against the cutting). Finally, after more than a year of struggle, the executive president of the IDA revoked the decision to clear-cut the forest. Instead, he donated the plots to the Ministry of Natural Resources, under whose authority they would be annexed to the Palo Verde National Park and would receive special and continuous protection.

The campaign to conserve the Mula represents an excellent example of how biologists and local people kept in regular communication until the decision to abort the cutting was made. It is also noteworthy that journalists had direct contact with government officials in San José and used these opportunities to influence their decision making, which in turn stemmed from the journalists' firsthand knowledge of the field situation through biologists and local people.

HOW TO REACH THE PRESS

From the example of the Mula, it is clear that conservation depends on three principal factors: the knowledge of biologists, awareness and action on the part of the public, and political support. The connecting link between these three factors, which coordinates and makes possible the actions of biologists, the public, and politicians, is the media. Use of the media is especially crucial in these times of economic globalization, powerful transnational companies, and movement of large capital throughout the world, in which the pressure to exploit natural resources currently protected has increased.

However, if the media are the crucial link, the scientists are responsible for the initial step in connecting this link—by aggressively pursuing the media and providing their information to interested journalists, as did the residents of Bagatzí in their attempt to save La Mula Creek. Some biologists do not address the media because they think journalists will not understand them or care about their situation or, even worse, will modify their statements. The popular image of journalists and reporters hustling to cover criminal events, politics, and economic swings and consequently having little time to think about nature is especially discouraging to these scientists. Yet, if it is true that journalists often seem to have little time to devote to environmental issues, it is not because they are not interested. It is certainly true that they live under constant pressure to find and publish the daily news. Bogged down with many interesting and newsworthy stories, these journalists need biologists to seek them out, to knock on the media doors and show them what is happening. When biologists encounter a situation that must be presented to the public eye, they must not hesitate to pick up a phone, send a fax, and communicate in any way possible. If their efforts are not fruitful the first time, they must try again. If one station or journal was unwilling to publish their story, then they must contact another one. In a word, persistence is the key to reaching the press (O'Brien 1993).

Moreover, biologists should not limit their contacts to one or two enthusiastic journalists but should try to identify journalists in several different media entities, such as radio, television, and newspapers, who write about the environment. The biologist should then formulate a list of these journalists for future reference. This list must be updated constantly because of the mobility of journalists and also because there are always new and enthusiastic reporters in each field. Scientists should call these journalists to establish an initial contact and should try to learn about their work specialty to see if biologist and journalist have interests in common. If so, biologists should make an effort to build a relationship with this journalist through consistent communication. Favorable contacts can easily be maintained by periodically sending the journalist a bulletin he or she can publish and even inviting him or her on a field trip to observe the biologist's work (Jukofsky and Wille 1993).

There are a number of media entities through which the concerned scientist can communicate with the public. Scientists should take advantage of as many of these channels as possible:

1. Bulletins

2. Interviews with the press

3. Press kits

4. Advertisements

5. Web pages

6. Press conferences

7. E-mail lists (Jacobson 1999)

Although preparation for each of these channels of communication varies slightly, some general guidelines can be pinpointed in the use of interviews and press bulletins.

HOW TO CONDUCT AN INTERVIEW

Those scientists who worry about misrepresentation of their evidence by the media have good reason. A good opportunity to report a threat to the environment to the media is often wasted because of the ignorance or lack of preparation of the reporter when interviewing the biologist. However, miscommunications can also easily be avoided by following a few simple guidelines. First, the biologist must understand that the journalist probably has no solid knowledge of the scientist's area of interest because the range of specialties is so wide. Taking this into account, the biologist can easily facilitate an effective and fluid interview, minus the dreaded distortion, by providing the journalist with preparatory material in anticipation of the interview. Such information could include location of the threatened area, type of habitat, affected animal and plant species, and who or what threatens them. It is also extremely important to "humanize" the report by indicating if people or settlements are affected and by making the value of the endangered land explicit.

If the area is threatened by the actions of a private firm, biologists should also provide phone numbers and names of people in charge, if available, so that the journalist's work can be facilitated with respect to the "balance," or fairness, of the report. They should also include information on how they can be reached, such as fax and cellular phone numbers or E-mail. Even a home phone number is necessary, since it is often during non–office hours when journalists have time to check these documents and search for newsworthy material.

Scientists should also prepare themselves beforehand for interviews with the media. Preparatory materials, such as maps, photographs, scientific data, statistics, charts, results from studies, and any other documents considered important to clarify or reaffirm concepts are absolutely necessary to support the scientist's words. Scientists planning for an interview should also anticipate questions, both negative and positive, that might be asked regarding the event in question, and they should prepare positive, precise, and direct answers. Time, for both journalist and biologist, is very valuable, and scientists should strive to say as much as possible in the amount of time available. In terms of content, there are two basic rules for every interview with a journalist: (1) Scientists should always tell the truth. Credibility is the most valuable possession the scientist has. (2) Scientists should avoid saying anything they do not want published. There is no such thing as off-the-record comments. When they are published, it will be too late for retraction. Finally, after the interview has taken place, the biologist must make sure that the journalist understood the concepts, magnitude of the problem, and terminology employed.

HOW TO DRAFT A PRESS BULLETIN

Another important mode of communication is the press bulletin. As previously mentioned, these bulletins are an effective way of developing a relationship with the press and educating people about their natural environment. The following are some key factors in the preparation of an effective press bulletin:

1. Know what you have to say. Make a rough draft of the points to be discussed and enumerate them from most important to least important. Jacobson (1999) has suggested that materials should be organized with the most significant information first, followed by key details added throughout the paper and ending with data that could be useful for the comprehension of the subject discussed.

2. Make your story newsworthy. Pinpoint why your story would interest the public. Avoid propaganda for yourself or your organization. If your information seems more like an advertisement, it will be ignored by the editing office.

3. Write in a simple, direct, and objective way. Present the situation in the least amount of words possible without losing coherence or making it incomprehensible. Any bulletin should not be longer than two double-spaced pages and should have short sentences and paragraphs that are easy to read. Set aside overly technical language that is incomprehensible. Extensive documents with difficult language scare away readers and journalists, who often do not have time to read them. More important, if the reporter cannot understand what the scientist is saying, then there will be no interest in publishing the story. These documents often end up in the trashcan. Even if the reporter does run the story, there is the risk of publishing incorrect data that will infuriate the environmental expert and create indifference from the public. Do not forget to include phone and fax numbers and other ways to contact you or your organization.

4. Emphasize the human side of the story. Always include the preoccupations, interests, or desires of the majority of people. The public will be interested when the problem touches the human aspect. Whenever possible, write your message as a story rather than as a scientific paper.

5. Send your story expeditiously. If there is an urgent event to communicate, do not wait to include it in your next bulletin; by then, the event may not be of interest anymore. Draft a special bulletin and distribute it immediately.

6. Make sure the bulletin reaches the right contact person. Do not send your story to just anyone who will receive it in the editing office. Always verify that your contacts still work in their organizations, and warn them of your incoming story.

7. Pay attention to the presentation of your bulletin. A document with inadequate diagrams, deficient composition, and poor handwriting will have difficulty attracting attention in the editing room. Make sure the bulletin is "clean," or not completely covered with text; leave some spaces blank so that the reader will have a chance to rest. If possible, use the stationery of the organization for the bulletin. Write double-spaced, only on one side of the paper, using wide margins and an appropriate letter size, not excessively small or large.

8. Include visual aids. Whenever possible, include colorful photographs and maps that will attract attention to your story. If the bulletin is for television, videos can also be used. Whenever possible, invite the media on a trip to the research area and offer room and board to the journalists, in addition to a guided tour of the area.

9. Follow up. When you wish to establish a relationship with a media organization, remember to follow up on your story even if your case was only published once. Keep the journalist regularly informed on the developments concerning your case, especially if he or she is far away from the case under study.

NEW DIRECTIONS

Aside from newspapers, radio, and television, scientists now have a new tool with which to reach large audiences: the Internet. Web pages are a new and effective channel for the diffusion of their campaigns. Not only is this form of communication now the fastest and most economical mode of distributing information of any used to date, but there are more than 67 million people worldwide navigating daily through the Internet. The Internet is also extremely versatile. It allows the mixing of text, photographs, audio, and video. It also allows for a special connection with the audience. "Visitors" to the site can simply obtain information from the computer screen or "download" documents of interest and save them. Direct communication with these visitors, who can respond immediately with feedback, is also possible through the use of E-mails listed on the Web site. The creation of Web pages is continuously becoming simpler; one no longer needs to be a computer expert to be able to create a Web page. Even now, there are Internet sites that provide complimentary manuals that can help interested scientists set up a more sophisticated and attractive page.

E-mail lists are also becoming more and more popular and can be targeted at specific groups of people. They allow one to communicate with one's colleagues and with media organizations and influential personalities of the entire world. E-mail lists also have some advantages over the Web. The information proceeds directly to the subscribers, who do not have to search for it on the Web, and the people who have subscribed are already interested in the information and are therefore much more receptive (see discussion in Jacobson 1999).

In conclusion, the experiences to date between biologists, the media, the general public, and decision makers indicate that planned channels of communication, perhaps coupled with a strategic plan, can produce positive results for conservation projects. Biologists have an important role to play in initiating and keeping the chan-

nels of communication open (O'Brien 1993). This will, of course, require biologists to invest some of their time and energy in the art of information transfer and perhaps to make other investments to enable their voices and points of view to be known and understood (Meffe 1998; Jacobson 1999). Many field biologists know a great deal about the biodiversity of their study areas and some of the consequences of losing it. There is a great need for more of them to come forward and share their knowledge and passion with others (Primack 1998).

REFERENCES

Carson, R. 1962. *Silent spring.* Boston: Houghton Mifflin. 368 pp.

Frankie, G. W., V. Solano, and M. McCoy. 1994. Una evaluación técnica del Corredor La Mula entre La Reserva Biológica Lomas Barbudal y El Parque Nacional Palo Verde. Bagaces: Amigos de Lomas Barbudal; Berkeley: University of California; and Heredia, Costa Rica: Universidad Nacional de Heredia. 126 pp. Contact frankie@nature.berkeley.edu for copies.

Jacobson, S. 1999. *Communication skills for conservation professionals.* Covelo, Calif.: Island Press. 351 pp.

Jukofsky, D., and C. Wille. 1993. *Difundan su mensaje, guía para conservacionistas.* San José and New York: Centro de Periodismo Ambiental, Proyecto de la Rainforest Alliance. 83 pp.

Meffe, G. K. 1998. Conservation biology: Into the millennium. *Conservation Biology* 12:1–3.

Nelson, P. 1994. *Diez recomendaciones prácticas para la investigación y redacción de reportajes sobre temas ambientales.* Washington, D.C.: International Center for Journalists. 63 pp. Contact: editor@icfj.org.

Noss, R. F., and A. Y. Cooperrider, eds. 1994. *Saving nature's legacy: Protecting and restoring biodiversity.* Covelo, Calif.: Island Press. 417 pp.

O'Brien, M. H. 1993. Being a scientist means taking sides. *BioScience* 43:706–8.

Primack, R. B. 1998. *Essentials of conservation biology.* 2d ed. Sunderland, Mass.: Sinauer Associates. 660 pp.

Soulé, M., ed. 1986. *Conservation biology: The science of scarcity and diversity.* Massachusetts: Sinauer Associates. 584 pp.

Tolan, S. 1990. *John Muir: Naturalist, writer, and guardian of the North American Wilderness.* Harrisburg, Pa.: Morehouse Publishing. 68 pp.

Wille, C., and D. Jukofsky. 1993. *Periodismo ambiental en América Central.* San José: Centro de Periodismo Ambiental, Rainforest Alliance. 53 pp. Contact: infotrop@racsa.co.cr.

CHAPTER 21

Threats to the Conservation of Tropical Dry Forest in Costa Rica

Mauricio Quesada and Kathryn E. Stoner

Approximately 550,000 km^2 of tropical dry forest covered the Pacific coast of Mesoamerica at the time that the Spaniards arrived. Today less than 2 percent of this forest remains (Janzen 1988), mostly in Mexico (Trejo and Dirzo 2000). It has been estimated that the only protected sites of tropical dry forest in Mesoamerica that are large enough to possibly sustain dry-forest ecosystems are Parque Nacional Santa Rosa and Parque Nacional Palo Verde in Guanacaste, Costa Rica, and the Chamela-Cuixmala Biosphere Reserve in Jalisco, Mexico (Hartshorn 1988).

Tropical dry forests in Costa Rica have almost disappeared. The total area of original dry forest in Costa Rica estimated before 1940 was approximately 400,000 ha (8% of the national territory), and by 1950 this area was reduced to 40,200 ha (Sader and Joyce 1988). The most recent Landsat TM satellite image analysis estimates that less than 0.1 percent of tropical dry forest remains in Costa Rica and recognizes this habitat as the most endangered within the country (Sánchez-Azofeifa 1997).

Eleven different conservation areas are recognized in Costa Rica today, and only two of these contain the ten national parks and reserves that protect tropical dry forest (Blanco and Mata 1994). Parque Nacional Guanacaste in the Guanacaste Conservation Area protects approximately 50,000 ha, and Parque Nacional Palo Verde and Reserva Biológica Lomas Barbudal in the Tempisque Conservation Area protect an additional 20,000 ha.

In this chapter we discuss the major factors that have affected tropical dry forests in Costa Rica and some of the effects that they have had on this ecosystem. We also discuss current management practices used by the Tempisque Conservation Area in Parque Nacional Palo Verde and Reserva Biológica Lomas Barbudal that may threaten the preservation of tropical dry forests.

Finally, we present some recommendations for the future successful conservation of tropical dry forest.

CAUSES OF DRY-FOREST CONVERSION IN COSTA RICA

CATTLE

Deforestation because of the cattle industry has been the main cause of tropical forest destruction throughout Mexico and Central America (Quesada-López-Calleja 1974; Toledo 1992; Maass 1995). Costa Rica is no exception, with the cattle industry contributing more to deforestation in the period before 1980 than all other economic activities combined including commercial logging (Lehmann 1992). On a countrywide basis, by 1973 more than one-third of the country's territory consisted of cattle pastures (Quesada-López-Calleja 1974; Lehmann 1992). The area of the country dedicated to pasture increased from 630,000 ha in 1950 to more than 2 million ha in 1994 (IICA 1995).

The first cattle ranch was founded in Guanacaste in the late 1500s (Janzen 1986), and extensive cattle ranches were established in this dry-forest area as early as 1800 (Boucher et al. 1983). The oldest post-Hispanic settlements in the dry forest were established along the Tempisque River Basin in Guanacaste with subsequent development of pastures and agriculture in this region. Data obtained from aerial photographs and satellite images indicate that approximately 46 percent (115,000 ha) of this region consisted of pastures by the mid-1950s (Maldonado et al. 1995).

Several factors affected the continued growth of the cattle industry in northern Costa Rica during the twentieth century. The construction of the Pan American Highway in the 1950s allowed easy access to the entire country, facilitating both settlement and marketing in the rest of Guanacaste (Williams 1986). Furthermore, expansion of the cattle industry was a major goal of the Costa Rican government in the 1950s in order to diversify export products. The exportation of live cattle began in 1954 and was soon replaced by the exportation of refrigerated beef (Hall 1985). The cattle business continued to grow as the government contributed with national and international credits to support the industry financially. It has been estimated that approximately 50 percent of all agricultural credit went to cattle in the early 1970s (Quesada-López-Calleja 1974; Leonard 1987). The Nicoya Peninsula and the land surrounding Liberia (the capital of Guanacaste) increased the area dedicated to pastures 151 percent from 1979 to 1992 as a result of economic incentives given to cattle owners (Canet et al. 1996).

In addition to forest destruction, another impact of the cattle industry on tropical dry forests is caused by the use of fire to maintain open pastures. Fire has been one of the single most detrimental effects on tropical dry-forest ecosystems in Costa Rica within this century (Janzen 1986). Natural fires in Neotropical ecosystems are extremely rare (but see Middleton et al. 1997); the majority of fires are caused by humans (Janzen 1986). Fires became a problem in Guanacaste because of the introduction of African star grass (*Hyparrhenia rufa*) in the 1920s (Parsons 1972). This grass is an aggressive self-seeding species, originally from the savannas of Africa, and is adapted to survive fire (Parsons 1972). Despite the widespread use of *H. rufa* as a source of food for cattle in Guanacaste, it is not an effective cattle feed. It has been demonstrated that cattle rarely consume this grass during the dry season, when it has a very low nutritional value (Daubenmire 1972a).

To minimize the impact of the cattle industry on the dry forest in Guanacaste, it will be necessary to change the current grazing practices and encourage alternative land uses for abandoned pastures. The Costa Rican government has already begun to encourage agricultural development in many degraded areas of formerly dry forest (see the section "Agriculture" later in this chapter). Continued efforts to minimize burning of pastures should be combined with the implementation of strong fire management programs both within protected areas and in adjacent areas. Fire management programs do exist in many of the protected areas in the dry forest, but a lack of adequate infrastructure (e.g., fire-fighting equipment) and sufficient trained personnel limit their effectiveness. One exception is the fire control program of the Guanacaste Conservation Area (Janzen 1986).

TIMBER

In 1943, Costa Rica still reported a forest cover of 70–75 percent of the national territory (Sader and Joyce 1988). However, large-scale deforestation was initiated in the 1950s, and by 1980 Costa Rica was experiencing 3.19 percent deforestation annually, one of the highest rates in the world (Leonard 1987). Forest destruction continued into the 1990s, and analysis of Landsat TM images revealed that by 1991 only 29 percent of the national territory remained covered with some type of forest (Sánchez-Azofeifa 1997). This same study estimated the rate of change of forest cover between 1986 and 1991 to be approximately 45,000 ha per year, which is equivalent to a 21 percent loss of the forest cover originally present in 1986. In contrast to Sánchez-Azofeifa (1997), a second recent study reported an increase of 10 percent forest cover between 1986 and 1997, which represents a reforestation rate of 83,300 ha per year. The government attributed this change to the success of reforestation programs and to the recovery of abandoned pastures (Castro and Arias 1998). Much debate has been generated over the interpretation of the Landsat TM images used in these studies primarily because Castro and Arias (1998) classified the forest cover uniformly and did not distinguish between the different levels of succession—abandoned pastures with some scattered trees and areas in reforestation programs (i.e., tree plantations) were categorized as forest. Even if the recent estimates provided by Castro and Arias (1998) were correct, the increase in forest cover is the result of secondary regeneration in the fragments of land that dominate the nation's landscape.

Most of the destruction of natural forests in Costa Rica has occurred because of a lack of government control and a philosophy oriented to provide economic incentives to transform forests into tree plantations, pastures, and agricultural fields. It was not until 1969, with the establishment of a forestry law, that a government office was created to enforce the protection of national parks and forest reserves. Despite this law, natural forests outside protected areas continued to be exploited without control, and economic incentives to maintain forest cover outside protected areas did not appear until 1979. The government developed a tax exemption program for landowners that adopted reforestation management within their property. This program has replanted only 0.8 percent of the national territory over the past 20 years (Canet et al. 1996). Other types of economic incentives were initiated after 1988 to encourage reforestation and include the following programs: Certificado de Abono Forestal, Certificado de Abono Forestal por Adelanto, Certificado de Abono Forestal para Manejo de Bosque, and Fondo de Desarrollo Forestal. Although these programs represented a creative initiative to protect tropical forests, a series of problems associated with insufficient monitoring, as well as changes in government administrations, have limited their success. Today, these reforestation programs (tree plantations) have replanted only 4 percent of the national territory and have received U.S. $98 million in economic incentives (Canet et al. 1996; Castro and Arias 1998).

Although the main purpose of these programs has been to promote the development of tree plantations in open and degraded areas, as well as the protection of natural forest in private hands, the government does not have the institutional capacity to monitor these agreements systematically. For example, a review of the national forestry policy indicated that several investment corporations sold or changed the use of land while continuing to receive economic incentives for reforestation (Rodríguez and Vargas 1988). Today, logging permits are issued to extract timber from plantations or on the basis of officially authorized management plans of natural forests; regulation is supposedly enforced through transportation controls (Kishor and Constantino 1993). Transportation controls do not monitor the impact of extraction on the natural forest or the ecological status of the exploited populations. In addition, it has been estimated that 50 percent of logging in Costa Rica is illegal, and logging trucks transport at night or on weekends when there are no controls (Kishor and Constantino 1993).

According to the current forestry policy (Gaceta 91, Resolution No. 323, 13 May 1998; Gaceta 100, Executive Decree No. 26977, 26 May 1998), the programs mentioned earlier have merged into a single program to compensate private landowners for the environmental services provided by the forest or trees within their property. This program is designed to provide the following economic incentives: (1) land devoted to reforestation with plantations will receive $576 per hectare over a five-year period (2) natural forests under management plans (i.e., selective logging) will receive $352 per hectare over a five-year period; and (3) natural forests under absolute protection will receive $224 per hectare over a five-year period. This policy is clearly oriented to stimulate the exploitation of natural forests outside protected areas by investing the funds obtained for conservation in economic incentives for deforestation.

Approximately 56 percent of timber harvested in Costa Rica in 1998 was obtained from forests; the rest came from pastures, remnant forests, and agricultural areas (Estado de la Nación 1999). Trees located in pastures and remnant forests accounted for 23 percent of the timber harvested in 1998, the same amount that was harvested from pastures and remnant forests in 1992 and 1993. This harvesting regime may have serious long-term consequences on the remaining natural forests in the country, since recent evidence has indicated the importance of isolated trees as "stepping-stones" for gene flow of tropical trees, especially in remnant forests that serve as

biological corridors (Aldrich and Hamrick 1998; Cascante et al. 2002; chapter 3). The sustainable use of tropical forests depends on the ability of trees to reproduce and regenerate under natural conditions; however, our current knowledge on these basic biological aspects is limited to only a few dry-forest timber trees (Cascante et al. 2002; Quesada et al. 2001).

Although much commercial logging today is accomplished within the legal framework of "forestry management plans," there is great variation in the degree of government control on management plans authorized by different conservation areas. For example, according to the Sistema Nacional de Areas de Conservación, between 1996 and 1997 the Tempisque Conservation Area approved management plans to exploit timber from tropical dry forests from an area of 607 ha (SINAC 1997). In contrast, the Guanacaste Conservation Area did not approve any forest areas for management plans in this same period (SINAC 1997). In Guanacaste today there are approximately 14 active sawmills with a capacity to process 47,000 m³ per day (Canet et al. 1996); much of the timber processed in these sawmills has been legally harvested through management plans authorized by the respective conservation areas. It is ironic that dry-forest timber species continue to be harvested today in Guanacaste, despite the fact that almost no natural forests are found outside protected areas.

The development of forest management plans by the government has not been effective in reducing the amount of deforestation but rather has provided a legal tool to facilitate the continued exploitation of the few remaining natural forests. A clear example of the damage that can be done, even when logging is conducted under the auspices of a management plan, is found in the area of the Osa Peninsula in southwestern Costa Rica. A recent study revealed that between 1997 and 1998, 164 forestry management plans were approved in this area, authorizing the cutting of more than 14,000 trees resulting in the deforestation of approximately 4,000 ha

TABLE 21.1

Commercially Important Native Timber Species from Costa Rica's Tropical Dry Forest That Are Legally Exploited Today, Market Value of the Wood, and Conservation Status of the Species

COMMON NAME	SCIENTIFIC NAME	FAMILY	VALUE[a]	STATUS[b]
Ron ron	*Astronium graveolens*	Anacardiaceae	233	T
Guayacan real	*Guaiacum sanctum*	Zygophyllaceae	233	E
Cocobola	*Dalbergia retusa*	Fabaceae	233	T
Guapinol	*Hymenea courbaril*	Caesalpinaceae	233	S
Cortez amarillo	*Tabebuia ochraceae*	Bignoniaceae	88	S
Cenizaro	*Samanea saman*	Mimosaceae	88	V
Pochote	*Pachira quinata*	Bombacaceae	88	V
Guanacaste	*Enterolobium cyclocarpum*	Mimosaceae	68	S
Guayaquil	*Albizzia guachapele*	Mimosaceae	68	S
Tempisque	*Sideroxylon capiri*	Sapotaceae	63	T
Roble sabana	Tabebuia rosea	Bignoniaceae	63	S

Source: Figures in "Value" column are from the official newspaper of the National Congress of Costa Rica, which published the approved law legalizing the exploitation, Gaceta 16, 23 January 1988, Executive Decree No. 26612-MINAE.

[a]Value in U.S. dollars for each cubic meter of wood of each tree species.
[b]Current status of each tree species according to Jiménez (1993): S = stable; E = endangered; T = threatened; V = vulnerable.

(Barrantes et al. 1999). This study documented that much of the logging is being conducted on the hills of watersheds of rivers and that many biological corridors are being destroyed. Furthermore, an evaluation of the approved management plans and field studies demonstrated that most of the requirements of the management plans are not being carried out in the field.

Deforestation to harvest trees for timber was one of the first activities that affected tropical dry forests in Costa Rica. Historically, extensive logging of economically important timber species such as brazilwood (*Caesalpinia* sp.), ironwood (*Guaicam sanctum*), mahogany (*Swietenia macrophylla*), rosewood (*Dalbergia retusa*), and Spanish cedar (*Cedrela odorata*) began in the early 1800s in northwestern Costa Rica as land was cleared for the development of cattle ranches (Boucher et al. 1983). The province of Guanacaste, owing to its geographical location and high number of economically important tree species, has greatly reduced most timber tree populations (Jiménez

1993). Table 21.1 shows a list of the most important commercial tree species that the government allows for trade (Gaceta 16, 23 January 1998, Executive Decree No. 26612-MINAE). One of these species has been recognized as in danger of extinction, three of these species are recognized as threatened, and two species are recognized as vulnerable (Jiménez 1993). Of these 11 species, only *Pachira quinata* is currently being used in plantations in reforestation programs; the other species are theoretically harvested from natural forests through management plans. Although these native tree species are important for the construction of furniture, buildings, and artisan wood crafts, the economic incentives for reforestation in plantations principally have been awarded for the use of exotic species such as melina (*Gmelina arborea*) and teak (*Tectona grandis*) (Canet et al. 1996). One exception to the pattern of using exotic species in plantations is the reforestation and research program being developed by the Guanacaste Conservation Area at

Horizontes Biological Station. An innovative program designed to evaluate the success of 12 native species in a variety of mixed plantations is under way (Brenes 1994). In addition, the Guanacaste Conservation Area has developed the only active program of natural regeneration of the tropical dry forest, and between 1979 and 1985 this program successfully restored approximately 2,100 ha of pasturelands into forest (Kramer 1997).

AGRICULTURE

Agricultural activities were conducted in Costa Rica in pre-Columbian times and perhaps were responsible for the first impact on tropical dry-forest ecosystems in Guanacaste (Quesada-López-Calleja 1980; Boucher et al. 1983). However, indigenous populations were reduced by as much as 95 percent (Parsons 1975) during the conquest beginning in 1560. The elimination of the native inhabitants, combined with the fact that Costa Rica remained sparsely populated until after independence (1821), allowed many formerly cultivated lands to regenerate into tropical forest. It is therefore unlikely that cultivation by indigenous groups had any long-lasting effect on the tropical dry forest in Guanacaste (Boucher et al. 1983).

Today in Costa Rica, the traditional crops of coffee, bananas, cacao, and sugarcane are the most important agricultural products, followed by rice, beans, and corn. Seventy-four percent of the land dedicated to agriculture is cultivated with these crops, and bananas and coffee remain as the most important sources of individual income (Estado de la Nación 1997, 1999). Most of these crops have not been produced in the tropical dry forest, and only recently has agriculture had an impact on natural forests in this area. Large-scale agricultural development in Guanacaste did not occur until prices for beef dropped in the 1980s and many landowners began to explore alternative uses for their land. Many former pastures were changed into agricultural fields in an attempt at economic solvency. Data from aerial photographs indicate that in the mid-1950s no agricultural crops were being produced in the Tempisque River Basin of Guanacaste, whereas in the early 1990s approximately 30 percent of this area consisted of agricultural fields (Maldonado et al. 1995). The most common crops today, sugarcane and rice, are produced in the artificially irrigated flatlands replacing pastures and dry forest. Approximately 17 percent of the land originally covered with dry forest in the Tempisque River Basin is cultivated with these crops (Maldonado et al. 1995).

Agricultural production in Guanacaste has been encouraged by the Servicio Nacional de Aguas Subterraneas Riego y Avenamiento (SENARA), which has developed the largest irrigation system in Costa Rica (SENARA 1998). The Proyecto de Riego de Arenal Tempisque transports water from the Arenal Lake (located in north-central Costa Rica in the Guanacaste Volcanic Mountain Range) in large cement canals to various areas in Guanacaste to provide irrigation water for agricultural crops. This program has incorporated approximately 15,000 ha into this irrigation network, investing a total of U.S. $38,460,000. Most of this project has been funded by loans from the Inter-American Bank for Development, the Venezuelan Inversion Fund, and local Costa Rican counterparts. It is estimated that approximately 336 agricultural producers have benefited from this irrigation system in Guanacaste (SENARA 1998).

Although agriculture may be a more financially productive use of former pasturelands in dry-forest habitats, efforts should be made to minimize the effects of agriculture on protected areas. One example of the agricultural area covered by the Proyecto de Riego de Arenal Tempisque irrigation system includes the rice fields contiguous with Parque Nacional Palo Verde and Reserva Biológica Lomas Barbudal. This agricultural development may affect the surrounding protected areas in several ways; for example, waterfowl and many native terrestrial animals from the protected areas nest or forage in the rice fields with high levels of insecticides (see chapter 5), and an increase in fires in the agricultural zone likely will increase fires in the adjacent protected areas. The development of buffer zones around protected lands should be enforced, and the use of these buffer zones should be monitored. Finally, the use of fire in agricultural fields adjacent to protected areas should be discouraged. Fire is often used during the production of sugarcane to burn the stems before harvesting. This practice is particularly dangerous in Guanacaste because sugarcane is harvested during the dry season, when the vegetation is dry and high winds often cause the fires to spread out of control.

TOURISM

The uncontrolled development of tourism is the most recent industry in Costa Rica affecting tropical dry-forest ecosystems (Estado de la Nación 1999). On a countrywide basis, international tourism is currently the main industry and has experienced a more than fourfold increase in income generated between 1986 and 1996 (Estado de la Nación 1997). In this same time period, the number of international tourists visiting the country increased from 261,000 (in 1986) to 779,000 (in 1996). Visitation of international tourists to the Costa Rican National Park system similarly has increased from 70,056 to 268,774 in this same time period.

In 1998, within the area recognized as tropical dry forest, more than 256 hotels and lodges with more than 5,150 rooms were dedicated to tourism (data summarized from Pariser 1998). Approximately 63 percent of these businesses primarily accommodate international tourists; the remaining facilities receive national and international visitors. The majority of these hotels (123) are located on the beaches of Guanacaste and Puntarenas (Pariser 1998), and consequently most of the international tourists who visit the dry forest of Costa Rica stay in beach hotels. Many of the tourists go on day trips to national parks or protected areas. Approximately one out of every three international tourists who came to Costa Rica in 1996 visited a national park or protected area (Estado de la Nación 1997). Therefore, the national parks and protected areas are an important attraction to many of the country's international tourists.

Within the dry forest, approximately 13,000 international tourists visited the Tempisque Conservation Area in 1996, and 26,643 visited the Guanacaste Conservation Area (SINAC 1996). With the increasing number of tourists visiting this endangered ecosystem and the subsequent income generated by this industry, it is imperative to assure that sufficient resources are invested in maintaining and improving protected areas.

To determine if the increase in tourism has led to a comparable increase in money generated by protected areas, we compare income generated by the hotel industry and by the conservation areas in the tropical dry forest. To estimate the income generated by the hotel sector, we divided the hotels into three categories based on price range during peak tourist season: (1) luxury hotel, more than $80 per room; (2) moderate hotel, from about $20–$80; and (3) economy hotels, less than $20. We conservatively assumed a 90 percent occupancy rate for four months during the peak season and a 50 percent occupancy rate for the other eight months. Average prices per room during the peak season for each category of hotel were $100, $50, and $20, respectively, for luxury, moderate, and economy hotels, and these prices were estimated as $80, $30, and $15 during the off season. Based on these data, a conservative estimate is that the hotel sector of tourism (not including food and entertainment) in the tropical dry forest generates approximately $73 million a year. This accounts for more than 10 percent of the total income generated by the entire tourist industry in all of Costa Rica during 1996 (Estado de la Nación 1997).

In contrast to the large income generated by tourism in the tropical dry forest by the private sector, in 1996 less than $165,000 was generated from tourism for the two conservation areas within this habitat (SINAC 1996). Despite the increase in tourists visiting protected areas, a similar investment has not been made for maintaining these areas in terms of infrastructure and personnel (Brandon 1996). Since the dry forest ecosystem is an important attraction for tourists, it should be compensated for this biological value. The hotel industry in Guanacaste could contribute by sharing the costs of protection and maintenance of protected areas within this area. Although theoretically the Instituto Costarricense de Turismo is responsible for monitoring the development of tourist accommodations, in 1999 a series of irregularities were discovered in the permits issued to this industry, especially in the coastal areas in Guanacaste and Puntarenas (Estado de la Nación 1999). Thus far in Costa Rica the development of tourism has largely been a private enterprise with little or no government regulations (Brandon 1996; Estado de la Nación 1999). Although the long-term cumulative effects of tourism on tropical dry-forest habitats are unknown, some of the potential effects include (1) damage to coastal and mangrove areas along the beach; (2) improper sewage and garbage disposal; (3) disturbance of nesting areas of endangered sea turtles; and (4) destruction of natural forests for tourist developments. To assure the continued well-being of tropical dry-forest ecosystems, it will be necessary for the government to implement and enforce stricter regulations for the development of the tourist industry.

WILDLIFE MANAGEMENT PLANS AND SUSTAINABLE DEVELOPMENT IN THE TROPICAL DRY FOREST: THEORY AND PRACTICE

HISTORY

Parque Nacional Palo Verde and Reserva Biológica Lomas Barbudal are located in the Tempisque River Basin in Guanacaste. These two protected sites cover an area of approximately 20,000 ha and encompass a variety of habitats including dry deciduous forest, regenerating dry deciduous forest of various ages, riparian and spring forests, savanna, mesic forest, mangrove forest, and wetlands (Frankie et al. 1993).

This area was historically a cattle ranch dating from 1926. In 1975 a portion of the land was expropriated by the Costa Rican government (Instituto de Tierras y Colonización) to develop

a new settlement program. In 1977, 4,800 ha of this land were declared as the Dr. Lucas Rodríguez Caballero National Wildlife Refuge (Executive Decree No. 6942-A, 18 April 1977). An area of approximately 10,000 ha adjacent to the refuge was protected as Parque Nacional Palo Verde in 1981 (Executive Decree No. 12765-A, 2 July 1981). The refuge and park were expanded several times during the next decade, and by 1990 Parque Nacional Palo Verde was expanded to include the refuge, Reserva Biológica Lomas Barbudal, and the connecting corridor for a total of approximately 20,000 ha (Executive decree No. 20033-MIRENEM, 9 November 1990).

Cattle have been present within this area under different densities for at least the past 80 years; however, the Stewart family removed them from Palo Verde in 1979 shortly after the creation of the wildlife refuge (D. A. Stewart interview). In 1987 some cattle were reintroduced into the Palo Verde Lagoon as part of a management program for the wetlands, and approximately 4,000 head of cattle were released into various lowland forested areas within the park in 1991 when a technical committee of the Tempisque Conservation Area decided to utilize cattle as a management tool to control fires and to manage the wetlands (Mozo 1995). In the following section we analyze the management plan and discuss some of its effects on this endangered ecosystem.

MANAGEMENT WITH CATTLE

The Tempisque Conservation Area, with support provided by the Inter-American Bank for Development as part of the funding to develop the irrigation project of SENARA (see the section "Agriculture" earlier in this chapter), facilitated the development of a wildlife management plan for Parque Nacional Palo Verde and Reserva Biológica Lomas Barbudal (Vaughan et al. 1995). This plan, in conjunction with a previously established program of the Tempisque Conservation Area, implemented the use of cattle within these protected areas with the intention of controlling fires and restoring the wetlands.

The management plan is currently using cattle in the Palo Verde wetlands as an attempt to maintain open waterbird habitat by eliminating cattails (*Typha dominguensis*) (Vaughan et al. 1995). This area historically has been one of the most important wetlands in Central America for more than 60 species of migratory and resident waterbirds and is currently recognized as a RAMSAR site (Vaughan et al. 1995). Since the 1980s, this marsh has experienced a series of successional changes that culminated in the reduction of open water and the establishment of large monospecific stands of cattails. Systematic reintroduction of cattle into the Palo Verde Lagoon began in 1991 with the objective of eliminating cattails and maintaining the waterbird habitat. According to McCoy (1994), cattle forage and trample on cattails, promoting open water. However, since the introduction of more than 500 head of cattle (1 cow per ha) in 1991, these wetlands are still dominated by monospecific stands of cattails. This observation is consistent with observations made by D. A. Stewart from more than 50 years of working with cattle in the Palo Verde Lagoon, during which time he never saw the cattle consuming cattails (D. A. Stewart interview).

The attempt to restore the Palo Verde Lagoon through the use of cattle has been implemented without conducting a systematic experiment to evaluate the impact and changes they may cause in this ecosystem. Although the current management plan assumes that cattle are the key element in maintaining the open marsh and reducing the number of cattails, many factors contribute to the spread of cattails and thus may be useful in controlling this species. The cattail is a fast-growing plant that successfully reproduces both sexually and asexually (McNaughton 1975). A single cattail head can produce up to 250,000 seeds, and the seeds may remain viable for almost 100 years with an approximately 100 percent germination rate (Sojda 1993). Previous research has demonstrated that the most effective methods for controlling cattails include increasing the water level and salinity (Kelley et al. 1993; Magee 1993; Sojda 1993).

While Palo Verde was part of the Stewart ranch, prior to 1979, five natural canals connected the Palo Verde Lagoon to the Tempisque River, allowing water to flood into the lagoon during high tide. Cement gates or weirs were used at the end of these natural canals to help regulate the water level in the lagoon. During the dry season these gates were regularly closed after high tide by the ranch hands to help maintain the lagoon flooded with salty water (D. A. Stewart interview). The weirs were not maintained once the ranch was removed from Palo Verde in 1979, and the natural canals silted in, contributing to the drying out of the lagoon and eliminating the entrance of brackish waters from the Tempisque River. These factors (and many others) should be evaluated because they undoubtedly contributed to the spread of cattails in the Palo Verde Lagoon during the following decades.

The decision of the management plan to use cattle to control fires and to promote regeneration of the forest was based on a poorly designed study (supported by the Area de Conservación Tempisque and the Organization for Tropical Studies) that concluded that cattle grazing reduces fires by controlling the expansion of pastures and favors the fast succession of dry forest (Barboza 1995, 1996). This study attempted to evaluate the effect of cattle grazing on the restoration of dry forest by comparing the following three treatments: (1) cattle grazing without fire; (2) no cattle grazing with fire; and (3) no cattle grazing without fire (control). Three replicates of each treatment were included in plots of 20 × 20 m. No standardized method of beginning each of the treatments at similar levels of regeneration was utilized, and the treatments were not randomly placed; the cattle without fire treatments were all closer to the seed source of the forest. In addition, the density of cattle within the treatments was not monitored. Since the density of cattle was low and variable during the study, it is possible that no cows were ever within the treatments designated as cattle grazing and that the proximity of these plots to the seed source (i.e., forest) was the principal contributing factor to the greater number of stems and species in this area. The conclusions of this study were based on qualitative interpretations only without any quantitative comparisons or statistical tests.

The study in Palo Verde also considered "controlled grazing" as a novel technique to generate economic benefits for local communities promoting sustainable development (Barboza 1996). Between 1991 and 1994, 14 people were given permission to have their cattle in the park. For each head of cattle, the participants were charged 100 colones (approximately 50 cents) per cow per month. In contrast, the approximate charge for pasture rental for cattle in the Guanacaste area at this time was approximately 600–900 colones ($3.00–$4.50) per cow per month. Thus, it appears that the few people that were participating in this program found it more economic to maintain their cows within the national park than within privately owned pastures. The cattle-grazing project was promoted as sustainable development presumably in terms of a way for local people to generate a constant income, but few people benefited from this program. In 1998 a similar number of people (15) received permission to maintain their cattle within the park for a rental fee of 200 colones (approximately 67 cents) per cow per month. The economic benefit for the Tempisque Conservation Area could not be estimated because of inadequate records documenting the collection of payments and the use of money (Mozo 1995). In sum, this program, which obtained much support because of its supposed qualities for sustainable development, has resulted in economic benefits for only a handful of local people and has not generated income for the park.

We conducted a preliminary study to evaluate the impact that the current management plan has on Palo Verde by comparing the floristic composition of an area within the cattle-grazing program with an area that had not been grazed over the past 15 years (Stern et al. 2003; chapter 5). A Shannon diversity index of the un-grazed area was significantly greater than the intermittently grazed sites ($t = 3.14$, d.f. = 743, $p < 0.001$). Janzen (1986) stated that the restoration of pastures to tropical dry forests is largely determined by the distance to the seed sources, the seed dispersal mode of the plant species, the proximity to the forest patches, and the number and species of animals involved. Once the seeds are established in the pasture, they have to outcompete the tall and dense grass community dominated by *H. rufa*. At this critical stage, livestock were originally used in certain areas of Parque Nacional Guanacaste, in low densities and for short periods of time to reduce the amount of grass. However, even under these controlled conditions, the resultant woody succession may have a different species structure than does succession without livestock (Janzen 1986). It is likely that cattle grazing controls the vertical expansion of *H. rufa*, but the horizontal growth continues and outcompetes other woody colonizers. This may be explained by the long evolutionary relationship between *H. rufa* and savanna grazers (Parsons 1972; McNaughton 1985; Milchunas et al. 1988). For the past several years, cattle have been completely eliminated from Parque Nacional Guanacaste and are not considered to be a viable management tool for controlling fires in this area.

It appears that the wildlife management plan for Palo Verde and Lomas Barbudal was developed without any systematic research and without reviewing the published information regarding the control of cattails (Kelley et al. 1993; Magee 1993; Sojda 1993) or the effect of cattle on vegetation (Daubenmire 1972a,b; Schulz and Leininger 1990; Bock et al. 1993). It has not been demonstrated that cattle reduce the number of cattails in the lagoon or that the use of cattle within the dry forest reduces the risk of fires or promotes "ecological restoration" of the forest. We suggest that systematic research be conducted to evaluate the effectiveness of cattle as a management tool, as well as the evaluation of other alternatives such as more and larger firebreaks or green breaks (Frere et al. 1992).

RECOMMENDATIONS FOR THE CONSERVATION OF TROPICAL DRY FOREST IN COSTA RICA

PROTECTION

The importance of complete protection of the few remaining tropical dry-forest habitats in Guanacaste cannot be over emphasized. Efforts must be made to purchase tropical dry-forest areas and to connect fragments of forest as well as protected areas. Deforestation affects many species of flora and fauna not only by eliminating their habitat but also by the inevitable fragmentation of habitats, which negatively affects population densities of many vertebrates and insects (Bierregaard and Stouffer 1997; Malcolm 1997). Furthermore, protection of elevational gradients is necessary for many species that annually migrate from tropical dry forests to alternative habitats (Janzen 1986; Stoner 2001; chapter 5). One example of a program connecting fragments over an elevational gradient is the Guanacaste Conservation Area. Parque Nacional Guanacaste now covers an elevational gradient from sea level up to the Cacao and Orosi volcanoes (1,100 meters above sea level). This innovative design should be taken as a model for other dry-forest areas in the Neotropics.

CATTLE AND FIRE

To minimize the impact of the cattle industry on the dry forest it will be necessary to change the current grazing practices that rely heavily on *H. rufa* and a regime of regular burning. Alternative feeds should be evaluated as potential sources of food for cattle. Continued efforts should be made to reduce fires in tropical dry forests. To achieve this goal it is essential that the conservation areas have the following: (1) a comprehensive system of firebreaks surrounding and within protected areas; (2) adequate personnel and equipment for fire fighting; and (3) a program of environmental education within the region. The effectiveness of this type of program may be seen in the success of Parque Nacional Guanacaste in recent years. The government (Ministry of Environment and Energy [MINAE])

should assure the Tempisque Conservation Area adequate resources to achieve this type of integrative program.

AGRICULTURAL AREAS AND BUFFER ZONES

Given the increase of land destined to be used as sugarcane and rice fields in the Guanacaste lowlands in the coming years, it is imperative that adequate buffer zones be created in areas surrounding parks and reserves. Buffer zones should reduce the impact on the protected areas they surround. Since previous studies have indicated that agricultural contamination, especially that from rice production, may have severe detrimental effects on the fauna within a region (see chapter 5), we do not recommend the continued development of agriculture in buffer zones. Land use that will be less harmful in buffer zones includes natural forest, forest plantations (preferably with native species), or regenerating forest. Monitoring of buffer zones should be conducted to assure that activities that may negatively affect the adjacent protected area are not initiated. Biological research should be encouraged in these areas to provide more information about the role of buffer zones and edge effects in the protection of parks.

RESTORATION ECOLOGY

If Costa Rica is to maintain and possibly increase forest cover within the dry forest, restoration and natural regeneration programs, equivalent to the projects developed by the Guanacaste Conservation Area, need to be implemented immediately, within both protected areas and privately owned lands. Furthermore, the largest economic incentives given for the environmental services provided by private landowners should be for total protection of existing natural forests, not for the development of forestry plantations. Finally, reforestation programs should concentrate on utilizing native timber species, not exotics. Today, the native tree species most wanted by loggers are mainly found in protected areas. Flores (1985) predicted that severe shortages in timber will result in a $350 million wood import bill by the beginning of the twenty-first century. If Costa Rica does not develop a program of plantations with its own timber species, the last logging frontier will begin and end in the national parks and protected areas of this small country.

TOURISM

The government should control the development of the tourism industry, and regulations should be implemented and monitored to assure that this industry does not destroy the dry-forest ecosystem in Guanacaste. A hotel tax should be imposed on hotels dedicated to the tourism industry. This tax should contribute to the maintenance and development of protected areas near the hotels (i.e., the areas most frequently visited by the hotel's clients).

CATTLE AS "MANAGEMENT TOOLS"

The use of cattle in Parque Nacional Palo Verde, Reserva Biológica Lomas Barbudal, and other protected areas of dry forest should be suspended until further research has evaluated the impact of this practice on the regeneration of the forest and the maintenance of wetlands. Alternative programs should be evaluated for controlling fires within the forest and for reducing the amount of *Typha* in the wetlands and restoring the marsh.

SCIENTIFIC PANELS TO EVALUATE WILDLIFE MANAGEMENT PLANS

The Costa Rican government and international organizations that provide funding for wildlife management plans should utilize scientific panels to evaluate the quality and potential effectiveness of these plans before implementation within protected areas. This review process is essential to evaluate and identify innovative ideas that may contribute to the protection of endangered habitats. Each conservation area within the country should have an independent scientific panel composed of Costa Rican and international biologists. The participants of this panel should be academic individuals who are independent of the government and the national park system. This panel can also identify and promote research within the respective conservation areas.

CONCLUSIONS

To accomplish any of these recommended goals, it will be necessary to have both sufficient economic resources and adequately trained personnel. Terborgh (1999: 161) stated that "tropical parks are failing in country after country because the institutions created to protect them are weak and ineffectual. Institutional weakness derives from many sources, but it arises ultimately from the low priority governments give to protection of parks." If tropical dry forests (and other habitats, as well) are to be successfully conserved within Costa Rica, the government must recognize the importance of this task and see it as one of its most important priorities within its administration. Many laws regarding the protection and use of biological resources have already been created (e.g., the new organic law for the environment), but the challenge lies in designating sufficient resources (both economic and personnel) to enforce them.

REFERENCES

Aldrich, P. R., and J. L. Hamrick. 1998. Reproductive dominance of pasture trees in a fragmented tropical forest mosaic. *Science* 281:103–5.

Barboza, G. 1995. *Pastoreo controlado para control de incendios y restauración de bosque tropical seco, en el Parque Nacional Palo Verde, Guanacaste, Costa Rica.* Informe de avance de resultados de monitoreo del proyecto, 12 de junio de 1995: San José: Organización para Estudios Tropicales. 7 pp.

———. 1996. Pastoreo controlado evita incendios y ayuda a ganaderos. *OET al Día* 1:4.

Barrantes, G., Q. Jiménez, J. Lobo, T. Maldonado, M. Quesada, and R. Quesada. 1999. *Evaluación de los planes de manejo forestal autorizados en el periodo 1997–1998 en la Peninsula de Osa. Cumplimiento de normas técnicas, ambientales e impacto sobre el bosque natural.* San José: Fundación Cecropia. 96 pp.

Bierregaard, R. O., Jr., and P. C. Stouffer. 1997. Understory birds and dynamic habitat mosaics in Amazonian rainforests. In *Tropical forest remnants: Ecology, management, and conservation of fragmented communities*, ed. W. H. Laurance and R. O. Bierregaard Jr., 138–55. Chicago: University of Chicago Press.

Blanco, O., and A. Mata. 1994. *La cuenca del Golfo de Nicoya: Un reto al desarrollo sostenible.* San José: Editorial de la Universidad de Costa Rica. 235 pp.

Bock, C. E., J. H. Bock, and H. M. Smith. 1993. Proposal for a system of federal livestock exclosures on public rangelands in the western United States. *Conservation Biology* 7:731–33.

Boucher, D. H., M. Hansen, S. Risch, and J. H. Vandermeer. 1983. Agriculture: Introduction. In *Costa Rican natural history,* ed. D. H. Janzen, 66–73. Chicago: University of Chicago Press.

Brandon, K. 1996. *Ecotourism and conservation: A review of key issues.* Environmental Department Papers, Global Environmental Division. Washington, D.C.: World Bank. 69 pp.

Brenes, G. 1994. *Descripción general del programa de restauración y silvicultura del bosque seco del Area de Conservación Guanacaste.* San José: Ministerio del Ambiente y Energia. 14 pp.

Canet, G., M. Chavarria, O. Gamboa, D. Garita, M. Jiménez, S. Lobo, P. Marín, L. Sevilla, Z. Trejos, and M. Valerio. 1996. *Informacíon estadística relevante sobre el sector forestal 1972–1995.* San José: Ministerio del Ambiente y Energía, Sistmea Nacional de Areas de Conservación, Area de Fomento. 54 pp.

Cascante, A., M. Quesada, J. A. Lobo, and E. Fuchs. 2002. Effects of dry tropical forest fragmentation on the reproductive success and genetic flow of the tree, *Samanea saman. Conservation Biology* 16:1–11.

Castro, R., and G. Arias. 1998. *Costa Rica: Hacia la sostenibilidad de sus recursos forestales.* San José: Ministerio del Ambiente y Energía y el Fondo Nacional de Finaciamiento Forestal. 23 pp.

Daubenmire, R. 1972a. Ecology of *Hyparrhenia rufa* (Nees) in derived savanna in north-western Costa Rica. *Journal of Applied Ecology* 9:11–23.

———. 1972b. Some ecological consequences of converting forest to savanna in northwestern Costa Rica. *Tropical Ecology* 13:31–51.

Estado de la Nación en Desarrollo Humano Sostenible. 1997. *Un analisis amplio y objetivo sobre la Costa Rica que tenemos a partir de los indicadores mas actuales (1996).* 1st ed. San José: Editorama S.A. 46 pp.

———. 1999. *Un analisis amplio y objetivo sobre la Costa Rica que tenemos a partir de los indicadores mas actuales (1998).* 1st ed. San José: Editorama S.A. 37 pp.

Flores, J. G. 1985. *Diagnóstico del sector industrial forestal.* San José: Editorial Universidad Estatal a Distancia. 72 pp.

Frankie, G. W., L. Newstrom, S. B. Vinson, and J. F. Barthell. 1993. Nesting-habit preferences of selected *Centris* bee species in Costan Rican dry forest. *Biotropica* 25:322–33.

Frere, E., P. Gandini, C. Hayslip, J. C. Martinez-Sanchez, and D. Milum. 1992. Aspects of biological management in Guanacaste National Park. *Institute for Environmental Studies* 12:1–29.

Garita, D. 1989. Mapa de cobertura boscosa. Report, Unidad de Cartografía y Topografía. San José: DGF and MIRENEM.

Hall, C. 1985. *Costa Rica: A geographical interpretation in historical perspective.* Boulder, Colo.: Westview Press. 348 pp.

Hartshorn, G. S. 1988. Tropical and subtropical vegetation of Meso-America. In *North American terrestrial vegetation,* ed. M. G. Barbour and W. D. Billings, 365–90. New York: Cambridge University Press.

IICA (Instituto Interamericano de Ciencias Agricolas). 1995. *Area de concentración I (Componente de política socioeconómica, comercio e inversiones).* San José: Ministereo de Agricultura.

Janzen, D. H. 1986. *Guanacaste National Park: Tropical ecological cultural restoration.* San José: Editorial Estatal a Distancia. 103 pp.

———. 1988. Tropical dry forests: The most endangered major tropical ecosystem. In *Biodiversity,* ed. E. O. Wilson, 130–37. Washington, D.C.: National Academy Press.

Jiménez, Q. 1993. *Arboles maderables en peligro de extinción en Costa Rica.* 1st ed. San José: INCAFO S.A. 121 pp.

Kelley, J. R., Jr., M. K. Laubhan, and F. A. Reid. 1993. Options for water-level control in developed wetlands. *Fish and Wildlife Leaflet* 13(4):1–7.

Kishor, N. M., and L. F. Constantino. 1993. Forest management and competing land uses: An economic analysis for Costa Rica. The World Bank, Latin America and Caribbean Region's Environmental Division (LATEN), Dissemination Note 7:1–30.

Kramer, E. 1997. Measuring landscape changes in remnant tropical dry forests. In *Tropical forest remnants: Ecology, management, and conservation of fragmented communities,* ed. W. H. Laurance and R. O. Bierregaard Jr., 386–99. Chicago: University of Chicago Press.

Lehmann, M. P. 1992. Deforestation and changing land-use patterns in Costa Rica. In *Changing tropical forests: Historical perspectives on today's challenges in Central and South America,* ed. H. K.

Steen and R. P. Tucker, 59–76. Durham, N.C.: Forest History Society.

Leonard, H. J. 1987. *Natural resources and economic development in Central America*. New Brunswick, N.J.: International Institute for Environment and Development, Rutgers University.

Maass, J. M. 1995. Conversion of tropical dry forest pasture and agriculture. In *Seasonally dry tropical forests*, ed. S. H. Bullock, H. A. Mooney, and E. Medina, 399–422. Cambridge: Cambridge University Press.

Magee, P. A. 1993. Detrital accumulation and processing in wetlands. *Fish and Wildlife Leaflet* 13(3):1–7.

Malcolm, J. R. 1997. Biomass and diversity of small mammals in Amazonian forest fragments. In *Tropical forest remnants: Ecology, management, and conservation of fragmented communities*, ed. W. H. Laurance and R. O. Bierregaard Jr., 207–21. Chicago: University of Chicago Press.

Maldonado, T., J. Bravo, G. Castro, Q. Jiménez, O. Saborio, and L. Paniagua. 1995. *Evaluación ecologica rapida región del Tempisque Guanacaste, Costa Rica*. San José: Fundación Neotropica, Centro de Estudios Ambientales y Politicas. 104 pp.

McCoy, M. B. 1994. Seasonal, freshwater marshes in the tropics: A case in which cattle grazing is not detrimental. In *Principles of conservation biology*, ed. G. K. Meffe and C. R. Carroll, 352–53. Sunderland, Mass.: Sinauer Associates.

McNaughton, S. J. 1975. "r" and "k" selection in *Typha*. *American Naturalist* 109:251–61.

———. 1985. Ecology of a grazing ecosystem: The Serengeti. *Ecological Monographs* 55:259–94.

Méndez, G. 1997. Centro de investigación del bosque tropical seco y estaciones biológicos: Una opción para el estudio, la investigación y el ecotourismo. *ACG Rothschildia Revista informativa* 4:9–10.

Middleton, B. A., E. Sánchez-Rojas, B. Suedmeyer, and A. Michels. 1997. Fire in a tropical dry forest of Central America: A natural part of the disturbance regime? *Biotropica* 29:515–17.

Milchunas, D. G., O. E. Sala, and W. K. Lauenroth. 1988. A generalized model of the effects of grazing by large herbivores on grassland community structure. *American Naturalist* 132:87–106.

Mozo, E. T. 1995. *Pastoreo con ganado vacuno, una alternativa del ACT para prevención de incendios forestales, recuperación de humedales y restauración del bosque tropical seco*. Bagaces, Costa Rica: Convenio MIRENEM–Opción Colombia, Universidad Sergio Arboleda. 66 pp.

Pariser, H. S. 1998. *Adventure guide to Costa Rica*. 3d ed. Edison, N.J.: Hunter Publishing. 546 pp.

Parsons, J. J. 1972. The spread of African pasture grasses into the New World tropics. *Journal of Range Management* 20:13–17.

———. 1975. The changing nature of New World tropical forests since European colonization. In *The use of ecological guidelines for development in the American humid tropics*, 28–38. IUCN Publications. Morges, Switzerland: IUCN.

Quesada, M., E. Fuchs, and J. Lobo. 2001. Pollen load size, reproductive success and progeny kinship of natural pollinated flowers of the tropical dry forest tree, *Pachira quinta. American Journal of Botany* 88:2113–18.

Quesada-López-Calleja, R. 1974. La forja de una nación, tomo II. Tesis de Licenciatura en Derecho, Universidad de Costa Rica.

———. 1980. *Costa Rica: La frontera sur de Mesoamérica*. 2d ed. San José: Instituto Costarricense de Turismo. 228 pp.

Rodríguez, R., and E. Vargas. 1988. *El recurso forestal en Costa Rica: Políticas públicas y sociedad*. Heredia, Costa Rica: Editorial de la Universidad Nacional. 61 pp.

Sader, S. A., and A. T. Joyce. 1988. Deforestation rates and trends in Costa Rica, 1940 to 1983. *Biotropica* 20:11–19.

Sánchez-Azofeifa, G. A. 1997. *Assessing land use/cover change in Costa Rica*. San José: Centro de Investigaciones en Desorrollo Sostenible, Universidad de Costa Rica. 181 pp.

Schulz, T. T., and W. C. Leininger. 1990. Differences in riparian vegetation structure between grazed areas and exclosures. *Journal of Range Management* 43:295–99.

SENARA (Servicio Nacional de Aguas Subterraneas Riego y Avenamiento). 1998. *Gestión institucional, 1994–1998*. Informe de las acciones implementadas en los programas y proyectos estrategicos del SENARA durante la administración Figueres Olsen. San José: SENARA. 19 pp.

SINAC (Sistema Nacional de Areas de Conservación). 1996. *Informe de ingresos*. San José: SINAC. 10 pp.

———. 1997. *Hectareas aprobadas para planes de manejo de bosque*. San José: SINAC. 15 pp.

Sojda, R. S. 1993. Management and control of cattails. *Fish and Wildlife Leaflet* 13(41):1–7.

Stern, M., M. Quesada, and K. E. Stoner. 2003. Changes in composition and structure of a tropical dry forest following intermittent cattle growing. *Revista de Biología Tropical* 50(3/4): 1021–34.

Stoner, K. E. 2001. Differential habitat use and reproductive patterns of tropical dry forest frugivorous and nectarivorous bats in northwestern Costa Rica. *Canadian Journal of Zoology* 79: 1626–33.

Terborgh, J. 1999. Why conservation in the tropics is failing: The need for a new paradigm. In *Requiem for nature*, 161–86. Washington, D.C.: Island Press/Shearwater Books.

Toledo, V. M. 1992. Bio-economic cost. In *Development or destruction? The conversion of tropical forest to pasture in Latin America*, ed. T. Downing, S. Hecht, and H. Pearson, 63–71. New York: Westview Press.

Trejo, I., and R. Dirzo. 2000. Deforestation of seasonally dry tropical forest: A national and local analysis in Mexico. *Biological Conservation* 94: 133–42.

Vaughan, C., M. McCoy, J. Fallas, H. Chaves, G. Barboza, G. Wong, M. Carbonell, J. Rau, and M. Carranza. 1995. *Plan de manejo y desarrollo del Parque Nacional Palo Verde y Reserva Biologica Lomas Barbudal*. Contrato SENARA-BID-MIRENEM-UNA. Heredia, Costa Rica: Universidad Nacional. 110 pp.

Williams, R. G. 1986. *Export agriculture and the crisis in Central America*. Chapel Hill: University of North Carolina Press. 52 pp.

CHAPTER 22

Environmental Law of Costa Rica

DEVELOPMENT AND ENFORCEMENT

Roxana Salazar

OVER THE PAST 20 YEARS, Costa Rica has kept pace with the evolution of environmental policy in the Central American region and the Caribbean, developing a fairly complete legal frame and, in general, a good set of policies. However, Costa Rica has also followed the general global trend, despite the importance that environmental issues have gained, by allowing the destruction of biodiversity to continue at an accelerated pace (see chapters 7, 12, 15, 21, and 23). Multiple declarations and agreements at the international level have not succeeded in stopping this worldwide destruction, as has been recognized by world authorities who attended the Ministers of the Environment World Forum (Ministers of the Environment World Forum 2000): "There is an alarming discrepancy between commitments and action. The goals and priorities agreed upon by the international community regarding sustainable development, like the adoption of national strategies and the in-creased help to developing countries, must go beyond what has been done until now." Further, it was pointed out that the main threats against the environment, which were discussed in Rio de Janeiro in 1992, are now global and have been sharpened by extreme consumer habits.

In Costa Rica, environmental destruction is, at least in part, the product of poor interpretation and lack of enforcement of the laws, as well as of shortcomings in the laws and public policies themselves. On the one hand, we must consider that attitude change begins with education and that sanctions and fines should be used as secondary measures. However, this change in attitude has yet to be systematically encouraged. The policies coming out of public institutions have been more of control and short-term responses than of prevention, education, and participation. The policies for biodiversity protection are also vertically controlled, which means that all respective duties are granted to only one ministry. As a result, laws and regulations are created that are inconsistent with social, economic, and/or cultural customs.

On the other hand, the judicial branch, which is responsible for exacting compliance with environmental law, lacks a basic understanding of ecology as well as of pertinent environmental issues. It thus has trouble identifying opportunities for legal actions. Another problem is that environmental offenses, and corresponding penalties, have not been classified. Without established categories of offenses and respective penalties, judges have difficulty assigning appropriate sanctions for the offender and compensation for damages committed against the environment. As a result, the judicial branch is often unable to carry out the intent of the law.

Enforcing environmental law is further hindered by a deficiency of clear policies, inadequate budgets and human resources, and lack of follow-up evaluation and verification mechanisms. An especially pernicious problem is the lack of coordinated actions between institutions of the public sector, as is the case for water resources management (see chapter 9), which means inefficiency in addressing ongoing environmental issues. This problem is evident in several well-known cases in which squatters who had invaded national wildlife refuges were already receiving utility services from national companies before anything was done to expel them. Although Costa Rica's environmental law frames are innovative and far-reaching in intent and have had an important presence in the country, there are many shortcomings that hinder their effectiveness.

This chapter presents the general legal frame for environmental and biodiversity protection in Costa Rica, identifying its weaknesses as well as important areas for action that must be considered for improvement of these conditions.

THE SPIRIT OF THE LAW

The Political Constitution of Costa Rica (GOCR 1984) grants a series of fundamental guarantees related to the environment. Among these is ar-

ticle 89, containing the cultural goals of the republic, which establishes the protection of natural beauty, conservation, and development of the historic and artistic heritage of the nation. Aside from protection of the environment for cultural purposes, the constitution also guarantees the right of each individual to "a healthy and ecologically balanced environment," which appears in article 50, amended in recent years to contain the following sentences: "The State will provide for the greater well-being of the inhabitants of the country, organizing and stimulating production and the most appropriate sharing of wealth" and " Every person has the right to a healthy and ecologically balanced environment. Therefore, he or she is justified in denouncing any act that infringes upon that right and claiming reparations for the damage caused."

In pursuit of these goals, the state has created several general guidelines for the environment's defense, including the "precautionary principle," or *in dubio pro natura,* and "the polluter pays." The first of these principles has been a persistent theme in the most important international environmental gatherings in the past decade, including the summit at Rio de Janeiro in 1992, the Biological Diversity Convention (UNEP 1992), and the Convention on Climate Change (Law 7414). Emphasizing preventive rather than reactive measures, the precautionary principle was formally adopted in Costa Rica's Biodiversity Law (Zeledón 1999c) in the 11th article: "2.—Precaution criterion or in dubio pro natura: Whenever there exists a danger of serious or irrevocable damage to biodiversity or to its associated knowledge, the absence of scientific certainty must not be used as a reason to postpone the adoption of effective measures for its protection."

The second principle, which demands that the polluter bear the cost of damage to the environment, also has roots in the declarations of internationally recognized conventions. Both the 16th principles of the Río Declaration and the Climatic Change Convention insisted that polluters internalize environmental costs and consider the public interest without distorting commerce and international investments. Costa Rica's variation is article 103d of the Biodiversity Law (Zeledón 1999c), which states that it is the obligation of the Ministry of Environment and Energy (MINAE) to eliminate negative incentives that encourage damage to the environment and to create disincentives that will promote environmental conservation.

One measure that puts this principle into practice is article 69 of the Forestry Law (Zeledón 1999b). Combining both a disincentive and an incentive to promote conservation, this law places a tax on fuels and compensates forestry plantation owners for the amount they spend on services that mitigate fuel emissions. However, there are many laws that do not follow the previously mentioned guidelines. For example, there is tax exemption for synthetic chemicals in certain percentages. This measure constitutes a "negative incentive" by encouraging the use of harmful synthetic chemicals without taking into consideration the high environmental or social costs that such use entails. Thus, even though the principles mentioned earlier are far-reaching in their intent, the laws themselves often distort the spirit of these guidelines, an issue that is discussed further in the following section.

THE LETTER OF THE LAW

The principles discussed earlier are the basis for some of the most important environmental laws produced by Costa Rica's Legislative Assembly. Establishing a series of general regulations for the environment's preservation, these are the Organic Environmental Law, the Forestry Law, the Biodiversity Law, the Wild Life Protection Law, and the Water Law (Zeledón 1999a–e).

ORGANIC ENVIRONMENTAL LAW

The Organic Environmental Law strives to provide Costa Ricans and the state with the necessary instruments for preserving a healthy and ecologically balanced environment. It is made up of three parts: environmental impact assessments (EIAs), territorial ordering plans, and restrictions on land use.

EIAs. This law forces economic parties to consider environmental costs in the design and execution of their projects and to take appropriate precautionary measures by requiring EIAs. These documents are then made public, allowing neighbors and interested parties to know the details of the project and to present their opinions for consideration before the project is authorized. When existing projects or activities do not comply with the terms under which they were approved, any interested party can denounce them before the National Environmental Technical Bureau, which is responsible for reviewing, approving, and monitoring these projects. However, despite this law's potential as an environmental defense mechanism, the success of EIAs in protecting the environment is highly questionable. The most serious problems lie in enforcement. The National Environmental Technical Bureau has too often approved EIAs for projects that clearly have strong negative environmental effects. In many areas, community participation in public hearings and consultations has become one more requisite with which to comply, and the challenges facing negatively affected communities are rarely taken into account.

Territorial Ordering Plans. The Organic Environmental Law encourages active participation from the inhabitants and organized society in the creation and application of territorial ordering plans and urban regulatory plans. These plans determine what type of industries, commercial establishments, or projects can be allowed in what areas and with what procedures. By participating in the creation of these plans, farmers, entrepreneurs, conservationist groups, and residents all have clear knowledge of the "rules of the game," and problems caused by an activity inappropriately placed can be avoided. Above all, this law requires that various administrative and local government entities cooperate to define special protection areas and work together for their true protection.

However, territorial ordering plans suffer from some of the same problems that affect environmental assessment plans: lack of proper enforcement. As in the case of the EIAs, experience shows that many county officials in charge of these plans do not exact compliance with their conditions. On the contrary, their refusal to enforce the plans is often tied to a deceitful agreement between the private owner and corrupt municipal representatives for their own private gain. *Limitations for Land and Forestry Property.* The Forestry Law defines as an essential and primary function of the state the conservation, protection, and administration of natural forests. It consists of a set of general regulations concerning the use and improvement of the nation's forest resources in accordance with the principle of correct and sustainable use of renewable natural resources. Put simply, the Forestry Law places restrictions on property use—even private property—and does not permit change of land use inside national forests.

Protecting the environment through restrictions on land use, however, has problems not only in its enforcement. It also conflicts with several important laws, especially those that protect private property. In response to these restrictions, some private landowners have insisted that the Forestry Law is contrary to the inviolability principle of property rights, granted by article 45 of the Constitution (GOCR 1984). Meanwhile, the Supreme Constitutional Court has maintained the position that forestry resources are protected in order to guarantee the integrity of the natural environment. Supreme Constitutional Court Vote 5893-1995 (Supreme Constitutional Court 1995) reemphasizes that the preservation of "forestry resources is not only, by itself, reasonable, but is constitutionally viable, its protection and rational exploitation being an obligation of the State." Although this interpretation has supported the importance of forest protection, it goes against long-established notions of private property and is met with much resistance.

NATIONAL PARKS AND WILDLIFE REFUGES

Conflict between laws, at least in the case of wildlife refuges, is really a management problem. The laws themselves are fairly straightforward. The government's executive branch is responsible for creating wildlife refuges (Zeledón 1999d: art. 82, p. 110) as well as classifying them as (1) state property, (2) mixed property, or (3) private property. No commercial activities are theoretically permitted in areas classified as state property; only authorized activities such as research and tourism are allowed, if properly controlled and with low impact. Private property is allowed in other management categories, but this is limited for environmental reasons. In fact, many wildlife refuges are mixed (article 82), such as those on the coast. In these refuges, the state owns the maritime-terrestrial zone, and private landowners may have properties in the rest of the refuge. Controlled development of private activities such as tourism and commerce is permitted in these private holdings. These activities must also be low impact and are subject to special regulations that guarantee compatibility between protection of the environment and right of property.

The institution in charge of these protected areas is the MINAE, in cooperation with the National System of Protected Areas, which clusters the National Park Service, the State Forestry Administration, the General Wildlife Bureau, and the Bureau of Geology and Mines. This agency, along with its associated organizations, is responsible for creating technical measures for the appropriate management and conservation of wild flora and fauna, recommending the establishment of national refuges, and requesting from respective competent authorities "the arrest of persons who invade property under the national wildlife refuge regime" (article 36 of the Forestry Law). Along with these responsibilities, the ministry has the power to authorize certain activities in refuges of mixed and private categories if their EIA is approved and as long as they continue to abide by strict sustainability criteria. According to article 81 of the bylaws, activities such as tourist development may be authorized if they are "in agreement with the principles of sustainable development established in the management plans."

It is the ministry's abuse of this power to authorize activities that creates conflict and ultimately threatens the national wildlife refuges. It is logical—and legal—for the ministry to approve permits in privately owned lands inside an officially declared refuge. However, even though the limits are not clearly defined and there are some contradictions in the bylaws, it is very clear that the state should not grant permission for developments in protected areas meant to conserve wildlife. Yet the ministry has allowed the invasion of protected state lands in several places, has even granted permits for construction in these protected areas, and has ignored, to a greater or lesser degree, the permission limits and agreements for activities in privately owned lands. The ministry has created bylaws that contradict state environmental law, introducing hotels into wildlife preserves, which were never intended to be tourist areas (Gandoca-Manzanillo National Wildlife Refuge and nearby coastal areas are an example of this contradictory policy. See Rossi 1992). As a result, Costa Rica's precious refuges and the biodiversity of wild species they contain have begun to be transformed, little by little, into tourist sites.

WATER PROTECTION

The conservation and sustainable use of water are a special case because protection of water is not only of environmental importance but also of social interest. Again, as with the Organic Environmental Law and wildlife refuges, the legal frame concerning water conservation is abundantly clear. Water is the property of the state, which is in charge of granting concessions for its use. The administration and management of water are the responsibility of the Water Department of the MINAE, which operates in the National Meteorological Institute. With respect to water pollution, article 132 clearly prohibits pouring wastewaters, solid wastes, or any other polluting substance in national waters. The Wildlife Conservation Law includes norms about water pollution (article 132, for example, prohibits water contamination) that have enabled citizens to file a number of complaints against industries that lack adequate waste treatment systems.

Despite these laws, the condition of the rivers that cross the Greater Metropolitan Area, although showing some improvements, continues to be deplorable (see chapter 9). The actions for the control and adequate emission of domestic wastes have not received proper attention, even though this is a serious problem that requires an urgent solution. Although citizens continue to denounce the condition of these public waters and laws are in place to enable actions against the perpetrators, the state has rarely responded. Part of the problem is that many different activities use water as a receptor of waste. In order for the state to enforce regulations it has to create new rules and controls for these activities—a politically risky business.

PROTECTION ZONES

Another special case is the protection zones or protection areas. The Forestry Law establishes that all Costa Rican lands with forests and especially those with the potential for forestry, whether they are state-owned or subject to private control, will fall under the coverage of the law. Of particular importance are forested areas adjacent to rivers, lagoons, or lakes. As with water, not only is conservation of these areas important for environmental reasons, but it also is necessary for preventing natural threats to civil works and building settlements. These areas have a propensity for landslides and floods, which have, every year, destroyed homes, bridges, highways, and other infrastructure, with serious consequences for the population. The slides have reached truly frightening dimensions, causing severe damages. To prevent these disasters, the state has declared forested areas along rivers, lagoons, and lakes "protection zones," entitled to special protections.

This law prohibits tree cutting in protection zones, and article 19 of the Forestry Law forbids land-use change. However, there are several exceptions to the law. The second paragraph of article 19 states that permits for logging and construction can be granted in forested areas with the objective of "carrying out infrastructure projects, state or private, that are of national convenience." This exception to the law is reiterated in article 34, which prohibits the cutting of trees in protection areas, except in those projects designated of "national convenience" by the executive branch.

The bylaws in the Forestry Law clarified what was meant by national convenience: "The activities of national convenience are those related to the study and execution of projects or activities of public interest carried out by the centralized State entities, independent institutions, or the private sector, which bring about benefits to all or a large part of society, such as: capture, transportation, and supply of water; pipelines; road construction; generation, transmission, and distribution of electricity; transportation; mining activities; irrigation and drainage channels; recovery of forestry vocation areas; conservation and sustainable use of forests; and others of the same nature to be determined by the Ministry of Energy and the Environment according to the needs of the country."

This definition largely refers to projects undertaken by the public sector. However, the state subsequently incorporated an article into the Biodiversity Law in which the activities of national convenience were defined as "activities carried out by centralized State entities, independent institutions, or the private sector, which have social benefits greater than the socio-environmental costs."

The threat to protection zones, as evidenced by the cited definitions, lies within the laws themselves. As various civilian groups, such as the AMBIO Foundation, have pointed out, the discretional power of the executive branch to interpret the law is far too wide. These groups have openly expressed their concern with this ruling, noting that almost any activity could be considered of "national convenience." Yet despite the danger to both the environment and civilian population living and working in these areas, logging and construction continue to occur in protection zones.

In summary, a broad and comprehensive constitutional and legal frame for the protection of the environment does exist in Costa Rica.

Moreover, it clearly reflects the spirit of Costa Rica's environmental principles. All three measures of the Organic Environmental Law as well as the establishment of protection zones seek to prevent damage to the environment by demarcating areas of protection, restricting land use, and requiring those who do intend to use their land to file EIAs. EIAs and water pollution laws have the added impact of forcing those planning projects to internalize costs to the environment by making them find alternatives to potentially damaging procedures.

However, effectiveness of these measures is dramatically diminished by the lack of proper enforcement by the institutions in charge of carrying out the laws. Conflicts between these laws and social policy only increase the opportunities for corrupt officials to neglect the conservation effort. Finally, problems exist within the laws themselves, as evidenced by laws that regulate land use in protection zones, allowing broad interpretations, which do not promote environmental preservation.

TWO CASES OF PARTIAL SUCCESS

It is useful to analyze two cases that reflect problems with the law and the institutions appointed to enforce them. The first of these concerns the Geest Caribbean (a British company) banana plantation, which began to expand its territories at the beginning of the 1990s. In doing so, the company failed to comply with various legal environmental requirements on some of its farms, clear-cutting trees near stream corridors that were officially protected and deviating streams in Tortuguero and the Santa Clara lowlands, in Costa Rica's northeastern Caribbean slope. The damages also affected the Tortuguero National Park and the Barra del Colorado Wildlife Refuge.

Although these areas were officially designated protected areas, the government at that time openly permitted the cutting of primary forest trees, considering agricultural expansion a national priority. The public was aware of these violations, however, and the state was sued by the general procurator (*procuraduria general*), legitimizing the claim presented by the non-governmental organization Justicia para la Naturaleza. In 1995 the penal process entered the judgment phase, and the Tropical Science Center, a nonprofit scientific organization based in San José, Costa Rica, was officially requested to conduct an EIA. Most of the economic evaluation (nonmarketing damages) was based on the United States' Clean Water Act, which permits an evaluation equal to the replacement costs (restoration of damaged resources), and the Oil Pollution Act of 1990, as well as on the cumulated experiences of the Tropical Science Center on EIAs and natural forest science.

In order to avoid a long process and a very possible larger penalty, the process ended in conciliation between parties. Although the penalty did not compensate all the damages, it established an important legal precedent in the history of Costa Rican legislation. The fine was to be employed in environmental restoration projects in the affected areas, as well as for legal and expertise expenses needed to complete them.

This case shows the importance of civil participation, but it also reveals, once again, the political influence of economic and development interests that prevent proper establishment of environmental and social frames. It also shows that enforcement is difficult to achieve for authorities because there are many interconnected interests associated with the activities. Finally, these authorities are often weak.

In the Gandoca-Manzanillo case, a group of investors began in 1992 to develop a tourist center on the Caribbean coast on a concession in the maritime zone granted by the Talamanca Municipality (province of Limón). Construction of the hotel complex was carried out with dramatic modifications to coastal resources. These damages included draining and filling wetlands for tennis courts, coral rock extraction for landfills, raw sewage dumped directly into the sea, and displacement and burying of official landmarks.

Local residents denounced the situation to the MINAE. After several years, the ministry was forced to investigate and finally to order demoli-tion of some of the already finished works—as always, after the damages against the environment were already done. Despite strong charges of habitat destruction and the obvious damages that were taking place, the constitutional procurator could not avoid the legal actions proposed by the interested companies, and the process was prolonged and continues to this very day. This case showed that MINAE action was weak and did not enforce rules until the damage was done. Part of the problem was that the EIA did not become compulsory until 1995, with the new Organic Environmental Law.

CONCLUSIONS AND RECOMMENDATIONS

For several decades, Costa Rica has encouraged the protection of natural areas, bringing the existing environmental legal frame up to date with the most current international law. Its commitment to preserving the environment and rich biodiversity of species it contains is reflected in a national system of conservation areas that enjoys international prestige. However, there are serious problems in the interpretation and enforcement of laws as well as in the structure of the laws themselves. In some instances, there is a clear lack of government interest in exacting compliance with the regulations.

Problems within institutions responsible for protecting the environment, such as the MINAE, are reflected in the lack of long-term policies and adequate budgets and human resources. Despite its mandate to monitor carefully all activities within conservation areas, the ministry lacks the follow-up, evaluation, and verification mechanisms that would prevent disasters such as that of the Gandoca case and others (see also chapter 23). Finally, the absence of coordinated actions between institutions of the public sector creates conflicts between laws that are not easily resolved.

All these problems have a direct effect on the health of the environment. There is also a very serious and continuing consequence to the quality of life of every Costa Rican citizen when the environment is seriously damaged or destroyed. Several mechanisms have been proposed to remedy these serious problems, but many have not offered even a glimmer of hope for the environment's protection. Thus, rather than adding new measures, it is urgently important that the current legal frame be reviewed and modified according to the following general recommendations:

1. Clear, long-term national environmental policies that focus on prevention rather than control of damages to the environment are urgently needed. It is necessary to classify environmental violations so that penalties and sanctions can be issued to violators. The loopholes that now exist in the legal frame, as evidenced in the Gandoca example, make enforcement of environmentally oriented laws an impossible task.

2. Once environmental laws have been created, they must be monitored and their efficiency and effectiveness evaluated. These laws must continue to be revised until they can guarantee the environment's protection.

3. It is important that social law and environmental law are compatible. Contradictions between private property rights and environmental law must be eliminated.

4. The judicial branch must have a basic understanding of both ecological processes and the environmental legal frame so that it can accurately interpret these environmental laws and can issue appropriate penalties (see also chapter 23).

5. It is necessary that all levels of action be horizontally integrated so that environmental law can be put into action. One institution (the MINAE) is not enough to regulate all activities in all conservation areas. Other institutions must be given the power to authorize activities and enforce legislation, and all institutions must work together to efficiently accomplish these tasks.

6. Citizens and citizens' organizations must be allowed to exercise their rights to a healthy environment by participating in conservation efforts, including the prevention, mitigation, and control of damages to the environment as well as its restoration after these damages have occurred.

7. Environmental education for the general public is absolutely necessary if they are to be involved in protecting the environment. Officials responsible for the environment need higher levels of education as well as specialized training to complete their obligations successfully.

REFERENCES

GOCR (Government of Costa Rica). 1984. *Political Constitution of the Republic of Costa Rica*. San José: National Printing Office. 100 pp.

———. 1994. Amendment to the constitution, by Law 7412 of May 24, 1994. *La Gazeta* (San José), 10 June 1994.

Ministers of the Environment World Forum. 2000. Malmoe Encounter, Sweden, 2000.

Rossi, A. 1992. *La loca de Gandoca*. San José: Editorial Universitaria Centroamericana. 140 pp.

Supreme Constitutional Court. 1995. Vote of 1995. Supreme Constitutional Court Archives, San José.

UNEP (United Nations Environmental Program). 1992. Biological Diversity Convention. Rio de Janeiro.

Zeledón, R., ed. 1999a. The Organic Environmental Law N°7554(10/4/95). In *Codigo ambiental*, 4. San José: Editorial Porvenir.

———. 1999b. The Forestry Law N°7575 (2/5/96), amended by laws N°7609 (6/11/96) and N°7788 (4/30/98). In *Codigo ambiental*, 31. San José: Editorial Porvenir.

———. 1999c. The Biodiversity Law N°7788 (4/30/98). In *Codigo ambiental*, 61. San José: Editorial Porvenir.

———. 1999d. The Wildlife Conservation Law N°7788 (4/30/98). In *Codigo ambiental*, 93. San José: Editorial Porvenir.

———. 1999e. The Water Law N°276 (8/27/42), amended by laws N°2332 (4/9/59), N°5046 (8/16/72) and N°5516 (5/2/74). In *Codigo ambiental*, 141. San José: Editorial Porvenir.

CHAPTER 23

Dispute over the Protection of the Environment in Costa Rica

Julio Alberto Bustos

ALTHOUGH THERE ARE many laws for the protection of the environment, there is also incongruity among them.

LEGAL PROTECTION OF BIODIVERSITY

INCONGRUITY OF ENVIRONMENTAL LAWS

The existence of a law for practically every environmental problem (forestry law, water law, biodiversity law, and so on) has led to an entanglement of laws that are often redundant, contradictory, and ambiguous and thus hinder cooperation between institutions and limit effective action. From its independence in 1821, Costa Rica has passed more than 19,000 laws for a country of fewer than 4 million inhabitants. More than 8,000 laws are currently in force, taking into consideration the abolition of some of these laws. Such a high figure suggests that, in Costa Rica, the solution for every problem is "passing a law" or increasing the sanctions provided in the existing laws. Whether these laws are in agreement with previous legislation is rarely considered, much less the requirements to put these laws into action, such as the economic and technical resources for their application, the establishment of specialized tribunals, and the instruction of judicial representatives in charge of administering justice in environmental matters.

Laws in general stumble into frequent legislative errors that leave loopholes through which perpetrators of environmental damages escape. For example, the legal norm in forestry law indicates that, independent of its vegetative cover, a plot is not a forest if it is smaller than 2 ha.[1] This allows for deforestation of small but vital

---

1. Forestry Law #7575 of 5 February 1996, art. 3, sec. d: "*Forest:* native or autochthonous ecosystem, intervened or non-regenerated by natural succession or other forestry techniques, occupying a surface of two more hectares."

forested areas, even if they protect a headwater or creek or are part of a larger biological corridor and their conservation is of utmost importance. Despite laws that prohibit the activity, there is no judicial sanction for dumping wastewaters, most of which are untreated, into rivers unless they contain heavy metals, trash, fuels, and sediments (see chapters 9 and 10). Thus, wastewaters from the Greater Metropolitan Area (San José and neighboring counties) are poured into the Tárcoles River at an annual volume of 35.2 million m^3, producing a yearlong index of critical contamination (see chapter 9). The Tempisque and Barranca Rivers are subject to similar contamination. A joint study by the National University (province of Heredia) and the Utrecht University (the Netherlands) regarding pollution of the Gulf of Nicoya established that the principal contaminator of the basin is the human population. Out of 41 municipalities in the area, only 22 dump their wastes in sanitary landfills and the rest in open dump sites.[2]

JUDGES' LACK OF ENVIRONMENTAL KNOWLEDGE

Even though there is a judicial school in Costa Rica that provides instruction to judges in the fields they oversee, there are always those who show a lack of consciousness and interest regarding protection of natural resources and their importance for public health. As a result, serious claims of destruction of specific natural resources are disregarded in the justice tribunals, starting with prosecutors who conduct pertinent investigations and ending with the final absolution from judges who perhaps do not understand the damage caused by cutting down trees or pouring toxic residues into a river (see chapters 9, 10, and 22).

ECONOMIC LIMITATIONS OF THE JUDICIAL POWER AND THE MINISTRY OF ENVIRONMENT AND ENERGY (MINAE)

There are many complaints concerning economic limitations for protecting the environment effectively. The environmental comptroller, in charge of the fiscalization of all laws related to the environment, has only one assistant and does not even have a vehicle for the appropriate duties of the post. The Environmental Prosecutor of the Public Ministry, the specialized office that tends to all cases pertaining to public action crimes that involve pollution, phytosanitary protection (e.g., quarantine and pest eradication), wildlife abuses, unregulated urban development, and the destruction or theft of archaeological heritage, has but three investigators to cover the entire country. The claims are actually received by assistant prosecutors around the country, who have shown an almost complete lack of knowledge regarding the environment's legal protections.

Costa Rica has theoretically protected 25 percent of its territory under the categories National Park, Forestry Reserve, or Wildlife Refuge and has achieved international prestige by elevating to a constitutional rank the right of its citizens to a healthy and ecologically balanced environment. This constitutional right allows every citizen to denounce acts that violate environmental law and to demand compensation for damages caused.[3] However, reality is different. Original private owners have not been paid in full for many lands expropriated by the government. These landowners exhibit a range of responses from patience to bitter frustration. Many, tired of waiting for promised compensation (sometimes for decades), exploit these lands as they

---

2. Economic-ecological appraisal of water deterioration in the Gulf of Nicoya, National University–Utrecht University, December 2000.

3. *Political Constitution of the Republic of Costa Rica*, art. 50, paras. 2, 3, 4: Every person has the right to a healthy and ecologically balanced environment. Therefore, they all

have the right to denounce actions that threaten this right and demand restoration of the damage caused.

The State will guarantee, defend, and preserve said right. The law will determine responsibilities and corresponding sanctions. (Article reformed by Law #7412 of 24 May 1994.)

see fit. Moreover, as private forests diminish, loggers are surreptitiously moving in on "protected" areas. There is a daily parade of logging trucks loaded with huge specimens from ancestral primary forests, especially during weekends or evenings when forest rangers are not on watch. MINAE estimates that 25 percent of the commercial wood in the country is extracted illegally.

MINAE, the institution responsible for stopping forest clear-cutting under a scheme of absolute protection, claims to have insufficient funds to hire enough park rangers to patrol the forests, much less supply them with the necessary equipment, such as vehicles and radios, for implementing their surveillance duties. At least that was its explanation when 3,000 ha from Tortuguero National Park were recently cut down right under its nose, without any inspector issuing a warning of the damages, as discussed later.

IMPUNITY OF VIOLATORS BEFORE ENVIRONMENTAL LAWS

Weakness of action, owing in part to lack of communication between controlling entities, strongly contributes to violators' evident impunity regarding environmental crimes. These crimes are currently denounced at the regional offices of MINAE, the Office of the Environmental Comptroller, the Environmental Tribunal, and any Prosecutor of the Republic, especially the Environmental Prosecutor, which is the specialized entity of the Public Ministry. Incredibly, these institutions do not communicate with one another, and there is no state entity that consolidates information on environmental damages at a national level.

The Environmental Prosecutor has records only of the number of submitted claims (137 in 1999 and 178 in 2000) but has no statistical follow-up of the dismissed cases and those that reached trial and ended in sentencing or absolution (J. A. Bustos pers. obs.). There is also no registry of repeat offenders—data that could determine the existence of professional delinquents in environmental crimes. Although there are no figures on environmental crimes that are punished with a sentence, ecologists, prosecutors, and the environmental comptroller agree that they are very few. In statements to the press, one well-known environmental prosecutor, José Pablo González, has suggested that the country is on the verge of total impunity with respect to environmental crimes.[4]

González and other prosecutors have blamed the lack of convictions and sentencing for environmental crimes on MINAE. This claim is only partially correct, as a lengthy legal process must be followed in order to prosecute a named party for an environmental crime. Investigation of an unlawful environmental act begins with MINAE and its initial collection of field evidence for possible prosecution of the case. As prosecutors have pointed out, the record shows that MINAE often does not conduct a thorough collection of field evidence in the vicinity of the alleged crime. Further, it does not present the evidence at a trial and commonly has little follow-up contact with the Public Ministry. These deficiencies often lead to poorly prepared cases of the prosecutors, resulting in acquittals. Clearly, the two ministries should be required to work more closely together.

The Public Ministry is the entity of the judicial power in Costa Rica that exercises the duties of plaintiff in the penal justice field. The Public Ministry must conduct the preparatory investigation in class action lawsuits and has complete functional independence in the exercise of its faculties and legal and regulatory credits.[5]

---

4. In Ernesto Rivera, "Weak Control of Environmental Crimes," *La Nación*, 31 December 2000, 4A, 5A.

5. Organic Law of the Public Ministry, #7442, 25 October 1994, modified by Judicial Reorganization Law #7728, 16 December 1997, arts. 1, 2, and 3.

Furthermore, Penal Procedural Code indicates that the Public Ministry will carry out penal action as established by law, exercise the pertinent and useful duties for determining the existence of an unlawful act, and will see to effective compliance with guarantees recognized by the Constitution and the existing international and community rights in the country and the law.[6] Therefore, determination of the existence of a crime and its investigation are the responsibility of the Public Ministry and not MINAE.

MINAE'S LACK OF ENFORCEMENT OF FORESTRY MANAGEMENT PLANS

Costa Rica has suffered a drastic loss in forested areas. Whereas 53 percent of the national territory was forested in 1961, by 1977 that figure had decreased to 31.1 percent. By late 1980, supposedly as a result of the Forestry Law of 1969, deforestation dropped from 50,000 ha per year to 22,000 ha. The figures are evidence that the country has suffered an accelerated disappearance of forests, with resulting ecological damages. Soils appropriate for forest production were converted to agricultural and cattle areas, segmenting the land into small farms and forest fragments. At the root of this destruction is Costa Rica's "forestry management plans," which have been strongly criticized and denounced by environmentalists, communities, and nongovernmental organizations.

The Forestry Law defines a forestry management plan as "a group of technical norms that will regulate activities in a forest or forestry plantation, a farm or part of it with the purpose of exploiting, preserving, and developing the existing or intended tree vegetation, in accordance with the principle of rational use of renewable natural resources that guarantees sustainability of the resource."[7] Despite its mandate to protect the sustainability of renewable resources, these plans have completely failed in their duties to-

ward the environment. This failure is the result not so much of flaws in the management plans themselves as of their lack of enforcement.

In response to numerous complaints, MINAE contracted and paid for forestry audits (mid-1990s) to evaluate "management plans" in the regions of Tortuguero, Osa, and Sarapiquí. The audits demonstrated that mechanisms and technical guidelines supporting forestry management have, for the most part, been entirely ignored by those companies that submitted plans and by MINAE itself. The following figures provide examples: 40 percent of the forestry files in the Sarapiquí region and 78 percent in the Tortuguero area (both in the Caribbean lowlands) were incomplete for one reason or another. Further, of those plans that had been approved, 40 percent in the Sarapiquí and 36 percent in Tortuguero were found to be incomplete. Other problems were also discovered. Forestry officials are supposed to adhere to the "60/40 logging criterion," whereby 60 percent or fewer of the inventoried trees in a given management plan may be cut but at least 40 percent must be left. In the Sarapiquí, this criterion was not observed in 60 percent of the cases; in Tortuguero, this figure was 44 percent. Cutting had exceeded the 60 percent limit at both locations. Finally, the forest inventories in both areas had statistical errors in about 40 percent of the cases.

Management plans must also include maps showing where trees scheduled for cutting and residual trees are located. Further, these maps are supposed to indicate the locations of prominent landmarks, boundaries, creeks, and roads to be used for accessing trees to be harvested. The auditors found that maps accompanying most management plans often did not agree with the field reality. Common problems included extra roads cut into forested areas, trails poorly sketched, and eroded soils due to excessive access routes, which were often wider than

---

6. *Penal Procedural Code,* Law #7594 of 26 March 1996. In force since 1 January 1998, arts. 62 and 63.

7. Forestry Law #7575, art. 3, sec. e.

permitted. Some trees were cut too low to the ground, which did not permit checking or marked locations on maps. "Mother or seed" trees were often cut. Yet, despite these problems, all examined plans had been approved, which indicates little effort had been made to follow up on proposed plans and enforce environmental laws when infractions were discovered.[8]

Once a management plan is approved, the Forestry Division allocates special tags to be attached to the cut logs for identification during transport to and receiving at the sawmill. The question that has arisen with regard to these tags is, Do cut logs correspond to specific tags that were allocated according to the submitted (and approved) plan? There is evidence that some logs come from other sites, including protected natural areas such as forest reserves and national parks. The current tree-tagging stage leaves wide open yet another avenue for avoiding full compliance with forestry law.

One reason that MINAE accepts and approves incomplete and illegal management plans is that its representatives, like the environmental judges, are ignorant of environmental processes and the laws that protect them. The following excerpts are taken from dendrologist Quírico Jiménez's article published in the national newspaper La Nación in 2000: "The lack of biological knowledge of the forest as an ecosystem of those in charge of executing the field management plans and those with approval power in the Environmental and Energy Ministry (MINAE) has made way for legalized deforestation." He argues further that "the political will to do something about it has been missing. Therefore, about 75,000 trees in protection areas have been sacrificed in two years of logging as a result of unclear management plans that do not feature even the minimum requirements. Corrections and sanctions have not been carried out, and impunity is prevalent."[9] Impunity before the law, according to Jiménez, is thus the result of MINAE's authorization of incomplete management plans as well as its refusal to enforce them once they have been authorized.

ABSENCE OF EDUCATIONAL CAMPAIGNS TO RAISE CONSCIOUSNESS

There is no better defender of the environment than a citizen who is conscious of the importance of preserving and protecting natural resources. Citizens who know and understand laws do not pollute and do not allow others to damage the environment. Thus, one of the main setbacks to an effective system of environmental protection in Costa Rica is the lack of educational campaigns in schools and for the general population (see also chapters 19 and 20). Although there is a law requiring environmental education in primary and secondary schools, the Education Ministry has made only marginal efforts to promote and advance environmental education. The same is true for MINAE's embarrassing program of environmental education (see also chapter 19). Environmental issues rarely appear in the media's daily agenda, being relegated to the lowest order of news, after sports, entertainment, events, and political news (see also chapter 20). In addition, weak environmental conscientiousness among Costa Rica's leaders does not lead to watchdog duties or educational media campaigns for the general population. Consequently, people commonly throw trash on the roads, dump waste in rivers, burn trash in neighborhoods without a care for the impact on surrounding homes, hunt in protected areas, and generally disrespect, out of their own ignorance, environmental laws.

THE CASE OF ALTOS DE LA BONITA

Altos de la Bonita is a farm located on the southern Pacific coast, facing Ballena Marine National Park in Puntarenas Province. The farm has steep,

8. Alpízar V. Edwin [forestry engineer, member of the Work Group on Forests and Forestry Products of FECON], "Forestry Regencies," Environmental Dialogues (trimester bulletin, June–August 2000).

9. Quírico M. Jiménez, "Legalized Deforestation," La Nación, 14 December 2000, 14/A.

clay soils, unsuitable for agriculture, and was completely covered with primary and secondary forests; the latter had not been disturbed for about 20 years. Because of its rugged slopes, the farm constituted an amphitheater for the park, with impressive scenic beauty provided by the abundance of trees and the mist that often rose slowly from the sea. It was the wish of the owner to preserve the farm in its natural state, without exploiting the trees. He had even requested a Certificate of Forest Protection, an incentive offered by MINAE to proprietors of private forests.

In 1996, the owner found evidence of logging that had taken place on the edge of a trail and immediately requested an inspection of the area from the ministry's regional office, which then submitted its claim to the Environmental Prosecutor. The claim, in brief, was as follows: "The purpose is and has been . . . to maintain the forest cover of the farm, especially to preserve the scenic value of said forests in front of Ballena Beach, declared Maritime Reserve, and to protect the Ballena, Mercedes, and Piñuela creeks, the latter a source of drinking water for the small settlement of Las Brisas. The first two creeks empty into Ballena Beach and the latter into Piñuelas Beach, which is part of the Reserve. The farm also protects Tortuguita Creek; it empties into the Tortuga River, itself a tributary near the mouth of the Balso River in a mangrove area. Conservation of the farm's forest cover is essential for future tourist developments and survival of the existing ecosystem."

Without protection of the trees, the headwaters would be in danger of drying up and torrential rains would drag clay sediments and deposit them in the coral reefs of the marine park, destroying them. The motion was presented before the Penal Tribunals of Pérez Zeledón, file #96-00430-195 PE, against Asdrúbal Cruz, who was charged by the owner of the farm with usurpation and illegal logging. The accused testified before the prosecutor's office in November 1996 and claimed that he was carrying out "agricultural ownership actions" (coffee crops and pastures for cattle) because "he requested a permit from the Platanares Rural Police [the town the farm is a part of], and was granted one." Although the rural police has never had the authority to grant land-use permits, the judicial authority carried out no actions to end the destruction, despite the proprietor's charges. Environmental deterioration and the consequent ecological damage continued to be sheltered by judicial inertia.

The investigation, taking place in March 1998, was done a year and a half after the claim was submitted and showed that the accused had remained on the farm and had already converted several hectares of forest into areas of perennial agricultural products. Further, there were burned areas, pasturelands, trails cut with heavy machinery, a storage yard with piles of wood that were being actively exploited, and land displacements that changed the property's nature. All of these infractions are detailed in the Forestry Law and punishable with a prison sentence.

The first trial took place on 6 November 1998. In the decision, the judge ignored the crimes verified through sight inspection, the report, and the photographic evidence supplied with the claim. Further, the judge demonstrated an inability to establish a chronological sequence of verified facts despite several reiterations of events. Although the usurper was sentenced for illegal logging, the previous Forestry Law, #7174, a law that had already been abolished but that the judge believed to be in force at the time of the events, was applied.

The usurper got away with a sanction of 500 colones per day for 200 days (slightly more than $300), even when the evaluation of 1998, with the new Forestry Law in full force, proved that the value of the extracted wood (to be used as firewood) exceeded the imposed fine by more than 11 times. Amazingly, the judge did not order the accused to vacate the farm in question, even though the usurper was not the legitimate owner. The accused was absolved of the usurpation charge by the *in dubio pro reo* principle (innocent until proven guilty), even when he himself admitted to having "worked" the farm without demonstrating any right of ownership. Finally, the Court of Final Appeal (cassation court) completely nullified the sentence and ordered a new trial.

Because of the grievous violations of due process and the errors when handing down the sentence, the judge was accused by the farm owner of the crimes of prevarication (issuing decisions contrary to law or based on false events), bias, and noncompliance of duties. However, the charge was dismissed, and a full discontinuance of the trial followed based on the decision that "the fact that the judge ignored logical reasoning does not translate into a crime as long as intent is not shown."[10]

When it was noted that damages continued on the farm, the owner again appeared before MINAE to request its involvement and to put an end to the systematic destruction of the ecosystem. The forestry inspector who visited the site reiterated the charge before the prosecutor of Pérez Zeledón. The prosecutor did not investigate the facts or attach the claim to the process already in progress but limited his involvement to requesting a final discontinuance in favor of the usurper and destroyer of the environment. In the analysis of events, the prosecutor maintained that "there is insufficient convincing evidence to require a trial." When requesting the absolution, the prosecutor declared that the forestry inspector "did not witness the accused logging" (hard to come by in an evidence inspection) and emphasized that no kind of outside investigation was carried out to determine that someone had executed the alleged logging, *even when the accused constantly admitted to engaging in these activities.* In response, the prosecutor announced that "the statements from the accused to the administrative authorities lack proof value."

The request for discontinuance in favor of the accused was treated as a new case, despite the efforts from the owner to attach the claim of the forestry inspector to the already existing process. The statements from the owner were registered by the prosecutor in a format file known as "Interview with a Witness," and the prosecutor himself, once the statement was signed and in the absence of the owner, committed the severe infraction of adding text to the statement to adjust it in accordance with the request for discontinuance.

The falsified document was presented before the Public Ministry's Prosecutor Investigation Unit, which absolved the prosecutor of all fault and responsibility. The investigators argued that the Document Analysis Section of the Judicial Investigation Bureau of Costa Rica lacked the technical means necessary to determine in what sequence the plaintiff's signature and the added writing occurred, although it was possible through simple observation to see the discontinuity between the last added part and the rest of the document.[11] They even excluded the evidence obtained through the use of a forensic study that left no doubt that part of the text had been added afterward.[12]

In distress, the owner of the farm personally appeared before Elizabeth Odio, the environmental minister, and asked for her cooperation in helping him to find justice and avoid further ecological destruction. After claiming in exasperation that "it was the one hundredth claim she received," the minister harshly stated that "she knew what had to be done," which she failed to demonstrate by doing absolutely nothing.

The second trial was held on 13 July 1999. Again the judge absolved the defendant of the

---

10. The final discontinuance in favor of Judge Franz Paniagua Mejía was issued at 4 P.M. on 26 May 2000 by Judge Hanz Roberto Leandro Carranza of the Penal Court of Pérez Zeledón. Prosecutor José Efraín Sanders Quesada made the request for discontinuance.

11. The accusation against Prosecutor Ronald Carmona González was filed as Administrative Cause #207-98 of the Prosecutor Investigation Unit and resolved by Vote #177-99

of the General Prosecutor of the Republic at 8 A.M. on 22 September 1999, signed by the general prosecutor, Carlos Arias Núñez, and by the assistant general prosecutor, Jorge Segura Román.

12. Discontinuance issued at 7:47 A.M. of 2 November 1999 by Judge Emilia Ureña Solis of the Penal Court of Pérez Zeledón.

charges of usurpation and Forestry Law infractions, based on a supposed "agricultural ownership" over which a penal judge has no decision power because such ownership must be established by agricultural judges. The Court of Final Appeal (Cassation) once again nullified sentencing of the farm invader. Finally, in a third trial, on 20 September 2000, more than four years after the claim was initially presented, the usurper was sentenced to one year in prison. However, the old abolished Forestry Law was applied, and a fine of 500 colones per day for 200 days was levied for the illegal logging, for a grand total of 100,000 colones (a little more than $300).[13]

Final restitution of the property to its rightful owners was ordered on 12 February 2001. However, there is a sad side note: As a result of the ignorance and total negligence of the authorities in charge of serving justice, there is probably irreversible destruction in a high-risk area that is part of a biological corridor and serves as buffer zone for a marine national park. After four years and three trials in court, during which the squatter continued to cut trees, plant coffee, and keep livestock, the court finally recognized the property's legal owner and penalized the squatter with a jail sentence and a fine to cover the damages. However, in a bizarre twist of fate, the squatter died shortly after this last trial, leaving no one to pay for the damages to the owner and to the environment, not only for the trees cut but also for the soil sediments that will now be transported to the coral reefs of Ballena Marine National Park.

The case in question clearly identified the possible culprit and provided substantial material evidence of environmental damage. The real problem begins with the obvious lack of knowledge on the part of the judges, whose ignorance of the environment and its protection and elementary knowledge of agricultural ownership, and how it is exercised, are overwhelming. The deficiencies in Costa Rica's environmental law

are more a case of "weak conduct" of the prosecutors, who commit crimes of omission and duty noncompliance, than of "weak claims" of the plaintiffs.

USURPATION AND LOGGING IN LANDS DONATED TO THE STATE

The second case illustrates the Costa Rican state's inability to protect areas guaranteed absolute protection by the national park system. The incapacity of judicial organizations allows for unchallenged destruction, but the government is also guilty of negligence in its obligations to donations from other countries of tremendously valuable ecosystems.

The case is more disheartening considering that part of the funds used to finance the purchase of lands donated to the Costa Rican state were collected by concerned students who wished to contribute to forest conservation. The Nepenthes Conservationist Group from Denmark collected and donated more than $300,000 so that the Neotropical Foundation could purchase and afterward donate lands to the Costa Rican state. These lands are part of the so-called Tortuguero–Barra del Colorado Biological Corridor and were to be added legally to the Tortuguero National Park to be forever protected.

Before the donation, the Neotropical Foundation fought for five years before the Justice Tribunals to expel illegal squatters who had invaded about 3,000 ha. Once the lands were delivered to the government of Costa Rica, MINAE was in charge of their administration and monitoring. Although the Nepenthes Foundation no longer had any power over these lands, some of its members visited the area in early February 2001 and were able to ascertain illegal actions such as wood extraction, use of land for production activities, and shifting of farm limits that encroach on the officially established limits. Representatives of MINAE were warned of the proven

---

13. Sentence #215-2000, passed by Judge Jaime Hernández Granillo, South Zone Court, Pérez Zeledón, at 12:30 hours of 20 September 2000.

irregularities and inspected the area on 19 March 2001. They discovered people living in ranches, evidence of illegal wood extraction, and indications of the existence of a sawmill in the area. In addition, there were planks tied together in the Tortuguero River channels, indicating that rivers were exploited for wood transportation and therefore that the perpetrators were eluding possible monitoring control on the roads.

The evidence further showed that logging was systematically carried out for more than a year. MINAE denounced before the Public Ministry those responsible for invading the area, and the drawn-out process in the tribunals began once again. MINAE's own excuse for overlooking the damages was a lack of personnel and transportation means, excuses exploited with exasperating regularity.

Representatives of the Nepenthes Conservationist Group have stated that "the government [of Costa Rica] seems incapable of protecting the national resources of the Costa Rican people."[14] A question remains: What would have happened if members of the Neotropical Foundation had not visited the donated lands? There may have been no notice of the invasion and flagrant destruction of a national park that is supposed to be constantly patrolled by park rangers.

RECOMMENDATIONS

These examples demonstrate that the accelerated deterioration of the Costa Rican environment and its biodiversity is a product of the impunity with which those who abuse and destroy natural resources are allowed to act. The farmer who takes over a plot and changes the land use, companies that contaminate aquifers, and the logging entrepreneur who hides behind an alleged "management plan" and uncontrollably destroys forests are only part of the problem. They can commit these acts only when law enforcement representatives do not carry out their duties and when the government itself neglects the lands it is called on to protect. All the laws in the world will be worthless unless there are effective means to apply them.

Recommendations are offered as possible solutions to this problem:

1. Costa Rica must comply with the obligation it assumed through the signing of the American Convention on Human Rights. In accordance with article 25 of said convention, Costa Rica must create "a quick and simple process or any other effective process before competent judges or tribunals that provides protection against actions that violate fundamental rights recognized by the Constitution, the law, or the present Convention, even when such violations are committed by people exercising their official functions." To date, there is no request for an injunction of constitutional violation against jurisdictional actions. Norms of the Organic Law of the Judicial Power, which prohibit acts in violation of the Constitution and the precedents and jurisprudence of the Supreme Constitutional Court, are only "paper" norms without established sanctions. There must be an awareness that the right to a healthy and ecologically balanced environment is a constitutional-level norm.

2. Judges presiding over environmental cases must have a more thorough knowledge of the environmental field. It is essential to know the difference between a primary forest, a secondary forest, and a forestry plantation, what levels of biodiversity each contains, and how each affects its ecosystem. Judges must be able to differentiate

---

14. Information given by Sonia González, administrative director of Neotrópica Foundation, and newspaper clip: Magaly Batista, "Danes Indignated with the Country," *Al Día*, 2 April 2001.

between a native, endangered, and common tree species in order to know what forests are most in need of protection. Finally, they must have a basic understanding of ecosystem theory, which describes the close relationship between soil, water, air, and wildlife, to defend the environment properly.

3. All institutions in charge of protecting the environment must be better integrated. The effective protection of biodiversity will not be achieved by increasing the number of laws and penalties but by integrating and coordinating them as an organic and congruent whole.

4. The Education Ministry and MINAE must make greater investments and commitments to educate the people of the country as to the importance of the environment and its relationship to their quality of life—on an individual and community level. In addition to preserving natural areas, the general topics of clean air, water, pollution, and improved public health must be stressed in all areas throughout the country.

CHAPTER 24

The Policy Context for Conservation in Costa Rica

MODEL OR MUDDLE?

Katrina Brandon

WORLDWIDE, a debate is under way over whether we can protect biodiversity *in situ*, whether we should bother to try, and whether these efforts should include any areas that limit human uses. Critics have claimed that protected areas are hard to manage and therefore we should not even try, that they are too small to make a difference, or that they are socially unfair and unjust (Brechin et al. 2002). Although these criticisms are mostly voiced by social scientists, alarmingly, some ecologists and policy makers, often those who work at levels far from the field, have echoed them (Sayer et al. 2000).

Within this debate, Costa Rica often features prominently and ironically—as an example of a country that has wholeheartedly embraced sustainable development with protected areas as the centerpiece or as a country with policies that fail to support conservation and parks too small to be ecologically viable. Much can be learned from examining the cases in this volume about the politics and policies surrounding biodiversity conservation; they not only present the situation as it exists within Costa Rica but also facilitate an understanding of the degree to which Costa Rica is, or is not, a model for other tropical countries.

This chapter builds from the other chapters in this book and examines Costa Rica's leadership as a "model" for conservation in other countries, expanding outward from dry forests to the broader issues of conservation in Costa Rica and how conservation in Costa Rica is linked to larger debates concerning biodiversity conservation worldwide. Although conservation can, and must, take place in many ways and at different scales, this chapter focuses on protected areas because they are the organizing nexus for biodiversity conservation efforts and offer the most concrete examples of how conservation actions occur.

COSTA RICA: A BRIEF REVIEW OF INNOVATION WITHIN CONSERVATION

In this chapter I identify the relevant contextual factors of scale, history, and social forces that have affected the development of both Costa Rican conservation policy and other policies that have affected Costa Rican conservation. Costa Rica is held up as a leader in three areas:

· Creating strong parks with a clear mission

· Linking protected areas with surrounding lands

· Politics, policies, and management affecting parks

CREATING STRONG PARKS WITH A CLEAR MISSION

Unlike remote areas in many parts of the world that have been protected, few, if any, areas of Costa Rica could be considered remote—even within the past 50 years. By the mid-1900s, most of the land suitable for agriculture in the central valley had been cleared, and settlers had begun to expand up the mountain slopes. In response to this expansion of the agricultural frontier, laws were passed as early as 1913 to protect wildlife and limit expansion into certain areas such as those around Poás Volcano. Other protected areas created prior to the 1950s generally emphasized scenic, historic, and recreational value—not biodiversity.

Costa Rica's modern system of parks started in 1969, when a major goal of the government was to establish new parks and protected areas rapidly, increase the size of existing areas, and increase support to the National Parks Service (Janzen 1983). A 1970 law set aside slightly more than 10 percent of the land in strictly protected areas and an additional 17 percent in "buffer zones" or forest reserves. Park creation continued during the 1980s, but a severe economic crisis struck the country, and the park system

entered a crisis phase. Although many parks had been created legally, there was no money to compensate landowners for land expropriated to create them and little money left to manage existing parks, and the high inflation rate meant that the buying power of colones was substantially reduced. Finally, International Monetary Fund requirements led to hiring freezes, leaving many parks with few managers or staff members. At the same time, threats to parks increased dramatically from multiple sources. Certain government ministries wanted to open parks to logging to generate cash, and the land titling and settlement agency saw parks as good areas for settlement of landless peasants. Landless peasants and unemployed banana workers also saw parks as commons areas available for colonization, and Corcovado National Park suffered a serious invasion by gold miners (Christen 1994).

The pressures on Costa Rica's tropical dry forest in the northwestern Pacific region of the country were intense, and forestland was rapidly being converted. By the mid-1980s, many conservationists were ready to give up on this area. Between 1979 and 1992, in the Liberia region, 119,712 ha of primary and secondary forests were transformed into pastures. During that time, Dan Janzen and Winnie Hallwachs acquired a 101,200-ha ranch and farm in the Guanacaste region and began the process of restoring it to wilderness (Janzen 1988).

It is vital to understand the policy context in which the parks were created. Deforestation was promoted both directly and indirectly by a set of government policies that favored conversion of forests to export-oriented commodities such as coffee, cattle, cacao, sugar, and bananas. The following statistics on deforestation are commonly cited:[1]

· Deforestation levels in Costa Rica were the highest in Latin America.

---

1. See World Bank (2000: 4–6) for a more complete discussion of the numbers, sources, and discrepancies.

- Between 1979 and 1992, primary forests declined by 38 percent and secondary forests by 8 percent.
- Rates decreased from approximately 46,500 ha per year in the 1950s, to less than 31,000 ha per year between 1979 and 1989, to about 16,000 ha per year in 1997 (World Bank 2000).

Protected areas within Costa Rica were established amid levels of deforestation and population growth that were among the highest in the world. Annual population growth rates reached 3.8 percent per year into the 1960s. Although the exact numbers are open to debate, it is clear that tremendous changes in land use have taken place in Costa Rica in the past 50 years.

As the economic crisis improved in the 1990s, the number of officially protected areas continued to increase: from 16.8 percent in 1990, to 23.8 percent in 1997, to 24.8 percent in 1999 (World Bank 2000: 12). Strictly protected areas (International Union for the Conservation of Nature [IUCN] categories I–V) amount to 14.2 percent of the national territory in 85 sites protecting approximately 723,000 ha (World Resources Institute 2000). The mission of Costa Rica's strictly protected areas overlapped with the IUCN's conceptions of "strictly" protected areas—recreational uses are allowed, extractive uses are not. There was an emphasis on conserving biodiversity within parks, since most parks were established specifically to help stop the transformation of the land and everything on it to other uses.

LINKING PROTECTED AREAS WITH SURROUNDING LANDS

Recognition is increasing that although protected areas should remain the cornerstone for the protection of biodiversity, "requiring them to carry the entire burden for biodiversity conservation is a recipe for ecological and social failure" (Brandon et al. 1998: 2). Costa Rica was one of the countries that first tried formally to link with surrounding lands the absolutely protected land (14%) and land in private hands but protected

(15%). In 1987, the Arias administration proposed creating a national system of conservation areas (the agency now known as Sistema Nacional de Areas de Conservación [SINAC]) to integrate protected area management and decentralize much of the decision-making power to regional levels (Umaña and Brandon 1992). The country was divided into nine Regional Conservation Units now called ARCs (Regional Conservation Areas) and sometimes called "megaparks." The current number of administrative units is now 11. Each ARC is composed of three land-use categories:

- *Core areas* subject to absolute protection, such as national parks
- *Buffer zones,* or multiple use areas, often forest or indigenous reserves, although some are highly populated or under agricultural use
- *Intensive extraction zones,* such as agricultural lands

Conceptually, the conservation objectives of the ARC system were to

- improve intersectoral coordination for each region;
- increase local participation in resource planning and use;
- create vertical linkages (between local people and government) within each region; and
- decentralize decision-making authority to regional levels.

All the ideas introduced under the ARC system were visionary at that time, and there was strong support from both international conservation organizations and the emerging ecotourism market. These ideas sought to minimize threats to parks from surrounding areas, increase local support for conservation, and prevent large-scale threats by government agencies while the system was in the early planning stages.

Costa Rica's emergence as an ecotourism destination supported these links in two ways.

First, the park system became the focal point for nature-based tourism, and "between 1990 and 1997, 38% of tourists visited national parks." At the national level, revenue from coffee, cane, cattle, and bananas was replaced by revenue from tourism. By 1999, tourism revenue reached $950 million, or 9 percent of gross domestic product (World Bank 2000: 23). Second, these links made private investment in ecotourism attractive to landowners with forests, particularly those with lands adjacent to parks. Private reserves adjacent to public areas extend ecosystem functions, expand habitats, and help attract tourists to areas, generating revenue through multiplier effects (Brandon 1996; Langholz et al. 2000). Privately managed reserves now total about 5 percent of the country's land area and 25 percent of the forested lands (World Bank 2000: 12–13).

POLITICS, POLICIES, AND MANAGEMENT AFFECTING PARKS

In the past 20 years, Costa Rica has also undertaken a broad-based set of political actions that were intended to support conservation. It has been considered a leader in a wide array of policies and actions that, broadly characterized, supported natural resource management, conservation, and biodiversity. Key policy actions have included

1. consolidating power for conservation by creating a new ministry;

2. creating new financing mechanisms to support conservation;

3. establishing the in-country technical capacity to catalog Costa Rica's tremendous biodiversity and identify potential uses; and

4. creating market-based incentives to support conservation.

In many Latin American countries, the greatest threats to parks and protected areas are from weak, inconsistent, poor, or conflictive government policy (Rudel and Roper 1996, 1997; Brandon et al. 1998). These weaknesses are largely due to the low level of import given to conserva-

tion relative to other government sectors, such as agriculture, forestry, mining, or public works. Recognizing this, the government consolidated a set of functions and in 1986 created a new ministry called the Ministerio de Recursos Naturales, Energía y Minas (MIREMEM) by transferring the Energy and Mines sections from the Ministry of Industry, Energy, and Mines and the National Park Service (NPS) and the General Forestry Directorate from the Ministry of Agriculture. Although it took nearly four years for the National Assembly to approve the creation of this ministry, MIRENEM operated in a de facto manner during the Arias administration. It is now known as the Ministry of Environment and Energy (MINAE).

Costa Rica has been viewed as a model also because of its innovation in financing arrangements to support conservation. In 1978, the government created the National Parks Foundation, an independent, private nonprofit foundation dedicated to the planning, management, protection, and development of national parks and reserves. It attracted donations from international conservation organizations and governments to support parks and played an important role in essentially privatizing the financing of the ARC system. Channeling financing through the foundation offered increased flexibility and responsiveness, and the financing was not subject to governmental constraints, such as the conditions imposed by the International Monetary Fund. Costa Rica began an intensive international fund-raising effort, whose success relied heavily on the participation of foundations, nongovernmental organizations, and private conservation groups. The country has also initiated a program of payment for environmental services, which include carbon sequestration, sustainable logging, ecotourism, hydroelectric power, water supply, bioprospecting, and payment in recognition of option and existence values (World Bank 1993). These actions are briefly described in the following paragraphs.

The country used debt-for-nature programs (debt swap) to turn a serious national problem into new opportunities for conservation. In mid-

1988 Costa Rica proposed a specific debt-for-nature swap with the Swedish government for the completion and endowment of Guanacaste National Park, a major conservation project in northern Costa Rica. Swedish students and private conservation groups supported the project, and a total of U.S. $3.5 million was allocated for debt conversion and targeted at Guanacaste National Park, out of a donated total of nearly $15 million, significant financing for the largest block of tropical dry forest in the country. Other debt swaps were channeled through the National Park Foundation to support a specific ARC. This is an example of how the ARC system was effectively privatized to facilitate fund-raising efforts and improve the regional disbursement of funds for conservation.

Through the National Biodiversity Institute (INBio), created in 1989, the country created the technical capacity to conduct an inventory of life forms in Costa Rica and is analyzing the central and potential contributions of biodiversity to society. A deal between INBio and Merck Pharmaceutical Company publicized the value in exploring the country's biodiversity in pursuit of marketable products, an area sometimes called ecoprospecting.

Costa Rica has also been an international leader in market-based mechanisms that support conservation, principally through payments for environmental services. In 1996, Costa Rica adopted a program for payment of environmental services to

1. eliminate subsidies that acted as perverse incentives for resource depletion;

2. collect revenue from users of environmental services to pay for them;

3. eliminate the dependence on the government for forest sector subsidies and get the forest sector to be viewed as providing services beyond wood;

4. fix the unequal distribution of benefits from many environmental services, which accrue nationally and internationally, not to the owner of land and forests; and

5. create incentives for improved forest management (World Bank 2000).

Payments for these services are from taxes on fossil fuel use; from an implicit resource transfer from urban to rural sector users; and from a sector that imposes high costs on the economy, in terms of foreign imports and pollution costs, to a sector that broadly provides services both nationally and internationally.

RHETORIC TO REALITY: IMPLEMENTATION OF POLICY REFORMS

Most of the rhetoric about Costa Rica portrays it as a progressive country, politically committed to sustainable development. The previous section outlined some of the actions that have led to this perception. This section briefly addresses how well this set of actions has been implemented in reality.

THE CONTEXT AND MISSION OF PARKS WITHIN COSTA RICA

Understanding how best to conserve tropical dry forest in Costa Rica can be only partially informed by ecological analyses, which provide information on *what* to conserve and *where* to conserve it. What is omitted by such ecological analysis is *how* to conserve it, which is not an ecological issue but a social and political one (Redford and Sanderson 1992; Brandon et al. 1998). The historical forces and social actors that shape the local context influence parks and the management they require. Just as biodiversity is scale-dependent, so too are the social forces that shape how biodiversity is used, managed, or destroyed. In any country and at any scale of analysis, it means that one must look at geographical scales (site to regional to national) and temporal scales (historical to present to the future) to understand the array of policies that affect biodiversity conservation. These policies include ones made at international levels (policies such as the Kyoto protocol) that in turn shape those decisions made at regional or provincial levels. Understanding these contexts—of scale, history, and social forces—is essential to developing lasting management approaches for a particular site.

Many of the protected areas established worldwide in the past 30 years have been established in areas that are geographically remote or viewed as a political backwater with little power. Parks were created in areas viewed as places with "nothing there," and the act of creating a park consisted of little more than drawing lines on maps to satisfy the clamoring of international conservation organizations. Yet consolidating the management of these types of areas is generally simple; the threats are locally based and often at low levels. Management can often be initiated by compensating people for lost access to land and resources, demarcating boundaries, educating people about conservation, and beginning what is more conventionally thought of as park management—the array of actions undertaken inside the park. The legacy of how a park is established influences the present-day management context (see Brandon 1998).

The social context in which Costa Rica's park system was created included the following elements:

- Rapid declaration of parks to protect areas of land from conversion to other uses

- Declaration of parks on the basis of what was socially and politically feasible, not on the basis of ecological criteria

- High levels of social hostility toward parks, resulting from expropriation without legally required compensation

- High levels of pressure on land proposed for parks to be converted to other uses—both at national levels for foreign exchange and at local levels for agriculture

The parks that were established, then, were created amid great social, economic, and demographic pressure. They were not developed based on a meaningful ecological framework— they were opportunistic expressions of what was possible at a given moment in time. In looking at Costa Rica, it is clear that most of the parks within the country were established with the realization that if any area was to be spared from chainsaws, it would have to be protected quickly. In such a context of rapid change, this was the only way that biodiversity conservation could have proceeded. Yet this context of creation has left many problems for Costa Rican parks— from both political and biodiversity conservation perspectives. It has meant that parks were not established

- with local support in a given area but to counter quickly pressures exerted at local levels;

- with sufficient area to protect the range of species that would be left within as parks became islands;

- as part of any regional land-use framework or strategy;

- with consideration to corridors or elevational gradients; or

- to represent the full spectrum of biodiversity (representation) to the greatest degree possible.[2]

All of this matters a great deal in understanding where Costa Rican parks, particularly those conserving tropical dry forests, fit into the international debates on parks. Although many view Costa Rica as an exemplar of park creation, in fact, in biodiversity terms, it represents a worst-case scenario. Costa Rican parks cannot serve as a model for other countries—except those with a similar set of social pressures: rapid land-use conversion, strong demographic pressure, rapid fragmentation of habitat, and relative ease of access to most parts of the country. When viewed from the context in which they were created, Costa Rican parks are *relatively* free from threats,

---

2. For excellent discussions of this, see Palminteri et al. (1999) and Powell et al. (2000, 2002).

particularly large-scale threats. But it is also impressive that in one generation, a relatively short amount of time, most Costa Ricans have come to value the park system. Costa Rican parks demonstrate that even areas established under difficult circumstances can function, if not flourish (Sanchez-Azofeifa et al. 1999). This is consistent with recent findings by a Conservation International team studying 93 parks (in 22 countries) that are more than 5,000 ha each, more than five years old, and subject to human pressure (Bruner et al. 2001). The study found that despite high levels of pressure, more than 80 percent of the parks had as much natural vegetative cover today as they did when they were first established, and a substantial percentage had more. There was also a notable difference in deforestation levels between parks and surrounding areas. The analysis of Costa Rica and this recent Conservation International study allow room for cautious optimism on the effectiveness of parks.

LINKING PARKS AND SURROUNDING LANDS

The model of how each of the regional conservation areas would operate is visionary. The idea of linking protected areas with their surrounding lands in order to improve intersectoral coordination, increase local participation in resource planning and use, create linkages between local people and government, and decentralize decision-making authority to regional levels is one that conceptually leads to better conservation. However, although the SINAC systems and each of the ARCs appear to be functional on paper, the system does not yet appear to have made substantial gains nationwide.

Part of the difficulty lies with stopping the existing forces leading to land-use change. As noted earlier, parks in Costa Rica were in large part created to be somewhat "separate" or "different" from the lands that surrounded them. It is worth exploring just how significant these differences are, as shown in table 24.1.

Table 24.1 shows that there has been a marked difference in deforestation rates between national parks and surrounding areas, including

TABLE 24.1
Deforestation Rates in Costa Rica's National Parks and outside Its Protected Areas

	IN NATIONAL PARKS (% PER YEAR)	OUTSIDE PROTECTED AREAS (% PER YEAR)
1976–86	0.56	3.6
1986–91	0.21	2.8
1991–95	0.16	3.2

Source: Adapted from World Bank (2000).

forest reserves (which have a less stringent protection status). What this demonstrates is that the parks have been relatively effective at halting land-use conversion, whereas the forested areas around them have been converted at high rates. This marked difference in deforestation rates also reflects the difficulties in making the kinds of links desired at the regional level.

Overall, the lack of available forests left to log has been a greater limiting factor for the conversion of forestland than any integrated plan under the SINAC. This volume contains numerous examples of activities taking place in or near a park that are clearly incompatible with the conservation uses within. For example, the Arenal-Tempisque Irrigation Project (see chapter 21) is clearly not a good neighbor for the park.

Other attempts to provide linkages between parks and surrounding areas have gone astray or been misinterpreted or have the potential to become problematic. For example, chapter 21 in this volume addresses the use of "controlled grazing" as a "novel technique to generate economic benefits for local communities providing sustainable development." Few have an image of cattle as a discriminating tool for weed management, fire control, and forest regeneration. It may well be that cattle can perform some of these services. However, decisions that should be rooted in science and range management quickly and easily become clouded when scientists and managers begin to focus on providing tangible, local, direct benefits to nearby residents. Since providing such benefits has become part of the mission of each of the ARCs, making decisions about park management quickly becomes entangled with making decisions that are popular at decentralized levels. Unfortunately, this often leads to weak outcomes for conservation—and to inequitable distributions of benefits, as well (see Brandon 1998, 2000). This volume also contains other examples that highlight the failure of conservation to be accorded importance equal to that of other sectors, even within the ARC system.

Increasingly, conservationists are identifying the kinds of uses that are likely to conserve biodiversity outside protected areas and act as sound buffers. Examples of areas that encourage consumptive and extractive uses but that can be "good neighbors" to parks include shade-grown coffee farms, organic cacao plantations, agro-ecosystem models, and extractive reserves. Clearly, there will be a need for what Boshier et al. (chapter 16) describe as *circa situm* efforts—even if those efforts focus on species conservation, as opposed to ecosystem processes. Such efforts are vital within the mosaic of landscape uses, but they do not negate the need for protected areas (Redford and Richter 1999). Yet we lack examples of functional, well-funded systems, such as the SINAC, in which decisions are made about landscape uses within regions in ways that preserve biodiversity and allow development, at appropriate levels of intensity and at appropriate scales, to take place. The SINAC system and ARCs are an attempt at this, but they are still a long way from demonstrating that effective integration of parks and surrounding areas is possible.

POLITICS, POLICIES, AND MANAGEMENT AFFECTING PARKS

Policies can affect parks directly in at least two ways. Policies designed to support conservation affect them favorably. Costa Rica's creation of an environmental ministry, implementation of policies to support financing for conservation,

development of a national-level technical capacity for conservation, and changes in forest sector policies are all examples of actions taken to support conservation. At the other extreme are policies that undermine conservation efforts, such as those promoting large-scale development activities or road construction, both of which often pose the most significant threats to biodiversity. A review of what Costa Rica intended by the actions described earlier and what actually took place when they were implemented reveals a vast discrepancy. Although Costa Rica established what could reasonably be called a broad set of "model" policies to support conservation, there have been substantial weaknesses in how these policies have been implemented in practical terms.

The creation of an environmental ministry has been an important action in attempting to elevate and integrate many of the diverse agencies that affect conservation. Simply putting these diverse agencies under one roof, however, has not led to better intergovernmental coordination within the ministry. It has also not given enough weight or political capital to MINAE for it to be a progressive advocate for change.

The World Bank concluded in a recent review: "Sustainable development is still not an official national objective. The government does not give support to forest management and conservation because it has not fully internalized the importance of forests to production, exports, employment, and a sound environment" (World Bank 2000: 61). This is largely due to politics and power. For example, under President Rodriguez's administration, MINAE lost significant power at the national level when the president reduced the overall number of ministers and assigned the second vice president dual responsibilities: that of second vice president and head of MINAE. This suggested that MINAE, and the functions under it, were viewed as less worthy of representation than other sectors of government. Furthermore, environmentalists had loudly complained that the second vice president lacked environmental credentials and was antienvironment. For example, despite the rhetoric given to ecotourism as a basis for supporting local-level development, government policies in fact support large-scale projects and put numerous obstacles in the way of small-scale tourism development (Honey 1999). Such political discussions have concrete ramifications that reach all the way to the site level, as evidenced in chapter 15.

Costa Rica has been viewed as a model in its innovative and creative financing arrangements, such as debt swaps, international fund-raising, the use of the National Parks Foundation and special relationships between donors and each ARC, and a system of payments for environmental services. Yet each innovative action has had difficulties when applied. Debt swaps were a great idea, but the market for them proved fairly short lived. Most were earmarked for a specific park or ARC. Costa Rica has benefited from high levels of international fund-raising, which was largely channeled through the National Parks Foundation. However, there were a number of problems with channeling support for conservation in this manner. First, obtaining external financing for conservation is reasonable when the premise is that most benefits are enjoyed internationally. But such a premise does little to instill national or local-level responsibilities or appreciation for the benefits that indeed are recognized at those levels. It also undermines arguments that biodiversity has high intrinsic value and that a range of localized conservation services are performed by forests and wild areas. It sets up an expectation that external support for conservation is the responsibility of the international community. This line of thinking, along with the high levels of funding given to the foundation for conservation, had the following consequences:

1. It created a "shadow" civil service whereby people hired by the foundation for conservation were paid much more than "real" civil servants, weakening the position of entities such as the National Park Service and

resulting in the loss of capable people from the public sector.

2. It created an impression that conservation should not be a mainline governmental responsibility, since it was not treated as such.

3. It created significant funding discrepancies between the popular ARCs, which were well supported, and those ARCs with less cachet.

4. It created a rapid influx of funds that raised local expectations and made people feel that they should directly benefit from the conservation sector.

The legacy of these problems, and the relatively weak political power that MINAE has, have meant that even when the policy framework for conservation has been great, implementation has been weak.

The most glaring current example of this discrepancy between policy and implementation is the 1996 law on payment for environmental services from fossil fuel taxes. The law allocates a third of the revenues from taxes on fossil fuels to conservation. For one 15-month period, $25 million should have been generated for conservation; however, the government used the money for other things, and only $7 million had been paid out to forest owner associations (World Bank 2000). Costa Rica's payments for environmental services, joint implementation for carbon sequestration, and the World Bank–funded "Ecomarkets" project are all examples of innovation. However, only when the implementation of these three innovations matches the rhetoric will Costa Rica truly be providing leadership in these areas.

Costa Rica's actions to develop a technical capacity for conservation are in fact exemplary. However, the high technical capacity can be traced as much to the abolition of the army and the investment in education as to other actions. With the creation of INBio, a wide variety of local people have been trained in parataxonomy;

helping to create local support for conservation within the ARCs. The country's technical capacity has also been bolstered by the huge number of students and researchers from other countries who have come to Costa Rica annually under the auspices of the Organization for Tropical Studies. As a result of their presence and the technical expertise they have brought, much of the research on the tropics has been generated in Costa Rica.[3] Other training that supports conservation has taken place in the ecotourism sector—this is one of the best ways in which local people have become directly involved and trained in areas that support conservation.

CONCLUSION

Costa Rica has won strong international acclaim for the fundamental action of creating a national system of parks. Yet, as this chapter demonstrates, there is little in the creation of these parks that serves as a model, other than the finding that boundary demarcation and enforcement, in a context in which land tenure is respected, can stop the rapid transformation of sites. The design of Costa Rica's parks was based on what was politically feasible, not on what was ecologically best. What remains, then, is a series of islands in the midst of a landscape undergoing transformation. Yet even those parks that are islands or fragments—and virtually all the unlinked parks are small enough to suffer the problems of fragmentation—have value. Although we may have lost keystone species in some fragments, we have learned that something valuable has been lost, and we are seeking to "rewild" and restore it (Soulé and Terborgh 1999).

The impressive gains made in the past 20 years in the Guanacaste ARC demonstrate this. The indomitable efforts of Dan Janzen and others, combined with a serendipitous drop in cattle prices and out-migration to the central valley, have taken a huge amount of pressure off the Guanacaste region for cattle ranching. This has made it possible to take a small park and expand it upward and outward so that it includes ecological gradients from the lowlands to the mountains and is a major wilderness area rather than a fragment. This example, which is of extreme importance in tropical dry-forest conservation, highlights the need to start with parks as anchors and then think at different scales of both space and time. Instead of giving up on conservation, even on a small scale, we must look at the contributions each park can make within the scale it occupies. From there, we must look to the future and think what might be possible if significant changes occur in an area.

Such an understanding of scale, on geographical and temporal levels, is important in both ecological and policy analysis. Many of the policies that Costa Rica has implemented look good in a particular place, at a particular level, or within a particular time period (see Cuello et al. 1998). As a result, innovative policies encouraging decentralization, which may work within one ARC, are captured by local-level politics and distorted in another ARC. Creative financing mechanisms defined for one park or ARC fail to materialize for others, leaving them as the destitute sibling ARCs. Creative ideas in one area make for bad policy in others. So when Dan Janzen decided to allow dumping of orange by-products from a juice factory in the Guanacaste Conservation Area in exchange for payments for ecosystem services (the by-products would degrade and create a well-fertilized area enhancing forest regeneration), problems quickly arose. How can a good idea such as this one be made to work across the system? What if oil palm or

---

3. The Organization for Tropical Studies began its activities in Costa Rica in 1963, and these helped provide a research foundation for many of the conservation actions taken.

coffee-processing wastes are dumped in an adjacent park for payment? What about pesticide loads? Who will speak for the park and ensure that what is dumped is sound? Policies can often ensure that damage is not done, but they are less good at encouraging good ideas at local levels. To discourage misuse, they must also discourage what might, in some cases, be good ideas.

The difficulty of scale arises again in looking at innovative national policies such as payments for ecosystem services. Despite the creation of the ARC system and the intention of linking parks with buffer areas, ARCs have had few concrete ways to do this. The law allowing fossil fuel taxes to be directed toward conservation could prove to be the best way of implementing ARCs—it provides immediate financing for forest protection in recognition of the services they provide. This in turn helps the country by ensuring a reasonable supply of future timber as well as biodiversity values and retains the quality of hydrological systems, vital in a country with an 83 percent dependence on energy from hydropower generation. What has eluded most of the ARCs, concrete ways to offer incentives to extend the ecosystem services of parks, would be possible for perhaps the first time. But at the national scale, MINAE enjoys limited political power, and there is not yet sufficient popular understanding of the law to demand that payments be made. This demonstrates the complexity and contradictions inherent in Costa Rican policies, a condition rampant in most countries (Barrett et al. 2001). At the national level, in terms of rhetoric and conceptual actions, Costa Rica has developed policies that are exemplary and could, with appropriate adaptation, serve as models within other countries. But in the implementation of these policies, Costa Rica's progress has been uneven. Therein lies the "muddle"—the contradictions, lack of application, and politicization that undermine sustainable development objectives. Yet there is hope that with the right framework and political will in place policy changes will lead to improvements and lasting conservation.

REFERENCES

Barrett, C. B., K. Brandon, C. Gibson, and H. Gjertsen. 2001. Conserving tropical biodiversity amid weak institutions. *BioScience* 51:497–502.

Brandon, K. 1996. *Ecotourism and conservation: A review of key issues.* Environment Department Paper 33. Washington, D.C.: World Bank. 70 pp.

———. 1998. Perils to parks: The social context of threats. In *Parks in peril: People, politics, and protected areas,* ed. K. Brandon, K. Redford, and S. Sanderson, 415–39. Covelo, Calif.: Island Press.

———. 2000. Moving beyond integrated conservation and development projects (ICDPs) to achieve biodiversity conservation. In *Tradeoffs or synergies? Agricultural intensification, economic development and the environment,* ed. D. R. Lee and C. B. Barrett, 417–32. Wallingford, England: CAB International.

Brandon, K., K. H. Redford, and S. E. Sanderson, eds. 1998. *Parks in peril: People, politics, and protected areas.* Covelo, Calif.: Island Press. 519 pp.

Brechin, S., P. R. Wilshusen, C. L. Fortwangler, and P. C. West. 2002. Beyond the square wheel: Toward a more comprehensive understanding of biodiversity conservation as a social and political process. *Society and Natural Resources* 15:41–64.

Bruner, A. G., R. E. Gullison, R. E. Rice, and G. A. da Fonseca. 2001. Effectiveness of parks in protecting tropical biodiversity. *Science* 291:125–28.

Christen, C. A. 1994. Development and conservation on Costa Rica's Osa Peninsula, 1937–1977: A regional case study of historical land use policy and practice in a small Neotropical country. Ph.D. diss., Johns Hopkins University.

Cuello, C. 1995. Sustainable development in theory and practice: Costa Rican thinking and experience on sustainability. Dissertation, University of Delaware.

Cuello, C., K. Brandon, and R. Margoluis. 1998. Costa Rica: Corcovado National Park. In *Parks in peril: People, politics, and protected areas,* ed. K. Brandon, K. Redford, and S. Sanderson, 143–92. Covelo, Calif.: Island Press.

Honey, M. 1999. Costa Rica: On the beaten path. In *Ecotourism and sustainable development: Who owns paradise?,* chap. 5. Washington, D.C.: Island Press.

Janzen, D., ed. 1983. *Costa Rican natural history.* Chicago: University of Chicago Press. 816 pp.

———. 1988. Buy Costa Rican Beef. *Oikos* 51: 257–58.

Langholz, J., J. Lassoie, and J. Schelhas. 2000. Incentives for biodiversity conservation: Lessons from Costa Rica's private wildlife refuge program. *Conservation Biology* 14:1735–43.

Palminteri, S., G. V. N. Powell, A. Fernandez, and D. Tovar. 1999. Talamanca Montane-Isthmian Pacific Ecoregion-based conservation plan: Preliminary reconnaissance phase. Unpublished WWF report.

Powell, G. V. N., J. Barborak, and S. Rodriguez. 2000. Assessing representativeness of protected natural areas in Costa Rica or conserving biodiversity: A preliminary gap analysis. *Biological Conservation* 93:9335–41.

Powell, G. V. N., S. Palminteri, B. Carlson, and M. Boza. 2002. Successes and failings of the Monteverde reserve complex and Costa Rica's system of national protected areas. In *Rescuing tropical nature: Making parks work*, ed. J. Terborgh, C. P. van Schaik, L. Davenport, and M. Rao, 156–71. Covelo, Calif.: Island Press.

Redford, K. H., and B. Richter. 1999. Conservation of biodiversity in a world of use. *Conservation Biology* 3:1246–56.

Redford, K. H., and S. E. Sanderson. 1992. The brief barren marriage of biodiversity and sustainability. *Bulletin of the Ecological Society of America* 73:36–39.

Rudel, T., and J. Roper. 1996. Regional patterns and historical trends in tropical deforestation, 1976–1990: A qualitative comparative analysis. *Ambio* 25(3):160–66.

———. 1997. The paths to rain forest destruction: Crossnational patterns of tropical deforestation, 1975–90. *World Development* 25:53–65.

Sanchez-Azofeifa, G. A., C. Quesada-Mateo, P. Gonzalez-Quesada, S. Dayanandan, and K. Bawa. 1999. Protected areas and conservation of biodiversity in the tropics. *Conservation Biology* 13:407–11.

Sayer, J., N. Ishwaran, J. Thorsell, and T. Sigaty. 2000. Tropical forest biodiversity and the World Heritage Convention. *Ambio* 29(6):302–13.

Soulé, M., and J. Terborgh, eds. 1999. Continental conservation: Scientific foundations of regional reserve networks. Covelo, Calif.: Island Press. 227 pp.

Umaña, A., and K. Brandon. 1992. Inventing institutions for conservation: Lessons from Costa Rica. In *Poverty, natural resources, and public policy in Central America*, ed. S. Annis, 85–107. Washington, D.C.: Overseas Development Council.

World Bank. 1993. *Costa Rica: Forest sector review.* Internal Division Reports, Agricultural Operations Report 13850. Washington, D.C.: Environment Department.

World Bank, Operations Evaluation Department. 2000. *Costa Rica: Forest strategy and the evolution of land use.* Internal report. Washington, D.C.: World Bank.

World Resources Institute, United Nations Development Programme, United Nations Environment Programme, World Bank. 2000. *World Resources: 2000–2001: People and ecosystems: The fraying web of life.* Washington, D.C.: World Resources Institute. 389 pp.

CHAPTER 25

Conclusion and Recommendations

Gordon W. Frankie, Alfonso Mata, and Katrina Brandon

IN ORDER TO SURVIVE, human beings must begin to consider the deterioration and destruction of natural resources as a capital loss, particularly for development and management options of future generations. Our choices are simple. Either we take care of our planet and its natural resources, or we continue to participate not only in our natural world's progressive deterioration but also in our self-destruction. The fundamental issue is that of appropriate environmental management, or in other words, how people can interact responsibly with nature. A friendly relation, nondestructive but sustainable, is something that *must* be accepted and adopted as a means of life and culture, and protecting and conserving nature is something that involves the whole of society. Thus, society needs to be informed about the potential and weaknesses of the environment in which humans live and work. The general scope of this book is to offer an interdisciplinary exploration, with an ecological basis, of Costa Rica's biodiversity and conservation focused in the tropical dry forest.

The biological, socioeconomic, cultural, and political knowledge presented in this volume suggests several general lessons for future projections on ecological restoration and biodiversity conservation. Interconnecting and underlying each of these lessons are the socioeconomic and political contexts that have developed around protected areas and the future of biodiversity conservation. In this final chapter we summarize the main biological and social lessons that are stated or, we believe, implied by the contributing authors. Where appropriate, we also include obvious recommendations for improvement on conserving biodiversity. The summary does not in any way suggest that individual lessons and recommendations pointed out in the various chapters are unimportant; they are all relevant and useful. We also looked for similarities in lessons that were shared with other regions of Costa Rica. Thus, most lessons offered here apply to the country as a whole and to other regions of Mesoamerica, as well.

LESSONS

Lesson 1. A great amount of information already exists for many prominent groups of plants and animals of the dry forest, but much more information is needed.

A wealth of knowledge already exists—in published scientific studies, unpublished reports, on-line sources, and semitechnical publications. Further, there are large collections of Costa Rican plants and animals in several museums. Most notable in Costa Rica are the Institute of Biodiversity (INBio) in Heredia, the National Museum in San José, and the University of Costa Rica in San Pedro. In the United States, large collections, especially of plants, are housed at the Missouri Botanical Garden in St. Louis and at the Chicago Field Museum. Additional sources of information are the many dry-forest researchers themselves and their ongoing studies, which continually produce new and useful findings. Many of these workers also regularly devote some of their time to educational outreach efforts.

Despite the accumulated and continuously emerging knowledge, there will always be the need and curiosity to obtain basic information. There will also be an increasing demand to apply existing knowledge to solve problems (Meffe 1998) and to obtain new information on how humans affect biodiversity (see chapters 1, 4, 7, 12, 15, 21, and 23). One important biological area in need of more research is that of monitoring selected taxonomic organisms to assess environmental health (chapters 4, 6, 9, 10, 12, and 15). Monitoring will also become increasingly necessary for surveying rare and endangered species (chapters 12 and 15). Another area that will require considerable new information and knowledgeable professionals is restoration ecology. However, before this knowledge can be applied, other new actions must be put into motion, as indicated in the lessons that follow.

Lesson 2. Studies on several groups of animals and habitats clearly indicate that the dry forest is ecologically linked to other, adjacent life zones and in some cases to geographical areas outside the country.

Many bird species (chapter 12) and sea turtles (chapter 15) regularly migrate long distances each year between the dry forest and other, widely separated geographical areas, and international treaties theoretically protect some of these well-known organisms. What is not generally recognized is that large numbers of diverse taxa also make regular migrations, most of which are seasonal, between dry and adjacent wetter forests of Costa Rica. The case for in-country migration of resident dry-forest animals is made for birds by Barrantes and Sanchez (chapter 15) and for bats by Stoner and Timm (chapter 5) and LaVal (chapter 13). Janzen (chapter 7) offers an introduction to the large numbers of phytophagous and some predator insect groups that travel seasonally between dry and wet forests. Haber and Stevenson (chapter 8) provide considerable survey information on three types of migrations that dry-forest butterfly species exhibit traveling between major biotic regions. Their survey also reveals that about half of all dry-forest butterfly species migrate!

Related to the organismal connectivity between dry and wet forests is another type of ecological connection. This can be readily observed in watersheds that traverse several life zones from high elevations to lower ones (chapter 9). These watersheds or corridors connecting diverse habitats have received little study to date. Yet they provide important aquatic and terrestrial environments for much biodiversity and, at the same time, important environmental services for humans (Daily 1997; see also chapters 9–11).

The important message of Lesson 2 is that the dry forest should not be considered as an island of special habitats and organisms. Rather, much of the dry-forest biota has evolved many different ecological relationships with wetter forests and in some cases with widely separated geographical areas. The relationships are complex and must be considered when developing effective legislation, local or regional management plans, and collaborations to protect them.

Lesson 3. Conserving biodiversity and the habitats that support it consists of many interacting biological, socioeconomic, political, policy, and organizational components, all of which are important and have a place in conservation.

In referring to programs for recovering endangered species in the United States, Clark et al. (1994: 419) state, "Regardless of the biological status of the species and its habitat, the ultimate causes of most species' endangerment lie in human values that are manifest in varying social, economic, and political institutions and activities." They expand on this fundamental proposition by pointing out that there is a basic need for holistic understanding of the problem, which should then receive interdisciplinary attention from the conservation community.

The same case can be made for projects to protect healthy species and habitats. Biologists and nonbiologists need to work together in a truly integrated manner to achieve stated goals (chapters 4, 9, 15–18, 20, 22, and 23). Working together has not been the rule in most conservation projects throughout the country (chapters 15, 17, 19, 21, and 23). The integrated approach requires more work through advanced planning, individual agreements among participants, frequent meetings to review and critique progress, and reports reflecting progress from all parties involved. Bringing participants together also requires new organizational structure, effective leadership, possibly additional funding, and group learning (Clark et al. 1994: 420; chapters 16 and 18).

There are a few caveats for increased collaboration, however. Although it is important for all relevant organizations to be informed about and consulted on what is happening, this does not mean that all should be involved in managing conservation programs. A recent study conducted by the Biodiversity Support Program (Margoluis et al. 2000) found that involving all relevant groups in conservation did not lead to the best conservation outcomes. What was most effective was having one strong lead organization that had a clear sense of mission and that was strategic in its collaboration with other organizations. One of the difficulties of having many organizations jointly develop a work plan is that they are each bound by their own policies and traditions (Clark et al. 1994). Multiple organizations without a shared sense of mission or clear goals often had difficulties working together. This study suggests that involvement of all relevant groups is essential but that complicated organizational structures to implement conservation projects may not lead to improved conservation outcomes. Clark et al. (1994: 421) came to a similar conclusion when considering species restoration projects, recommending that high-performance teams (i.e., lead groups) conduct the actual conservation work.

Lesson 4. Gaps in transferring information from biologists to databases (large and small) to policy makers and land managers/stewards must be recognized and bridged.

Conserving biodiversity implies that there is an orderly transfer process, which entails knowing the organisms (naming), their biologies and ecologies, and how to get this information to the people who will decide on plans for managing the organisms and their habitats. Hanson (chapter 17) states that "the sequence of information transfer that needs to occur is systematics [leading to] ecology [leading to] conservation"— a logical concept. We know most of the prominent organisms of the dry forest and something of their ecologies, but numerous accounts in this volume indicate that we have a serious problem in the transfer of knowledge to the practice of conservation. Actually, the problem is a multifaceted one. We have identified the most obvious gaps in information transfer: (a) between biologists and government officials (decision makers) charged with protecting biodiversity and the environment in the field as well as in the Ministry of Environment and Energy (MINAE) in the capital, San José; (b) between biologists and the media; (c) between biologists and local people adjacent to protected areas; (d) between local people and government officials; and (e) between the laws and their effective implementation.

These are extremely important gaps that confront professionals who wish to see biological knowledge invested in the most productive ways in order to protect biodiversity. Each of these gaps is discussed in the lessons that follow.

Lesson 5. Officials in the central government as well as field directors charged with protecting biodiversity and the environment must be better educated and trained. Upgrading capacities and careful hiring of committed personnel are a necessity.

As pointed out in Stoner and Timm (chapter 5), the vast majority (98%) of government officials charged with protecting biodiversity and the environment in MINAE have never received any university education or training, and many of them are lacking basic ecoethical values, environmental commitments, or a minimal motivation for protecting the environment. Yet these individuals are charged with the huge task of protecting the country's biodiversity and environment—a complex and difficult proposition by any measure. The deficiencies in understanding, much less protecting, biodiversity are pointed out with clear examples in chapters 7, 9, 12, 15, 17, 19, and 21–24. This scenario is further complicated if corrupt situations are involved, especially in relation to land-use permits in protected areas (chapters 22 and 23).

The obvious remedy seems clear enough. Hire a large number of university graduates over a period of time and screen personnel for their commitment to conservation and understanding of its importance. These individuals should have bachelor's and master's degrees in a wide variety of biological and social fields in order to deal with the many complex problems that occur in conservation (chapters 15, 19, 21–24). A good case could easily be developed to justify this change. However, it would not be easy to implement for many reasons. First, there is tremendous inertia in MINAE, which is not unexpected (Clark et al. 1994). Second, this change must have leadership and support at the highest political level of the government. As Brandon points out in chapter 24, the central government has not been recently inclined to support conservation in effective ways. Third, more money would be needed support the new salaries that

would have to be offered to attract good professional people. Last, if new people are hired, they would need to be effectively incorporated into the system.

Hiring more qualified people would represent a big step in the right direction. In addition, this change would allow for more effective communication and collaboration between biologists and directors of the large conservation areas (chapters 1 and 24). At the present time, with a few exceptions, many biologists shy away from working in parks and reserves because of the difficulties of working with government officials and their cumbersome regulations (see Lesson 6). This is unfortunate because protected areas need biologists. In addition, it seems that the decentralization of MINAE into conservation areas permitted laxity in leadership, poor enforcement of the law, and a lack of monitoring of violations (chapters 21–23), with corruption in the form of granting government permissions for forest cutting and land-use permits (e.g., Playa Grande and Ostional wildlife refuges).

There is also a disconnection in academia between biology and conservation. Many academic biologists feel that if they pursue applied aspects of conservation, they will not be taken seriously or granted tenure. This has been a subject of debate within the Society for Conservation Biology and also holds true throughout Latin America. Another key element is that the courses and training most biologists receive have little to do with applied conservation (Meffe 1998).

Lesson 6. More collaborative partnerships must be built between the public and private sectors in conserving biodiversity. The private sector, including biologists, nongovernmental organizations, and private landowners, has a great role to play in biodiversity conservation.

The need for more collaboration in conservation work has never been greater. Collaboration is at the core of truly integrated, multidisciplinary conservation projects (Lesson 3), and it depends largely on effective information transfer (Lesson 4). Collaborations can be simple agreements or more complex contracts, but regardless of their form, it is highly desirable to view these relationships as partnerships (see Wondolleck and Yaffee 2000).

There are many types of collaborations that need to be developed or strengthened, including (a) government agency to government agency; (b) government agency to biologists; (c) government agency to private organizations, especially nongovernmental organizations (NGOs); (d) government agency to private landowners; and (e) government to local associations and other civic groups.

In this lesson, attention is focused on the government and its many relationships because it plays a major role in the protection and regulation of biodiversity by virtue of its authority. Yet its record of collaborations within its own structure and with the private sector falls far short of what it could be (chapters 7, 12, 15, 19, and 21–23), and this deficiency in collaboration is negatively affecting biodiversity in a variety of ways (chapters 21–24). To emphasize the importance of the potential for more effective collaborations between government and the private sector, we focus on biologists, NGOs, and private landowners.

NONGOVERNMENTAL BIOLOGISTS

As mentioned in Lesson 1, professional biologists have worked for years in Costa Rica to produce a vast amount of biological knowledge (Janzen 1983). Yet most biologists are aware that their best science is not being applied to protect biodiversity in protected areas (chapters 7, 12, 15, 17, 19, 21, 23, and 24). Further, only rarely are they being asked to contribute directly to problem solving and overall management (see chapter 17).

Collaborations between biologists and government land stewards need to increase quickly because species are being lost and more will be lost in the future (chapter 7, 12, and 15; see also Lesson 11). Several accounts in this volume suggest that a greater effort be made by government officials to attract and work more closely with biologists (Lessons 4 and 5), and government incentives to encourage collaborations would rep-

resent a good start. Private biologists and government land stewards should form special teams or committees that work together to produce management plans, and biologists must be assured that their contributions will be appropriately represented (O'Brien 1993). Finally, professional biologists must be invited periodically to review management plans critically (Lesson 9).

NONGOVERNMENTAL CONSERVATION ORGANIZATIONS

NGOs that focus on conservation and environmental issues have played a considerable role in protecting the country's biodiversity. Their work is, however, not always recognized, mostly because of their small size and lack of media attention. Collaborations between government and NGOs are gradually increasing in the country, but many more need to be established. Further, government incentives need to be offered, especially to those organizations that become legally registered in the country.

Small nonprofit organizations have several advantages over government agencies: they can organize and mobilize quickly, require little start-up money, are staffed with dedicated workers, often have leaders with bachelor's or higher degrees, are in contact with a concerned segment of society, often have many available volunteers, and can serve as advocacy groups to offer alternate viewpoints on the health of the environment. Their big disadvantage is that they are always desperately short on funds (chapter 19).

Large international NGOs such as the World Wildlife Fund (WWF), World Wide Fund for Nature (WWF), Conservation International (CI), and the Nature Conservancy (TNC) have occasionally contributed directly to protecting biodiversity, but these organizations and their funds are often targeted early on toward specific projects. They can be an excellent source of targeted assistance, but they are often reluctant to speak out forcefully and publicly on inappropriate government actions. Even though much of conservation is in fact political, it has to happen behind the scenes. In several countries, large international NGOs seen to be publicly taking strong stands on issues would likely be asked to leave the country. For this reason, they often have networks of in-country NGOs that they work with and support, which can take stronger stances on issues of national importance.

The first Costa Rican association for the conservation of nature (ASCONA), now FECON (Costa Rican Federation for Environmental Conservationists), was founded at the Tropical Science Center (TSC), a private NGO in San José; almost all members of the TSC were members of ASCONA. In contrast, Fundación de Parques Nacionales (NPF) and Fundación Neotropica (NF) have programs favoring conservation, but they do not participate openly in defense of conservation and in denouncing transgressions or corruption cases. NGOs such as the Organization for Tropical Studies (OTS), TSC, and Monteverde Conservation League (MCL); York University; and a few other private institutions manage considerable areas with strict protection and also are dedicated to research and ecotourism activities. Projects such as AMISCONDE (Wille 1994), in the southern part of Costa Rica, which have shown to be very successful, have been sponsored by private companies such as McDonald's and Nestle through the intermediacy and technical guidance of CI and the TSC.

PRIVATE LANDOWNERS

The flora and fauna of Costa Rica do not recognize societal and political boundaries. Obviously, only part of the country's biodiversity is contained within the boundaries of national parks and reserves. What needs to be taken into consideration is the surrounding areas and their capacity and potential to conserve biodiversity (chapters 16 and 17) or their capacity to serve as a buffer for effects by human activities. Another important consideration is what the government is doing to encourage biodiversity protection on adjacent public and private lands. See Bustos (chapter 23) and a theoretical discussion of this topic in Brandon (chapter 24) and Brandon et al. (1998).

Collaborations between government land stewards and adjacent landowners have been mixed throughout the dry forest. Relationships vary from tolerance to outright distrust and disregard. This is unfortunate because many private landowners still have much intact habitat on their properties, and if they are approached in a professional manner with proposals, many could be effective partners in biodiversity conservation. Consider also, for example, that many landowners like wildlife, stream corridors, and trees (see chapter 19) and that they discourage hunters, control fire on their properties, and in general love the land they work. Many also want their hard work and family legacy passed on to their offspring.

These landowners are mostly responsible stewards who could be doing more to protect their lands if there were effective collaborations with the government. These could range from simple agreements with landowners to more involved projects in which resources and personnel are shared for clearly stated goals. Further, some landowners are in the process of considering conservation easements (Gustanski and Squires 2000) to protect their properties from further development. Conservation easements are just beginning to play a role in biodiversity conservation in Costa Rica. These facts suggest a great potential for collaborations that would further protect biodiversity. However, there must be a change in attitude on the part of government personnel to be able to negotiate these collaborations. We recommend that new government personnel, trained in public relations and other socioeconomic skills, be directed to work with landowners on new conservation projects. Private biologists and NGOs may need to be invited to facilitate and implement agreements.

Lesson 7. Conserving biodiversity requires environmental education of many different public and private audiences.

Several authors expressed the need for increased environmental education to expand the knowledge base concerning the natural and human-altered environments of Costa Rica (chapters 5, 6, 9, 10, 13–16, 19, 21, and 23). The contributions on water by Mata (chapter 9) and Vargas and Mata (chapter 10) are extremely important in this regard because they relate to environmental issues of human health and food supply. They point out important relations between environmental impacts, human health, and environmental stress and stability on the one hand and economic activities, quality of life, and ecological restoration on the other and how education is necessary to improve the general scenario.

Knowing the characteristics of target audiences is a fundamental component of environmental education (Jacobson 1999), and a few authors have focused on selected audiences (chapters 9, 17, and 19). Aburto (chapter 20) addresses another important audience in need of special environmental education—the biologists themselves. She stresses the need for biologists to learn how to communicate their important findings to the media, with the goal of transferring new information to the public. Bustos (chapter 23) points out the need for more environmental education of judges who preside over biodiversity and environmental laws (chapter 22), about which they know little.

The media also need to be better informed about environmental issues. For groups such as the media and judges, what they need to know consists of two components. The first is environmental education. The second, although related to the first, is a more complex understanding of economics, politics, and environmental issues. For example, an increase in oil prices in San José is not only an economic issue but also an environmental issue—from increased revenue for payment for ecosystem services, to foreign exchange needs, to sprawl, congestion, and pollution in the Central Valley. Many issues in Costa Rica have environmental repercussions, but, as in the United States, there is often no interest or general understanding of how these issues are related to one another. The OTS offers courses on this topic for U.S. decision makers, who visit Costa Rica for a week to learn about rain forests, primary forests, energy issues, global

warming and climate change, protected areas, and payments for environmental services. Palo Verde National Park in the dry forest is an exceptional site to demonstrate biological links between the United States and other countries, given its importance as a site for migratory waterfowl (chapter 12). It also provides a window on the complexities of park management amid government programs aimed at promoting development. Courses of this type should be greatly expanded to include more Costa Rican decision makers, an issue raised in the National Strategy of Conservation of Costa Rica (Quesada-Mateo 1990).

The need for environmental education can be easily justified—with such education, all audiences associated with biodiversity conservation will be better informed. The critical question is whether appropriate investments by government and private groups will be made to better inform the citizenry of the country. To date, individual private groups have mostly recognized the need for environmental education and have taken the initiative to implement programs. The government, through MINAE, has yet to make significant investments in meaningful environmental education programs (G. Frankie pers. obs.), and much more should be expected from the Ministry of Education. We strongly recommend that the government increase spending for environmental education to a variety of audiences. See also Holl et al. (1995).

Lesson 8. Connections between biodiversity, natural resources and their use, and ecosystem services—as well as economic expenditures and accounting—need to be made explicit and clearly understood, from the highest government level to the local level.

This lesson has many components. The first is that biodiversity conservation is not necessarily synonymous with natural resource management or ecosystem services. One can have well-forested watersheds that provide stable sources of timber and abundant clean water but that are devoid of the multiplicity of species that once resided there. In many parts of Latin America, this "empty forest" syndrome has already been recognized—forests that lack viable populations of characteristic fauna (Redford and Sanderson 1992).

Well-managed natural resources can exist without biodiversity—they represent areas where the ultimate management objective is to ensure a continuous stream of resources for human use. Ecosystem services can be thought of as a broader set of processes that act as the foundation for life—they represent clean air, clean water, fertile soils, and the like (Daily 1997). Both natural resource management and ecosystem services can occur at reasonable levels without maintaining the biodiversity that was once intact in an area (see Redford and Richter 1999). Sound natural resource management policies and policies that ensure ecosystem services represent the context within which biodiversity conservation must occur.

Managing for biodiversity implies putting existence values ahead of use values. In our changing world, it may mean being active land and biodiversity managers in ways not thought of a decade ago. For example, we now know that Costa Rica's fabled golden toad is probably extinct because the level of the cloud forests has receded, and the toads were unable to change habitats quickly and move upslope to areas that retained the humidity they needed. Now, golden toads are famous for being the first species whose probable extinction is directly linked to climate change. Keeping viable populations of amphibians in this setting means either carrying frogs and toads up the steep slopes in Monteverde or figuring out how to get moist clouds to linger lower for longer periods of time. Are we ready to do this? Is this a requirement of actively managing for biodiversity?

A second key lesson in this is that we can attach values to the many ecosystem services provided. These values do not appear in anyone's accounting. Although there have been huge advances in the past decade among ecological and environmental economists in how to measure the value of these services and include them in our measures of productivity (e.g., green GDP) and our national accounting systems (green accounting), politicians have had little use for these numbers. Politically, it is to the benefit of most politicians to boost exports and generate foreign exchange—even if these come from unsustainable resources practices. The political benefits are immediate, and by the time the damage begins to exact a toll on the economy, voters rarely remember who did what, and the politician is long gone. Circumventing this means incorporating these green measures into standard ways of measuring productivity and expenditures in order to understand how well we are managing natural capital. Yet, as demonstrated by the case of Costa Rica with the payment for environmental services from fossil fuel taxes, understanding is not equivalent to action (chapter 24). If Costa Rica is exceptional in that it has made the first strides at least to establish this, it is all the more saddening and sobering that actions that make good economic and environmental sense are still ignored.

Lesson 9. There is an urgent need to use ecoregional planning as the basis for land-use management countrywide, to make parks the anchors for biodiversity within each ecoregion, and to monitor these actions continuously.

Many lessons within this chapter have more than one dimension to them. This lesson addresses the need to (a) move toward ecoregional actions; (b) reinforce the necessity for parks to be the cornerstone of biodiversity conservation; and (c) ensure that both planning and implementation of development activities are compatible with conservation. Within the conservation community, there has been a dramatic shift to thinking at larger scales than parks, owing to a variety of ecological problems that are raised in numerous chapters in this book and elsewhere (e.g., Soulé and Terborgh 1999).

Costa Rica developed the Regional Conservation Areas (ARC) system to be responsive to the need to link protected areas with the surrounding lands. Unfortunately, the ARC system has not led to better coordination or to actions that are consistent with biodiversity conservation.

Some might question why biodiversity conservation should serve as the basis for regional planning within the country. There are several answers to this, but the bottom line is money. It is only within the past few years that products of the Intel plant in the Central Valley have surpassed other exports. But the fact remains that, aside from Intel, Costa Rica's economy depends on tourism and agriculture. Within the rural sector, these two and biodiversity are inextricably linked. Costa Rica has developed a strong reputation as an ecotourism destination, a position that could easily be lost without strong management of protected areas. We are increasingly seeing shifts to forms of both tourism and agriculture that are not sustainable. Negative effects in one area—such as pesticide runoff and wildfires—affect not only biodiversity but also tourism and the overall health of the general population (chapters 5, 9, and 19).

Many of Costa Rica's parks are too small to be ecologically viable for what they seek to protect (e.g., see Cuello et al. 1998). Either these areas should be enlarged, or they need to have adjacent lands in compatible management forms (chapters 14 and 16). Ecologically, this is paramount, but it is socially important, as well. Smaller-scale entrepreneurial activities, such as nature-based tourism lodges and shade-grown organic coffee, offer a chance for people to be owners and managers. This differs vastly from employment in commercial tourism, which often provides only seasonal work in low-paying, menial categories.

Strong ecoregional plans with participation by different government agencies, plans that include green accounting and provide a realistic understanding of the inherent economic and ecological trade-offs, are likely to lead to good planning—from social, economic, and environmental sides. The challenge is to see if the political will exists for their implementation. Scientifically based management plans are absolutely necessary to place clear boundaries on economic interests related to tourist businesses. Here again, there is a paradox in the definition of policies: that conservation is meant for future development, that is, for ecotourism, and therefore land-use permits can be granted to hotels in protected refuges.

Lesson 10. Biodiversity and environmental laws and policies need periodic critical review to identify those that work and those that do not work and why. Implementation must be reviewed critically.

Laws and policies need to represent the best science and highest certainty of implementation. This often creates deep conflicts between science and policy. As Mata notes in chapter 9, a recent Costa Rican forestry law (No. 75757, 1996) bans tree cutting along riparian corridors using categorically defined distance measures that reflect urban versus rural and type of topography. He notes that "the appropriate measurement should be determined by practical and scientific observations of the stream's conditions: its role in local ecological processes, the amount of biodiversity it contains, stream dynamics, and the equilibrium [relationships] of related ecosystems."

Unfortunately, laws cannot be established this way because they would quickly become arbitrary. Neither can they be precise enough to specify every eventuality. They must be blunt instruments, established in ways that represent the "best science" (or "best guess") and the best chance that the laws will be implemented. So in this case, 50 m represented the best science or guess and the best hope that it would be followed. Finding the balance between science and the reality of what people will do is tricky. In general, because many environmental problems cannot be reversed, it is better to be more cautious on the "science" side and give a greater push toward implementation (see also Soulé 1986: 6).

Like indicators in a good research design, laws and policies must be precise, measurable, consistent, and sensitive. Precision is an extremely important criterion—there must be a way to tell if the law or policy applies to a particular issue or condition. Within this volume are numerous examples in which laws and policies were formulated with insufficient clarity and consequently were open to a variety of interpretations.

Precision is desirable unless one is guaranteed that the direction of interpretation will always be pro-environment, an unlikely case. Measurability is important because it determines whether the law or policy is accomplishing what it was intended to accomplish. In general, simple measures work best. Consistency is important, as well—the policy or law should apply every time in an equal situation or for all cases. This brings us to Dan Janzen's attempt to generate revenue for Guanacaste National Park by allowing orange by-products to be dumped in it (see chapter 24). Although the idea was a good one—economically and ecologically—how can a law allowing the dumping of by-products be applied consistently without harmful effects in other cases? Great ideas often die because the policy and legal context rejected them; but the trade-off for the lack of progress (and in this case revenue) is protection from misuse of a law opening parks to such uses. The last criterion of a law or policy is sensitivity—its ability to capture the variety of changes or conditions that are relevant to the issue at hand.

Laws and policies can quickly be evaluated to determine if they meet these standards and if the standards capture the best available science. Implementation is the second part of the equation—there must be a basis on which people *want* or *need* to act in the specified manner. Wanting to act in a specified manner can be promoted in a variety of ways, from church sermons to television advertisements. Needing to act a certain way is more likely to come about from a deterrence or incentive point of view. Because implementation is malleable, laws that are a few degrees harsher than one might expect should be pushed. All of this necessitates reviewing and revising laws as needed—there is nothing sacred in laws and policies. The tricky element, however, is to get good laws implemented, and that requires political will.

Lesson 11. Biologists have warned that species have recently been lost from the country and that more will be lost unless new steps are taken to avert these projected losses.

Biologists have certainly posted their warnings, but the general public and decision makers probably have not heard and understood these warnings very well. Many scientists generally couch their findings in ways that are appropriate to academia, referring to limitations of the data and what can and cannot be extrapolated from findings (Soulé 1986). However, what may be appropriate within the scientific community is generally inaccessible to others because key conclusions are buried in jargon. Scientists also often wait for the media to come to them, rather than being proactive (chapter 20).

Reed Noss (1995: 701–3) writes, "We should not be so assured that the degradation of nature is general knowledge." Evidence of this lack of knowledge dates from Leopold: "Much of the damage inflicted on land is quite invisible to laymen" (Leopold in Noss 1995: 701). If damage on land is invisible, how difficult must it be to detect very subtle changes in insects, birds, fish, and mammals? Biologists can, and must, become much more vocal with their findings (O'Brien 1993; chapters 7, 9, 20, 21, and 23). For those doing research in Costa Rica, it means taking more dramatic action than publishing in the journals *TREE* or *Conservation Biology*. It means bringing the findings to a Costa Rican NGO, a television station, and the offices of *La Nación* (Costa Rica's largest newspaper). It means asking to speak at a local school. It may even mean buying a round of drinks in the local cantina near a research site on a Saturday night and giving an emotional speech (chapters 18–21 and 23).

There is good news here—evidence suggests that crisis leads to action (Brandon et al. 1998). Two of the strongest allies for conservation are pride and a sense of ownership. People react when something they care about may be lost; however, people need to be told what is being lost and what they can do about it. One study within Costa Rica found that even when people had some idea about an environmental problem, they seldom knew what action they should take, if any. There was, even among different socioeconomic groups, a very high (91%) willingness to pay more for services such as water and electricity if the money was used to protect biodiversity (Holl et al. 1995). This suggests a set of findings: (a) we need to craft messages that are clearer and louder about the impending species losses and how these affect every citizen; (b) biologists must take a more proactive role in this process (chapter 19); (c) there is generalized support for environmental and biodiversity protection; (d) financial support for biodiversity conservation exits in Costa Rica but it is not allocated; and (e) greater public political awareness and outcry are needed to relate environmental issues to quality of life—clean air and water, food, and recreation (chapter 20).

Lesson 12. National politics concerning larger social issues and international conservation trends have played, and will continue to play, a great role in determining policies for conserving Costa Rica's biodiversity.

In the coming decade, many factors will influence how well biodiversity is conserved, protected areas are maintained, and ecosystems function. These factors are both direct and indirect. The most important direct factor will be how well the laws and policies that are already on the books are implemented (chapters 22 and 23). Indirect factors will shape conservation, as well—in more subtle and hard-to-measure ways. But the bottom line is that even proactive measures designed to support conservation indirectly will have little impact if direct implementation is not improved. Equivalently, negative actions will exert a negative impact. In the universe of indirect effects, lack of implementation of sound policies and practices generally is a lose-lose proposition.

The role of international conservation organizations has been significant in the development of Costa Rica's conservation policies and programs; however, this has been a two-way street. Many policy reforms that Costa Rica has undertaken have been initiatives that started within Costa Rica and have in turn shaped the international conservation community.

Costa Rica has exerted strong leadership in a large number of environmental arenas. The forestry law has been frequently revised as needed to attempt to control deforestation. Early efforts at decentralization have been made. INBio has been a model for bioprospecting and training committed local naturalists (parataxonomists) (see chapter 17). Debt-for-nature swaps and other financing mechanisms have been significant in what they have accomplished. Costa Rica helped to define the potential for international ecotourism. Notable also has been the law allowing payment for environmental services. All of these actions have served as a model in some form and have influenced the overall trajectory of international conservation. What has been missing, however, is consistent and effective implementation.

CONCLUDING REMARKS

The defense and appropriate management of protected areas are crucial for the future of biodiversity. In the case of Costa Rica, which is a politically and socially stable country, we can derive from this chapter's lessons four major principles that are indispensable in order to protect ecosystems effectively:

1. Clear (political) definitions of the national concepts of "protection" and "natural patrimony" are needed to consolidate the integrity of what is already gained, territorially and institutionally.

2. Strong, governmentally backed institutions should be in charge of this protection, with clear goals and obligations toward effective conservation.

3. Any corruption in these institutions must be controlled and environmental ethics developed, especially for those in charge.

4. Active citizen participation is needed.

A clear definition of "protection" is lacking, even in the bylaws. Despite several mishaps (e.g., Gandoca, Nosara, Tamarindo, Osa), "developments" and resource extraction or land-use permits are still officially granted in areas that have been declared refuges, protected areas, or reserves (see example in Rossi 1999). The legal protection of an especially diverse area, by decree or by law, is not a guarantee by itself. Although creation of protected areas is a necessary first step, appropriate management by strong institutions and dedicated functionaries are the most important factors. The critical opinion and monitoring eye of citizens are also important and may become a key element of supervision and protection.

Priorities in conservation efforts are also necessary. For example, environmental protection does not make sense unless ecosystems, whose processes are inextricably linked to one another, can be rescued intact. Costa Rica is at a critical juncture. The coming decade will largely decide what wildlife and which wildlands will endure in the future. Far from being a total success, conservation in Costa Rica still needs a final and effective push toward consolidation and even restoration. Many important and effective laws already exist; but a large part of the solution to problems lies in strong implementation and enforcement, with the backing of wise political decisions at the highest level.

Biologists, conservationists, and informed citizens have major roles to play in ensuring that protected areas serve as the cornerstones of biodiversity conservation, that laws are strictly enforced, that parks and lands around them are better managed, that the general public is well informed, and that conservation receives its due within the political process. There is still the potential to take action; however, doing so will require the coordination of many specialists and their colleagues. Doing less than this will certainly lead to the demise of tropical dry forests and their unique biodiversity.

REFERENCES

Brandon, K. 1996. *Ecotourism and conservation: A review of key issues.* Environment Department Paper 33. Washington, D.C.: World Bank. 70 pp.

Brandon, K., K. H. Redford, and S. E. Sanderson, eds. 1998. *Parks in peril: People, politics, and protected areas.* Covelo, Calif.: Island Press. 519 pp.

Clark, T. W., R. P. Reading, and A. L. Clarke, eds. 1994. *Endangered species recovery: Finding the lessons, improving the process.* Covelo, Calif.: Island Press. 450 pp.

Cuello, C., K. Brandon, and R. Margoluis. 1998. Costa Rica: Corcovado National Park. In *Parks in peril: People, politics, and protected areas,* ed. K. Brandon, K. Redford, and S. Sanderson, 142–91. Covelo, Calif.: Island Press.

Daily, G. C., ed.. 1997. *Nature's services: Societal dependence on natural ecosystems.* Covelo, Calif.: Island Press. 392 pp.

Frankie, G. W., V. Solano, and M. McCoy. 1994. *Una evaluación técnica del Corredor La Mula entre La Reserva Biológica Lomas Barbudal y El Parque Nacional Palo Verde.* Bagaces: Amigos de Lomas Barbudal; Berkeley: University of California; and Heredia, Costa Rica: Universidad Nacional de Heredia. 126 pp. Contact frankie@nature.berkeley.edu for copies.

Gustanski, J. A., and R. H. Squires, eds. 2000. *Protecting the land: Conservation easements past, present, and future.* Covelo, Calif.: Island Press. 566 pp.

Holl, K. D., G. C. Daily, and P. R. Ehrlich. 1995. Knowledge and perception in Costa Rica regarding environment, population, and biodiversity issues. *Conservation Biology* 9:1548–57.

Jacobson, S. K. 1999. *Communication skills for conservation professionals.* Covelo, Calif.: Island Press. 351 pp.

Janzen, D. H. 1983. *Costa Rican natural history.* Chicago: University of Chicago Press. 816 pp.

———. 1986. *Guanacaste National Park: Tropical ecological and cultural restoration.* San José: Editorial Universidad Estatal A Distancia. 103 pp.

Margoluis, R., C. Margoluis, K. Brandon, and N. Salafsky. 2000. *In good company: Effective alliances for conservation.* Washington, D.C.: Biodiversity Support Program.

Meffe, G. K. 1998. Conservation biology: Into the millennium. *Conservation Biology* 12:1–3.

Noss, R. 1995. The perils of Pollyannas. *Conservation Biology* 9:701–3.

O'Brien, M. H. 1993. The professional biologist: Being a scientist means taking sides. *BioScience* 43:706–8.

Quesada-Mateo, C., ed. 1990. *Estrategia de conservación para el desarrollo sostenible.* San José: Servicios Litograficos. 180 pp.

Redford, K. H., and B. Richter. 1999. Conservation of biodiversity in a world of use. *Conservation Biology* 3:1246–56.

Redford, K. H., and S. E. Sanderson. 1992. The brief barren marriage of biodiversity and sustainability. *Bulletin of the Ecological Society of America* 73:36–39.

Rossi, A. 1999. *La loca de Gandoca*. San José: Editorial Universitaria Centroamericana—EDUCA. 138 pp. Contact: educacr@sol.rasca.co.cr.

Soulé, M., ed. 1986. *Conservation biology: The science of scarcity and diversity*. Sunderland, Mass.: Sinauer Associates. 584 pp.

Soulé, M., and J. Terborgh, eds. 1999. *Continental conservation: Scientific foundations of regional reserve networks*. Covelo, Calif.: Island Press. 238 pp.

Terborgh, J. 1999. *Requiem for nature*. Covelo, Calif.: Island Press. 224 pp.

Wille, C. 1994. Nature's hothouse: Can we save the Neotropics? *American Birds* 48:56.

Wondolleck, J. M., and S. L. Yaffee. 2000. *Making collaborations work: Lessons from Innovation in Natural Resource Management*. Covelo, Calif.: Island Press. 277 pp.

CONTRIBUTORS

GILDA ABURTO San José, Costa Rica

VICTORIA J. APSIT Biology Department, University of Missouri, St. Louis, Missouri

ADRIAN J. BARRANCE Overseas Development Institute, London

GILBERT BARRANTES Escuela de Biología, Universidad de Costa Rica, San Pedro, Costa Rica

KAMALJIT S. BAWA Department of Biology, University of Massachusetts, Boston, Massachusetts

FEDERICO BOLAÑOS Escuela de Biología, Universidad de Costa Rica, San Pedro, Costa Rica

DAVID H. BOSHIER Department of Plant Sciences, Oxford Forestry Institute, University of Oxford, Oxford, England

KATRINA BRANDON Center for Applied Biodiversity Science, Conservation International, Washington, D.C.

JULIO ALBERTO BUSTOS San José, Costa Rica

JAIME ECHEVERRÍA Centro Scientifico Tropical, San José, Costa Rica

GORDON W. FRANKIE Division of Insect Biology—College of Natural Resources, University of California, Berkeley, California

GREGORY A. GIUSTI University of California, Cooperative Extension, Ukiah, California

JAMES E. GORDON Department of Plant Sciences, University of Oxford, Oxford, England

WILLIAM A. HABER Monteverde, Puntarenas, Costa Rica, and Missouri Botanical Garden, St. Louis, Missouri

JAMES L. HAMRICK Departments of Botany and Genetics, University of Georgia, Athens, Georgia

PAUL HANSON Escuela de Biología, Universidad de Costa Rica, San Pedro, Costa Rica

DANIEL H. JANZEN Department of Biology, University of Pennsylvania, Philadelphia, Pennsylvania

JORGE A. JIMÉNEZ Organization for Tropical Studies, San Pedro, Costa Rica

RICHARD K. LAVAL Monteverde, Puntarenas, Costa Rica

ALFONSO MATA Centro Scientifico Tropical, San José, Costa Rica

SEAN T. O'KEEFE Department of Biological and Environmental Sciences, Morehead State University, Morehead, Kentucky

FRANK V. PALADINO Department of Biology, Indiana-Purdue University, Fort Wayne, Indiana

MAURICIO QUESADA Departamento de Ecología de los Recursos Naturales, Instituto de Ecología, Universidad Nacional Autónoma de México (UNAM), Morelia, Michoacán, Mexico

PETER S. RONCHI Amigos de Lomas Barbudal, Bagaces, Guanacaste, Costa Rica

ROXANA SALAZAR Fundación Ambio, San José, Costa Rica

JULIO E. SÁNCHEZ Museo Nacional de Costa Rica, San José, Costa Rica

MAHMOOD SASA Organization for Tropical Studies, San Pedro, Costa Rica, and Instituto Clodomiro Picado, Universidad de Costa Rica, San Pedro, Costa Rica

JAMES R. SPOTILA School of Environmental Science, Engineering, and Policy, Drexel University, Philadelphia, Pennsylvania

ROBERT D. STEVENSON Department of Biology, University of Massachusetts, Boston, Massachusetts

KATHRYN E. STONER Departamento de Ecología de los Recursos Naturales, Instituto de Ecología, Universidad Nacional Autónoma de México (UNAM), Morelia, Michoacán, Mexico

ROBERT M. TIMM Department of Ecology and Evolutionary Biology, University of Kansas Natural History Museum, Lawrence, Kansas

JOSÉ A. VARGAS Centro de Investigación en Ciencias del Mar y Limnología (CIMAR), Universidad de Costa Rica, San Pedro, Costa Rica

S. BRADLEIGH VINSON Department of Entomology, Texas A&M University, College Station, Texas

NELSON ZAMORA Instituto de Biodiversidad (INBio), Santo Domingo, Heredia, Costa Rica

INDEX

PROJECT MANAGEMENT, COPYEDITING,
INDEXING, AND COMPOSITION: Princeton Editorial Associates, Inc.
TEXT: Scala
DISPLAY: Scala Sans and Scala Sans Caps
PRINTER AND BINDER: Malloy Lithographing, Inc.